MME

LIKE IT

Produced by ESMÉ CHURCH

Scenery and Costumes by MOLLY McARTHUR

Orchestra under the direction of HERBERT MENGES

Leader of the Orchestra DAVID CARL TAYLOR

Music arranged by HERBERT MENGES

Wrestling arranged by GIBSON-COWAN

Dance arranged by ROLLO GAMBLE

Crossbows kindly lent by BARTY'S

Wigs by " BERT "

Flowers and fruit by WINDRAMS

Stage Director	...	GEORGE CHAMBERLAIN
Stage Manager	...	JAMES HOYLE
Press Representative	...	DOROTHY DRAKE
Electrician ...	...	J. EGAN
Scene painting directed by	...	GEORGE WIGGINS
Wardrobe Mistress	...	MRS. NEWMAN
Wardrobe Master	...	O. WHITEHEAD

Business Manager and Treasurer — BRUCE WORSLEY

THE COUNTRY WIFE

PROGRAMME

In Association with GILBERT MILLER

(WYCHERLEY)

Produced by TYRONE GUTHRIE

Designed by OLIVER MESSEL

SEASON 1936—37

THE OLD VIC
RUN IN CONNECTION WITH
SADLER'S WELLS

Lessee and Manager of both Theatres :

LILIAN BAYLIS, C.H., M.A., Oxon. (Hon.), LL.D., Birm. (Hon.)

23rd CONSECUTIVE SEASON of DRAMA at the OLD VIC

TUESDAY, OCTOBER 6th at 8

In association with Gilbert Miller

The Country Wife

(Wycherley)

Nightly at 8

Extra Performance, Mondays at 8

Matinees, Wednesdays and Saturdays, at 2.30

Programme—PRICE THREEPENCE

IN MY MIND'S I

MICHAEL REDGRAVE

IN MY MIND'S I

AN ACTOR'S AUTOBIOGRAPHY

THE VIKING PRESS   NEW YORK

To Corin

Copyright © 1983 by Michael Redgrave Productions Limited
All rights reserved
Published in 1983 by The Viking Press
40 West 23rd Street, New York, N.Y. 10010
Published simultaneously in Canada by
Penguin Books Canada Limited

LIBRARY OF CONGRESS CATALOGING IN PUBLICATION DATA
Redgrave, Michael, Sir.
In my mind's I.
1. Redgrave, Michael, Sir.
2. Actors—Great Britain—Biography.   I. Title
PN2598.R42A29   1983   792'.028'0924   [B]   83-47930
ISBN 0-670-14233-6

Published in Great Britain under the title *In My Mind's Eye*.

Grateful acknowledgment is made to the following for permission to reprint copy-
righted material:
Executors of the Estate of the late Dame Edith Evans: Selections from the letters of Dame
Edith Evans to Sir Michael Redgrave. Copyright © 1983 by the Executors of the
Estate of the late Dame Edith Evans. *Harcourt Brace Jovanovich, Inc., and Faber and
Faber Publishers*: A two-line excerpt from *The Family Reunion*, by T. S. Eliot. Copy-
right 1939 by T. S. Eliot. Copyright renewed 1967 by Esme Valerie Eliot. *David
Higham Associates Limited*: A selection from *For Johnny: Poems of World War Two*, by
John Pudney, published by Walwyn. *Hughes Massie Limited*: Selections from a letter
of Tyrone Guthrie to Sir Michael Redgrave. Copyright © 1983 by Hughes Massie
Limited, Copyright Agents. *Joan M. Ling, as Agent for Michael Asquith and Mrs.
Vivien Asquith*: Selections from a letter of Sir James Matthew Barrie, Bart., to Sir
Michael Redgrave. Copyright © 1983 by Michael Asquith and Mrs. Vivien Asquith,
copyright Proprietors of the works and letters of J. M. Barrie. *The New Yorker*: An
excerpt from "The Player, Part I," by Lillian Ross, from the October 21, 1961, issue
of *The New Yorker*. Copyright © 1961 by The New Yorker Magazine, Inc. *Dr. Jan
Van Loewen Ltd., Exclusive Agents for the Estate of Noël Coward*: Lyrics to "Could You
Please Oblige Us with a Bren Gun." Copyright © Noël Coward Estate. All rights
reserved.

The programmes for productions of *The Country Wife*, *Three Sisters*, and *As You Like
It* are reproduced courtesy of The Old Vic Ltd., and The Queen's Theatre, London.
The early part of the list of performances is based on that in Richard Findlater's
Michael Redgrave: Actor (1956). Unless otherwise credited in the list of illustrations,
all photographs are from the author's album.

Printed in the United States of America
Set in Bembo

LIST OF ILLUSTRATIONS

A List of Performances and Productions follows page 237.

IN MY MIND'S I

I

I T WAS after breakfast, and Aunt Mabel and I were alone in the
dining-room of my stepfather's house off Belgrave Square. She
had been telling me stories about Roy, my father, whom I did not
remember, and of whom I knew next to nothing, and little good.

My stepfather had left for the City at nine-thirty, as usual. He had
been a tea and rubber planter in Ceylon, and now was a director of
various companies. My actress mother, when not rehearsing, usually
had her breakfast in bed. Mabel, my actress aunt, with her cigarette
bobbing up and down as she spoke, would now and then whisk her
hand over her blouse whether ash had fallen there or not. Mother
was always alarmed by Mabel's habit of smoking in bed.

Aunt Mabel – or 'Miggles' as Mother called her because her name
began with an 'M' (Mabel called Mother 'Diggles' because her name
was Daisy) – had just finished telling me of how my father had gone
down a street at night, tearing the knockers off the front doors. It
was understood, of course, that he had been drunk.

I murmured something. As Bacchus, my legendary father was
nothing new to me. I had not pictured him as Hercules.

'Oh, yes,' said Mabel and giggled. 'You know,' she added, as if
offering an official stamp to what she had just told me, 'I think Roy
only touched Diggles once, and you, my dearest little Micky
Doodlums, were the result.'

To Mabel's news I feel sure I said nothing. When deeply interested
I frequently say nothing. Those who know me well say that at such
moments expression drains slowly from my face and I am the
picture of boredom. It was certainly quite a moment. As I recall it I
can almost taste the Ceylon 'Breakfast' tea, see again the gloomy
light of that dining-room, with its dark red damask curtains, its
embossed wallpaper looking like crocodile skin, the Persian carpets,

the electrified alabaster bowl which hung above the oddly square dining-table and cast such a waxy light on the faces of the diners, the rows of books bought by the yard, Dickens and Scott in Library Editions, *The Beaux and Belles of England* in half-leather bindings which all too neatly filled the glazed upper parts of the huge three-piece secretaire whose lower parts housed the best tea service and the cut-glass tumblers and wineglasses, the large, handsome sideboards, the heavy decanters of whisky and port, the epergne shaped like a cluster of tall tropical trees with a cut-glass fruit bowl resting in their delicate silver branches and a Singalese shepherd reclining in their shade (a gift to my stepfather from the Ceylon and Eastern Agency when he retired). All these, I feel, as I remember Aunt Mabel that day, might still be there, if only I did not know for certain that they are not. Still there, still kept in spotless order by Mary, the parlourmaid from County Wicklow, mute witnesses of dining-room conversations that were usually strained, because nothing unpleasant, no discomfortable fact, must ever be mentioned, and long silences, even at breakfast, were not allowed. It was the one room in the house which I really hated; it was so hard to escape from it.

On occasional Sunday evenings, when guests came, I remember it seemed far less gloomy and the faces beneath the light from the alabaster bowl looked less strained. 'The Captain', my stepfather – he had kept his Army rank after the war – was a kind man, a good and a just man, and a charming host. He was also a very conventional man. I feared him. Yes, a charming host. But for most of the year that dining-room in the house off Belgrave Square was a terrible room.

But that morning, Aunt Mabel's information, though somewhat stunning, elated me. My father now seemed a sort of Jove, descending lustfully on his unsuspecting love. I became a Perseus or a Minos, chance offspring of one improbable but gaudy night. This, at the time, did not seem to conflict in any way with the fact that Mother had more than once told me that my father, Roy, was a wonderful lover, or that she had attended seances to get in touch with him after his death, or that they had, after all, cohabited off and on for nearly three years. (The seances proved somewhat inconclusive. Roy, through the medium, informed Mother that he had never forgotten, simply couldn't bear, in fact, her way of sitting with her hands folded, as if silently reproaching him. It seemed very convincing, until Mother remembered that she had been sitting, just so, with her hands folded, throughout the seance.)

For her part, Mother, in her rare confidences to me on the subject, though she extolled his charm, his physical allure, and his acting talent, managed to implant in my mind at an early age the knowledge of her chief fear: that I might grow up to be like him. 'He used to point at things with his middle, instead of his index, finger, and once when you were about four you pointed at something with your middle finger and I nearly screamed.'

Not knowing a hundredth part of all I now know about my parents' marriage, and being aware that the two half-sisters were close to each other, I accepted Mabel's fantastic surmises with bewilderment but without question. Mother had already told me Roy had been married before, to an actress called Judith Kyrle, who had three children by him.

'"Judith Kyrle,"' I exclaimed, 'what a beautiful name!'

'She was a beautiful woman. *Not,*' Mother added with slight acerbity, 'a very good actress.'

There had been a divorce.

Roy had met my mother, Daisy Scudamore, in a theatrical 'stock' company at Brighton in the summer of 1907. Daisy was in her mid-twenties and Roy was thirty-six. She married him, she once told me, because she thought she could 'save' him. 'Men loved him,' she said, 'and women adored him.'

Mabel's version of the marriage was less romantic. Shortly before they met, said Mabel, Roy had had an affair with the wife of a well-to-do newspaper proprietor. The husband was to divorce his wife, citing the actor as co-respondent. Roy, according to Mabel, took what seemed the easiest way of preserving his 'quaint honour' and married the young actress in haste even if it meant repentance at leisure.

Little can be found to support this story of Mabel's. Nevertheless, there was certainly a third woman and, moreover, another child, a boy of whom Roy was passionately fond. The woman was referred to as 'Miss C.' or 'the lady'. There is no evidence that Roy wanted to marry Miss C., but his love of the child – his fourth – battled with his infatuation for Daisy.

> How strange [wrote Daisy] that you should see 'the lady' in the train. Well dear, nasty or not, it doesn't matter now, it's all over and done with, and she's only herself to blame. Happiness was easily within her reach, and she's thrown herself and it away. Am glad to hear the boy is getting on so well, it will do you the world of good to see him; you must get him to yourself as often as you can. I do hope *she* won't be anywhere near at the time. We're doing wretched business here.

The jaunty tone of this letter is misleading, I fancy.

Men and women in love, writing to each other once or even twice a day, often do not date their letters beyond writing the name of the day. But some short time after Daisy's chirpy letter there is one from Roy which must have struck fear into her heart. He says in it that Miss C.'s divorce will soon be through and that 'my first duty is to her and the boy . . . my name of course figures in the case and I shall marry her as soon as she is free.' He goes on to say that it will seem brutal to Daisy for him to write in this way, but that it is the only 'right thing' he can do. 'Heaven knows,' he exclaims, 'how this other trouble of yours hurts me and you know I shall do all I possibly can to straighten matters.'

'This other trouble' was, presumably, myself, to whom he refers later as 'the future event'. I can only conjecture Daisy's answer to this, but I am certain that few men would have wanted to be in Roy's shoes when he received it. Whatever it was, it won the day, game and set, if not, as it turned out, match. It produced a complete volte-face from, as he signed himself, 'your old worried Roy'.

He had surely much reason to be worried. His liaison with Miss C., whoever she was – and here perhaps Aunt Mabel was right, though I'm inclined to think that she, too, was an actress – was over, but from numerous references it is clear that he adored the son she had given him and that this love was returned by the child.

My dearest,
    I am writing this at the theatre. Have come down early this evening. I have just wired you and shall be restless until I get your reply. I don't know why, but I've been so restless all day, and now I've finally made up my mind.
    If you reply saying you will have me, then dear we will be married the next time we meet in Glasgow.
    I know I love you. I believe you love me and if you will bear with me I will do my level best by you. I know I am not a saint but dear, with the right hand at the helm I can and will steer straight. I can say no more. Believe me I have not come to this conclusion in a hurry. I have thought and thought all ways. I can see *no other* way but this. I feel sure this *is* right.
    I think we shall both feel happier when we have things settled. Believe me I appreciate the sacrifice you make – or would make – for me. I think you know the sacrifice I have made.
    I *can't* have the boy. We must have our own.
        My love dear wife
        Your
        Roy

The sacrifice he had made refers, I can only suppose, to his having, by his decision to marry Daisy, given up his rights to his son by Miss C. What Daisy's sacrifice could have been I am not so sure. Perhaps that is just conventional gallantry. 'I *can't* have the boy. We must have our own,' is a fine curtain line of the period.

The letter is written in his neatest, most well-shaped, and soberest hand. His writing varied much, as do most handwritings, I guess. Daisy's reply is written in the bold, large, generous script she maintained to the end of her life:

> My Roy, my dear dear Roy,
>
> Your wire came just as I was going on the stage. I read it and went on in an excited dream – not conscious of one word I uttered during the prologue.
>
> Oh my dearest your message tonight is the most sacred of all you have ever given me – whether I am your wife in name matters not – but that you call me so in your heart – means, oh my darling, it means all the universe to me.
>
> I am going to bed tonight the happiest woman in the world. It seems all too good to be true that you love me so much and yet I know it is true – but I feel – oh I feel I want to shout it tonight from the housetops. I love you and you love me.
>
> Dearest, say it again in your letters and whisper it to me when we meet. Wife, wife, don't you know – can't you guess what it means? My darling my darling – God bless a thousand times –
> Daisy

Roy's next letter is strange, to say the least. Having dragged his feet over marrying Daisy, he now appears anxious to be married in all possible haste, in a form of marriage designed for 'mariners, travellers, etc.', which, he assures her, will be 'legal and binding the world over'. It has the great advantage that he can be simply labelled 'divorced', without having to produce any papers to show how, when, or why. Could this be, I wonder, because he never had, in fact, been divorced from his first wife, Judith Kyrle, so that his marriage to Daisy was bigamous?

> 2 Birnam Terrace
> Craighton Road
> Govan
>
> Thursday
>
> My dear love,
> I have just returned from Glasgow. Have had a good long talk with the registrar and now beg – fair lady – to make my report.

I have *settled* nothing! Nor can I do so until I hear from you. That's why I want you to particularly *understand* this letter and wire me by 12 tomorrow. *Because* (now the explanation) we can, if you like and are still willing, be married on Monday *next* before Sheriff MacKenzie. I have been all through it with him this morning and he says that if we can produce two witnesses to say we have both lived in Scotland for 21 days prior to the ceremony he will manage to get it through early for us on Monday, so as to enable me to catch my train for Bradford. Now I can't very well keep any of our crowd behind to act as witnesses, can *you* manage that part? It doesn't matter who they are really, so long as they don't mind signing their names 4 or 5 times to different affidavits and being – *for sure* – at the Registrar's in Minerva Street, Glasgow by 10.30 on Monday morning. The whole affair will be over by 11.30 and is as binding for all in *any* part of the world as though we gave the 21 days' notice and had the clergyman etc. I have gone well into the thing myself with him and am sure it is just as good and binding and as legal. The only thing is it is a bit more expensive. I enclose you a form which he has marked for me and which I have to fill up (I have a copy). This special marriage ceremony I may tell you is *allowed by a special revision of the marriage laws made last June* and I want you dear to decide for yourself. Personally I am quite satisfied, but if you would prefer it, make enquiries – you can do it at any Registrar's in Dundee on receipt of this. Mention the paragraph I've underlined because I believe that until this revision was made in June this particular law was only for Scotland. It has been repealed and revised for the benefit of those – such as mariners, travellers etc. – who are not 21 days in residence at one place, to hold legal and binding the world over.

This procedure of marriage has the *great* advantage that *I* am just labelled 'divorced' and need not necessarily produce papers etc., shewing when, how, date etc., which will take trouble and money and time to get. . . .

We can come into Glasgow early Monday, go to the registrar's with our witnesses at 10.30 and the whole thing will be done in an hour, in fact just in time for me to get away and our honeymoon will have to be postponed.

Thus by Monday midday you will be Mrs Redgrave and I shall be 'with you – with you'.

I want you to wire me yes or no – as near 12 tomorrow Friday as possible. I shall be at the theatre from 11.30 till 12.30 on the watch. Address Lyceum Theatre, Govan. . . .

A good idea – could you not get that friend you wrote me about to be one of the witnesses? We don't want any more 'outside members' than we can help to know the exact date of our marriage on account of the future event. I shall be all excitement till I hear from you. I've given you till 12 in case you want to go round to the Registrar's yourself.

That's all settled now, isn't it?

Now dearie, about myself. I am quite like my old self again today, quite lively and bright. So glad to hear my dearest is still keeping well. . . .

Well dearest and best of girls I must off to catch the mail. My best and fondest love to you dear love.

　　　Your devoted husband and lover
　　　Roy

These letters come from two dress-boxes marked 'Woollands, Knightsbridge', a shop where in later, palmier, if less halcyon days, my mother bought many of her clothes. The boxes were sent to me from Stanmore, where she lived in a nursing home during the last few years of her life. She sent me the boxes after she had started writing her 'notebooks', school copy-books I had sent her, suggesting that since she remembered so much about the theatre of her days it should be recorded. 'Don't write what you thought of this or that actor or actress,' I said, 'so much as what you were paid, working conditions, landladies, Sunday "train-calls" and the rest of it.'

She had been a good seamstress when young – you had to be if you were a touring leading lady on five pounds a week, finding all your own clothes – but she had lost the knack and the patience. In later days she had no use for cards, except for telling fortunes, or for crossword puzzles, or knitting. She still read avidly, mostly memoirs, but it irritated her not to be able to remember what she had just read. I hoped that the notebooks would provide some sort of occupational therapy. She completed nearly five of them.

The contents of the boxes are what must be all my father's letters to her, some telegrams, a few press-cuttings recording his death in Australia at the age of fifty, and her letters to him before and shortly after their marriage. One telegram, however, is missing, if we are to believe Aunt Mabel.

'You know,' she said on that dark morning in that dark dining-room, 'Roy only acted in the West End once. He preferred to be a big fish in a small pond. But shortly before you were born he did get a West End engagement. Daisy didn't hear a word from him when you were born, but suddenly a few days later he wired her, saying, "Come at once and bring the boy."' Aunt Mabel paused here, I think, for I remember her looking at me to see how I was taking it. She added, 'You see, his play had flopped.'

7

She went on to tell me other and even more scarifying things about Roy. Some of them I cannot entirely disbelieve. Although that curt telegram is not among the rest – and surely it would be if it existed, for it seems Mother kept everything – Roy's letter which greets her first letter about his new son can hardly have been the one which Daisy had hoped for. After not getting a letter at the house (lodgings in Clapham), he was, he writes, 'a little fidgety in case' she should not be well, and delighted therefore to find a letter waiting for him at the theatre where he was rehearsing.

The theatre was the Pavilion in Mile End Road, 'hitherto known as "The Drury Lane of the East"', says a newspaper cutting of 22 March 1908, whose 'traditions' would be again revived on 28 March, when, 'entirely redecorated, the theatre will be re-opened. The new management intend to spare neither money nor effort in providing the best possible entertainment that can be placed before the public of the eastern portion of the metropolis, and will produce on the opening night an adaptation by Mr Alfred Dampier of Rolf Bolder-wood's famous novel, *Robbery Under Arms*, which has not been seen in London for some fourteen years. Mr Roy Redgrave, so long the favourite of the Britannia Theatre, Hoxton, will appear as Captain Starlight.'

The cutting is dated two days after my birth in 'digs' above a paper shop on St Michael's Hill in Bristol. Mabel, it seems, was mistaken about the West End engagement – or perhaps it was I who was mistaken; perhaps she said a London engagement. Anyway, *Robbery Under Arms* was a big success in its way. Roy had indeed been a favourite at the 'Brit', as it was called. 'It was an institution,' writes W. Macqueen-Pope. It had

> its own traditions, and its history is unique in London's theatrical annals. No theatre had ever been so long under one management. Authors wrote for it exclusively, actors joined it as boys and remained until old age. Its main support came from people of the surrounding neighbourhood, who loved it and revered its manageress, Sara Lane. In its pantomimes (which always ran until Easter) she played the Principal Boy until she was in her seventies. ... The Britannia was the last London theatre to give up its own local and democratic drama and take in touring companies. After the death of Mrs Lane, mourned by the entire neighbourhood, the theatre passed into the hands of relatives and became a cinema.

It was a cinema when I first saw it. Quite by chance – for I had no idea that what I used to think of as 'my father's old theatre' still existed – I was strolling jubilantly down the High Street of Hoxton, returning from seeing the showing of my first screen test, at the old Gainsborough Studios in Islington, which had resulted in my being offered a film contract starting at what to me seemed the dizzy sum of one hundred and fifty pounds a week. It was a fine late afternoon in the early winter of 1938, and I was walking to look for a telephone box from which to call home to tell Rachel, my wife, that I had overcome my scruples and accepted the contract. I did not have much doubt about her reaction, but I was less sure of what my dear friend Edith Evans and my colleagues at the Queen's Theatre, John Gielgud and Peggy Ashcroft and Glen Byam Shaw, would say. Films were frowned upon by many 'serious' artists in the theatre in those days, and it should be remembered that, with a few memorable exceptions, British films before 1939 were regarded as something of a laughing-stock in England and were almost unknown abroad. Among the exceptions, of course, were the films of Asquith and Hitchcock, and it was with the promise that Hitchcock would direct my first picture – *The Lady Vanishes* – and the to me all-important clause that I should have absolute freedom to work in the theatre for six months every year, that I had agreed to the contract.

I was feeling extremely pleased with myself as I strode along Hoxton's High Street. Suddenly I saw the posters outside a cinema. It was the old Brit, my legendary father's legendary theatre. I paid and went in. It was difficult to see much of the auditorium in the dark. It seemed huge. As I came out I went into a corner pub, ordered a drink, and asked if I could use the telephone. As I drank I asked the barmaid, 'How long has the Brit been a cinema? I didn't know it still existed.'

She called towards the other bar. 'Fred! How long have they had flicks at the Brit?' While he was scratching his head she went on: 'You see, my husband and I met at the Brit. I was a dresser and he was a stage-hand. A scene-shifter, you know.'

'My father used to act there . . . Roy Redgrave.'

'You're *Roy Redgrave*'s son?'

After several drinks I left them. It was clear that they adored Roy. I could not resist telling them of the film contract. I told them I would be filming in Islington quite a lot in the years to come and would look in to see them.

I never did. I made only one film at the Islington Studios and during the making of that I was acting at the Queen's Theatre at night, and a year later the Second World War came, and during the Blitz the Brit was bombed.

I had for some time one relic of it: a rolled-gold signet ring given to my father by Sara Lane, the old actress-manageress, whose picture as a young girl in the role of Columbine can be seen in old 'tuppence-coloured' prints. But during the Blitz our house was burgled, and among the things which disappeared was Sara Lane's ring. It was worth no more than five bob or so but was, apart from a few photos, the only possession I had which was a link with Roy.

He had acted at the Brit for many seasons – everything, it would seem, that a leading man could play: Marcus Superbus in *The Sign of the Cross*, Hamlet, the lot. I don't know if he was still there when the old lady died, in 1899. He must have made his first marriage by then.

I have only two memories of my father. The first is of a tall man bending down to press the toe of my new shoe. I cannot be sure that it was Roy and not a shop assistant or some other grown-up. Yet something about this man in my mind's eye convinces me that it was he. The second is only slightly less fragmentary. I am looking through the bars of my cot. There is a fire in the grate, and standing in front of it are a man and a woman, arguing. Their voices are raised and he seems to be scolding her. Perhaps Roy and Daisy were rehearsing a scene from a play, but it seems all too probable that this was a real argument.

Both recollections must date from Australia, where Mother had taken me to join Roy. In the spring of 1909 they had been touring together, in England, in a melodrama called *The Christian*, and I was in the care of Auntie May, one of the numerous aunties who looked after me when Mother was away. After I was born, Roy, Mother told me in the notebooks, had been 'fairly well-behaved' – which, I fear, he all too rarely was after the first months of their marriage. But suddenly he had announced that he was off to Australia again: 'That's where the money is.' And off he went. (He had played there before, according to a newspaper obituary, in the company of a popular Australian actress, Minnie Titell Brune.) The tour of *The Christian* came to an end, and Mother was left penniless and alone.

It was not, it seems, Roy's intention to desert her. He wrote a letter a day from the boat on the journey out, some of them fully as passionate as the letters of his courtship. But Daisy knew all too well what would be the effect of a long separation. Both for my sake and for her own she was determined not to give him up for lost. Finding the money to follow him to Australia, however, was an almost insoluble problem. By a stroke of astonishingly good fortune she learned that a Mr Phillipson, the very manager who had hired Roy for his company in Australia, had recently come to England, so she sought him out and persuaded him to hire her as well. This must have taken some doing, as Phillipson had already engaged a leading lady and had a full complement of players for his company, but somehow she prevailed upon him to take her on as well, and even to advance her twenty pounds.

Besides these two memories of my father, I remember very little of Australia: the trams in Melbourne; standing beneath the hosepipe in some backyard whilst the landlady hosed me down and left me to dry fully-clothed in the scorching summer's sun; and a furious fight with a young boy named Cyril. He was a plain little boy, but with gorgeous flaxen curls which someone had been tactless enough to praise in my hearing. I was already well-accustomed to being the centre of attention. A terrific squawking was heard from the hens in the fowl run at the bottom of the yard, and terrified cries from Cyril, whose hair I was mercilessly pulling.

It can't have been a happy time. J. C. Williamson, the most successful Australian impresario, regularly imported English actors to play the leading parts, but this was the first time that the Phillipson management had done so. Roy was a big hit with Australian audiences, Daisy rather less successful. Her fellow-players she found wanting in accomplishment and apt to resent her.

Audiences in the outback and in the mining towns were rumbustious and highly vocal in their likes and dislikes. In one of the bush dramas, *The Squatter's Daughter*, Mother had to wrestle with the two villains who were trying to steal some title deeds to land with buried treasure. Accidentally she clipped one on the chin, sending him sprawling into the footlights, and the audience rose and roared their approval. Next she had to scale a mountainside and make good her escape across a log bridge spanning a ravine. The Australian productions were immensely lavish and costly, with real sheep, real horses, and, in this play, a real waterfall à la Beerbohm Tree. Missing her footing on the log bridge, she fell twenty feet into the water tank below, making a spectacular splash and miraculously avoiding the edges of the tank. This brought the house down.

But she was fighting a losing battle to keep her hold on Roy's wayward affections. He had met us off the *Orsova* at Fremantle, and for a while, she writes, 'the old joy was there'. But eventually, what with women and wine – though Roy was, I'm certain, always highly professional despite his legendary drinking habits – the battle proved too unequal. Moreover, she says, 'he did not really care for you. The only child he ever really loved was Robin,' his son by Judith Kyrle.

Perhaps so, although he also doted on the son he had had by Miss C., and I fancy that in his erratic way Roy could have been a delightful, if seldom seen, father. Looking at him now in the two photographs I have of him, I see a tall, lean, muscular man, with the wry smile of the rover he knew himself to be. In one, a studio portrait taken in the costume of one of his bush dramas, he sits on a log, his bush ranger's hat perched on the back of his head, with curly, slightly receding hair, pipe in one hand, poking the embers of the fire with his stick in the other: wry, philosophic, manly, and sentimental.

As for me, he can have seen little of me in the sixteen months between my birth in Bristol and our meeting off the boat in Fremantle. Roy, I'm sure, would have liked to make me laugh, and that must have proved inordinately difficult. I was a very serious baby, and a solemn child, easily moved to floods of tears. Mother remarks that, when someone at the quayside asked, 'Well, Michael, and were you sick on the boat?' I answered, 'No, I was sick on the pillow.'

The tears proved very successful on my debut on the Australian stage at two years of age. I was to run on at the end of a monologue by Roy and cry out, 'Daddy!' Instead, after some agonizing pushing and cajoling from Mother and the stage management, I ran on, clung to his legs, and cried piteously. Apparently this went down tremendously well with the audience, though that certainly wasn't what Roy intended. The monologue is addressed to 'Little X':

> Oh X! Little X! Is it quite understood
> When you make your appearance, you'll have to be good?
> Great parcels of love are awaitin' yer comin'
> An' leave it to Dad for to set the house hummin'.
> There is no one 'in front' but shall know that you're here
> So just you take it quietly and 'leave the stage clear'.
> An' then when your poppa's exhausted your praises,
> *Then* throw out your chest an' yell at 'em like blazes.
> But it ain't etiquette in our bus'ness, that's flat,
> For to give 'em 'sensations' right in the 'first act'.
> Just you study Brer Rabbit; pretend to lie low
> 'Cos too much at the starting'll ruin the show.
> Mind, of all the 'big parts' a 'good character's' best

So strike out for that line, boy, and leave them the rest.
The drama called 'Life' you have got to appear in
Has plenty of howlin' and lots more of cheerin'
And althou' but a 'call boy' to start with you'll need
To remember that some day you're sure to be 'lead'.
Then, when pa and ma's played out, an' you see 'em pause
And you walk to the centre and hear the applause
Don't forget lad – in front – maybe 'up in the gods',
The old folk will be watching – you jest bet the odds,
And amid the applause that your ear then devours
You will hear them both whisper, 'He's splendid! He's ours!'

Roy was the author of several melodramas containing fat parts for himself. None, so far as I know, has survived. Of his verses I have – besides the monologue to 'Little X' – only two examples. The first is a ballad called 'Ghosts'. It is signed 'R.R., Kalgoorlie, 1905', the period of his first visit to Australia, and is the only piece of paper in his handwriting which dates from before the time he met Daisy. To whom it is written is not easy to guess, except that in 1907 he was writing to Daisy that he had had six years with Miss C.

Dear, is the daylight come so soon
Is yon pale gleam the dawn?
Oh say 'tis a glimpse of the pallid moon
Thro' the curtains closely drawn.

More light, more wine: let the music chime
And the feast again begin.
With song, with kiss, keep back the time
When day and ghosts come in.

For there in the dawn stand spectres twain
That will not be charmed away;
The ghosts of two in the night-time slain
And they only walk by day.

A fair white maid and a man with her
Like a murdered king and queen:
The ghosts of the woman that once you were
And the man I might have been.

I would – if pressed – part with most of the few mementoes I possess except for this one, so redolent of Roy, and of the morals and gestures of his time.

The other poem is Roy's own epitaph. Amongst the letters preserved by Mother, I found a cutting from the Sydney *Morning Herald*, headed ROY REDGRAVE'S RETROSPECT – DEAD ACTOR'S LAST LINES.

Shortly before his death in a Sydney hospital on May 25th [1922], Roy Redgrave, the popular actor, wrote the following:

> One of the best! Held his own 'in a crowd',
> Lived like the rest (when finances allowed),
> Slapped on the back as a jolly fine sport,
> Drank any tack from bad whisky to port.
> Fool to himself – that's the worst you can say;
> Cruel to himself, for the health has to pay.
> Months back he died, and we've only just heard,
> No friends by his side just to say the kind word.
> No relatives near and no assets at all,
> Quite lonely, I fear, when he answered the call.
> One of the best. Held his own while he could.
> Died like the rest, just when life seemed so good.

II

A YEAR after our arrival in Australia, Mother and I were on the P. & O. liner, second class, returning home. It must have been a hard decision for Daisy to leave Australia. She had reached the end of her contract with the Phillipson management. If she renewed it, they would no longer be obliged to pay her passage home, and she knew she could never save enough to pay for it herself. Roy was hopeless with money, and Daisy was regularly having to settle his debts. If she left, she was sure she would never see Roy again. Was it perhaps the image of me, peering through the bars of my cot, which tipped the scales?

Roy wrote to her only once after her return to England, the one letter of his which she never kept.

Returning home also on the ship were a company of English actors. They had been in a comedy which had failed. One of them, an actor called Kenyon Musgrove, was a friend of the actor-manager Arthur Bourchier, who owned the Strand Theatre in London. Musgrove and his company were travelling first class, but the Captain allowed us to join them in the first-class compartments, except at mealtimes. Mother and Musgrove made friends, and he promised her an introduction to Bourchier when we reached England.

When the ship put in at Colombo, Mother made another acquaintance, which was to change both our lives. J. P. Anderson had gone out to Ceylon as a young man of eighteen in the employ of the Ceylon and Eastern Agency, and, now in his late forties, was returning home. He had made his money; he was 'well off' – though with a person so unostentatious, estimations of the actual size of his 'small fortune' varied. 'Andy', one may be sure, was commendably reticent about Roy, and in her notebooks Daisy claims that she 'never reviled him'. Andy did, however, ask Daisy about her marriage and, one night in the Mediterranean, over a brandy, confided that he had lived with a native woman in Ceylon whom he had since provided with an income which would at least ensure that she would never want, and that she and her two daughters would live, by Singalese standards, very comfortably.

He presented Mother with a Maltese lace handkerchief, first prize for a fancy-dress competition on board in which she appeared as Trilby and I as a pierrot. By the end of the voyage he had given her the address of his London club, and said that he would like to meet her again.

They did meet, two weeks later, at the Café Royal. Mother wore a stage frock and borrowed three and sixpence for a taxi from our landlady. With mounting anxiety she watched the taxi meter as the fare clicked up; but all was well, Andy – 'good man' – paid the fare at the other end, and paid her return fare, too.

There were many of 'our calling', as Mother's friend Allan Aynesworth would say, at Mrs Gold's establishment in Faunce Street, Kennington. I remember Mother – how beautiful I thought she was, and beautifully-dressed! – standing on the pavement outside our lodging, handing out sweets to the boys from the neighbourhood. For years I used to think of that pavement as unusually broad. In fact, as a recent visit showed, it is of the usual narrow dimensions, and Mrs Gold's must have been small and cramped. But to Mother and me it was the best of all possible digs. We shared a bed in a room at the back on the first floor. Every morning Florrie, the maid, would come pounding up the stairs with our breakfast and I would pinch Mother awake, shouting, 'Here comes Florrie with the breakfast!' It seemed heaven.

Mrs Gold was a wonderful gossip, and there was plenty for Mother and her to catch up with – the tragedy of Mother's parting with Roy in Australia, her anxieties about the future, what had happened in the theatre in her absence.

We were penniless, and Mother desperately needed work. A pall seemed to hang over the house in Faunce Street. Many of Mrs Gold's other lodgers were in the same plight, and, after a day of traipsing round the offices of theatrical managements, the actor's expressive face could tell 'volumes in folio'. But at last a job lifted its head, and in five minutes all woe had been forgotten. Adderley Howard, Roy's stepfather, not a noted actor but quite a successful one, gave Mother a part in one of his sketches. That tided us over for a few weeks, and then came a tour with a melodrama, *Two Little Vagabonds*.

First date on the tour was Sunderland. It was winter and bitterly cold. I was swathed in an overcoat many sizes too large, lent me by kind Mrs Gold. There must have been another play in town, because all the usual digs were full. Eventually, after hours of tramping about fruitlessly, we came to a pub where the publican's wife took us in and gave us a huge four-poster bed with a feather mattress, which we fell into. There had been a party for a working-men's club that night, and the landlady served us a supper of fish and cockle sauce – nothing had ever tasted better than that cockle sauce. We huddled up under the eiderdown and to get me to sleep Mother recited, as she often did, sometimes Shakespeare, sometimes Tennyson. 'A fool, a fool, I met a fool in the forest' – I loved that fool – and 'You must wake and call me early, call me early, Mother dear.'

Sundays was the 'train-call', when every actress on tour would put on her glad rags, hoping that some manager would spot her whilst she was changing trains at Crewe Junction.

We moved south, to Brighton. For the first time I was allowed to see a performance. At the curtain of the second act of *Two Little Vagabonds*, Mother had to take into her arms a small boy called Dick and, sobbing, cry out, 'Dick! My son! My son!' This was too much for me. With all the wrath of a four-year-old, I rose from my seat and cried out, 'He's not your son! I'm your son!' When telling this anecdote, Mother said that the other actors on stage 'corpsed' to a man, while a kind lady in the pit tried to lure me away by shaking a bottle of sweets, rattling it like a tambourine.

Our shipboard acquaintance, Kenyon Musgrove, proved as good as his word. Mother got her introduction to Arthur Bourchier, and was engaged to understudy his wife, Violet Vanbrugh, at the Garrick Theatre in the Charing Cross Road. A better job than it might sound, for it brought her within a step or two of the West End stage, and in those days, as she complains bitterly in her notebooks, it was immensely difficult for a 'provincial' actor to gain a toehold in the West End. Fortunately, ailments were plentiful, and actors more inclined then than nowadays to take a night off if they were ill, so Mother managed to go on for Miss Vanbrugh on several occasions.

What a strange place the theatre seemed – those garishly-painted faces. I am backstage in my mother's dressing-room. So many women in varying states of dress and undress. One of them bends down to pick me up and I start to cry. Was it, as Mother said, fright at the strangeness of her make-up? Or the fear of a small boy that he might not recognize his mother in that gallery of painted faces?

Frightening, but fascinating. In those days the company manager would always give fellow-professionals free seats for the matinée if the house was not full. Tom Pitt, the company manager at the Globe and a great favourite of Mother's, gave us seats for *The Chocolate Soldier* in the stage box, and a nice programme-seller gave me an extra hassock on my chair to perch on, so I had a fine view of the stage. Half-way through the play, I could no longer resist the impulse to join in, and started to clamber over the side of the box onto the stage, only to be hauled away, protesting, by Mother and the programme-seller. Tom Pitt made amends after the show by pinching my cheek and saying, 'I can see you'll be an actor, Michael.'

We moved to a flat in Battersea, and a Miss Holland came to look after me. We were walking one afternoon in Prince of Wales Drive when an old lady stopped us, pointing with a shocked expression at my headgear. Though otherwise presentable, I had, so Mother thought, rather prominent ears, and she devised a sort of rugby player's scrum cap to flatten them.

'Did the little man hurt himself?'

I was about to reply when, without waiting for an answer, the old lady dived into her purse and produced a new penny, which she handed me. The incident must have made its impression on me. It was the first time I had been paid for dressing-up.

Mother now had a more regular income, though still very small, and for a while life was more orderly and settled. But it was a strain having to leave me in 'Mummy' Holland's care whilst she was at the theatre every night: there was the night she came home to find me delirious with fever; there were the nightmares of our house burning down. Was it for this reason that I was sent away to stay with relations? No doubt, though there was also another reason, of which I was to remain ignorant for some time.

Fortunately the Scudamores were very numerous. There was Auntie May, in Sheffield, which I remember only for the river Don and for the layer of soot which always coated the leaves. There were Uncle Norman and Auntie Bea at Wem, in Shropshire. Norman was a farmer, and the high spot of my stay with them was walking Ruth the cow to the county fair at Shrewsbury. Their daughter Joan was about my age, and we would play together, singing songs at the piano. Or, rather, I sang and played, and Joan, though I think she could play as well as I, would listen, since I insisted on an audience.

Together we would dress up, which was always my favourite game, making fantastic costumes out of crêpe paper. An old shed was our theatre. We must have been careless about tidying away our costumes, for I remember Norman in a fury at finding crêpe paper strewn all over the manger. It was the first time a grown-up had been angry with me, and it came as a shock, as Norman was usually so gentle and even-tempered.

Best of all, there was Portsmouth. Mother would tie a label, 'M. S. Redgrave, Portsmouth', on my lapel, and I would travel in the guard's van (safer and cheaper, she thought, to send me as a parcel than with a third-class ticket in a compartment). It was a grand way to travel. You could run about, dance even, or sit on the guard's stool watching the fields pelt by through his little bay window. And for additional company there were usually animals, or sometimes a pair of pigeons.

No 8 Victory Villas, Portsea, Portsmouth, Hants, was one of a row of terraced houses, back-to-back, with an outside lavatory and a tin bath in the scullery. But it seemed to offer everything a boy of six could wish for. There was Grannie Clara, and Auntie Annie, waiting on the doorstep to smother me with kisses. The Scudamores, all except for Grandpa, were great ones for kissing. And when all the hugs and kisses were done, everyone had to move to the front parlour, where the piano stood, and I was bidden on Mother's written instructions to play my parlour piece, Grieg's 'The Watchman's Song'.

Only Grandpa William, a retired shipwright, was excused this custom. It was understood that he was too old to want to negotiate the narrow passage which separated the front parlour from the kitchen, where he sat in his armchair by the window, reading that best of all monthlies, the *Strand* magazine.

Grandpa was awesomely silent. He was also awesomely deaf. A formidable character. Only once did I provoke a reaction from him. Auntie Annie had a second-hand-clothes shop on the corner of our street, and used to let me dress up in a suit, or long dresses, smelling strongly of mothballs. I put on a bonnet, cape, and skirt, found myself a stick, and hobbled back to our house, just as Grandpa was about to come out for his walk. The corridor was so dark that he didn't see at once who I was. Then, realizing it was I, he uttered a strange growl and raised his stick as if to smite me into the ground. Grandma appeared from nowhere to rescue me from Grandpa's sudden, amazing wrath. I thought she would scold him, but no – for the first and only time, she scolded me. Even Uncle Willie, whom I adored, was unusually silent that night.

Uncle Willie, a wainwright in the dockyards, was the bread-winner of the family. Two or three times a week he would give me twopence to see the pierrots on Clarence Pier. I loved the pierrots. But best of all was our trip to the music-hall on Saturday nights. Uncle Willie was a real theatre-goer. He used to hum a lot to himself, and on Saturday evenings, when he was shaving before setting off to the theatre, he became especially melodious, and his face, as we set off to see George Robey or Houdini or Little Tich, gleamed with excitement. Sitting in the gallery, I would roll up my programme and clasp it to my eye like a telescope, so that all I could see when the curtain rose was one face in the chorus. A sort of concentrated excitement gradually unfolded and flooded over me as I unfurled my programme wide enough to see the whole stage.

The War had started. Portsmouth, they said, with its naval dock-yards would be a prime target for the Germans, so I was sent to a boys' boarding school at Leigh on Sea, on the East Coast. Robert Blatchford, the socialist writer and the editor of the *Clarion*, lived next door. Mother was a socialist and admired Blatchford, so to Leigh on Sea I went, where the Headmaster gave me a sort of entrance examination.

He produced a shallow basket in which were tufts of different-coloured wool. He held up one of these and gently de-manded, 'Now, what colour is this, Michael?'

Though mystified, I gave a prompt answer. 'Red.'

'And this?'

'Blue.'

'Yes. Pretty colours, aren't they? Now what is this?' He dangled a mauve-coloured tuft before me.

I hesitated. 'It's a sort of blue.'

'*What* sort of blue?'

'Well . . . blue.'

'Dear me, the boy's colour-blind,' said the Headmaster. 'Now, I'd like him to meet my assistant, Mrs Joce. If he comes here, he'll mostly be taught by her. We'll just see . . . she may be busy. . . .'

He rose and conducted us to his study. Although it was a bright summer's afternoon, the blinds were drawn and the atmosphere was oppressively warm. Three or four boys were gathered round a lighted candle. Mrs Joce held a golf ball, which she twirled with three fingers whilst slowly revolving it around the candle.

'You see,' she said triumphantly, 'this is the way the earth moves round the sun. We call it the earth's *orbit*.' She went on describing the earth's daily journey, but one of the boys seemed to be trying to say something.

'What is it, Peter?'

'I'm sorry, Mrs Joce,' the boy called Peter mumbled, and then was neatly sick over his shoes.

Scarcely had Mother returned to London and her theatre when the Germans started shelling the East Coast, and she rushed back in a panic. She next deposited me at Cricklewood, in north-west London, where two maiden ladies, Auntie Lou and Auntie Gwen, took me in as a boarder. No 2 St Paul's Avenue was a large Victorian gabled building, housing about eight or ten young lodgers, who on the whole were a lively lot. There was Frank Bear, who was a nice boy with whom I shared a bedroom; and his sister, who was fun; and Peggy, a little girl of four who was so backward she could hardly speak, and whom we didn't include in our games because she seemed so slow on the uptake.

There remained the problem of my education. There was a convent of St Ursula in Cricklewood, with school attached. My acquaintance with it did not have much time to develop. It was the beginning of term, and newcomers to the convent school were each in turn introduced to the Mother Superior. When it came to my turn, I was determined to show myself at my best and, in a futile effort to be amiable, I put on a broad grin and uttered one word: 'Mummy.'

For three or four seconds everything went silent. Then the nun who seemed to be conducting the interview burst out (bobbing a curtsy to the Mother Superior), 'No, no, young man, that will not do! One addresses Mother Superior with respect. It is not a joke.'

I mumbled something.

'What's that you say? Speak up, young man.'

'I said, "Mummy".'

The Mother Superior's eyes closed in deep pain. With a low voice she murmured, 'Take him home. Someone must take him home.'

Some weeks elapsed before my next school was found for me. It was known as Mr Dove's and was not far from 2 St Paul's Avenue.

Auntie Lou was putting on my coat and scarf. We were getting ready for her to take me for my first morning at Mr Dove's.

'They say you're backward. But I don't believe that. It's just that they don't understand your jokes. They're Belgian, you see.' She chuckled at her own joke. 'But don't call the Headmaster "Daddy",' she cautioned.

On arrival at Mr Dove's, I found a huge classroom with some fifteen or twenty boys who did not seem to be paying much attention to the master. But Mr Micklethwaite knew what he was doing.

'I'm going to give you someone to help you. He's passed his exam, so he can teach you to read and write.'

He put me at the back of the class, where I was joined by Skipton, a jolly boy carrying an armful of books. 'Now, take your pick,' he said. 'You know your alphabet, I suppose? Here, take one of these. It's not difficult, you know. I'll soon teach you.' Skipton was as good as his word, and in a month I could read tolerably well.

I went to sleep clutching one of G. A. Henty's adventure stories, and, waking in the early morning, I was still clutching it and began to read on where I had left off. No word in my vocabulary then could describe my feelings as I absorbed Mr Henty's bluff magic. Reaching the end of the tale, I immediately turned back to the first page and imagined myself *Out in the Pampas* all over again. I remember my pleasure at my accomplishment in reading a whole book was strangely mixed with indignation that Mr Henty had somehow duped me. How dared he bring his novel to a close?

It would be fitting if I could claim that I had read all of the author's other works. After all, it was he and Skipton who had opened the gate to this new existence. But in fact I jilted him and transferred my affections to James Fenimore Cooper, and to the authors of *A Boy of the Limberlost, A Girl of the Limberlost*, and *Daddy-Long-Legs*. Frank Bear told me that stories like *Daddy-Long-Legs* were 'soppy' and meant only for soppy girls. But that did not shake my admiration one jot.

Amidst this plethora of words, two were missing: my name. And I decided to write a story myself. There was a children's paper called *Puck*, which I noticed was prepared to give two prizes for essays describing 'My Christmas Holidays'. I entered the competition and was awarded the second prize of half-a-crown. The paper's illustrator drew a picture of me, together with a picture of the girl who had won the first prize of five shillings. He did not manage to make much of a likeness. I had to be content with a back view of myself. But my main object was achieved. There ought to be a special word for people who like seeing their name in print.

My next effort was more ambitious. Mother was playing in H. B. Irving's company at the Savoy Theatre, in J. M. Barrie's *The Professor's Love Story*. When we met Barrie in the street outside the Adelphi, she introduced me to him, and asked if she could send him a story I had written. Permission was granted, and we waited to hear what the famous author thought. His reply, when it came, was a model of tact:

My dear Michael,
Your wicked witch put a lot of books on top of your story so I lost sight of it, but i have found it now and i like it very much. I am sending it back to u with many thanks for letting me read it, and some day i expect u will be the author of printed books if there is nothing better for u to do.
your fellow scribe
J. M. Barrie

One Saturday afternoon near Christmas, Mother collected me as usual from Auntie Lou's and took me on the bus to the Garrick Theatre. The show we saw that afternoon was a bewildering entertainment called *The CockyOllyBird*. After the show we went backstage to the girls' dressing-room. My eyes opened wide as, for the first time in my life, I saw a host of females undressing. But one in particular caught my attention, Joan Carr, a girl of fourteen or so with a mass of golden curls, like Mary Pickford's, and an enchanting smile. She had tea with us and afterwards took the bus back with us to Cricklewood. There, at Auntie Lou's, I kissed Mother goodbye till next weekend, and was hoping that Joan would kiss me too, when, to my astonishment, Mother kissed Joan goodbye, and I realized that she was going to stay.

'Your mother says you play the piano very nicely, Michael,' said Auntie Lou that night, tucking me into bed. 'Tomorrow Joan shall play for you.'

'That'll be nice,' I thought. But I little guessed what an influence this pretty child was to have on me. Within a few days she had become a sort of fairy godmother, and everything she did or said was remarkable in my eyes.

The next day, after breakfast, Auntie Lou, as promised, asked Joan to play for me; but Joan refused, saying she wasn't ready to perform at that time of day. Towards evening she relented, however, and played Rachmaninoff's most famous prelude. In later years she was to deny ever having played that hackneyed piece, but I know she did, and I remember the three opening chords as she played them that evening, which sent shivers down my spine. When she'd finished, I didn't know what to say. I gazed at her, dumbstruck. I had never heard music of that kind played 'live', as we would say now. When the time came for Joan to go to the theatre I begged Auntie Lou to let me accompany her, but she said, 'Another day.' Another day came and went, and day after day my wonder at such a magical human being grew. I remember with particular affection the sight of Joan, one January morning, wrapped in scarf and thick overcoat, holding a little box. What was in the box, I asked. 'Feel it,' she said. I put my hand to pick it up and nearly dropped it in surprise; it was a little charcoal burner, which Joan held in her muff. She was going to the rehearsal rooms of Rosenthal in South Audley Street for her weekly lesson.

She was a wonderfully accomplished pianist, and liked acting, too. She and I improvised ballets to the music of an old gramophone which Allan Aynsworth, Mother's actor friend, had given me, and plays, too, which we would write together. No two youngsters can ever have been more stage-struck. We knew what was on and who were the stars at every London theatre, learning the list off by heart from the daily papers.

One day she was absent from breakfast. I was told she wasn't very well, and that after breakfast I might tap on her door and hope she would soon be better. I raced upstairs and tapped rather loudly.

'Come in,' said a feeble voice.

'Auntie Lou said I could give you a kiss and hope that you'll soon be better.'

She was lying stiff and straight, and to signify that permission was granted she pursed her lips and closed her eyes. I tiptoed to the side of her bed. When I reached it she flung out her arms – still keeping her eyes closed – clasped me to her, and gave me the juiciest kiss I had ever received. When I recovered from this, I asked her what was the matter with her.

'I don't think you'd understand. You have to be grown-up to understand.'

'Grown-up?'

'Yes. Listen,' she whispered. 'I know how babies come into the world.' I didn't know what to say. 'I'll tell you one day.'

I was bitterly disappointed. I couldn't have cared less how babies came into the world.

'You may kiss me again.' Perhaps she sensed my disappointment. It was the first and only time she ever implied the difference in our ages.

The time came when Joan left Cricklewood. She was training to become a professional pianist. She promised that she would come back and see me from time to time, and would take me out to tea or to a cinema. I missed her greatly. There was no one to take her place, not even Hilda Bayley, an actress in H. B. Irving's company who treated me like a grown-up. I made one attempt to get in touch with Joan. Having somehow obtained her telephone number, I rang her up and asked her if she would like to come and play in the afternoon. She answered that she would have loved to, but that she was getting married on Wednesday. Some time later I asked Mother if she knew where Joan now was. 'She married a violinist. An Australian, I think.' Later I heard it said that she had gone into the theatre and was one of the sensational totem chorus in *Rose Marie*. Then the *Daily Mail* mentioned her name and said that she was in Hollywood. At the start of the Second World War her name figured prominently in the announcement of the BBC's newly-formed repertory company. And then there was an advertisement for Pond's facial cream, which stated that she used no other – she being by now dark-haired, so the picture in the advertisement suggested, and, what was more, a well-known society beauty. 'Viscountess Moore', said the caption. Could it be the same Joan I had known at 2 St Paul's Avenue? It could. It was.

Without Joan, life at St Paul's Avenue seemed rather flat. And then one day a car pulled up, driven by 'Uncle' Andy in his uniform of Captain in the Middlesex regiment. (He was too old for active service, of course.) He and I had had only a nodding acquaintance since meeting on the ship home from Australia. There had been a dinner one evening at the Café Royal, made memorable by the creamed rice pudding with a plentiful topping of hundreds-and-thousands they gave me. And then, early one morning, when we lived at the flat in Battersea, I glimpsed him in his uniform as he was leaving. And again one afternoon when Mother and I visited the barracks of the Middlesex regiment and Andy showed us round. 'So this is the son and heir!' had said a fellow-officer to Andy as we walked through the mess. Son and heir?

And here he was again, in a big black motor car with its hood up, calling for me at St Paul's Avenue.

The motor car was the symbol of another life, something very grown-up and very sophisticated. And good heavens, look at Peggy, what was she dressed like that for? Poor dumb Peg, so backward she could still hardly speak and was never allowed to join our games, dressed heaven knows why in a party frock.

'Would you both like to go to the Trocadero tonight ... or tomorrow?' asked Andy.

'Troca-what?' I asked. Andy laughed. 'Is it Tamil? Ask me if I can speak Tamil, Uncle Andy.'

'Can you speak Tamil, Michael?' he asked, dutifully.

'*Collipa pumbli, collipa ambli, collipa ahl,*' I said triumphantly.

'Fancy your remembering that.'

I examined the car and sounded the rubber bulb of the horn several times until Auntie Lou told me to stop. It made a noise like a sick cow, reminding me of Ruth, one of Uncle Norman's cows at Wem.

The two aunts waved us goodbye.

'Where are we going?' I asked Uncle Andy.

'You'll see.'

'Where's Mother?'

'At home. Shan't be long now,' Andy replied.

I imagined he must mean Shepherd Market in Mayfair, where Mother had rooms and I would visit her at weekends. But no, we drew up outside a different house, 9 Chapel Street, with Mother waiting for us on the doorstep. I was bewildered. Mother looked worried, and so did Uncle Andy as he brought in our bits and pieces of luggage. In this he was aided by a young woman with a strange head-dress of crinkly white linen. I had never seen a domestic servant before, but Mother seemed to know her quite well, and called her 'Mary'.

'Now,' said Mother, when we were all in the house, 'would you like Mary to show you your room?'

Mary led the way up the stairs. 'This is the drawing-room,' she said, 'and here's a fine piano for you to play on. You'll like that, won't you, Master Michael?'

'It's a grand piano,' I said.

'So it is. So it is,' said Mary, who came from County Wicklow.

We went further upstairs, to a room at the back of the house, which Mary said was to be a nursery. Then she said, 'And here's your room, Master Michael.' It was a small room, with a brand-new, smart-looking bed and chest of drawers. Next to this we entered another bedroom, with two beds in it. The furniture here was altogether different, a bright white, with pretty transfers of butterflies and birds and cheerful children. 'And this is Miss Peggy's room,' said Mary.

I didn't like to ask why there was a room for Peggy. But when Mother and I were in the nursery alone, I was to discover. Mother sat in a big chair and drew me to her, brushing my forelock off my forehead. (For some years afterwards I was to bridle when she made this gesture.) She gathered me into her arms and we sat together in the big chair, and for a moment or two I thought she was about to cry.

When she spoke, her voice was soft and low. 'You see,' she said, 'Peggy is your sister. Your half-sister,' she corrected herself. 'And Uncle Andy and I, for better or worse, are married.'

I did not at once make out what this meant. She must have seen my bewilderment and, putting on a stauncher tone of voice, she extolled some of Andy's excellent virtues, his kindness, his honesty : 'He is . . . a man you can trust.'

After a long silence I hesitantly said, 'Are we going back to Australia, then ?'

'No, my darling, no,' she said, and hugged me. 'Now,' she said, 'I want you to go downstairs to the morning-room, where Uncle Andy is, and sit on his knee, and give him a kiss, and call him Daddy.'

I do not remember what Andy said when I perched myself on his knee and kissed him on his tobacco-smelling moustache.

As for Peggy, my half-sister, how and when had she come on the scene ? I remembered that, some time before, when Mother and I were staying at a friend's house in Pinner one weekend, I had said, 'Race me !' and set off down the lawn. I had looked back at Mother, and noticed how heavy she had become, and out of breath, though still beautiful. But that was long before Joan Carr offered to teach me the facts of life, and I had thought nothing of it.

The other occupant of the white night-nursery, furnished by Heal's of Tottenham Court Road, turned out to be a formidable lady with leg-of-mutton sleeves, long since out of fashion, and a way of giving emphasis to platitudes which I thought plain silly. I ragged Miss Goss unmercifully. She insisted on reading to me, despite the fact, as I reminded her, that I was now quite capable of reading for myself. But nemesis was near at hand.

The Germans started to bomb London again, driving the population underground and into the Tubes. Andy decided that the whole household at Chapel Street should huddle under the kitchen stairs in the basement. I rather enjoyed this, and knitted half a balaclava helmet, while Mary the parlourmaid kept us amused with tales of County 'Wickerlow'.

Miss Goss was given her notice. Why, I don't know. She reacted waspishly. 'Your name is Scudamore . . . a foreign name, isn't it ? One has to be so careful these days, don't you think ?' (A wave of xenophobia swept London in the War, especially after the bombing.)

Mother came swiftly to the defence of the Scudamores. 'It's a French name. The French are our allies. The name means "shield of love" – *scutum amoris.*' Mother was very proud of her name. On the landing at Chapel Street hung a photograph of 'Poor Dadda', Fortunatus Augustin Scudamore, in the regalia of the Norman Conquest. Harris Scudamore, another relation, had almost bankrupted himself trying to prove that we latter-day Scudamores were descended from the Norman invaders.

It was about this time that Mother changed her name from Daisy to Margaret, more suitable for the West End actress she wanted to become, and which, at this time, she gave every promise of becoming. When she played Lady Bracknell at the Theatre Royal, Haymarket, however, in the first revival of Wilde's masterpiece, *The Importance of Being Earnest*, she was considered too young. She never, in fact, became a leading lady.

As for Andy, he never really came to terms with the theatre. Unfortunately for his and my relationship, I cared for little else.

Best of all, I loved my visits to the Savoy Theatre, when Mother was in H. B. Irving's company. I had the unique experience of watching H. B. playing his father's most celebrated role, Mathias in *The Bells*, from the flies. I could sit up there with a couple of stage-hands, behind the great double doors of Mathias's inn. Far below was the figure of Irving, bent double, agonizing in the front of the stage. Even the big black satin head-dress which, from my vantage point, completely obscured my mother's face, became a symbol for my imagination. Was not that paper snowstorm, falling gently from the flies, part of my creation?

It was a Sunday afternoon in autumn. Andy was away in Scotland, fishing or shooting. Mother was out. Peggy was staying with friends. I was an inquisitive boy. Some impulse prompted me to satisfy my curiosity by looking in Andy's bedroom. It was dull and sombre, in its way as forbidding a place as the dining-room. I saw it each day before school, when Peggy and I had to wish Andy good morning, but at other times it was – without, of course, anyone's saying so – out of bounds.

It smelled, faintly, of Andy, of the Gold Flake cigarettes he smoked through a cherrywood holder. On the mantelpiece were twelve elephants, carved in ivory. I used to picture their originals sitting in a row in front of his bungalow in Ceylon, trumpeting for Andy. Indeed there was a touch of the elephant about Andy himself, with his long Scots nose and heavy feet. On the chest of drawers was a medicine bottle with some colourful pills. These dated from the occasion when Andy had had hiccups for three days running, and we had to tiptoe into his bedroom to pay our last respects, and Mary and the staff crossed themselves and spoke with lowered voices, for it was understood that after the second day of hiccups a man might die.

The wardrobe contained Andy's suits, overcoats, shoes, and, on the top shelf, two or three hats. In the chest of drawers I found gloves, scarves, etc. I had never seen Andy wear spats, but there were two pairs of them. And what was this – a watch-glass? Screwed rather clumsily into my eye – an eyeglass! The monocle effected an instant change in my personality. I grabbed a grey Homburg hat, which, somehow, besides being too big for me, failed to produce the dashing effect that such a hat can bestow. But when I turned down one half of the brim and set the hat at as rakish an angle as it could bear without actually falling off, a character began to emerge. I turned my attention to the spats.

> I'm Gilbert, the Filber , the knut with a 'K',
> The pride of Piccadilly, the ladies' roué . . .

I stood back from the long mirror to see the total effect. Spiffing! I raced downstairs, nearly forgetting an essential prop – you couldn't be a knut without a cane. I selected a Malacca walking-stick from the hall hatstand and strolled up Chapel Street to Belgrave Square. There were very few people about in the Square – in fact the only time I ever saw a crowd in Mr Cubitt's masterpiece was on the day of the peace procession – so I shifted my ground to Grosvenor Gardens, and then into Hyde Park. On a Sunday morning, surely, they would be riding in Rotten Row? They were, but neither riders nor pedestrians took the slightest notice of me. It was all rather disheartening. I strode on to Piccadilly, intending to walk as far in an easterly direction as Lyons' Corner House, where I would treat myself to a Snowflake Sundae – ice cream, whipped cream, and shredded coconut, with a white grape on top. Here I got a polite nod from an old lady – I always seemed to attract old ladies – who stopped stock-still, looked at me, smiled, and shook her head. Not at all the effect I was hoping for. Crestfallen, I tried limping. But now I had become self-conscious, and cutting short my walk I scuttled back to Chapel Street. I tried to enter unnoticed by the basement door, but was met by Mary the parlourmaid. 'You've missed your tea. I'm off to confession.'

Andy had his two clubs, the Badminton and the Junior Athenaeum, and doubtless he had friends there. But in the evenings, alone with his beloved P.G.Wodehouse, that most prolific of authors whom Andy would curse for not writing enough books, he seemed to have no friends to invite to dinner. No one ever 'dropped in' to see Andy. Even on Peace Night, when every room in Chapel Street was crammed with friends, I remember only one friend of Andy's, a Major Papillon.

No, he didn't care for the theatre. Mother would book seats for the three of us, Andy, Peggy, and me, for plays such as *The Cat and the Canary*, or musicals like *Lady Be Good*, or *Hit the Deck*, and these were thought to be sensationally good. But not by Andy, who found them noisy, and who didn't much care for an American accent wherever he found it.

'Yes,' he would say, 'I liked it very much ... but you know it can't compare with the musical comedies I saw when I was a young man on leave.'

'What were they, Daddy?'

'Oh, you know ... things like *Les Cloches de Corneville* ... Ah yes, now! I'd give the whole lot of your American comedies for one night at *Les Cloches de Corneville*.'

Later, when I was an undergraduate, we had the chance to prove the worth of this exchange, for a season of old operettas was announced for the London Casino Theatre in Soho, and to open the season was dear old *Les Cloches de Corneville*. I bought two tickets and offered to take Andy as a birthday present. The curtain rose on the first act and my heart sank. The scenery was out of date and looked as though it needed more than one new coat of paint. The star of the show, Hayden Coffin, had no doubt shone in the original English production, but time had not dealt kindly with him. Nor did his name – no fault of his – do much to set the bells of Corneville ringing. The male chorus, representing the male population of Corneville, seemed embarrassed at the endless 'ding-dongs' of the show's hit number. Somehow we sat it through to the end. 'Those fisher-folk were rather fishy,' I said as we left, trying to cheer Andy up.

'Times change,' said Andy – sadly, I thought.

III

A T CHAPEL Street a new school had to be found for me. It turned out to be Gladstone's, a preparatory school for about fifty boys, conveniently nearby, in Eaton Gate. There was a mistress who taught the smaller boys; a Mr Vipan; and Mr Gladstone himself, a sweet man who seemed to find something humorous in the art of teaching boys. In winter afternoons, just before dusk, whilst we were finishing our essays, he would turn on the light on his desk and his gentle voice would strike a musical note as he said, 'Come ... with me.' A gratified murmur would run through the class. It was the signal for a story, or reading from some history book for about half an hour, and that was the end of work for the day.

We played soccer in a field somewhere near Acton. In summer we went to the Buckingham Palace Road baths (now demolished). Once or twice a term we went to the Natural History Museum, and at Christmas time, together with another school, we were treated to a performance by Maskelyne and Devant at their theatre in Langham Place. Once we went to the Chiswick Empire and saw a rough-and-ready performance by Ben Greet and his company of *Macbeth*.

The question of a public school eventually presented itself. This posed a slight difficulty. None of Mother's relations had been to a public school and Andy had spent too long away from England to feel confident of choosing a school himself. The question was referred, as often such questions were, to a friend of Mother's, Ruthie Harker, a pretty, jolly woman whose son Geoffrey was at Clifton and was said to be quite happy there. So I was put down for Clifton for the same House that Geoffrey was in.

Mr Gladstone sent a pleasant reference to my new school:

31

M. S. Redgrave has been a pupil of this school for the past two years and six months.

His conduct during that time has been excellent. He works well and is fairly advanced for his age.

He has great musical talent.

Nothing in that is remarkable, except perhaps the last sentence, and that needs some qualification.

At one of the concerts which my piano teacher, Miss Smith, organized for her best pupils, Mother, who was always very fair, asked why the audience hadn't applauded John Casson (the son of Sybil Thorndike and Lewis Casson) more than me. 'Surely he played better than Michael?' Mother asked.

Miss Smith agreed. 'But, you see,' she added, 'when Michael gets up to play, he starts to *act*!'

I did progress at the piano, however, and I was sent to the Royal Academy of Music in Marylebone to study with Harold Craxton. The great teacher approved of my playing but found that I had an almost insuperable problem. I was stiff at the wrists. To get expert advice on this disability I was sent to Tobias Matthay, who sat close to me on the piano stool and, when I was least expecting it, dealt a sharp blow from underneath at my forearms. Matthay showed me how they should fly up, if they were relaxed, so that only the weight of the hand went into the keyboard, allowing the wrists to rotate freely.

Richard Prescott Keigwin was the Housemaster of my House, Dakyn's, at Clifton. He combined the best mixture of scholar and athlete. He had been 'capped' at university for cricket and hockey and he was one of the few masters who had any semblance of being up with the times. His own house adjoined Dakyn's, and a small queue of new boys had formed in the passage connecting the two. A House Prefect organized the introductions.

'Ah, Redgrave,' said Keigwin, 'how is my old friend Gladstone? And that reminds me,' he went on, addressing the Prefect, 'the piano in the library badly needs tuning. I don't think our friend Redgrave would condescend to play on such an instrument.' He laughed in an easy, relaxed sort of way.

'You've been studying under Mr Craxton. Let's see ... what games do you play?'

'Soccer, of course. Oh! and cricket. I bowl a bit.'

'Good, good, splendid. It's rugger here, actually, as I expect you know. Well, you'd better run along. You'll be in the small dormitory. Our friend Bissell will keep an eye on you.'

'Thank you, sir.'

'Which study is he in, Bissell?'

'"D," sir. With Cundy, Charters, Clayton minor, and Wong.'

'Right,' said Bissell, as we left Keigwin's study, 'now for Gee-Gee.'

'Gee-Gee?'

'Mr Gee to you. Assistant Housemaster. An awful swank. But don't say I said so.' He knocked on Mr Gee's door.

'Enter!' said a sharp voice. Mr Gee was seated on a sofa with a cup and saucer in his hand. At his side was a big box of Bourbon biscuits. 'Have a biscuit,' said Gee. 'Take two.'

I did so.

Mr Gee seemed to have no wish to prolong the interview. 'That's all right,' he said, waving us away, 'show him his study.'

'This is the largest study,' explained Bissell. 'That's because it's for five people. You'll like Wong. He's the best three-quarter in the business.'

Wong was sitting on a window-seat. 'I've bagged this,' he said. 'I'd bag a chair if I were you. Have you seen our dormitory?'

Standing by a bed in the small dormitory was the Matron, who had already unpacked most of my clothes. 'Where did you get this?' she asked. Mother had packed my clothes in a theatrical skip, instead of the prescribed trunk, insisting that it would last for years. It looked like a large laundry basket, with my name, 'M. S. Redgrave', painted in big bold black letters on its lid.

'Mother thought it would be more practical,' I mumbled.

'Are you fond of animals?'

'Um . . . yes.'

'Good. I've put you on "Zoo-side".' She indicated which was to be my bed, and at that moment a piercing cry came from over the road. 'Peacock,' said Matron.

'Zoo-side' was so called because it bordered the Clifton Zoo.

'Which reminds me,' she continued, 'how old are you, Wong?'

'Thirteen,' said Wong.

'I shall leave the light on in the passage . . . just in case . . . ' said Matron as she bade us good night. 'You'll soon get used to the menagerie.'

Later, when we were all in bed, we talked in hushed voices, and Charters and Cundy answered questions from the new boys.

Soon the others fell asleep. I was kept awake by the cries of the peacocks. For some reason I was reminded of one of Mother's favourite poems, Blake's 'Tyger! Tyger! burning bright / In the forests of the night.' (She had never been able to make me understand what 'fearful symmetry' meant.) There was no mistaking the sound which came from across the road. It was a huge belch proceeding from the cavernous jaws of a big cat, as if a clap of thunder had split the little dormitory, and there was I marching into the forests of the night.

I lost no time in writing home:

Dear Mother,

I am getting on fairly well. I didn't sleep at all well last night and woke up with a ghastly headache. There are four other boys besides myself in my study called Charters, Cundy, Clayton and Wong. Charters and Cundy are old boys who have been here for some terms, but Clayton is a new boy. I evidently don't have to have an order for my clothes, but the school shop is closed this afternoon.

I have not seen Geoff anywhere today.

I am by far the youngest in my form and am finding things rather difficult. It all seems like a dream and it seems very funny to wake up in the middle of the night and wonder where I am. We have a nice little study and everything is comfy barring the beds! They are rather like the bare ground!

I was tried for the choir this morning but they didn't quite think my voice was strong enough but I think I am in the choral society. This afternoon I went to the music school and played a few things to Mr Beachcroft and I am to go on Monday to arrange about my music lessons. We had to prepare Lesson 27 in the Old Testament this evening.

Auntie Bea's cake and tart are ripping and are much appreciated.

It was freezingly cold today and we went for a long run (compulsory) this afternoon, with nothing but a thin vest and short pair of trousers. It is absolutely true that when I came in afterwards I fell on my bed and did not move for five minutes because I was so cold and tired.

I have nothing else to say (except that I shall write to Daddy tomorrow) so here I will close.

      your loving son
      Michael

'Ah! The very chap I was looking for! You're Redgrave, aren't you? A little bird tells me that we have here the rival of the Divine Sarah. Are you she? Myself I am but a lowly stage-manager. But where would you be without me? Up the spout! One turn of the switch and you are plunged in darkness. What do you say?'

McOstrich was the humorist of the House, the wag. He saw that I was carrying a book, which he took from me.

'What have we got here? Mathematics! Who wants mathematics?' He went back into his study, saying, 'Come in here. Would you like to be in the school play?'

'Is there a school play?'

'Oh yes. One a year at Commem. This year, *The Critic*, by Richard Brinsley Sheridan. Produced by A. C. K. Toms. Lighting by McO., another Irish genius. Come in here. Shut the door.'

In exchange for my maths book, he showed me a book of his own. 'Now there! A fifth Irish genius, the greatest man in the English theatre, the scourge of the critics, the one and only George Bernard Shaw!' He sat down and burst into wild applause. And then abruptly dropped the bantering tone. 'Are you thinking of going on the stage?'

'Good Lord, no!' I said. 'My stepfather would have a fit.'

'But your mother's an actress, isn't she?'

'Yes, but that's different.'

'I tell you what,' said McOstrich, 'you come and do your early prep in here, seven o'clock every morning, and I'll introduce you to Toms. He listens to my words. *De Toms en Toms.*'

Mr Toms cast me as the second niece.

'Big School', a vast, cavernous building, with its painful acoustics and difficult sightlines, was totally unsuited for the presentation of plays of any period. The ventilation was almost non-existent. That summer we performed the school play in a heat wave, with bath-tubs filled with huge blocks of ice, and electric fans playing across them, assisting the general inaudibility. But none of these defects prevented me from having, as they said, a whale of a time. My only disappointment was that Mother, who was acting in the West End, could not be there. The second niece is not a very rewarding part, but I played her 'up to the hilt, and somewhat more,' said Mr Taylor, the geography master, who had a sarcastic tongue. He added that the second niece was undoubtedly pretty, though her looks were rather those of *une fille de joie*.

The part of the second niece would not make anyone's fortune, but Mr Toms was sufficiently impressed with my acting to promote me in the commemoration festivities the following year. As Lady Mary in Barrie's *The Admirable Crichton*, I made a discovery. Lady Mary is the eldest of Lord Loam's three daughters and, when the family is shipwrecked on a Pacific island, Crichton – the butler – takes over as chieftain, and Loam and his daughters and sons-in-law find their social roles reversed. Lady Mary, with bow and arrow, becomes the huntress and falls in love with Crichton. When finally a ship is sighted off the island, Crichton makes ready to signal to it. Lady Mary in an outburst of passion begs him to let the ship go, but Crichton is firm, and the family return to England and to their former social status. Accompanying them to the ship is a rescue party of marines, who arrive just as Lady Mary has made her passionate plea – 'Let the ship go, Guv! Let the ship go!' I found on the first performance – there were only two – that I was shedding Lady Mary's tears. At the second performance, the marine nearest me on-stage saw that I was crying and whispered from the corner of his mouth, 'Blubbing again!' I discovered that I could turn on the water taps at will. Laurence Olivier calls it 'the gift of tears'. A very doubtful gift: unless the text specifically calls for tears, they are better left unshed.

The day before the end of my second term, McOstrich told me there was going to be a grand party in the senior dormitory that night. He had thought of inviting me, he said, but had decided against it because if I were to be asked the others in the junior dormitory might feel left out. There was to be wine, and candlelight, and formal invitations, and it was thought that Barlow had shown a pretty wit in his acceptance: 'Yours, to the last cork.'

It was impossible to go to sleep that night with so much conspiracy seething up in the darkness. A sentinel had been posted to tiptoe up and down the staircase which led to Keigwin's part of the house.

McOstrich put his head round the door of my dormitory and beckoned. 'Come and look,' he said. The senior dormitory by candlelight looked like a scene from *Peter Pan*, with some of the revellers in masks, and I was disinclined to go back to the small dormitory. But McOstrich said no, I was not to be involved in any way and, rather to my surprise, kissed me on the forehead, something he had never done before. Then, with a gentle pat, he ushered me back to my own bed. He seemed perfectly sober then. This could hardly be said of him later.

I do not know how long I slept, but I was woken by someone sitting on my bed. 'Hello, McOstrich,' I whispered.

'It's not McOstrich, you silly little fool.' It was Simpson, the butt of the House. He leant over me and said, 'Bloody good party.' His breath smelt absolutely foul.

'Yes,' I said, feebly, 'was it?'

His voice went on mumbling. 'Look here, I'm getting cold. Let me get into bed.'

I managed to slip out the other side of the bed and start for the 'rears'. I shut the door, bolted myself in, and waited for Simpson to go away. But he only became more insistent.

'Don't be afraid. I wasn't going to do anything.' He kept this up for about five minutes in loud whispers. 'Come on out. Come on, don't be silly.'

Suddenly there was another voice. 'Bugger off, Simpson.' It was McOstrich, sounding so drunk that I still didn't dare to unbolt the door. I could hear the sound of a scuffle. It became more vigorous and sounded as if at any moment it might develop into a brawl. There was the sound of a body falling on the floor and a groan from McOstrich, and the outer door of the 'rears' slammed. I swiftly unbolted the door of my cubicle and knelt down beside McOstrich, shaking him by his shoulders. I could smell the wine on his breath and, prig that I was, became angry with him. I slapped his face two or three times. To my surprise it seemed to rally him a little.

'Don't do that,' he said, 'stop it.'

'You're drunk,' I said.

'Of course I am. Bloody good party.'

'Come along, Mac, get up.' With difficulty I hoisted him to his feet.

McOstrich suddenly laughed.

'What are you laughing at?'

'You. Helping me. You don't know how funny that is.'

Mother was able to see me in only one of the three remaining plays during my time at Clifton (as Lady Macbeth, Mrs Hardcastle in *She Stoops to Conquer*, and Captain Absolute in *The Rivals*), and it may be that my performance as Lady Macbeth made her think twice about my becoming a professional actor. In her notebook she recalls a piece of business from the sleep-walking scene: 'you not only really seemed to be asleep, you bowed your head just before the end of the scene and your head seemed to drop as though you were tired to death. . . . It was a lovely bit of business.' Yet she had always been firmly against my becoming an actor. I was 'too tall', the stage was 'no life for a man'. This last, of course, referred to Roy. The shadow of my father haunted her until she was an old woman. I have already mentioned her fear that I might become like him. And to this was added her concern for what might displease my stepfather: 'the

37

master who produced the plays was terribly keen on your being an actor and begged me to send you to Oxford or Cambridge and then let you go on the stage. Good advice, I am sure, but I knew Andy would be against it, so I did not encourage the idea.'

IV

I F I SET aside my early trip to Australia and back, I suppose my first foreign holiday occurred when I was about sixteen, when Mother, Andy, Peggy, and I went to Normandy, to the small, delightfully-named watering-place Veules-les-Roses, where we stayed at the important-sounding Hôtel des Bains et de la Plage, a small, second-rate hotel near the sea. The bathing was poor, off a shingle beach, backed by chalk cliffs. The hotel food was sometimes suspected of being of equine origin, dressed up with watercress.

But it was 'abroad'. There were charming, poppy-sprinkled walks through the fields at the top of the cliffs. There was a 'casino': a rather shabby affair where one could dance to a trio, and an inner room where the grown-ups could gamble for small stakes. 'Yes, We Have No Bananas' was the rage of Veules that year and I danced to it evening after evening with a beautiful, tall, dark American girl with the Shakespearian name of Mary Arden Stead. I imagined myself to be in love with her, and I do not think she was averse to me. She was, perhaps, three or four years older than I, and several years more worldly-wise. On an excursion to Rouen I bought her a bracelet of olivewood, marked 'Jerusalem'. Her embarrassment at being presented with this dismal object must have been keen, but she concealed it well enough and certainly wore it that evening. A very sweet young woman.

However, she was not to be the visiting star of that holiday. When we had been at Veules-les-Roses for about a week, Andy broke the news that the son of the British Prime Minister, Stanley Baldwin, was expected.

Oliver Baldwin was a socialist and had been canvassing as a Labour candidate for Dudley, a constituency close to his father's. That he was known to be Labour was sufficient to damn him in my stepfather's opinion; that he should attempt to win a seat on the

39

opposite side of the House to his father, the Prime Minister, placed him, as Andy put it, 'beyond the pale'. This was enough to make me prepared to like him.

In a day or two he arrived. Tall, with straight, reddish-gold, silky hair, a trim officer's moustache, and pale but piercing blue eyes, he had an air of distinction and, indeed, beauty which would not have disgraced a pre-Raphaelite hero. He was accompanied by two other young men. The elder of these was a florid, merry-looking fellow of about Oliver Baldwin's age. The younger looked very singular. It appeared as if his head had been shaved or closely cropped. He looked what later would have been called 'butch', but 'butch' with a difference. That long scarf, flung round his neck, those birdlike, roving eyes, the drop of his hand over the back of the dining-room chair . . . he seemed a singular travelling companion for the two stalwart men.

One afternoon I was strumming away on the piano in one of the lounges of the hotel, sight-reading some simple music which I had found in the piano stool. When I stopped for a moment, a light voice from behind me said, 'You play very well. Do go on.' I turned and found 'Master Silk Scarf' (as Andy had dubbed him) sitting in an armchair with his feet curled up under him.

I thanked him and added that I could play only with the printed music in front of me. Not from memory or by ear. He disregarded this and, rising from the chair, threw his scarf over his other shoulder. 'Play me some Chopin,' he said.

'No, really, I can't. Not without music.'

'Do you know any of the *Valses*?'

'Yes, but I'm afraid I can't play any without –'

He cut me short by leaning forward and spreading his hands on the keys. I slid off the piano stool to make room for him. He sat and started to play.

He played very well in what, to my thinking, was rather a florid manner. His head and shoulders swayed and, for several seconds at a time, he would close his eyes during a few bars of rubato. I was rather given to rubato myself in my own playing and was inclined to over-indulge myself with the soft pedal. I thought he went altogether too far. I had yet to discover how far he was prepared to go.

He finished playing the Chopin waltz and paused for a moment or two. I hardly had time to say something in the way of praise before he started playing again, this time Rachmaninoff's showy and pianistic 'Polichinelle'.

'Oh, I play that,' I interjected.

He stopped immediately. 'Then *you* play it.' He rose abruptly from the piano.

'It's no good,' I said, 'I can't – '

' – without music, I know. But I don't know that I believe you. You're too timid, that's what's the matter with you, my friend.' In almost the same breath he said, 'Come on. Let's go for a walk.' He redraped his scarf.

The word 'timid' had done the trick. No boy likes to be called timid. I did not particularly want to go for a walk with this rather extravagant-looking young man. Suppose I were to meet one of the family? How could I introduce him, not knowing his name or anything about him except his piano-playing?

We walked up the chine of Veules-les-Roses on to a road hedged with poplars running between fields of corn and poppies. He asked me my name, where I lived, where I went to school, who my family were: He told me he lived at Sidmouth with his mother. I asked him how he came to know the Prime Minister's son.

'Oh, don't!' he said, rather petulantly. Then, suddenly, 'Oh, God, I am *so tired*. Let's sit down somewhere.'

There was no comfortable place to sit down except against a haystack. I thought for a moment, Aha! Here we are, back at school again. But the word 'timid' still had a slight sting. We sat down and leant our backs against the haystack.

'Why are you so tired?' I asked, politely.

'They talk all night and I can hear them through the wall.'

'Who talks all night?'

'*They* do. My two gaolers.'

'Do you mean – '

'Yes. Johnnie and Oliver. They're supposed to be looking after me. But they talk all night and then wake me up at seven to order breakfast for them. You see, neither of them can speak French, even though they were at Eton together. They had all my hair cut off – I don't know what my mother would say if she knew. Shaven and shorn I was, like a lamb.'

'How awful. Why don't you tell her? Then you could go back home.'

'Mother paid for their so-called holiday – fares, hotel bills, everything. They were supposed to be looking after me, but they treat me like a skivvy. Oh, it's too tedious. I can't *tell* you.'

Looking back, I cannot imagine how I believed all this. The words 'pathological' and 'paranoiac' were unknown to me and, I fancy, to all but a minority in those days. Pansies were for thoughts.

I felt myself moved and indignant on Sidney's behalf. That was his name: Sidney from Sidmouth. It was not long before I was disillusioned.

Coming downstairs before dinner that evening, I heard footsteps behind me. They were accompanied by a grave, gentle, but authoritative voice.

'Redgrave. I wouldn't believe everything that young man tells you. Not if I were you.'

I stopped and turned and found myself facing the dastardly Baldwin.

'Well, I think it's rotten, *rotten*, the way you've treated him.' There was a tremor in my voice, and he smiled.

He did not speak for several seconds but seemed to be weighing the situation up. My outburst had left me slightly shaky with emotion.

'Would you like an orangeade before dinner?' he asked at last. The wind was immediately and completely taken out of my sails.

'All right. Thank you.'

We sat in the gravelled courtyard and he ordered two orangeades. Waiting for these to be served, he asked me what school I went to, how long I and my family were staying in France, and other politenesses. I told him that my father had been an actor. I said I thought Roy was dead. And then he explained about Sidney.

Sidney's mother, a widow and an invalid, seemingly doted on her only child. She wanted him to travel but could not accompany him. Baldwin had been a friend of her family for some years. She was also a friend of Rudyard Kipling, who was Oliver's godfather. (This impressed me vastly.) Hearing that Baldwin was going to France, she besought him to take Sidney along. This, said Baldwin, was easier said than done. The youth was not only a congenital liar, but his appearance, even on his home ground, was considerably daunting. On a tour of Normandy and Brittany there was only one word for it: impossible. The mother's request was acceded to, but on conditions. Sidney could not be given a complete *laisser-aller*: he must first of all cut very short his artificially-bright golden hair and promise not to make up his face. Not even in the evenings.

'You see,' said Baldwin, 'he was known as the "Painted Lady of Sidmouth".'

I was so taken up with this glimpse of a mode of life so different from that of my stepfather's house and the purlieus of Belgrave Square that I was late for dinner.

42

I was not questioned about either of my acquaintances, which was a relief, but an ominous silence prevailed until Mother, who was always the first to try to break the dreaded pauses, asked me what I had been doing all day. As it happened, the great *Lieder* singer Sir George Henschel was staying at the hotel with his wife and daughter, and I had met Georgina, the girl, that morning when we had discussed the idea of getting up some charades in the lounge one evening. It was my idea. Inflamed by my success as Lady Macbeth in the school play, not to mention an hysterical Clarence in the murder scene from *Richard III* in the Christmas-term House Play, and a French maid in one of my Housemaster's one-act French plays, entitled *Par un Jour de Pluie*, I was always thinking in terms of 'theatricals', as Andy called them.

I revealed my and Georgina's general plan.

'You'd like that, wouldn't you, Peg?' said Mother.

I had not even thought of including my half-sister in the project. Peg was shy, but game.

'*Rather!*' was all she replied, without great conviction.

'When are you going to play this game?' asked Andy.

'Oh, it isn't a game exactly. More like a performance. We shall rehearse it all first.'

'A performance! Who's going to watch?'

'The residents.'

'You mean French people?'

'If they want to. There are heaps of English in the hotel. Of course, they'll have to pay. Same as the English.'

'Pay!' Consternation mounted. 'You won't get many if you make them pay.'

'On the contrary. Lots more.'

Mother reverted for a moment to being a 'pro'. 'There's something in what he says, Andy.'

There was a pause. Then Andy said, 'What will you do with the money?'

I hadn't thought of that. 'We haven't decided. We shall only charge a few centimes, anyway.'

For the rest of the meal I talked about Georgina's father, Sir George, who, it was reputed, at the age of seventy and even though he smoked cigars, could still sing 'Erlkönig'. When I told Georgina that my Housemaster had a record of him singing 'Erlkönig', she persuaded him to sit at the piano and sing it for me. His cigar lay in an ashtray and was still alight when he finished. His voice sounded much the same as on the old record, the cries of the dying child as passionate. 'When you have learned to sing a song properly, you can always sing it,' the old man said. 'It's like riding a bicycle. A bit rusty, perhaps, but it still goes.'

Georgina and I invented and rehearsed the charades. I had put up a notice in the lobby and we had a full house. (No cinema and, of course, no television. Nothing much else for the guests of an evening.) After the performance, when the audience was dispersing, Baldwin invited the cast to orangeade and ices in the courtyard. He asked us if any of us liked ghost-stories. 'Oh, yes!' some of us said.

We were all elated by the success of our charades, and the beach-huts were only a few yards down the road. About eight of us packed into one of them. It was completely dark, and there were squeals of pretended fear and some giggles. Baldwin waited until we were all seated on the floor.

'No whispering,' he commanded. The whispers died and he held a long pause.

The stories he told us were simple and in themselves not very alarming, but his voice had mesmeric overtones and he cleverly underplayed his narrative and would make a slight hesitation before each climax. When he thought we had had enough he was begged for more, but he said it was time some of us were in bed. He would tell us another story the next evening.

As we sauntered back to the hotel, I plucked up the nerve to say to him, 'You ought to have been an actor, Oliver, don't you think so?'

'As a matter of fact, yes, I do. If I could be smuggled into England as, shall we say, a well-known Polish actor, I'd show them how to play Richard the Second, or Hamlet.'

'Yes! Wouldn't that be marvellous?'

'I'm not serious, Michael. It would be impossible, anyway. For better or worse I'm too well-known. Anyway, I have other things that have to be done.'

I sensed that this meant politics and thought it better to keep my mouth shut about these.

'I suppose you're a Tory, like your stepfather?' he asked.

'Well . . . I don't think about it very much.'

'We can talk about it some time, if you'd like to. Shall we go for a walk tomorrow, after lunch?'

During this conversation the others had called good night or simply disappeared. Johnnie Boyle came up to us as we reached the hotel.

'Michael thinks I should play Richard II,' said Oliver.

'He'd be not bad, you know. Marvellous, in fact. He's read me a lot of it, especially the prison scene. But then he knows all about prisons. Or should do, by now.'

'We won't go into that,' said Oliver. 'But there's one thing I'm sure of.'

'What's that?'

'Michael should be an actor.'

The next day, the three of us set out for a walk. I did not ask where Sidney was, but Johnnie implied that he had gone or been sent home. We walked along the top of the cliffs in the direction of Saint-Valéry. We talked of this and that. But suddenly, Oliver, who was marching along strongly, almost like the Guards' officer he had been, sat down on a milestone and said, 'Don't wait for me. I'll sit down for a minute. I'll catch you up.'

I was for stopping and waiting for him, but Johnnie tugged at my sleeve and said, 'Come on.'

As we passed out of earshot he said it was nothing to worry about, but that 'Noll' was not as robust as he looked. Not surprisingly, he said, after what 'Noll' had been through. I enquired, tentatively, what that might be.

After the Great War, when he had served in the Brigade of Guards, he had become deeply and actively involved in the fate of what Johnnie called 'poor, bloody Armenia'. He had risen to the rank of Lieutenant-Colonel in the Armenian Army and had been captured by both the Turks and the Bolsheviks, and incarcerated in six different prisons. From one prison he had been marched out to be shot and then, for lack of ammunition, marched in again. As a result of these experiences, Johnnie concluded, Oliver had a serious set-back in health. He would wake up in a nightmare every night, or groan and call out in his sleep. They had chosen to holiday at Veules-les-Roses as the best place for his recuperation because of its quiet.

I was knocked sideways by this brief résumé of Oliver's heroism and sufferings. I looked back to where he had sat down. He was already on his feet and walking towards us. We waited for him to catch us up.

When he came abreast with us he said, with a smile, 'No gossip, I hope, Johnnie.'

'I was telling him about your book.'

'Oh, that.'

I thought it was about time I said something. 'What's it called, your book?' I asked.

There was a pause. Johnnie answered: 'This one's called *Six Prisons and Two Revolutions*.'

I forget what Oliver said but he abruptly and firmly changed the subject.

Later, back at the Bains et Plage, an awkward little incident blew up which was embarrassing to all concerned and agonizing for me until it blew over.

It seemed that my stepfather had struck up a bar-room acquaintance with a friend of Oliver's. Andy's strong Tory prejudices still resented the mere presence of the young Baldwin in the same hotel, and I dare say something had reached him about the beach-hut entertainments. That the 'Bolshie' should be placed 'beyond the pale' was no longer strong enough. He should be 'horse-whipped'. The other man expostulated, presumably, and Andy calmed down sufficiently to say he would like to talk to the feller and would the friend convey an invitation from Andy asking the deluded young man to have a drink with him, even if this amounted to asking Oliver to step inside the 'pale' for a few minutes.

'Your stepfather has invited me to have a drink with him.'

'Oh, dear!'

'Don't worry. I shan't go, of course.'

My anxiety was by no means relieved at this. Oliver's non-appearance might be taken as a 'cut' and lead to anything.

He then related what was supposed to have taken place.

I was panic-stricken. 'Are you going to tell him why you can't go?'

He explained that, since the invitation had not been issued in person and had threats attached, he thought it better to ignore it. What he had seen of war and revolution had made him a pacifist.

'When the next war comes, as it will, I shall be proud to lead a regiment of young men sharing my convictions into prison.'

Good Lord, I thought, it's just as well if he *doesn't* meet Andy.

But when we met for dinner that evening, the dreaded subject of Oliver was never mentioned. I can only suppose that the friendly go-between had told Andy about his war service when under age, and his career as a Lieutenant-Colonel in the Armenian Army in the war, which had dragged on and which few spoke about because comparatively few had ever heard about it.

Then, one day, all too suddenly, Oliver and Johnnie left Veules-les-Roses. Life became very dull. Mary Arden Stead had found a new cavalier. The Henschels had gone.

But what I chiefly suffered from was not loneliness but impatience. For before they left, Johnnie had asked me to stay with them for a week during the remainder of the 'hols'. To apprise Andy of this, as things were, I should have had to pluck up more courage than I think I possessed. But Johnnie took the matter in hand. He was, if anything, more socialite than socialist and he had a very jolly way with him. He explained that their little house was in Oxfordshire, at Shirburn, quite close to his sister's place, Shirburn Castle – on the same land, in fact. Did Andy know the Macclesfields?

I do not mean that it was only this mention of his aristocratic relations that did the trick. Not entirely. For John Boyle, when he set out to charm, seldom had a failure. He remembered that I had said Andy usually went shooting or fishing at the suitable times. 'Where are you shooting this year?' he asked. That was what did it, though I think the Earl and Countess helped.

My stepfather simply said, 'Have you told your mother?' I said I hadn't, yet.

But Johnnie had another card up his sleeve. 'We must take him over to Chequers some evening.'

Chequers, I fancy, was brought in not only for Andy's but for Oliver's sake. Many people must have assumed that the Baldwins *père et fils* could not be on speaking terms, which was scarcely the case (as Keith Middlemas and John Barnes testify in *Baldwin: A Biography*, published in 1969).

Anyway, we did go to Chequers, as one of my childishly-written diaries records: 'This morning Oliver and I had a long talk about many things. In the evening we went to Checquers [*sic*] to dine.'

What we talked about that morning was Socialism and Sex. We were sitting in a little hut at the end of the garden, a place Oliver used for his painting and in summer for writing. A peacock and peahen were on the lawn.

'I have a question for you,' said Oliver, 'but I'm not sure you'll like it. Shall we toss a coin for it? If you win, you don't have to answer.'

For a moment I thought he was joking, but he looked deadly serious. 'All right,' I said, thinking it would be unsporting not to agree; besides, I was curious.

'Shall I ask you the question first or shall we toss first? I think toss first, don't you?'

This, I was too slow to perceive, was cunning of him, because if I won the toss I should be agog to know the undivulged question. So, like a fool, I said, 'Yes, let's toss first.'

I won the toss.

Oliver smiled. He knew he only had to wait. 'Well, then, I'll ask you another question: Do you believe in socialism?'

I hesitated and then said, 'I suppose so.'

'It's not a question of supposing, it's a question of belief. It's a positive question.'

'I don't know.'

'You haven't really thought about it, have you? You would believe whatever the last person told you, wouldn't you?'

'Oh, I don't know about that. . . .'

'Well, I do. But I could make you believe in socialism without much talk or argument. I could *show* you and you'd have to believe your eyes.'

'How?'

'Come with me for a day, or even a few hours, to Dudley. I'd show you the living conditions. I'd show you the difference between the privileged and the people.'

I couldn't help looking at the peacocks.

'Before Mother married Andy I used to see lots of poor people. In Portsmouth and . . .'

'It isn't poverty I'm talking about. I'm talking about misery. Britain is Two Nations: the Rich and the Poor.'

I expect Oliver may have used Disraeli's famous tag on countless platforms. He can seldom have found a more receptive listener than myself, ignoramus that I was. But from that day I could not politically call myself anything but a socialist.

When I returned home I was already a different fellow to what I was before I visited Shirburn. Of course, I played Shirburn Castle and Chequers for all they were worth and skirted round Andy's awkward and dreaded question 'Was the PM there for dinner?' with a line I had thought up on the train back to London: 'Oh, I would think he has far too much on his plate at the moment. Wouldn't you?'

Betting on the chance that Andy had no more idea of what the Prime Minister had on his plate than I had, I thought discussion of Chequers was closed. There was a pause in the conversation. 'What's he got on his plate?' asked Andy suddenly.

'Oh, you know,' I replied limply.

When I was reading in bed later that evening, I was surprised that Mother came into my room. She sat on the bed and her hand patted mine.

'Don't let him think you've become a socialist,' she said, with an anxious smile, 'it only makes things more difficult.'

'Yes, I know.'

'Well, don't, then. There's a dear. It upsets him terribly. He doesn't understand that one has these convictions when one is young. I used to be a socialist. Do you remember how I introduced you to Robert Blatchford when you were a little boy? He was a fine man.'

'Yes, I remember, vaguely.'

'You were only six.' She kissed me and I hugged her.

On the mantelpiece stood a framed photo of herself. Carelessly I had used it to prop up a photo of Oliver in front of it. As she rose to leave, it caught her eye. She looked at it and picked it up. I thought she was going to say something, but she didn't. She just laid it flat on the mantelpiece and said good night. I had not leant Oliver's photo there with any purpose of defacing hers. But there it was and there was nothing I could say without making matters worse.

Oliver was my first hero, and for a time he could in my eyes do no wrong.

My later memories of him are scattered, but somehow he always remained 'in character'. One characteristic was his desire to shock. Of this I became aware when gnawing curiosity made me ask him to put the question to me which I had escaped by the turn of the coin. I had thought he might be going to ask me something portentous.

And he did.

'Have you ever been to bed with a woman?'

I shook my head slowly.

'I think, if I were you, I would.'

V

IN THE 1920s it was commercial death for any manager to mount a production of Shakespeare in London, and no West End actor would want to be called 'Shakespearian'. Nor would Mother, I think, have cared for the label. Yet it was she who was largely responsible for the 'Fellowship of Players', an admirable enterprise which set out to perform, in London, the entire Shakespearian canon. The plays were cast from out-of-work actors, and sometimes leading actors if they could spare the rehearsal time. There were two performances: one on Sunday evening, and a matinée on Monday.

I was at a loose end. I had left Clifton in the summer of 1926 with no job to go to, and no particular prospects. When Mother suggested I might 'walk on' in *The Taming of the Shrew* as one of Petruchio's servants, I was over the moon, especially when I heard that Robert Loraine was to play Petruchio. Though not such a beautiful man as Henry Ainley, whom I revered and, alas, never met, Loraine was a wonderfully magnetic actor and a great favourite. The production, if you could call it that, was by Ben Greet, the staunch and much-loved Shakespearian.

I was told that I was to play the cook. Not much of a part, really, but Greet had inherited a surefire piece of business where the cook, on his name being called, was sent twirling from one servant to another until, at the end of the line, he almost fell into the arms of the dread Petruchio.

This I performed at the dress rehearsal to Loraine's satisfaction, I suppose. But at the first performance I was inspired to try something a little more vivid. Instead of being caught by Petruchio, I eluded his grasp, fell flat on my face, and lay winded and panting at his feet. This produced a big laugh. Loraine, I thought, mistook it for a genuinely accidental fall, though I was told by his dresser that he could see I was an actor's son by the way I held the fall and got a much bigger laugh. At the second performance I was all set to elaborate my pratfall, but Loraine was too quick for me: as I reached him he started to speak the next line and walked away a pace or two with a broad smile, taking the audience's interest with him.

Many years later I undertook Strindberg's *The Father*, which had not been seen in the West End since Loraine had made a tremendous success in it. My notices were good; some very good. Some, though good, said that my performance had not erased the memory of Loraine's. I myself could still picture Loraine vividly in the part. I was puzzled, however, by a mental image of him seated in a wheelchair. This I placed as coming from a curtain-raiser – Barrie's *Barbara's Wedding*. But why had he thought a curtain-raiser necessary? *Barbara's Wedding* played for at least half an hour, and *The Father* was long enough in itself.

I was haunted by Loraine. After the last matinée performance at the Duchess Theatre, I was visited by Loraine's widow. I asked her why Robert had needed a curtain-raiser. 'He didn't. But he thought he did.' He couldn't, she said, bear to be thought of as a weak man, even on the stage. So he cut every line of the Captain's which showed his weakness, thus turning the play upside down.

'But the critics . . . ?' I exclaimed.

'Ah, yes, the critics. Most of them, you see, had never read the play.'

And now, I thought, their knowledge of the play, for the most part, was the imagined remembrance of Robert's rugged, forceful, and highly-effective performance, which many of them had not even seen.

The results of my School Certificate examination arrived. I had failed. Andy, who had borne the expense of my five years' public schooling – and all for nothing, it seemed – never once reproached me for this dismal failure. In fact, he scarcely ever reprimanded me. He was never angry, and he tried hard not to be impatient; but one by one, every little thing that went wrong, or wouldn't work, came to seem – even if obliquely – my fault.

Two newspapers were delivered at number 9: *The Times* and the *Daily Mail*. The *Mail* was for the whole household; *The Times*, it was understood, was exclusively Andy's. One morning he was a little late taking his bath and I dared to take *The Times* into the lavatory with me. Something must have caught my eye, for I sat there quite a while, reading. As I emerged from the cubiculo I collided with Andy, who had been searching for his newspaper beneath the breakfast table.

'Oh, sorry, Dad,' I said, handing him the paper. Suppressed anger made his hand shake as he seized it from me. 'Sorry, Dad,' I said again.

'I suppose you know,' he said at last, 'that you would be turfed out of any London club for that?'

Mother produced a sort of careers brochure for school-leavers, and she, Andy, and I worked our way through its suggestions. Accountancy, architecture, bee-keeping (bee-keeping?) ... catering management, draughtsmanship, engineering ... The trouble was that to embark on any one of them I should need some qualifications, and I had none. As I leafed through the catalogue, the realization dawned on me that really I should like nothing so much as to do nothing at all.

Andy gave a sigh. 'Of course, there's always that.' He pointed towards the mantelpiece, to a watercolour of a Ceylonese scene. I looked at Mother in some astonishment. Andy caught my look. 'Of course, you're too young. But I dare say the Agency might stretch a point.'

There were a few seconds of silence. Andy went on: 'We could wangle it somehow, I'm sure. It's a fine life. You'd have your own bungalow, and servants. And the climate, well ... it's not like India. A beautiful place, really.'

'Sounds idyllic,' I said. So it did.

'Of course,' Andy went on, 'you'd have to ride twenty miles for your game of bridge.'

There was a long silence.

'Never mind,' said Andy, 'just a suggestion. Not the life for Michael, really.'

'Don't worry,' I said. 'I'll find something.'

I had, in point of fact, found something; or, at least, there was something there for the taking. It was Margot Dempster, back from Hollywood, full of vitality and 'oomph'. Margot was a friend of Mother's; in her late thirties, an independent woman whose job, I knew, had something to do with films. We had met the year before, on holiday at Pornic in France. She invited me to her flat and I arrived with a pot of chrysanthemums.

'You've grown,' she said.

'Everyone says that.'

Her manner had much changed. At Pornic, she had seemed always to be holding back. Here, in London, and with the aura of glamorous Hollywood still about her, she startled me at first. Before, she had kissed me on the cheek. Now she kissed me full on the lips, and went straight into a monologue about Gary Cooper, Norma Shearer, Clara Bow, Chaplin, and other personalities. She spoke with a hint of an American accent, an assumption which I found immensely pleasing.

'And what about you, Mike,' she asked, 'what are you doing?'

'Nothing very much.'

'British studios! You know they really take the cake! They keep you hanging about for hours. They've no idea of the value of publicity.'

'No ... I dare say,' I said.

'I'm seeing this man at Teddington on Wednesday. Now, if this were Hollywood, they'd have some creature to follow me around, carry my camera, run errands, look up telephone numbers. Chaplin always sent a car for me ...' Suddenly it seemed as if some important thought had crossed her mind. 'What are you doing Wednesday? Or Tuesday, for that matter?'

'Nothing,' I said.

'Well, would you do that for me? You know, run errands, look after me? How are you off for money? What does Andy give you?'

'Oh, well ... you know. ... '

'Strictly professional,' she said, slipping a five-pound note into my breast pocket.

A few days later she gave a cocktail party – 'Just a few chums. You must come, Mike.'

It was all so unlike Chapel Street, where a cocktail meant a rather weak Martini. At Margot's, cocktails were cocktails: Tom Collinses or Clover Clubs, served with Hollywood showmanship, the rim of the cocktail glass neatly coated with sugar. I downed three or four in rather quick succession. Suddenly Chapel Street seemed very far away, and very hard to get to.

'I'd sit down for a moment if I were you, Mike.'

'I think I'd better.' The other guests had all departed.

'I could put you up for the night.'

She wore black silk stockings, which were new to me; flesh-coloured stockings were the fashion then. I asked her why. 'I've a friend who likes me in them,' she said.

What followed, on the carpet in front of the fire, was new to me also, and would never have occurred to me without her guidance. Many years later, on a trip to Pompeii, I was reminded of it – at the *gabinetto pornografico*, where our guide tactfully dismissed the children. He pointed at one of the frescoes. 'You see?' he said. *'La donna è sopra.'*

It was Mother who procured half a dozen letters of introduction for me to take round Fleet Street, in hopes that one at least might provide the entrée to a career in letters. I gave *Punch* the privilege of first choice, and I felt quite cheerful as I entered a handsomely-furnished room – could it have been the boardroom? – where a smartly-dressed, youngish man shook my hand warmly and invited me to sit down. It was all very gentlemanly, and we spent a few minutes talking about the world in general; and when we had done with the world, he focussed my attention upon me. By degrees his suave manner changed, and he became rather brisk. He asked me what I thought *Punch* could do for me. I chuckled to show that I was quite up to the sub-compliment. A pause followed.

'Have you brought anything which I might read?'

I thought of poor feeble Mr Bate of Billingsgate, with his twenty-five rhymes on the syllable 'hate', and rejected him hastily.

'No, I'm sorry ... I wasn't expecting ... '

His manner became even more brisk. 'I'll tell you what,' he said, 'you send me a few things of yours, and I'll drop you a line when I've read them. Then, perhaps, we could meet again.' He rose and opened the door for me and shook my hand.

A telephone call put me in touch with Sir Ernest Benn, a big noise in Fleet Street, who, like the young man from *Punch*, was most cordial. After a little chit-chat he said, 'Now, let's talk about you. You have, of course, your School Certificate?'

'Er ... no, I'm afraid not.'

'Oh dear! It's rather a yardstick, you know, the School Certificate. Never mind, we'll soon find out. ... Tell you what, I'll give you a job on the *Western Farmer's Journal*. You won't like it, but it'll give you a toehold in Fleet Street, and that's the main thing. ... '

Next on my list was the publisher Mr Ivor Nicholson of *Nash's* Magazine, who was about to launch the firm of Nicholson and Watson. He was just leaving his office when I asked to speak to him, but he made time to see me the next day. I told him what Sir Ernest had said, and asked his advice about the *Western Farmer's Journal*.

'He's quite right, of course,' Nicholson said, 'you'd hate it there, I fancy. What are your languages up to?'

'To be honest, not much.'

'The trouble is,' he said, 'you have nothing to offer. Who sent you
to Clifton?'

'My stepfather.'

'Couldn't he send you to France and Germany for a few months?'

'I don't like to ask him,' I said. 'He suggested I be a tea and rubber
planter, though I don't think he's too keen on that, either. I really
don't think I can ask him to send me abroad.'

'Has he money?' asked Nicholson.

'Yes, he's well off.'

'Well, then, *I'll* ask him.'

To my surprise, Andy received Nicholson's suggestion with
something like enthusiasm. Later it occurred to me that he didn't in
the least mind parting with some cash – not such a lot by today's
standards, anyway – if it meant getting me out of the way. The
Orbachs were called in. George Orbach and his wife lived just round
the corner from us, in Chesham Street. With immense zest, George,
being German, went into the salient characteristics of Munich,
Berlin, Leipzig, Mannheim, Hamburg. 'But of course,' he concluded, 'Michael would not be happy in any of these places. Let us
think of the smaller, artistic milieu, such as he would find – say – in
the Black Forest ... or Heidelberg. Aha!' he said, as he slapped his
plump thighs. 'Yes, Heidelberg! That is the place for Michael!'

If Ivor Nicholson's kindly interference had filled me with happy
expectation, George's enthusiasm for Heidelberg was like strong
drink. I couldn't contain myself; I danced round the supper table.

'You seem damned anxious to get away from us,' said Andy.

'Oh, no!' I said, suddenly realizing how much the whole project
depended on Andy's generosity. And it was hard to tell from his
look whether he was not suffering from some distemper, whereas
George – who, come to think of it, always took my side – was
wreathed in eupeptic smiles. He started to sing, '*Alt Heidelberg du
feine, du Stadt an Ehren reich ...* '

It was all so sudden. Had anyone ever sung before at that
forbidding table?

Mother came up to kiss me good night.

'Won't it be wonderful?' I said.

'It hasn't happened yet,' she said, 'but yes, it will be good for you
... for both of you.'

It came with something of a jolt to realize that she meant it would
be a relief for Andy, as well as for me. For a very brief moment I had
a glimpse of my own selfishness. The idea of Ernest Benn's offer,

though I felt I had to be polite about it, had filled me with distaste; worse, with rank boredom. And then I must have fallen asleep.

'Today, my friend Chichele Waterston and I went skiing in the Black Forest,' I wrote to Mother. We had set off in a train starting at about four in the morning, with a party of students from Heidelberg. Now, we were back in the acetylene-lighted hut which served as an hotel, waiting to pile into the truck which was to return us to the station.

The students started to sing, '*Ich weiss nicht was soll es bedeuten, dass ich so traurig bin.*' I felt rather *traurig* myself. What a waste the day had been. Another wasted day! For the hundred and first time, I resolved to work harder. Not for me, I thought, this suicidal sport. Better use could be made of my money by going to the theatre, or even the cinema. Better by far to steep myself in Goethe's mighty lines.

And who better to speak them than Maria Andor, grave of face and sweet of tongue, the leading actress at the Stadttheater? I wished a thousand times for the nerve to present myself at her stage door. I tried hanging about near the theatre, but never succeeded in exchanging a single word with her.

Later, when I left Heidelberg, I did catch a glimpse of her on the next platform, waiting for a train going in the opposite direction. I was on my way to Mainz, at the order of Andy. I was to bring my half-sister, Peg, back from Germany to England, with all possible speed. Peg, I should explain, had asked to be sent to Germany in my wake. Why she wanted to go I cannot now remember, nor why she had chosen Mainz. But now it appeared that she had fallen in love with a German doctor and was talking about marriage. She had written to Andy about this, and Andy had gone up in smoke. Peggy must return at once. It was arranged that he and I together should fetch her.

She met us at the station at Mainz, accompanied by an agreeable-looking fair-haired individual of very German countenance. Peggy immediately let forth a torrent of German, smiling and laughing till I thought Andy would burst. It came as something of a shock to realize that she spoke German far more fluently and idiomatically than I. Peg was staying at a small but rather elegant pension, while Andy and I were to share a room at the Vier Jahreszeiten Hotel. The four of us met for dinner, where again Peg kept up a stream of fluent German, Andy demanding of me all the while, 'What's she saying? What was that?' The trouble was I couldn't always follow what they were saying, and when this occurred, I was obliged to improvise.

Andy announced that they would return home in three days' time. I was ordered to organize the return journey through an itinerary which included Paris. This was intended to sweeten the prospect of Peg's enforced departure.

I was fond of my half-sister in a 'dear old Peg' sort of way, and was quite unprepared for the sight of the truly tragic young woman who presented herself on the station platform on the morning of departure. She had not shown, or I had not noticed, any great grief the previous three days, but now her tears and strange, choking, wailing sounds made me think that surely Andy would relent, or at least permit some stay of execution.

Feverishly she looked about for her doctor, and at last he appeared, running down the platform. As he approached, the train started slowly to move. It was all too much for Andy, who uttered the unfortunate expletive 'Good grief!' The train quickened its pace. Peg's doctor was left standing. He called out, in perfect English, 'Don't forget! Write to me!'

I returned to Heidelberg. But life at Fräulein Rauch's Pension Sylvaner now seemed humdrum. My fellow-lodger Chichele Waterston had gone for two months' skiing. I missed him. He continually used words which were unfamiliar to me ('occlusion', 'increment') and had a way, which I was to copy when I came to Cambridge, of always carrying a book under his arm.

Christmas came and my German lessons were suspended. What command of the language I had acquired with the help of Professor Wildhagen, my tutor – a dear old creature of incredibly dirty appearance, whose passion was translating Turgenev – began to ebb away.

New Year came, and with it David Loveday, who had been the Assistant Chaplain at Clifton.

Before he left he had put forward a bold scheme. Someone should persuade Andy to send me to Cambridge. I had been a late developer, he said, but now I was at the stage where university might set me on my feet intellectually. Would Andy agree to this prospect? I said I strongly doubted it. David announced his intention of talking it over with him. I was to return home in a few weeks, and it was arranged that David would visit us at Chapel Street.

He was a nervous man but not a timid one. He pressed his case very clearly and sympathetically. And Andy, though far from timid himself, was perhaps a little awed by the Cloth and the 'Reverend'. After about half an hour it was settled. What clinched the matter was David's offer to coach me himself for the entrance exam. I would spend six weeks at Bristol. He would coach me in Latin, and a mathematician from Bristol University would be persuaded to 'cram' me with maths. This would be followed by three months in France to improve my French, the idea being that I should read Modern Languages. The thought of my being coached in this way at no extra cost so appealed to Andy that he even swallowed France without blinking.

Monsieur Sémézies, who was entrusted with the task of burnishing my French, was styled *ancien professeur de l'École Berlitz*. I took this to mean that he was ancient, or ageing, half-expecting a Gallic version of my Professor Wildhagen, and was surprised to find a young man, with a very attractive young wife. They lived at the Château l'Estiou on the Loire, near Beaugency. There were three other pensionnaires – two German boys and Luis, a Spaniard, who spoke very fast and incomprehensibly.

Word came from David, who had friends at Magdalene, that I had passed the entrance exam in Latin and English, and that the College would take me provided I had achieved a pass mark in Maths.

In the afternoons I would walk across the fields to the river. The German boys would appear in their boat, constructed by a former pensionnaire, a wonderful punt with a carpet for a sail. The Loire was very shallow at this point, and the current strong. Upstream, with a breeze behind us, our little craft would manage about four hundred yards an hour. Downstream, it covered the same distance in about ten minutes. I would hang on to the boat, and they would pull me up very slowly to the top of the beach. Two of us would bathe, while the third held the boat. Then we would skim back downstream, moor her in a backwater, and walk back across the fields.

After dinner we would play the gramophone. Or sometimes I would play the piano, or accompany M. Fritz, one of the German boys, on his cello; and then go to bed.

We were playing croquet on the gravel in the back garden one afternoon when the postman appeared with a telegram for me. *Accepté par la Madeleine*, it said. Years of public school French and a month with M. Sémézies and his wife had not prepared me for instant translation. La Madeleine? That big church in Paris? Or the little cake which, according to Chichele Waterston, Proust dipped in his tea? It took me a minute or two, sitting in the garden of the Château l'Estiou, to realize that here was the key to the next three – or, as it turned out, four – years at Cambridge.

VI

My first year in Magdalene, in 1928, I had rooms in Bridge Street, only a few yards from the entrance to the College, over the bridge. In the rooms above me was Robin Fedden, a fellow-Cliftonian. It was thought for that reason that we should like to be boarded together. In fact, we scarcely knew each other, since at School we had been in different houses.

Robin's sitting-room or study was graced with watercolours by his artist father, Romilly Fedden; mine with coloured reproductions of ballet designs by Bakst, taken from *L'Illustration* and framed in passe-partout.

I hired an upright piano and bought gramophone records of Beethoven's last quartets. There was often a vase of flowers on a table by the window.

At midday the bus to Newnham would stop opposite my window, and the Newnham girls on the top deck would be able to look straight into my sitting-room on the first floor, where they could see me, playing the piano or seated at the table piled high with dictionaries and colourful books, casually looking up to see if any one of them was interested. None of them ever looked back. I could not think why. Too well brought up, I supposed.

During the first week or so, several characters called on me. During my last summer term at Clifton I had taken up rowing. I did not care for rowing. I had taken it up chiefly because of a romantic affection for a small boy who was a cox, and a marked loathing for the game of cricket. I told my first visitor that I had a dicky heart. A totally unnecessary lie. But how was I to declare what was indeed the truth: that I had already taken up, perhaps unwittingly, the role of a University aesthete?

My next visitor brought with him the proposal of athletics. In spite of my 'dicky heart', I received him with a show of warmth. I really enjoyed running, especially cross-country. I told the second caller that I might be of some slight use as a long-distance runner. My distances at Fenners, the University playing fields, were the mile and three miles. Both were run in the same afternoon, and I managed to scrape into third place twice, for which, to my surprise, I won two bronze medals. These were delivered to me when a voice from a window the other side of Magdalene Bridge called out my name. I looked up to see Richard Bonham-Carter, who called down, 'Half a minute. You'd better have these,' and chucked the medals into the street.

My third visitor was from the Amateur Dramatic Club; he had heard, from some old Cliftonians, of my renditions of Lady Macbeth, Mrs Hardcastle, Captain Absolute, etc., in the school plays. Rather to my surprise I heard myself saying that, until I had completed the first part of my Modern Language tripos, I could not think about theatricals. But of course I was grateful for being asked.

I cannot say that I worked hard my first year. But I did work. I biked to tutorials and attended most of the lectures on French or German literature. I gained an Upper Second (2.1) in the first part of the Modern Languages tripos, which was not discreditable, and the College gave me a bursary of twenty (or was it ten?) pounds. Next year, I thought, I'd really get down to it. Meanwhile, I had two weeks before the start of the long vacation to do as I pleased.

Early on the first morning of this fortnight I received a visit from Frank Birch, a professional actor and producer. He was directing a production of the Goldoni comedy *The Servant of Two Masters* for the Amateur Dramatic Club, and the part of the romantic lover, Florindo, had fallen vacant due to a sudden illness. Would I take over, with one week's rehearsal? I said I must ask my tutor at Magdalene for permission. This was easily granted. And so began a delightful and hectic six days of rehearsals, followed by a week of performances in May Week.

Until this ADC production I had resisted the lure of the footlights at Cambridge. But I had undertaken a number of activities which in no way assisted me in the Modern Language tripos.

I do not remember how I got myself on the staff of the University magazine *Granta*, but I did and was appointed chief film critic. There were five cinemas in Cambridge at that time. The 'talkies' had not yet reached the Fen country. A small orchestra, a piano or His Master's Voice accompanied the films with what was frequently wildly inappropriate music, often rendered inaudible by the comments and derisory noises of the undergraduates. At the cinema in Market Square the audience achieved a ceaseless running commentary of laughter, cheers, ribald remarks, and rude noises. The favourite stars of the moment – Clara Bow and Laura La Plante – came in for much adoring dirt. It was not easy to review the films in which these two delectable stars appeared.

One day, towards the end of our first year, Robin Fedden and I went for a walk to Grantchester. It may have been the evocative place-name and the legend of Rupert Brooke that set us talking of poets and poetry, of which, certainly at that time, we both knew not very much. What Cambridge needed, we had decided, was a literary magazine.

So shallow was our editorial experience that it came quickly to the boil: as we returned, a rough plan was made, and before we were back in College even the name of the magazine had been chosen: *The Venture*. Not a very bold title, perhaps, but not too pretentious. It hardly occurred to us that the project might not be financially viable. After all, *Granta* and *The Cambridge Review* appeared weekly and had successfully done so for many years. Was there not room for another periodical?

My first approach was to the printers R. I. Severs. This proved to be a very fortunate choice. Severs was not only enthusiastic but patient. Four years later I was still paying off my debt to them, my co-editors having from the start perforce waived all financial responsibility.

It had never occurred to us that there might not be enough poets and writers blushing unseen but bursting to appear in print. I began the search for potential contributors by writing round to the editors of the college magazines and of *The Cambridge Review*. The response was not very promising. I also wrote to Oliver Baldwin. I remembered that, framed above the piano in Oliver's cottage in Oxfordshire, was a sonnet by John Drinkwater, which I asked his permission to print. Then Mother, off her own bat, persuaded Clemence Dane to contribute a short story, 'The Youth Who Longed to Shudder'. From Oliver, again, came an introduction to J. R. Ackerley, who sent us a short poem. Why my fellow-editors did not stamp on these three contributions whilst the first number was going into print, I don't know. They were enough to sink any literary magazine. Perhaps, like me, they were too polite to reject them.

It was Robin who suggested we should have a third editor. He put forward the name of a young post-graduate student at Trinity, Anthony Blunt. I never got to know Anthony well, and he did not, as I recall, take a very active part in editorship, but his contributions to *The Venture* – 'Self-consciousness in Modern Art', 'John Michael Fischer and the Bavarian Rococo' – lent a real and much-needed note of distinction.

The day of publication was at hand. Excitement ran moderately high. Never had my desire to see my name in print come so near to satisfaction. There it was, beneath the title, as Editor, and amongst the list of contributors as author of 'The Widows', a short prose fragment. (I was much given to fragments in those days.) I hired a barrow with a large poster to be parked in various strategic spots, and a dozen sandwichmen were paid to walk up and down King's Parade.

The Venture sold fairly well at its first appearance. But what nearly eclipsed that first edition was the arrival, at much the same time, of another literary magazine, edited by Jacob Bronowski and William Empson. I thought poorly of some of the poems which our competitors had printed: Empson's 'She cleaned her teeth into the lake', for instance, seemed too self-consciously anti-poetic. But *Experiment*, as the rival magazine was called, *was* genuinely experimental. In its light *The Venture* was shown clearly to be what it was – a farrago of juvenile trifles.

Nevertheless, we persevered and improved, publishing six issues, one a term, for two years, and in the course of these we published several writers who subsequently made their mark: Malcolm Lowry, John Lehmann, Julian Bell, and John Davenport.

The rivalry that was supposed to exist between *The Venture* and *Experiment* was more the invention of *The Cambridge Review* than of our making. In fact, I had come to admire Empson tremendously. When he was sent down, or 'rusticated,' on account – it was said – of contraceptives being found in his rooms, all literary Cambridge exploded. John Davenport, Hugh Sykes Davies, and I hired the Masonic Hall. Dressed *à la Bohème*, with a jug of beer on a candle-lit table, three mugs, and a pile of manuscripts, we read or declaimed Empson's poems for the best part of an afternoon before an enthusiastically partisan audience.

'He's really rather a nice old chap. But he will not go to bed. You must sit up with him until the early hours of the morning or he becomes a bit tetchy. But the food and wine are first-rate, and he has some nice pictures. I think you could do worse than to spend ten days or so with him.' It was my friend Francis Cook telling me about an elderly man, an invalid, who lived on Lake Garda. It was the long vacation in 1928, and as I would be returning from Sicily through Italy, it seemed a simple matter to break the Journey at Verona and catch the train on to Lake Garda, and it was duly arranged that I should be a guest with Fothergill Robinson.

He was standing on the steps of the villa, waiting to greet me. He was dressed in a sort of pyjama suit. Both his hands were heavily bandaged. He was rather charmingly effusive. He wanted to hear all about Sicily, which he said he had not visited for years.

'Would you like to bathe?' he asked.

'Just what I was hoping you would say.'

'We shall get on famously, I can see that,' said he.

Tea was served by a man in a white jacket.

'I must introduce you to Marco. He is my butler, my valet, my amanuensis. He also plays the piano, not very well, but quite pleasingly. Don't you, Marco?'

'My name's not Marco,' said the latter. 'Never was. He likes to pretend I'm Italian. I ask you, do I look Italian?'

'You do, a bit,' I said, smiling.

'Ah, there! You see?' said Fothergill Robinson. 'He's on my side!'

During the following ten days I found myself frequently on Marco's side. But I seldom liked to contradict F.R., as he preferred to be called. Marco's real name was Sam, and he had been a chorister at a church in Leamington when F.R., as a young clergyman, had been incumbent there. The two of them pursued a seemingly endless bickering. Yet, from time to time, a great affection could be seen.

'Thank God you're here, sir,' said Marco after dinner that first evening. 'There are times when I think I'm going potty. You will sit up with him, won't you, and listen to his talk? When he was young he knew everybody, and it irritates him when I don't know half the people he's talking about. Oh, and don't forget, if you should find yourself dropping off, try not to let him see it. He can be very funny that way.'

Fothergill Robinson had been in holy orders as a young cleric in a fashionable church. He had had, as a boy, a pleasing treble voice, which had ripened into a very fine tenor. He had been a very handsome man, and some of the ladies of Leamington had 'shot many an amorous dart in my direction', as he put it. The time came when, bolder than the rest, a beautiful Leamingtonian young lady, who happened to have a comfortable income, proposed to him and was joyously accepted. It was a Society wedding, and among F.R.'s friends, believe it or not, was the painter Romilly Fedden (father to my friend and co-editor, Robin). There were some very handsome presents, among them a portrait by Fedden of the bride.

It was now two o'clock in the morning. We were sitting on the porch. He had been talking for almost three hours. At the mention of the portrait, the old man's voice shrank almost to a whisper. There was a long pause while he lit a Turkish cigarette. The pause grew so long that I thought I should say something.

'Was it a good portrait?' I asked.

'Technically, yes. A good likeness. The painting of the dress of broderie anglaise brilliantly executed. But there was something about the picture which I did not like and which she – my wife – found most displeasing.'

There was another pause.

'What was it?' I asked.

The pause this time was so long that I feared he had gone to sleep. So I asked again, 'What was it in the portrait you didn't like?'

'Epilepsy. I charged Fedden with this, and he said that it wrung his heart, but that if he were to paint the same sitter for a hundred years, he would see it the same.'

'What did you do about it?' I asked.

'Poor Hilda. Her health deteriorated rapidly and she had to be sent to a nursing home. In those days divorce was not granted on the basis of physical ailments.'

There was another pause.

'What time is it?' he asked.

'Nearly three.'

'Is that all?' he said, to my dismay. 'Well, it's your first night here. I never tire, but I suppose you do. Better go to bed.'

Life at the Villa Rampolla was smooth enough. *Modo sic, modo sic. Ita vita truditur*, F.R. would say. He had a fondness for Petronius and a wealth of Latin tags. The days passed slowly, and the nights were interminable. In the mornings I would write poems, much under the influence of Arthur Waley and his translations from the Chinese. At midday I would go for a swim, sleep in the afternoons, and in the evenings listen to F.R.

Lake Garda is a long stretch of water, and one day, towards the end of my stay, I took one of the steamers and sailed round the lake, stopping at the various landing-stages. When the steamer reached the last but one port of call, there was some merriment going on. A wedding was in progress, and the happy couple and their retinue were dancing to the tune of an accordion. It was all very jolly. And then I began to realize that I might be late for dinner.

As I came in through the front door, an unmistakable voice said, 'Is that you? Where have you been?'

'Shan't be long,' I called out. I hurried upstairs to change for dinner.

Sam was hovering nervously on the landing. 'I think you'd better go down and break the ice, sir. He's in one of his moods.'

'You must find it rather dull here,' said F.R.

'Oh, not a bit!' I said. 'I'm terribly sorry, I . . .'

'No, don't apologize. It is dull, isn't it, Marco?'

'It comes and goes,' agreed the latter.

'It wasn't so always. A lot of people used to come here. All sorts of people, every summer. But they're mostly dead now. I've enjoyed your stay very much.'

'So have I,' I said emphatically. I felt very guilty. That night F.R. suddenly terminated our conversation after brandy and insisted that we go to bed. It was not even midnight.

And then something happened. Next morning, I was in the bathroom, shaving; F.R. was in bed, writing letters. I was singing – bits of Schumann and Schubert, echoes of Heidelberg, among them Schumann's superb setting of Heine's 'The Two Grenadiers', a song which asks as much from the actor as from the singer. I was just leaving the house for my morning bathe when he appeared in the doorway of his room.

'Sing that again,' he said.

I put down my towel and bathing costume.

'Have you had any training?'

'A little,' I said, 'nothing much.'

'Who taught you?'

'No one, really. I've always loved singing.'

He walked about the room impatiently.

'Has anyone ever told you that you have the makings of a fine voice?'

'No.'

'A very fine voice. I don't mean an operatic tenor, but a fine tenor-baritone. Like Steuart Wilson, or . . . sing the Schumann again. You know, I know what I'm talking about. I was a member of The English Singers for years. Agnes Nicholls, Dora Labette . . . I'll tell you what I want you to do. I will send you to Munich so that Beibig may hear you. And what would please me most would be that you should work under him. Don't worry about the money. I have plenty.'

'But,' I said, 'I don't think I love music enough to want to devote myself to it entirely.'

'My dear fellow, you surely don't suppose that singers have to think, do you? Or even love music? What are you hoping to be if not a singer?'

'Well, I really want to be a poet.'

'A *what*?'

'A poet.'

'What have you written? Go on, fetch something.'

I went to my room and found a poem which I had finished that morning.

'Read it to me,' he said.

I read:

> Like an actor in an antique tragedy
> The young cat creeps out onto the porch steps,
> And then returns into the dark house
> To look for the birthplace of her children.
> The ugly cat stalks out of the ferns,
> Pauses on the steps, turns at some sound,
> Showing the dull red wound in his neck,
> And walks on into the flowers, which hide him,
> Hateful, and humiliated, and alone.
> The grey one is just seen in the dark doorway,
> Easing herself of her burden on the ground.
> These actors speak a foreign tongue,
> Only the gist of the play is understood;
> Stripped of softening, explanatory speeches
> And accompanied by the thin squeak of bats,
> Their mime touches me more than a play.

'Rubbish,' he said. 'Oh . . . I know how it is when one is young. They think they can do anything, and they go frittering their time and their talent away, and it's only when it's too late that they sit down and think. I would not be telling you the truth if I encouraged you to be a poet. We'll talk about it after dinner tonight.'

We talked until about three o'clock in the morning. The old man's tenacity was most disturbing. Again and again he would almost convince me that I had to be something bigger than my present existence allowed for, and that such stature could come only through music. Finally the situation became impossible even for him, and he told me – or, rather, commanded me – to go to bed.

I was very tired and I slept poorly. Next morning I had an urge to sing. I wanted to sing very much, but I checked myself to a pianissimo in case the sound of my voice should prompt him to start all over again. I left the house early for a swim. As I walked through the garden, across the road, and down the pebbly beach to the water's edge, I could hear the sound of F. R.'s gramophone, *La Marechiare . . . la Marechiare . . .*

I paused and listened to the end of the song.

The water was cool and clear. I thought of Heidelberg . . . of Munich . . . *I don't mean an operatic tenor, but a fine tenor-baritone. Like Steuart Wilson, or . . .*

As I walked back through the garden, F. R. stumbled out of the house.

'That song you were playing,' I said, 'it's lovely! *La Marechiare . . .* who was it singing?'

'Tito Schipa,' he said. 'Have you packed? Your train leaves at eight.'

As I sat in the train I thought, 'Poor old man. Kind old chap. A sick man wanting to be in the swim again. Sitting up in bed at the Villa, sending cheques to me, or to Beibig. . . . '

And yet . . . and yet . . . could it be arranged, I wondered, that I should meet Beibig? All those framed photographs in the morning-room of the Villa Rampolla . . . Caruso . . . McCormack . . . I had given them only a casual glance. I had the same urge as in the morning: I wanted to sing. The train carriage was full. I stepped into the corridor and sang, quietly at first, 'The Lass with the Delicate Air'. I looked around to see if I was being overheard. They were all reading, or admiring the sunset. I tried a bar or so of *La Donna è mobile*, and decided that I was aiming too high. Then, no doubt to the astonishment of my fellow-travellers, I launched into my version of 'Every valley shall be exalted'. The noise of the train prevented me from sounding at my best. But I was not displeased with myself. When I dried up, having gone as far into the valley as I could remember, I came out with a medley of songs from *The Beggar's Opera*. I was more satisfied. 'Let us take the road' . . . good! 'Fill every glass' . . . Aha!

Nevertheless, as our train rolled on through Italy and into France, I was brought back, by degrees, to my first conclusion: that there was a world of difference between the professional and the amateur.

Chantmesle, my next port of call, twenty miles or so from Paris, had once belonged to Charles Conder, the English impressionist painter.

My first visit there, to stay with Robin Fedden and his parents, had not been an unqualified success. I had chattered on interminably about the Château l'Estiou, intoxicated with the sound of my own conversation. The bedroom walls upstairs were thin, and, going to bed that night, I overheard Mrs Fedden saying, 'Does that young man never stop talking?' I was horribly crestfallen, and the following day, on a trip to Chartres, I tried to make amends, asking, as I hoped, all the right questions and confining my remarks to expressions of polite interest such as a model guest might make. I succeeded in being more dull than the night before.

So when Robin asked me to stay again, after the Villa Rampolla, I murmured something about things being very busy, and privately decided not to go. Impressions were very important to me, and I feared I had made a very poor impression on that first visit. I wrote from the Villa Rampolla to say that, no, I should not be able to make it to Chantmesle that summer.

But Robin was not to be put off. He wrote back to say that he hoped I would change my mind, especially since Margaret Coss and her sister Mary would be staying, and Mary was dying to meet me again. 'Mary', said Robin, 'says she has fallen in love with you.' This put a very different complexion on the invitation. I wrote back at once to say that, after all, I would be delighted to come, if only for a day or two.

Margaret and Mary Coss were Americans who had been sent by their parents to Europe that summer in search of culture. Margaret, though attractive, was a rather over-earnest intellectual, at least in her appearance. Robin, I thought, was keen on her. Mary was strikingly beautiful. So much I knew from having met her at tea one afternoon in Robin's rooms at Cambridge. She had said nothing, but had looked at me once, very thoughtfully. She had wide-open, very dark brown eyes.

We were sitting on a low stone wall, backed with vines, on the road to La Rocheguyon. All evening I had tried to summon the courage to ask her to come for a walk. Robin had tactfully disappeared to put the car away. The other guests had gone out to welcome a late-comer, whose arrival had caused a minor commotion, but I was seized with panic and remained tongue-tied.

Then, when everyone had come back, and I realized I had lost my chance, I blurted out: 'I think it's very hot in here. Who says a walk? Mary, will you come for a walk?'

'I'd love to,' she said.

Now in the moonlight we were talking of Cambridge. She told me that Bill Empson had reported me as 'one of the nicest people there'. This surprised and delighted me more than I could say. It emboldened me to talk about the first time I had seen her, at the tea-party in Robin's rooms.

'You were beautifully dressed in brown, with a golden chain round your neck. You sat down in an armchair opposite me.'

'I know,' she said. She spoke in a low, deep voice. 'I came to see you.'

'You'd never seen me before, had you?'

'Yes, I had. Margaret and I were walking in Magdalene Fellows' Garden, with a dreadful man – I forget his name – oh, an awful man. Suddenly you came across the lawn. You had a book in your hand. I said, "Who's that?" and Margaret said it was you. I thought any man who could look so beautiful in glasses was the one for me. I decided that I must meet you. So it was arranged, and I came to call for Margaret at Robin's rooms fifteen minutes too soon. Then Robin said that he would ask you here. Then came a long letter of his to Margaret. On the last page he said, "Michael cannot come." I was so miserable I didn't know what to do. Then we found he had written a P.S. saying, "Michael *is* coming."'

There was a pause and I took her hand.

She leant towards me. I kissed her. A sweetness, a tenderness I had never felt before. We walked along the road, stopping every other moment to embrace. The moon had gone down. I carried her for twenty yards. A dog barked at us, a little terrier, filling the whole country with its noise. Eventually we reached Chantmesle. It was half-past three in the morning, and as we stood outside the gate, a bird was singing. It was already dawn.

At breakfast she appeared wearing a lovely brown dress with a deep collar and a long scarf trailing from her shoulder. After breakfast I suggested a walk. She told me she was coming back to Europe the next year to learn French. Good, somehow I would get to France then, to see her. And after that – she would spend three years at university in America. Three years! I protested: Too long! I could get a Commonwealth scholarship, she suggested. Yes, but that would hardly bring us closer together. America seemed so vast. I hinted that I would always wait for her and tried to show her how I saw my life for years to come. How difficult but how necessary it would be to break from my family if I were to dedicate my life to poetry. How – and here the picture I painted was heavily fringed with melodrama – my home life had been overshadowed by a stepfather who misunderstood me. Such envy, hatred, malice, uncharitableness – I laid it on thick.

She looked at me, her eyes full of compassion and understanding.

'And you, Michael,' she asked, without the slightest trace of irony, as if I really might be perfect, 'have you no faults?'

'But of course I have,' I said, magnanimously.

'Tell them me.'

'I am selfish. Proud. Weak in needing encouragement. Living too much in the present . . . sensual . . . and vain,' I added.

She smiled, and nodded, and with all the wisdom in the world, I thought, said nothing.

After lunch we took a boat up the Seine to bathe, I rowing as impressively as I was able.

'And you?' I asked her, 'What will you do?'

'I shall read, and I shall work, and work, and work. And then one day I shall come back to England and we shall go to a tea-party together, and I shall astound you with my knowledge.'

I felt a little frightened by this. I must have overawed her, I realized, with my description of my life to come. Now she would spend the next three years trying to catch up with me. This would never do.

'Oh, don't worry, Michael,' she teased, 'I shall never be more brilliant than you. And don't,' she added, 'worry so much about how you talk. You talk quite brilliantly enough.'

We were silent all the way back to the house. I tried to hum 'Fain would I change that note', but the effort was beyond me.

Tea was a dismal affair. The girls went upstairs to get ready, and came down in their travelling clothes.

'Goodbye, Mrs Fedden,' Mary said, 'and thank you so very much.'

At the station, sister Margaret, with her lorgnettes, bought the tickets. Robin and I carried their bags to the platform. Mary was silent and miserable. The train arrived and we found them two corner seats. I shook hands with the sister first – 'Goodbye, Margaret' – then, 'Goodbye, Mary.' Her look was haunting. We got out on to the platform and watched them through the window, smiling a little.

Robin and I drank in a café in silence. On the drive back, over the hill, stopping on the way to send telegrams, I was unable to control my tears. Robin said nothing, but took my arm, and we walked the last part of the journey arm in arm back to Chantmesle.

Mary returned to Cambridge the following year. In America, Margaret told me, she had cut her hair very short and unbecomingly, so as not to attract any of the sophomores. Though not a Cambridge undergraduate, she attended almost all the lectures. She accompanied me every opening night to the Festival Theatre when I went as drama critic for *The Cambridge Review*. Without anything being said, or written, the two of us found ourselves out of love and not in the least missing it.

She returned to Philadelphia, where Francis Cook, on a Commonwealth Fellowship, met her. 'She's very beautiful,' I had told him, 'and I charge you not to fall in love with her.' A year or so later came a letter from Francis saying that, despite my half-earnest injunction, he and Mary had married. And then, I cannot remember how, I learned that she had joined the Communist Party and was selling their paper on street corners, and she and Francis had parted.

After the Goldoni comedy my taste for acting and all things theatrical was given a broad scope. Dennis Arundell, who was a great figure in University theatre, asked me to play the Soldier in the first performance in England in 1928 of Stravinsky's *The Tale of a Soldier*, to be staged at the ADC Theatre. Maynard Keynes, the economist, was married to the Russian ballerina Lydia Lopokova, and he and balletomane Arnold Haskell backed the venture, which, even in those days and especially in that tiny theatre, must have been an expensive trifle. Lydia played – or, rather, danced – the part of the Princess; Hedley Briggs, a talented young actor-dancer who had distinguished himself in Norman Marshall's season at the Cambridge Festival Theatre, played the showy part of the Devil. Arundell directed and spoke the words of the Narrator, and Boris Ord, the organist at King's College chapel, conducted the orchestra of eight picked professionals. Costumes were designed by Duncan Grant and the sets by Humphrey Jennings, to whose pioneering documentaries the British cinema owes so much. (One of them, *Diary for Timothy*, was to be the occasion for my renewing acquaintance with Jennings towards the end of the War. He asked me to record the commentary for it written by E.M. Forster.)

After the prestige of *The Tale of a Soldier* there was no stopping me. George ('Dadie') Rylands, a young don at King's, put on a reading of scenes from *Comus* in his rooms, himself playing the name part, with Robert Eddison and myself playing the brothers, and Lydia as the Lady. Eddison, a fine actor and a brilliant cabaret performer, excelled in our university productions in what were known as 'breeches' parts, in which the woman plays the man, with the double irony in Robert's case of the man, and an elegant, six-foot man at that, playing the woman playing the man. In the audience for *Comus* were Virginia and Leonard Woolf. I was much in awe of the beautiful Virginia, who asked me if I was nervous when acting. I replied, 'Yes, hideously.' I do not know why, for as an amateur I was seldom, if ever, nervous on the stage.

There was another performance of this programme at the Keyneses' house in Gordon Square before a scintillating audience of, largely, Bloomsbury artists and writers, including Walter Sickert, who for some unknown reason addressed Robert and myself in French: '*Messieurs, vous étiez délicieux!*'

Lopokova's broken English was adorable, but it was an acquired taste. Especially in Milton. Nevertheless, Maynard must have believed in her powers as an actress, for he took the Arts Theatre in London for a programme consisting of *A Lover's Complaint*, the scenes from *Comus*, excerpts from *Paradise Lost*, and, to end the evening, a *divertissement* of ballet. In the last item, to the music of William Boyce arranged and conducted by Constant Lambert, she was supported by Frederick Ashton and Harold Turner. The critic of the *New Statesman*, Raymond Mortimer, dubbed this 'a blue-blooded evening'.

To be acting in a real theatre, even if was only a club theatre, filled me with a comfortable conceit and, to cap it all, there was Maynard Keynes handing each member of the company a crisp five-pound note.

Among the starry audience at Gordon Square was a woman who introduced herself to me as Hilda Matheson of the BBC. She asked me if I would like to do a test for reading on the radio. Term had not then begun, and it was arranged that I should do the test one morning at Savoy Hill, where the BBC first set up shop. I was received by a tall, smiling man who looked as if he would burst into giggles at any moment. His name was Lionel Fielden.

He listened to whatever it was I had prepared and, still smiling, drawled, 'Yes, that will do *very* nicely.' I thought he was sending me up. However, within a few days, a contract from the BBC arrived by post and, by hand, an edition of Lord Chesterfield's *Letters*. I was to read from the *Letters* for three Saturday evenings, each time, I think, for about twenty minutes. It seems unlikely, now, that the BBC would put out such material even for one Saturday evening.

More improbable still that I should be allowed to make my own choice of the excerpts. But so it was, and I was paid two guineas a time. Later I was asked to read poetry, amongst other things T.S. Eliot's *The Waste Land*. This poem I did not well understand, and I wrote to Eliot asking if he could tell me the kind of delivery he thought most suitable. I received a letter from his secretary saying that Mr Eliot suggested I use as *little expression* as possible. This I did to the best of my ability, only to receive a letter from a clergyman criticizing me for my unpoetic, flat delivery. He said he had switched off after five minutes.

I did many readings for Fielden during my time at Cambridge. His sardonic humour, his air of treating the work as if it were a great lark, must have concealed a deep concern for the future of broadcasting. His entry in *Who's Who* gave as his recreation 'trying to avoid being organized'. Nevertheless, he was made Controller of Broadcasting in India, a post he held for five years. We met by chance in Italy some time later, and I lunched with him at the farm to which he had retired, not without some disgust, it seemed. He made languid scorn of everything: Right, Left, and Centre. I remembered that his Brasenose smile had always been worse than his bite.

High on the list of activities during my four years at Magdalene were the reading parties organized by a don, Francis Turner, each Easter, when some six or eight of us would meet for about a fortnight and study. We lodged in the Castle Rock Hotel, Mortehoe, in North Devon. Perched on a cliff, half-way up the hill to the village, the old Victorian building looks out to distant Lundy Island, and on one side of the hotel a cliff path leads to Morte Point, providing an excellent track for a run, up and down, down and up, round the Point and back. On the other side, after one crosses the long beach, Woolacombe Sands, is another headland, Baggy Point, which offers as pleasant a walk as one may ask.

Mornings for work, evenings for chess or card games, afternoons for walks or rustic hockey or 'waterworks' on the sands, to the pub sometimes ... plenty of exercise, plain food, no talk of war ... *Love's Labour's Lost*, Act One, Scene One.

It was Francis Turner who steered me in the direction of what, for a brief moment, might have been an academic life. After a year of Modern Languages I had embarked on the English tripos. I had achieved a satisfactory Upper Second degree in my finals, but still I had no more idea of what to do with my life than when I first went up to Magdalene. Francis suggested I should stay on for a fourth year and read for the Le Bas prize. The winning text was always published by the Cambridge University Press, and the prize carried some kudos. Francis himself had won it, and the £100 that went with it, with a treatise on *Irony*. Clearly he thought an academic career was indicated for me, and I was by no means averse to the idea.

The day came when, without trumpets, the examiners announced the set subject for the Le Bas, and my spirits took a definite and deep drop. I could hardly believe that some obscure don had wasted his midnight oil thinking up such a musty subject: 'The Idea of a Victorian University.'

As I look back on it, the subject was perhaps an interesting one, but it called for an orderly mind and I had no idea where to begin. I browsed in the library, hoping that inspiration might come. I dipped into Cardinal Newman, but it seemed that this eminent Victorian had said all that could be said on the matter.

I called on my tutor, 'Dadie' Rylands, to ask his advice, and it was agreed that I should abandon the Le Bas and read instead for the second part of the English tripos. Such merciful release went to my head. Two whole terms now stretched before me, offering renewed scope for all my extracurricular activities, and I availed myself of it greedily.

I brought the life of *The Venture* to a not discreditable end and took up editorship of *The Cambridge Review*. Boldly I broke with tradition by not printing the University Sermon, replacing it with articles such as Basil Wright's on the new movement in the German cinema. No one rebuked me. None of my friends noticed the loss. Not until the end of my stint as editor did someone think to tell me that subscriptions to *The Cambridge Review*, under my aegis, had shown a somewhat drastic decline. Parsons up and down the country, I was informed, relied upon cribbing from the University Sermon for their weekly pulpit orations.

I developed a warm friendship with John Davenport, and together we edited for the Hogarth Press two volumes of Cambridge poetry.

Davenport had the enviable gift of a photographic memory, and I was what is known as a 'quick study'. Hearing that two members of the cast in Peter Hannen's production of *The Voysey Inheritance* would have to miss one performance in order to register their votes in a Union debate, for a lark John and I learned their parts and took their place for that one performance. Somehow I also found time to write and direct a two-act operetta called *The Battle of the Book*, in which I appeared as Samuel Pepys. All this stretched the patience of our tutors a little too far. I was sent for by Dadie, and was told to stop fooling around and get down to work. Too late. I had almost forgotten what work meant.

For my last appearance in May Week at the ADC, I took the name part in Shaw's *Captain Brassbound's Conversion*, with sets designed by Guy Burgess. Very good sets, too. Burgess was one of the bright stars of the University scene, with a reputation for being able to turn his hand to anything. Alistair Cooke reviewed our production, none too favourably. He was appearing in something put on by another Cambridge dramatic society, The Mummers, and I sharpened my pen and took my revenge. 'Mr Cooke,' I wrote, 'knows all the tricks but, unfortunately, can do none of them.' I had forgotten this squib until, many years later, Cooke quoted it when introducing me on a television programme in New York.

It was the first and, as it turned out, the last time I ever acted in Shaw in the theatre. Shaw claimed, correctly, that his characters are 'actor-proof'. I think that is why I have always resisted playing them. (Gabriel Pascal came near to persuading me to play Dubedat in a film of *The Doctor's Dilemma* and, later, Apollodorus in *Caesar and Cleopatra*, but I was playing in *Uncle Harry* in the West End at the time and after seven months in a heavy dramatic part I thought that the strain of filming in the day would have been too great, so I backed out.) Shaw had the last word. He sent one of his famous postcards to Mother: 'What!!! So Michael is your son? I must re-write *Coriolanus* for the two of you.'

VII

THE YEAR I left Cambridge – 1931 – was hardly the most propitious time to find a job: the year of the run on the pound; the fall of the Ramsay MacDonald Labour government; the election of the National government, which cut the dole and established the means test for the two and a half million unemployed. But I had my Bachelor of Arts degree. Failing all else, I thought, I could teach. I went, like many another penniless graduate, to the Gabbitas Thring Agency and presented myself and my B.A. Hons (Cantab.). I had pictured an offer to teach French, German, and English in a beautiful old school somewhere on the South Downs. What I was offered was the tutelage of a small Brazilian boy, aged twelve, called Miguel. His guardian put at our disposal a room in the Piccadilly Hotel.

Miguel was a charming boy, and spoke almost perfect English. After a fortnight, our hotel room and the same walk each day around St James's Park became rather constricting, and Miguel suggested we might try the cinema. This wrecked the whole thing. One morning Miguel's guardian apprehended me in the hotel lobby and addressed me with thinly-disguised annoyance.

'Miguel tells me you amuse yourself with visits to the cinema. I have nothing against the cinema, please understand, but it is not my idea of how English should be learnt.'

He paid me my fee, and that was that. It was back to Gabbitas Thring.

As it happened, they had something more substantial to offer me. Highgate Grammar School wanted an assistant master to teach Modern Languages, French and German, able to help out with hockey, and ready to start within a week. 'They'll want a reference, of course.' I thought at once of David Loveday, whose helping

77

hand had got me to Cambridge. David, I knew, had left his old post at Clifton as assistant chaplain and taken up the Headmastership at Cranleigh School, in Surrey.

'I don't really intend to teach,' I told Loveday, 'not for long, anyway. I don't really know what I want to do.'

'Why don't you come and give this place a try? I've a post here for a Modern Languages master. Stay a couple of terms. It won't make your fortune, but what will, nowadays?'

And so began another beginning. The salary was not, indeed, princely: £225 a year. But with bed and board for eight months of the year, it could hardly be sneezed at. The school, Victorian Gothic, built for the education of the younger sons of well-to-do clergymen, was – another point in its favour – conveniently close to London.

It is customary, in tales of schoolmasters and their lives, that one should be a young Olympian, another a crabbed and dangerous character – *Mr Perrin and Mr Traill*, *The Browning Version*, etc. Perhaps I was fortunate. My contemporaries in the Common Room seemed as pleasant a bunch of men as one could hope to find in such surroundings. Only one, Frank Devonshire, who had been at Cambridge with me, seemed out of his depth. Frank, an Etonian and a brilliant scholar, had a fatal lack of confidence, which instantly conveyed itself to the boys he was attempting to teach. After a day or two, murmuring and muffled laughter could be heard beyond the thin partition which separated his form room from mine, giving way to howls of incredulity, shouts, guffaws, and a hammering of desk tops. My class looked at me to see if my nerve would crack.

My disability was of a different kind, though no less fatal to serious teaching in the long run. I could not resist playing for a laugh. The room was a little overheated, and I took hold of the cord of one of the transom windows. There was nothing to attach it to. I stood there, cord in hand, and asked, with my most dead-pan expression, 'What do I do with this? Stand here all morning?' The form laughed. Redgrave, it seemed, was all right.

One of the set books for the Higher Certificate was Milton's *Samson Agonistes*. My sixth-form class, usually a very lively lot, were making heavy weather of it. Not even Robert Bridge's excellent guide, *Milton's Prosody*, could loosen its adamantine chains. We came to the messenger's speech. I remembered that in Greek drama the messenger speech is often the most vivid moment of the play, and so it is in *Samson*. Suddenly I threw my textbook into the air and said, 'Let's learn it.' There were a few subdued groans.

'We'll learn it,' I said, 'and act it. Here in the school library. We'll do it Sunday fortnight.'

I rigged up some costumes of buckram tabards, a beard for Manoa, a spear for the giant. Mr Bowyer, the Classics master, a dear man and a very accomplished composer, wrote some excellent music. I elected to play Samson and treated myself to a wig from Fox's Costumiers; the hair was not quite as long as Samson's should have been, but time was short. When the day came for our first performance, my class was quite cheerful, I even more so. What did it matter if Milton had ordained that his poem should not be performed? I believed that I had tumbled on an unacknowledged theatrical treasure:

> O dark, dark, dark, amid the blaze of noon,
> Irrecoverably dark, total eclipse
> Without all hope of day!

The awesome weight of Milton had been lifted.

Cranleigh, before my arrival, had the reputation of being a 'tough' school with no theatrical tradition. Perhaps it was a chance over-heard remark of some German visitors who had strayed into a rehearsal of *Hamlet* and left muttering, '*Nur Kultur und Liebe*', which riled me and helped to nurture a secret ambition that Cranleigh might have its own tradition that would bring scholars and amateurs of the theatre, in the way that the Greek play performed at Bradfield attracted classical scholars to that school.

It remained – fortunately, perhaps – a secret ambition. Another, more peremptory ambition was forming itself during my three years as a schoolmaster. In all I did six productions at Cranleigh: *HMS Pinafore*, *As You Like It*, *Hamlet*, *The Tempest*, *Samson Agonistes*, and *King Lear*, and played the leading part in five of them. Besides, only a few miles away, there was the semi-professional Guildford Repertory Company, where somehow or other I managed to squeeze in Menelaus in *The Trojan Women*, Young Marlow in *She Stoops to Conquer*, Ernest in *The Importance of Being Earnest*, Robert Browning in *The Barretts of Wimpole Street*, and Clive Champion-Cheney in Maugham's *The Circle*.

Loveday had given me every encouragement, turning a blind eye when needed to the amount of time spent on our 'theatricals', as the Bursar called them. But the inspiration which decided me came from

79

another quarter. During the spring term, in my second year at Cranleigh, I had taken my French class to London to see La Compagnie des Quinze. The Quinze had grown out of Jacques Copeau's troupe, Les Copiaus, a young company which he had formed and trained in a village in Burgundy after his retirement from the Théâtre du Vieux Colombier. But after five years, expecting an invitation to the Comédie Française, Copeau, who, despite his dedication to the idea of a theatre without stars, had more than a touch of the *grand seigneur* about him, disbanded Les Copiaus, who thereupon regrouped themselves as La Compagnie des Quinze. They had an author, André Obey, to write for them plays such as *Noah* and *The Rape of Lucrece*; they had a collapsible rostrum with surrounding tent for a stage; they were jugglers, mimes, acrobats; their productions, wrote Tyrone Guthrie, 'were like a ballet, only they had fifty times more content than any ballet ever had'; above all they had – or, rather, they found – an audience, for Copeau in the last years at Pernand-Vergelesses had starved his company of performance. Bronson Albery had brought them to London for a short season at the Arts Theatre the previous year, and such was their success that he was able to transfer their productions to the Ambassadors and the New, and then bring them back to Wyndham's Theatre the following two years, 1932 and 1933.

What my French class made of our excursions I am not sure, though no doubt they flattered me into thinking that six seats in the gallery at Wyndham's had not harmed their chances in the School Certificate. For me, the Quinze were a revelation. There were fine actors in the company, and Pierre Fresnay gave a glittering performance in *Don Juan*. But the French actors showed us an ensemble with a style and a dedication for which there was no English equivalent. In their bright light, all obstacles – my stepfather's disapproval, the warnings that I was 'too tall', the insecurity which I would be exchanging for a safe job and a permanent salary – melted away. I gave in my notice to leave at the end of the summer term of 1934.

Andy's reaction, when I broke the news to him, was contrary to all expectation. He raised no objection at all. Perhaps he was relieved. For so many years he had paid for my education, an investment which, to his prudent way of thinking, must have seemed to yield a lamentably small return. And to make matters worse, though he never complained about it, he had had to pick up the debts I ran up at Cambridge and at Cranleigh. Perhaps, as

Mother conjectured, 'he had been salmon fishing all that month in Scotland and had had much luck, and due to that he did not seem to mind very much that you had decided to become an actor.'

Mother, at any rate, was delighted and rushed up from Windsor, where she was playing in repertory, to see Lilian Baylis at the Old Vic Theatre. Baylis, the founder and manageress of the Vic, had asked Mother to be on the committee of the sister theatre, Sadler's Wells, and would have liked her to come to the Vic, 'but I knew', Mother wrote, 'that that would mean *living* at the Vic.'

I was granted an audition, and summoned to present myself at the stage door in Waterloo Road at 10.40 a.m. The time being so specified rather daunted me, implying the presence of many other hopefuls besides myself. Listening to them, as I waited my turn to be called, I thought they were rather good. The season we were auditioning for was to be directed by Henry Cass, built around the personality of Maurice Evans, who had made a notable success at the Vic.

I had chosen one of the lesser-known soliloquies from the canon, Rumour's prologue to *Henry IV, Part II*, which I had played for the Cambridge Marlowe Society, doubling it with Prince Hal, in a very stylized performance, with much waving of arms. I thought it unlikely any of the other contestants would choose it. I was quite right. Most of them had chosen one or other of Hamlet's soliloquies. I had completed only about half a dozen lines when a voice from the stalls called out, loud and clear, 'yes, thank you. *Thank* you.' I was badly rattled. The others had been allowed to go on for about five minutes.

'I can't see anything but hands,' said the voice from the stalls. It was Lilian Baylis. 'Do something else. Can't you do anything *not* Shakespeare?'

'A little onward lend thy guiding hand / To these dark steps, a little further on ... ' I launched myself into Samson's lines, shuffling forward, arms outstretched, not pausing to reflect that Samson, as I had played him, was even more balletic of gesture than Rumour. I had spoken hardly three lines when she interrupted me again. 'You'll have to learn to use your hands, y'know,' she said, adding, 'I couldn't pay you anything. I have to pay the actors who carry the show.'

'She's trying to get you to come for nothing,' whispered Cass. 'Don't!'

I'd accept an offer of three shillings a week, I thought – anything to be able to say, 'I'm an actor at the Old Vic.'

I said, 'Yes, I will come if you'll give me something to do. I'm too old to carry a spear or wave a flag.'

'My dear boy,' said Cass, 'if you can play Romeo, you shall play Romeo. But I can't promise anything.'

As I left the stage door, Murray Macdonald, who was to be the season's stage director, walked with me a few steps and said, 'I expect you'll be with us. I hope you'll be with us.'

In spite of Murray's kindly words I heard nothing from the Vic. I went back to Cranleigh for my final term, disappointed but not downcast, thinking that I must spread my net wider, and wondering whom I should invite to come down and see what I could make of *Lear*. The Whitsun holiday arrived. Still no word from the Vic. I had written a note to William Armstrong at the Liverpool Playhouse, saying that I would be coming up to see the Saturday matinée, and would he please give me an interview. Before catching the train to Liverpool I called at Chapel Street to collect some photographs. There was no one at home, but I found two letters for me, and one of them was from the Old Vic, offering me a contract for the next season for three pounds a week.

Armstrong was polite, but seemed rather abstracted, more or less pushing my photos aside.

'I know your mother, of course, a delightful actress, but, you see, my company is nearly filled. I have some very good young men – oh, and an excellent new young assistant director – you have some experience of directing, didn't you say? – but I'll let you know.'

'When could you let me know, Mr Armstrong?' – and here I made as if to reach into my breast pocket. 'When could you let me know? Because, you see, I have a contract for the Old Vic.' I paused.

Willie looked at me with something like alarm. 'A contract for the Vic?' he said. 'How much for?'

'Three pounds a week,' I said.

'I'll give you four,' said Willie. And four it was. For an instant I regretted my honesty, as I told Willie later, having the impression that if I'd said seven, he would have capped it with eight.

The Liverpool Playhouse theatre had just been redecorated. It was, and is, one of the most attractive old theatres in England. I saw the matinée, of a play by John Van Druten, and enjoyed it. The company seemed to play to a high standard. But my mind kept wandering to the photographs in front of the theatre. How, I wondered, would mine look amongst them?

I bought myself another ticket for the evening performance, and that, too, proved a great stroke of luck, for in the audience was a very popular actor, Lyn Harding. We were introduced, and Willie mentioned that I would be joining the Playhouse for the next season. As we parted at the end of the second interval, Harding said suddenly, 'By the way, Redgrave, never let them tell you you're too tall. I was told that many times.' (Triumphantly my mind flashed to my mother's warnings, and I longed to tell her what Harding had just said. And I remembered an evening at the Savoy, where Lionel Fielden had taken me after a broadcast. Tyrone Guthrie was there. He was planning a new season. 'You should have Michael,' Fielden said. 'Michael should be an actor.' 'Far too tall,' said Guthrie.)

'How tall are you?' Harding went on.

'Six foot three.'

'Same height as Lucien Guitry. A wonderfully graceful actor. You never noticed his height when he was on stage.'

VIII

OUR FIRST production was *Counsellor-at-Law* by Elmer Rice, an excellent choice of play for a repertory company. It had first been done in 1931 in New York by the Group Theatre. The Group had Clifford Odets and Elmer Rice to write for them, and such as John Garfield, Margaret Sullavan and Luther Adler in their company. But there were no 'stars' in the Group. *Counsellor-at-Law* had, as they say, something for everyone.

In our Liverpool production James Stephenson played the Counsellor. Rather an English counsellor he seemed to me, but then we had not long had the talkies to teach us what we should sound like, and none of us except Deirdre Doyle – who could switch accents at the drop of a hat – had spent any time in America. Ena Burrill was our leading lady, but wasn't to join us until the next play, so the part of the secretary went to another actress, Lindisfarne Hamilton. Netta Westcott, who had played the part in London, was the counsellor's wife, whom I, as a 'lounge lizard', had to seduce. Netta was somewhat older, and complained that she felt a little less seduceable each day, till at the dress rehearsal I, like so many another young actor in his first part in repertory, assumed another twenty years by larding my hair with 'Number 20'.

William Armstrong, one of the most beloved figures in the English theatre, had made a reputation for the Liverpool Playhouse which, together with the Birmingham Repertory Theatre, was at that time outstanding. He was mocked, imitated, and adored. At the end of a scene in rehearsal, his voice could be heard from the back of the stalls saying, 'Oh! It's so beautiful! So moving!'

Just before he died, in 1952, he broadcast his memoirs for the BBC. He had been a leading man with Mrs Patrick Campbell, and one of his favourite stories, based on Mrs Pat, can still be heard in truncated form in King's Road, Chelsea, or anywhere that so-and-so has set up his camp. The original, according to William, concerned two young actors who appeared to be more wrapped up in each other than was strictly necessary. On hearing of them Mrs Pat remarked: 'I don't care what they do, so long as they don't do it in the street and frighten the horses.' Today the catch-phrase survives, rather as Edith Evans's inflection of 'a handbag!' is echoed by those far too young to have seen or heard the original.

I began to take stock of the company. Of all the young men, Geoffrey Edwards and Robert Flemyng seemed likely to be my chief rivals. Bobby was an expert light comedian who could shoulder broad comedy parts as well, but he was no one's idea – least of all his own – of a classical actor. Geoffrey, however, was to play Hamlet, and I confess I was not altogether pleased to learn that I should play his Horatio. I don't know if there was not a little spite one evening when, as I cradled the dying Hamlet in my arms, I contrived to weep and a large splash of warm mascara fell on Hamlet's chin. But on the whole it was a happy company. Once Deirdre Doyle tried to kill a laugh by upstaging me, but for that I had learned from Mother a surefire remedy. You simply walked upstage with the culprit until you reached the backcloth. 'They'll never do it again,' Mother had said, 'at least, not to you.' She was right.

There was James Stephenson, who had been with the company for two years, with no previous experience of acting. A dark horse if ever there was one. To most of us he seemed an honest, earnest nonentity. Towards the end of the year he was cast as the lead opposite Ena Burrill in S. N. Behrman's *Biography*. 'What's he like to act with?' I asked Ena. 'Well,' she said, 'he's *clean*, and do you notice he always wears patent-leather shoes? That's so as the audience will think he's polished them well, I suppose. Oh, James is all right . . . the girls find him attractive.'

But the camera could discern something in James which none of us at Liverpool, except perhaps Willie, had noticed. James left to try his luck in London. He photographed very well, and almost immediately landed a part in a picture at Teddington studios, and had hardly finished that when he was offered a contract in Hollywood, and off he shipped himself with his young wife, to play a long string of parts, including a notable performance, opposite Bette Davis, as the defending counsel in *The Letter*.

There was Ena Burrill, our leading lady. Ena was something of a riddle. Very tall, weighty without being fat, and with a dazzling smile, she would scarcely bother to characterize a part, was almost lazy at times, and yet could walk on to a stage and command an audience's attention by the sheer force of her personality.

There was Deirdre Doyle, who was a mistress of make-up and could look at will remarkably like Marie Tempest, or Sara Allgood, or anyone she chose. Most of what I learned about make-up was from Deirdre. One trick in particular, very useful for middle-aged or elderly parts : you etched in the lines round the eye with the milled edge of a silver coin, after powdering the foundation. It produced a delicate, soft, feathery wrinkle.

There were the Sangsters, Alfred and Pauline, who were the parent figures of our company. Alfred had written several plays, one of which, *The Brontës*, had some success. He lived in hopes that Willie would stage it, and I, who had a strange ambition to play the Reverend Nicholls in it – very strange, now I come to think of it, because there is scarcely anything for the reverend gentleman to do – pleaded its case with Willie, too. But Willie resisted, probably because it needed three girls of really star quality, and Willie, expert in diplomacy, could foresee the ructions that might cause in his company. To each of his actresses he conveyed the impression that, all things being equal, and were it only a matter of his choice, she would be leading lady next season.

There was Hannah Daniel, who was determined to be a great actress, and if determination were sufficient, she would have been. There was something very touching about Hannah. She lived, breathed, and, indeed, entirely existed for the boards. A while after I had left Liverpool I bumped into her at a theatre and tentatively asked her what she was doing. She burst into tears on the spot. 'Oh, Michael, I'm married, I'm going to have a baby!'

I remembered walking her back to her digs one night after a performance, in which she had, in fact, been very effective, of Pirandello's *The Man with a Flower in His Mouth*. She kept stopping and breathing deeply, as if not wanting that precious moment to be lost. Suddenly she burst out, 'It's all so precarious! A lot of people get on just by having a pretty face. I'm not pretty, but I *know* I can act if I'm given a chance. It's so unfair.'

'Yes, isn't it?' I said.

'Oh *you*.' She sounded almost exasperated. 'You've got nothing to worry about.'

'I don't know,' I said, 'sometimes I get very worried.'

'What on earth about?'

'Well . . . I've had three successes in a row now, and I wonder if I can keep it up.'

I blush to recall my conceit.

There was little Larry Shipston, who, apart from his lack of inches, was truly unprepossessing in appearance. I shall never forget the zeal with which he pounded the Green Room table one morning, insisting that any actor ought to be able to play any part no matter what he looked like.

And there was I, who almost by luck had fallen into a job in the Playhouse, and was loving every minute of it. After three or four plays I was given my first really good part, Melchior Feydak, a Hungarian composer of musicals, in *Biography*. Speaking S. N. Behrman's excellent dialogue and accompanying myself on the piano, I felt like Noël Coward and Ivor Novello rolled into one. On a sudden impulse I bearded Willie in his office as he was writing a letter. 'Willie,' I said, 'I'm worth more than four pounds a week.'

'I know you are,' he replied, without looking up. 'I'll give you six.'

A painted sign above a rather dingy-looking staircase said: GYM. NEL TARLETON. I walked up to the top floor. Liverpool was a city of sharp contrasts. My rooms in Falkner Street were almost next door to the cathedral. Chinatown was five minutes' walk away. Bold Street was the Bond Street of Liverpool, yet it housed this dirty-looking entrance to the workshop of the Featherweight Champion of England.

Tarleton himself appeared, and I explained that I wanted to enrol myself at his gym. He seemed pleased. 'When would you like to start?' 'Now!' I answered and ran back to my rooms to get the right clothes. My eagerness seemed to amuse him. He put me through a brief work-out of exercises, skipping and punching, and afterwards filled a bath for me and washed my back. I told him how I had seen his title fight at Bellevue, Manchester, the year before. I vowed to myself I would train each day.

There was still the problem of height. So many years of being told I was too tall for an actor had had its effect on me.

We were to do John Van Druten's play *Flowers of the Forest* in March 1935. Ena and Bobby Flemyng were leaving the company to go to London in a new play, so the coast was clear for me and – and who? I was courting a young actress, Ruth Lodge, and was keen to get her into the company. I invited her up to Liverpool, where we waylaid Willie Armstrong.

'Oh!' he said. 'Oh, dear! I've already cast the part. Rachel Kempson.'

87

'But she's much too short,' I said.

On a visit to Stratford the year before, I had been very taken with the actress playing Hero in *Much Ado About Nothing*, Phoebe in *As You Like It*, and Ariel in *The Tempest*. Perhaps it had something to do with the Spanish costumes in *Much Ado*, with the Velásquez wigs and pannier skirts, but somehow I had got the impression she was rather short.

'I should have to go down on my knees to kiss her,' I protested.

The first night was proceeding quite smoothly, until we came to the love scene in Act Two. There was some business with a standard lamp, which I had to switch off in the middle of the scene. One thing which every aspiring actor learns in repertory is how to turn off a standard lamp: you remember to keep your finger on the switch until the light is turned off by the electrician at the switchboard. I went to the lamp and mimed switching it off, but it refused to go out. Another thing you learn is you cannot play a love scene with one hand on a standard lamp. So I left the wretched light and continued the scene as best I could and, at the very moment when I took Rachel in my arms, the lamp went out. Big laugh. I dare say we played the scene adequately. The audience were polite and laughed only once or twice. The curtain fell and we fell into each other's arms.

'Oh!' said Willie. 'Oh, dear!' We had waited until we were sure he would engage us both for the following season before breaking the news that we were to marry. 'You see,' he sighed, 'all the girls in the audience want to sleep with Michael, and all the men want to take Rachel out to supper. . . . However, if you're *quite* determined . . . ' He kissed us both, and a tear ran down his cheek.

Breaking the news to Willie was a sight easier than facing our respective parents. Of one thing we could be certain, we said: we did not want a church wedding with all that fuss and expense. We were soon to learn, however, how many things and people change their specific gravity when it's a question of a wedding. For instance, in the question of whom to invite, and whom not, the protagonists are shown in very different lights. And one may be sure that among them is one who will think the whole idea misplaced. How were we going to live – what would we live on? Was J. P. Anderson solvent, and if so, for how long? In short, every delaying tactic short of Tybalt's death was to hand. Tears were not uncommon. Even threats, of a kind. I was told there was a certain window in the Royal

My father, Roy Redgrave, in an Australian bush drama.

My mother, Daisy Scudamore, as Glory Quayle in the popular melodrama *The Christian* (about 1909).

Daisy (now Mrs. J. P. Anderson) on her wedding day (1922).

Margaret Scudamore (no longer Daisy) as Lady Bracknell in the first revival of *The Importance of Being Earnest* after Oscar Wilde's imprisonment and death.

My stepfather Andy (*centre*) and some friends at a shoot.

F. A. Scudamore (Daisy's real father) in the 1880s.

In my sailor hat, in either 1911 or 1912.

(*Left*) As Lady Macbeth, at Clifton. 'A little bird tells me that we have here the rival of the Divine Sarah. Are you thinking of going on the stage?' 'Good Lord, no!' I said (1925). (*Right*) As Captain Absolute in *The Rivals*, at Clifton (1926).

With Arthur Marshall as the female lead in *Captain Brassbound's Conversion*, at the Amateur Dramatic Club in Cambridge. The first and, as it turned out, the last time I ever acted in Shaw in the theatre. He claimed, correctly, that his characters are 'actor-proof' (1931).

With Mother, Andy, and Viscount Falkland on Degree Day at Cambridge (1931).

As Hamlet, at Cranleigh. This first attempt owed so much to Gielgud's performance in 1930 that I must have seemed like his understudy (1933).

As King Lear, at Cranleigh (1934).

With Rachel at Liverpool – an engagement photograph (1935).

With Alfred Sangster, Rachel, Deirdre Doyle and Eileen Douglas in *Miss Linley of Bath* (1935).

With Lloyd Pearson and Jane Baxter in *A Hundred Years Old* (1935).

With Denis Webb, Rachel, Deirdre Doyle and Cyril Lister in *The Wind and the Rain* (1935).

Naval College at Dartmouth – Rachel's father was Headmaster – where certain cadets were keeping up a constant menacing watch for Redgrave coming up the drive. Privately, I doubted this. After all, Redgrave would have been no more recognizable to any of them than the Barber of Seville.

Years afterwards Rachel and I simultaneously confessed that there had been a weakening of resolve on both sides. Eric, Rachel's father, most sympathetically, had gone so far as to say that it could still be called off. And there were moments when I would have been only too glad to hear that it had been. But I funked the role of the jilter.

According to custom, the wedding gifts were put on view in the drawing-room. Needless to say, there were more presents from the bride's friends than from the groom's. So far, so good. But my best man, Dick Green, my closest friend at Cambridge, had asked me what I wanted, and I had chosen a print by Maillol, one of a series of nudes. I was not present at the moment when Rachel's mother, Beatrice, saw the print, but Rachel told me there followed a short, serious discussion as to whose feelings would be more offended: the guests', if the nude were to remain on display, or the best man's and the groom's, if it were not (it being impossible, of course, to please both parties at once). The nude was turned to the wall.

After this, the wedding ceremony itself was plain sailing. I had not spent all those years as a chorister at Clifton for nothing, and sang lustily. Cyril Maude, an expert light-comedy actor, was the guest of honour, and made the speech. The Dartmouth cadets crossed swords and were given a half-holiday.

The time came for Rachel to put on travelling clothes, amidst renewed signs of tearfulness from mothers and aunts. We had been lent a comfortable old Morris by Rachel's father and, during the last two weeks of the Playhouse season, I had attempted to pass the driving test. My examiner professed to be an ardent fan of everyone at the Playhouse and knew that I was going to be married, and somehow I thought this might prejudice him in my favour. No such luck. With a broad grin he said, 'Sorry, old man, I'd sooner see you both come back in one piece. Failed.'

So it was arranged that a hired Daimler with chauffeur would drive us from the College to Totnes, where the old Morris would be waiting for us with 'learner plates' attached. I drove fairly competently, buoyed up with champagne, until we got to Exeter. Then Rachel, who was an expert driver, drove us through the town.

The most lavish of all our gifts was the cottage we were lent on the river Hamble, together with an excellent cook. But it was thought we would not reach the cottage in one swoop, so a double room had been booked at a hotel in Lyme Regis.

Rachel seemed rather nervous, I thought, so I volunteered to go down to the bar and have a drink while she changed upstairs. The wedding champagne was having a soporific effect on me, and two dry sherries in the bar somehow failed to produce the amorous, seductive character I was hoping to become. I thought of Margot, but that didn't help much, either. We were both eager to get into bed, yet I knew for a certainty that when we did, I, for one, would fall asleep. And so it happened. But it was a very happy awakening for both of us.

A delightful actress joined the company for the second season: a rather surprising engagement, since Jane Baxter was already a star performer. She had played leading parts in London and had made two films in Hollywood. She was every undergraduate's ideal of an English rose. I viewed her arrival with some alarm, wondering how it might affect the parts Rachel would play. But there was no need. The opportunities William gave his Company were well judged, as I might have known they would be.

There was to be a double bill: *The Copy*, by the Scandinavian playwright Helge Krog, and *A Hundred Years Old*, by the Quintero brothers. To my delight I was given the leading part in both plays. In the Krog piece I played a Schnitzlerian, worldly cynic (with a beard, to show I was cynical). The Liverpool evening paper, which always published a photo of the play after the first night, pleased my vanity by printing my picture above the caption 'Redgrave – with a beard.' To be referred to, not as 'Mr Redgrave', not as 'Michael Redgrave', but as 'Redgrave' *tout court*!

A few nights later, after the curtain call, on our way back to our dressing-rooms, Jane called to me, 'Michael, have you got a second?' She introduced me to a tall, sauve, very English Englishman, Bill Linnit. He was her agent, and had invited himself up to Liverpool to see how she was getting on. He asked me if I were going to be in any of the shows to come. I mentioned, among others, *Richard of Bordeaux*. I said I wasn't sure that I would get the part, but that it was whispered that I would.

'Ah,' said Mr Linnit, 'if you're not sure, then there is some hope for my project.'

He went on to say that watching the performance that night he had had it in mind to offer me one of the leads in Henry Bernstein's *L'Espoir* in London, 'unless, of course, you want to stay here to play Richard. I think you'd be wise to do so.' He asked me if I had an agent, and said that if he could help me in that respect, he'd be very happy to do so.

I thanked him profusely. I longed to stay and question Jane, but instinct said it was better to make a quick exit. A day later he repeated his offer by letter. But again he stressed that if I were offered Richard I should be wise to stay on at Liverpool. He would come up and see me in it. There would be many other offers.

That night Rachel and I sat up till two in the morning, by which time I had played the lead in *Richard of Bordeaux*, acquired the lease to His Majesty's, commissioned T. S. Eliot to write a play for both of us ... and what was *L'Espoir* anyway?

Linnit was as good as his word. A few weeks later he sent me a note saying that he was coming to Liverpool to see *Richard of Bordeaux*, bringing Hugh Beaumont with him. The name meant nothing to me.

Bill's face as he entered my dressing-room after the performance looked tired and sad, and for an awful moment I thought he had been disappointed. But no, his car had broken down outside Chester, and he had seen only the last two scenes of the play. In came a young man: 'Bill has told you? I *am* sorry. I *am* sorry. *What* a shame.' Almost at once he asked where the telephone was, and then began a series of telephone calls to London, and from these I gathered that this Mr Beaumont had something to do with the theatre. I looked around for Willie Armstrong, but he had fled the building. Two such stars could not keep their orbits in one sphere.

Rachel and I had decided that, rather than take them to supper at the Adelphi Hotel, it would be more chic for us to give them white wine and smoked salmon at our rooms in Falkner Street. Mr Beaumont, we learned, was a new but powerful producer, whose other name seemed to be 'Binkie'. Did I know *The Ante-Room* by the Irish writer Kate O'Brien, he asked. No, I didn't. 'Pity,' said Binkie, 'I was thinking of asking you if you would care to play the leading male part in a dramatization of it.' Diana Wynyard was to play the lead. Diana was a very big star at that moment, having done some Hollywood pictures. She was also well-remembered in Liverpool, where she had played for a season at the Playhouse. The play would be directed by Guthrie McClintic, Katharine Cornell's husband.

At nine the next morning Rachel and I were up and out, searching every bookshop in Liverpool for Kate O'Brien's novel.

My part, if the novel was to be trusted, was a good one, and the prospect of landing such a leading role in the West End was immensely pleasing. Meanwhile, arrangements would be made, said Binkie, and a script would be sent as soon as it was ready.

But, before I received it, another important person arrived unexpectedly in Liverpool whose visit was to change the course of my young career and put in the shade such ambition as I had of landing feet first in the West End – Tyrone Guthrie.

IX

I FIRST met Tyrone Guthrie in Cambridge days. I doubt whether he noticed my presence much, though his presence was unmistakable. He was a giant of a man, even taller than I, with a short military moustache and a funny, light head-voice – nowadays it would be called 'camp', though he was far from 'camp' – with which to deliver devastating one-line judgements. At the Festival Theatre just outside Cambridge, he staged witty, inventive, very theatrical productions. When you saw them you realized that times had changed.

I wrote to him several times during my interlude as a schoolmaster at Cranleigh, inviting him to come down and see my productions. He would reply expressing regret – genuine, I felt – that he was unable to come. For my final production, *King Lear*, I wrote again, and received the usual kind reply, thanking me for the notices I had sent in the hope that they might tempt him. Yes, he had heard the production was 'brilliant'; he wished me luck in my forthcoming job at the Liverpool Playhouse; but no, regretfully, he couldn't come. I made one last desperate attempt and rang him. Telephoning from school was no easy matter. There was chapel at nine, followed by lessons throughout the morning, and the only available phone was in the music master's rooms. Guthrie at eight-thirty in the morning was a little less urbane than usual. Wasn't I 'a bit of a mug' to be giving up my safe job as a schoolmaster? He wished me luck but, again, was sorry that he wasn't able to come.

It was two years before I heard from Guthrie again. We were nearing the end of our second season at Liverpool, and Rachel and I were playing the young leads in a James Bridie play, *Storm in a Teacup*. It was 1 May 1936, the sort of morning which makes Liverpool – to us who loved Liverpool – look its sootiest and most appealing. We walked, as usual, to the theatre for rehearsals for

Twelfth Night, the last play of the season, in which Rachel was to play Viola and I, Malvolio. The letter at the stage door had been delivered by hand that morning, from the Adelphi Hotel.

> I saw your show last night [wrote Guthrie], and enjoyed it very much. We are en route for Ireland for a short holiday. I saw William Armstrong and he tells me you have several alluring offers in view, so I don't suppose there is much likelihood of my being able to persuade you and your wife to come to the Old Vic with me next autumn. The money we can offer you will *not* compare favourably with a West End salary. But the work would, I think, be more interesting, and possibly, at a long view, more profitable even in a worldly sense. I know in Rep. one has neither time nor energy for writing, so enclose an addressed postcard which may save bother.

Malvolio that morning smiled and smiled, and Viola positively danced through rehearsal.

I did, it was true, have one other offer in view: *The Ante-Room*. This had no doubt been elaborated and added to by Willie Armstrong so as to paint a picture for Guthrie of West End managers queueing for our services. When we had told him that we wanted to leave at the end of the season, he had done his utmost to dissuade us. But now, having reconciled himself to our leaving, he was not going to allow Guthrie to think he was discovering any ordinary actors.

The postcard enclosed with Guthrie's letter read:

> We are / are not interested in the idea of an Old Vic season. We are / are not available. If your salesman calls (in plain van) around May 25 we can / cannot discuss the matter fully.

We lunched at the Bon Marché, wondering what parts Guthrie might offer us. It seemed too lucky to be true, that we should have the chance to go on working together. Supposing Binkie had brought a script of *The Ante-Room* with him, and I had already signed a contract? Supposing Guthrie had seen us in less good parts in another play? We wrote to him that afternoon.

He replied by return of post. He couldn't yet promise an exact list of parts, he said. He was in negotiation with Edith Evans, and after Christmas, Laurence Olivier would probably join the company, so the final list of plays and parts would have to wait on their acceptances.

> Olivier and you might a little tend to want the same parts, but I'm inclined to think that even with Olivier there would be enough for you to do in order to show yourself to the public and the critics in the best way e.g.

94

Horatio, *not* Hamlet, in the noted tragedy of that name. I think that from your point of view it would be wiser to make a very favourable impression in a few leading roles (not the big classic parts) and in good second parts, rather than take the risk of appearing straight off in the big parts in which you eventually want to make your name. I think the honest summary of the position is that I would like to use you two as the *juvenile leads* not as the *stars* of the season; though we should 'star' you in the billing. I can't say exactly about the money but it wouldn't be much – top salary is £20 per week. I expect you'd get that or somewhere near it. The following list of plays and parts is strictly provisional, but I think I can say that it represents the sort of stuff you would be asked to do. If there were any part or parts you particularly wanted I would gladly make an effort to arrange things to make it possible.

The Merchant of Venice	Portia
	Bassanio
Antony and Cleopatra	Charmian
	Caesar
Ghosts	Regina
	Oswald
Hamlet	Ophelia
	Horatio
Love's Labour's Lost	King
	Princess
Witch of Edmonton	
Within the Gates	leading juvenile parts

(produced by Michel Saint-Denis)

He ended by suggesting, 'If you want to play it we might try to do *Richard II*,' and promising, 'I anticipate getting money to spend on the productions, so the scenery and costumes will not, I hope, be tatty.'

(Lilian Baylis was notoriously tight-fisted: £25 was the budget for scenery and costumes for each production until Guthrie arrived, though, of course, it should be remembered that the theatre then had no subsidy and each play had to pay its way for its four or five weeks' run. Guthrie as director and his leading actors were engaged for the season, the supporting players from play to play, and all were on rock-bottom salaries. Baylis herself, of course, never directed, but hers was the dominant presence at the Vic throughout her life. She could hardly be said to have had a 'policy', still less a 'house style'. But more important than policy or style are vision and purpose. Baylis's vision of a popular theatre presenting its classics to a local audience was heroic. The Vic in her day never talked down to its audience, never imposed on them, and never tried to overawe them. As a result, it won their respect and their fierce loyalty to a degree unsurpassed by any other theatre.)

My reply to Guthrie was a mixture of shrewdness and sheer cheek:

The prospect of Oswald is tremendously attractive to me, especially playing with Miss Evans. [So it was: I always wanted to play Oswald, and never did.] But I imagine this would almost certainly be one of the plays which would drop out if Miss Evans did not come. [My instinct was right: Edith did come, but didn't want to play Mrs. Alving, and *Ghosts* was dropped.] I feel that supposing I played just those parts you mention, but not Oswald, I should be like a card player who has a fair hand, one to play an intelligent-enough game, but with which he could not possibly win. This is due, of course, to the fact that juveniles are, often as not, rather unexciting parts, and the exciting ones, except Oswald, would all be played by Olivier. And I wondered whether you had not perhaps noticed something of the sort when you suggest I should play *Richard II*? Your list of parts, given the plays, and Olivier, are certainly varied, but with the exception of Oswald I could play them on my head, as the saying goes. If you can find some way to give me one or two parts I could really get my teeth into, I should be very happy. I expect you want someone for Claudius with more weight than I could be supposed to assume – but I should very much like to play Laertes rather than Horatio. It seems to me that Laertes should be a young soldier, very forceful and physically bigger than Hamlet, bursting with health and proper pride, and so untouched by sorrow that his reactions to Ophelia's madness become, as they easily might, selfish, conventional, and a little unreal. I imagine that is how Matheson Lang must have played him when he was young. Then, if you would consider me as Macduff rather than Malcolm [Guthrie had said that Olivier, if he came, was keen to play Macbeth], and Archer, rather than the attendant without in *The Beaux' Stratagem* [another possibility, if Edith Evans were to come], I should feel I was really getting somewhere.

The cocksure tone of this letter, from a young actor who had yet to prove himself outside provincial repertory, is outrageous, though Guthrie, to his credit, took it in his stride. ('Laertes by all means if you prefer, though *I'd* call Horatio the better part.') I had no conception then that I could possibly fail in a part. I set no bounds on what I could do. I scarcely knew what it was like to feel nervous on-stage.

96

Love's Labour's Lost opened in September 1936 at the Old Vic to good notices, though rather poor houses. The stars, Evans and Olivier, had yet to join the company, and we were a very young group, with Guthrie putting us through our paces. Alec Guinness was Boyet; Alec Clunes, Berowne; Rachel was the Princess of France and I was the King of Navarre. Guthrie, introducing us in the Vic-Wells magazine, sounded rather like the *maître d'école* assessing his newest intake:

> Incidentally, the small permanent company includes two young men for whose future we have the highest hopes. Alec Clunes is not unknown to Old Vic audiences. He is still very young, but the promise of great gifts is apparent: and when time has a little mellowed and ripened them there is the possibility of great things.
>
> Michael Redgrave is a few years older. He comes with the reputation of two very fine seasons of work at Liverpool Repertory, the nursery of so many excellent actors. We believe he has the equipment of a potential star. He has refused more lucrative offers, both on stage and screen, because he preferred to work at the Vic in plays of quality. It is our hope that this season will establish him as a new leading man.

Clunes had the most beautiful voice I had heard in a young actor and was an excellent Berowne. Nevertheless, I couldn't help thinking that he and I might be rivals, and wondering why Guthrie had passed me over for Berowne. Ferdinand, as I had told him, was one of those parts I thought I could play on my head. Guinness, as Boyet, had a rather tiresome part, and succeeded against the odds in bringing it to life. He had, and still has, that most valuable asset for comedy: the appearance of possessing an impenetrable secret.

And the promise of money to spend on the productions had not materialized, at least not yet. There was a real fountain centre stage, as there had been in Guthrie's last production of the play. But at the Vic the set had a distinctly utilitarian appearance. The skycloth had seen far better days, and a gauze had to be hung in front of it to hide its wrinkles and gashes, giving the whole play an autumnal, hazy look quite at odds with its springtime theme. And I hated my costume. It was absurdly frilly and over-pretty, marabout edged in lace, like an illustration to a child's history book. Here, perhaps, was the chink in my seeming armour of self-confidence. I had a slight secret fear that I might look effeminate, that out there in the audience someone would say, 'He's a bit of a "nancy".' I would counter this by charging myself up in the wings to strike what Macready calls 'the firm manly tone'.

Besides this half-acknowledged fear, I had an inhibition, quite evident in my photographs of this period, about smiling. 'You should use your smile more, dear,' my mother would say, 'you have such a charming smile.' But I couldn't. I was embarrassed about showing my teeth. I went to the dentist to have them filed down, but it was little help. Later, in my first film part, they plugged a gap between my teeth with gutta-percha, which was constantly falling out but seemed to overcome the problem.

But these were small clouds, easily overlooked. Rachel and I had taken a small furnished flat in Greycoat Mansions, off Victoria Street. Soon we should need a larger flat because Rachel was pregnant. That much we knew, but in all other respects we were thoroughly ignorant. So when someone recommended a doctor who advised a vegetarian diet for Rachel, we accepted this as if it were the latest medical wisdom and became regular customers at the Vega Restaurant near Leicester Square, never questioning the fact that Rachel became more and more hungry and weak throughout her pregnancy.

'Have you read *The Country Wife*?' asked Guthrie, one of our first visitors at Greycoat Mansions. 'Read it, and see what you think of Horner.' He explained it would be done in co-production with an American management, and would transfer to Broadway after a six-week run at the Vic. 'I think it would be rather chic for a young actor in his first season in London to go straight to New York, don't you?'

On the first day of rehearsal of *The Country Wife* – the 'read-through' – the entire company was assembled, and there was a kind of quiver in the air; for an actor no other occasion can match this, except perhaps the first night. One or two nonsenses were spoken in asides to each other by the cast. One of the student actors whispers, 'I've got two lines – "Yes, Madam" and "No, Madam" – I'm simply terrified.' 'No need,' says another, knowledgeably. 'You'll see. Guthrie always invents the best business for his extras. He's wizard.' After the introductions were over, all eyes turned to the American actress Ruth Gordon – the unknown quantity. Miss Gordon seemed supremely confident. Well she might be; her knowledge of the play exceeded all of ours, including the director's. She had played it with resounding success in summer theatre, and she clearly knew more than her lines.

The whole production was to be far more costly than had ever before been mounted at the Old Vic. Never had the old boards creaked under the tread of such expensive shoes. The leading actors may have agreed to play for a low salary, but Oliver Messel, the designer, had it in his contract that if anything in the set or costumes did not meet with his approval, it should be changed. With no argument.

Gilbert Miller, the American impresario, and Helen Hayes, a close friend of Ruth's, had raised the money to mount the production first in England, before transferring it to New York. It had, I suspect, always been an ambition of Ruth's to be acknowledged as a classical actress, and though it might be stretching a point to claim that Wycherley's *The Country Wife* is the pure serene of the classical temple, it was nevertheless a minor classic and would serve as a 'classic' vehicle for Miss Gordon. She took it greedily and joyously with both hands. Not for her to revert to giving a mere reading. Her bright, bird-like eyes twinkled. She put down her script, having no need to consult it, and launched into a full-scale performance. Did I say I was never nervous? I was that morning.

I was conscious during the reading that those bird-like eyes were fixed to some extent on me. And every now and then she would shoot a glance at me which did not bode too well. What was to be decided was whether I was mature enough to play the lead in such a company. I felt miserable and uncomfortable. But apart from me, the cast read with great spirit. Edith Evans, as Lady Fidget, was in her element. Altogether it seemed certain that, when Guthrie had got to work on the play, all would be well.

My difficulty was that, when giving me the play to read, Guthrie had given me no indication of how he wanted me to play Horner, who, it will be remembered, feigns impotence in order to deceive the husbands and seduce the wives. Once rehearsals proper had begun, I thought I had found a clue to his character, but at each attempt of mine to fix the salaciousness of the part, Guthrie would shake his head. I did not know then, nor did I learn until the play was already in performance, that I was being directed to soften the ugly contours of the play, to placate the Old Vic's Board of Governors. Guthrie had told Lilian Baylis that such was my youthful charm that not one of them would see a jot of harm in the antics of this pleasant young scoundrel. This ploy succeeded admirably so far as the Governors were concerned. As Lord Lytton, the Chairman, wrote in a letter to the *Daily Telegraph*: 'The coarseness of the play can only be redeemed by the rendering of the part of Horner. The fact that he is performed at the Old Vic by an artist whose inherent niceness is so transparent, makes the whole thing a clean and not a dirty entertainment.' Right you are if you think you are. But it left me hopelessly at sea as rehearsals progressed.

When, three weeks later, it came to the dress rehearsal, all attack had left me. My voice sounded soft, my motions apologetic. Jed Harris, Ruth's common-law second husband, who had come over to vet the production, drew me aside and said, 'You know, Mike, if I were playing your part, I'd start with Horner in bed, and during his first scene with the doctor I'd start to dress and try and make myself more alluring. I'd maybe put him in corsets, and apply a patch to each cheek. . . . '

I listened, but couldn't think what to say. I was sure that Charles Laughton, who had come over with Jed, was working on Lilian Baylis. 'Let me play the part,' I could almost hear him saying, adding, no doubt, 'At the same salary. Just to show you how it should be done.'

To cap it all, Tony Guthrie gave me at the final dress rehearsal an almost impossible piece of business to cover a scene change. Rather than lower an act drop, he wanted me to walk across the stage laughing throughout the length of time it took to change the set. It was like corporal punishment. I was already sufficiently despairing about my capacity as a laughter-raiser, let alone a life-giver. But Tony, as always once he had set his mind on something, refused to acknowledge any difficulty. 'Go on, Mike, laugh!'

Leaving my dressing-room that night, I found my mother, tearful. 'Murray Macdonald [the stage director] says you don't appear to be even trying. What's the matter?'

'I don't know what Tony wants me to do.'

'And you should smile more, dear.'

Just then we met Edith Evans coming from her dressing-room. Mother didn't greatly admire Edith. She called her 'a spurious actress', a 'clever woman' who had somehow fooled the critics. But at this moment Edith said something which, for the moment, pushed away my fears. I had sprained my ankle at the last but one performance of *Love's Labour's Lost* and was still limping.

'Here's the hero of the evening,' said Edith, 'still soldiering on.'

'Well, dear,' said Mother, cutting Edith short, 'remember what I said. It'll be fine. It'll be fine.'

Edith's words gave me a much-needed lift. When we assembled for notes the following morning, she gave me a radiant smile, and presently she said something more, which took my breath away. In her most honeyed tones, almost a whisper, as if she and I were old friends of long standing, she said, 'You don't want to go to New York to play Horner on Broadway' – she made it sound as if only a

great booby could possibly want such a thing – 'you want to stay
here and play Orlando with me.' All that day I was buoyed up with
the excitement her words had given me. But then, just before the
curtain went up, I overheard two stage-hands talking: 'I hear
Charlie Laughton's in front.' I felt as though all the wind had
been taken from my sails. I could see Laughton out there saying,
'That boy's no good.' Even the elementary sense not to break an
audience's laugh, which I must certainly have acquired after two years
at Liverpool, clean deserted me. Guthrie had devised some simple
business where I had to push Edith, as Lady Fidget, down on to a
settee and she, thoroughly predatory, had to pull me on top of her.
It got a huge laugh from the first-night audience. Almost oblivious
of this, I was rising to continue the scene when I felt Edith's hands
grip me at the waist with what seemed enormous strength, holding
me there on top of her until the laughter had subsided. Somehow I
braced myself to bluff my way through the remainder of the
evening, and I fancy that in some measure my performance strengthened.

Certainly it strengthened sufficiently during the three weeks
playing for the Gilbert Miller management to change their minds
about me. I knew they had had their eye on another actor, Roger
Livesey, for the Broadway production. But now they thought that
perhaps they should give me a second chance. I was sent for to
Miller's offices in the St James's Theatre to discuss a contract, and
he came out with the suggestion that I should play the part in New
York for the same salary as I was getting at the Vic, £20 a week. I
pointed out that Edith and Ruth could probably afford to play for
such a small sum, but that I could not, and I said this in sufficiently
positive and final a manner for Miller to be taken aback. He
dithered for a few moments. 'Well,' he said, eventually, 'time is
short, but all you have to do is to make up your mind.' I made up
my mind there and then. I would stay and play Orlando with
Edith.

Ever since, I have marvelled at my good luck. Had I gone to
New York at that stage, and been exposed to New York critics and
audiences, heaven knows how long it might have taken me to
recover. Not that I was afraid of such exposure. After a few weeks'
playing I had more or less recovered my nerve, and a portion of my
conceit. The London critics had been kind enough, and perhaps
ignorant of the play's real intentions, to praise me quite warmly.
Only James Agate in the *Sunday Times* seemed to have detected

what was wrong: 'Mr Redgrave was neither old enough, nor experienced enough, nor sardonic enough, and was altogether much too nice a youth to hit upon this play's ugly and middle-aged invention.'

The rehearsal room at the Vic – too hot in summer and too cold in winter – has witnessed some remarkable scenes. Unlike so many rehearsal rooms, it seems to take on the character of the actors who are at work in it.

During the rehearsals of *As You Like It*, its walls resounded to the cascade of merriment which was Edith Evans's voice. Her voice was very particular to her. She had studied with Elsie Fogerty, the great teacher-healer. (Much could be written of Fogerty's ability to divine the source of an actor's problems. Once, when in trouble with a part, Edith went to Fogerty, who said, 'Well, of course you can't act it in those shoes.' 'So,' said Edith, 'I took them off and that was all there was to it. I had no more trouble after that.')

Each day she had lunch in her dressing-room. She was dieting to reduce her weight. She was a sturdily-built woman, and now she needed to do what she had done so successfully as Millamant in *The Way of the World*, when she is reputed to have said to some admirer, 'I just say to myself, "You are the most beautiful woman in London"' – and so, for the nonce, she was. Unkind critics, not the professional ones, would remark that the three best actresses in London were 'Bosseye', 'Popeye', and 'Dropeye'. 'Dropeye', of course, referred to Edith, whose drooping eyelid can be seen in Sickert's portrait of her. She didn't follow fashion. The works of Schiaparelli and company had no allure for her. At first glance, indeed, one could describe her manner of dressing truthfully, if not charitably, as dowdy. And now that she was forty-eight, even her most devoted admirers feared that she had left it too late to play Rosalind again.

The Country Wife had been as big a success as it promised to be, and was still playing to packed houses. The advance bookings for *As You Like It* seemed, by comparison, thin. Even some of Edith's closest friends had not booked seats for the first night.

None of these perilous thoughts seemed to touch her. Only in the first scenes were her fears evident. As Rosalind the girl, she was less than persuasive. But when she changed into a boy her whole being seemed transformed. It was not that she looked in the least like a boy. The Watteau style which the designer had imposed upon the play was most unbecoming to her. But nothing mattered except her spell – even when, once, she 'dried'. She simply laughed, in the most assured way, and one could have sworn that the word that eluded her mattered far less than the music of her laughter. She waltzed across to the prompt corner, took her prompt, and waltzed back, laughing.

I had fallen under this spell when we were half-way through rehearsals. We had worked together all morning. When we came to the exit in Act Three – 'Will you go?' says Rosalind. 'With all my heart, good youth,' says Orlando. 'Nay, you must call me Rosalind' – at this point, when we were sitting close to each other on the ground, I leant forwards and, taking her in my arms, kissed her.

For several days Edith made no reference to the incident in the rehearsal room. Then, one morning, during a break, she asked me to have dinner with her at the Café Royal, a place which still offered an atmosphere of bohemianism.

'Tell me,' she said that night, 'why did you kiss me?'

I tried to shrug it off with a laugh. 'Because I wanted to. Did you mind?'

'That makes me feel quite sick.'

I felt like a man who goes out to paddle at the water's edge, and finds himself up to his neck in deep waters. We were silent for several moments. 'Is that a new hat?'

'Yes.' She smiled. 'Do you like it?'

I realized that I was completely out of my depth. Still I floundered on. 'You have a farm? Where is it?'

She told me about the farm. Thirteenth century. Moated. Guy's pride and joy. 'You must come down and see it one weekend. What about next weekend?'

'I'd love to.'

She had surprised me again by referring to her husband. I had no idea she had been married. Very few people knew of her marriage to George (Guy) Booth, a childhood friend, who had died tragically the year before.

The following day at rehearsal I asked her, 'Would you care to try the Café Royal again?'

'I was hoping you'd say that. Why not come to my flat? What do you like to eat?'

'Scrambled eggs would be very nice.'

That night after the show we went to her flat in West Halkin Street. 'There's something I wanted to show you.'

On the mantelpiece was a photograph of Guy pruning an apple tree.

'You see, I was in New York when he died. Playing the nurse in *Romeo* with Kit Cornell. I knew nothing of his illness until after his death. But it's there, do you see? There's death in that face.'

She asked me about my family – Mother, Andy, Peggy. She was particularly interested in my Portsmouth relations. I asked her about her Welsh origins.

'I'm not really,' she said. 'Not *really* Welsh. I just let them think that because of the name.'

'I do hope that you have no notion whatever of living your life without me,' she wrote. 'You simply couldn't do it. We have such beautiful things in common. Oh – so very common. Rice pudding on the hearth rug and coats over the back of the chair. Darling, please don't alter. I love you shamelessly.'

What with rehearsals of *As You Like It* by day and performances of *The Country Wife* at night, we hoped to conceal major indiscretions with a host of minor fibs and prevarications. When, in response to her invitation that night at the Café Royal, I went to stay for the weekend at her farm in Biddenden, Alec Guinness accompanied us. A photo, taken by her chauffeur, shows Guinness, a very young man, with a few sparse curls still lingering on his crown, arm in arm with Edith on her left hand; I, windblown, laughing, a head taller than my companions, arm in arm on Edith's right; and Edith, between us, her slacks tucked into woollen socks, like a land-girl, is smiling triumphantly as if saying, 'Aha! Look what I've got!'

That evening, after our walk on the Romney Marshes, Edith asked us both, 'What is your idea of a theatre?' Alec, answering first, talked gently but cogently about a company, like the Moscow Arts Theatre, working together, developing its own repertoire and style. And I answered in similar terms. Both of us had been inspired by the theatre of Jacques Copeau and La Compagnie des Quinze. A theatre without stars. 'But what,' asked Edith, 'would there be for me in such a theatre?'

I fell head over heels in love with Edith, and she with me. She had chosen me, a young actor floundering helplessly in his first leading role, to play Orlando to her Rosalind.

Esmé Church, our producer, was of the 'Yes, dear, that'll be lovely, let's do it again' school. I cannot for the life of me recall a single note she gave me during our four weeks' rehearsal, or whether she gave me a note at all. Nor do I think it mattered. I can think of one prescription only for any young actor who is to play Orlando: fall in love with your Rosalind. And if that should fail? Try again.

After six weeks at the Old Vic, and another four weeks when Edith played the Witch in Dekker's *The Witch of Edmonton* with me in the part of Warbeck, *As You Like It* transferred to the New Theatre, where it ran for a further three months, a very respectable run for Shakespeare then. I think Bronson Albery, the New's manager, must have known about our affair. He was casting for *The Taming of the Shrew* with Edith as Kate and Leslie Banks as Petruchio, and offered me the part of Biondello, probably thinking that we wanted to continue playing together. But I, thinking that Biondello was a very insignificant part after Orlando, turned it down with some amazement that it had even been suggested. I went into *The Bat*, a once highly successful thriller, with Eva Moore, which came and went with scarcely a flutter, to be followed by two more West End plays, which disappeared with equal dispatch. And then I joined John Gielgud's company at the Queen's Theatre to play Bolingbroke in *Richard II*.

'More and more I want us to be together in the theatre,' wrote Edith, on tour with Mother in St John Ervine's play *Robert's Wife* in the autumn of 1937 whilst I was rehearsing at the Queen's. 'Murray was full of praise for your Bolingbroke and, oh, how my heart jumps with pride when people speak well of you. The situation here is so odd, and would be unbearable over a length of time. Your mother and about six of us meet every night at supper, and I feel that the home possessive atmosphere of you, not wrongfully, is very strong, and there I am sitting in the midst, my heart singing for joy because of my share in your life, and nobody knows.'

I confided in my friend from Cambridge days, Paddy Railton. Under the pen name of 'Patrick Carleton' he had published several novels, including a fine historical novel, *Under the Hog*, which gave me the idea he might write something for Edith and myself. 'I told Paddy,' I wrote to Edith, 'and boy! was he excited! He looked like Armado in *Love's Labour's* – "I'm for whole volumes in folios." You'll find yourself with a Plantagenet trilogy on your hands if you're not careful!' But Paddy was by now suffering chronically from tuberculosis and wasn't able to complete the play.

'Isn't love extraordinary,' she wrote, 'the way it releases energy?' It was so, for her. She took up riding and then, having been chauffeured for years, learned to drive and passed her test. And her dress, very ordinary and everyday before, became distinctly smart and fashionable.

Though I never learned to ride nor to drive – I had given over driving to Rachel ever since our honeymoon – I nevertheless felt immeasurably strengthened by Edith's love. She had accepted me at a very early, critical stage in my career. One day, at the start of rehearsals for *As You Like It*, she had asked me, 'What do you want in the theatre? Everyone knows what Larry stands for, and what Peggy and John and I stand for. But what sort of an actor do you want to be?' Suddenly I realized that she was suggesting that I might, if I chose, and applied myself, and put thought and passion into it, find my place in such company. It took my breath away.

Her remarks about my acting, and acting in general, were brief, but illuminating: 'I am told you are going to be most excellent as Sir Andrew.' (It was the summer of 1938 and I was rehearsing in Michel Saint-Denis's production of *Twelfth Night* at the Phoenix.) 'It doesn't surprise me. I saw all the seeds of your acting when we were so much together. A look here, a look there, told me all I wanted. I just knew that you required stability of character to hold your talents in place.' Written in pencil, these last words are scored in so heavily as almost to break the pencil lead. 'If you want things enough, you can't compromise. To like them enough you must have passion. If you want to be first-class you must grow in loving and passion.'

Years later, in America, I gave an interview to Lillian Ross of *The New Yorker*, in which I spoke about Edith. It conveys, I think, the essence of our relationship:

> For me, Edith Evans has the authentic magic. Claptrap word though 'magic' may be, it's the only word for the stage. When she comes onstage, the stage lights up. She's a very strict person about her own profession and is without any of the nonsense. She's a real and dedicated artist. Her art is her life. Everything she does on the stage is interpreted through her own morality. It's the way Picasso paints. It's the way Beethoven composed. It's the thing the great artist has that makes him different from other people. I don't mean morality in a pettifogging way. I mean moral values, without which nothing is achieved, and nothing created. Part of it is caring enough about what you do to achieve something beyond the mundane.
>
> Acting with Edith Evans was heaven. It was like being in your mother's arms, like knowing how to swim, like riding a bicycle. You're safe. The late Michael Chekhov said once that there were three ways to act: for yourself, for the audience, and to your partner. Some of the

newer theorists say that if it's true for yourself, it's truthful, which is not so. The majority of actors act for themselves or for the audience. I believe that the only way to act is to your partner. As a partner Edith Evans was like a great conductor who allows a soloist as much latitude as is needed, but always keeps everything strict. It's strict but free. Never is anything too set, too rigid. The stage relationship always leaves enough room to improvise. For the first time in my life, acting in *As You Like It*, I felt completely unselfconscious. Acting with her made me feel, oh, it's so easy. You don't start acting, she told me, until you stop *trying* to act. It doesn't leave the ground until you don't have to think about it. The play and our stage relationship in it always had the same shape. It was entirely well-proportioned and yet, in many respects, it was all fluid. In the forest scenes between Orlando and Rosalind, she would encourage me to do almost anything that came into my head. Yet, if I had done anything excessive she would have stopped it by the simplest means. Somehow it didn't occur to me to do anything excessive. For the first time, onstage or off, I felt completely free.

After *As You Like It*, we saw each other only infrequently. It was Edith who ended it. Rachel and I, for what reason I forget, had had an argument and I, in a fit of temper, stayed out all night. Rachel rang Edith in desperation. She came round immediately and spent the night with Rachel, comforting her. Days later she wrote me a letter of farewell. She was incapable of jealousy and hated deception. And she was very fond of Rachel. She would always write, at the end of her letters, 'My love to your two ladies.'

The other lady, of course, was Vanessa, who was born towards the end of my first season at the Vic. It was the last Saturday in January 1937, a matinée performance of *Hamlet* in its entirety. I, as Laertes, could hardly put one foot in front of another. In the wings the other actors whispered, 'Any news?' I shook my head.

'If it's a girl, we can't call her Sarah,' Rachel had insisted. 'She'll end up being called Sally.' We had been sitting up late at night in our flat. Outside, it was snowing heavily. We were waiting to see whether the pangs which Rachel had felt an hour or two before should prove, yet again, a false alarm. From the bookshelf I picked out at random *Men and Memories* by William Rothenstein and, flipping through the index, I came upon the entry 'Bell, Vanessa'. That would do, we decided, and immediately, as if in answer, the pangs came with redoubled force, and we bundled off to Blackheath. There, as the night wore on more or less sleeplessly and the pains subsided, it seemed we were in for another delay.

In the duel scene at the matinée, Olivier placed his foil against mine with infinite care and we pit-patted our way through the fight as in slow motion. Then, between the shows, came a telephone call from Blackheath, and the evening performance flew. When it came to the duel, though Laertes was far from steady on his feet, the fight was fast and brilliant. Larry at the curtain-call made a speech, as was the custom at the Vic on Saturdays, and announced, 'Ladies and gentlemen, tonight a great actress has been born. Laertes has a daughter.' The gallery roared their approval, and from the wings the student actors wheeled on a barrow of flowers with the message 'To Rachel and Michael – Love's Labour's Not Lost.' And after the show, at the Moulin d'Or, a favourite haunt for actors, Larry and Bobby Flemyng cleared a path for me through the tables, throwing flowers to the astonished diners and singing out, 'He's had a daughter.'

X

IN 1928, during my first year at Cambridge, I read that there was to be a performance by the French actor-director Jacques Copeau, founder and creator of what came to be called La Compagnie des Quinze, entitled *L'Illusion*. It was, as its title promised, an exploration of theatrical magic in its simplest and most potent terms, as if a great craftsman, having made a crystal vase, had deliberately shattered it by letting it fall to the ground, and then, with one swoop of his hands, had reassembled the beautiful object in a new and yet more perfect form – the truth, as seen by the illusionist, becoming the truth, at that moment, for the spectator. Actors came forward inviting the audience to a game: 'We can make you believe in anything – and show you it's only an illusion.'

Then, when I was teaching at Cranleigh, came the visit of La Compagnie des Quinze with *Noah*, *Don Juan*, and *The Rape of Lucrece*, followed by a rarefied piece called *Loire*, in which the actors appeared as owls, grass-snakes, and wolves, impersonating the spirit of the great river. It was a revelation: now I knew what I wanted to do.

In *Don Juan*, the actor playing the Don's servant, Leporello, was of a sturdy, pleasant appearance, not so brilliant nor so rib-tickling as Leporellos sometimes strive to be, but fitting with ease into the pattern of a production which was graceful without being mannered, and funny without seeming to ask for laughs. He was Copeau's nephew, Michel Saint-Denis. He was to become, both as director and as teacher, an acknowledged hero of two generations of English actors – that of Gielgud and Ashcroft, and that of his students at the London Theatre School – and a hero of his countrymen, to whom he broadcast daily throughout the Second World War.

I was overjoyed to hear from Guthrie that Michel would be directing Dekker's *The Witch of Edmonton*, the play that was to follow *As You Like It* at the Old Vic, but dismayed to find, when the casting was announced, that Marius Goring, who had acted with the Quinze in France, had been chosen to play the juvenile lead, whilst I had been assigned a thankless role, off the stage almost before I had set foot on it – at all events, nothing to bring me to the notice of Michel. I was so riled at having to play this minuscule part, after my success as Orlando, that in desperation I begged Michel to allow me to swap parts with another actor, Leonard Sachs. It seemed to me that his part, although small, had at least a grain of evil in him. Michel raised an eyebrow at my request, but agreed to the swap, though in such manner as to suggest that there was not a halfpenny difference between the two roles or the two actors.

During the performances I would sit through my long waits with Edith in her dressing-room, with scarcely a thought for the play, neglected for the past three hundred years and soon, I thought, to be consigned once more to well-deserved oblivion. The critics patronized it with faint praise. Something of the quality which the Quinze had shown us in *Loire* kept bursting through, but not often enough. Edith, though praised for her performance as Mother Sawyer, the witch, found it very hard to discard Rosalind. There was always the sense that this old beldam concealed a joyous girl wanting to be out. She wore a bald wig with one sinister raven's feather, seeming one moment to beckon and the next to threaten. She begged me not to look at her.

Michel's first job in London, after the Quinze had disbanded in 1935, had been a production of Obey's *Noah* with John Gielgud. It ran for ten weeks and was respectfully received, but, as with our *Witch of Edmonton* the following year, some of the joy of the Quinze production was missing. There was a *Macbeth* with Olivier at the Old Vic. And then, in the autumn of 1937, Gielgud invited Michel to direct *Three Sisters* for his season at the Queen's Theatre.

John G. had assembled a company which was unique at that time; it not only glittered but was remarkable for being a team. His season was to consist of four plays, *Richard II*, Sheridan's *The School for Scandal*, Chekhov's *Three Sisters*, and *The Merchant of Venice*. I was to play Bolingbroke to John's Richard; Charles Surface in *The School for Scandal*; and last, but least, Bassanio in *The Merchant*. I was to be paid £25 a week, rising to £30 if the box office went above £1,200. So much I knew. But my request to be allowed to play Andrei in *Three Sisters* was stonewalled. Michel, said John, must be allowed to choose his own cast. He would see us working together in *Richard* and then make his choice, and whatever the outcome I should not be too disappointed – all the parts in *Three Sisters* were good.

We assembled for the first reading of *Richard II*. I felt proud to be a member of such a company: Gielgud as Richard; Peggy Ashcroft as the Queen; Leon Quartermaine as John of Gaunt; Frederick Lloyd; Harcourt Williams; Dorothy Green; beside them Anthony Quayle, Alec Guinness, Glen Byam Shaw, and George Devine. Gielgud himself was directing. He was only three or four years my senior, but I was still a comparative newcomer, with only three years' professional experience behind me; Gielgud had been a leading actor for more than a decade. It would be an exaggeration to say that I was in awe of Peggy Ashcroft. She was so thoroughly unpretentious and friendly. But I admired her greatly, from the time when, as a schoolmaster, I had seen her again and again in Komisarjevsky's production of *The Seagull*. (I have seen several actresses play Nina since, and it would be foolish to try to grade them either in technique or personality, though I must add that my daughter Vanessa would not have to fight her way into any list. But the memory of Peggy's performance is indelible.)

It was a nerve-racking occasion. I raced through Bolingbroke's first speech without difficulty, but when I came to his entrance in the lists – 'Harry of Hereford, Lancaster, and Derby am I' – I tripped over my tongue, pronounced 'Hereford' as 'Hertford', and came to a halt. 'That was wrong, wasn't it?' 'Quite wrong,' said John, smiling. I took a deep breath and began again.

John, even at the first reading, was as near perfect as I could wish or imagine. Ninety per cent of the beauty of his acting was the beauty of his voice. To this day I can see no way of improving on the dazzling virtuosity of phrasing and breathing which was Gielgud's in the cadenza beginning:

> Draw near,
> And list what with our council we have done.

English actors, observed the great French actor Coquelin, have turned into its own defect their national virtue, a passion for originality. Yet Irving, when he was about to play a part made famous by Frédéric Lemaitre, could write to a friend: 'You said you might have a few bits of business of the immortal Frederick. I never saw that great actor, but everything he did would be well worth consideration.' Fourteen years after the Queen's season, when I played *Richard II* at Stratford, some reviewers – amongst them Ivor Brown – found traces of Gielgud in my performance. I do not see how it could have been otherwise.

A passion for originality seized Guthrie, who directed *The School for Scandal*. There was a tendency for a director who wished to impose his mark upon a classical play to set the action in some different era from that in which it was written. Tony set *The School for Scandal* in the 1790s, so that one could almost hear the distant rattle of tumbrils. One thing bothered me considerably: John, as Joseph Surface, was faultlessly dressed in grey watered silk, while I, as his younger brother, Charles, appeared as a 'bumpkin come to town', as one critic put it. And yet Joseph expressly says that he is a fop 'only in his books', and Charles is said to be in debt owing to his extravagance, amongst other things, in his dress.

Once again, as in *The Country Wife*, I found myself at odds with myself. It was on such occasions that I found that, despite what discipline I had learned at Liverpool, my amateur training was still a distinct handicap. I was used to the easy approach of four or five months in which to rehearse.

I was, I suppose, scarcely surprised when John informed me that Michel wanted me to play Baron Tusenbach in *Three Sisters*. Michel, said John, wanted Tusenbach played as a character part. 'Fine,' I said, thinking that Michel obviously did not want me as Andrei and perhaps not particularly as Tusenbach. It would have been absurd to say that I was disappointed with the part. John himself had played the Baron in Komisarjevsky's production. Komis had directed the play with his usual sleight-of-hand, but since he was a Russian, everyone took his word as gospel. His *Three Sisters* was a highly romantic affair, with the ladies in crinolines and Gielgud as a handsome young lover who is killed in a duel.

We gathered together for the first reading. There are certain plays whose beginnings have an echoing quality. I can never listen to the opening of *Hamlet* without a shiver running down my spine:

> Who's there?
> Nay, answer me. Stand and unfold yourself.

'Unfold' has a resonance and depth of meaning which is almost wasted in this opening exchange. The same lambent quality is to be found in the opening few moments of *Three Sisters*. (The very number 'three' has an incantatory magic.) Listening to Gwen Ffrangcon-Davies as Olga that morning, I felt the same authentic thrill as when, a small boy in the gallery at Portsmouth with Uncle Willie, I had glued my eye to my rolled-up programme, waiting for the curtain to rise.

My own reading was rather sentimental and banal. I tried to apply to the part everything I had learned from my reading of Stanislavsky. I wanted more than anything to impress Michel. But as the days went by, I could see that he thought very little of my work. When he gave me a note or asked me a question, I would answer with a show of brightness but with a miserable lack of confidence within myself.

One day, when I came to Tusenbach's speech about migratory birds in Act Two, Michel stopped me abruptly. I had assumed the voice and stance of a lecturer, rather pedantic, beside his magic lantern. Michel gestured at me impatiently with his pipe-stem, bringing me to a halt. 'No, no, my friend. You speak as if the lines were important. You speak as if you wanted to make it all intelligible, as if it all made sense.'

'Isn't that what an actor is supposed to do?' I asked, somewhat tartly.

'No,' said Michel.

I thought, to hell with it, and read the speech again, throwing it all away. At once it came to life.

Michel's reaction was immediate: 'There! You see? You 'ave eet!'

I think I was near tears to have this commendation.

From that moment I seemed to grow in Michel's approval. When we came to the dress rehearsal I had a toupée, and a slight paunch, and a pair of gold-rimmed spectacles, which, besides giving me a slightly owlish countenance, twisted my ears forward. I also painted spots on my face. The effect of this disguise on the company was startling and gratifying. Michel continued to guide me. A week or so after we had opened, he took me aside, pointing out how I had begun to exaggerate certain effects. 'It's beautifully done,' he said, 'but you are underlining, and once you start underlining, it's not art.' No one in the theatre had ever spoken to me like that before.

Rachel had seen an advertisement for a mill and miller's cottage in Essex. We drove down to find a huge tower mill, in about three-quarters of an acre of garden, to be sold for £750. The sails were broken, there were no main services, and the well was not improved by a drum of oil which had fallen down it, obliging us to walk to a pump the other side of the village to fetch pails of water. But we knew we should be happy there.

I had signed the film contract with Gainsborough Pictures, with that all-important clause that I must have six months in every year free for theatre work. During the run of *Three Sisters* Michel had spoken to me about forming a company, mentioning the possibility of *Twelfth Night* and asking what I thought of it. I replied that *Twelfth Night* should be given a long rest. It had been so overworked that that most exquisite of comedies was in need of a holiday. 'Ah!' said Michel. I said I thought it would be impossible to find an adequate cast for the play. Michel smiled and said, 'But what would you think of Peggy as Viola, Ralph as Sir Toby, Larry as Malvolio, Stephen Haggard as Feste, and you as Orsino . . . or Sir Andrew?' That, I said, would be an entirely different matter.

I was doing my second film when Michel sent me the script of a Russian play by Mikhail Bulgakov. Called originally *The Last Days of the Turbins*, it was now retitled *The White Guard* in an adaptation by Rodney Ackland, and was to open the season with Michel's company at the Phoenix. It contained a number of excellent parts which might have been written for the company of *Three Sisters* and which perfectly suited Michel's talent for poetic naturalism. There was a wonderful part for Peggy and a fine heroic one for me.

It was a brilliant production but unfortunately it coincided with the Munich Conference and Chamberlain's 'peace in our time', and the play, which dealt with the fortunes and misfortunes of a bourgeois family in the civil war after the Russian Revolution, had to be withdrawn after three weeks. This was a serious setback to our hopes and plans. Bronson Albery had found the financial backing to launch our season. But to convince the backers, still sceptical about the prospects of a permanent company in the West End, we needed the kind of financial success as well as the esteem which *Three Sisters* had enjoyed.

26 October 1937

Michel [I wrote in my diary] came down to the Mill after the matinée last Saturday afternoon. *Twelfth Night*, having to be put into rehearsal so soon, has taken him by surprise and he has not prepared it fully. He prepares extremely thoroughly. A large notebook contains his notes for moves and motives, etc., no random jotting in the margin of a small text, no improvising. His moves and business, though altered sometimes, are nearly always right, very practicable, and never effective at the expense of some other point.

We rang up the Postmistress with elaborate instructions for the invaluable Mrs Brittain [our daily help]. I bought a cheese and some coffee at the French shop behind the Queen's for Michel to take down, feeling that it was important that these things, at least, should be good. Vera drove down with us after the play at night [Vera Lindsay, Michel's friend, a member of the company]. We kept imagining Michel inquiring the way in his delightful and astonishing accent. A very mature and positive person in every way, there is nevertheless something vulnerable about him on which one's affections fasten eagerly, so that one could not bear anything to happen to him. It was a glorious starry night when we arrived.

On Sunday morning it was fine and warm. Michel was in great spirits. I showed him over the Mill. The view from the top door, leading on to the fantail platform, was more stupendous than ever. The clover field opposite the house has been ploughed in the finest straight furrows and looks rich. *Il a un air maritime*, said Michel.

The Sunday papers arrived, which we seized on, to see if Edith's, John's, Sybil's and Emlyn Williams' letter defending *The White Guard* had been printed. It had, but under the heading 'A Helping Hand', which, as Michel said, gave more the impression of what fine chaps the writers were than a leg-up for our play.

Lunch came upon us suddenly. It was all delightful that day. Some time back I should have been so anxious to please Michel that I should have been self-conscious and boring. Now, since quite recently, I feel so much more certain of myself. Knowing his respect for me has helped almost as much as anything.

Vera is the most enchanting creature. In blue trousers, with a sweater and Russian handkerchief on her head, she transforms herself again : she always looks different and always lovely. She and Rachel set each other off like a red and white rose. I thought this when the three of us packed into Michel's car that afternoon. The peace of sitting there with Rachel, whom I have never loved more than these last few days . . . '

When we came to rehearse *Twelfth Night*, we found we had a good cast but not a brilliant one. Peggy was Viola. I was Sir Andrew Aguecheek, the part which Jouvet had played in Copeau's famous 1914 production, *Une Nuit des Rois*, brilliantly decorated with business derived from the *commedia dell'arte*. Drawing on everything which Michel remembered of Jouvet, we painted a character who is not simply the butt of all around him, but an ass who knows he is an ass and takes the utmost delight in it. James Agate, the doyen of Fleet Street theatre critics, called me a 'giddy, witty maypole' and spoke of my 'glorious clowning', and then wrote a second review, revising his opinion and saying that, no matter how glorious, my Aguecheek unbalanced the play. Quoting Lamb, Hazlitt, and a great deal of the play, Agate upheld the traditional interpretation of Aguecheek as a butt. I would still defend the perspective we found for the character. But I confess there was some truth in Agate's stricture that it unbalanced the production, if not the play.

Twelfth Night, all in all, was a failure. Michel, a very independent person in all other respects, was still in thrall to Copeau, and his production faithfully followed all Copeau's business. And without the brilliant cast Michel had hoped for – though it was a good cast – his production seemed overloaded and fussy. Audiences were poor; our backers took flight. All our plans for the remainder of the season had to be shelved.

There were several more weekends at the Mill with Michel and Vera. One I remember particularly, after *Twelfth Night* had opened and failed. The plans, the avoiding of excuses, or at least the disguising of them – how happy I felt, underneath my disappointment, to be implicated with such people in misfortune. Or rather I was unhappy, aware that I was unhappy, and content to be so, having good cause, though I had made a personal success and had none of the usual responsibility. Michel, a totally complete and honest character, was neither glum nor dull, as in his shoes I might have been. We only felt he had some secret information about life which he couldn't tell us. That day I remember as clearly in mood as I recall Vera crying and laughing at dinner 'about nothing'. Crying and talking and smiling, and trying to defend herself from Michel's teasing, all at the same time.

With the promise of another addition to the family we left our flat in Bayswater and took a long lease of a house in Clifton Hill, St John's Wood, with a garden in the front, and in the back a magnificent pear tree. I was now being paid well for films, and spent far too extravagantly on satin curtains and fitted carpets, not to mention two chandeliers.

It was here, in the spring of 1939, that we gave a party for the cast after the first night of T.S.Eliot's *The Family Reunion* at the Westminster. Michel was there, and of all the opinions to be voiced that night, it was his I valued most. All our guests having arrived, I took the opportunity of walking him into the garden to hear what he had to say about the production and of my part in it.

Michel had first brought Eliot's play to me, one weekend at the Mill, during the run of *Twelfth Night*. I told him how, after he and the others had gone to bed, I had stood reading the play, tears of fright pouring down my cheeks, so excited that I wanted to wake him up there and then.

> It is possible you are the consciousness of your unhappy family
> Its bird sent flying through the purgatorial flame . . .

It was, to say the least, a difficult play, not the least of whose difficulties was the hero's first entrance. As Lord Harry Monchensey, a modern version of Orestes, I was required to enter into the drawing-room of Wishwood, the family seat, where my family were assembled, not having seen them for eight years, and immediately be transfixed with fear at the sight of the Furies, who have pursued me. Eliot himself has written amusingly about those damned Eumenides:

> We tried every possible method of presenting them. We put them on the stage, and they looked like uninvited guests who had strayed in from a fancy-dress ball. We concealed them behind gauze, and they looked like a 'still' out of a Walt Disney film. We made them dimmer, and they looked just like shrubbery outside the window. I have seen other expedients tried: I have seen them signalling from across the garden, or swarming onto the stage like a football team, and they are never right. They never succeed in being either Greek goddesses or modern spooks. But their failure is merely a symptom of the failure to adjust the ancient with the modern.

And their problem, it might be added, is also the problem of the actor who is haunted by them. Only once, late in rehearsal, did I manage to get this extraordinarily difficult entrance right, to convey the fear and the suffering which are necessary without being merely melodramatic. But the harder I tried to recapture the emotion I had experienced at that rehearsal, the more difficult it became. I religiously got myself ready for the entrance well ahead of time, keeping as much as possible out of earshot of the actors playing the preceding scene. I scrupulously followed Komisarjevsky's tip about examining the texture of some object: he had advised his pupils, before they went on stage, to feel very carefully the texture of something – a piece of wood, some canvas – or the temperature of some metal object to achieve that 'circle of concentration' which the actor requires to master his nerves and alert his senses. But the harder I tried, the more completely I failed. Where I should have looked tragic, I looked merely worried. The reason was, quite simply, that I was trying too hard. Michel had told me during the run of *Twelfth Night*, 'You have both comic and tragic possibilities, but at the moment mainly comic.' There and then I had decided that I would be a tragic actor even if I died in the attempt.

I mentioned all this to Michel. He spoke kindly of my performance in *The Family Reunion*, and said that my difficulties were not all of my own making. The director, he felt, had made a great mistake in underlining the Greek origins of the play by the use of white Ionic columns and other stylized allusions to the Greece of Aeschylus and Sophocles. And, especially in the latter half of the play, there was a failure of imagination on Eliot's part. Where do Lord Monchensey and his chauffeur go at the end of the play?

I had wrestled with this question in rehearsal for some days before daring to broach it to Eliot himself. 'Well,' he said, 'I think they would probably go off and find jobs in the East End.' They might, but from the tone of his reply it was apparent that he wasn't at all sure.

Eliot had been present throughout our rehearsals. Very occasionally he glanced at the stage, but most of the time his face was buried in the text, as if it were a musical score. Not a word or a line was changed or cut. Once, I ventured to suggest to the director, Martin Browne, that a certain line might sound more human if it were turned around. 'Michael,' he said, with a forgiving smile, '*everything that man does is human.*'

It was at Clifton Hill, in July 1939, that our son, Corin, was born – Corin, the shepherd in *As You Like It*, and (another link with the same play) William, in case Corin should seem too fancy and because William is the most euphonious of all masculine names. We talked of calling him Cornelius, another sweet-sounding name, after his great-grandfather, Roy's father. That Cornelius had a tobacco shop in Drury Lane, and sold tickets for the two licensed theatres. When the authorities tried to stop this anticipation of Keith Prowse, Cornelius gathered his cronies in the stalls of Drury Lane, where at an appointed signal they all raised their newspapers, thus obscuring the stage and nearly causing a riot. Wisely, the authorities gave in.

Monday, 17 July

I got home earlier from the studios [Twickenham, *The Stars Look Down*] on Saturday, and found Rachel not so well, saying she thought she had a chill, feeling 'stopped up' and aching. She went to bed shortly after and had bread and milk for supper. After dinner, with 'Mac' [the nurse who looked after Rachel at Stonefield when she had Vanessa], I went up to her, brought the wicker chair down from the nursery and read her two chapters of *Lark Rise*, an enchanting book which Edith was reading when I saw her last. We said goodnight at 10.30, but I was some time getting to bed and not inclined to sleep, having a free day the next day for the first time for a fortnight.

At about 11.15 I went in to see Rachel again as her light was still on, and she said she thought she had started, as she had had pains, tightening and definite, twice since 10.45. We waited and talked, wide awake and now full of excitement, until about twenty minutes off midnight, when the pains recurred, regularly. So I called Mac, who had been asleep about three-quarters of an hour. She and I arranged the room, with oilcloth one side of the bed. I stayed up till one. Mac dressed, in uniform now.

Then I thought I'd better sleep a little, expecting I'd be woken within the next few hours. But it was 8 by the time I woke. Rachel had had pains regularly all night, dozing between, but increasing in power. We decided to ring for Dr Broadbridge. He came just before 9, a jolly little man in Wellington boots and a tennis shirt under his mac.

I had some breakfast. Shortly after, he came down and said it was all going fine and would be over in about an hour. At first I heard nothing but feet moving about, but when I went into the hall I could hear my darling Rachel crying with pain, not loud, high and suppressed. I wandered about, looking out into the garden, thinking the silliest thoughts, including the observation that I was watching myself, which I detested. I kept being sure it was a girl coming, to forestall my disappointment. Then I heard Rachel's voice groaning, very low and hoarse, like an animal. Then she said, in the middle of a cry, 'I'm so sorry,' which wrung my heart. The housemaid kept going up and down the stairs, as about her job. Each time I heard her coming down I thought it was the doctor or the nurse, and went into the hall. Then there was a lull, and I heard the baby crying, and thought, they know what it is, but I don't, I must know, they must tell me.

There was no sound from Rachel for some minutes, and I stood in the hall. Then I heard her voice, no longer in agony, and began to go upstairs. At last I couldn't wait any more, and hearing her say my name, called out, 'Rachel.' Then again. Then the doctor came to the door and said I could come in: 'It's a fine boy.'

Rachel and I hugged each other, crying with happiness and relief. And I saw him in the cot, wrapped round in a woollen sheet, wrinkled and ugly and matted with the thick paste he had been lying in. Rachel couldn't see him from the bed and we lifted the basket down for her.

Later I saw him bathed for the first time, saw his cord tied a second time, and wrapped up in a little package on his tummy. His little tongue was bright red like a wood strawberry, and his parts seemed enormous compared to the rest of him. He weighed 8 pounds less ¼ oz.

XI

FROM THE moment of my arrival in London I had been pursued by the films. But for a time I had resolutely refused all temptations from that quarter. Not that I had any objection to films as films. Quite the contrary; I had been addicted to them ever since the days when I was taken to see Annette Kellerman, the aquatic actress, emoting under water in a stuffy bioscope which had formerly been Terry's Theatre in the Strand. Towards the end of the First World War I saw *Intolerance* at the Stoll Opera House in Kingsway and walked home with Mother whilst searchlights picked out the German aircraft overhead, which somehow seemed much less real than Griffith's masterpiece. *The Rink*, *The Tramp*, *Shoulder Arms*, *The Kid*, Rod La Rocque, Laura La Plante, and the early Garbo pictures which, later as a schoolboy at Clifton, I saw at the cinema in Whiteladies Road – all these and many others I saw and loved.

As an undergraduate film critic on *Granta* I solemnly predicted that talkies would never last or, if they did, that they would be the ruin of the cinema. It was here that I came into contact with two good friends, Humphrey Jennings and Basil Wright, later to become great names in the documentary films of the 1940s. I remember vividly certain scenes of what must have been Wright's first film, which he shot himself – with, I suppose, some help, for he was also the protagonist – in sixteen-millimetre. It was a naïve little story of a young fellow from the country who came up to town for the day and got so confused by the London traffic and the noise and all the rest of it that he lost his nerve, his reason – represented by a taut frayed string which broke – and finally his life, when he was knocked down by a motor vehicle of some sort – a bus, I fancy – somewhere near Hyde Park Corner. I wish this piece of juvenilia still existed. I remember the general impression vividly, and it had a few of the lyrical touches which distinguish some of Wright's mature work, such as in *The Song of Ceylon*.

As Mr Horner to Edith Evans's Lady Fidget in *The Country Wife* at the Old Vic (1936).

With Edith Evans in *As You Like It*, at the Old Vic. I can think of one prescription only for any young actor who is to play Orlando: fall in love with your Rosalind (1936).

Edith Evans as Rosalind. 'You don't start acting', she told me, 'until you stop *trying* to act. It doesn't leave the ground until you don't have to think about it' (1936).

As Laertes, duelling with Olivier's Hamlet, under Tyrone Guthrie's direction (1937).

With Peggy Ashcroft in *The Three Sisters*. My chief emotion when acting with her was the same as when acting with Edith: a feeling of great safety and great freedom (1938).

With Margaret Lockwood in my first film, *The Lady Vanishes*. I, who believed that in good acting there must be a continual stream of improvisation, began to think that this business of hitting chalk marks was a very mechanical, second-best thing indeed. From Hitchcock I learned to do as I was told and not to worry too much (1938).

As Charleston in *Thunder Rock* at the Globe Theatre (1940).

In the Royal Navy. I'm the troop leader, sitting in the first row, centre (1941).

With Anatol de Grunwald, Paul Sherriff, Anthony Asquith, John Mills, Terence Rattigan and Basil Radford on the set of *The Way to the Stars* (1944).

The Redgraves.

Being welcomed to Hollywood by Fritz Lang. There must have been a dozen or more photographers who had made the journey out to Pasadena to photograph Fritz in his camel-hair coat and off-white fedora and me in my brand-new suit from Saks Fifth Avenue (1947).

In *Secret Beyond the Door*. Even Fritz Lang couldn't make a silk purse out of a sow's ear, and this was a sow's ear and a half. I could never bring myself to see it (1947).

Around the corner from Wright's rooms, the Cambridge Union Film Society showed us some of the great Russian silent-film classics, and I think I saw most of these. I remember an especial fondness for *Turk-Sib*, a documentary about the creation of the Turkestan-Siberian railway, with its remarkable shots of the irrigation of the desert and the steady push forward of the iron way across the barren wastes. Before this, as a student at Heidelberg, I had seen, several times, *The Student of Prague*, *The Golem*, the Fritz Lang *Nibelungen* saga, the early silent films of the demonic, elegant Conrad Veidt, and the astonishing, unforgettable young Elisabeth Bergner.

I do not wish to give the impression that I was solely addicted to the great Continental silent classics. If I mention them more than the *Ben-Hur*s, the *Big Parade*s, the Clara Bows, which I devoured just as avidly, it is simply because, in some aspects, they are more memorable.

With all this it may seem a little odd that when at last I decided to become an actor, I should have been so aloof towards the cinema.

But I was a stage actor, and at that time there was a gulf between the stage and the screen. Not an unbridgeable gulf: Olivier and Ralph Richardson made films, but only Charles Laughton took films, especially English films, seriously. Films, Ralph wrote to me when he heard that I'd been offered a contract, 'are where you sell what you've learned on the stage'. And besides, the actors I most admired – Edith Evans, Peggy Ashcroft, John Gielgud – had either done no films at all or only one or two, and those one or two had done nothing to enhance their great reputations.

I was playing in *Three Sisters* when at last I agreed to do a test, for *The Lady Vanishes*, which was to be directed by Alfred Hitchcock in a few weeks' time at Islington Studios. Having taken my decision, I spent a sleepless night on it. With the proviso that I should have six months a year free for stage work, I succumbed and signed a contract.

Of course, to do this I had to have Gielgud's permission, since it would mean leaving the company before the last play of the season, *The Merchant of Venice*. I asked Peggy Ashcroft whether she thought John would mind. She begged me to think again. John cautioned me that it might be thought that I was leaving having played my best parts. (True, only Bassanio was to come, and I didn't relish Bassanio.) But the more that they and other members of the company sought to make me change my mind, the more I thought I had the right to go ahead, provided Gielgud should not positively say no. Edith lamented, 'I'm disappointed only because you do not see that *all that* [films] will come later,' and she thought there was no sense in rushing things. Michel was not so censorious. The French cinema, after all, had its great directors – Renoir, Ophüls, René Clair – and great actors like Jouvet had given many fine performances on film. But he warned me to be careful. He had seen many actors, he said, who had signed film contracts grow to expect a life of luxury and accept parts which were not worthy of them.

All of this was good advice in its way, and I have repeated it myself to younger actors many times since. But I stuck to my decision. I must resist the temptation now to justify it overmuch with hindsight. To say that *The Lady Vanishes* became one of the classics of the screen; that the British cinema was soon to enjoy a renaissance; that the theatre in 1938, with honourable exceptions, of which the Queen's company was undoubtedly one, was at a low ebb, and that for years to come it would continue to suffer for want of an infusion of new creative writing – all this would be true, yet I felt at the time, for all the stubbornness with which, having made up my mind, I stuck to it, that I had made a mistake.

Having at last succumbed to the blandishments of Gainsborough Pictures (1928) Ltd, I found from reading my papers that I was to be 'teamed' with a very popular actress who was soon to head every annual popularity poll for the cinema and to acquire the sobriquet of 'the first lady of our screen'. This was somewhat alarming to me and, I dare say, to Margaret Lockwood.

We were introduced at a charity film ball at the Royal Albert Hall, where we danced together and were photographed in a tight embrace which suggested that, to say the least, we knew each other quite well. My first day's work at Islington consisted of a scene which was designed to show how boy meets girl and, as everybody who has ever seen Hitchcock's films knows, boy must meet girl in a way that is unusual and, if possible, 'cute'. The girl, a rich heiress stranded in a Middle European hotel, has been arrogant enough to persuade the manager to turn the young man out because he, a student of folk music, and his companions have been making far too much noise dancing in his room, which is above hers. The young man is evicted and, in revenge, makes his way into the girl's room, announcing, with a degree of arrogance and bad taste which certainly caps hers, that he is going to spend the night there.

Cinema-goers today are much wiser in the techniques and mysteries of film-making than we were then. I had no idea how fortunate I was, on my first day's work in the studio, to be given a scene from the beginning of the film and not to have to plunge into some climactic adventure three-quarters of the way through the film. What I did discover that first morning was the want of that quality essential to good acting on the stage: the rapport between artists who have worked together for at least as long as the rehearsal period. From the actor's point of view, it is possibly the gravest disadvantage of acting for the camera that one must do an important scene with someone one has never acted with, perhaps never even met, or, as with Margaret Lockwood and myself, met only briefly and in somewhat artificial circumstances. After some initial parrying, Margaret and I got along well, though we remained suspicious of each other for some time. She must have understood, though she was too kind to reproach me for it, that my mind and my feelings were a long way away from acting in films. I respected her professionalism, as I respected Hitchcock's, yet secretly I saw little to praise in it.

The next thing I learned on this my first morning was rather surprising to me; indeed, I expected the very opposite. It is generally supposed that acting for the stage involves a number of artificial gestures and movements which the actors cannot conceivably use in everyday life, but that is not so. In the theatre it is not only possible but essential for the actor to find a sequence of physical movements which – allowing for certain conventions such as raising the voice when playing upstage – seems completely natural to him. Indeed, a break in the flow of his physical movements can destroy the stage actor's sense of inner reality. It was not at all the same in front of the camera. I soon learned that one was frequently obliged to stand much closer to one's partner than one would ever do in ordinary life, or balance one's voice to a more even level because the microphone could not 'take' a sudden change of volume. Not only that, but every movement and every position, from one camera angle to the next, was subject to a series of slight variations, or 'cheats', to compensate for the disorientation which the spectator in the cinema would otherwise feel as the camera shifted from one place to another. Again, this would not be news to a generation of film-goers who take it for granted that if Alan Ladd kissed Sophia Loren he would be standing on a box, or if Robert Ryan shook hands with James Cagney he might be half-buried in a trench. But it was news to me, and rather disconcerting; I fancy that the amount of such 'cheating' which the camera requires in practice would surprise even the most experienced film-goer.

No one, on that first morning, bothered to explain to me the elementary grammar of filming. On my second morning I felt inspired to give a little lift to one of my takes with some improvised business. 'Cut,' said Hitchcock; and then, when the camera had stopped rolling and the scene had frozen to a halt, 'You can't do that.'

'Why ever not?' I asked. I had thought my business was rather a happy invention. But, it was explained, it would not match the business of the previous take.

So this is filming, I thought, schooling myself to try to repeat exactly what I had done before. I, who believed that in good acting there must be a continual stream of improvisation, began to think that this business of hitting chalk marks, adjusting one's gaze to right and left of camera in order to get the 'eyeline' right, and all the rest of the paraphernalia of filming, was a very mechanical, second-best thing indeed. Today, after many films, good and bad, I would no longer find these constraints inhibiting. I would seek, and on happy occasions I would find, within these necessary conventions, the freedom to improvise and find the creative mood. Then and there, however, I thought, Just say the lines and get on with it.

I have learned most of what little I know about film through my directors. From Hitchcock I learned to do as I was told and not to worry too much. Towards the end of *The Lady Vanishes* there is a short scene in which a foreign agent mentions that his perfect command of English is due to his having been educated at Oxford. Whereupon my character picks up a chair and crashes it down on the unsuspecting agent's head. 'Why did you do that?' exclaims an onlooker. My reply – 'I was at Cambridge' – seemed to me so utterly hackneyed and puerile that I should have dearly liked to ask Hitch to cut it. It was perhaps the biggest laugh in the picture.

Being the brilliant master of the technical side of his script that he was, he knew he could get a performance out of me by his own skill in cutting. He knew that mine was a very good part, that I was more or less the right type for it, that I was sufficiently trained to be able to rattle off my lines, and that, mercifully, since I was aware that not even the cleverest cameraman in the world could make me look like Robert Taylor, I was never particularly camera-conscious. But he also sensed that I found the whole atmosphere of filming uncongenial, to say the least, compared to the theatre, where I was playing every night with a remarkable cast. Besides his trick of casting against type, which he managed often with great success, he would use 'shock' tactics, believing, nót always correctly, that actors take themselves too seriously, and that those who have an infinite capacity for taking praise will sometimes perform better if they are humorously insulted. He evidently thought I had a romantic reverence for the theatre, and he could see that I had the newcomer's disdain for the working conditions of the studio. I do not know whether his famous 'Actors are cattle' remark was coined for my benefit, but I well remember his saying it in my presence. In time I grew to like him, though I confess I never warmed to the peculiarly dead-pan humour which was his hallmark, on screen and off.

By general consent . The Lady Vanishes is the masterpiece of Hitchcock's English period, possibly of all his films. Yet I confess I saw it through mud-coloured spectacles. The melodramatic touches – a hand pushing a flowerpot off the edge of a balcony, so that it lands precisely on an unseen person's head, the lifting of a nun's skirt to reveal a pair of shoes from the Rue de la Paix – all this seemed . . . no, I had a prejudice against Hitchcock.

I was sitting in the make-up chair on my third morning, brushing the sleep from my eyes, when a voice behind me said, 'They tell me this is your first film. I have made fourteen in Hollywood, and boy! is it a grind!'

It was Paul Lukas, an actor I greatly admired and liked, and in the long waits between each set-up, he and I discussed the horrors of film-making.

One morning when the film was well-advanced, Paul found me again in the make-up room. He came towards me with a severe frown on his face and then, with elaborate courtesy, took my hand and kissed it. English actors are not accustomed to kissing hands at seven-thirty in the morning. The gesture arrested me, as did, even more so, his next remark.

'You're a real actor! Why did no one tell me? I saw you in Three Sisters last night, and boy! you're a great actor. But here, my friend, you're not even trying.'

'No,' I said, 'as a matter of fact I find it intensely boring.'

'But, my dear boy, it's all going in the can. Once the director has taken the last shot of a scene it's too late to wish you could do it again. It's all in the can!'

From that moment I started to act. I could not bring myself to see the film until fifteen years later, but when I did I could detect, even at that distance of time, the moment when Paul had pulled me up and I had started to try.

After the disenchantment of working with Hitchcock, I was almost drowned in the milk of human kindness proffered me by Paul Czinner. Remembering those happy hours in the dingy little cinemas of Heidelberg, I could hardly believe that his wife, Elisabeth Bergner, one of my goddesses, should be there beside me on set. Paul sensed this and did everything possible to put me at my ease, flattering me in a thousand subtle ways to make me believe I was good enough to play opposite my adored Elisabeth. It was Gainsborough Pictures, when they leased me out to Paramount for *Stolen Life*, that insisted I should have equal billing with Bergner, even though not a single foot of film on me had been yet shown in public. To my embarrassment Paramount agreed. To my even greater embarrassment they agreed to Gainsborough's other stipulation that I should be paid a huge sum, almost ten times my salary with Gainsborough, the difference to be shared between Gainsborough and me. This almost wrecked the deal. I was so shocked by these manoeuvres that I told Paramount I wasn't interested in the money, I simply wanted to do the film, and I should be returning my half of the ransom which Gainsborough had extracted. This I did for several weeks, until someone pointed out that I should still have to pay income tax on it and might find myself at the end of the year regretting my gesture. It was my first introduction to the sometimes lunatic economics of the cinema.

Czinner was an imperfect perfectionist. He explained very carefully to me his view of the relationship between the actor and the camera, which was, roughly speaking, that if you shot sufficient feet of film, some of them must be in the right direction. He printed all the takes, and there were usually a great many, of all the shots. He said that by frequent close cutting and the selection of a look from one take, a line from another, and a particular, though perhaps quite irrelevant, expression from a third, a performance was very often much richer than the actor felt it to be, even in his best take. He personally directed the editing of the film, and no editing was begun until the entire shooting was completed.

Most of these feet were, quite naturally, focussed on Elisabeth. In common with most great artists, she demanded excessive consideration. In her case this meant above all the right not to face the camera until the sun was well over the yard-arm. Those brimming eyes and childlike features demanded many hours of lying in bed. Such conduct made her the subject of much exasperation, as it did years later with another great Hollywood actress. But not from me.

The publicity and the huge posters linking my name in letters ten feet high with this goddess went to my head. It is hard to describe the impact of a large poster on a little conceit. I know that in my case I was first flattered and then alarmed to find fans fighting in the gutter for my cigarette stub when I went to open a new cinema in Slough. Not one of my pictures had yet been shown. Perhaps not much harm is done if one retains a sense of humour. It was Sam Behrman who remarked – he, Rachel, and I were driving into Leicester Square for the gala opening of my picture *The Years Between*, and as we rounded the corner a frenzied cheering began and the full force of a searchlight hit me square in the face – 'Wonderful the way they get so much on the head of a sixpence.'

XII

THE OLD VIC in the autumn of 1939, on the eve of the Second World War, was to present its programme in 'a new repertory system', alternating its plays on different nights throughout the week. Not only that, but – was there no limit to Guthrie's experiments ? – the same leading part would be played on different nights by different actors. I was to share the main parts with Robert Donat and would be, said the *Evening News*, 'the youngest star ever to lead the company at the Vic'.

The approach of war brought with it the finest summer we had enjoyed for years. Donat and Constance Cummings were to open the season in August. I was to join the company in January, having completed my film commitments. Meanwhile I was eager to begin my preparations.

I remembered that Michel had told us how, when he was preparing *Three Sisters*, he had consulted Stanislavsky's widow in Paris. One of my parts was to be Uncle Vanya, and I decided to follow Michel's example by making a pilgrimage to Paris to consult Idyanova.

I had become a disciple of Stanislavsky by chance some two years before. Opposite the Victoria and Albert Museum was a bookshop which specialized in theatre books and magazines such as the American *Theatre Arts Monthly*. It was there that I stumbled on a copy of Stanislavsky's *An Actor Prepares*, which was to light my way for many nights to come. The effect was instantaneous.

I was playing the part of a doctor at the time – it was May 1937 – in *A Ship Comes Home* at the St Martin's. It was the second of three plays I did in quick succession after *As You Like It*, and I felt I was having to learn the art of making bricks without straw.

The single set of the play represented the doctor's consulting room, which the director had dressed with a clutter of objects strewn about in profusion. I was half-way through a matinée performance, in the middle of a love scene, when I looked at the mess around me and thought, this won't do, a doctor should be tidy, and set about tidying my room, to the consternation of my leading lady. I was, without knowing it, making the mistake of certain 'Method' actors who say, 'If it's true for yourself, it's true.'

Stanislavsky's widow, I had been warned, spoke very little French and no English, so I took Michel's friend Vera Lindsay, who was Russian by birth, to act as interpreter. We found Idyanova in what was left of Stanislavsky's apartment, sitting by a small table near the window, with her back to the light, which streamed on to me. She had been told that I was to play Vanya at the Vic, and was said to be very excited at the prospect of *un comédien célèbre anglais* coming to ask her advice. Her reaction was immediate. With a kind of sob she put both hands to her cheeks, a gesture much favoured by actresses of all nationalities, sobbed again, and then, with the utmost force, cried out, 'No! No!' My heart sank. 'No! No! No!' she repeated, 'No Vanya!' She approached me, and for a moment I thought she was going to lunge at me. Then her face unclouded and she stretched out her arms towards me, and with even greater force repeated, 'No Vanya! Astrov!'

Then all was laughter and tears. Astrov, the young doctor, after all, had been *his* part. For the next three days I took my interleaved copy of *Uncle Vanya* to work in Idyanova's apartment, or to walk in the Bois de Boulogne. I would ply her with questions: 'Why in Act One does Astrov say . . . ?' 'What does he mean by . . . ?' And Vera and she would go into a huddle, and after a great deal of talk to and fro, Vera would extricate some meaning, as often as not sibylline in its simplicity: 'Because he is bored.'

However, not only did I not play in *Uncle Vanya*, but the whole season turned out to be a season that never was. As devised by Guthrie, Donat was to have played Macbeth and Romeo, and I, besides doing Richard II and Vanya, should take over one of Donat's parts for the second half of the season. Uncertain which to choose, I asked Michel's advice and he plumped for Romeo. Edith thought I should take the more difficult choice and play Macbeth.

War came and put an end to my indecision. The nearest I came to playing Romeo was in a much-cut version for television at Alexandra Palace, with Jean Forbes-Robertson, and later, in 1940, at a charity matinée at the Palace Theatre, when Peggy Ashcroft and I flitted across the stage to the satisfaction of James Agate, who wrote, 'Michael Redgrave, with his swift turn of heel, may well turn out to be the Romeo of his generation.'

It was Peggy who suggested me to John Gielgud for Macheath in *The Beggar's Opera*. Rachel and I used to sing at Peggy's house in Campden Hill Road in Kensington, and hearing that John was thinking of an actor-singer for the lead in the Glyndebourne production of Gay's ballad opera, she said, 'Why don't you have Michael? He sings.' It was the winter of 1939. The war had started and no one would go to Glyndebourne, so Glyndebourne was coming to London, to the Haymarket. John agreed to Peggy's suggestion. Glyndebourne, however, needed convincing.

Rudolf Bing, who was to direct the production, came to Southport, where I was touring in *Springtime for Henry* with Rachel, Roger Livesey, and his wife, Ursula Jeans. It was the period known as the Phoney War, and theatres in London, which had closed overnight when war was declared, had now reopened. But there was little chance of our play, which had already had a big success in London and Broadway, coming to the West End.

So I stood on the stage, with an accompanist in the pit, facing Bing and John Christie, the founder of Glyndebourne Opera, in the stalls, and launched into Schubert, then Brahms, then some English folk-songs, and finally Macheath. 'Yes,' said Bing at the end, 'I think you can sing it. But could you sing it eight times a week without losing your voice?' I hadn't considered that. Bing continued, 'I'd like you to work with our voice coach, Jani Strasser.' I thought of Fothergill Robinson, and Munich, and Beibig, and said, 'Well, but I've known people with "natural" voices who ruined them by too much coaching.'

'We won't do that,' said Bing.

And so Jani stayed with me for the remainder of the tour. I took to him tremendously. 'You must have a continual flow of air,' he explained, 'like a waterwheel.' Jani taught through metaphor. His principle was breathing, that you must never sing on a dying breath. When you were getting to the end of a breath, and before you had exhausted it, you deliberately expelled the remainder. In other words, in order to breathe in properly, you had to breathe out. 'Amateur singers,' Jani would say, 'often think a volume of sound must come from the throat. Quite wrong.' He demonstrated. Like some teachers, he had a rather harsh, grating voice, though he would never admit it. 'It's as if you were fishing. You cast your line and start to fish. That's where your note comes from, the end of your line.'

I found Jani's metaphors illuminating, though they were not everyone's cup of tea. Years later, when Olivier was to sing Macheath in Peter Brook's film of *The Beggar's Opera*, I recommended Jani to him.

'That chap you sent me to,' complained Larry, 'says I've got a palm tree growing out of my forehead.'

Macheath has what is known as a well-built-up entrance at the end of Act One. For almost forty minutes, the other principals do little else than sing about him and talk about him, and to top all this expectation John had devised as sensational an entrance for me as anyone could wish: from a cupboard high on the landing, where I was concealed, pistols cocked, I took a leap over the banisters on to the counter of Peachum's shop, another jump to the stage, and straight into the duet 'Pretty Polly say'. This was followed by a short spoken scene, a solo, and then Polly and I sang what may be termed the show's hit number, 'Where I laid on Greenland's coast'. Then, with a few strides to the window, I looked out, tossed a huge red rose to Polly, and blew her a kiss. Exit. Curtain.

We were in our third week at the Haymarket and I was sitting in my dressing-room in the first interval, thinking how lucky I was to have 'got away' with Macheath. I had been too much preoccupied with the singing to lay the proper foundations for my character. John had muddled me in rehearsal, giving me one direction one day and countermanding it the next. On tour I had burned the candle at both ends, sitting up night after night with Ivor and friends from the cast of *Perchance to Dream*, tiring my throat and, against all advice, staying up when I should have gone to bed and called the doctor. And then, to cap it all, I had heard from Rachel that Edith Evans had said my work was suffering. This rumour, I thought, could only have come from John, who had dropped in to see a particularly bad matinée. Why, I wondered peevishly, did he have to choose that matinée?

Never mind, I thought, for the past ten days my acting had been truer and freer than ever before. Preparing to go on for Act Two, I gave myself a quick last-moment appraisal in the mirror: eyes slightly slanted, the corners of my eyes pulled back by two pieces of transparent gauze glued to my temples, joined to a piece of strong elastic beneath my wig.

The Second Act curtain goes up revealing all Macheath's accomplices. Very picturesque they look, too. I come in. They go out, singing 'Let us take the road'. As they go I seize a chair, and sitting astride it in that beloved old swashbuckling posture, chair back to front, with an amber in the fireplace to light me, I peel off my gloves to sing Macheath's best-loved solo, 'If the heart of a man'. It is at such moments, when an actor feels he has the audience in the palm of his hand, that his concentration slips and he hears things which at other times he would ignore. In that split-second pause between the last note of the orchestra's introduction and the first note of the verse I heard a voice from the Circle say, in a stage whisper worthy of Mrs Pat, 'And *who* is this?'

It was a Sunday early in May 1940 during the run of *The Beggar's Opera*:

> As I had breakfast in the dining room, Van was playing by herself in the garden. First she would rearrange the two bald dolls sitting in the dolls' pram, then wander round the pear tree in a rhythmic sort of way. She bounced a ball, found two sticks, came up the steps to the dining-room window, and asked to be let in.
>
> When I had to go she wanted to be taken to the nursery, and cried a little at being told to stay in the garden. I had to say a firm 'no'; any attempt to compromise brings on a real temperamental fit of tears.
>
> Rachel and I catch the 10.50 train to Great Missenden, to see Andy and Mother at Chapel Farm. We had got up after being telephoned by Cochran, who rang to say that Shaw had recommended me for a part in a musical version of *The Importance of Being Earnest*. Flattering indeed. I had woken very cross and tired, partly because Rachel had cried when we woke, and partly because we had sat up till 3 or so in the morning, talking things out. For two nights before I had not been home, and though I imagined that Rachel knew where I was and accepted it, I find that I have caused her two days of agony. I felt in despair with myself at my cruelty.
>
> I told Rachel all about Roy and his end: always it returns to this question of a split personality, and I cannot feel that it would be right – even if I had the will-power, which I have not – to cut off or starve the other side of my nature. I complained, weakly, but with some sense, that whereas people go to see plays like *Mourning Becomes Electra* and *The Family Reunion*, they nevertheless think a person morbid who feels as those characters feel and I felt last night, and have felt obscurely before, that
>
>> It is possible you are the consciousness of your unhappy family
>> Its bird sent flying through the purgatorial flame ...
>
> Chapel Farm is looking wonderful. The skyline of the Chilterns – a great gentle bowl – is now all the tenderest green. Some fruit blossom is still out; there are smells of woodsmoke from the chimney, and sturdy wallflowers in the front beds.
>
> Andy and Mother are very glad to see us. We walk and sit in the brilliant sun, with cocktails, before lunch, and afterwards sleep in deckchairs in the rose garden, while Andy retires indoors. Presently Rachel, Mother and I walk down the lane to a favourite gate. The

hedgerows are full of violets, speedwell, bluebells, yellownettles, and pretty things I know no name for.

The winter here was intense, Mother says, they spent all their energies keeping fires alight and themselves warm. Each has been ill in turn. She says that a week or so ago Andy looked very shaky. Two friends, Nellie and Joan, died recently. The house in Edinburgh has been sold.

Peggy's child John is very timid. He needs to be left alone more, and less notice taken of him. His eyes are a beautiful agate colour and his hair pure gold. Mother spoils him and tries too hard to amuse him. He is very fond of her, though. I thought of myself as a child in her arms, and oddly enough I don't remember her being especially affectionate, though always calm and gracious and beautiful.

I sit on the lawn behind the house writing this, and the shadow of the yew hedge round the rose garden has rolled itself like a dark carpet across the lawn. 6 pm. I don't dare face the wireless news. The others have been listening to it, and now Andy, with hat and stick, sits far away at the other end of the lawn. An impressive character.

One Sunday, later in that May of 1940, I was at the Mill by myself, recovering from a bad cold which I had tried and failed to shake off, losing my voice. I used the time to read a play that Herbert Marshall had sent me, Robert Ardrey's *Thunder Rock*. Marshall had worked with Stanislavsky in Moscow, and was now the director of The Neighbourhood, a tiny theatre in South Kensington.

The play's hero, Charleston, has secluded himself in a lighthouse on Lake Michigan, disgusted with a world he sees being helplessly driven towards a catastrophic war. His isolation is invaded by the ghosts of men and women who drowned ninety years before when their ship foundered. Immigrants to America, fleeing from hunger and persecution in Europe, they died believing that all they longed for had been lost. Their despair rouses Charleston. He shows them how, since their death, the battles they fought against exploitation, prejudice, and ignorance have been won, and, in so doing, he discovers new courage and hope. Marshall warned me that *Thunder Rock* had closed in New York after a week, having failed dismally. I thought it one of the most exciting plays I had read.

The air raids had begun, and for a while London's night-life almost came to a stop. All but two West End theatres were 'dark' in the week we opened in June. Crammed into The Neighbourhood's two hundred seats, beneath a perilous glass roof, our audience found a play which seemed perfectly to catch their mood. The critics heaped praise on us, as a sort of national asset. 'A tonic to the mind, and a bath to the spirit,' said the *News Chronicle*. Diana and Duff

Cooper came, and urged that *Thunder Rock* be transferred to a larger theatre. I said that we should like to transfer, and that I would put up my own money if necessary. Duff Cooper said he would see if he could use his new post in the Ministry of Information to help.

Next day came a call inviting me to the Treasury. Two officials met me, and assured me, 'Mr Cooper is very interested in your play.' They would make enquiries to see what could be done to help in the way of finance, though, 'Mark you, if this comes up in the House, we should simply deny it.' Their enquiries proved fruitful; and *Thunder Rock*, transferred to the Globe, was so successful that the Treasury was repaid.

The Blitz began in earnest. The sirens would sound, and we would stop the play. I would step down to the front of the stage and explain to the audience where they could find the nearest shelter if they wished to leave; we would resume the play when the raid was over; meanwhile, for those who wished to stay, we would have a sing-song. I would sing and lead the audience in the choruses, with the indefatigable Kitty Black, Binkie Beaumont's secretary, at the piano. Soon these interludes became almost as popular as the play itself, with audiences from the other theatres round about coming to join in.

Who's Who wrote to me for the first time, asking for an entry. A well-known hostess invited me to her luncheons. *Picture Post* put me on their front page. I felt I had arrived.

XIII

ARLY IN 1941 I was sitting under the pear tree in our back garden at Clifton Hill when I opened what appeared to be a circular. It was a manifesto of sorts against the War, and two slogans caught my attention (as well they might): 'a people's war' and 'a people's peace'. These were points 9 and 10 of what was an appeal to rally the forces of common sense to 'a People's Convention'.

I thought, Here's a good socialist document. I had no idea of being a pacifist. My first reaction to the War had been, 'What a nuisance, what an interruption', but I expected to be called up when my age group was due and I was intending to join the Navy. I thought of myself as a socialist, though an inactive one. I signed the manifesto.

I did not have long to wait before I was put to the test. I learned that it was rumoured that all signatories to the People's Convention would be banned from broadcasting by the BBC. Sure enough, I was bidden to present myself for an interview at Broadcasting House, where two very polite gentlemen met me in the lobby.

I recorded our conversation, and the events of the next few days, as fully as I could in my diary. The affair itself was short-lived, but for some years to come I was haunted by the words 'People's Convention'.

Tuesday, 25 February

Day off. [I was filming *Atlantic Ferry* at the time.] I called at Bentinck House, an annexe of the BBC, where I was met by a Mr Streeton and another official, a lawyer presumably. I knew what they wanted because Lew Stone, who is also a supporter of the People's Convention, had already been to see them. They said that the Governors had decided that the People's Convention was not in the national interest and would like to know where I stood regarding it; that I need not answer at once, could have time, etc.

I replied that I didn't need time, and that I took the view that since the People's Convention is not suppressed by the Government, but is a perfectly legal, constitutional method for the People of England to express themselves, it was not for the BBC to censor it. The official thanked me for making my position so clear.

I said, 'I take it that that being the case, you do not wish to use me as a broadcaster?'

'Yes.'

'And how does that affect my contract on Sunday to sing?'

'Oh . . . I was not aware of any outstanding contract – but *that* will be *quite* all right, Mr Redgrave.'

We shook hands very amicably and I was seen to the lift.

I had a moment or two of regret afterwards that I had made the going so easy for them, and as usual a crowd of things came into my head that I might have said. But perhaps it was best so.

Rehearsed with Berkeley Fase [composer, supporter of the People's Convention] at Weekes. Actually we talked indignantly most of the time. Then lunch, then Marlene Dietrich in *Seven Sinners* and, after dinner at Scotts restaurant, to *A Long Voyage Home* [film] with him and Geoffrey Parsons. Then to a drab little nightclub, the Nightlight, with subdued light, subdued talk. The proprietress, who used to run the Torch, made much of me. Told me that Barbara Mullen had been in, who had said that the revival of *Thunder Rock* was awful. She didn't think Walter Hudd would be good in my part, as he was 'too political to be an artist'. I was almost too bored with this old theme to argue and knew that she'd only said it because it was the sort of thing she thought I'd like her to say.

Wednesday, 26 February

At the studio. The opening sequence, launching the *Gigantic*. Read Lenin's *Socialism and War*. My eyes, already strained by those two films yesterday, look very bloodshot under the arcs.

Thursday, 27 February

With Marione Everall [later married to Feliks Topolski] to lunch at Café Royal, where we sat with Lionel Fielden and his Indian friend, whose name, even after asking twice, I cannot get. We talked of the People's Convention. Both Lionel and friend were very scornful of anything that had to do with Pritt [D.N.Pritt, K.C., one of the leading sponsors of the People's Convention, and a well-known fellow-traveller with the Communist Party]. They were very interesting on India, but it was quaint to notice that the Indian, who seemed a great advocate of democracy, became almost feudal on the question of servants. He despised the English for asking their servants, 'Would you please do this; might I have that,' and said that at home he ate when he liked, even if it were in the middle of the night, and no questions asked. They talked of Nehru as the only man who could unite India, of Ram Gopal, whom I've never seen, and Uday Shankar.

Lionel said the BBC ban would make no difference, and that I must do some records for him. But it was depressing to find him, with all his knowledge, initiative, and I am sure, guts, apparently believing that nothing could be done to get us all a bit straighter. . . .

Marione and I went to some bookshops. She wanted *Socialism and War*, but Collet's was closed. Then to the National Gallery to see the exhibition of war paintings, monstrous for the most part, though some of Topolski's are superb. He compares very well with most, and noticeably well with Ardizzone, whose pictures in the mass – and there were a mass of them – show how slickly he composes. No life or movement. It is painful to see such an accomplished artist struggling to express movement. Amidst the general Royal Academy level I found the right perspective for the Henry Moore shelter pictures, which I couldn't 'get' before.

Sunday, 2 March

Rehearse at the Scala, broadcast at 12.30 (farewell!) with Debroy Somers, etc. Sang 'If the heart of a man' and Berkeley's 'Smile from a stranger'. A good reception.

Monday, 3 March

Work again. Only two days' work last week – when will this picture end? Paper (*News Chronicle*) rings up about the People's Convention.

Tuesday, 4 March

News of the BBC ban! The *News Chronicle* gives it front page top headline with a photo of me, pushing Moscow's warning to Bulgaria into second place. A bit breathtaking. There's no mention in the *Telegraph*, though they rang after midnight, wanting confirmation of the *News Chronicle* story and expecting Rachel to wake me up.

The phone goes all day. A meeting is arranged at the Workers' Music Association at 6 o'clock for a protest. Larry Olivier rings up – not having seen the papers – to ask if it's true. He says, 'I thought that sort of thing was what we were fighting against. It's certainly what I came home to fight against.' Benn Levy [playwright, author of *Springtime for Henry*] also most sympathetic.

Silence on the subject at the studio. They had been sufficiently worried by Jonah Barrington's article in the *Express* some weeks back which foreshadowed the ban, written in that good *Express* style that by ellipsis made it sound as if one were both pacifist and communist.

Now I can see them whispering about it, but not one person except Culley Forde [wife of Walter Forde, *Atlantic Ferry*'s director] speaks of it to me.

Rachel goes to the meeting in my stead, and says it goes well.

Wednesday, 5 March

Front page again, with picture of Rachel at Workers' Music Association meeting. The Council for Civil Liberties is to hold a protest meeting.

Jack Dunfee [my film agent] says that Black and Ostrer [producers of *Atlantic Ferry*] are 'wild' and don't know what to do. He suggests that I meet them at Claridges for a drink this evening, but there, in Jack's room, I found only Marcel Hellman [Hellman was to produce my next film, *Jeannie*].

I make my position clear, that I know what I'm doing. Black and Ostrer have said it's like the Gracie Fields case. [There had been a great patriotic hue and cry against Fields in the press when she went to live in America with her Italian husband.] Hellman doesn't agree. He says I have the chance to become 'the most popular man in England'. Every one of them says, 'They are using you.'

Hellman is very nice on the whole. I offer him back the *Jeannie* contract. He says he would hate to have to think of such a thing. He says, 'We must do something.' Suggests drafting a statement, getting Oscar Deutsch [part-owner and managing director of the Odeon circuit] to invite the press to a cocktail party on Monday to tell them about my joining the Navy, etc. I don't think this will help but I agree to let him go ahead.

Dinner with Rachel at Café Royal. David Henley, Rank's press officer, most sympathetic – says he will organize Donat, Olivier, [Leslie] Howard, Vivien Leigh, etc., not to broadcast. Somehow I doubt this also.

Thursday, 6 March

A late call for the studio. I attempt to go to the *Star* office in Bouverie Street with my letter, but the driver has no idea of the direction and I'm afraid of being late, so I phone the letter from the Post Office in Euston Road.

At the studio I find I'm not wanted (of course) till after lunch. About two shots, of *Anne of Liverpool* deck scenes. Someone has chalked 'Make Peace' between my names on my canvas chair. I laugh this off, but do not sit in the chair. Presently it is wiped off.

The *Star* contains my letter in full, with photo and large heading: 'Michael Redgrave replies'. Nothing in the other papers – no mention of the ban at all.

Call at Grosvenor Square to see Carol Reed [he had just directed me in *Kipps*], who is kind and sympathetic. Collette Harrison, Rex's wife, is there, also Harold French, who is to direct *Jeannie*. I explain how sorry I feel for Carol, because of possible bad publicity for *Kipps*, and that I know I'm committing a sort of professional suicide.

To the Ivy, to meet Rachel and Marcel Hellman. I find them outside in the dark as the Ivy doesn't open in the evenings nowadays. With them is Joseph Pole. Dinner at Hungarian Czardas. Pole – who handles publicity at United Artists – talks at great length about the Communist Party and the People's Convention. He's worked in the Labour Party – I think – for years, and was a Conscientious Objector in the last war. He says that he and his wife knew, just as everyone in the Labour Party knew, when first they saw the list of signatories, that it was a C.P. affair. He explains how they always use another organization, and then drop it when it suits them. I listen with alarm, he obviously knows what he is talking about. He shows me a letter he has drafted. Although very tired I take it home and rewrite it.

Friday, 7 March

Telephone the *News Chronicle* to hold my letter, similar to the one I wrote to the *Star*. Rachel takes the new letter to be typed at Marcel Hellman's office.

Meet Geoffrey Parsons and Berkeley Fase at the Nightlight, where I am not so well received as before, but maybe I'm imagining this.

I tell Geoffrey that I must make my position clear, and explain about my letter to the papers. He talks more or less convincingly. Says that it all looks hopeless, but these things so often do until the moment comes when they change. I charge him, as a member of the C.P., with their being liable to drop the People's Convention when they have no further use for it. He says, 'So what? Aren't the Government "using" the Labour leaders, and won't they drop them when it suits them?' These sorts of arguments and parallels exhaust me and I begin to distrust them.

Saturday, 8 March

My letter in the *News Chronicle*, beneath a protest from 40 M.P.s, J.B. Priestley, Harold Laski, etc.

In the afternoon to studio for tedious and tiring post-synching. Culley Forde very angry about the 'Make Peace' episode, about which Rachel had rung her up.

I was becoming more and more irresolute about the stand I had taken. At first I thought, I'll see this through, and for all the studio's anxiety about my future – and their investment – I was inclined to stick to my guns. But the more I thought about the People's Convention, the more ambiguous it seemed. What was its attitude to the War? What would it advocate supposing we were invaded by Germany? How could one answer the charge that it was a C.P. front, on orders from Moscow, following the line of the Molotov-Ribbentrop pact?

One of those who tried to reassure me was the famous geneticist J.B.S.Haldane. A great big burly man, he arrived one afternoon unannounced at my dressing-room at Denham Studios and asked if we could talk. He told me about his experiments on the human body, using himself as a guinea-pig, to determine how far and under what conditions it could withstand temperatures of extreme cold. I knew Haldane was on the board of the *Daily Worker*. I didn't know then, and neither did anyone except the War Office, that he was their leading expert on submarine escape. As to the People's Convention, of which he was also a signatory, I remember little of what he said, except one thing: 'People will soon forget what it was that you put your foot down about. The main thing is that you put it down.'

Another who tried to answer my doubts was D.N.Pritt, who wrote that he had read my letter in the *Chronicle*, and suggested we meet to talk it over.

Saturday, 15 March

To Reading to lunch with Pritt, who meets me in a smart yellow and black car. Reading very peacetime-looking. Pritt very amiable, rather like a schoolmaster. A pleasant drive to a lovely house. Mrs Pritt is warm and friendly, with a rosy face like a nice winter apple. She knows a lot about gardening – they have a beautiful garden with a stream and pond.

We sit in the open, drinking Cinzano. Cold breeze but warm sun. Then lunch, lovely Russian plates on the walls, 'biscuit' from the old Imperial potteries, with Soviet designs. Then coffee in the drawing-room (Russian picture papers with views of marble Metro, Mayakovsky, etc.).

After coffee Pritt and I walk in the garden, including many times round the lawn, talking of the People's Convention. He quotes some alarming rumours of Churchill saying, 'There'll be a few people after this war who'll need machine-gunning,' and says it is thought the Canadians and Poles are being kept for this.

I raise my position re films. He says there's nothing he can do to help. I suggest that the People's Convention must make clear where it stands on the war effort. He agrees, and says the Dean of Canterbury has raised the same point and been convinced. Says it will be good if he can say that the Dean and I are reassured on this point and still staunch.

I quote Geoffrey Parsons' answer when I said that it was held that the C.P. were using the People's Convention as a blind – which was 'So what?' 'So what indeed?' says Pritt. On the way back to the station, referring to actors and politics, and to my present position, he says, 'Well, never mind – perhaps you'll one day be an honoured Artist of the Republic.' Significant remark. Of course it's just the sort of daydream which flatters and pleases me but I think, even at the time, 'No, this is England, not Russia, I think you have got Russia on the brain.'

At home, I confess to Rachel that I'm not much clearer than when I started. In the evening to the Convention dance at the Royal Hotel. A friendly, jolly, atmosphere. . . .

I sing a song, and give the prizes, and there is much applause whenever I am mentioned.

Home, and the 'all clear' goes before twelve to absolve us from fire-watching. A mercy.

Sunday, 16 March

To the Royal Hotel for Convention. A long depressing day, full of disappointment and dismay. I can see very well why the movement is charged with revolutionary defeatism. Everyone who speaks, airs a grievance. . . . I long several times to get up and say, 'But what about the War? What is our attitude to the possibility of defeat? Friendship with the USSR certainly – but England must do better than that.'

The chairman makes a snarling speech, referring obscurely to my letter to the press. At the collection I foolishly give a cheque for 15 guineas, I cannot now think why, but not until the next day did I see the necessity of leaving this false set-up.

My singing record for the Workers' Music Association is played about a dozen times, and I sign about sixty copies.

After dinner I write my speech for tomorrow.

O a sad day.

Monday, 17 March

Lunch at Claridges with Marcel Hellman and Harold French, who express surprise at the 15 guineas – it's all over the front page of the *Daily Mail* – and I can't explain. Black and Ostrer are in the other restaurant but we avoid them. From Marcel's hints of what they have said, I'm furious with them. Ostrer had tried to scare Marcel out of using me for *Jeannie*, really in order that I should do *Spitfire* for him, and *Spitfire* is now off anyway.

Then to Conway Hall for the Council for Civil Liberties meeting. E. M. Forster speaks, Beatrix Lehmann, the Archdeacon of Westminster, and myself. My speech goes well, especially the crack about, 'I've searched hard for a precedent for a politically-conscious actor, and the only one I can find is John Wilkes Booth, who murdered Lincoln.' Both the Ediths – Evans and Hargraves – are there, Rachel, Roger Livesey and Ursula, Benn Levy and Connie Cummings, bless them.

Wednesday, 19 March

Bromyard. [The children were evacuated to Bromyard in Herefordshire to stay with Rachel's cousin Lucy Kempson.] Vanessa calls on me in bed very early, and recites and sings long verses of a hymn, something about 'precious blood', which occurs a lot. Corin wakes me up at 7.30 and yells at his potting. Rachel leaves by the early train for a film test at Ealing Studios, and I get the children up. Corin won't eat much breakfast. He likes everything to be 'in order' and can't understand why I'm there.

We go for a walk, and Vanessa insists on taking her tricycle down into town, which is far too steep, and then up the old road to Mrs Ware's, also too steep. I sing 'Daisy, Daisy', 'Lovely to Look at', and 'Old Man River', vaguely thinking this may counteract 'precious blood'.

Lunch, and Corin consents to eat a jam pancake on my lap. Then to play in the garden, where Vanessa keeps saying she is getting a cold too. I say 'Rubbish' very firmly. She also insists she has something in her toe. I say 'Rubbish' to this, too. After about the fourth complaint, I say, 'All right then, take your shoe and sock off and see what it is.' It is a large thorn. A cold, rather windy day. Nurse Dulcie arrives back just as I am beginning not to cope.

After dinner I persuade Lucy to go to a Spencer Tracy–Hedy Lamarr film, which I know will be bad, by saying that he is always interesting. He is, too. He does some remarkable things.

To study to write letters, to Adams and Pritt, asking that my name be withdrawn from the list of People's Convention supporters.

Churchill made a speech opposing the BBC's broadcasting ban, and it was dropped. The careers of those of us who signed the People's Convention were, so far as I know, unaffected by all the fuss and consternation. The film *Kipps*, about which I had expressed alarm to Carol Reed for fear that its chances of success might be ruined by so much adverse publicity, was well-received. (Years later I detected an echo of the furore which attended my participation in the People's Convention. I was playing Hector in Giraudoux's *Tiger at the Gates* on Broadway in 1956, when I received a request for an interview with someone from the State Department. Obliquely I was given to understand that the subject of our interview would be politics. Somewhat amazed, for the matter had never been raised before on any of my previous visits to the States, I heard myself refer to my C.B.E. 'Was it really likely,' I wondered aloud, 'was it really likely, that Her Majesty would confer membership of such an Order on an *untrustworthy* subject?' This, and a wounded voice, seemed to dispose of the matter.)

Kipps was the third film I made with Carol Reed. He was the gentlest of directors, so quiet that his 'Action!' was almost inaudible. Yet underneath that gentle touch was an iron will which eleven times out of twelve would have its own way. I found that admirable. With Reed I learned for the first time how subtle the relationship between an actor and a director could be. The theatre and acting were in his blood and he was able, with infinite pains and care, to bestow on his actors the feeling that everything was up to them and that all he was doing was to make sure that they were seen to their best advantage.

I cannot say that I became aware of this all at once. Our first film, *Climbing High*, which I made in 1938, a few weeks after *Stolen Life*, had been intended as a song-and-dance vehicle for Jessie Matthews. But the Studio had lost money on her previous film and were looking for economies, so somehow the dances and most of the songs got lost, and what was left could hardly have been redeemed by the combined charms of Cary Grant and David Niven. Certainly my presence as the young millionaire hero didn't help much.

The Stars Look Down, which we shot in the summer of 1939, was much more suited to both our talents. A warm and friendly feeling prevailed, and Reed encouraged me to feel that I had assisted him in the preparation of the film.

He often asked for my suggestions and usually, I think, adopted them in his own fashion. One such occasion was when we were shooting in a narrow street of miners' cottages in Cumberland and I noticed a child sweeping a puddle in the road with a look of rapt determination in its face and sensuous pleasure in every sweep of the broom. Whether this detail is in the finished film I cannot now recall, for by the time the camera came to turn on her the girl's mother had changed her out of her grimy smock into her Sunday best and put ribbons in her hair. I do remember Reed being infinitely tactful about this. He was inordinately considerate and attentive to people's feelings. He had a way of plying you with questions and watching as you answered, his big blue eyes as wide as a child's. His seeming ingenuousness and his repeated exclamations of surprise or incredulity – 'Do you really?' 'That's fascinating!' 'How true!' – would strike one as naïve to the point of absurdity if after a short time one did not become aware that these simple and direct questions were not so simple nor so direct as they seemed. Unwittingly you had supplied him with an answer or a clue to a different question.

Carol ate, drank, and slept cinema. *Kipps* was shot at the Shepherd's Bush studios throughout the 1940 Blitz, and for the duration of the shooting we both took flats in a solid, steel-girdered building, Number 20 Grosvenor Square (now part of the American Embassy), so that we could meet and talk in the evenings. It was a time I remember above all for its divorce from any reality except that of imaginative work for to face the cameras each morning as a younger man than myself I was obliged to take sleeping pills each night in order to sleep through the noise of the bombardment. And there in the morning on the set would be Diana Wynyard, who had driven through the tail-end of a long raid to have her hair washed and be made up, ready to appear at eight o'clock, ravishingly gowned by Cecil Beaton.

Carol and I sat up late one night discussing Diana, then at the height of her mature beauty. Carol maintained that she had yet to come to terms with her looks, that she was at arm's length from her beauty. 'She needs some man to wake her to the realization of her glorious self. You could help her do that. Why don't you have a shot, Michael? Go on, wake her up, wake her up!' The next day Diana casually informed me that she and Carol had been married a few days before. It was not I who woke her up, if, indeed, such a thing was necessary. But we began a long friendship.

In the evenings we left the Studio ten minutes before blackout and, as we drove home in the dusk, the sirens would start. If they did not, I remember, we were faintly worried. No wonder that my memory of the Blitz is largely of a fictitious Folkestone in Edwardian dress.

It was on one such evening at the end of a day's shooting that my film agent, Jack Dunfee, appeared with a briefcase full of papers. He wanted 'a few signatures', he said, and as we drove home he explained what these were all about. There had been a flourishing British film industry at the start of the First World War, he said, but during the war we had lost the initiative to the Americans, who had snatched the opportunity to swallow up the home product. The

Government was determined not to let this happen again, and wanted to put key actors and technicians under contract.

The papers were to do with a contract for me whereby my call-up would be indefinitely postponed provided I made myself available for whatever films might come my way. I told Jack that I was about to undergo my medical. He pointed out that, at my age, it might prove more useful to make films than mark time in one of the Services. He urged me to accept the contract, and was rather surprised when I insisted that I intended to join the Navy when my age group was called.

'But,' I said, 'I'm not going into the Army.'

'You are, you know,' said the officer, scanning my papers. 'You expressed no preference.'

'I wasn't asked.' And here I stamped my naked foot. Stamping one's foot is always an ineffectual gesture, but to stamp it when starkers is the height of folly. 'It's not too late to change, is it?'

'Why don't you want to join the Army? What Service do you favour?' he said, with heavy sarcasm. 'You're a bit old for the RAF.'

'I know that.'

'Why the Navy? Any special reason?'

'Yes, my wife's family are naval. Her father is the Headmaster of the Royal Naval College at Dartmouth.'

He was clearly a bit impressed by this, so I followed up with 'One of her brothers is a naval lieutenant' – I could see him weakening – 'My wife and I were married in the Royal Naval College chapel at Dartmouth.'

That shook him. 'Were you really? Look,' he said, pointing to the other end of the drill hall, 'you'd better have a word with the Colonel over there. Better put your clothes on first.'

I dressed and looked around for the Colonel. He turned out to be a Colonel of the Marines, and was civility itself. He seemed amused about something.

'You look frustrated,' he said. 'What is it you want?'

I told him, briefly.

'Yes, well,' he said, 'that's simple enough. Only, my dear fellow, you ought to learn that it's one thing to put your foot down, and another thing to stamp it.'

When my call-up papers came, in June 1941, I was in the middle of another film, *Jeannie*. Rachel and I had taken a short lease of a farmhouse owned by the director Gabriel Pascal near Denham

Studios in Buckinghamshire, where I was filming, so that I could spend as much time with the family as possible. Various friends came and stayed with us a few nights. One of them brought news that Paddy Railton, one of my closest friends from Cambridge days, was dying of tuberculosis in a sanatorium in North Wales, and that weekend I took the opportunity of going to see him. His death would leave a dark shadow.

I took the train to Manchester and arranged for a car to take me on to Ruthven the next day. I had asked the Studio to book a ticket for whatever was on at the theatre that night, and was delighted to find that I was to see the second performance of Noël Coward's new comedy, *Blithe Spirit*.

I was on my way to my hotel room when I heard a familiar voice. I did not know Noël, except from one meeting of The Actors' Orphanage committee, of which I was a member and he was President, but now he invited me to join him and the actress Joyce Carey that night in his box. He disappeared during the first interval, and when he came back he seemed rather highly-strung. I ventured to remark with special praise on the actress who played Madame Arcati. Apparently it was the last thing I should have done. Margaret Rutherford was not yet the almost national figure she later became. Noël slaughtered her in one clipped word – 'Amateur!' The house lights went down. A merciful eclipse.

Afterwards we went backstage and Noël introduced me to his other guests. When I told him that I was going into the Navy his manner became suddenly serious and he said that I must come and see him at the Savoy before the Navy swallowed me up. I promised to do so.

XIV

O N THE night train to Plymouth I slept most of the way. I wondered if I should shave, but decided that my shipmates would almost certainly do no such thing. As I stepped out of the station the sun hit me forcibly as if it were midday, and I blinked as I looked around me. My throat was parched and I longed for a cup of tea. I could not see a café, so I peered inquisitively through the windows of a pub, the Royal Standard, but the blackout curtains had not yet been drawn.

Just as I turned away, a woman appeared at the door with a cup in her hand. 'Want something?' she asked.

'Do you know where I could get a cup of tea?'

For a second or two she looked at me as if trying to identify me. Then she tapped her cup and shot the tea-leaves into the gutter. 'Come on in.'

Inside the dark bar she said, 'I don't make a habit of this, as you can *well* imagine.' I started to say something, but she cut me short. 'Don't tell me,' she said abruptly, 'I know you. I *know* you, very well. It's your face. Well, fancy seeing you. You been on leave?'

'Not exactly. It's my first day.'

'Well ... fancy that.' She moved to where a kettle was boiling. 'They won't believe me when I say I had Michael Redgrave ... There! That's the name, isn't it? ... That I had Michael Redgrave to tea at seven o'clock on a nice fine morning.' She suddenly burst into a short gale of laughter. 'My husband'll have something to say about this.' There were sounds of footsteps coming downstairs. 'Here he is. Bert, look at this gentleman. He's a bloody film star. It's his first day over the road.'

I peered past the blackout curtain and saw a sailor going through the gates of the barracks. 'I think I'd better go and present myself.'

147

'That's right. We mustn't keep you waiting, must we, Bert? Finish your tea, don't worry, the first four days are the worst, so they say. Then they'll send you to HMS *Raleigh*. Why do some of them call it "*Raw*leigh"?' she added.

'Pleased to meet you, Michael,' said Bert.

Once inside the gate I was given over to a nice young Ordinary Seaman, who told me cheerful details of the air raids as he took me over to the kitting-up mess, a sort of hut building, where about fifty or sixty young men, stokers-to-be, sat about playing cards and reading papers, while at a table two very affable Petty Officers were taking down particulars.

'Oh hello, Michael,' said one, 'sit down and put your bag over there. Have you got a little gas mask? Well, take it out.' He handed me a copy of the Regulations.

'Just arrived, did you?' one of the stokers asked me. 'We've been here three weeks and there's still no clothes.'

The other Petty Officer came up with a Wren on his arm, whom he introduced as his young lady.

'Here's Michael.'

'I know,' she said, 'I wrote to you.'

I thought she meant a fan letter.

'Yes, she sent you your call-up papers.'

'Oh. Thanks.'

'I like your pictures,' she said.

That afternoon, and almost every day for the next two months, I wrote to Rachel.

1 July

An extremely nice rating called Siddall took me for a stroll around. The noise and the general confusion . . . it doesn't look as if one would ever make sense of it. Have intimated to a Petty Officer that I don't want to be a coder. He's told me the procedure.

I was warned that unless I fought for it I should find myself without anything to eat at lunch. But this wasn't so, or at any rate I seemed to do all right. Lunch was in fact pretty much what I'd expected.

Afterwards I was introduced to one Needle, who is not a very nice piece of work. Interesting, though. Full of dodges, has a secret hoard of sugar and cigarettes, and warns me to beware of scroungers. Except that Gilbert and Sullivan is the height of his culture, he's like Chester Coote in *Kipps*.

I can sleep out any alternate night (being over 21) – except that in Plymouth there's nowhere to stay. But Needle knows all the places round about where you could come and stay.

Now I'm sitting outside the kitting-up mess and it's very nice and hot. Some of the lads go bathing at Plymouth Hoe in the evening. Not a bad idea at that. The dreaded continual wireless has started. The first four days, as the lady in the pub warned, seem likely to be the worst.

2 July

I leave the kitting-up mess today to go to HMS *Raleigh*, a training barracks across the water. I had been entered as a coder, but got that changed yesterday to an ordinary seaman, which is a tougher job but will lead to a commission eventually. (I put in a request for one yesterday – you have to put in a request for everything, including leave, in the Navy, or else you don't get it.) *Raleigh* is said to be a picnic compared to *Drake* where I am now. Certainly the kitting-up mess is no picnic (though I've had no actual *work* to do as yet). But it's funny, I already feel sentimental about leaving it. The friendliness is indescribable, it could make anything bearable. The ubiquitous, the unfailing Needle goes with me. I begin to like him a lot. An amazing character – a Jew, and I think I told you a Russian by descent – he had been a soldier in the Grenadiers for nine years, and for many years since then a cab driver. His general knowledge astounds me and puts me to shame. Still, I learn quite a lot.

Yesterday we went ashore to the Hoe. Plymouth is beyond belief. London may have greater areas of square feet of devastation, but Plymouth is almost entirely *flat*. But, incredibly, there are still people about, and singing in the pubs, and bathing at the Hoe, and in the evenings dancing on the Hoe.

The attendant at the beachpool told us they no longer hire trunks and towels so we had to watch, and watching soon made us thirsty, so we went for a drink at the Grand. Into the very quiet bar came two lieutenants RNVR, and presently when I went to get an evening paper one of them spoke to me:

'What are you doing in these parts? I didn't know there was a theatre open.'

When I told him, he said, 'Oh, God! how ghastly,' and promptly invited me aboard his ship, which is some sort of motor launch. Name of Bailey.

Yesterday the PO in charge of the kitting-up mess took me aside during a little diversion which consisted of everyone putting on gas masks for half an hour – (an ideal day for it, really 'brillig'. I was reading Pushkin and feeling sorry for the poor buggers who were doing work) – and told me to be careful at *Raleigh*. Because of my height and reputation, he said, I'd be watched more carefully than the other lads, and Newton's example (don't repeat) had to be lived down. Everyone in barracks, it seems, knows about him. But I'm inclined to think it will be easier to follow him than some sort of shining model – by contrast I may seem quite serious and efficient. [Bobby Newton had earned himself a thoroughly black mark, at least in the eyes of the officers. He had managed to gatecrash an officers' party, and when they asked him what he was doing there, he slapped them on the back, saying, 'It's all right, I'm Robert Newton.' Apparently it wasn't all right.]

8 July

Yesterday and today we started in earnest and it's at first quite tough going, especially on the *feet*! I really love most of it, though my new job as class leader takes some of the freedom to enjoy it all away. It's hard to have so much new to learn, as well as getting used to new surroundings, and also to have to assume responsibility for thirty others. I have to see the mess is kept clean, appoint cleaners and cooks (not real cooks – just blokes to hand out the stuff and stow away the plates, etc.), keep order in the mess and also, which is what plagues me most at the moment, relearn all the parade words of command of a section leader so as to march my class past in Divisions. I suppose it will be all right 'when I know the lines'. And the thirty are so mixed, from Needle, who is thirty-six and was in the Grenadier Guards, to some rather half-baked youngsters who don't have any idea of discipline yet. But what is wonderful is to see the classes who have been here only three or four weeks, and which were obviously as mixed as mine, and who are now really very trim and smart.

13 July

Today is the first day I've felt really low since I came here. It's partly thinking of you being so near at Dartmouth, and so disappointing that we can't meet. And it's raining, after a fortnight of brilliant sunshine.

I'm supposed to compère and sing in a foc's'le concert on Thursday, which would be enjoyable if only one had time to do it properly. As it is, we can only hope. I've spent part of the afternoon coaching a very earnest seaman to do 'All the world's a stage'. He wanted to do Richard II and Richard III also, but I dissuaded him.

I had not long been in barracks when I was approached by the Entertainments Officer. From my first morning I had found that attitudes to me fell broadly into two categories: those who were naïvely flattered to meet me, and those who made it clear that whoever I was I could expect no special privileges. But Lieutenant Green, the Entertainments Officer, was in a category of his own.

'We shall *have* to organize a ship's concert,' he said, looking at me with a gleam of hope. 'Could you do anything?'

'Everything, if you like.'

'Splendid.' He seemed very relieved. 'I can leave it to you, then?'

Which he did, entirely. I wrote to Noël asking if he had any new songs which I might sing, and by return post came a package containing three or four songs copied out in manuscript, including one – 'Could you please oblige us with a Bren Gun?' – which seemed to fit the bill perfectly. The trouble was there was neither time nor place during the day where I could learn the words quietly by myself. I was obliged to learn them in the lavatory after lights-out:

> Colonel McNamara who/Was in Calcutta in ninety-two
> Emerged from his retirement for the war.
> He wasn't very pleased with what he heard and what he saw.
> But whatever he felt,/He tightened his belt –
> And organized a corps . . .

It was a 'patter' song and very difficult to learn. I had just about mastered it when a telegram arrived from Noël: PLEASE CHANGE MCNAMARA TO MONTMORENCY STOP THERE IS A REAL AND VERY ANGRY MCNAMARA IN THE WAR OFFICE.

The package that contained the songs also carried a letter which told of a meeting between Coward and Mountbatten, where Noël had praised the beginnings of my nautical career so warmly that 'Dickie' had 'requested' me for his new command, the aircraft carrier *Illustrious*.

30 July

Didn't tell you of my interview last Friday with the Divisional Commander [Jeremy Hutchinson, Peggy Ashcroft's husband]? He told me he was going to relieve me of being class leader as Menzies had to be tried. He said, 'I'm thoroughly satisfied with your performance and have put you down as commission-worthy. It's just that Menzies, you see, is secretary to the Duke of Atholl and we have had a little pressure!'

10 August

Your letters are more lovely to get than you can imagine. I love your news, and of Van and Corin. 'V for Vanessa' it certainly shall be. I hate this 'V for Victory' nonsense. Did you ever hear the like of the press now that Russia is 'on our side'? Disgusting.

Did you hear my broadcast last night? I do hope you did. It was the greatest fun to do. Edith [Edith Hargraves, my voluntary secretary] and I – Edith, as I think I told you, has been taking her holidays at Crafthole – went round on the Friday and saw the Henry Hall Variety Show at the Palace from the wings. You can imagine with what nostalgia. Oh, the smell of those old provincial theatres! Actually I don't think I've ever been backstage during variety before, except once at the Coliseum during the last war when Mother was playing with Potash and Perlmutter. I always remember the thrill of sitting on a skip and revolving with the stage.

At the Palace there is a serving-hatch in the wings through to the stalls bar, which makes it delightful for a stage-door Jack who can drink himself silly while watching the show. A rattling good show it was, too. A marvellous man called Owen McGiverney played *all the parts* in the scene from *Oliver Twist* where Nancy is murdered. He did complete changes in less than two seconds. A gorgeous ham of an actor – but you could learn something from watching what can be done in the matter of quick changes if you've a mind (and muscle) to do it.

I didn't actually know Henry Hall but shamefully pretended we had met and knew that we'd see the show somehow that way. (All the best seats were sold – he's done record business at the Palace this week. In 1941, think of that!) He was really charming. He asked me to go on and take a bow, but I, wisely I think, thought not. I need hardly tell you it was Edith who suggested to him that I should sing in his Guest Broadcast the following night. Actually, as I guessed, and as he confessed after-wards, he'd no idea I sang at all and was a bit doubtful in his mind.

I was very nimble the next morning, and got permission to go ashore in the afternoon, having found a substitute for my duties. (All very formal. A request, an interview, etc.) I also wired Noël for permission to sing 'London Pride'.

So I got into my tiddly suit in a lavatory at the Grand and went along to rehearse at 2.30. Then Edith and I had tea. Then I slept in the lounge of the Grand. Then a sherry. No smoking. It was like old times. I wasn't a bit nervous, but very keyed up. I knew I'd get a good reception, the uniform would settle that if nothing else, but I must say it was terrific. Did you hear it? I long to know. I sent a wire to Mother and another to Noël. The band had already played 'London Pride' and performed really well. It's the first time I've had proper support from a dance band. Usually they're very scraggy.

Commodore's inspection this morning. About an hour standing rigid on the parade ground, while the Marine Band played 'Roses of Picardy', 'Because', etc., plus their own special derangement of 'Bitter Sweet'. You can't imagine what Ivy St Helier's 'If Love Were All' sounds like when played by a Marine Band on Church Parade. Or perhaps you can . . .

That September I was on my first leave in London when Noël called me to his house, where I found him in a serious mood, talking to a Colonel Buchanan of the Marines. Noël introduced us and said, 'Buchanan has something to tell you.'

'You'll be very disappointed,' said the Colonel, 'if I tell you that Mountbatten has now been appointed C.-in-C. Joint Ops. So I'm afraid you won't be able to serve under him.'

I had a choice, he explained, between joining HMS *Illustrious* where she lay refitting in Norfolk, Virginia, or waiting to be drafted elsewhere. If the latter, it might mean a long wait. Mountbatten had suggested I might join a Commander Morrison, but his destroyer was still at sea. 'You could be kicking your heels about in barracks for several months,' said Buchanan. On the other hand, I could join *Illustrious* almost immediately.

I chose *Illustrious*. It *was* disappointing that Mountbatten would no longer be commanding her, but, besides the fact, as the Colonel had pointed out, that I could join her within a few weeks, and so put in the three months at sea which were needed before one could be trained for a commission, there was another enticing factor: New York!

It was no secret that *Illustrious* was being refitted in the States. There were pictures of her on the front page of *Picture Post*. But how were we to get there? If you're an Ordinary Seaman, the Navy never tell you anything. I went with a small draft of seamen, accompanied by a Master-at-Arms, to Birmingham, where we stopped for something to eat, and then on to Gourock, on the west coast of Scotland, which seemed a very hot, busy, bustling place, the September sunshine making our kitbags and ditty boxes unbearably heavy. We were directed to the SS *Pasteur*, newly-painted in camouflage. She had been designed for the South American luxury trade, we were told, and now, crammed to many times her normal capacity, mainly with RAF troops bound for training in Pensacola, Florida, she was making her first transatlantic voyage.

Once again my film face was noticed, and amongst those who sought me out were some of the stewards of the White Star Line, who invited me to their mess. The *Pasteur*, it seemed, was a 'dry' ship, but not for them. Their company, and the two ship's concerts I organized, helped to pass the time.

'What kind of a climate is it?' I asked my companion, an American Air Force man. We were in calm waters now, sailing down the

St Lawrence River to Lake Erie; the same route, I thought, as the refugees in *Thunder Rock* had taken when escaping from the oppressions of Europe. The *Pasteur*'s deck was once more thronging with passengers, after the rolling in the Atlantic which had driven all but a few of us below.

'Virginia? Well, let's see. It's kinda damp.'

'Oh, dear.' I had hoped, I said, to have left that sort of thing behind in England.

'Well,' he said, 'it's not like English damp.' And here he paused for reflection. 'It's a kind of a *dry* damp.'

'I see.'

'Yes sir,' he said, warming to his theme, 'you get all kinds of damp there, *and* all kinds of sunshine.'

And then, the longest train ride I had ever taken, from Montreal to Norfolk, Virginia.

I was in a deep sleep in our coach [I wrote to Rachel] when I was woken by a PO who said there was a party forrard in the Pullman with some Air Force and other worthies and that I was requested to come and sing. I looked at him sleepily, but the next word I caught was 'whisky' and was on my feet in a flash (you know the Redgrave flash) and we found one very pie-eyed Air Force bloke and an assorted Pullman full of people, all moderately fried. I was introduced, whereupon instead of saying howdo they did what I always thought was a convention of Hollywood and clapped my entrance in a polite, if as I say slightly-fried, fashion. So hey presto I sang 'London Pride', of course, and several others.

My overriding obsession was to visit New York, and at about noon the next day that truly fabulous skyline came into view, as if hurling itself out of the ground. A night in New York, perhaps, or even a few hours? The Navy, as was the Navy's practice, had told us nothing at all about our movements. And then, while I was still gasping and craning, the train suddenly took to earth, and we changed trains underground. Twenty minutes later we were on our way again, with one last tantalizing glimpse of Manhattan. I almost wept. The train rumbled on all day. By nightfall we arrived at Cape Charles, where we disembarked, exhausted, and then changed trains to a local which took us through the streets of Norfolk, uttering that strange wailing that goes with American railways.

2 November

Well, this is a ship, and some ship. There seems at first glance no chance of ever getting to know one's way about, it's so vast and complicated. But I have tried to learn various routes systematically, and can find my way unaided to the lavatory and the washplace, and with great concentration to the foc's'le (I am a foc's'leman), and the flight deck. And by dint of walking about at an angle of forty-five degrees I have so far avoided braining myself.

The first morning after Divisions I was dispatched with a clutch of other ratings to a remote place where we were issued with paint cans and brushes, and an Able Seaman (as distinct from the Ordinary kind) was put in charge of us and our cans. 'How many cans of paint does she require?' I asked facetiously. No reply. We halted by the forward end of the flight deck and were detailed into pairs. I followed my companion to a porthole tucked away under a flange of the flight deck. Nimble as a squirrel, he leapt through the porthole to where a board some four feet long and a foot wide was slung, bumping against the ship's side. I attempted to copy him, but as I looked down I could see that we were slung not over the water but the concrete paving of the pier, scores of feet below.

'Don't look down,' shouted my companion. 'There's no hurry. You can take the whole morning if you want.'

The days extended into weeks, and still *Illustrious* was not ready to sail. Her refitting was taking longer than predicted. I began to regret my decision at Noël's house that morning, and to wish I could have my choice over again. None of this time at Norfolk would count as time at sea, and for me it seemed a waste.

Norfolk, Virginia, one might think, was not so bad a place for a sailor. It was so clean, so smooth, so shipshape . . . but so dull. And the damp which my companion on the *Pasteur* had promised – 'you get all kinds of damp there' – turned out to be a very damp damp, sticky and rather enervating. No liquor, of course, which did not make for gaiety. Norfolk at that time was a quiet town indeed, a far cry from Devonport, or from the Portsmouth of my childhood – where, in the pubs, so Uncle Willie told me, especially on Saturday nights, merry hell was apt to break loose. True, the cinemas were free, but one had the feeling they were subsidized only to keep the boys off the streets. And yet in this dear, dull town I made some dear friends.

A note from the ship's padre had suggested I might like to meet some people he knew, natives of Norfolk. And so I made the acquaintance of the Masyngylls. They had an old-fashioned wooden house, very simple, furnished with a nice conservative taste. Harold Masyngyll was one of those few people of whose goodness one is immediately and utterly convinced. But then he was so charming, so courteous and kind, that one wondered if it could be true. And then again, after a short while, one came back to one's first conviction: he was just plain damned good. They had a son of eighteen, Harold junior, known as 'Bud', very bright, healthy, and rather artistic.

The first evening I went to the Masyngylls', Harold's wife, Carole, said, 'You just come any time, there'll always be a place laid for you.'

And so I believe there was, though I never tested it, but always telephoned first.

We'd play the piano, or talk, and Harold would mix his mysterious 'Old-Fashioneds' quietly and powerfully, and by the end of each evening we'd be a little stinking, and pulling out photographs, and albums, and chatting about our children.

When Manhattan's skyline had disappeared from view on our train ride down south, I had made up my mind that, come what may, I would not let New York slip through my fingers again. But there were all kinds of difficulties. I found out that you had to get a letter inviting you there. That part was simple enough. Letters of invitation from Paul Lukas and Ruth Gordon arrived by return of post. And then by adding the name of Rachel's aunt, Nora McMullen, who had married Andrew Mellon, and laying it on thickly that Ruth had offered to take Vanessa and Corin, I got 'relative's leave'. We had only been allowed to take £10 out of England, which was just enough to get an aeroplane ticket. The train would have been cheaper, but I was determined to enjoy as many moments in New York as I could, and counted on someone lending me money when I got there.

Over the marshes and broad rivers of Virginia to Washington, D.C., changing planes at the most beautiful airport I'd ever seen, like some highly-dramatic modern temple, and then taking off for New York – it seemed the most gay, enchanting, and improbable journey of my life. Ruth Gordon met me at the airport and said, 'Darling, I'm not just going to show you New York, I'm going to show you *theatrical* New York.' And so she did.

In those three days Ruth and Paul and Daisy Lukas took me to all the smartest restaurants and clubs and we had a whale of a time. Ruth had asked what show I wanted to see and I'd said *Watch on the Rhine* which Paul is in and is a fine play, and Helen Hayes in the new Maxwell Anderson play, *Candle in the Wind*. I'd always longed to see Helen Hayes. The play was awful, as I thought it would be – I don't like Maxwell Anderson – but I loved Helen, saw her afterwards, and drove with her to her rehearsal at the broadcasting studio. She asked me to broadcast with her the next day in *The Last of Mrs Cheyney*, but I didn't know how that would go down with my Captain, so I thought it best to refuse.

Then we saw the new Garbo picture, *Two-Faced Woman*, which Ruth is in. She had MGM run it for us. And the people I met! Ronald Colman, Edna Best, Jack Warner, Rouben Mamoulian [head of MGM], Gaby Pascal – who wanted me to go to Hollywood and act in an episode of the British War Relief film, with Charlie Chaplin of all people – tea with Robert Sherwood and his wife, oh, and hosts of other celebrities!

On Sunday night (the shows can open Sunday if they want to) we went to *Pal Joey*. I've never seen a musical so well done, except when I visited New York two weeks later and saw *Let's Face It*, the new smash hit.

The second visit was even more amazing than the first. I came to do two broadcasts, one for British War Relief and the other for 'Bundles for Britain'. The first was a bad play with Flora Robson, the second a terrifying quiz programme called *45 Questions on Broadway* with Ruth, Jessie Matthews, and that marvellous, eccentric character actor Mischa Auer. We were sat at a table, and there was a large and very excited audience who backed their favourites and who were very pro-me, mostly on account of my uniform, of course, but also because I had fans there, which I'll tell you about in a minute. Ruth won, which pleased Jones very much – Jones is her son, aged twelve – because, he said, 'she never wins anything'.

Well – the fans! It started the first evening of my second visit. No, before that, because a popular columnist had written in his column the time before that I was in New York, and some of the fans had written to *Illustrious*.

The Stars Look Down had only just been shown here, and was still playing at what they call the neighbourhood theatres. Also, *The Lady Vanishes*, which is always being revived here – it's just about the most popular English picture in New York.

Well, as I said, on the first evening of the second visit, Mr and Mrs Tyrone Power had given Ruth four seats for the new Cole Porter musical, *Let's Face It*, which is such a hit that I doubt whether even Cole Porter could get in. And as we were coming out some 'standees' recognized me and asked for autographs. I told them I was broadcasting and they said, 'We'll be there!' I thought they meant they'd listen in. But no, they found out the times of rehearsal, and next day at Radio City about six of them were there when I went in, and slightly more when I came out. And at the broadcast that night they were about a dozen strong. They'd gone off and bought stills of *Stolen Life* and *The Lady Vanishes* and gave me notes and walked along with me until, in self-preservation, I got into a taxi and said, 'Go to the Alvin,' where Gertie Lawrence is playing in *Lady in the Dark*. I heard them take up the cry, 'The Alvin!' And off I went, gaily waving and thinking I'd seen the last of them. I went into the Alvin and stood for about twenty-five minutes of Gertie's show, which although everyone says they loathe it, is a big hit. Came out – and there were the faithful, massed across the street, and now about two dozen of them, including a huge coloured woman who with overwhelming sincerity told me that *The Stars Look Down* was etc., etc. I went from the Alvin to see the last two acts of Ethel Barrymore in *The Corn Is Green* and damme if they weren't still there when I got out of that. After that I had the sense to say I was going home to bed.

But they turned up again on the Sunday at the quiz programme, and whenever I got a question right, which I did very occasionally, they cheered me lustily.

Well, I'd always heard that in England you have to fight to get publicity, and in America fight harder to avoid it, and I guess it's true. The moment I landed in Canada someone from the press came aboard. And at Norfolk whenever I gave a concert, they'd make a great song and dance of it and there'd be a two-column story about me.

It's taken rather longer to describe than I meant to, but I thought you'd like to hear it. Together with meeting all the stage folk and hearing the gossip and everyone [then, before Pearl Harbor] carrying on as if there wasn't a war, it made me homesick to act again.

The other play I saw was *Life with Father*, which I stood for and would stand on my head to see again. It came in quietly in November 1939 and no one thought it would be much to write home about, with no stars and taken from a book by Clarence Day, very popular but with not a shred of plot in it. It has become almost an American institution. I laughed and cried and have since reread the play twice. You shall read it when I get back. It's just about the most human, funny, touching and enjoyable thing I ever did see.

I met lots more people this second trip of course, but I shall chiefly remember the Saturday night, after seeing *Life with Father*, when Ruth gave a dinner party for Ludmilla Pitoëff, Lillian Gish and Thornton Wilder. That was a real actor's evening.

And so was my last evening in New York. Guthrie McClintic had asked us to dinner, but I had to fly back that night to rejoin the ship. So he said come along as soon as we'd done the quiz broadcast. So about six o'clock we went to his lovely house in Beekman Place, overlooking the East River. Katharine Cornell, his wife, was on tour with *The Doctor's Dilemma*, so unfortunately I didn't meet her. I had an early dinner on a tray and then, at about eight, when I had to go, the party began to arrive: Ethel Barrymore, Mildred Natwick, Aubrey Smith and his wife and their nephew – a naval commander whom they'd not heard of since Crete and who had turned up suddenly on their doorstep. It was horrid having to leave that party. But next day, very suddenly, we went to sea, so the anti-climax was not so bad.

I had intended to borrow some money from business friends of Noël's, and the hope was not ill-founded. I did not have to ask. Several people would hang on to a handshake long enough to tell me there was money in the hand, and when I left I was several hundred dollars to the good. I was even contemplating a third trip to New York when the gunnery officer called us together to tell us we were going for our gunnery trials off Jamaica.

To my surprise and excitement I was posted to the bridge, where I was to relay commands to the starboard batteries. I had no idea of what these consisted, beyond a recollection of about eight 'pom-poms' and some other very powerful-looking guns. I had been chosen to be on the bridge, I supposed, because it would be assumed that my professional diction would be useful.

And then began what seemed to be a game. Suddenly the sky spat out black smudges against the deep Caribbean blue. I could not understand why we seemed to be firing at American targets. Beside me on the bridge stood the gunnery officer. I could not understand why 'Guns' kept on giving the same command, 'Follow Evershed', which I relayed. We were being mock-bombed by squadrons of American planes. Repeatedly this same command, 'Follow Evershed', rang out, first from the throat of the gunnery officer, and then from mine as I echoed him. I could not imagine what or who Evershed was. Some daredevil Errol Flynnish pilot, no doubt. Though of course I knew that this was only practice and that Evershed would live to tell the tale.

And then came news that out there in the Pacific the *Prince of Wales* had received a mortal hit. I knew that Rachel's younger brother, Robin, was on board.

XV

REFITTING ACCOMPLISHED, *Illustrious* sped home. After the excitement of the gunnery trials, the night watches in the Atlantic seemed almost dangerously uneventful, the most imminent danger being to fall asleep. To prevent this catastrophe, I found a remedy. I would take some point in my life – say, 1921, the season at Stratford. Usually at such an hour my thoughts would run or rumble around any old how, but standing up there on the bridge in the dark, during the long middle watch – midnight to four a.m. – I trained my mind deliberately to follow certain sequences, trying to fit each detail and development to the next. Stratford, 1921, when Mother was a member of the company. . . . I started with my sister, Peg, and me arriving at the station. It was a hot, sunny day. Near the station there were posters of the Festival. . . . Mother wearing a hat with a broad brim: 'It's *The Wives* tonight [Mistress Page was her favourite part], you'll be able to go.' . . . The little house she had taken, with a piano in the front room, where the dining-room was redolent of lime juice and a-buzz with wasps. . . . Marion Phillips, a young actress, coming to stay and saying she was an atheist, which shocked my conventional mind very much at the time, not so much because of her atheism as because she should want to tell me about it. . . . Percy Rhodes's son and I fishing up the Avon . . . a wonderful night when we lashed the punts together by lantern-light. . . . I tried to visualize the geography of the theatre, the stage door, bicycles stacked outside it, Mother's dressing-room . . . an all-woman production of *Henry V* which cracked a few breastplates . . . the last night of the season after *Antony and Cleopatra*, when we carried the flowers home and the stars were so bright that the Milky Way looked newly-spilt across the sky. . . .

When I had pursued these recollections as far as I could, I tried a different tack. I made a list of all the places I had always wanted to visit but had never had the opportunity, and chief amongst these loomed, for some reason, the Ritz Hotel in London.

I had developed a severe ache and stiffness in my right elbow. No one could say for sure how I had come by it, but it was thought that it was perhaps due to some injury sustained whilst ammunitioning ship in Norfolk, and our ship's doctor promised to send me to the Liverpool Hospital when we landed. My view was that I was suffering from a surfeit of bananas. When we left Jamaica, where we had anchored during our gunnery trials, a local banana merchant, to show his appreciation of *Illustrious* and all who sailed in her, presented the ship with as many bananas as could be hung on the cable deck. The ship's company was encouraged to eat as many as they could swallow, and they tucked in with a will, but they very soon grew satiated with bananas, which then began to rot. I was one of the party, stripped to the waist and armed with huge shovels, which was detailed to jettison the evil-smelling debris.

Once back at Liverpool, I went to the David Lewis Hospital for treatment to my arm. I was expecting some brilliant manipulation or some radiant heat, at least an X-ray. But after some rather limp massage I was told to return next morning and was then turned loose on the streets of Liverpool.

Liverpool without the Playhouse company was like a foreign city. I treated myself to lunch at the Adelphi Brasserie, where the woman who served me failed to recognize me. In the afternoon I started by browsing in a bookshop, but I found myself very tired and, for the first time, allowed the thought that I was too old for a sailor's life to come uppermost in my mind. There was a 'flea-pit' cinema up the hill from the Adelphi. Indeed, Liverpool was rich in its number of cinemas, and I think I must have fallen asleep in each one of them in turn. I really must be tired, I told myself. I took myself back to the Adelphi and booked a room for a rest. Every morning, after Divisions, I presented myself at the hospital for massage, and every afternoon I repeated, with minor variations, my aimless wanderings about Liverpool, punctuated at some point by a snooze at the Adelphi. It was a far cry from the young Lochinvar who was to have served under Mountbatten.

My arm was showing no signs of improvement. I saw myself spending the remainder of the war in barracks in Liverpool, and the rest of my career playing Richard III. I requested to see the Captain, and was told he was on leave and would not be back for some weeks.

The ship's doctor suggested that as I myself was due for leave in a week or two, I should have a specialist in London look at my arm. I began to yearn for London.

The Head Porter at the Ritz greeted me warmly. 'What do you want, mate?'

'A room.' I advanced towards the desk. It was eight in the morning. I had just got off the train from Liverpool and was still wearing my Ordinary Seaman's uniform and carrying my kitbag.

He must have thought I was drunk, or joking. A few minutes later I found myself across the road, trying a slightly different tack at the Berkeley. But my polished posh accent failed to do the trick, and I found myself on the pavement again, walking towards Jermyn Street.

I seemed to recollect a pleasant evening at the Cavendish Hotel with Dick Green and some painter friends, Robert Beulah and his wife, Eric O'Dea, Lucien Freud – now there, I felt sure, they would let me have a room, if only for the night.

'What do you want?' said a voice, seeming to belong to a pair of legs: it was Rosa Lewis, legendary proprietress of the Cavendish, caricatured as Lottie Crump in Evelyn Waugh's novels and post-humously commemorated as 'the Duchess of Duke Street', half-hidden in her famous wicker chair, 'having her feet done', as she put it. Very pretty feet, too.

'Good morning, Mrs Lewis,' I said.

'You're early, aren't you?' she replied. 'Sure you've come to the right place?'

'Quite sure, if you've got a room I could have for a few nights.'

She hesitated a moment, and then called into her office, 'Edith, show the sailor into – you know the room I mean.'

The room she meant was at the end of a long, dark corridor. There was no running water, only an enamel jug and a china basin. The bathroom was at the other end of the corridor. I returned to the lobby to find Mrs Lewis casually glancing at the label on my kitbag. Still, her manner betrayed no particular interest in who I was or what I was doing.

'It's all I've got for the moment,' she said firmly, 'Will you take it?'

'It'll do for the present,' I said, 'and perhaps, when I've had a bath, say round about eleven o'clock, you'll help me crack a bottle of the Widow?' (Despite all wartime shortages, the Cavendish somehow maintained a fairly well-stocked cellar. Rosa showed it me one night.

'These,' she said, gesturing at thousands of empty champagne bottles, 'are my *ruins*.')

Later, over champagne, she became less guarded. Soon she was calling me by my Christian name, and by midday she had corralled some more guests who were about to leave, and more champagne was opened. It was clear she had taken a shine to me. 'Think of it,' she said to the assembled company. 'Here's Michael, with a wife and two children, and has to pay for all of this' – and here she made a sweeping gesture, as if to embrace not only the Cavendish Hotel but all of Jermyn Street as well – '*all* of this on two and sixpence a day.'

I made my headquarters at the Cavendish Hotel for the next three months. Rachel was on tour; I was on leave. Our third child, Lynn, who was born in March 1943, was already on the way. I had seen a specialist within a day or so of my arrival in London, he had indicated that the injury to my arm might be a permanent disability, and had undertaken to inform the Admiralty. And then a telegram arrived from that quarter informing me that my leave was to be indefinitely prolonged.

Bill Linnit, who had been so helpful in forming my stage career, sent me a play to direct. It was called *Lifeline*, and depicted the voyage of a tanker in wartime across the Atlantic. The four leading characters had already been cast, and I thought to myself that if I could direct Wilfred Lawson, Frank Pettingell, Arthur Sinclair, and Terence de Marney, each one of them a good actor, but collectively four of the more eccentric actors in London, I could direct anything.

I set about trying to put the play's rather loose script on more solid foundations. I practically rewrote the play. The authoress seemed grateful. I obtained permission to spend several days in the London docks. I got to know Wilfred Lawson and something of his pattern of self-destruction. It was after the first run-through, and we had adjourned, as was our custom, to a neighbouring pub in Drury Lane, when Wilfred with his perennial grin casually informed me that my ambitions as an actor were doomed. He had been at a midnight performance of *Three Sisters*, he told me, and my performance as Tusenbach was not worth talking about, *but* – this was said with great candour and sincerity – 'you really ought to take up directing, you have something of a talent for that. *Not* acting.'

'Not acting?'

'*Not* acting.'

Lifeline opened and closed within a fortnight, and any lingering hopes I had had that the notices would proclaim a triumph of realism proved ill-founded. Still, most of them were respectful, and meanwhile Linnit had other plans for me: a play by Patrick Hamilton, *The Duke in Darkness*, a costume melodrama, with a bravura part for Leslie Banks as the Duke and for me as his tailor, Gribaud. I enjoyed playing the tailor and, best of all, I could take real satisfaction in the production. Yet this play, too, despite our good notices, failed. Perhaps it was too sombre for its time.

Meanwhile I had received another telegram from Their Lordships at the Admiralty, requiring me to present myself in uniform at Chatham Barracks at eight-thirty in the morning. Not in uniform, I thought, they'll keep you for good. I wore a suit, trusting to luck that no one would notice.

I was on the point of jumping on to the train to take me down to Chatham, when I felt a hand slap me on the back. I turned round to find Needle.

'Mike! Where are you off to? No, don't tell me, let me guess. Chatham?'

'Yes . . . '

'Oughtn't you to be wearing your uniform? You naughty boy, you've been up to something. Am I right?'

'Not really . . . '

The whistle blew and we climbed in. I had reconciled myself to the thought of sharing the compartment with Needle for the journey, but instead he dived off past me down the corridor, pausing only to explain in a stage whisper, 'I suppose you heard I was married? No? Terrible mistake!' – leaving me to rehearse my coming interview.

I had guessed right about the uniform. No one so much as asked me why I wasn't wearing it.

The interview with the Surgeon-Admiral, X-rays included, was brisk and business-like.

'Well, it certainly seems that you would be of more use making films than giving ship's concerts. Rather a pity, but there it is. What do you think?'

'Well, sir, I don't want to sit in barracks till the end of the War running messages. I've had enough of that.'

'I dare say. Could you scramble down the side of a sinking ship?'

'I doubt it, sir.'

'I doubt it, too. Very well. Thank you.'

An awful thought occurred to me: 'They won't call me up into the Army, will they, sir?'

'Frankly,' he said, with a ghost of a smile, 'I doubt if they will. Don't you?'

A few weeks later, in November 1942, a year almost to the day since I had boarded *Illustrious* in Norfolk, Virginia, I was discharged from the Navy. I began to look around me.

I first made acquaintance with Turgenev's 'summer' play, *A Month in the Country*, at the Cambridge Festival Theatre, where it was played in a sad, though very effective, key. I had always wanted to see its comic side, and now plans were afoot for me to do it with Peggy Ashcroft. Everything was set – the cast, the theatre, the designer, the director (Emlyn Williams) – everything. And then, on the first day of rehearsal, Peggy trapped her foot in a taxi door; the doctor said it would take several weeks to recover from her injury; and we were without a Natalya Petrovna.

Valerie Taylor's name was suggested. The only part I could remember seeing her play was Nina in *The Seagull*. Binkie said he would release her from *Watch on the Rhine*, in which she was playing at the time, and the general opinion seemed to be that Valerie would be ideal. It was arranged that I should see *Watch on the Rhine*, and, when I did, two things happened. One, Valerie gave a beautiful, tragic performance, and two, she missed her first entrance, causing Athene Seyler and the rest of the cast to improvise innocuous lines – 'Whatever can have happened to the girl?' 'Darling, are you coming?' and, finally, 'It's getting late, dear!'

If I mention Valerie's missed entrance in *Watch on the Rhine*, it is to remind myself how everything, within the picture frame that dominated our theatre for two centuries, is done to sustain an illusion. And yet the very completeness of that illusion, or suspension of disbelief, can numb the audience, and can induce in the actor a false sense of security. It was in the course of a matinée performance of *A Month in the Country* at the St James's, half-way through our long run, and I was settling down to the first undisturbed duologue between the heroine and myself, looking up at Valerie with eyes brimful of affection and love, when I heard a lady in the stalls whisper to her companion, 'I like *her*.' I was noticeably quicker on my cues after that.

There are those who think that the advent of films, and then of television, where the reactions of the spectator cannot affect the spectacle, has made audiences more insensitive and noisier. Personally

I doubt this. For what it is worth, I have noticed throughout my career a marked increase of concentration in audiences. Perhaps a part of this is due to the general prohibition on smoking. And the deplorable custom of drinking tea off trays on the lap, which was so prevalent in the English theatre, especially at matinées, has now – so far as I know – disappeared.

It was thanks to a tea drinker in a matinée of *A Month in the Country*, when we were on tour in Liverpool, that I lost my temper and shattered the illusion by addressing the audience. After a fifteen-minute interval during which teas were served, the Second Act began with its long soliloquy from the heroine, after which I had to enter for an impassioned scene between us. I could hear, as I stood in the wings, the rattle of teacups, and this annoyed me, more particularly as I had recently complained that fifteen minutes was surely long enough for people to drink a cup of tea and the manager had promised to do something about it.

As I waited, my irritation mounted, and I forced myself to remember what Edith Evans had once told me. She recalled how, when she once was playing *The Way of the World*, the local Hammersmith boys would come and bang on the metal scene-dock doors out of pure mischief, which used to throw her out of gear, and Robert Loraine, seeing her distress, had advised, 'If there is a disturbance which you can stop, have it stopped. If you can't stop it, take no notice.' I reminded myself of this and said to myself that I must make my entrance and be especially good and that then the audience would forget about their teacups. I entered and, as it happened, the noise of teacups ceased for several minutes – how fatal it is to be pleased with oneself! – but suddenly a noise that sounded as if three trays of tea had been dashed to the ground echoed round the theatre. I was about to take Valerie in my arms when the incident occurred. Instead, I dropped her as suddenly, if not as noisily, as the tea-trays and, turning to the audience, said with the kind of frigid authority of which, amongst actors, Coward alone was the master, 'When *you* have all finished with your teas, *we* shall go on with the play.'

Of course, far worse things have been said by actors to audiences. It was in Liverpool also, I believe, that George Frederick Cooke, when playing Othello, was hissed by an audience probably more versed in the ways of melodrama than in Shakespeare, though it is also possible that in Cooke's production there was not so great a distinction between the two. He stopped in mid-sentence and turned on them in fury, saying, 'So ye hiss George Frederick Cooke, do ye? Let me tell you that every stone of your damned city was cemented by the blood of a Negro.' One would dearly love to have seen the audience's reaction to that.

In my own case the audience's response was instructive. My rebuke reduced them to such a cowed silence that although the play is termed a comedy, and our production – as I fondly hoped – had succeeded in bringing out its comic side, no one, least of all myself, succeeded in getting another laugh for the rest of the Act. As another actor in the cast, Michael Shepley, said to me afterwards, 'I rather admire you for having done that, but you'll never want to do it again, will you?' He was right.

At the back of my mind, since Liverpool days, was the ambition to work with a permanent company. Kindled by the visit of La Compagnie des Quinze, it had flared up during the Gielgud season at the Queen's and blazed like a meteor after working with Michel. Wartime was no time to start such a project. But one could make plans for the future, and I began to think about forming a company.

Rachel and I had seen Sonia Dresdel in *Hedda Gabler*. 'There's your leading lady,' whispered Rachel. There are certain people who have what we please to call 'star quality', which compels you to look at them whether you want to or no. Sonia was a highly-talented actress. She was also, I discovered, her own worst enemy.

I outlined to her the sort of work I had in mind. One of the plays I wanted to revive was Goldoni's *La Locandiera* – *The Mistress of the Inn* – in which Duse had had one of her greatest successes.

'Oh, I could never play that,' said Sonia, handing me back the script.

'Why ever not?'

'I haven't the charm.'

I was very shocked by this remark. I did not then believe, as I do now, that nine-tenths of a good performance lies in good casting. I believed that a strong director could always wring a good performance out of his actors. I thought that all my geese were swans.

I wanted to get as much varied experience of directing as possible. During the year-long run of *A Month in the Country* I directed three plays: Henri Becque's *La Parisienne*, with Sonia and myself in the leading parts, for six special matinées at the St James's; Peter Ustinov's second play, *Blow Your Own Trumpet*; and Maxwell Anderson's *Wingless Victory*.

Ustinov's first play had raised great expectations for his second. He had created some memorable character parts for elderly actors, but, in both plays, it was noticeable that his characterization of young, or younger, people was not so effective, and in *Blow Your Own Trumpet* the two young people had a love scene that was positively embarrassing. I decided to ask Ustinov to rewrite it, which he agreed to do, and in due course he came back with his rewritten scene written on the backs of envelopes. I asked the stage management to arrange for the revision to be typed. When I read it I was somewhat puzzled. There was no difference between the 'write' and the 'rewrite'; not a word had been changed.

Blow Your Own Trumpet closed after a fortnight. I was stung by the dismissive reviews of Ustinov's play. With all its faults it had ambition, and I felt it had deserved better treatment from its reviewers.

With eight performances a week of the Turgenev, rehearsals of *Wingless Victory* were bound to suffer. The first time I saw it in performance was at a matinée at Oxford, during the pre-London tour, where a scant and unappreciative house made me fear that Anderson's play would fare no better with the critics than Ustinov's. Perched on someone else's suitcase in the crowded corridor of the train going back to London, I started writing a piece which I labelled 'An Actor to the Critics'.

Wingless Victory had some of that strain of thin high-mindedness – the legacy of Ralph Waldo Emerson – that I had so disliked in *Winterset*. But it had a worthwhile theme. Its setting was almost the same as in Arthur Miller's *The Crucible*. The heroine and hero, a woman from the Fiji Islands and her rich white husband, incur at sight the wrath of the citizens of Salem, amongst whom is the hero's mother.

Unknown to me, though guessed at, forces were at work that almost guaranteed the failure of Anderson's play. I had been obliged to fire the first actress who played the racist mother when, during early rehearsals, I could see that, like many an older actress, she was not prepared to be totally unsympathetic. I told her that the play simply couldn't work unless the citizens of Salem displayed their bigotry without reservation. The actress had been at the Savoy with my mother in H.B.Irving's company, and my feelings can be imagined when I had to tell her to go. Another actress was approached, and I explained to her the need for the villainess to be a villainess. She nodded and said she could quite see what I meant, and set about giving a serviceable interpretation of the role. Yet the matinée at Oxford had revived my fears. She simply could not help trying to ingratiate herself with the audience.

On the first night in London, as soon as the curtain was down on the Turgenev, I skipped with a heart of lead over to the Phoenix Theatre to hear how *Wingless Victory* had gone.

The actress who played the Fijian heroine was almost in tears, and it was confirmed by other members of the company that it would have been almost impossible for the audience not to take sides against her when her opponent was all sweetness and light. I raced up the stairs to the dressing-room of the actress playing the mother, but she had fled. I called the company for notes the next morning, but their hearts were not in it, nor was mine.

Meanwhile, 'An Actor to the Critics' had been published in the *New Statesman*. So that it should have extra impact, I arranged that a copy should be sent to critics of all the leading newspapers. I was invited to address the Critics' Circle, which I did, and spoke heatedly and badly, and a journalist named Beverley Baxter rounded off the debate by praising me for taking the theatre seriously but begging me not to take myself too seriously. And that seemed to sum up the general reaction: I must not take myself too seriously.

As to the points which my article proposed by way of improvement to the general run of theatrical criticism – that newspapers should reserve space for their reviews at the end of the week, so that a critic would not be obliged to dash off his review by telephone, sometimes even before the curtain had fallen on the first performance; that critics should sometimes avail themselves of a study of good dramatic criticism, such as Hazlitt's, or G. H. Lewes's (again a note of frigid authority, I fear) – these were accepted with good grace but dismissed as impractical. 'Mr Redgrave,' wrote Harold Hobson, 'can write most of London's critics off their heads and into the middle of next week,' but he doubted whether my outburst would have much influence.

(Some years later, when I published a second book of essays on acting and the theatre, *Mask or Face*, Mr Hobson – whom we referred to in the family circle as 'Handsome Harold' for a good notice and 'Horrid' or 'Hobnailed' for a bad one – reviewed the book in terms so lavish that all the actors in the profession could have been forgiven for sending me to Coventry for bribery. I had asked my secretary to send advance copies to some of my friends in the theatre. I had jotted down a list of names, with a suitable dedication attached, including one addressed to 'Harold, from whom I have learned so much'. I had recently been playing in Giraudoux's *Tiger at the Gates*, and I could truthfully say that I had learned a lot from the American director Harold Clurman, for whom the copy was intended. It would have been churlish, of course, having discovered the mistake, to have attempted to correct it. One does, after all, in the long run, learn something from one's critics.)

When *A Month in the Country* finally closed at the St James's, I was looking for a play to take on tour for ENSA, the Entertainments National Services Association, and the Turgenev was considered too heavy for consumption by the troops. Meeting Beatrix Lehmann outside the theatre, I asked her about the melodrama *Uncle Harry*, which for some reason had folded on the road the previous year. Beatrix was not only a good actress; she had – as might be expected of John and Rosamond Lehmann's sister – an incisive mind. I trusted her judgement. She said it was a fine play and Eric Portman a fine actor, but that Willie Armstrong had misdirected the play. The central character was an amateur painter, a facet which was over-stressed, making Harry into an artist *manqué*. Moreover, the play needed two sets, and a revolve to make the two sets work. Beatrix gave me the script of the play, and that evening, having read it, I rang her up and asked her if she would be prepared to do it again in a different production.

Beatrix was very well cast as the younger sister. As Lucy, the girl who jilted Uncle Harry, I cast Rachel. She and I had planned to act together whenever possible, but after our season at Liverpool the plan had met with a set-back. No statistics can convey how many gifted young actresses have suffered such set-backs with the birth of children, set-backs from which their careers never quite recover. At Stratford, before we met, Rachel had had a great success as Juliet, and after Liverpool she was to have played Ophelia to Larry Olivier's Hamlet at the Old Vic, and Viola. She had not, of course, been idle since Vanessa's birth, but she had not had the chances she deserved. Now, she and I would have the key scene of the play.

We did the customary six weeks' ENSA tour, which with a lesser play might have been a chore, yet it was evident even at the beginning that *Uncle Harry* was going to be a huge success.

On the morning of the opening night in London, 29 March 1944, I woke, terrified by a sore throat. At lunch, at the club, Leslie Banks wouldn't sit next to me: 'Because you have a first night.' Then, in the afternoon, I tried to sleep at the Garrick Theatre in my dressing-room, which was filled with telegrams and flowers, without success. That flat, deadly calm, my form of 'nerves', invaded me. And then the temperamental member of the company threw her tantrum, which gave me a dose of adrenalin, and I started the First Act angry. The lights were wrong; there were no bar bells to summon the audience back for the Second Act; the house lights were left on too long. It was not, could not be, as good a performance as the dress rehearsal had been, when I had said to myself, This is your best performance, *don't* try to repeat this tomorrow – which, of course, was exactly what I did, all the while thinking of the critics in front.

At the end, a great reception. James Agate came round 'to pay his respects'. He said, 'Now you can stop being an intellectual and start being a real actor,' and wrote in his review: 'Here and now I take the opportunity of advising him to give up the intellectual drama and devote himself to the profession (the secret of intellectual drama is that anyone can do it).'

'Algebra in wigs,' John Mason Brown called it, referring to the ingenuity of *Uncle Harry*'s construction. After ten years in the theatre, I had my first 'commercial' success in the West End. I had intended to play in *Uncle Harry* for three months, but I agreed to extend the run, and by the end of the year I felt close to a nervous breakdown. Harry was an unnerving part, not only for the audience but for the actor. I would take to delaying my arrival at the theatre as long as possible, rushing in at the 'quarter', leaving myself just sufficient time to make ready for my entrance. At the end of the performance I felt fit for nothing. It was a year of hurly-burly, Benzedrine, and colonic irrigations: illnesses real and imaginary.

The air raids suddenly became intense, and the theatres began to close. Binkie was determined not to let a little thing like that stop the progress of *Uncle Harry*, and he booked us for a long tour of the provinces, playing mainly the big Northern towns where the bombing had almost ceased.

We were in Hull on the second week of our tour when Anthony Asquith and Terence Rattigan appeared on the scene. They were about to make *The Way to the Stars* and wanted to offer me a short part in it if matters could be arranged with Binkie. Flight Lieutenant Archdale was killed in action so early in the story that one was tempted to dub it 'One of Our Actors Is Missing', but the part was well-written, with the promise of enough distinction to make his presence felt even after his departure. Shooting was to begin on location at Catterick, in Yorkshire, the following week and, amazingly, within forty-eight hours it had been agreed that the cast of *Uncle Harry* would be retained on full salary – an almost unheard-of arrangement then – while I took three weeks' leave of absence for the location scenes.

At Hull station the following Monday, Rachel and I parted, she to join the children in Herefordshire; I to catch the twelve-twenty to York. 'A right *clever* train,' said the porter, '*if* it comes.' I had my Everyman copy of *Doctor Thorne*. I had become addicted, during that short tour, to the novels of Trollope (and am so still), an admirable antidote to the high tension of *Uncle Harry*. No hurry, I thought. This will be a holiday.

And so it was. Rattigan's story commemorated a way of life that was vanishing while the film was being made and was past by the time it appeared in July 1945. His script was superb. Not that there was anything so exceptional in his characters, but the ingenuity, the contrast of characters and situation were masterly. And his story contained a strong, clear idea, one to which the makers of *Yanks* returned recently: the conflict of temperament between the British and Americans in time of war.

Our location at Catterick was a real, though no longer operational, RAF camp, its corridors spotlessly painted in regulation cream, its narrow beds hard and yet unbelievably comfortable, like the bunks of my dormitory at HMS *Raleigh*. To tumble into such a bed at night after an evening spent in the Sergeants' Mess, or with the WAAFs in the village pub, was to be transported back two and a half years to the first few weeks of my naval training at Plymouth. The same indescribable friendliness, the same wartime atmosphere of living for the moment, yet without the underlying anxiety because now the end of the war was in sight and I was no longer an actor having to prove myself as an Ordinary Seaman.

Shooting proceeded in fits and starts. Hours of enforced leisure, waiting for the sun to appear; playing snooker with the C.O.; taking driving lessons with Johnnie Mills round and round the perimeter in an old Aston Martin, and discovering that I was only slightly more incompetent than on my honeymoon nine years before; bicycling down long, straight Yorkshire roads, criss-crossed by one-track railway lines. Days of anxious waiting for my moustache to arrive. (I had decided, reluctantly, that Archdale must wear a moustache. It makes one look and feel older than one's years, as

RAF pilots tended to look.) It was to be flown direct to Catterick –
no, it was awaiting collection in the parcels office at York. And then,
while all eyes were turned to York, it appeared mysteriously
blowing along the platform at Darlington.

At half past five in the afternoon the sun would put in an
appearance and we would scramble into activity. After three weeks
at such a tempo the actor began to feel he had earned his uniform, if
not his medals.

The success of *The Way to the Stars* was largely owing to the
atmosphere of those three weeks at Catterick, which could never
have been created in a studio. I remember 'Puffin' Asquith calling at
my room at the end of the second day's shooting and lending me
Donald Tovey's book on the Concerto, which has the following:
'One of the first essentials of creative art is the habit of imagining the
most familiar things as vividly as the most surprising.' I cannot now
recall whether it was he or I who underlined those words, but they
sum up rather well what he did and what made the film memorable,
as did John Pudney's poem, written for my character, with its
strong socialist undercurrent:

> Do not despair
> For Johnny Head-in-air,
> He sleeps as sound
> As Johnny underground.
>
> Better by far
> For Johnny-the-Bright-Star
> To keep your head
> And see his children fed.

Before we had finished shooting *The Way to the Stars* I was
approached by Ealing Studios to play in an episodic film about the
supernatural called *Dead of Night*. It was to be directed by Alberto
Cavalcanti, and I was to play a schizophrenic ventriloquist. It was
not an easy part. For one thing, the ventriloquist has to remember to
keep his mouth open. I managed that all right, but still I wanted an
entirely different voice, though my own, for the dummy. I asked a
friend, Diana Graves, to help. I would speak the dummy's lines; she
would copy me, following as closely as possible my inflections and
timing; then I would copy her copying me.

For the dummy itself I enlisted the help of the ventriloquist Peter
Brough, who was, strange to say, an almost national figure on radio.
Cavalcanti's first idea was that the dummy should be modelled to

look like me. I wanted a figure which would look as different to me as possible, a caricature of a cheeky overgrown schoolboy, like Brough's Archie Andrews. Some people think this is my best film – especially on the Continent, where for a time the success of *Au Coeur de la Nuit* meant that I was greeted by total strangers as a long-lost brother.

XVI

I T W A S Jean Gabin, I believe, who answered when someone asked
him what he looked for in a film, *L'histoire! L'histoire!* I might have
done well to consider this before accepting *The Secret Beyond the Door*. It
had a story, to be sure, a mystery of sorts, pseudo-pathological and
pretentious. But it was to be directed by Fritz Lang, a hero of mine since
those far-off student days when I watched the *Nibelungen* in a dingy,
smoke-filled cinema in Heidelberg. And it was to be made in
Hollywood.

It was not that I had ever been especially keen to visit Hollywood *qua*
Hollywood. When I began making films in the late 1930s, at a time
when our home-grown product was considered almost a laughing-
stock and most young English actors eager to make their way in the
cinema looked towards the States, I frequently had to rebut rumours
that I had a one-way ticket to Hollywood in my breast pocket. And my
love affair with the States, which began, I think, in boyhood, with the
arrival in London of those fabulous American musicals like *Hit the
Deck*, was principally a love affair with New York.

But I loved travel. And sunshine. As I motored back and forth from
our home in Chiswick to the film studios at Denham in the first week of
January 1947, anxiously surveying each day's schedule to see whether
we should complete *Fame Is the Spur* in time for me to catch Saturday's
sailing of the *America*, Hollywood seemed infinitely far away and
infinitely attractive. The pea-souper fogs (long since swept from
London by Clean Air regulations) were so dense that the short distance
from Chiswick to Denham was frequently stretched out to a two-hour
journey. At times the fog was so thick that I was obliged to walk on the
pavement a pace or two ahead of my car, holding an open book in my
hands, its white pages guiding my driver like a beacon.

Fritz Lang met me off the *Super Chief* at Pasadena station, an act of old-world courtesy not lost on me as I blinked in the Californian sun at eight o'clock in the morning. I tried to arrange my face for the photographers. 'Now in Hollywood they understand the value of publicity,' I remembered Margot Dempster saying. They did, too. There must have been a dozen or more photographers who had made the journey out to Pasadena to photograph Fritz in his camel-hair coat and off-white fedora and me in my brand-new suit from Saks Fifth Avenue. (Clothes, like everything else, were still rationed in England. I had spent all my clothing coupons before I left London, thinking I ought to look the part of a visiting English 'star'. But in New York I was met by someone from Universal International and whisked to a suite in the Sherry Netherland. I was given a fistful of dollars for expenses. My navy blue chalk-stripe suit and ill-fitting dinner jacket were jettisoned and I acquired an entirely new wardrobe.)

We drove from Pasadena to Bel Air, our chauffeur pointing out the sights along the way: 'This used to be John A.'s place.'

'Oh? Whose is it now?'

'John B.'s.'

Hollywood seemed to be changing hands with bewildering speed.

'That's Cromwell's place,' Fritz told me, pointing to a ramshackle old house in the middle of the Sunset Strip. Richard Cromwell, he explained, was a long-standing member of Hollywood's English colony, a successful feature player who had had the good sense, before he retired, to buy himself an avocado orchard in what was soon to become one of Hollywood's most expensive pieces of real estate. He lived there still, tucked away amidst the expensive restaurants and the bright lights, half a dozen avocado trees all that remained of his orchard now.

'Take in the church, Joan honey. Give a glance at the ceiling. You're waiting for Michael – be a little apprehensive!'

We were shooting our first scene, in a Mexican church. Joan Bennett seemed a little distressed, I thought, as Fritz kept up a continual running commentary from behind the camera.

'Don't close your mouth, Joan. No, *don't* close your mouth! I said *don't*. Cut! Do you think you could leave your mouth a little open, Joan honey?'

'He treats me like a puppet,' muttered Joan as she walked off the set to her caravan after the shot. But he must know what he's doing, I thought. In his two previous films she had given very polished performances.

Lang had proved with his first Hollywood film, *Fury*, that he, like Renoir in his *Swamp Water* and *The Southerner*, could successfully absorb material which was not native to him. But neither Lang nor Renoir could make a silk purse out of a sow's ear, and *The Secret Beyond the Door* was a sow's ear and a half. I could never bring myself to see it.

I learned from Lang what it is like to be caught up in the Hollywood machine, working in studios where even your personal telephone calls might be tapped. He would often ask me about working in England. I urged him to come and direct Dylan Thomas's *The Doctor and the Devils*, which I had persuaded the Rank Organization to buy for me. He never came, unfortunately, and Thomas's script was never made. I tried hard to have it filmed, but was told it was impossible because a 'B' movie on the subject of the body snatchers had been made a year or two previously.

Hollywood produced its share, perhaps more than its share, of eccentrics, most of whom seemed, in my short stay, to be of the imported variety. I was lying by the hotel pool one day when I heard the clatter of heavy feet approaching, making a considerable noise. Their owner was dressed in high boots and a trench coat. He smoked a pipe, and I noticed he conspicuously avoided taking a shower before jumping into the pool. It was Evelyn Waugh.

As it happened, we were both invited to the studio that afternoon, where they were running a preview of Carol Reed's *Odd Man Out*. More by accident than by design, we sat next to each other.

'Who is that young man wearing a Guards' tie?' asked Waugh. It was Greer Garson's husband, Richard Ney. He repeated the question in a rather louder voice. 'Who is that young man?'

'I don't know,' I said, making as if to get up, but there was no other seat.

'Surely that is a Guards' tie?'

'Probably,' I said, weakly.

The lights went out. The picture had been running about a quarter of an hour when Waugh nudged me. 'What did you say the name of this film was?'

'*Odd Man Out.*'

'Do you think we've missed something at the beginning?'

'No, I don't think so.'

'But it doesn't make sense.'

'It will,' I said, rather flustered.

Another five minutes elapsed. Suddenly we heard a delicate high-pitched chiming sound, and a few heads turned round from the rows in front. Waugh had pulled out his repeater watch. 'This is a very *long* film,' he said.

'Now in Hollywood they understand the value of publicity. ... ' Yes, but not always how to get the best value for their money. For the Lang film, Universal's publicity department worked hard to promote me as the clean-limbed, all-weather type of Englishman. 'He's tall – he's rangy,' began one of their handouts.

For *Mourning Becomes Electra*, which I began in April 1947, RKO set about restoring the image of the English classical actor, pipe-smoking, reclusive, deeply philosophical. Nothing is so serious as Hollywood when it takes itself seriously, and when it tackles a Great American Classic, it takes itself very seriously indeed. There had been several attempts to put Eugene O'Neill's play on the screen, but he had refused them all. But at last, with the promise that it would be filmed with the utmost fidelity to the original, and that the direction would be entrusted to Dudley Nichols, a fine scriptwriter and a personal friend of O'Neill's, RKO had finally secured the rights.

The production was unique in one respect, I believe. The film was shot in strict continuity. No doubt this was in deference to O'Neill, though whether he had actually requested it, I don't know. It meant that all the sets – and they were very heavy – had to remain standing throughout the shooting period, which must have added consider-ably to the production's costs. It also highlighted what was wrong with the film: it was simply too faithful to the original. O'Neill had ransacked Greek myth to make a modern American myth, based on Freud's incest wish. By the same token the film needed to take some of the liberties with O'Neill that O'Neill took with Aeschylus. But Nichols's script scrupulously avoided all temptation to take his camera beyond the walls of the New England mansion which is the play's setting. Though it shortened the play's four hours' traffic to two and a half hours' screen time, it was very faithful to the text. The camera remained fixed on the face of whichever actor was speaking, often in very long close-up, as if hardly daring to look beyond for fear that the audience might not concentrate on the speech.

These were minor problems, however, compared to the problem of casting. Rosalind Russell was an excellent comedienne, but the very qualities of sanity and wholesomeness which lit up her comedy worked against her as Lavinia / Electra. Mourning did *not* become her. On the first day's shooting she greeted me with 'Hi, Michael! I hear you dig deep into your part. Not me, I'm afraid. I like to have a laugh with the boys in the gantry, know what I mean?' I thought it wiser not to pursue this too far.

Leo Genn, another English actor, with a very fine voice and a soothing manner, was a pillar of rectitude as Adam/Aegisthus, the raffish sea captain who is adored by mother and daughter. To the part of the heavy father, Ezra/Agamemnon, Raymond Massey brought all his personal charm, which was considerable, but made nonsense of the plot, so that his part of the story – like Leo's – was, as it were, scuttled. But the biggest disappointment was Katina Paxinou, the Greek actress who had won an Oscar for her performance in *For Whom the Bell Tolls*. As Hemingway's peasant woman Pilar, she had been splendid, but as Christine/Clytemnestra, with O'Neill's dialogue to speak, she was bowled out by the very thing which had helped her before, a heavy Greek accent and a very imperfect command of the English language.

Why, I wondered, should such a multi-accented cast be assembled for a story about a New England family at the end of the Civil War? I was concerned on my own account to manage the New England accent. I consulted George Cukor, who opined that I had a 'lazy upper lip', and sent me to a well-known studio dialogue/accent coach. She listened to my upper lip, but told me that New England English must have been as close as dammit to English English seventy years ago, so I should carry on just as I was. The one piece of casting I could not quarrel with was that of a sturdy young American with a corncrake voice, Kirk Douglas. He and I got along well until the end of the film, when I made a bad blunder. Browsing in a Los Angeles bookshop I came across a theatrical pamphlet published some time in the 1840s, which offered advice to the aspiring young actor on how to behave towards his older, more experienced colleagues. I bought it for a joke and gave it to Kirk. My idea of a joke was obviously not the same as his. He shot me a glance which more than justified his casting in his next picture as a boxing champion.

Mourning Becomes Electra didn't reach England until five years later. It hadn't done good box office in the States, though it won me an American award, from the National Board of Film Review, and a nomination for an Oscar. The English exhibitors cold-shouldered it altogether, until in 1952 BBC television broadcast the play and to everyone's surprise it proved very popular. Whereupon an independent exhibitor in Manchester booked our film for a screening and the notices in the national newspapers were so good that the exhibitors in Wardour Street rather shamefacedly dusted it off their shelves and screened it in London, where it was publicized as 'the film they didn't want you to see!'

George Cukor was on the telephone. He was organizing an 'English Lunch' and, since Ethel Barrymore was getting too old and frail to go out to lunch, it was to be given at her house in Pacific Palisades.

It was arranged that Katharine Hepburn should give me a lift. She was playing tennis at the Beverly Hills Hotel when I called there to pick her up. She appeared to be beating the bejesus out of her opponents. When she had finally disposed of them, she disappeared to take a shower, and emerged about five minutes later looking as fresh as a daisy. I had met Miss Hepburn before, in London. She asked me if I could see Fanny Brice anywhere. This lady was, as usual, pretty easy to see, and hear.

Katie drove and Miss Brice listened. But not for long. In about five minutes both ladies were talking at the tops of their voices, the only difference being that Hepburn gesticulated somewhat more than Brice. This seemed to unnerve the latter.

'Do you think it would help if you occasionally took hold of the wheel?' she demanded.

Hepburn did not hear this, and we continued to hover between life and death until we reached Pacific Palisades.

Some of the guests had already arrived. Ivor Novello was the guest of honour. Bobby Andrews, Dorothy Dickson, Beatrice Lillie, Gladys Cooper, and – surprise, surprise – Miss Greta Garbo.

Cukor was an accomplished host, subtly steering the conversation from one guest to another. I was so overcome by meeting Garbo that I did not venture to produce my camera, which I had left in the hall. At one point in the afternoon there was a lull in the conversation. Cukor's voice quietly put an end to this with a remark that woke everybody up: 'What do you suppose would be the combined salaries for this afternoon?'

Someone coughed discreetly.

Garbo had never seen Bea Lillie perform, and Cukor persuaded the *diseuse* to do 'I've been to a marvellous party'. She went through what must have been half her repertoire. It was a joy to see Garbo laughing with the same abandon as in *Ninotchka*.

When the time came for the guests to leave I found that by a stroke of luck I was in the same car as Garbo and sitting directly behind her. Cukor was driving. There was a pause. Suddenly he addressed himself to me. He asked when Rachel was arriving. Before I had time to answer, Garbo turned round in her seat and, smiling as if in great wonderment, said, 'Ooh, you are married?'

The question caught me unawares and I do not remember how I answered. I tried to think of something to prolong the conversation. She continued to smile, and all I could think of was her astounding eyes.

After a few long seconds she spoke again. 'How is Mr Rank?'

'Blooming,' I answered.

She continued to look in my direction as if wishing to help me say something. She spoke again. 'Is there much Buddhism in England?'

Everyone who knows anything about the lady knows of her interest in Eastern religions. I was quite ready to worship at her shrine. What, then, was the matter with me that I should have said the one thing that would make her drop me like a hot brick? 'Not a great deal, I think. And what little we have, we have exported to the States.'

The great blue eyes turned to ice and she returned her gaze to the Californian landscape.

News came that Andy, my stepfather, had died. Towards the end of his life he had become almost blind. I had overcome my childhood resentment of him, and had come to like him and respect him increasingly ever since the time when, as I was leaving Cambridge, he said one day, 'You know, Michael, you and I don't speak the same language.' An admirable man.

I invited Mother to come and stay with us. Rachel, who had joined me in Hollywood at the beginning of March, was busy preparing a film she was to do with Charles Boyer. Mother had rather a dull time. The O'Neill film was in full swing. The few amongst the English colony who knew her would invite her to tea or drinks, and she would regale them with an endless flow of theatrical gossip from the distant past. I found it was almost impossible to persuade her to go to bed, and what with early calls to the studio nearly every morning, I found myself snapping at her. Both my films were turning out to be disappointments. Rachel and I had reached a turning point in our marriage, and all things seemed aggravated by being in Hollywood.

At last, in July, the end was in sight. J. Arthur Rank was in Hollywood for the christening of a grandchild, and we were invited to the christening party. There was something rather dynastic about the event, as the newcomer to the Rank empire gurgled happily alongside a replica of himself and his cot modelled in ice. Rank introduced me to one of his henchmen and instructed him to acquaint me with the situation: audiences, it seemed, were not yet responding as they should to all the talent and money which J. Arthur was pouring into British films, and as for the Commonwealth, no one had heard of us. J. Arthur thought it regrettable that so many fine English actors and actresses who had made films in Hollywood simply bypassed Canada. I was returning to England shortly, was I not? Would I consider returning via Canada, to do some personal appearances?

Why on earth did I succumb to this proposition so easily? True, Rank was the leading British producer and I was under contract to him at the time, and had made several films for him; but I was under no obligation to undertake this kind of publicity venture. But Rachel was still filming *A Woman's Vengeance* with Boyer. Mother had already returned home. I accepted, with the proviso that I should have two weeks in New York before setting off, and that I should have someone who would accompany me and look after me every inch of the way in Canada.

We started at Niagara Falls. An irritating lapse of nature. In addition to the humid summer climate – no one had mentioned to me that Eastern Canada in summer was renowned for its humidity – the spray from the Falls could be detected for miles around. After half an hour or so, one would be soaked. 'Shirts for Mr Redgrave.' Someone was sent to purchase a quantity of shirts, and I would be ferried to my hotel to put on a clean dry one, and then back to the Falls again.

Next stop, Belleville, Ontario, where I had my first real check. I had asked that someone should get me a drink and was told that it just wasn't possible unless I bought a bottle from a licensed liquor store. Canada's liquor laws – another thing they had forgotten to mention. I began to feel rather irritable.

And on to Hamilton. 'Michael Redgrave drives a Buick in Hamilton,' proclaimed an advertisement in the local daily paper. They evidently didn't realize that I couldn't drive (still can't). I glanced at a copy of the tour itinerary. 'Mounted Police,' it said, 'to guard back door of hotel.' I was to be taken in by the back staircase, hold a press conference, and, at the conclusion, address the crowd from a first-floor balcony. The hotel was opposite a new Odeon cinema. 'What makes you think', I asked my guide, 'that there are going to be crowds? We didn't see anything like that in Belleville.'

'You're forgetting', said my guide, 'the power of local radio. We've been putting out on this for three days, and I can tell you the interest in you is quite something.' He said this very seriously.

'We'll see,' I muttered.

He was right. I stepped out on to the balcony, to find a huge crowd filling the square. I spoke for ten minutes; heaven knows what about. They clapped me politely, and I set off for Toronto. A visit to a veterans' hospital, three personal appearances, and then I was in Montreal. Three more personal appearances, this time in French.

In all these capers I was accompanied by a young American, Bob Michell, who offered to come to England with me in the hopes of working there. Try as we might, a work permit couldn't be arranged. But Bob stayed with us, a dear friend to me and to the whole family, for nearly twelve years. Then he went home, married, and had two delightful children. He died in 1975 while I was touring America in *Shakespeare's People*. Shortly before his death I flew to see him and his wife and children at their home in Reno. As I entered the departure lounge to leave, he scribbled on the notebook that he used, lacking the power of speech: 'I won't stay to wave you off. I know I should start crying.'

XVII

OR THE latter part of my stay in Hollywood the studio had rented a house for me. Its walls were lined with books and a priceless collection of magazines and periodicals – copies of the *Illustrated London News* dating back to the first issue. The owner, John Balderston, had been a distinguished war correspondent in the First World War. He had also collaborated with J. C. Squire on the play *Berkeley Square*, a very successful adaptation of Henry James's *A Sense of the Past*. It was there that I began to think about James and the theatre.

The following year, holidaying with Rachel and the children at Bexhill-on-Sea, I began an adaptation of James's story *The Aspern Papers*. It had been a busy year. I had played Macbeth on Broadway in the spring of 1948, an enterprise which takes some nerve, as other actors have discovered. I had translated and adapted, with Diana Gould, a French play by Georges de Porto-Riche, *Amoureuse*, which we called *A Woman in Love*. I had introduced Diana to Yehudi Menuhin, whom she later married. I needed a rest and a change. In the mornings I worked on *The Aspern Papers*, letting James's words transport me from hydrangea-besotted Bexhill to the Venice of the 1880s. In the afternoon I dug sandcastles and 'waterworks' with the children on the beach.

Eleven years and many versions later, *The Aspern Papers* reached the stage, with Flora Robson as Miss Tina, Beatrix Lehmann as Miss Bordereau, and myself as H. J., the story's narrator. Some surprise was expressed by reviewers that James, whose long and notorious courtship of the theatre had been so unsuccessful in his lifetime, should find success posthumously with an adaptation of such an 'untheatrical' story.

No such thought occurred to me at Bexhill. Here, I thought, were at least half a dozen capital scenes which could be lifted almost straight

As Macbeth at the Aldwych Theatre in London and the National Theatre in New York (1947–48).

On holiday at Bexhill, Sussex (1948).

With Nancy Coleman, Kirk Douglas and Katina Paxinou in *Mourning Becomes Electra*. Nothing is so serious as Hollywood when it takes itself seriously, and when it tackles a Great American Classic, it takes itself very seriously indeed. I won an Oscar nomination (1951).

With Brian Smith in *The Browning Version*, directed by Anthony Asquith. Rattigan's script was a marvel of its kind – one of those scripts where every line seems so right that you do not have to learn them. For Crocker-Harris I won the prize for best performance at the Cannes Film Festival, the first English actor to do so (1950).

As Antony in the Shakespeare Memorial Theatre Company's *Antony and Cleopatra*. There is no plain sailing in Antony, no point of rest where the words will carry you along. It is a part that calls on all the strength one possesses and tests out every weakness (1953).

The Redgraves at Chiswick, our home for twelve years. Vanessa was fourteen, Lynn eight, and Corin eleven (1951).

As Hector in *Tiger at the Gates* at the Apollo Theatre (1955).

With Diana Wynyard and Vanessa in *A Touch of the Sun*. This was Vanessa's first appearance in London, and our first together (1958). 'Be severe, demanding, a person of taste. That leads to success in our work.' No young actress could have taken Bernhardt's injunction more seriously.

The Redgraves in 1962. We were now all on the stage and, as Vanessa once said, 'Ours is a family that rejoices in each other.'

At Angkor Thom, Cambodia, a break from shooting *The Quiet American* in Saigon (1957).

As Hamlet with the Shakespeare Memorial Company in Moscow. It was the last Hamlet I ever gave, and the best (1958).

With Maggie Smith in *The Master Builder* at the National Theatre, London (1963–64).

(*Below left*) As Samson in *Samson Agonistes*, Yvonne Arnaud Theatre, Guildford, and (*below right*) with Ingrid Bergman and Emlyn Williams in *A Month in the Country*, Cambridge Theatre, London (1965).

As Uncle Vanya. Antony and Vanya are the two performances I am proudest of (1962–63).

In *Hobson's Choice* at the National Theatre (1963–64).

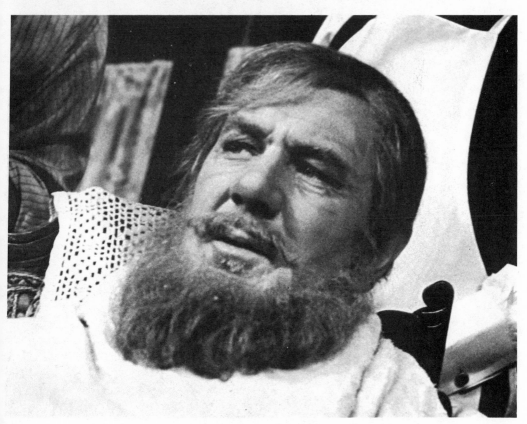

As King Lear, with Vanessa, at the Roundhouse in London (1982).

on to the stage. What was more, two strong Jamesian forces gave promise of holding these scenes together: situation and suspense. The suspense might be finely-drawn, almost imperceptible, but it was there. And where there was suspense, there was theatre.

Snapshots galore. From my earliest experiments with a Brownie box camera I have thousands of snaps of the children. Corin did not take to the camera at first. In a group photograph he can usually be seen shielding his eyes from the sun or looking in a different direction. The Lynn of those early photos is a plump little dumpling: hard to associate with the svelte, out-giving Broadway star, mother of three, now settled in California. Vanessa's joyous smile she inherits in large part from her mother.

This was the time when Vanessa, fending off some interviewer anxious to know if she would be 'following in her parents' footsteps', replied with devastating frankness, 'Good God, no!' Yet it was evident, I thought, that she was bound for the theatre. We took it for granted and seldom talked about it. At the age of about ten she favoured ballet, accepting the fact that she might grow too tall for it. She was almost too tall already. But Marie Rambert, to whom I took Vanessa, said that she would be glad to have her as a pupil. At some point, tall girls stop growing, and if she were to go into the theatre the grace of ballet training would not come amiss.

I pointed out to Vanessa the examples of Edith Evans, Margaret Leighton, and other tall women who had built fine stage careers in spite of their inches. I encouraged her to stand up straight. 'Be severe, demanding, a person of taste. That leads to success in our work.' No young actress could have taken Bernhardt's injunction more seriously.

'Hugh Hunt telephoned while you were out,' said Rachel. 'He asked if you could ring him back.'

'I know what that's about,' I said. Michael Benthall had told me about Hugh's plans for the 1949 season at the Old Vic, in which he was to direct *She Stoops to Conquer*. Hunt had been director of Dublin's Abbey Theatre before the War, and later of the Bristol Old Vic. The next season was to be his first as the newly-appointed director of the Old Vic in London.

I telephoned Hugh, who suggested that we meet for lunch. Was it about the season at the Vic? I asked. It was. Were the plays to be *Love's Labour's Lost, She Stoops to Conquer, A Month in the Country*, and Molière's *The Miser*? Yes.

'And what's the fifth play?'

'I don't know,' said Hugh, 'but it will probably have to be another Shakespeare.'

'There's no need to take me to lunch. Make the fifth play *Hamlet* and I'll play as cast.' (I remembered meeting Robert Helpmann at a party not long before. 'And when are you going to give us your Hamlet, Mr Redgrave?' 'When someone asks me, I suppose.' 'If I'd waited to be asked, I'd *never* have played Hamlet,' said Helpmann.)

There was a moment's pause.

'Haven't we had rather a lot of Hamlets lately?' Hugh asked.

'No,' I said, firmly.

'I'll have to talk to the Governors.'

Within twenty-four hours it was settled. I would play Berowne in *Love's Labour's Lost*, Young Marlow in *She Stoops*, Rakitin in *A Month in the Country*, and Hamlet.

Meanwhile, I had to earn some money. It was the summer of 1949. We should not be playing at the Old Vic until the autumn, and I knew that my salary there would not go far.

Another unexpected telephone call: Noël Coward.

'They're making a film of *The Astonished Heart* and you've got the part.'

'Oh, yes?' I didn't even know that I was being considered for it.

'Yes. There are only two actors who could play it: you and I.'

In that case, I thought, I wonder that you don't play it yourself. But I put the thought out of mind and waited for the script. Noël, it appeared, was tired and in need of a holiday in Jamaica.

The screenplay, by Muriel Box, was very faithful to Noël's play. One thing troubled me. The hero, an eminent psychiatrist, put an end to his life by throwing himself from the roof of the Dorchester Hotel. Surely, I asked the producer, Sydney Box, a great man in such a profession would choose almost any other exit than that? It was agreed that Noël should be asked if this could be changed. Word came back very smartly: nothing doing. But by then I had persuaded myself to accept the film. Celia Johnson and Margaret Leighton, two of the greatest leading ladies, I thought, were to be my co-stars.

We rehearsed at Denham Studios. Asquith, whom I liked and trusted, was directing. But soon he and I began to lose confidence. I tried changing my words. Noël had insisted that not one word should be altered, but he was on holiday and didn't want to be disturbed. I did not yet know that his contract said that his judgement on any matter of shooting or script was irreversible. I was soon to find out.

On the day after his return from holiday a great commotion could be heard in Denham's corridors, and soon Noël himself swept in like a whirlwind. I had expected him to invite me to lunch, but no such thing.

'What do you look like in a moustache?' he asked. I had decided that I needed a moustache to make me look older. In any case, a moustache was indicated in the script.

'Like this,' I said, pulling out an eyebrow pencil and drawing one across my lip.

'No moustache!' said Noël.

'But it's in the . . .'

'No moustache!'

After a fortnight or so of shooting I was in a quandary, and requested a meeting with the producers. Sydney Box came, and Tony Darnborough, and Noël. As best I could, I explained that I simply couldn't see myself in the part. This seemed to cause a mild sensation. (Afterwards I reflected — and the point is made in Coward's diaries — that Noël himself had probably engineered this situation as the most tactful way of replacing me.)

'We'll have to find another actor,' said Sydney.

I suggested one or two, including Stewart Granger.

'No,' said Noël, very firmly, 'I'd rather have Mike.'

There was a silence, whilst we turned the pages of *Spotlight*, the casting directory.

'I *could* play the part,' said Noël eventually, adding quickly, 'But of course Mike mustn't lose a penny.'

'Of course,' agreed Sydney.

I could not resist seeing the film, nor help noticing that Noël had taken more pains over the script than in the version which had given me such difficulty. Nor could I help the feeling that my doubts about the story had been confirmed in the result, though there was not much joy in that.

Until we came to play it on the Continent, *She Stoops to Conquer* was only a moderate success. But for me it was a second homecoming. Like the arrival of an Albert Finney or a Peter O'Toole from the provinces, my first appearance in London at the Old Vic years before had caused a considerable stir of excitement, not least because it was known, or rumoured, that I had already turned down several glamorous offers to play in the West End. And after the success of *As You Like It* I was praised to the skies, besieged with invitations to play this, that, and the other. No part seemed beyond my reach. Whatever leading role was to be cast, I was every producer's first choice. Once, as I entered the room at the Garrick Club where Seymour Hicks was giving a party, Godfrey Tearle, a most commanding figure in the theatre then, said, in his most distinguished voice, 'And here's the great white hope.'

For all that, I paid a penalty. As Terence Rattigan once told me, 'When you've had three good notices in a row, get ready for a bad one.' This was not by any means an entirely cynical remark; critics will always find ample time to repent their over-enthusiasm. Their reaction to me as time went on was to find my performances too studied, too elaborate, too 'intellectual'. And no doubt there was some truth in this. As Remond de St Albine, an eighteenth-century author of a treatise on acting, puts it: 'The reason why we sometimes discover the study'd action of the player, is not because he has been at pains studying it beforehand, but because he has not studied it enough: the last touches of his application in this kind, should be those employed to conceal that there was ever any labour bestow'd at all upon what he is doing; and the rest, without this, always hurts instead of pleasing us.' This may be simple but it is profound.

Since *A Month in the Country* at the St James's in 1943, I had played very little comedy. For that, strangely enough, the critic James Agate was partly responsible. He had written that I succeeded best in parts that had a touch of the 'morbid' in them, that I lacked light-heartedness. 'For Michael Redgrave to play Young Marlow,' he wrote, 'would be as unprofitable as for Bob Hope to play King Lear.'

Now Agate was dead, and Michael Benthall, our director, had the happy knack of convincing me that I was a great comic actor. Rehearsals for *She Stoops* went smoothly and well. I seized on a fragment of text – 'This stammer in my address' – to justify playing the young man with a stammer. I found that by holding back on the letter 'm', letting the audience attune themselves to the stammer, I could pause as long as I liked before the line 'Madam, will you marry me?'and the longer I paused, the greater the laugh.

The audience reception was warm. Next morning I lay in bed and heard *The Times* and the *News Chronicle* drop like time bombs through the letter-box. Should I, or shouldn't I? Yes, I should read them and face the worst, and to hell with Agate. Had he still been among the living, I would have been neither so eager nor so nervous.

I had no need to quail before his ghost. The notices were excellent.
'A performance accurately pitched on a note of high comedy,' said
The Times. High comedy ! ? I raced upstairs to show Rachel the good
news. 'What's the matter, darling, why are you crying ?' she said.
(The reader will have noticed that the Scudamores cry very easily.)
We read the reviews over and over. 'The part of Young Marlow,'
wrote Eric Keown, 'is a pretty good test of an actor. . . . He who
plays him must be constantly changing gear. He must be hesitant
and tongue-tied, though not quite a boor, and the next moment a
warm young amorist still palpably a gentleman. The success of the
play depends upon his mastery of these diverse elements, and the
success of this production is Mr Michael Redgrave. . . . It is a fine
piece of gentle comedy, and Mr Redgrave has a way of locking his
lips mulishly on an "M" that puts him among the great stage
stammerers.'

And to hell with Agate now!

Despite Hugh Hunt's 'Haven't we had rather a lot of Hamlets
lately ?' there had, in fact, been rather few. There was the Stratford
Hamlet in 1948, with Bobby Helpmann and Paul Scofield alternating
in the part, and Robert Eddison's at the Bristol Old Vic. But in those
days *Hamlet*, as befitted one of the peaks – if not *the* peak – of dramatic
literature, was not performed as it is now, in season and out. To play
Hamlet was the supreme test of an actor's quality.

I think Hugh, who had a military background, appreciated the
dash with which I had insisted on Hamlet before accepting the other
parts he had to offer. Probably that, more than anything, convinced
him that I could play it. At all events, he said something at our first
meeting after that telephone conversation which puzzled and intri-
gued me : 'You are a misunderstood actor.'

'What does he mean ?' I asked Rachel.

'He's right,' she answered, 'but for that you have only yourself to
blame.'

We gathered together for the first read-through. Wanda Rotha was
to play the Queen, at my suggestion. The Queen needs a quality of
over-ripe sensuality. This, Wanda had. What was more, she spoke
perfect English but with a trace of a German accent, and the Queen's
line, 'O, this is counter, you false Danish dogs,' suggested to me, which
I had never noticed in any commentary, that she must be a foreign
queen. Yvonne Mitchell was to play Ophelia – a very happy choice. For
Laertes I had insisted on a good fencer, Peter Copley, remembering
how I as Laertes had cut Larry's forehead thirteen years before.

Hugh opened the proceedings with a specially-prepared lecture, as he had for *Love's Labour's Lost*. On that occasion most of the actors, unfamiliar with the play, had congratulated him warmly. For *Hamlet* his lecture was rather longer and the actors seemed restless, feeling that they knew the play and wanted to get on with it. No one pressed forward at the end to thank him except myself, feeling that I had to. Perhaps they were right. The difficulties of *Hamlet* are many, but none so difficult in performance as they are on paper.

'Roy,' says Mother in one of her notebooks, 'could never be bothered with Shakespeare and the poets. He told a story of how he was going to play Hamlet when he was at Mrs Lane's theatre and had not troubled to read it till he heard one of the costers reciting some of it, and then he thought he'd better get on with the words.' Good or bad, Roy's Hamlet was his own. My first attempt, as a schoolmaster at Cranleigh, owed so much to Gielgud's performance in the part in 1930 that I must have seemed like Gielgud's understudy. So much so that I obliged myself not to see any of his later interpretations, knowing that if I were to play the part myself I should want to clear my imagination of his presence.

When we came to rehearse *Hamlet* I brought with me only a few preconceptions, most of them of a negative kind. *Hamlet* was not, I thought, as the Olivier film had suggested, 'the tragedy of a man who could not make up his mind'. On the contrary, he *did* make up his mind, as thoroughly as anyone in his unique circumstances could. To take another example, I so strongly rejected the 'pathological' interpretation of Hamlet, as in some way the victim of an Oedipus complex, that I used every possible occasion to stress his love for his father.

For the actor, the difficulties of Hamlet are those which reveal themselves only when one starts to act him. How, for example, to greet the ghost, when several other characters have already met him twice? Garrick, we know, made great play with his hands, and for years after, his business was copied by successive Hamlets, becoming almost a test of an actor's skill. It seemed to me that the solution was to do nothing. Just as in the cinema Eisenstein showed that by skilful editing a close-up of an actor without any expression will reveal by suggestion what the audience wants it to reveal, so there are moments in the theatre when the actor is able to do nothing, and even feel nothing, and yet the audience will see in him all that they want or need to see.

In the closet scene, I imported a piece of business from William Poel's production of *Fratricide Punished*, in which Mother had played the Queen to Esmé Percy's Hamlet. A maidservant placed the Queen's chestnut-red wig on a block, and the Queen was seen to have grey hair.

(*Fratricide Punished* deserves, and has probably received elsewhere, a chapter to itself. It was a simplified version of *Hamlet* performed on the Continent by English actors in the 1650s, when Cromwell had closed the theatres.)

For 'Look here upon this picture, and on this, / The counterfeit presentment of two brothers,' I drew a coin from my pocket with Claudius's head on it, and holding it side by side with a miniature portrait of Hamlet's father which I wore in a locket, I thrust them at the Queen, almost ramming them in her face:

> . . . Have you eyes?
> Could you on this fair mountain leave to feed,
> And batten on this moor? Ha! have you eyes?

Since the 'rogue and peasant slave' soliloquy brought the curtain down on the first half, I thought some theatrical effect was called for there. The troupe of players had brought on a large theatrical skip, so on the words 'O, vengeance', with the players' sword held in both hands, I did a forward fall as if stabbing Claudius. I spoke the remainder of the soliloquy very quietly until the last two lines. Then, rising to my feet, holding a crown from the players' prop basket at arm's length above my head, and with the other arm swirling a red cloak about me, I gave a joyous shout, as if, for the first time, Hamlet knew what to do:

> . . . The play's the thing
> Wherein I'll catch the conscience of the king.

Yvonne Mitchell had waited in the wings till the end of the Act before returning to her dressing-room, and when the applause subsided, she gave me a radiant smile, as much as to say 'What did I tell you?' As I reached the stairs, my dresser met me. He said he had just been telephoned by Olivier's dresser at the St James's, where Larry was playing with Rachel in Christopher Fry's *Venus Observed*. 'Sir Laurence wants to know how it's going.'

In the scores of times I have played Hamlet, it seems to me that I never gave the same performance twice. Not that the theatre-goer who came on Wednesday would see something very different to what he would have seen on Tuesday, but that I was always open to a new effect. This was not, for me, a matter of pride or deliberate choice. I could admire, if not envy, those actors who prided themselves on repeating in each performance what they had done on previous occasions. I admired Donald Wolfit, who knew exactly how he had mapped his part and would stick to that territory through thick and thin.

'Michael,' he once said to me, 'you've worked with Guthrie. What's he like?'

We were at the Garrick Club. Wolfit, I knew, was going to the Vic to play Tamburlaine, in which he would be very fine, and Lear (though the latter never materialized).

'Well,' I said, choosing my words carefully, 'he's very stimulating.'

Wolfit brushed this aside, as I thought he might. 'Yes, yes, I dare say, but what's he like?'

I was a little nonplussed. 'Did you see – ' I asked, and reeled off some of Tony's productions.

Donald's face clouded. It was clear he had seen none of them, and the bare mention of them seemed to deepen his disquiet. 'Because, you see,' he said, 'I have thirteen effects in my Lear, and *I don't intend to lose one of them.*'

No notices, however good, can ever quite satisfy an actor. No applause is ever quite long enough. At the end of a reception, no matter how tumultuous, one part of an actor's vanity must ask, 'Yes, but why have you stopped?'

Only in Leningrad and Moscow, where, eight years later, in 1958, I gave my last performances of Hamlet with the Shakespeare Memorial Company, did the applause, which lasted several minutes, silence almost all my doubts and questions. I was fifty, an age at which one can start, like Solness, to look over one's shoulder at the next generation pressing on one's heels. The young and brilliant Ian Holm was my understudy. He would watch every scene from the wings, which is right and conscientious for an understudy, but I could not help imagining him saying to himself, 'Yes, but just let me play it.'

Once I came off after the battlements scene and passed him in the wings, as usual, and he whispered, 'What you are doing out there is absolutely incredible.' I flew, I walked on air for the rest of that performance. It was the last I ever gave. And the best.

Something else happened on that tour. When our plane landed in Moscow, from amongst the press corps waiting to photograph us on arrival an English journalist took me aside and said he had a message for me: 'Guy Burgess wants to know if you would agree to meet him.'

'Guy Burgess? Yes, of course.'

I'd not seen Burgess since we had been together at Cambridge. He had designed the sets for a play I was in. I had a general recollection that he was amusing. He had a very lively mind.

On the first night of *Hamlet* in Moscow a rather noisy group of English newspapermen were gathered outside my dressing-room door. Out of their hubbub came one voice I thought I recognized. It could be Guy's – it was. He swept into my dressing-room, extending both arms to greet me. He had been crying. 'Oh, Michael! Those words, those words! You can imagine how they carry me back. Magic!'

His face underwent a sort of convulsion; he lurched past me and, with what looked like practised accuracy, was sick into the basin. An athletic-looking young man who had come in with Guy waved his hands in apology. 'Oh, Guy, you are a *peeg*,' he said, with considerable force.

When Guy had recovered, which he did almost immediately, he introduced the young man: a factory worker, studying ballet at evening classes, whom Guy had persuaded to leave work early to see my Hamlet.

Next day, Guy called for me and we drove through the snowy suburbs to lunch at his flat. He seemed anxious to impress. He was wearing his old Etonian tie; his suit was well worn and a bit shiny; he was stouter than he used to be.

His flat was tidy and comfortable. Placed on the coffee-table in order to catch my eye was the current *New Statesman*: equally eye-catching was a pot of pâté de foie gras from France. Lunch was served by a cook-housekeeper. She appeared to speak no English, though Guy in her presence said that she understood every word, adding as she left the room, 'She reports on me, of course.'

We sat down to eat the foie gras. Or, rather, I sat alone at the table whilst Guy, who was already too drunk to eat, paced up and down the room, talking. The second course was a hare, but the cook-housekeeper had omitted to remove the gallbladder, and it was totally inedible. Guy apologized profusely, but there was nothing else to eat except the remains of the foie gras.

After lunch we walked. We passed a nearby basilica which he said he often visited: 'They have wonderful music.' He told me 'they' had only wanted him to deliver Donald Maclean; he repeated this more than once.

He came to see us several times at the theatre and made friends with Coral Browne, who played the Queen in *Hamlet*. She agreed to order him some clothes at Simpsons in Piccadilly when we got back. He said he still had some money in England.

On the day we were leaving he came to see us off at the hotel. As we drove away, he was near tears. 'Write to me,' he said, 'it's bloody lonely here, you know.'

'And which is *your* favourite film?' A favourite question, this, and a difficult one to answer. Among the fifty or so pictures I have made are some that would hardly appear in anyone's selection of memorable films, yet I loved every moment of making them. There have been times, working with Orson Welles on *Confidential Report* (1955), for example, when even at three-thirty in the morning I have not wanted to stop. And I have seldom been happier than when working with Gene Kelly in Paris on *The Happy Road* (1956).

One thing I learned from working with Fritz Lang – or, rather, relearned, for I think I knew it already – was that not only should a film have a strong central idea, but its idea should be such as can be conveyed in a single sentence. Not all good films, I realize, conform to this criterion. But I have found when answering that other favourite question, 'What's it about?' that if you can awaken the interest of your questioner in a sentence or two – 'It's about a ventriloquist who thinks he's possessed by his dummy,' 'It's about an embittered schoolmaster whose defences break down because someone, unexpectedly, is kind to him' – it's a fair, though not complete, test of the appeal that your film will have at large.

So it was with *The Browning Version*. In 1950 I found myself, unexpectedly, at a loose end, when the money ran out for a film I was making with Anouk Aimée in the South of France. I returned home to another surprise. 'Puffin Asquith wants you for *The Browning Version*,' I was told. Eric Portman had created the part of Crocker-Harris with great success. Now Eric was unavailable for the film, and at short notice I took on the part. (Sometimes two actors' careers become strangely enmeshed. Eric had taken over my part in *The 49th Parallel*, a war-effort movie that Michael Powell shot in the early days of the war.)

The 'look' of a part is always highly important, especially in films, where once the first scenes are in the can it is too late and too expensive to make any substantial changes in one's appearance. For *The Browning Version* I did a number of camera tests. There was the question of spectacles. I was in two minds about this. Spectacles are the first thing that actors lay hold of when they have to play an academic character. So I thought, *I* won't wear spectacles. I tried one camera test without. Then another, with : the first pair concealed too much of the expression in my eyes, so I asked them to make me another without rims to the lenses, and then, when these seemed to suit, a spare pair for safety's sake.

I also asked for camera tests with sound. I wanted a light head-voice for Crocker-Harris, and I knew that when one first assumes a pitch or an accent different from one's own, it is hard to get a true impression of what it will sound like to an audience because the sound in one's own ear at first is often very exaggerated.

I lightened my hair with very strong peroxide, which in black-and-white photography would give a look of hair that was fading and turning grey. I also had the hairdresser shave the crown of my head (though to my annoyance this bald patch was seen in only one shot in the film).

Despite these preparations it was a terrible beginning. We had to do the last shots first, and these last scenes were very emotional. There were none of the scenes of minor importance which one usually did first so as to work one's way into the film. I can still see perfectly clearly in that film where the camera angle changes during a scene, where my make-up changes; even my weight changes from scene to scene. (At that time I could gain weight and shed it almost at will, which was very useful for certain character parts, because even a slight change of weight would show immediately in my face, altering its expression. But in taking on *The Browning Version* at such short notice, I had not had time to lose as much weight as I wanted at the start.)

In the scene with the headmaster at the cricket match, there is another mistake in my playing, which shows if one looks for it. Not many in the audience would spot it, I think, but C. A. Lejeune, the *Observer* critic at the time, who had been bowled over by Portman's performance in the part, noticed it immediately. 'For such a big man,' she wrote of me, 'his performance is wonderfully delicate' – ominous compliment – 'but it is the delicacy of a floorwalker rather than a scholar.' And, as far as the cricket-match scene went, she was right. At the last minute, and to my surprise, Wilfrid Hyde-White had been cast as the headmaster. A very successful actor in his chosen field, but too smooth and urbane, I thought, for this part. I tried to adjust myself, but in doing so I somehow slipped into a manner that was too deferential, almost obsequious, where my character should have stood his own ground more firmly. 'The delicacy of a floor-walker' – how one phrase like that remains in the memory long after recollections of the most lavish praise have faded, and all the more so if one recognizes its partial truth.

Rattigan's script was a marvel of its kind. There are scripts, now and then, where every line seems so right that you do not have to learn them. It is enough to repeat the words a few times for every line to fall into place. Rattigan's script also gave me that rare opportunity, such as I had in *Dead of Night*, and would have again as Barnes Wallis in *The Dam Busters*, to create a character totally different from my own. This is not necessarily the highest achievement of acting. I could equally, if not more, admire a Garbo, who could change her mood in a score of different ways without ever changing character. Nevertheless, it is one of the most satisfying.

It was Barnes Wallis himself, incidentally, who gave me the clue to my performance in *The Dam Busters*, a film which I enjoyed making more than any since *The Browning Version*. We were introduced, and Wallis, who was a good deal shorter than I and rather slim, burst out laughing. We 'clicked' at once. At our second meeting I said, 'I'm not going to mimic you, you know.' His reply was interesting, not so much because he was evidently relieved as for what it showed of the method he would use to tackle a problem, even in the field of acting.

'No, of course. Your problem is not to imitate a person, but to create him.'

It illustrated, I thought, his scientific approach to the very essence of what he was considering. A quality – not at all to be confused with the stereotype of the absent-minded professor – of setting aside everything but the essential, which must have driven him on and sustained him through countless set-backs and disappointments.

XVIII

THE MEMORIAL Theatre had been expensively refurbished for the hundreds of thousands of visitors who were expected at Stratford in 1951, the year of the Festival of Britain. Shakespeare's history plays were to be produced, from *Richard II* to *Henry V*. Anthony Quayle, the actor-director of the Memorial Theatre, was to play Falstaff. The young Welsh actor Richard Burton was Hal. My parts were Richard, Hotspur, and Chorus in *Henry V*. Also Prospero – a Stratford season at that time consisted of five productions, and at my request *The Tempest* was chosen as the fifth play.

Memories of the season when Mother played Mistress Page buzzed about my head as I bicycled to rehearsal every morning. The old theatre, where I had been allowed to walk-on in *Henry IV, Part II* to swell the tiny crowd of extras who cheered Maurice Colbourne as Prince Hal in the coronation scene, burnt to the ground in 1926 – set alight by the Flower family, it was said in jest. The Flowers, that munificent family of Warwickshire brewers whose ancestor built the first theatre at Stratford in the 1890s, had long wanted a modern theatre in its place, and built one in 1933, and were rewarded for their pains by the universal 'ya-boos' which greeted the new design, red brick upon red brick, 'the Jam Factory'.

Stratford was much changed. The Stratford of my boyhood was a little market town. Sheep Street in the town centre was memorable for its tea-shop, where they sold wonderful lemon cakes. The season was divided into two parts, with nine or ten productions in all. Ten days or a fortnight was considered sufficient time to rehearse a production, though rehearsals in those days, when Actors' Equity was only a gleam in the eyes of a few, would frequently go on till the players dropped from exhaustion. There were fine actors at Stratford then, but no one expected to make his reputation or his fortune there.

Nor for that matter were fortunes to be made now, at least not by the actors. The top salary was £60 a week, the minimum £9. But the quarter of a million visitors who would come to the theatre this season would keep the cash tills ringing, and the box office was confidently expected to recoup the £75,000 spent on enlarging and improving the auditorium.

In its own prestige, and the reputation it could bestow upon its actors, Stratford was totally changed. Anthony Quayle had seen to that, almost single-handedly. Since the War, Robert Helpmann and Paul Scofield had played there, as had Godfrey Tearle, Diana Wynyard, John Gielgud, and Peggy Ashcroft.

The 1951 season was the first in anyone's memory when the history plays were produced as a cycle. Quayle and I discussed how this might alter and define our view of the chief characters, for characters and events change their meaning when the plays are seen as a whole. Richard II, for instance, was customarily played as a figure of tragedy and Bolingbroke as a ruthless schemer when the play was performed on its own. Indeed, to Bolingbroke's opponents in the later plays that is how he appears in retrospect: 'Richard, that sweet lovely rose'. Yet it seemed essential that Richard's vanity and cruelty, so evident in his treatment of John of Gaunt, be given full measure if Bolingbroke's usurping the Crown were to be understood not merely as a crime but as a *necessary* crime. Having some responsibility for the cycle (I was to direct *Henry IV, Part II*), I laid some emphasis on Richard's pettiness and hysteria in the first half of the play – too much emphasis, in fact, in my anxiety that the audience should get the point.

Hotspur, says Lady Percy, was 'thick of speech'. That, and some of Hotspur's own lines, suggested to me that he was a rough, ragged rascal, unversed in the ways of the Court. At Quayle's suggestion I had gone up to Northumberland in search of a convincing accent for Hotspur – not the Tyneside 'Geordie' but the Northumbrian country accent. Somehow this had got into the press, and amongst those who came forward offering help and tuition was the Duke of Northumberland, who invited me to dinner at Alnwick and introduced me to Jack Armstrong, who had the honorary title of the Duke's Piper.

So, armed with the cumbersome wire recorder of those days, I acquired something that passed for Northumbrian, with its burred 'r' almost like the French guttural 'r' sound. I found the accent an enormous help. It took me outside myself and made the strongest possible contrast with the tones of Richard II, which I had been playing in each preceding performance. Of course, no amount of argument or textual justification would have carried the day if the accent had not been felt by audiences to come off. On the whole I think it did. Perhaps the greatest compliment paid me on that account was by two Northumbrian friends of Quayle's.

'What did you think of Redgrave's accent?' he asked them after a performance.

'Ooh, right, yes, bang on. Alnwick,' said one.

'Ye-es, very good,' said the other, 'but I'd say more Wooler than Alnwick.' Wooler and Alnwick are less than twenty miles apart.

Traditionally, Hotspur was the romantic hero of *Henry IV, Part I*. But in the cycle as a whole, Quayle and I decided Burton's Hal must emerge as the hero, whose final justification and expiation comes at Agincourt.

I had, I suppose, a slight possessive feeling for Prince Hal, having played him for the Marlowe Society at Cambridge. But I was fascinated by the ease with which Richard Burton slipped into the part without even appearing to try. My Hotspur in the preceding play was, I thought, the best thing I had done. Yet it was over-shadowed to some degree by Burton's Hal. He had 'arrived', as I had fourteen years before, and taken everyone by storm.

'You must be more competitive!' Mother used to warn me. But I wasn't. I saw no need to compete. I felt as sure of myself at this time as I had ever felt, secure in the knowledge that those whom I most admired – Michel, Peggy, George Devine – respected my work.

I think I got on well with Burton, and would have got on better had not a caucus of inflammable Welshmen been moved by his mere presence to take sides between the two of us. With so many Welsh members in the company, especially in the Glendower scene, the atmosphere of a Rugby final at Cardiff Arms Park was never far away.

'Would you mind,' asked Olivier, 'if I made a film of *The Beggar's Opera*?'

'Not in the least.'

We were staying at Notley Abbey, Olivier's country house near Thame, one weekend towards the end of my Stratford season. I had a question for him.

'What would you think of a film of *The Importance of Being Earnest*?'

'Who's directing?'

'Puffin.' It would be my third film with Asquith and there were few directors I would have sooner worked for, but, 'Do you think he has the incisive style necessary for such a production?'

'Do you?' Olivier parried.

Edith would recreate her definitive Lady Bracknell. I would play Ernest, Joan Greenwood would be Gwendolen, but ... but ... for the time being I put it out of my mind. And then a week later I thought what nonsense, of course I must do it.

When I saw the first screening five months later in a private viewing theatre in Wardour Street I was very disappointed. The tempo, which it is true must not be hurried, was ponderous, and sometimes the players, as Shaw noted of the original production, were too much in awe of Wilde to give their lines the air of conversation. I missed the response of an audience terribly. Wilde's epigrams demand their tribute of laughter and, without it, both the actors and the story seemed very vulnerable.

Since then I have seen the film three or four times on television, and each time I like it more. I find, in general, with a few obstinate exceptions, that I like my films more the further in time it is from the making of them. But with *The Importance of Being Earnest* time has restored a truer and certainly a more generous consideration of its qualities.

The scenes between Gwendolen and Cecily are the best I have ever seen them done. (I had asked for Dorothy Tutin to play Cecily, her first film part. I later adored her Sally Bowles in *I Am a Camera*.) And, of course, there was Edith as Lady Bracknell. It was not and could not be quite the performance she gave in Gielgud's unforgettable revival at the Haymarket in 1940, but it was unmistakably there.

We had been nervous, she and I, at our first meeting on the set of *The Importance of Being Earnest* and a little shy of each other. Not so, however, for our last film together. It was in Dublin, where we went to make *Young Cassidy*, a film biography of Sean O'Casey. We were on location and the players had been allocated a sitting-room in one of the nearby buildings. I was playing the middle-aged W. B. Yeats. Miss Horniman was played by Edith, no less. The part of O'Casey was entrusted to the capable hands of Rod Taylor, an excellent actor if a trifle too robust for the poet.

I came into the sitting-room and found myself face to face with Edith. I was expecting to meet her in the course of filming, but for an instant I was caught by surprise. Edith rose to her feet and, swooping down on me, hugged me and kissed me. Rod Taylor scrutinized this and remarked, 'I didn't get anything like that when I came in.'

'Ah,' said Edith, and let out a short peal of laughter, hugged me again and said with that famous dive in her voice, 'Ah, but you see Mike and I are *old* lovers.'

Amongst the plays I had been sent whilst I was filming *The Importance of Being Earnest* were Arthur Miller's adaptation of *An Enemy of the People*, Lillian Hellman's *The Autumn Garden*, and a play by Clifford Odets about the theatre. Originally called *The Country Girl*, it was now retitled *Winter Journey*.

A young Broadway director wants, against all advice, to cast in the leading part in his production an older actor whose career is almost finished. The part of Frank Elgin, the actor, had a touch of Barrymore about him which appealed to me. Years before I had been sent a play about Barrymore, *Goodnight, Sweet Prince*, a horrifying cautionary tale, though an unconvincing play. But *Winter Journey* is authentic in its portrayal of actors and theatre people. Elgin is an extreme contradiction. He is said to be a great actor, and whoever plays him must convince the audience of that. He is also abominably sly, vain, self-deluding and an alcoholic.

I couldn't make up my mind. The Third Act, though well written, was sentimental and rather hollow. I asked the young American Sam Wanamaker, who was to play the director and to direct the play, to give me a week to decide. I had spent a year at Stratford and now, after *The Importance of Being Earnest*, I wanted to do a modern part – but I wasn't sure. I had also been offered the part of the Judge in Rattigan's *The Deep Blue Sea*, which had all the hallmarks of a box-office success about it.

Friday came and I was still uncertain of my answer. During a break in shooting I wandered over to another sound stage to pay a call on Alec Guinness. We had been friends since our first season at the Old Vic in 1936 – not close friends, but liking one another and respecting each other's work. We were near neighbours: I at Chiswick Mall, Guinness at St Peter's Square, in one of a terrace of Regency houses built from public subscription for the victorious generals of Wellington's army at Waterloo. Our sons played together. There was very little sense in which Alec and I could be considered rivals. Yet, as I waited for him to appear – he was somewhere in the studio, no one was quite sure where – I had the peculiar sensation that he was avoiding me. And this in turn was followed by the notion that perhaps he wanted to play Elgin in

Winter Journey. He would be an excellent choice, I thought, and at that moment I wanted to play the part more than anything else and made up my mind to do it.

Later that day we shared a car home, and it turned out that I was right. Alec not only wanted the part, he had been offered it. I made some senseless apology and Alec, the soul of politeness, said, 'Not at all. I'm only wondering how much I can sue the producer for.'

It was a strange beginning, but rehearsals went smoothly enough, with no more than their fair share of disagreements. Wanamaker was a devotee of Stanislavsky, more so than I at that time, and suggested that he, I and Googie Withers, who played my wife, should write down the prehistory of our characters, before the moment they are first seen in the play. I thought this a useful exercise for students, but impractical for us, or for me at any rate. I had no wish to commit myself to a definite preconception of Elgin until I'd had a chance to explore him more fully in rehearsal. On the other hand, when the suggestion arose that a certain part of the first scene should be improvised at each performance, I agreed readily. It would not be easy, I thought. In improvisation it is usually simpler to lead than to follow, and Elgin in this scene had to follow. Moreover, I should have to sustain my New York accent, which is harder to do in improvisation than in lines one has learned. But it would help to keep our performances fresh each night.

Late one night, after we had opened at the St James's Theatre and had been playing for about three weeks, Wanamaker rang me in a fury.

'You called me a kike.'

'When?'

'Tonight. On stage.'

'No,' I said, 'I called you a tyke.' This is a Yorkshire term, half insult and half admiration, for someone who is like a bull terrier. Not at all New York, but there it was, I'd used it. Wanamaker would have none of it.

'I've got three witnesses.'

With all the finality I could muster I suggested he should stuff his three witnesses.

From that moment on, for the rest of our six months' run, we were not on speaking terms. Neither of us said anything about it in public, but word got out and each night, as the gallery queue formed on the pavement outside my dressing-room window, I could hear them talking about it. Perhaps it contributed something to the atmosphere of the play and served to neutralize its sentimentality, but it was horrible. I had always loathed quarrelling with those I worked with, and now every performance seemed like a contest. During one of my speeches in the Second Act, I became convinced that Wanamaker was scraping a chair across the floor to upset me, though no doubt in his own mind there was a perfectly adequate reason for it. I glared at him night after night till I could stand it no longer, and the next night, as the scraping began, I grasped the back of the chair with both hands so firmly that we would have stopped the play altogether if he'd tried to wrestle it from me. We obviously couldn't continue doing that every night without an absurd, undignified scramble to see who could reach the chair first. For the next few performances nothing happened. Then the scraping began again. I halted in mid-speech.

'Don't do that!' I yelled.

'Why not?' asked Sam, rather taken by surprise I fancy.

'Because it goes *right through my head*!'

It didn't happen again.

Wanamaker was excellent in the play, and his direction was first class. I owed a good deal of my own performance to him. We've met since then once or twice, and drawn a veil over *Winter Journey*. Like all clashes of personality, it was agonizing at the time and afterwards it is hard to imagine how it happened.

My 'An Actor to the Critics' and other articles which had been published from time to time in theatrical magazines had brought me a number of invitations to lecture or to write a book about acting. I had refused them all. Two considerations held me back, the first being that whatever a player may say about his work, it is by his work, by what he projects on-stage, that he is judged. In England, especially in the English theatre, there is an ingrained prejudice against any attempt at an analysis of acting. Agate's 'Now you can stop being an intellectual and start being a real actor' summed up this attitude.

An invitation from Bristol University to deliver the Rockefeller Foundation lectures on the subject of acting changed my mind. It was 1952, my nineteenth year on the stage – not quite the twenty years that by tradition are said to make an actor, but near enough. I had a strong sense that it was now or never. And besides, Bristol was my birthplace.

I took the opportunity to pay a fleeting visit to Clifton. The paper shop on St Michael's Hill was still the paper shop on St Michael's Hill. The cinema in Whiteladies Road was still 'the flicks'.

I was to give four lectures. The first, in the University's largest auditorium, before an audience of a thousand or so, was open to the public. The last three were for University members only. This suited me rather well, for it allowed me to approach my subject by a discursive, circuitous route, with all the necessary disclaimers. I was aware, I told my audience, that my questions were far more plentiful than my answers, and that my answers, in most cases, were implied far more than they were stated.

As I sat down to prepare a framework for the lectures, which came very readily, and then to undertake the much more difficult task of sifting my material to fill my framework, I was aware of another constraint. Six months from then, I realized, when the lectures were published, I might well be thinking very differently about my subject. An actor can add up many or most of the figures on his professional ledger, but it is in the nature of his work that he should never attempt a final sum. Moreover, as in higher mathematics, where two and two need not necessarily make four, his sums may come out differently on different occasions. The title I chose, *An Actor's Ways and Means*, was itself a kind of disclaimer, for it suggested to me the sort of day-to-day account which in the conditions of the theatre then – the English theatre of the 1940s and 1950s – was very much the way a professional actor had to live and work.

The book sold slowly, but it sold steadily. A quarter of a century hurtled by, and I was asked to write a preface to a new paperback edition. Re-reading it I found, with surprise, that there was very little I wished to change. Something, surely? 'The actor must create his own luck.' That was a statement which had provoked understandable annoyance in some quarters. Yet I believe it to be true. Edith Evans's remark 'You only really begin to act when you leave off trying' annoys some people still. It contains, I think, as much truth as many paradoxes, and more than most. For it goes almost without saying that to achieve that sense of effortlessness which is a hallmark of good acting, much discipline and effort are necessary.

'Unless the actor is on that particular evening wishing above everything else to act, that performance may be reasonably good but it is unlikely to be his best. To act well and to act well repeatedly has to become an obsession.' *There* was something I wished to withdraw. For the actor may and sometimes does give of his best on those evenings when he feels ill, or tired, or even slightly bored. Reading those lines, I remembered a young actor, playing Laertes at the Vic, who discovered that in the 'eternity', or uncut, version of *Hamlet* there are some two hours between his exit in Act Two and his reappearance in Act Four. He tried staying in his dressing-room, keeping in the mood. That lasted for about twenty minutes. He tried sitting in a nearby cabman's shelter, drinking innumerable cups of coffee. That gave him sleepless nights. Then he remembered that at the end of Waterloo Road was Waterloo Bridge, and beyond Waterloo Bridge stood the Gaiety Theatre, where Leslie Henson, one of the great comedians, was playing nightly in *Seeing Stars*. Taking careful note of the time, he set off at a run for the Gaiety – a strange figure, no doubt, in his raincoat, green tights, and flaming red wig. Reaching the gallery entrance door, he slipped inside, climbed the long gallery, and took his seat unobserved in the 'gods', to watch the great Leslie.

That strange tall figure was, of course, myself. At that age I took many things for granted. Yet I dare say I was even then as 'obsessed' as any with the ambition of acting well, and I doubt whether these nightly excursions did any harm to my performance – they may even have done it good.

Edward Thompson, of Heinemann's, who had started the ball rolling by asking me to write a book about acting (an offer I had always refused), pressed me, after the publication of *An Actor's Ways and Means*, to write another. I refused again. I've done enough, I thought. And anyway, that book had grown naturally out of the lectures. But Thompson persisted, and the result was *Mask or Face*, in which almost everything else I had written or lectured about on acting, including the Theodore Spencer lecture at Harvard, was collected into a book of essays, subtitled *Reflections in an Actor's Mirror*.

Three years later, in 1958, I was at Stratford again, playing Hamlet and Benedick. August came round, and with it the annual series of lectures in the Conference Hall given by Shakespearian scholars, directors, and actors. As usual I was asked to lecture, and as usual I agreed. And then I thought, But I've nothing to say. Surely I had said all I wanted to say in 'Shakespeare and the Actors'? Even on that occasion I had found it necessary to fill up my matter with a quantity of art: my lecture had included a monstrously long quotation from *The Tempest*. It had pleased my audience, for I had spoken it with much feeling, but on paper it looked like padding, which it was.

Going for a walk in the country, I began to ruminate on the question 'What makes an actor "tick"?' and realized I might put it into fiction. By the end of my walk I had the outline of my story. Two weeks later I read it at Stratford in the Conference Hall, before an audience surprised, and then delighted, to find themselves listening to a story instead of a lecture. That winter I read it in Vienna to an audience in the Auditorium Maximum, having prefaced it with a speech in German to soften them up. A year later it became a short novel, *The Mountebank's Tale*: 'Joseph was a classical actor in the unusual but real sense of the word. He never altered the balance of a part, consciously or unconsciously, to suit his own style or personality. He scrupulously measured each part in relation to the text and the author's meaning.' Joseph, I might add, is not myself. But he is the type of actor whom in *An Actor's Ways and Means* I dubbed 'protean' or, in Jouvet's terms, a *comédien*. The novel says as much about acting, I think, as either of my two previous books. Like them, it ends with a question.

It is 1953. At Stratford again. We assemble for the first read-through of *Antony and Cleopatra*. It is the third play of the season. We know that, whatever its success or failure, nearly every performance will be sold out for the next three months. Stratford is *still* the unofficial national theatre.

Do I detect a hint of nervousness in Peggy's reading? Perhaps. A trace. In my own? No, having reluctantly agreed to play the part, I go for it hammer and tongs. It's *not* a part I would have chosen to play. Come to think of it, of my three parts this season, only Lear, which is yet to come, accords completely with my own choice. Shylock, they said, was a question of money. If I wouldn't play Shylock, another leading actor would have to be engaged, and the annual budget couldn't stretch to that.

But Shylock was easy. Antony is another question. I declined the part two years ago when Peggy invited me to play it with her at the Vic. 'Do you really want to play Cleopatra?' I had asked her.

'We-ll ...' She thought, and after a moment said, 'It would be a *challenge*.'

'In that case, Peg,' I replied, 'I don't think so.'

And the idea had been dropped.

Of all the plays of Shakespeare's maturity, *Antony and Cleopatra* is the least often performed. There had been only two major productions since the War: Godfrey Tearle's with Edith Evans, and the Oliviers' at the St James's. Neither was notably successful. Indeed, looking back, since the days of Benson no actor's reputation had been enhanced by playing Antony. Now, reading through the play, I think I can see why. There is no plain sailing in Antony, no point of rest where the words will carry you along, no safe haven until the very end, at Antony's death. It is a part that calls on all the strength one possesses and tests out every weakness.

No creative artist is complete without a fatal flaw. In life, as in art, he is paradoxically only at full strength when his spirit grapples with this flaw. He may not be aware of it – indeed, he must not be too aware of it. But the battle has begun.

I make a stupid mistake. I allow myself to become convinced that Antony is difficult to learn. I ask Godfrey Tearle over lunch at the Garrick Club whether he, too, found the text of Antony peculiarly difficult to commit to memory. He tells me that he learned all the great Shakespearian roles by watching his father play them – all except Antony. 'It's the very devil,' he says.

I compound this mistake by asking Olivier the same question. 'Difficult? You must be joking,' he says, with a wry smile.

I have never had any difficulty in learning a part until this moment. Now, every evening I sit with Glen Byam Shaw, the director, who hears me the lines, and by the end of the evening I know them; but the next day the difficulty returns. At the dress rehearsal I hesitate, fluff, and dry with mounting panic.

On the first night I wait for my entrance with my usual feeling of deadly calm, hearing rather than listening to the opening lines: 'Nay, but this dotage of our general's o'erflows the measure . . . ' A typical opening, this, for one of Shakespeare's great tragedies. A note of doubt or questioning, conversational in tone, almost conspiratorial, as if deliberately to counterpoint the splendour of the chief characters' first appearance. At each dress rehearsal our two actors playing Philo and Demetrius have been warned against 'ponging' their lines.

'You're signalling to the audience that it's the start of the play. You're trying to give it a lift. Don't!' says Glen. 'Say it quietly, as if you don't want to be overheard.'

And tonight they get it right. I give a final twitch to my costume and run on with Peggy. I had suggested this entrance to Glen. Cleopatra has a sort of giant daisy-chain, a long rope of water-lilies, and snares Antony with them on the line 'If it be love indeed, tell me how much.'

The entrance goes well. From the word go, from my first line, I sail through the performance without a single fluff or dry. Only to be trapped at the winning-post by an alliteration. As Antony breathes his last, buoyed up with confidence and a wondrous sense of relief, I decide to give him a really good send-off, and on the line 'A Roman, by a Roman valiantly vanquished,' I gave him literally an extra dying breath by pausing naturalistically, as if searching for the adjective. The prompter, who has sat all evening in his corner feeling thwarted after what happened at the dress rehearsal, seizes this briefest of pauses to ply his trade, and his voice rings out loud and strong.

'Never, *ever*, prompt me again,' I curse at him, poor fellow, after the curtain-call, with mingled exasperation and relief, 'even if you have to wait an eternity.'

Acting together, Peggy and I succeeded. Writing of her performance, Kenneth Tynan, who at this stage of his career had adopted the role of the theatre's chief iconoclast, used the opprobrious term 'Kensington', meaning, of course, that her accent was too 'refined'. And, true, if you wanted to listen for it, her vowel sounds would have given her away. But her acting was on a level which takes no account of vowel sounds. With no other actress since Edith Evans had I found such support and mutual help as I found with Peggy. Acting with her my chief emotion was the same as when acting with Edith: a feeling of great safety, and great freedom.

After *Antony and Cleopatra* had finished its season at Stratford and a six-week season in London, we did a short Continental tour. At The Hague the audiences were ecstatic. But on our first night in Paris, as Peggy and I came running on for our entrance, I was alarmed by the sound of a distinct chuckle. Was it our clothes? 'Peggy must have some new costumes,' I had warned Glen, for though I had never played in Paris until that night, I knew how in the French theatre the actress would put in the programme: *Mlle Telle-et-telle, habillée sur la scène et en ville par Tel-et-tel*, and I feared lest French audiences should find us dowdy. The laughter subsided and we continued, slightly shaken.

(An untoward laugh can temporarily wreck an otherwise fine performance. I remember an unfortunate Macbeth who listened to Lennox's gory catalogue of disasters in Act Two, Scene Three, thinking, My God, this fellow's slow, and snapping impatiently at the poor actor, ''Twas a rough night.' He must have overlooked the obvious double meaning which the adjective *rough* might have for an American audience. There was no mistaking their reaction. It was in New York, and I was the unfortunate Macbeth.)

After the performance, at supper given in our honour by some of the actors from the Comédie Française, I found myself seated at table next to a celebrated poetess. I asked why the audience had laughed at that particular point. 'Ah that!' She smiled. 'It's very simple. In France, in tragedy, *on ne court jamais*. You *never* run!'

XIX

I HAD long wanted to play Hector, Jouvet's part, in Giraudoux's play *La Guerre de Troie n'aura pas lieu* (*Tiger at the Gates*, in Christopher Fry's translation). It was one of the plays Michel Saint-Denis had had in mind for our season at the Phoenix before the War, where I had played another of Jouvet's roles, Sir Andrew Aguecheek in *Twelfth Night*. Giraudoux himself came to London, reportedly to satisfy himself that I was mature enough to play Hector, but then came the Munich agreement, which seemed to put a temporary question mark over Giraudoux's parable on the inevitability of war. And soon after that our finances ran out, and all our plans for the company were shelved.

Since then there had been one or two vague offers from across the Atlantic, but they had not materialized. And now my eye caught a paragraph in one of our trade papers: the American impresario Roger Stevens, it said, was planning a production of Giraudoux's play in London and New York; Harold Clurman would be directing the play; Clurman was coming to England, hoping to persuade me to play Hector. Clurman ... the Group Theatre ... *The Fervent Years*! Admiration made me shy at the thought of meeting him. There was no need. Whatever I had expected, Clurman's warmth, humour, and knowledge of the theatre dispelled my shyness at once. Within an hour we were friends and colleagues. No one since Michel had made me so sure that this was where I wanted to be, this was what I wanted to do. There are directors in the theatre who say a lot and achieve little. And those, more rare, like Clurman, who seem by their presence to extract the very best their cast is capable of. What I got from Clurman is all-important: the feeling that he was getting something from me, and that it pleased him.

He agreed with me that the American translation, which had been going the rounds for years, was quite inadequate, and suggested that Christopher Fry do a new translation, to which I agreed at once. We also agreed, with scarcely a demur, on the casting. (At rehearsals I began to have some doubts about Diane Cilento's playing Helen of Troy. I wondered how an audience would react to her flat Australian vowels and her direct, high-voltage sex appeal – an English audience, that is, conditioned in their response to Helen by Christopher Marlowe's 'Was this the face that launched a thousand ships . . .' to expect abstract beauty rather than sex appeal. Harold said, 'I know what you mean, but wait until the first night in New York.' He was proved entirely right. From the moment she began to speak, the American audience was with her.)

Unknown to me, Vanessa and Corin had asked Clurman if they could watch rehearsals. He gave his permission, so long as they remained out of sight. And this they did, sitting each day discreetly at the back of the stalls in the darkened auditorium of the Apollo. It was the school holidays. I had expected they would soon find something else to do, but to my surprise they came each day of the four-week rehearsal period. Vanessa was eighteen now, and without question too tall for the ballet. At my insistence that she should learn another language, she had spent six months in Italy. She had come back, closeted herself in her room for another three months, and passed her A-level exam in Italian. Now she was in her first year at drama school. The most I could say at this stage was that I knew she would be an actress. I had seen one of her last school plays, something written by her, in which, because she was the tallest, she played a man's part. I was impressed by an immensely long pause she made, and held, and afterwards asked her was it art, or was it a dry?

'Art, of course.'

'I'm not sure that I believe you.'

She made an impromptu show of being hurt at my disbelief, and then laughed and confessed it was a dry. That impressed me even more.

In London, *Tiger at the Gates* was successful. That is to say, the applause was generous, in that English way which Irving, knowing that audiences need encouragement, would fill out by having his drummer in the pit sustain it and swell it with a sostenuto roll on the bass kettledrum. The notices were excellent – though of that English kind which makes an actor say, 'Yes, but is that all?' and which made Garrick and Irving buy their own periodicals in which to praise their own performances and answer their detractors. On the whole

the English actor will not complain, for audiences in London repay
him for any lack of warmth in their ovation by their loyalty and by
their long memories.

In New York we were a 'hit'. I recall Leonard Bernstein's flinging
his arms around me: 'Oh, Michael, you're a doll!' I recall Ruth
Gordon's note to me on the first night. I rarely read wires or notes
before the first performance. This one I read; it said, 'Remember,
they are longing to like it!'

The same good wishes would have been more to the point before
the first night of my next production, Terence Rattigan's *The
Sleeping Prince*. By ill fortune we opened on Broadway in the autumn
of 1956, when the twin crises of Eden's Suez adventure and the
Hungarian revolution were in full flood. In the play's First Act the
young King, who suspects his father, the Prince Regent, of plotting
behind his back, bursts out, 'I will not have my country made the
pawn of British imperialism and French greed.' At this, an audible
frisson ran through the audience. The performance had not started
well and proceeded from bad to worse. When the Prince Regent
airily remarks that the music which is coming from beyond the door
is 'probably some Hungarian violinist', our doom was sealed. I had
suggested to Rattigan that these lines might, perhaps, given the
circumstances, be cut. But Terry, convinced that art outlives contemporary events, was insistent that they be spoken. Not for the first
time, contemporary events proved themselves the stronger.

And yet my contribution was perhaps principally to be blamed for
our lack of success. *The Sleeping Prince*, subtitled *A Ruritanian
Comedy*, is an impudently light-weight play whose characters, like
insects on the water's surface, are borne aloft by nothing more than
surface tension and the skill of the principal performers. How easy it
is for an actor, tempted by the kind of success which only Broadway
can offer, to choose such a vehicle for his next appearance. Especially
when six uniforms, specially designed for him by Bermans in
London, each one more gorgeous than the last, add their lustre to the
possibilities of self-deception. We had opened in New Haven before
a largely student audience from Yale which had roared with
laughter. Yet even before the first performance in New York I was
reminded that between the poles of success and failure in that city
there is scarcely any middle ground. The management did something which I have never encountered before or since. Two days
before the opening night I was met at the theatre by a representative
from the management who suggested with no visible embarrass-

ment that another actor might be brought in to rehearse my part with me in the hope that it would help me get more laughs. Whom, I asked, politely, did they have in mind?

'Well,' they said, 'it would have to be a British actor. How about Cyril Ritchard?'

'But surely Cyril will not want to take on such a job at two days' notice. Besides, would he be free?'

'He's here, and free,' came the reply.

'And waiting in the lobby?'

'Exactly. He's in the lobby. Shall we ask him up?'

'It would be discourteous not to,' I said.

Cyril Ritchard, an old friend of mine, came into the room, embarrassment writ large across his usually cheerful face. I could not help thinking how good he would have been in the part. He stayed and chatted for a few awkward moments, in what was clearly an untenable situation, and made his departure, offering his apologies if he had wasted anybody's time.

The first night was a disaster. Yet at this distance of time I am inclined to shoulder at least half the blame. When one is half the management, the director, *and* the leading actor, one can but say, *La débâcle, c'est moi.*

The Sleeping Prince was due to end its run after ten weeks, and I was expecting to be home for Christmas, when I was offered a television 'spectacular': *Ruggles of Red Gap.*

I had never learned very much about television; I had had little opportunity to do so. My first acquaintance with TV cameras, in 1936, with Jean Forbes-Robertson in *Scenes from Romeo and Juliet* at Alexandra Palace, was something that, in later years, I found useful as a conversation-stopper whenever the 'old boys' at Television Centre began to reminisce, but of little practical value apart from that. Few people could have witnessed this spirited pioneering attempt to put Shakespeare on the box. To see it, Rachel had had to visit Selfridges in Oxford Street, where they had a demonstration TV set.

On another occasion, but with the same cultural urge, I attempted Chekhov's famous one-acter *The Bear* on television. It was 1948, and I was playing Macbeth on Broadway. Of *The Bear*, which is virtually a monologue, I recollect only that it suffered for lack of rehearsal. According to my great friend Norris Houghton it was a lesson, brilliant of its kind, in improvisation.

Ruggles was to be a musical, with a delightful score, specially commissioned from Jule Styne, and a starry cast. It sounded like a busman's holiday, and I agreed to do it. And then my agent phoned with the bad news. A film company was competing for my services, and it rather looked as though the television company would win. The film was Graham Greene's *The Quiet American*. They wanted me to play Fowler – 'Just about the best part this year,' my agent said. I have never taken kindly to any attempt to thwart me from something I wanted to do, and I very much wanted to play Fowler. No contracts had been signed, I pleaded. The answer came back that the verbal agreement I had given was, of course, sufficiently binding. Couldn't the film company wait a few days? I asked. Very difficult, came the answer. Locations were to be in Saigon, and Joseph Mankiewicz, the director, wanted to use scenes of the Indo-Chinese New Year, so the schedule was tight. By now I heartily wished I had never heard of *Ruggles*. Even if, by some unlikely good fortune, the film company could accommodate the dates, the last thing I could wish for, before a film as heavy as this, would be to be up to my ears in a TV spectacular – a 'live' spectacular, as all TV productions were then. In desperation, I hired a lawyer – 'the very best', I was told, for this kind of job, a real shark. Within twenty-four hours he rang me back. 'I've fixed it. You can do them both.'

4 February 1957

The morning run-through wasn't too bad. Then I sat at the local restaurant for fifty minutes and was given an almost uneatable steak. Lack of food and too much vodka made me sleepy and cross. The dress rehearsal seemed endless and dismal. After the morning run congratulations poured in effusively; after the afternoon – none. I haven't yet been through a performance without 'drying', and indeed cutting chunks of the almost unspeakable script.

Take a shower and shave and chew a few mouthfuls of dry chopped steak. Very nervous. I have the feeling that with my illnesses and absences and lack of precision I have turned all the cast against me, including sweet little Jane Powell, whose acting is, it is true, of the 'do-it-by-numbers' style.

But the performance goes – it goes. Imogene Coca does her damnedest and is pretty good. David Wayne also nervous but as always keeps a definite pattern and is reliable. Peter Lawford very nervous. The only people really relaxed and good are the dancers and singers. There was a party afterwards at which everyone *seemed* elated.

So by car to Idlewild, and at last off to Saigon. Our plane is a little late leaving and there is a nervous moment when we are told 'the field is closed.'

6 February

Not a very comfortable berth. Too short, and sleeping diagonally was uncomfortable. I sat up late with David Wayne, who told me of his experiences in the 8th Army, and his love of the British. We became close, though a bit alcoholic.

He gets out at Los Angeles, sunny and warm. I give two of my hand luggage pieces for someone to send along, not realizing that the plane is an hour late, and that I have only one hour to catch the plane on to 'Frisco. Get fussed and wonder why airports always assume you know what that Big Sister voice means.

On to 'Frisco sitting next to a vivacious pregnant woman who shows me photographs and talks (with enthusiasm!) about *Ruggles*.

At 'Frisco I have twenty-five minutes, and no baggage problems. The air is crisp and the sun warm. We fly on to Seattle, which is overcast and drizzly. Here I am given an executive suite which has everything but a bed.

After a good dinner back to the airport. A long wait before the plane leaves, an hour and a half late.

7 February

It appears we take a northerly route to Anchorage, Alaska, and Shemya before heading for Tokyo. I take two Doridon, and then another in the night in hot milk, and sleep – I have no idea for how long, as my watch says twelve and is still going, which looks as if I had at least ten hours. Is that possible?

The sun is up and we are still flying about the north. We touched down at Anchorage but not at Shemya, they say, not yet.

There were several wires on the first night – what am I talking about? – the first *and last* night of *Ruggles*, though Alexander Cohen [the New York impresario] *has* in fact inquired as to my interest in a Broadway version for the fall – including one with the strangest signature 'From Saigon'. Joe Mankiewicz? DEAREST MICHAEL AT A MOMENT LIKE THIS THERE IS SO LITTLE WE CAN SAY STOP CHIN UP BE BRAVE REMEMBER REMEMBER THAT THIS TOO SHALL PASS AWAY STOP COME TO US QUICKLY STOP NOT NECESSARY KNOW OUR LINES BUT FOR HEAVENS SAKE FORGET PRESENT ONES ALL LOVE THE QUIET AND DISQUIETED.

It looks sunny down below. 'Will passengers please fasten their seatbelts at this time in preparation for landing at Shemya, Alaska.'

Suddenly we are in dense cloud, and I think of *The Night My Number Came Up*. No wonder all these people who make a living out of flying seem so calm.

Why at this moment should I think of Paul Dehn? I must write to him this afternoon. I suppose it's because I have written this as I haven't for ages written anything, and remember my postcard to him from Eze about why Mme de Sévigné or whatever her married name was had no time to write to her mother. . . .

Alex Cohen told me in a recent letter that Mankiewicz had told him 'in strict secrecy' about plans for filming *Twelfth Night* in Rome in November. I wonder how I shall greet this when it is properly broached to me. (Maybe it won't be, though, for I am by no means sure I'll be able to do Fowler to J.M.'s satisfaction or to mine.) Come to think of it, it's not the first time this project has been mooted. I put the idea to John Huston once. He was very excited. We talked of casting. Orson, Danny Kaye, self ... Next morning I met him: 'How did you sleep?' 'Great! Dreaming about *Twelfth Night*.' 'Yes?' 'Yes. Orson was Sir Toby, Kaye was Sir Andrew and you ... ' 'Yes?' 'Funny ... you weren't in it.' ...

Now we have Japanese stewardesses, and one has just given a lifebelt demonstration which seemed calculated to make one forget the practical side of the matter. We have been in the air for about twenty minutes. Tokyo by night from the air resembles the slums of Los Angeles. The whole personality of the aircraft, if such a thing has such a thing, seems changed.

I realize after several sips of gin and tonic that what is depressing me, apart from tiredness, is that the whole personality of the aircraft has *not* changed. It's only that before I had a large berth, and a Mr Eugen Johannsen, of Kristiansand, Norway, and I had this whole rear cabin to ourselves and now I am surrounded – surrounded? There are only six others, mainly Japanese, with me. But I'm feeling foolish and resentful because the company didn't book a berth for me for this part of the journey, and I didn't feel like parting with fifty-five dollars in travellers' cheques even if I could reclaim them. . . .

At Manila Airport, after all my dread about baggage, money, health certificates, and Customs, I sailed through, thanks to a Filipino official who looked about 15½ and said, 'I've seen *all* your films.'

Audie Murphy, the most highly decorated soldier in the States, was to be my co-star in *The Quiet American*. I was eager to meet him. But the first news that greeted me as I stepped off the plane at Saigon was that Murphy had contracted some germ or other in Hong Kong, and was confined to hospital there. The numerous shots of penicillin he had received during the War made it unwise and, indeed, useless for him to receive any more.

So, leaving Audie to fend for himself, and with no thought of jet lag on my part (it had not yet been invented), we started shooting.

Vietnam, following the Geneva peace conference three years before, was a divided country. Saigon, with its pleasant tree-lined boulevards from the days of French colonial rule, was now like a shabby French provincial town. There seemed little trace of the war that had been fought or the war that was to come. Americans we met were mostly attached to the diplomatic service. They talked eagerly about the film, in the manner of those who seek distraction from the boredom of service in a routine provincial posting.

Only once did we see a sign of conflict. It was whilst we were shooting the scenes of the Indo-Chinese New Year. Placards borne aloft in a religious demonstration were suddenly turned around, revealing on their reverse side anti-Government slogans. When this was pointed out and interpreted for us, someone suggested we should have to cut those shots, or else reshoot them. 'Leave them in,' said Joe. An erudite, frequently witty man, he also cultivated a 'tough guy' image. 'What the hell? No one'll know what they mean.'

21 March

[We were in Rome now, at Cinecittà, for the interiors.] A miserable day for it seems to me I'll never adjust to the problem of acting with someone like Murphy, a 'natural' with a mass of experience but no technique. Joe seems unaware of the problem; perhaps for him it *isn't* a problem. I feel like telling him it's one thing to get a performance out of an amateur, another thing to give a performance with one.

I have a streaming cold. At the end of the day Joe annoys me with, 'Take care of that cold,' to which I reply, 'What do you *think* I'm going to do with it?'

27 March

Vexed from the word go. Joe meets me on the stairs and says in his peculiar 'tough' way, 'Well, how y'a feeling?' and I am so exhausted and stopped-up with cold that I feel a sort of baleful dislike of him and the whole set-up.

28 March

Everything seems much better today. My cold less heavy – irritation less. Only once in the morning do I feel ragingly impatient with Joe. After doing the 'Continental' scene with Audie for three hours, right on form, I think, we eventually get to my close-up. Audie's off-camera lines are not very stirringly delivered, to put it mildly; the need not to 'overlap' the lines in a close shot also slows the scene up, and Joe impatiently says, 'No, cut! Start again – it's getting spongey.' Spongey! For a moment I feel like telling him what I think of this, but decide to 'use' my irritation in the playing of the scene.

20 May

A letter from my agent, Cecil Tennant. I look at the date. It was dictated and sent on April 25th. That was mysterious enough. But the conclusion of the letter is hideously depressing, crowning my misery at Joan's [my secretary, Joan Hirst] information that the reason we have only £2,000 in the bank is that £8,000 of the *Quiet American* cheque went to the bloody tax people. But Cecil's letter is worse, for he advises, after this, two films, or at least one Hollywood film, and certainly not more than two plays at Stratford, and why not Stratford in '59 rather than '58?

This makes all my plans for Stratford next year, following a play in London, mere wishful thinking. And here I have been encouraging Glen [Glen Byam Shaw, Stratford's director] that there may be hope of three plays at Stratford, and writing to Peter Hall – though I could still not post the letter – that I might like to do John Whiting's *The Gates of Summer*, which he sent me, together with [Jean Anouilh's] *Ornifle*.

Oh, Lord, it is so disappointing to feel I'm back on the treadmill, or certainly will be if I don't follow Cecil's advice. Yet if I do follow it, it means not doing what I want to do.

All the same, it's all very well of Glennie to quote Irving saying to his financiers, 'Gentlemen, I was not sent on earth to make money.' I know that, even if I have not always the same belief in myself to phrase it so. The point is, Irving paid 6d – or was it a shilling in the pound? – income tax.

5 June

A happy day, because a cable came from Rachel this morning saying that Vanessa shares the Sybil Thorndike prize for best performance by a girl at Central School. I've been childishly happy ever since.

I'm still waiting to hear from Glen, though I've made my mind up, I think. I shall have to do Stratford. I can't let him down. And after all, it's what I wanted to do. The advantages Glen offers, £60 a week for me plus £40 for Rachel, plus the main house at Avoncliffe, plus *quelques choses* – well, all very well. But somehow, because of V's prize, I feel all the more inclined to do what, after all, I want to do.

Joe thinks, and Cecil thinks, that I shall be what is known as 'hot' after this movie, may get an Oscar, etc., and I know I'll probably never have such a chance again. But one's career teaches one that blind gropes in the dark are the ones which pay best in the end.

XX

I T WAS the autumn of 1957. I had not acted in London since *Tiger at the Gates*, two years before. I was looking for a play, and I was faced with a number of choices. And then a script arrived from Binkie Beaumont, a new play by N.C. Hunter. This puzzling work read as if Norman Hunter, tired of being called 'the English Chekhov', had decided to be the English Ibsen. It was concerned with money, and the effect which a sudden glimpse of wealth, in the shape of rich relations, has on a not-so-well-to-do schoolmaster's family. But so unremittingly was this theme driven home that it quickly became very boring, and the principal character, the schoolmaster, insufferably priggish.

I made these points in a letter to Binkie, who relayed its contents to Hunter. To my surprise Hunter sat down and rewrote the play in the shape of my suggestions. In its new form, *A Touch of the Sun* appealed to me. All the parts were good acting parts, which is never to be sniffed at – and there was a nice part for the schoolmaster's daughter. It crossed my mind that Norman might have written it for Vanessa. A short tour was planned, and then into the Saville, which someone said was an 'unlucky' theatre, but I said, rather arrogantly perhaps, 'No theatre is unlucky when it's filled to the brim.'

At Blackpool we went our separate ways – I to my hotel, Vanessa to her digs. From the start of rehearsals, though she was still living at home, we would as a rule travel separately to and from the theatre. Occasionally, and usually only when she asked for it, I would give her a note. She listened gravely and attentively. Vanessa is great on gravity. In Robert Beulah's portrait of her as a little girl, she looks severe, almost cross. Gravity can be mistaken for severity.

The first performance went well, astonishingly well. 'Vanessa a distinct hit with the audience (and with Binkie),' I noted in my diary.

At a supper party after the show, Ronnie Squire, who played the father, immaculately, told me he was bequeathing me Irving's powder box.

After the first night at the Saville, Binkie reminded me of Larry's curtain speech at the Vic on the night Vanessa was born: 'A great actress has been born.' 'Great?' I asked, thrilled but not fishing for compliments. 'Yes, great. A remarkable actress.'

We had known since she was a baby that she had an actress's gift. It flowered early, and beyond expectation. But great? About such matters one must be careful not to exaggerate. And not to underestimate. In Robert Bolt's *The Tiger and the Horse*, in which we played together in 1960, I recall being almost thrown by the force of her concentration. Hers was a part that required concentration, certainly, and it was there, bang, unmistakably there. That is one half of the gift of acting. The other half, no less important, though more rare, she had also: the ability to switch oneself off, to absent oneself from a scene that belongs to someone else. So many actors, finding that they have been given little to do in a certain scene, start inventing bits of business, nods and becks and wreathed smiles, when they should simply absent themselves awhile.

It is hard for the child of whom great things are expected, but harder by far for the one who is adorable and sweet, and of whom no one expects anything very much. Lynn, growing up in the shadows of her elder sister and brother, spent much of her time with Rosalinda, the pony which her godmother, Edith Hargraves, had given her. There was even talk of her joining Pat Smythe's stable and taking up horse-riding. One afternoon at Stratford, when she was sixteen, Lynn arranged a small hurdle for her pony to jump. She had won dozens of rosettes for jumping and gymkhanas, but now – probably because she was fraught with doubts and confusion – she fell and lay there winded. I was about twenty yards off and it took me some time to realize that she wasn't moving. Perhaps that fall tipped the balance between horse-riding and the theatre.

She had said nothing about the theatre. But, next year, staying with Vanessa at Stratford, she surprised us all by suddenly announcing that she was going to act. She bundled off to Central School, where Vanessa had been. I went with some apprehension to the Embassy Theatre to see her first public performance there. The image of this divided, decidedly plump young girl troubled me. Memory insists that it was a scene from a Shaw play, though I recall no telephone in Shaw and in this there was certainly a telephone. Lynn came on and, for a split second, looked exactly like Rachel. I had never been able to see the likeness till that occasion. I was astounded. This was a mature young woman, and the last thing I had expected of Lynn was that she was capable of suggesting maturity.

Such early images are haunting. Time has overlaid them with later images: the pride and thrill of seeing her on Broadway in *My Fat Friend*, when the audience applauded as she removed her coat in the final act and revealed a graceful woman. But, for a while, it was as though I could not quite synchronize with Lynn and her achievements. I went to see her at Southsea in *Billy Liar* when she was nineteen, and had to leave after the first act to get back to Chichester. There were about fifteen people in the house, and a very brash young actor was playing the lead. 'Very good,' I told her, 'but of course impossible to play with a young man like that,' only to find that the young man in question was standing beside me.

Something unfortunate happened also on the occasion I went to see her in her first West End play, *The Tulip Tree*, which, as it happened, was also by N. C. Hunter. She played a young girl who longs to be a dancer, and had a touching scene to herself where she brought on a gramophone and danced to it, and was then surprised in the act by another character. She played it very truthfully, moving the audience by the concentration with which she danced as well as she could, where another actress might have played for sympathy or laughs by exaggerating the young girl's awkwardness. But at the appointed moment the other actor failed to appear. Lynn danced on, improvising her steps as best she could. 'Very good,' I comforted her, 'the way you carried on dancing.' And so it was, though for her the scene was ruined.

Like myself, Corin, when he arrived at school, coming from a theatrical family, was expected to take the leading women's parts. When he played Portia, topped off with a bird's nest of a wig, there were moments when a promising actor shone through the insecurities inevitable in a school production. A little later I heard him at home, in a next-door room, practising some speech to a tape recorder. Fragments of Mark Antony reached me and caught my attention. That's good, I thought, very good, and wondered whether to go in and tell him, then thought better of it.

As Palaestrio in Plautus' *Miles Gloriosus* in his school's annual Latin play, he was impressive. True, a foreign language, especially Latin, might be said to smooth an actor's path, for the audience is bound to think, How clever, but there was no mistaking two attributes which proclaim an actor in the making: personality and authority.

At Cambridge, which was noted for the number of amateur actors straining to go on the boards, he did his share of acting and production. At the end of his third year George Devine offered him a job as an assistant artistic director at the Royal Court and for a moment it seemed that one of the children would do something other than act. But within a month or so he, too, was acting, with Lynn in *A Midsummer Night's Dream*.

Parents and children were now all on the stage. We had arrived at the intersection of our private and our public lives. There was pleasure and satisfaction in that, each supporting the other. As Vanessa once said, 'Ours is a family that rejoices in each other.' Some loss, too. No longer the Redgrave family, but the family Redgrave, a being in the public eye which interrupts the normal flow, the ups and downs of personal relationships.

It was in 1958, during my last season at Stratford, that Mother died. They called me in the morning and I held her hand whilst she was semi-conscious. It was a matinée day, but I went back between the shows – and she had died.

I thought of the last time we had been at Stratford together, the last and happiest time, clouded over since by the squabbles and scenes, hurtful and sometimes alarming, of her final illness. It had been during the history cycle in 1951. Mother was playing in *Man and Superman* under John Clements's management, and he was about to begin rehearsals of a new play. Most surprisingly he offered Mother a part in it, which would mean her coming off after Act One of the Shaw, taking a taxi to another theatre, and appearing there in Act Three of *And This Was Odd*. 'The most chic thing you can do,' I told her, 'is to appear in London in two plays at once.'

Mother had immense respect for Clements, and he had infinite tact and patience with her. Just as well, for she was inclined to interrupt him, as he was describing the new play to her, with, 'Now I'll tell you a play you ought to do, *much* more suitable than this.' She agreed, somewhat reluctantly, to John's proposal. She was dissatisfied with small parts, but found it increasingly difficult to learn new ones, and was beginning to lose her way on-stage.

Clements suggested she should take a week off from the Shaw, and I proposed that she should spend it with me at Stratford. I could hear her in the early mornings, reciting her new lines, and I would make her a cup of tea. Our talk was nearly all of the theatre. She had an astonishing memory for names, especially actors' names, and that week at Avoncliffe those names came flooding into our memories. Dorothy Green, an excellent Cleopatra; Edmund Willard, a fine Macbeth; Baliol Holloway, 'There was an actor'; Vivienne Bennett, who could play boys' parts . . . and further back in time to the old Savoy Theatre with H.B.Irving. That week at Stratford, thanks to Clements, made it possible to forget the unhappiness of the last years of her illness.

'What on earth are those kids of yours up to now?'

My questioner, an elderly member of the Garrick Club, clearly doesn't expect an answer. He presses on, outraged. Have I heard, did I know, that they're invading people's dressing-rooms, haranguing them by the hour?

I have grown accustomed to such stories. I shrug and raise my eyebrows. I rather like being buttonholed about my children. I do not understand their politics, but I like the revolutionary flavour.

Only once, I recall, did I try to influence their outlook. Their nanny was a staunch reader of the Tory *Daily Mail*. Under her influence, and the *Daily Mail*'s, they seemed to be growing up as little Conservatives, and I felt I should try to redress the balance. 'If you're going to read *that*,' I said, bursting into their nursery, 'you ought to read *this* as well,' and I handed them a copy of the liberal *News Chronicle*. They looked understandably baffled.

Since the days of Oliver Baldwin, I had considered myself a socialist – and still do. As a young schoolmaster at Cranleigh I had had modest success in encouraging the boys to talk about politics, rubbing it into them that the views of their parents need not necessarily be their own. As a young actor I made no attempt to disguise my left-wing opinions, when asked. It was during the Depression, and for an actor to be a socialist was not unpopular. When I signed the People's Convention, I was asked to stand for Parliament. 'You could be the most popular actor in England,' someone said. I toyed with the idea for all of twenty minutes before rejecting it, knowing perfectly well that I could never carry it through. But my political development stopped with the People's Convention. The fear that I had been used by people and a party I did not wholly trust, for a cause I did not fully understand, made me cautious, and in time my caution turned to conservatism, though with a small 'c'.

I had the same fear for Vanessa and Corin at first. On two or three occasions I went to Hyde Park to hear Vanessa speak for her party, standing at a distance so as not to be seen by her. I remember thinking that, as yet, she was more persuasive as an actress than as a public speaker. But to those who seemed to think that her politics would diminish her acting, I would reply that, on the contrary, each strengthened the other and both were strengthened by her sense of purpose. As she grew up, her life became a study in purpose. How many parents could say of their children, I thought, that they had purpose?

Not long before the final season at Stratford, the tax collector and my own financial imprudence caught up with me. I was forced to do six films in succession to pay my arrears, and then to sell our house in Chiswick.

The human condition postulates some anchorage or other, and in this we were blessed beyond an actor's dreams. Rachel was given Wilks Water, an eighteenth-century farm labourer's cottage set among the fields and woods of what was once a Hampshire estate. For this gift three generations of Redgraves and Kempsons have now rejoiced for more than twenty-five years. Rachel poured her talent for making a family, and all that a family demands, into a haven which would be the envy of any theatrical country-lover.

Much as I love New York, California, and the lengthy tours which have taken up such a large part of my later life, I cannot now imagine an existence which did not contain something like Wilks Water, nor Wilks Water without Rachel running out of the front door to meet me.

As an actress matures, it often happens that she finds roles which deepen her gifts. Rachel left the Royal Academy of Dramatic Art in 1933 with an exciting vista of beautiful young parts ahead of her. In her first professional engagement at Stratford that year, she played everything from Juliet to a witch in Komisarjevsky's production of *Macbeth*.

The births of our children were joyous events, but they cannot be said to have enlarged her theatrical horizon. She made a modest, but definite, success as Charles Boyer's wife in the Hollywood film *A Woman's Vengeance* from Aldous Huxley's *The Gioconda Smile*, in Christopher Fry's *Venus Observed* with Olivier at the St James's in 1949, and in a variety of parts in George Devine's first season at the Royal Court. But the real showing of her talent has come later, as

Somerset Maugham's *Jane* on television, and only a year or two ago as the irascible elderly social worker *Kate, the Good Neighbour*.

When she is in a play in the West End, I selfishly hope it will not run too long, for that means she will stay at the cottage only from Saturday night till Monday afternoon. But often – too often – it does.

XXI

WHEN THE phone call came from Larry Olivier suggesting
Uncle Vanya for the opening season at the Chichester Theatre
Festival in 1961, I said yes at once.

Rehearsals began in a drill hall behind Sloane Square. 'I know you
think there's no such thing as a definitive performance, but *this* . . . '
Larry murmured in my ear at the first reading as he closed the book
on the last page. It was rumoured that he had insured the Festival
against loss, and looking about one at the cast he had assembled for
Vanya, I thought, What an insurance! Joan Plowright, Sybil Thorndike and Lewis Casson, Joan Greenwood, André Morell, Peter
Woodthorpe; and Larry himself as Astrov.

The first two plays, *The Broken Heart* by Ford, and *The Chances* by
Beaumont and Fletcher, gave little promise of what was to come.
But there was no mistaking the triumph of *Vanya*. Even those who
vowed that Chekhov could never work on Chichester's open stage
were dumbfounded.

Larry and I had not worked together since *Hamlet* in 1937. During
the War, while I was acting in *A Month in the Country* at the
St James's, Alan Dent, the critic and theatre historian, had brought me
a message from Olivier asking if I would like to play the Dauphin in
his film of *Henry V*. At that time I was firmly of the opinion that any
film of Shakespeare was doomed to failure, and I helpfully gave Dent
the reasons for my prejudice, the gist of which was that, in the
unequal fight between the image and the word, the image must
always triumph at the expense of the word, and – 'Stop! Stop!' cried
Dent. 'If I'm not careful you'll persuade me to think likewise.'

After the War, Rachel and I stayed several weekends with the
Oliviers at Notley Abbey. Larry's energy was impressive. Quite
early on a Sunday morning he would be pruning what he called a

'where'er you walk' of pleached hornbeams or beech. A big party would assemble in the afternoon, some twenty or more guests. It was the heyday of the game called 'the Game'.

One evening at Chichester, as we were going out to supper, Olivier said, 'I think we'll have to keep *Vanya* going next year.' It may have been that evening also that he told me, in the way he had of dropping such hints, that Chichester was to be the launching pad for the National Theatre, and that he and I would lead the company in the National's first season. I was overjoyed. I showed Larry a photograph of the model of what was to be, at some distant future date, the Yvonne Arnaud Theatre at Guildford; I had been asked to direct their opening festival. Laughingly I said, 'You've got your theatre, and I've got mine.'

'Would ya keer ta swap?' said Larry.

Those two seasons at Chichester rank amongst my happiest times in the theatre. I was proud of my work, proud of Larry's company. In the 1940s and 1950s I had been sometimes boosted in the press as Olivier's rival, and, it is said, by Sally Beauman in a recent history of the Royal Shakespeare Company, though on what authority I don't know, that Larry was conscious of this. At Chichester we worked together in complete harmony. I thought his Astrov faultless. I wished fervently that Mother could have lived to see our *Uncle Vanya*. No actor alive could meet her expectations, but of them all, Olivier came nearest to everything which she thought an actor should be, and which I should try harder to outstrip, though that was never my intention.

'The National Theatre at the Old Vic' was now the proud blazon across the façade of the dear old building in Waterloo Road. Denys Lasdun's building on the South Bank was, as yet, only a forest of girders, cement, and holes in the ground in the autumn of 1963, and for some time to come the Old Vic was to be our home. It was given a face-lift in honour of the occasion. Some noisy alterations were in progress, and a revolving stage was being installed, making our opening rehearsals very difficult.

At Chichester Olivier had opened the proceedings with two almost unknown Jacobean plays, as if to give his company a chance to stretch their limbs in unfamiliar surroundings. But for the National's first production we were to start at full throttle. *Hamlet* was to be the first production, with Peter O'Toole, directed by Larry himself. I was to play the King.

'We'll e'en fly at it like French falconers.' Good advice, if only one could take it. But somehow I couldn't. For my first entrance, with

Diana Wynyard as the Queen, I had to descend an immense flight of stairs, from the flies to the stage. Heights have always unnerved me, and I dearly wished for another, simpler entrance. But Diana didn't seem too nervous, so I thought I'd better persevere. By the time I reached the bottom step, all attack had deserted me.

Larry had indicated that the King and Queen should come to rest on two blocks – presumably thrones – at the foot of the staircase. Somehow my feet always seemed to carry me to the throne nearer stage centre. Time and again we made our entrance, and time and again I heard Larry's voice saying, 'The other throne, Michael. The *other* throne.' Poor Diana! After a while, when it must have looked as if I would never get the move right, she came storming into my dressing-room, saying, 'Michael, do you realize you've got that move wrong seventeen times?' 'Oh, sorry,' I said, privately thinking, Well, if an actor makes the wrong move so many times, it must be because the move itself is wrong. And then Larry said the same thing. Next day, giving notes, he said, 'When you came on as Macbeth, it was as if you were saying, "Fuck you, I *am* Macbeth." As Claudius you are *dim*.' These were portents.

We opened in November to indifferent notices all round. Performance after performance, I ploughed heavily through the part of the King and, as time went on, I thought I was neither so bad nor so ineffective as I had thought myself at the beginning. I no longer remember the details of my performance. I remember only a great feeling of tiredness. I frequently caught myself looking at some object, fixedly staring. I began to think that I was ill.

Our next play was *Hobson's Choice*. When Larry had asked me over the phone to play Hobson, my first reaction was 'What on earth makes you think I could play that?' 'You're a good character actor,' Larry said.

Harold Brighouse's play is a Lancashire comedy, as much of its time and place as the Neapolitan comedies of Eduardo da Filippo. Its humour lies, to a large extent, in its observation of status. Hobson is a Salford shopkeeper, but a tyrant in his own world. My chief difficulty was with the dialect. Usually I had no trouble with accents. But Hobson's demands a Lancashire accent, something with a strong bite to it, and when in rehearsal I tried to apply the 'bite', I thought I sounded slightly absurd. One of my fellow-actors gave up part of his Sundays to help me with it. Still it sounded off-key. Possibly not to everyone, but even the kindliest Lancastrian in the audience, I thought, would have awarded me no more than '2' for trying. Perhaps I could also plead that, but for the demands of repertory, I would never have been cast in the part of a North Country bully.

None of these excuses could be applied to Solness in *The Master Builder*, a part which might be said to be right up my street. Yet, once again, the lines would not stick. I had the feeling that the rest of the company were whispering about me. More and more I retreated into myself.

Diana was playing Mrs Solness. One afternoon after rehearsal a number of the cast were crowded into my dressing-room, making a slight hubbub, when in came Diana from her dressing-room next door, almost frantic with distress, saying, 'Oh, do be quiet, please, please be quiet.' She died the next day. She had become, after Edith, my closest woman friend. From the time we first worked together through the Blitz in *Kipps* I loved her for her beauty, her gaiety, and the sense of light-heartedness she unleashed in me.

Celia Johnson took over Diana's part. Rehearsals continued. I found myself at odds with everything, hating the production, hating the set. I could see the look of bewilderment on the faces of my fellow-actors when, in the final runs-through, I tried to apologize for not knowing my lines. I could hardly have blamed them if they thought that the serious memory gaps I began to suffer were due to the demon drink. I partly thought so myself.

On the first night I managed without a prompter, but my unease communicated itself to the audience, as it must have to the rest of the cast.

I kept telling myself when I woke up on Ibsen days that tonight I would get it right. Yet, as I taxied to the theatre, my confidence always slowly ebbed away, and as the taxi crossed Waterloo Bridge I would begin to tremble.

The season came to an end, and new contracts had to be drawn up. *Vanya* was to be withdrawn from the repertoire. It was assumed that I would go on playing my other three parts. But I stood firm on Solness. I would not take on that part again. Larry said that *The Master Builder* had been an expensive production and had to be revived, and that if I would not do Solness he would have to undertake it himself. I knew that he was loath to do this because of the heavy parts, including Othello, which he had coming up, but I was obstinate. So he took on the part. On his first night I sent him a wire quoting Solness's famous line 'It will be wonderful, wonderful, wonderful.' And so I was sure he would be, though I could never bring myself to see his performance.

For the opening festival of the Yvonne Arnaud Theatre at Guildford in 1965, I played safe by choosing parts which I had played before and therefore knew already. In the case of *Samson Agonistes*, which I had played at Cranleigh, this proved to be a mistake. It was one thing to ignore Milton's damnation of the theatre by rigging up an impromptu performance in the school library, but quite another to present it as a play to the citizens of Guildford. They came, audibly bracing themselves for the ordeal. But *A Month in the Country*, which I had played twice before and directed in New York, paid off very well. It was not the best-acted version I had been in, but the presence of Ingrid Bergman made it, whatever its shortcomings, a joyous occasion. We had acted together not long before in a television production of *Hedda Gabler*, and at the suggestion of a friend I had rung her, asking her to come to Guildford to play Natalya Petrovna. She agreed there and then, and the success of the season was assured.

It should be easy to describe Ingrid Bergman's art, and perhaps for that very reason it is difficult. In *A Month in the Country*, truth to say, she was not at the top of her form, but in most people's opinion and in mine it simply didn't matter. Her capacious good nature shone through everything she did. She was a lovely paradox: a very private person whose whole personality was on display.

It was a happy season, followed by a very successful six months' run of the Turgenev at the Cambridge Theatre in London. I had put the National Theatre behind me and out of mind. I was in good spirits and good health, or so it seemed. The only symptom that anything was amiss was an occasional spell of dizziness, and that could be put down to poor circulation.

I realize now that my loss of memory at the National, the shaking as I crossed Waterloo Bridge before *The Master Builder*, and the feeling I had that the company – 'they' – were against me, were all symptoms of the onset of Parkinson's disease. Yet the disease itself was not diagnosed for another nine years.

Parkinson's disease takes so many forms that no two cases are ever identical. It can strike so severely that its victim is completely incapacitated, or so lightly as to leave him in full possession of all his faculties, with nothing but the faintest tremor to indicate its presence. It is as old as recorded history. References to it are found in Galen, and in the Bible, where, in the Authorized Version, it is called 'the Palsy'. The physician James Parkinson, in honour of whose work the disease takes its name, called it the 'shaking palsy'. *Paralysis agitans*, its Latin title, expresses its nature and its essence better than any other, for the disease exhibits itself as a sharp and sometimes painful contradiction: it impels a person into bouts of restless movement, and yet paralyses him at that point where he *wants* to move.

The next period of my life remains, therefore, a grey expanse, with intermittent shafts of light. For much of this time my abiding feeling was simply of an absence of well-being. Weeks and sometimes months would pass pleasantly enough, but without my being able to summon the energy to accomplish anything very much. At such times it seemed as though my old enemy, procrastination, now ruled my life. Not an unprofitable drifting, at least not financially. Numerous films came along, some very good, like *The Go-Between*. Unconsciously, I sought to avoid situations where the symptoms I had felt at the National might recur. When I did return to the stage, in 1971, it was not, as I recall, from a conscious deliberation that I should do so. Simply that I liked the play, and thought, Why not?

I was happy enough rehearsing William Trevor's play *The Old Boys* with Sylvia Coleridge at the Mermaid Theatre in 1971. Happy enough to think that all was going well. Which it patently wasn't. At the dress rehearsal in the afternoon, I met Josephine Miles, the wife of the Mermaid's director, at the stage door. Or, rather, we bumped into each other. Till then she had appeared to be avoiding me. 'It's a very funny play, isn't it?' I said. 'Will your husband be out front?'

'Very funny,' she said. I noticed she was blowing her nose. I looked again, and saw that she was crying. 'Yes, a very funny play,' she repeated. I looked at her intently. The play wasn't as funny as all that. At that moment Bernard Miles appeared. 'I've sent for one of those contraptions,' he said. 'I think it might help you.'

When it arrived we spent some time practising how to use it. It seemed to be some sort of hearing-aid. Turn it up, and the prompter's voice bellowed and crackled in my ear; turn it down, and it murmured inaudibly. I ploughed through the dress rehearsal as best I could, with Sylvia doing her utmost to help me. I had not till that moment thought that anything was wrong. At the first performance I decided to brave it out. But unfortunately Sylvia and I, in a bit of rough-and-tumble, were more energetic than was strictly necessary, and the hearing-aid, making a few squawks, disintegrated and scattered in pieces around me. The loyal Sylvia started picking them up. 'I'm afraid it's broken, darling,' she muttered in a stage whisper.

At the Hospital for Nervous Diseases in Queen's Square, Professor Watkins diagnosed Parkinson's and prescribed L-dopa. I started taking it and was surprised at how cheerful I felt. I put this down to my cheerful nature; then I found it was an effect of the drug.

L-dopa by this time (1972) had been in use for some five years. At first it had been hailed as a miracle drug. Perfectly healthy people experimented with it in California in the belief that it was the elixir of life. Like all drugs, it is a stopgap, and until such time as the cause of the cell damage which is Parkinson's is understood and can be cured or prevented, L-dopa, or some derivative grandchild of L-dopa, will probably continue to be used. It is certainly useful, but it bestows its benefits in a capricious way. After the cheerfulness came sudden bouts of nausea. Later came hallucinations – voices from the next-door room, the corridor outside, or the pavement beyond my window, whispering about me or against me. The drug needed periodical fine-tuning of its dosage to overcome these unpleasant side-effects.

'I think that, after all, an operation won't be necessary,' said Dr Cooper. I felt relieved and rewarded. I had come to the Bronx at the suggestion of Lynn and her husband, John Clark, to be treated at St Barnabas Hospital, where Dr Irving Cooper had performed a number of operations on Parkinsonian patients, with some success. I had had numerous tests and observations. So impressed was I with the efficiency of this hospital and the wonders of modern medicine that I had gradually put myself in a frame of mind where I was ready for the operation on the morrow. To be told now that it wasn't necessary was like an unexpected reward for my bravery. 'Fine,' I said. But what next?

Illness played tricks with my memory. I found I could still retain large chunks of parts I had played before, but could not memorize new ones. I began to think I should be confined to radio broadcasts for the rest of my working life. Not an invigorating prospect, much as I enjoy broadcasting from time to time.

Suddenly, in July 1973, came an unexpected bonus. Would I care to accompany Peggy Ashcroft and others to Central City, Colorado, for a few performances at its festival of *The Hollow Crown*? This was an anthology devised by John Barton for the Royal Shakespeare Company about the kings and queens of England. Originally intended as a one-off divertissement in 1960, it had proved so successful and durable that it remained in the repertoire on and off for the next twelve years. It made an interesting, varied recital of pieces as diverse as Richard II's return from Ireland and the nine-year-old Jane Austen's potted history of England. They were divided among four actors, with good parts for all, and there was the added advantage of a production which allowed us to carry our scripts so as to read our parts when necessary.

We performed for two weeks in the neat little Opera House in the ruins of the city of the great Gold Rush. From there we moved to Washington, D.C., where we played another two weeks in the Opera House of the Kennedy Center. It was the beginning of the 'Save Michael' campaign, for the following year a new tour was mounted of *The Hollow Crown*, and the year after, another, and for the next three years there were tours of *Shakespeare's People*. One hundred and twenty-six theatres in one hundred and fifteen towns across four continents.

The date is 15 April 1974; Brooklyn; towards midnight. A dark and almost deserted place. We have just finished our first performance of *The Hollow Crown* in the Opera House of the Brooklyn Academy. Next week, Nazareth College, Rochester. Then Princeton. Then Harvard. (The emphasis seems to be on academic dates.) But then we travel west, to towns with charming names like Spokane, Tucson, Flagstaff . . .

The temperature rises, but, thank heavens, the bus is air-conditioned.

> Our driver's name is Mr OSCAR BRADFORD. The following rules have been found to be mutually beneficial, and we hope they will enable everyone to enjoy what is in effect our home for the next eleven weeks – 'THE BUS'.
>
> The bus will be divided into SMOKING and NON-SMOKING areas.
>
> Each member of the company will have a double seat to themselves, and that seat should be the same for the duration of the tour. When leaving the hotel in the morning it is customary that the first few hours of travel take place in silence, thus enabling the 'slow wakers' to do just that. Games that rattle or bang must be avoided.
>
> *Time Changes*: We will announce the fact when we go through a time change. After this announcement you will each be responsible for responding to calls on the new time.

1975. A marvellous homecoming. Our final performance of *The Hollow Crown*, newly-returned from the Antipodes, is at the

Redgrave Theatre in Farnham, Surrey. All that hectic fund-raising seems light-years away. The result is delightful, a tonic to the spirit of one who has never grown out of the childlike pleasure of seeing his own name in print.

The year is 1976. The programme of *Shakespeare's People* consists, for my part, entirely of pieces which I have known and played so often that I do not need a script. And who could resist a tour whose itinerary begins: 'September 20–24: Rehearse at Prince of Wales pub, Drury Lane. September 28: Depart Heathrow. September 29: Arrive Rio de Janeiro'?

The performance goes especially well in Rio. The Teatro João Caetano turns out to be a fine, sumptuously-appointed opera house of the 1860s, perfectly proportioned, with a row of boxes surrounding what was once the pit, each furnished with its little ante-room where ladies could retire or entertain.

No audience anywhere, at any time, is ever 'typical', but this one in Rio cannot be, for our brief stay – two nights – will attract only the English-speaking, the Shakespeare-lovers, those who want to see, and those who want to be seen. The applause is deafening, especially for *Macbeth*, Act One, Scene Three. Rosalind Shanks is a very attractive Lady Macbeth. There are five of us in *Shakespeare's People* – Ros and I, David Dodimead, Philip Bowen, and Rod Willmott and his lute – all on stage together throughout the evening. At the end of the performance the applause outdoes anything in any other continent. Cheers, stamping feet, flowers from the gallery...

It is 1977. Behind us are Indianapolis, Chattanooga, Knoxville. Ahead: London, Ontario, where I first played Macbeth before opening on Broadway twenty-nine years ago, and where once again we'll have to suffer Canada's liquor laws: 'The consumption of alcoholic beverages on public highways is illegal. Alcohol may be transported on the bus, but must not be consumed while we are in transit. No open bottles will be permitted when entering Canada, so you should plan accordingly.' After London: Kalamazoo; Bloomington; and Normal, Illinois. Tonight: Terre Haute, Indiana, in the Tilson Music Hall. If I close my eyes, as I frequently do on the bus, I can picture Terre Haute as a two-horse town with its dusty main street, John Wayne stepping out of the saloon bar, and gaily made-up ladies leaning against the piano of the Tilson Music Hall. But no, there will be a Howard Johnson's motel, and the Music Hall will be a large, well-equipped theatre. I *like* Howard Johnson's motels, for their sameness and efficiency. I like touring – love touring, in fact. No letters, no phone calls, no messages. Ideal – were it not for the loneliness.

I get to the theatre just before the 'half' and take a look at the stage. An actor with experience instinctively knows if it's a good auditorium to be seen and heard in : 'If in doubt, shout.' The university theatres have immense auditoriums, so large that only a small percentage of the audience can possibly see one's expression. But university audiences are amongst the best. The most fascinating theatre on this tour was Frank Lloyd Wright's building at Tempe, Arizona : round, pink, situated in a vast open space, and with a delightful impromptu air, despite the comfort and expense of all its fittings.

In my dressing-room I sing a little, to bring the voice forward. The 'five' is called. I put on my costume – a dark, full-sleeved Hamlet shirt, dark trousers.

The performance goes well. This is the third year of *Shakespeare's People* and my performance doesn't vary a great deal. On each tour I've tried to simplify it. 'The cardinal labour of composition is excision,' says Virginia Woolf, which in the language of acting means learning to do less.

There are a few visitors after the performance. It's nice to have visitors, of course, with their congratulations, but it's embarrassing somewhat, because unless they are professionals they find it very hard to leave. I've found it best to help them, and myself, by standing in the doorway of my dressing-room holding something over my arm, making as if I'm in a bit of a hurry. In the distance one can hear the stage staff packing the furniture, and over the public address system comes the stage-manager's voice announcing the time of departure for our next port of call, across the border and into Canada. The dramatic critic of Terre Haute's newspaper will be at work on his review, but we shan't be there to read it. Strange – notices are part of our addiction to receiving praise or blame, but when you're hurtling from one place to the next in a bus, it's amazing how well you manage without them.

'Would you prefer to cancel the performance tonight, Sir Michael? You may find it difficult to keep your feet.'

'Then we'll sit. No, we won't cancel it.'

The *QE2* is rolling heavily in rough weather. Half the passengers have kept to their bunks, and the other half have crowded into every corner of the main ballroom. An audience mainly middle-aged, middle-class, middle-brow, many of whom would not have come had the play been performed in their home town in England, but who come tonight because it's something different on board a ship, and find, to their surprise, that they enjoy every moment of it. 'I can't wait to get home and read it all again,' says one, with tears in her eyes. It's a comment I've heard before – typical, I think, of many of our audiences in the English-speaking countries. 'Did you find the audiences varied enormously?' I'm asked. True, we have played it across three continents. But no, the answer is no. Performances vary, and no audience is ever quite the same as the previous one. But essentially audiences, whatever the country, laugh when they're amused, and are amused in much the same way; sit silent when they're absorbed, and are restless when they're not; and are absorbed by what we, the actors, do, when it's done well and truthfully.

XXII

SCUDAMORES, REDGRAVES ... Dockyard workers, wain-
wrights ... Fortunatus Augustin Scudamore, his actor children
Dolly and Lionel ... A distinguished cleric, Roy's uncle, the
Reverend Henry Hymer Redgrave, who lived well into his nineties,
performed a christening service for Lynn, and in his extreme old age
was still working on a concordance to the Bible ... Grace, his
daughter, an acrobatic dancer ...

Nor should the offspring of Roy's first marriage be overlooked.
Judith Kyrle, Roy's first wife, gave up the stage and married a man
whose financial prospects were a great deal more stable than she
could have hoped for during her marriage to Roy. As a wedding
present, her new father-in-law gave her an oil well in Rumania.
Their son Robin, my half-brother, I met more than once, the air on
such occasions being filled with conjecture and surmise. The grandson, christened Roy, a General when I met him, on leave from
command of Her Majesty's forces in Hong Kong ...

Mabel, my actress aunt, who signed all her letters to me with the
drawing of a little imp. 'Impy' was a little ragged doll made out of
hairpins, with a goblin cap and a red bobble on it, and even now I
have only to say 'Impy with his knitty wire hand' to be back in the
days of my childhood and Mrs Gold.

I last saw Mabel when I was an undergraduate. A letter arrived
saying that she and her husband's company were playing at Saffron
Walden, and would I care to come over from Cambridge to see a
performance. I had not seen Mabel since the days when, with the
help of her dressmaker, Mother had fitted her up with the costumes
for *A Royal Divorce*, in which she played the Empress Josephine with
her husband as Napoleon. But those were the palmy days.

The Woman Always Pays, said the poster outside the village hall.

No mention was made of the author. Inside I found Mabel in the box office selling tickets. She greeted me with a cheerful smile and hurried backstage.

The play – seeming strangely familiar – was performed at a brisk pace. Henry Beckett, Mabel's second husband, was a fine actor who had played many seasons at Bridport.

'Did you like it?' asked Mabel.

'Yes, very much.'

'We had to change the title, of course. Good, don't you think? Good for the box office.'

'But what is the real title?' I asked.

'*Hindle Wakes*. Didn't you recognize it? Good little play, but of course we couldn't afford the royalties.'

'We live and learn,' said Mabel.

Mother said, 'What do you mean?'

Mabel fell silent. But not for long. 'At least,' she said, 'we learn who are our friends and who are not.'

'Nonsense.' Mother had a real sweetness of her own, but in her old age she could not stand nonsense.

Mabel continued. 'Who was it who said it would be better if we were born old and grew young?'

'I can't imagine.'

'Who said that? That dreadful man who thought you could find the truth by turning everything upside-down – you know, you hate me quoting him . . . ?'

'*What* about it?'

'Well, try another favourite of yours, Goethe's *Poetry and Truth*: "What a man wants in his youth he gets in plenty in his old age." What about that?'

'It's all relative,' said Mother. 'Relatively there is progress, absolutely there is no such thing.'

'What do you think, Michael?' I had been listening.

'"The sixth age shifts into the lean and slippered pantaloon . . . "' I began.

'That's enough, Michael. We don't want to know what the old idiot does or doesn't. That's enough.'

LIST OF PERFORMANCES AND PRODUCTIONS

Films are listed by their general release date.
Plays produced/directed by Michael Redgrave are asterisked.

AMATEUR AND SEMI-AMATEUR

Date		Character	Play or Film and Author, etc.	Theatre
1921	July	Walked on	Henry IV, Part 2 (Shakespeare)	Memorial Theatre, Stratford-on-Avon
1922	June	Second Niece	The Critic (Sheridan)	Clifton College
	December	She	A Pair of Lunatics	
		Barbara	The Private Detective (J. A. O. Muirhead)	
1923	June	Lady Mary	The Admirable Crichton (Barrie)	
	December	Cosmo Lennox	The Refugee (J. A. O. Muirhead)	
1924	June	Mrs Hardcastle	She Stoops to Conquer (Goldsmith)	
	December	Clarence	Richard III (Shakespeare)	
1925	June	Lady Macbeth	Macbeth (Shakespeare)	
	December	Reginald	Pigs in Straw (M. Redgrave)	
1926	June	The Young Man	The Bathroom Door (Gertrude Jennings)	Orthopaedic Hospital
		The Old Man	The Maker of Dreams (Harold Chapin)	
		Captain Absolute	The Rivals (Sheridan)	Clifton College
	August	The Young Man	The Bathroom Door (Gertrude Jennings)	Duke of York's Camp
1928	October	The Cook	The Taming of the Shrew (Shakespeare)	Apollo
	June	Florindo	The Servant of Two Masters (Goldoni)	A.D.C., Cambridge
	November	The Soldier	The Soldier's Tale (Ramuz-Stravinsky)	
		The Lover	A Lover's Complaint (Shakespeare)	

Date	Character	Play or Film and Author, etc.	Theatre
1929 March	Edgar	King Lear (Shakespeare)	King's College, Cambridge, and 46 Gordon Sq., London
November	Mr Voysey	The Voysey Inheritance (Harley Granville-Barker)	
December	Second Brother	Comus (Milton)	
1930 February	Rumour and Prince Hal	Henry IV, Part 2 (Shakespeare)	A.D.C., Cambridge
March	Mr Pepys	The Battle of the Book (Redgrave–Turner)★	
December	The Lover	A Lover's Complaint (Shakespeare)	Arts, London
	Second Brother	Comus (Milton)	
1931 June	Captain Brassbound	Captain Brassbound's Conversion (Shaw)	A.D.C., Cambridge
1932 June	Hymen	As You Like It (Shakespeare)★	Cranleigh School
November	Ralph Rackstraw	H.M.S. Pinafore (Gilbert–Sullivan)★	
1933 March	Samson	Samson Agonistes (Milton)★	
June	Hamlet	Hamlet (Shakespeare)★	Guildford Rep. Co.
October	John Worthing	The Importance of Being Earnest (Oscar Wilde)	
November	Menelaus	The Trojan Women (Euripides)	Cranleigh School
	Prospero	The Tempest (Shakespeare)★	Guildford Rep. Co.
1934 February	Clive Champion Cheney	The Circle (W. S. Maugham)	
March	Young Marlow	She Stoops to Conquer (Goldsmith)	Cranleigh School
June	Lear	King Lear (Shakespeare)★	Guildford Rep. Co.
July	Mr Browning	The Barretts of Wimpole Street (Rudolph Besier)	

PROFESSIONAL

Date	Character	Play or Film and Author, etc.	Theatre
August	Roy Darwin	Counsellor at Law (Elmer Rice)	Liverpool Playhouse
September	Charles Hubbard	The Distaff Side (John van Druten)	
October	Dr Purley	A Sleeping Clergyman (James Bridie)	
	The Man	The Perfect Plot (Aubrey Ensor)	
November	Mr Bolton	Sheppey (W. S. Maugham)	Liverpool Playhouse
December	Ernest Hubbard	Heaven on Earth (Philip Johnson)	

Date		Character	Play or Film and Author, etc.	Theatre
1935	January	Melchior Feydak	Biography (S. N. Behrman)	
	February	Gaston	Villa for Sale (Sacha Guitry)	
	March	Sir Mark Loddon	Libel (Edward Wooll)	
		Richard Newton Clare	Flowers of the Forest (John van Druten)	Winter Gardens, New Brighton
	April	Horatio	Hamlet (Shakespeare)	
	May	Bill Clarke	Too Young to Marry (Martin Flavin)	
	June	Oliver Maitland	The Matriarch (G. B. Stern)	
		Sir Mark Loddon	Libel (Edward Wooll)	
	July	Charles McFadden	Counsellor at Law (Elmer Rice)	Liverpool Playhouse
		Bill Clarke	Too Young to Marry (Martin Flavin)	
	August	Randolph Warrender	Youth at the Helm (Hubert Griffith)	
	September	Richard Barnet	Barnet's Folly (Jan Stewer)	
	October	Robert Murrison	Cornelius (J. B. Priestley)	
		Richard Brinsley Sheridan	Miss Linley of Bath (Mary D. Sheridan)	
	November	Max	The Copy (Helge Krog)	
		Trino	A Hundred Years Old (Quintero Brothers)	
	December	Gilbert Raymond	The Wind and the Rain (Merton Hodge)	
		BBC Official	Circus Boy (Michael Redgrave)	
1936	February	Rev Ernest Dunwoody	Boyd's Shop (St John Ervine)	
	March	A Radio Announcer	And So To War (Joe Corrie)	
	April	Richard II	Richard of Bordeaux (Gordon Daviot)	
		Richard Burdon	Storm in a Teacup (James Bridie)	
	May	Tom Lambert	Painted Sparrows (Guy Paxton and Edward V. Hoile)	
	June	Malvolio	Twelfth Night (Shakespeare)	
	September	Ferdinand, King of Navarre	Love's Labour's Lost (Shakespeare)	Old Vic
	October	Mr Horner	The Country Wife (Wycherley)	
	November	Orlando	As You Like It (Shakespeare)	
	December	Warbeck	The Witch of Edmonton (Dekker)	
1937	January	Laertes	Hamlet (Shakespeare)	

Date	Character	Play or Film and Author, etc.	Theatre
February	Orlando	*As You Like It* (Shakespeare)	New
March	Anderson	*The Bat* (Mary Roberts Rinehart and Avery Hopwood)	Embassy
April	Iachimo	Scene from *Cymbeline* (Shakespeare)	Old Vic
	Chorus	*Henry V* (Shakespeare)	
May	Christopher Drew	*A Ship Comes Home* (Daisy Fisher)	St Martin's
June	Larry Starr	*Three Set Out* (Philip Leaver)	Embassy
September	Bolingbroke	*Richard II* (Shakespeare)	Queen's
November	Charles Surface	*The School for Scandal* (Sheridan)	Queen's
1938 January	Baron Tusenbach	*The Three Sisters* (Chekhov)	
April	Chorus	*Henry V* (Shakespeare)	Old Vic
July	Orlando	Scenes from *As You Like It* (Shakespeare)	The Barn, Smallhythe
October	Alexei Turbin	*The White Guard* (Michael Bulgakov, adapted by Rodney Ackland)	Phœnix
December	Sir Andrew Aguecheek	*Twelfth Night* (Shakespeare)	Phœnix
1939 January	Gilbert	*The Lady Vanishes* (dir. Alfred Hitchcock)	Film
March	Lord Harry Monchensey	*The Family Reunion* (T. S. Eliot)	Westminster
April	Alan Mackenzie	*Stolen Life* (dir. Paul Czinner)	Film
May	Nicholas Brooke	*Climbing High* (dir. Carol Reed)	Film
October	Henry Dewlip	*Springtime for Henry* (Benn W. Levy)	Provincial tour
1940 February	David Fenwick	*The Stars Look Down* (dir. Carol Reed)	Film
March	Captain Macheath	*The Beggar's Opera* (John Gay)	Haymarket
	Romeo	Scene from *Romeo and Juliet* (Shakespeare)	Palace
June	Peter	*A Window in London* (dir. Herbert Mason)	Film
	Charleston	*Thunder Rock* (Robert Ardrey)	Neighbourhood
July	Charleston	*Thunder Rock* (Robert Ardrey)	Globe
1941 June	Kipps	*Kipps* (dir. Carol Reed)	Film
July	Entered Royal Navy		
September	Charles MacIver	*Atlantic Ferry* (dir. Walter Forde)	Film
	Stanley Smith	*Jeannie* (dir. Harold French)	Film

Date		Character	Play or Film and Author, etc.	Theatre
1942	March	The Russian	The Big Blockade (dir. Charles Frend)	Film
	July		Lifeline (Norman Armstrong)★	Duchess
	October	Gribaud	The Duke in Darkness (Patrick Hamilton)	St James's
1943	February	Charleston	Thunder Rock (dir. Roy Boulting)	Film
	June	Rakitin	A Month in the Country (Turgenev)	St James's
	August	Lafont	Parisienne (Henry Becque, adapted by Ashley Dukes)	St James's
	September		Blow Your Own Trumpet (Peter Ustinov)★	Playhouse
1944	March	Harry	The Wingless Victory (Maxwell Anderson)★	Phoenix
1945	June	The Colonel	Uncle Harry (Thomas Job)★	Garrick
			Jacobowsky and the Colonel (Franz Werfel and S. N. Behrman)★	Piccadilly
1946	July	Flight Lieut. Archdale	The Way to the Stars (dir. Anthony Asquith)	Film
	October	Maxwell Frere	Dead of Night (Sequence dir. Alberto Cavalcanti)	Film
	April	Karel Hasek	The Captive Heart (dir. Basil Dearden)	Film
	July	Michael Wentworth	The Years Between (dir. Compton Bennett)	Film
1947	May	Carlyon	The Man Within (dir. Bernard Knowles)	Film
	November	Hamer Radshaw	Fame is the Spur (dir. Roy Boulting)	Film
	December	Macbeth	Macbeth (Shakespeare)	Aldwych
1948	March	Macbeth	Macbeth (Shakespeare)	National, New York
	November	The Captain	The Father (Strindberg)	Embassy
	December	Mark Lamphere	Secret Beyond the Door (dir. Fritz Lang)	Film
1949	January	The Captain	The Father (Strindberg)	Duchess
	April	Etienne	A Woman in Love (M. Redgrave and Diana Gould, from G. de Porto-Riche)★	Embassy
	October	Berowne	Love's Labour's Lost (Shakespeare)	New
		Young Marlow	She Stoops to Conquer (Shakespeare)	
1950	November	Rakitin	A Month in the Country (Turgenev)	New
	February	Hamlet	Hamlet (Shakespeare)	New
	June	Hamlet	Hamlet	Kronborg Castle
	November	Filmer Jesson	Scene from His House in Order (Pinero)	Drury Lane

Date	*Character*	*Play or Film and Author, etc.*	*Theatre*
December	Solo performances of Shakespeare		Holland
1951 March	Richard II	*Richard II* (Shakespeare)	Stratford-on-Avon
April	Hotspur	*Henry IV, Part 1* (Shakespeare)	
	Andrew Crocker-Harris	*The Browning Version* (dir. Anthony Asquith)★	*Film*
May		*Henry IV, Part 2* (Shakespeare)	Stratford-on-Avon
June	Prospero	*The Tempest* (Shakespeare)	Holland Festival
July	Solo performances of Shakespeare		
July	Chorus	*Henry V* (Shakespeare)	Stratford-on-Avon
	Mr Lege	*The Magic Box* (dir. John Boulting)	
1952 April	Frank Elgin	*Winter Journey* (Clifford Odets)	St James's
July	John Worthing	*The Importance of Being Earnest* (dir. Anthony Asquith)	*Film*
July	Orin Mannon	*Mourning Becomes Electra* (dir. Dudley Nichols; released New York 1947)	*Film*
1953 March	Shylock	*The Merchant of Venice* (Shakespeare)	Stratford-on-Avon
April	Antony	*Antony and Cleopatra* (Shakespeare)	Princes
July	Lear	*King Lear* (Shakespeare)	
November	Antony	*Antony and Cleopatra* (Shakespeare)	The Hague, Amsterdam, Antwerp, Brussels and Paris
1954 January	Antony	*Antony and Cleopatra* (Shakespeare)	
September	Maître Déliot	*The Green Scarf* (dir. George More O'Ferrall)	*Film*
1955 January	Air Commodore Waltby	*The Sea Shall Not Have Them* (dir. Lewis Gilbert)	*Film*
	Colonel Eisenstein	*Oh, Rosalinda!* (dir. Michael Powell and Emeric Pressburger)	*Film*
April	The Air Marshal	*The Night My Number Came Up* (dir. Leslie Norman)	*Film*
June	Barnes Wallis	*The Dam Busters* (dir. Michael Anderson)	*Film*

Date	*Character*	*Play or Film and Author, etc.*	*Theatre*
	Hector	Tiger at the Gates (Jean Giraudoux, trans. Christopher Fry)	Apollo
October	Hector	Tiger at the Gates	Plymouth, New York
1956 November	Trebitsch	Confidential Report (dir. Orson Welles)	Film
December	Shylock	Tubal scene in The Merchant of Venice (Shakespeare)★	Waldorf-Astoria
March	O'Connor	1984 (dir. Michael Anderson)	Film
April		A Month in the Country (Turgenev)★	Phœnix, New York
November	The Regent	The Sleeping Prince (Terence Rattigan)	Coronet, New York
1957 January	Ruggles	Ruggles of Red Gap	NBC TV
March	David Graham	Time Without Pity (dir. Joseph Losey)	Film
June	General Medworth	The Happy Road (dir. Gene Kelly)	Film
September	Narrator	Vanishing Cornwall (Christian Browning)	Film
1958 January	Philip Lester	A Touch of the Sun (N. C. Hunter)	Saville
March	Fowler	The Quiet American (dir. Joseph L. Mankiewicz)	Film
June	Hamlet	Hamlet (Shakespeare (Director) Glen Byam Shaw)	Stratford-on-Avon
	Percy	Law and Disorder (dir. Charles Crichton)	Film
August	Benedick	Much Ado About Nothing (Shakespeare)	Stratford-on-Avon
October	Narrator	The Immortal Land (dir. Basil Wright)	Film
November	Hamlet	Hamlet	Palace of Culture, Leningrad and Moscow Art Theatre, Moscow
	Sir Arthur Benson Gray	Behind the Mask (dir. Brian Desmond Hurst)	Film
1959 August	H.J.	The Aspern Papers (Henry James: adapted by MR)★	Queens
May	Michael Collins	Shake Hands with the Devil (dir. Michael Anderson)	Film
December	Mr Nyland	The Wreck of the Mary Deare (dir. Michael Anderson)	Film
1960 April	Solo performances of Shakespeare		Ordry, Budapest
August	Jack Dean	The Tiger and the Horse (Robert Bolt)	Queen's

Date	Character	Play or Film and Author, etc.	Theatre
1961 June	Solo performances of Shakespeare and Hans Andersen		Bath Festival
August	Sir Matthew Carr	No, My Darling Daughter (dir. Betty Box and Ralph Thomas)	Film
November	The Uncle	The Innocents (dir. Jack Clayton)	Film
	Victor Rhodes	The Complaisant Lover (Graham Greene)	Ethel Barrymore, New York
1962 July	Vanya	Uncle Vanya (Chekhov)	Chichester Festival
September	Governor	The Loneliness of the Long-Distance Runner (dir. Tony Richardson)	Film
November	Lancelot Dodd	Out of Bounds (Arthur Watkyn)	Wyndham's
December	Tesman	Hedda Gabler (Ibsen)	BBC TV
1963 May	General Cavendish	Return to the Regiment (dir. John Moxey)	ITV
July	Vanya	Uncle Vanya (Chekhov)	Chichester Festival
October	Claudius	Hamlet (Shakespeare)	Old Vic (National Theatre)
November	Vanya	Uncle Vanya (Chekhov)	
1964 January	Henry Hobson	Hobson's Choice (Harold Brighouse)	BBC TV
April	Narrator	The Great War (John Terraine and Corelli Barnett)	
June	Solness	The Master Builder (Ibsen)	Old Vic (National Theatre)
1965 November	Reader	Tribute to President Kennedy	ABC TV
March	W. B. Yeats	Young Cassidy (dir. Jack Cardiff)	Film
May	Rakitin	A Month in the Country (Turgenev)	Yvonne Arnaud, Guildford
June	Samson	Samson Agonistes (Milton)	
	Uncle	The Heroes of Telemark (dir. Anthony Mann)	Film
	The M.O.	The Hill (dir. Sidney Lumet)	Film
September	Rakitin	A Month in the Country (Turgenev)	Cambridge, London

Date	Character	Play or Film and Author, etc.	Theatre
1966 June		Werther (Massenet)★	Glyndebourne Opera
October	Narrator	The Lost Peace (John Terraine)	BBC TV
December	The Blue Caterpillar	Alice in Wonderland (Lewis Carroll)	BBC TV
1967 June		La Bohème (Puccini)★	Glyndebourne Opera
November	Commentary	October Revolution (Fred Nossif)	BBC Radio
December	Charles Dickens	Mr Dickens of London (Barry Morse)	ABC TV
1968 January	Monsieur Barnett	Monsieur Barnett (Jean Anouilh)	BBC TV
	Harris	Assignment K (dir. Val Guest)	Film
May	Reading from the Huntingdonshire Cabmen	World of Beachcomber	BBC TV
	Prospero	The Tempest (Shakespeare)	BBC TV
	The Ghost	The Canterville Ghost	ABC TV
November	Grandfather	Heidi	NBC TV
1969 April	General Wilson	Oh, What A Lovely War (dir. Richard Attenborough)	Film
September	Air Vice Marshal Evill	Battle of Britain (dir. Guy Hamilton)	Film
November	The Headmaster	Goodbye, Mr Chips (dir. Herbert Ross)	Film
1970 March	Mr Peggotty	David Copperfield (dir. Delbert Mann)	Film
August	The MP	Goodbye Gemini (dir. Alan Gibson)	Film
1971 April	The Commander	Hell scene from Man and Superman (G. B. Shaw)	BBC TV
April	Polonius	Hamlet (Shakespeare)	TV, USA; BBC TV, UK
May	James Wallraven	Connecting Rooms (dir. Franklin Gollings)	Film
July	Mr Jaraby	The Old Boys (William Trevor)	Mermaid Theatre London
1972 August	Father	A Voyage Round My Father (John Mortimer)	Haymarket
September	Leo when older	The Go-Between (dir. Joseph Losey)	Film
April	Grand Duke	Nicholas and Alexandra (dir. Franklin Shaffner)	Film
September		A Voyage Round My Father (John Mortimer)	Tour of Canada and Australia
December	John	The Pump (James Cameron)	BBC Radio
	Erik Fritsch	The Last Target (dir. George Spenton-Foster)	Film

Date	Character	Play or Film and Author, etc.	Theatre
1973 August		Reading of *Child's Christmas in Wales* for the National Theatre of the Deaf	CBS
		Reading *The Hollow Crown* (Shakespeare)	Central City, Denver and Opera House, Washington
1974		Reading *The Hollow Crown* (Shakespeare) and *Pleasure and Repentance* (programme of poetry, prose and songs)	USA Tour
1975 January		Reading *The Hollow Crown* (Shakespeare) and *Pleasure and Repentance* (poetry, prose and songs)	World Tour
August		Reading *Shakespeare's People* (Shakespeare)	South Africa
1976 October		Reading *Shakespeare's People* (Shakespeare)	Tour of South America and Canada
November	Reading	*The Wheel of Fire* (Shakespeare)	Theatre Royal, Windsor, and English Tour
1977 March		Reading *Shakespeare's People* (Shakespeare)	Tour of Denmark, Canada, New Zealand and USA
1978 January		Reading *Shakespeare's People* (Shakespeare)	Bermuda Festival
April		Reading from Hans Andersen	Palaects Lesser Hall, Copenhagen
September		Reading *Shakespeare's People* (Shakespeare)	Arts Theatre, Cambridge
1979 May	Jasper	*Close of Play* (Simon Gray) Directed by Harold Pinter	National Theatre, London
October		*Close of Play* (Simon Gray)	Royal, Bath
		Close of Play (Simon Gray)	Olympia, Dublin
1982		Scene from *King Lear* (Shakespeare)	Roundhouse

INDEX

MR stands for Michael Redgrave

Early Modern Germany, 1477–1806
Michael Hughes

Attempts to present a coherent account of early modern German history are often hampered by the German equivalent of the Whig theory of history, by which all useful roads lead up to the creation of the nineteenth-century power state *(Machstaat)* or institutional state *(Anstaltstaat)*. In this kind of historiography, there are large "blank" areas between the "important" events like the Reformation, the Thirty Years War, the Seven Years War, and the French Revolution. During the intervals of apparent stagnation between these events, "Germany" seems to disappear, to be replaced by states such as Prussia and Austria, Saxony, Bavaria, and the Palatinate. Substantial areas are ignored, and groups such as the parliamentary Estates which stood in the way of state-building are virtually written out of most accounts.

Rather than focusing on the separate histories of the individual German states, Michael Hughes looks to the structure of the Holy Roman Empire in its final centuries and writes an account of Germany as a functioning, federative state, with institutions capable of reform and modernization.

For nineteenth- and early twentieth-century historians, the Empire was seen as the embodiment of division and weakness. But by examining the first *Reich*, Hughes reveals the persistence of the idea of Germanness and German national feeling during a period when, according to most accounts, Germany had virtually ceased to exist. At the same time, he examines "the element of continuity in Germany's development ... in an attempt to discover how far back in Germany's past it is necessary to go to find the roots of the 'German problem,' the Germans' search for a political expression of their strongly developed awareness of cultural unity."

EARLY MODERN GERMANY, 1477–1806

Early Modern
Germany, 1477–1806

MICHAEL HUGHES

uɲɲ

University of Pennsylvania Press
Philadelphia

Copyright © 1992 by Michael Hughes

First published 1992 by
Macmillan Education Ltd

First published in the United States 1992 by the
University of Pennsylvania Press

Library of Congress Cataloging-in-Publication Data
Hughes, Michael.
    Early modern Germany, 1477–1806 / Michael Hughes.
       p. cm.
    Includes bibliographical references (p.) and index.
    ISBN 0–8122–3182–1. — ISBN 0–8122–1427–7 (pbk.)
     1. Germany—History—1517–1871. 2. Germany—History—Frederick
III, 1440–1493. 3. Germany—History—Maximilian I, 1493–1519.
I. Title.
DD175.H84   1992
943'.028—dc20   91–41377
                                                     CIP

Printed in Hong Kong

For Yvonne

Contents

Preface

This is a study of Germany in the Early Modern period. It is a story of the failure of a feudal Empire to find unity, except in the loosest of federations, and the failure of a nation to create a state for itself. The basic aim of the book is to investigate the survival of the idea of Germanness, or German national feeling, during a period when, according to traditional accounts, Germany as a state had virtually ceased to exist. The element of continuity in Germany's development will also be examined in an attempt to discover how far back in Germany's past it is necessary to go to find the roots of the "German problem", the Germans' search for a political expression of their strongly developed awareness of cultural unity, which was to have important consequences for the rest of Europe in the late nineteenth and twentieth centuries. It is not a collective history of individual German states but an attempt to show that an all-German dimension persisted until the end of the Holy Roman Empire in 1806. Only then did Germany cease to exist, except as a geographical expression and an idea in men's minds, until its re-creation in the Confederation of 1815.

The Germans were themselves responsible for the long neglect of the Holy Roman Empire, the first *Reich*, the German political organization in the Early Modern period, is a traditionally state-centred historiography. For nineteenth- and early twentieth-century historians, progress in German history meant progress towards national unity. The Empire was seen as the embodiment of division and weakness and seemed to lack all the essential characteristics of a real state. Viewed with hindsight the Empire for a long time seemed exotic and too often it was remembered in the aphorisms of critics like Pufendorf and Voltaire. Understandably perhaps, after 1945 views of

Germany's past seemed to be overshadowed by recent events and there was a tendency to scour German history to discover the roots of the events of 1933 to 1945. This has produced a concentration on nineteenth- and twentieth-century history and contributed to a pessimistic interpretation of that history derived from the underlying assumption that Germany's problems stemmed from her arrested development and divergence from the rest of Western Europe. Germany's slide into disunity and impotence in the Early Modern period was compared with the simultaneous rise of powerful unified states, like France and England. Germany was rather to be compared to Poland and escaped a similar fate, partition and extinction, only through a combination of fortunate circumstances. This was echoed in the traditional German view, taught in German schools until 1945, which attributed Germany's division and weakness and all that flowed from them to the Thirty Years' War and the treaties of Westphalia. After 1919 it was very convenient to link this to the Treaty of Versailles and blame all Germany's problems on foreigners.

Any attempt to present a manageable account of German history after 1648 runs up against serious problems. The German equivalent of the Whig theory of history — a concentration on state-building combined with a belief that Germany after 1648 was no longer a state but a collection of states — has produced a fragmentary approach. The concept of the state was identified almost exclusively with the nineteenth-century power state (*Machtstaat*) or institutional state (*Anstaltstaat*). In traditional historiography there are large "blank" areas between the important events like the Reformation, the Thirty Years' War, the Seven Years' War and the French Revolution. During these intervals of "stagnation", such as the periods 1555 to 1600 and 1648 to 1740, nothing of note seemed to be happening. "Germany" apparently disappeared, to be replaced by states like Prussia, Austria and, a long way behind, Saxony, Bavaria and the Palatinate. Substantial areas of Germany and all-German history were ignored. In the same way those groups which apparently stood in the way of state-building, for example the parliamentary Estates, were written out of German history. It is the object of this book to examine some of these blanks. An alternative to the all-German approach in the past was to study what is essentially local history, the developments in the individual little states. Not only is this extremely complex but it also involves the risk of sliding into a narrow antiquarianism. In the same way study of the daily lives of "ordinary" Germans can become folkloric. Too many traditional histories of "Germany" tended to deal only with developments in Prussia and, when written by Austrian historians, in Austria, as the real "growth points" in German history. One problem was that a separate Austrian "national" historiography developed early and reflected the long-standing ambivalent relationship between Austria and Germany.

There has been particular concentration on Prussia, a result of the development of the so-called Borussian legend in the nineteenth century, the notion that it was Prussia's manifest destiny from the seventeenth century to lead and unite Germany. The Borussian legend is remarkably tenacious in popular views of German history. One example among many will serve to illustrate the distorting effect of this. Between 1907 and 1909 a commission of thirty-two historians of the Württemberg Historical and Antiquarian Society published a large and sumptuous two-volume study of Duke Charles Eugene of Württemberg (1744–93) and his times. The introductory chapter praised Frederick II of Prussia to the skies, portraying him as the pioneer of a new and creative state idea and the founder of a state which acted as a beacon for the whole German nation. Among the king's manifold achievements one in particular was highlighted: Frederick prevented the creation of a German-Austrian great power and began the process of excluding Austria from German affairs.

There has been some change in approach in recent years. The significance of the Empire is increasingly recognized in recent histo-riography, which has taken a much more favourable view of it than used to be the case. In recent years, when the whole future shape of Germany has again become the subject of debate and the search for a new *Modell Deutschland* has become current, there has been a new interest in the old *Reich*. The tradition of federalism in German history, long neglected, is again the object of serious study. It is now recognized that, though pre-modern in essence, the *Reich* did show evidence of growth, vitality and progress and can no longer be seen as a nation in aspic. The looseness of the German constitution provided opportunities for a great variety of different evolutions and there was nothing inevitable about developments. Perhaps the pendulum has swung too far: there is some danger now of a new form of anachro-nism, a new *Reichsromantik* or *Reichspathos*, with the Holy Roman Empire being portrayed as a combination of the European Court of Human Rights, the United Nations and the EEC. The fact that the Empire was, at least in part, devoted to peace, freedom and justice derived as much from external factors as from a conscious choice of its inhabitants. This idealization of the old *Reich* is itself part of the "new nationalism" seen recently in Germany.

It is now possible to trace some trends which affected the whole of
Germany (though there are always exceptions to any generalization).
It is the object of this study to describe these trends and to attempt to
provide a genuine history of Germany as a whole in the last century
and a half of the Holy Roman Empire. The experience of individual
states will be used to illustrate general developments but it will very
quickly become clear that there was no typical German state. One of
the most striking characteristics of the Empire was its enormous
complexity and the great variety of developments within its component parts. There is a widespread but mistaken belief that everything
was more simple in earlier centuries and that things have become
more complicated as a result of industrialization and the dawning of
the mass age. In reality the opposite is the case: uniformity and
standardization are characteristics of the modern age. The Holy
Roman Empire was a system which sheltered a very wide variety of
political systems, local self-government, clerical rule, urban republicanism, parliamentary government, limited monarchy and absolute
monarchy. Traditional interpretations can be misleading in other
ways. The Empire was not uniformly stagnant. Modernization took
place within it although there were great differences between developments in the individual states. The period was not dominated by the
rise of absolutism and religious antagonism.

Throughout the period studied foreign influence was of great
importance in Germany's development. The "German question" was
always also a European question. At the beginning Germany was
involved in the rivalry between the Habsburgs and the Valois and at
the end French influence and control became paramount. Germany's
involvement in European affairs will be an important element in this
study.

The keynote of this period in German history is the interplay
between dualities, between unity and diversity in politics, in economic
and social development and in culture, between the Empire and the
states, the Emperor and the princes, rulers and their subjects, after
the Reformation between two faiths and from the later eighteenth
century between Prussia and Austria. While Germany as a whole did
not progress from a feudal collection of provinces to a centrally
administered total state (*Gesamtstaat*), individual German states progressed a long way along that road. State-building in the individual
states prevented state-building in the Empire but the fact that the
Empire retained some state-like functions prevented the states from
exercising total sovereignty.

The approach adopted in the book is chronological and it employs a mixture of narrative and analysis. It is written with sixth-form and undergraduate students of history and general readers wanting to understand the background of the "German question" in mind. It is primarily a political history which concentrates on key developments producing substantial change within a remarkably stable constitutional framework established in the late fifteenth and early sixteenth centuries. Economic and social developments will be introduced only as background to analysis of the political situation; artistic, musical and literary aspects are not covered. A case will be made for the legitimacy of writing about "Germany" even when it was deeply fragmented. A political Germany existed in the *Reich*, much more important than used to be thought. There was no economic Germany but there was no economic France either. A spiritual or intellectual Germany was always there, as was a Germany of the mind. Germany as an employment common market also continued to exist, even if it was weakened by the confessionalization of life which followed the Reformation.

I must thank all those who have contributed to the writing of this book. I am particularly grateful to the University College of Wales for leave of absence and financial help, to the U.C.W. Hugh Owen Library and the library of the German Historical Institute, London, to Dr Jeremy Black of the University of Durham, Mr M. D. Hughes and Dr and Mrs J. Marek.

Michael Hughes

List of Abbreviations

AmHR	*American Historical Review*
CEH	*Central European History*
EcHR	*Economic History Review*
EHR	*English Historical Review*
EHQ	*European History Quarterly*
ESR	*European Studies Review*
HJ	*Historical Journal*
JCH	*Journal of Contemporary History*
JEcH	*Journal of Economic History*
JMH	*Journal of Modern History*
PandP	*Past and Present*
TRHS	*Transactions of the Royal Historical Society*

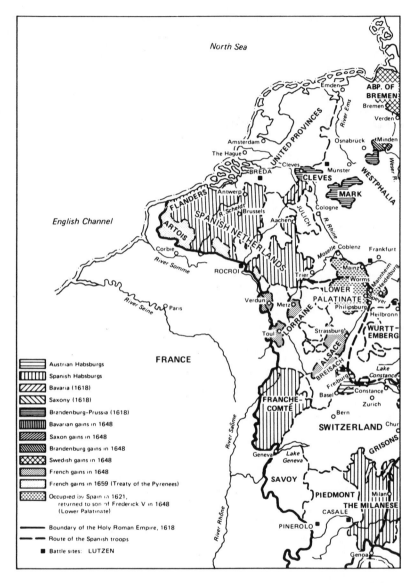

Map 1   The Holy Roman Empire during the Thirty Years' War

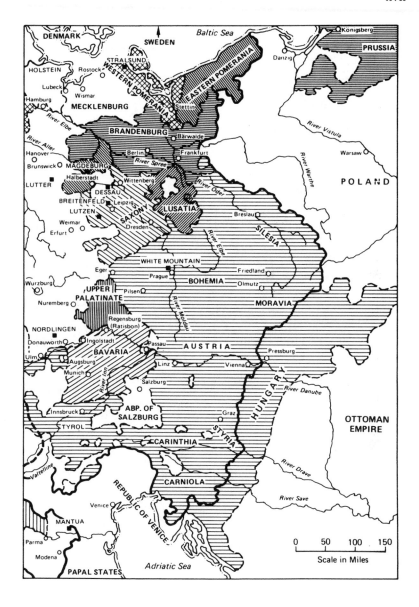

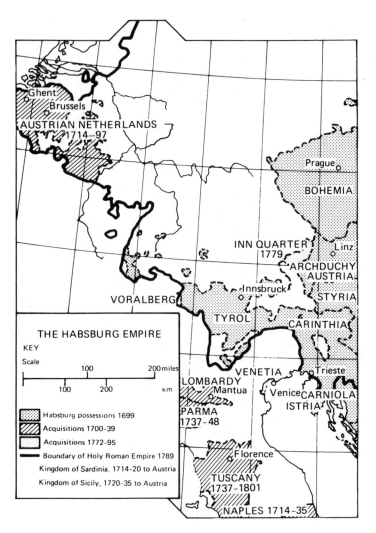

Map 2　　The Habsburg Empire

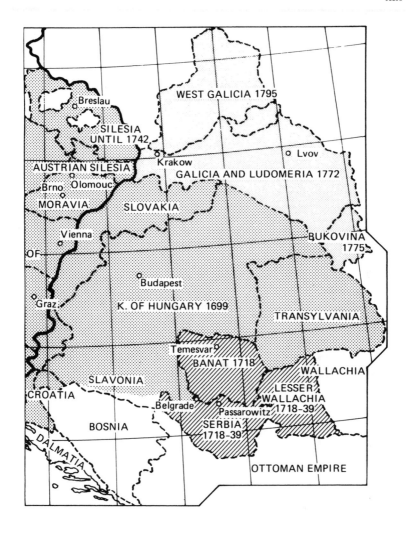

Breslau

WEST GALICIA 1795

SILESIA
UNTIL 1742

AUSTRIAN SILESIA

Krakow

o Lvov

GALICIA AND LUDOMERIA 1772

Brno Olomouc

MORAVIA

SLOVAKIA

Vienna

BUKOVINA
1775

OF

Budapest

Graz

K. OF HUNGARY 1699

TRANSYLVANIA

Temesvar

BANAT 1718

WALLACHIA

SLAVONIA

LESSER
WALLACHIA
1718-39

CROATIA

Belgrade

Passarowitz

SERBIA
1718-39

BOSNIA

DALMATIA

OTTOMAN EMPIRE

1 Introduction

On 21 April 1477 in the Brabant city of Malines Maximilian of Habsburg, son of the Holy Roman Emperor Frederick III, married by proxy, Mary, sole heiress to the Burgundian territories, including the Netherlands and the county of Burgundy, after the death of her father Charles the Bold, Duke of Burgundy. The Habsburgs had only recently taken a great step forward when, through the marriage of Albert of Austria, Frederick III's predecessor, to the daughter of the Luxemburg Emperor Sigismund, they acquired a claim to Hungary and Bohemia. This second marriage opened for them the marvellous prospect of a huge new territorial base from which to strike at their main dynastic rival, the King of France, and to launch a bid to strengthen their position in Germany. The marriage coincided with a growing popular campaign within Germany for a revival or renewal of the Holy Roman Empire (*renovatio imperii*) as a means of solving Germany's many problems. Both hopes, dynastic and national, were destined to be cruelly disappointed.

This study begins with an examination of Germany on the eve of the Protestant Reformation. The most striking feature of the country at that time was its fragmentation into the famous patchwork quilt of states, which is probably the best-remembered aspect of the Holy Roman Empire. In order to understand the conditions of the time, it is necessary to make a quick tour of earlier German history. [1] Between the tenth and twelfth centuries there were signs of the growth of national self-consciousness in the German lands, associated with a revival of the Holy Roman Empire, which suggested that the first European national state might be emerging there. The Empire was the centre of gravity in Europe and the Emperor shared with the ruler of Byzantium the great prestige associated with the inheritance of

1

imperial Rome and the Frankish empire of Charlemagne. During the eleventh, twelfth and thirteenth centuries Germany really mattered in Europe. Under the greatest emperors of the Middle Ages, Frederick I Barbarossa and his grandson Frederick II, both from the House of Hohenstaufen, Germany seemed united and strong. It was economically vital and had a large population. It enjoyed a fortunate geographical position astride the major European trade routes at a time when the bulk of trade was carried by road or on navigable waterways. Germany was a more urban society than most areas of Europe. Urban growth and the social mobility associated with it were particularly marked and there were strong concentrations of powerful and prosperous towns in the Baltic region, the Rhine valley and the south. It is estimated that on the eve of the Reformation ten per cent of the population lived in towns.

The early promise was not fulfilled. The first signs of decline began to appear in the fourteenth century, and then in the fifteenth Germany seemed to enter a long period of economic, political and social decay, which lasted until the early nineteenth century. For some five hundred years Germany was to be a negative quantity in Europe, which had things done to it but which was able to achieve little. It became the anvil when it should have been the hammer.

In reality the political cohesion and strength of Germany in the Middle Ages were illusory. The Hohenstaufen period, especially the reign of Frederick Barbarossa (1155–90), is traditionally regarded as the zenith of medieval German power. In fact apparent success only masked a number of well-established and damaging trends in Germany's political development. With the death of the last Hohenstaufen, Conrad IV, in 1254, these trends resumed. The Great Interregnum, "the terrible time without an Emperor", followed until 1273 and then there was a succession of weak rulers, minorities and double elections. These accelerated certain constitutional developments visible from the beginning of the thirteenth century, as a result of which Germany began to diverge increasingly from many of her neighbours. While elsewhere rulers were beginning the process of subordinating their great feudatories, depriving them of their semi-independent status, the German nobility began to take powers from their king. A number of acts marked Germany's progress down this road — for example in 1231–2 Frederick II issued the Statute in Favour of the Princes — though these were only the early steps in a long process. Later Henry VII (1308–13) deliberately gave away many important royal rights to the great nobles in order to buy their support for his campaigns in Italy. He also had hopes of persuading them to agree to the ending of the elective nature of the German crown by making concessions but they rejected this, instinctively sensing the danger an hereditary monarchy represented to their position.

Some of the reasons for Germany's problems were obvious and, while they help to explain what happened, they do not tell the whole story, as many of the same factors were present in other countries without producing the same results. Germany was big, sprawling and dislocated. As a result the monarchy, which initially relied on rule through personal contacts, was unable to penetrate into some parts. Germany lacked geographical unity and natural frontiers. The relics of an older tribal consciousness were also present in the "tribal" or "stem" duchies (*Stammherzogtümer*) Swabia, Franconia, Saxony, Bavaria and Austria, whose dukes had earlier elected one of their number as German king. More important, the medieval kings and emperors (the latter title was taken by the rulers crowned by the pope) were unable to establish strong and effective government. The reasons for this were many. There were frequent changes of dynasty as the German crown remained elective. The Saxon dynasty ruled from 919 to 1024, the Salians from 1024 to 1125 and the Staufer or Hohenstaufen from 1138 to 1254. The absence of an hereditary German royal dynasty meant that German national consciousness lacked a point of focus around which it could coalesce.

There is no simple explanation as to why the elective monarchy persisted in Germany. Among the factors must be listed the already mentioned survival of tribal consciousness and its associated tradition of elected leaders. The long drawn-out conflict between the papacy and the German crown in the eleventh century, known as the Investiture Contest, also played an important part. In 1076 the pope excommunicated Henry IV, giving the king's political opponents in Germany an excuse to elect another king. By the mid-thirteenth century the electoral system had solidified to the extent that seven hereditary electorates had emerged and it was accepted that their consent was required for a valid election.

There is dispute concerning the basis of the special status of the seven electors. The three ecclesiastics, the Archbishops of Mainz, Trier and Cologne, were the senior prelates of the German Church. It has been suggested that the four lay electors, Saxony, Bohemia, Brandenburg and the Palatinate, owed their status to descent from the daughters of Emperor Otto I or to the fact that they were political allies of the Emperor Charles IV, in whose reign the Golden Bull, which finalised electoral arrangements, was issued.[2] Previously the right to participate in royal elections had been undefined and varied from time to time. Some of the other great nobles continued to claim a say in elections and confusion continued until the whole process was systematized in great detail in the Golden Bull of 1356, which, after the election of King Sigismund in 1410, remained in force until the end of the Empire. The superior status of the electors was symbolized by recognition that the lands of the four lay rulers were indivisible primogenitures and by the grant to each of the seven of a special ceremonial function at the coronation of the king/Emperor. Details of this were also laid down in the Bull. The towns were forbidden to accept the electors' subjects as citizens. The Bull also proposed annual meetings of the electors to share the government of the Empire with the king/Emperor, but such a permanent council did not come into existence in the form envisaged.

In order to secure election, candidates for the German crown had to make concessions to the electors. This aggravated the second inherent weakness of the German crown, its inability to control its own nominal servants. The size of Germany and the many threats to its borders made it essential for the kings to delegate power but a combination of circumstances made it possible for men originally commissioned as royal officials to turn their territories into hereditary fiefs, especially when they coincided with the older tribal dukedoms (*Stammherzogtümer*). The offices of count (*Graf*) and imperial steward (*Reichsvogt*), established as instruments of royal control, were easily turned into hereditary territorial possessions. This feudalization led to the emergence of a group of intermediate rulers between the king/Emperor and the mass of Germans, who became only indirect subjects of their monarch. These rulers, usually for convenience described as "the princes", were able gradually to pare away more and more royal rights and royal lands, especially the major accumulation of the Hohenstaufens in the south west and Franconia, either by seizing them or as a result of grants from the crown, until they became as good as sovereign in their own territories.

There were very heavy losses during the Interregnum, which lasted from 1256 until 1273. As a result of losses the German monarchs became dependent on their nominal inferiors and the overmighty subject became permanently institutionalized in German political life. A wide gulf therefore opened between the king/Emperor's claims to enjoy the plenitude of power of the Roman Caesars and the real and manifest weakness of his position. The power of the German princes became institutionalized not only in the elective monarchy but also in the imperial diet (*Hoftag* later *Reichstag*). Its form was becoming systematized by the thirteenth century, though its membership and composition were not finally fixed until the seventeenth. It was accepted early that the consent of the *Reichstag* was essential for legislation: Germany became a dualistic state in which power was shared between the crown and the nobility, with the balance shifting increasingly in favour of the latter. The same process was to become apparent in many of the individual German states with the rise of parliamentary Estates, though in the great majority the crown eventually emasculated the Estates, the exact opposite of the all-German situation. Some German monarchs did make efforts to reverse this process but in vain.

Unlike many of the fellow rulers, the German monarchs were unable to make use of a policy of divide and rule to strengthen their position. In the Middle Ages German kings and Emperors, in order to achieve short-term aims, too readily abandoned groups who might have been their natural allies. Too many were, for example, obsessed with the recovery of shadowy imperial authority in Italy, which was richer than Germany, had a more pleasant climate and contained Rome, and were prepared to sacrifice their German interests. Germany was seen as no more than a source of men and money and the nobility were best able to provide both. Frederick II, known as the Wonder of the World and a great German ruler, spent all of his time and effort in Italy. Only in the later thirteenth century did these Italian ambitions gradually become less important though non-German affairs continued to occupy the attention of German rulers. The damaging Investiture Contest arose from papal fear of a revival of imperial power in Italy, which led successive popes to support the Emperor's enemies in Germany. It also deprived the Emperors of the support of the clergy, elsewhere often useful allies of the monarchy. The German Church became feudalized and its higher offices, bishoprics, great abbeys and their chapters, a near monopoly of the nobility.

Another such group were the *ministeriales*, a class of royal servants which became part of the nobility in the course of the twelfth century. At that time there was a fluid situation within the German aristocracy with plenty of opportunities to rise. New families were elbowing their way up while others were falling or dying out. By the sixteenth century the whole system had settled down and very few new major ruling families emerged thereafter.

The towns, whose growth was at first encouraged by German rulers as a counterweight to the nobility and a vital source of revenues, were completely sacrificed for the kings' Italian ambitions. For example, in the Statute in Favour of the Princes, Frederick II gave the princes the right of chartering towns. Great towns like Cologne, Strasburg, Augsburg, Nuremberg and Lübeck were powerful enough to retain their autonomy but the majority were very vulnerable. In the course of the fifteenth century many previously self-governing towns fell under the control of neighbouring rulers, such as Mainz and Erfurt, and the process continued into the sixteenth century.

Some kings deliberately weakened the crown. There was a substantial loss of royal power under Charles IV (1346–78), later to be seen as a brilliant ruler. In fact he concentrated on furthering the interests of Bohemia, which became a great power under him, and of his Luxemburg dynasty. In the process Germany was seriously damaged. Within thirty years of his death the Great Schism split Christendom and the Hussite conflict, religious and ethnic civil wars, ravaged Bohemia. Charles also made the financial problems of the German crown much worse. Before his reign royal lands and rights had been gradually alienated to reward followers or to raise ready cash. Often the land was leased but it proved very difficult for the crown to recover land at the termination of the lease, as shown by the proverb *Pfand gibt oft Land* (roughly, "a lease often gives ownership"). The Hohenstaufen plan to create a belt of imperial territory across Germany as the basis for a revival of royal power came to nothing. There was no imperial treasury; at a time when individual states were beginning to rationalize their financial administrations, the *Reich* did not. During his reign Charles IV gave away large amounts of land and rights. His motive was buy votes for his son's election and deliberately to impoverish the German crown in order to make the title hereditary in the House of Luxemburg, enriched by the silver of Bohemia. No potential rival would, he calculated, have the resources to sustain the imperial dignity.

The desire to secure the election of his son Wenceslas was a major motive behind the issue of the Golden Bull. He failed to create an hereditary monarchy. His plans for the creation of a powerful state came to nothing: he partitioned his lands among his five sons and nephews and all died without male heirs. His son Wenceslas was deposed by the German rulers in 1400 as incompetent and five years later the League of Marbach declared the right of the princes to share the Emperor's power and to depose an Emperor they disapproved of.

Charles had effectively deprived later emperors of anything but very scant revenues from the Empire. Emperors were forced to draw on the resources of their own personal possessions, if they were available, to fund imperial policies in Germany.

As a consequence of their lack of resources German monarchs were unable to fulfil the basic functions of government, strong administration and the maintenance of law and order. This led in the fourteenth century to bouts of anarchy and petty wars, which damaged the economy. Serious damage was caused by chronic rivalry between the Habsburg, Wittelsbach and Luxemburg families, all ambitious for more land and the royal title. As a result Germany entered a vicious circle: the weakness of the central government forced the substantial local nobles to take over more functions of government themselves, further weakening central authority. The local nobles needed more money to sustain their governments and therefore they took over more imperial revenues and rights. In the fifteenth century another period of prolonged anarchy led the towns of the south west to form leagues to protect themselves and their commerce. They acted nominally as the agents of the Emperor but in reality the self-help strategy embodied in these leagues symbolized imperial weakness. The first Swabian League was established in 1376 as a defensive organization and was a sign of growing friction between the towns and the nobility. The greatest league was the Swabian League of 1488 to 1534, made up of towns and small and ecclesiastical states. It was very powerful and a source of serious concern to the German nobility. It eventually broke up as a result of religious disputes. Its collapse destroyed another institution which might have balanced the power of the princes or prevented their total victory. The leagues were temporary as it was impossible to establish permanent cohesion between the towns.

In addition to the above factors, certain basic divisions within Germany were well-established before the fifteenth century. The survival of regionalism has already been mentioned. There were broad differences between north and south, separated by the Main river, in geography and agriculture. One reason for this was the absence of navigable waterways, on which bulk goods were moved, linking north and south. The main south German rivers, the Main and the Danube, flowed west and east. There were marked differences in the German spoken in the two regions. The Teutonic Order began to disintegrate, among other factors, because of rivalry between speakers of High and Low German.

The social and economic differences between east and west, divided by the Elbe river, were also growing. [3] The east gradually diverged from the west and remained backward in its development. There is some danger in over-emphasizing the contrast in the period before the fifteenth century. In the twelfth and early thirteenth centuries Germany, along with the rest of Western Europe, experienced a population rise and the peasants lost their bargaining power. As a result, serfdom became established by 1200. The continuing population rise and a desire to escape serfdom led to a great migration of Germans eastwards into sparsely populated areas. Recruiters known as *locatores* collected settlers from as far west as Flanders and assembled great German wagon trains, which rolled eastwards. The native Slav populations were driven out or Germanized. This became combined with a Christianizing mission among the heathen Slavs organized first by the Cistercians and later the Teutonic Knights, the Knights of St Mary's Hospital in Jerusalem, who were thrown out of the Holy Land by the Moslems and eventually set up their new headquarters in Königsberg. They subsequently moved to the great fortress of Marienburg in Prussia, where they were given large areas of land to subdue and settle. Many new towns were established with German municipal law and a high degree of self-government. They also became centres of Germanization. German commercial power, embodied most spectacularly in the Hanseatic League, stretched out, with German towns, along the Baltic coast and southwards into Poland, Bohemia and Hungary, though German dominance in the last areas became weaker from the fifteenth century as natives began to displace the former German urban ruling class. New German states emerged from this eastwards expansion, including Mecklenburg, Brandenburg, Pomerania and Silesia. In contrast to the west, the east was markedly free. By the mid-fourteenth century the east was still thinly populated and labourers, a rare commodity, were able to retain their freedom. There was little or no feudalization, village and town self-government through popular assemblies was common and most peasants held their land as free tenants or in return for light labour services.

Circumstances began to change with the coming of the Black Death in Western Europe from the mid-fourteenth to the fifteenth century. This precipitated an agrarian crisis caused by a sudden population fall, made worse by earlier emigration. In the west the epidemic caused the decay of feudalism: the fifteenth century was the Golden Age of the western peasant, with rising living standards. It also produced the lord-tenant system known as *Grundherrschaft*, under which the lords left the farming of the bulk of the land to tenants in return for payments. In the east *Gutsherrschaft* became predominant. Under that system the lords farmed most of the land directly to produce a surplus, using the labour of unfree tenants who were allowed a small plot from which to feed their families. Landlords, including the Teutonic Order, responded to the labour shortage with a new policy, the imposition of unfreedom on their tenants, taking advantage of weak rulers to do so. Serfdom began to become established in the east and was further strengthened in the sixteenth and seventeenth centuries with the emergence of a class of noble capitalist farmers, the *Junkers*, who made themselves rich by selling surplus grain to Western Europe. They were able to make themselves politically dominant over their rulers, to destroy the great majority of the towns and to exact high labour services from their serfs. Serfdom lingered on in the east into the nineteenth century. As industry developed in the west, Eastern Europe, including Germany east of the Elbe, was organized to feed the growing urban centres of the Netherlands, north eastern France and south eastern England. Danzig developed as a great centre for the shipment of grain drawn to it from the Vistula river basin. The cultivation of the grain was based on serf labour. There was therefore no market in the east for imported manufactures except luxuries for the landowners. Industry was restricted to the nobles' estates. In the absence of a developed urban class, the nobles remained economically and socially dominant. The distinction between east and west was to remain politically significant in Germany into the twentieth century.

2 Germany on the Eve of the Reformation

In the late fifteenth century the Holy Roman Empire was changing in two important ways.[1] First it was shedding its international or supranational image and becoming more self-consciously German in character. Secondly, it was entering a prolonged period of political, social, religious and economic unrest which coincided with growing threats from outside. These problems reached a crisis point simultaneously in the years around 1500.

In the late fifteenth century Germany entered a period of chronic instability which produced a wave of millenarianism, an expectation that the end of the world was approaching. Turkish attacks on Europe were viewed as part of a pattern of divine punishment for men's sins. There was an excited and restless spirit abroad. The times seemed "out of joint" and there was a real fear of imminent catastrophe. Among the symptoms of this were serious social divisions, growing violence, including frequent rioting and rampant anti-Semitism, and more extreme religious observance. Men's need for reassurance about the availability of salvation and the rush to achieve it, if possible by a short-cut, took many forms, traditional and new, including a frenzy of charitable works, the spread of superstitious practices, frantic efforts to see as many holy relics as possible, pilgrimages and the emergence of wild preachers. The last was seen especially in overpopulated areas like Bohemia, Westphalia and the Netherlands, where they gained a following among groups on the margins of society. Such an excess of religion was easily explained: pictorial representations of religious themes were everywhere in churches, in paintings, sculptures and stained-glass windows, which were used during services to point up the religious message. Wood-block prints containing religious themes were very popular.

These problems were made worse by the absence of a strong central authority in Germany and there were fears that the weakness of the Empire threatened the stability of the individual German states. In the fifteenth century many anonymous pamphlets appeared calling for a fundamental reform of the Empire and often for social and economic reforms, including secularization of Church property, the abolition of the nobility, a married clergy and the fixing of fair prices. This overlapping of political, social and spiritual grievances, the blending of anti-clericalism, anti-noble sentiments and an idealization of the Empire, was typical. Some predicted the emergence of a messianic leader from the lower orders to head a movement to restore the Emperor to all his powers as a strict but just father of his people. Revolutionary and reactionary sentiments were often mixed: a social, political and religious revolution was envisaged, a violent overturning of society portrayed as the gateway to a new Golden Age. At the same time there was a yearning for a return to the society of the past, the memory of which was gilded by remoteness and myth. Anger against innovations and talk of the "good old days" were frequent.

Economic problems played a major part in all this. Germany was, on the surface, still enjoying the prosperity seen in the later Middle Ages but some parts of the economy were finding it hard to adapt to new methods and new circumstances and strains were beginning to show. The effects were patchy but certain trends were clear. The whole economic structure of Europe was changing to Germany's disadvantage in the first third of the sixteenth century. The Hanseatic League, after reaching the peak of its prosperity in the fifteenth century, began to decline as powerful foreign interests, in particular the rising Scandinavian states, England and the Netherlands, encroached in the Baltic. The lack of German fleet and natural accidents like the migration of the herring shoals from the Baltic into the North Sea compounded the situation. Germany also experienced a relative decline in population in comparison with her neighbours, especially France. The Mediterranean and Baltic were beginning to lose their economic primacy, on which Germany, due to its central position, had grown prosperous, and the rise of the "Atlantic economy" was beginning to move the centres of European economic activity decisively away from Germany to cities like Antwerp, Seville and Lisbon. The movement of goods on the great land and river routes across the continent declined after reaching a peak around 1500.

The overall economic picture was very mixed, with examples of growth and expansion alongside stagnation and decline. Some

German towns saw their predominance beginning to disappear, as silver mines became exhausted and foreign competitors began to undercut them. In the sixteenth century, as if to illustrate the decline in enterprise, many of the south German cities, previously centres of commerce and manufacturing, became financial centres. Popular mentalities remained rooted in a pre-capitalist age in medieval notions of a moral economy; monopolies and "usury" reemained the object of considerable popular hostility, seen in many complaints against them in the *Reichstag*. The falling behind of Germany was made worse by the political fragmentation of the country and the emergence of distinct and self-centred state economies. The ability of the *Reich* to regulate the all-German economy, if it had ever existed, was disappearing.

The population of Germany rose between the late fifteenth and the early seventeenth centuries, though estimates of the figures vary between 12 and 18 millions in 1500 and 16 and 21 millions in 1618. There were clear local variations within the overall picture: growth was strongest in the west and south. Growing demand for food pushed up prices and this, combined with the injection into the European economy of large quantities of silver from South America, produced the unprecedented price inflation known as the Price Revolution, which lasted from the 1470s to the 1620s. Initially, while it was mild, the inflation stimulated production and Germany benefited.

Towns were the main beneficiaries. There were about 4000 towns and cities in Germany at the beginning of the sixteenth century. "Towns" were defined by a special legal status rather than economic activities; the majority were in reality walled villages dependent on the agricultural production of land outside the walls but some were more. The largest towns were commercial centres like Cologne, Nuremberg, Strasburg, Augsburg, Vienna, Lübeck and Magdeburg. The early sixteenth century saw a boom in the Hanseatic cities and the great manufacturing centres of the south and central Germany, whose capitalist enterprises in banking, long-distance trade, textiles, metalwork and mining did very well. The growth of centres like Hamburg, Prague, Nuremberg and the Saxon mining towns was revealed in sharp rises in their populations, reflecting both their attractiveness to immigrants and growing demographic pressures in the rural areas. Individual entrepreneurs, many of them former guild members, made fortunes producing cheap textiles and other items of mass consumption. Augsburg, seat of the huge Fugger enterprise, was a major textile centre until the early seventeenth century and its prosperity spread far beyond its walls as a result of the employment of substantial numbers of out-workers in the countryside to spin and weave. This was symbolized most splendidly in the person of Jacob Fugger, known as the Rich, who died in 1525.

In the Harz, Thuringia and the Alps new methods enabled previously inaccessible veins of lead, copper and silver ore to be worked. Such enterprises needed substantial capital and were vulnerable to changes in demand. With the arrival of substantial imports from South America, Germany lost its position as the major source of silver in Europe. Capital generated by mining and manufacturing funded an expanding financial business in Germany, toppling the Italians from their earlier dominant position. Houses like the Fuggers used their immense financial power to obtain trade monopolies and other favours. Charles V, notoriously, owed his ability to bribe the German electors to vote for him as Emperor to massive loans from the Fuggers. The great south German finance houses such as the Fuggers and Welsers at first joined in the growing colonial trade with bases in southern Spain. In the early 1520s there were plans for a great German investment in South American trade and manufacturing but it came to nothing. Major rivals appeared. By the middle of the sixteenth century the Germans had been ousted and first Antwerp and later Amsterdam supplanted them. By about the middle of the sixteenth century the Dutch had overtaken the Hanseatic League in Baltic trade. Only towns which were able to maintain links with centres of the Atlantic economy remained buoyant. Hamburg and Frankfurt benefited from the talents of refugees they welcomed within their walls, such as Sephardic Jews from Spain and Portugal and people from the Netherlands.

Demographic and economic changes promoted growing social mobility, with enhanced opportunities to rise and fall. Within each social class there was a widening gulf between the rich, who seemed to be growing richer, and the poor, whose conditions seemed to be worsening, leading to serious social tension. The situation was made worse by visible displays of luxury and conspicuous consumption on the part of the new rich. From about 1530 the price inflation was to become obvious and added substantially to the crisis mentality. It was beyond the comprehension of most men and there seemed no way of dealing with it. Real incomes for the majority were falling but government efforts to deal with the problem had no effect because governments were as ignorant of the real causes as the masses. The rise of the money economy was another cause of instability. It was said that only monopolists and usurers were flourishing. It seemed everything was for sale. Even the Church was not immune, being seen as riddled with simony and nothing more than a great bureaucratic money-making machine. Hostility to early manifestations of the market economy and economic individualism were subsumed in a general attack on "monopoly", a shorthand term for a whole range of objectionable economic practices. They were frequently attacked in the imperial diet and on his election as Emperor Charles V had to promise to bring them to a stop. It was easy to blame everything on divine wrath or wicked men.

In particular the peasants in many parts of the country felt themselves under pressure. Agriculture and forestry were the over-whelmingly dominant sectors of the economy in terms of employment and as sources of revenue for governments, the Church and the nobility, of capital and of food, fuel, building materials and com-modities used in manufactures. In the fourteenth and fifteenth centuries landlords and governments suffered increasing financial difficulties and this led to a large-scale conversion of labour services into money rents. A very complex system of tenures, based on mutual rights and obligations of lords and tenants, emerged, the balance of which changed according to circumstances. Serfdom survived in most parts of western Germany only in the form of relics but even these were seen as increasingly burdensome by the peasantry. From about 1500 the sharp population rise contributed to new economic and social difficulties. Some parts of Germany saw mounting land hunger. At first this was partly relieved by various methods of making extra land available for cultivation, such as using mountain pastures or reclaiming land from the sea, but, apart from a few favoured areas like the Tyrol and East Frisia, this was a solution with limited possibilities. Subdivision of existing holdings was another short-term answer.

A fundamental problem was the inflexibility of agriculture. Yields in the bulk of German agriculture were very low, giving, typically, a return of about 5:1 of the sowing, and it was very hard to convert from subsistence farming to production for the market. Where growing market opportunities appeared, for example from the expansion of town populations, attempts to exploit them often added to conflicts between lords and tenants and between different groups of tenants. The divisions between peasants with substantial holdings (*Vollbauer*), and those with smaller plots or with no land at all, known by a variety of names (*Halbbauer, Insten, Gärtner, Kossäten*), became deeper. Only the more fortunate peasants were able to cash in on the price rise but in most cases the landlords, the nobles, the Church, townsmen or the state were the main beneficiaries.

The position of the lower nobility was ambivalent. Some could benefit from new opportunities offered by economic change and were able to retain social and political power but this opportunity was available to few. The social, economic and political trends of the time seemed to be undermining the status of the free imperial knights. In the medieval period, as heavy armoured cavalry, they had formed the core of armies and their castles, of which there were an estimated 10 000 in Germany, had given them power. By 1500 they were clearly outdated, their military uselessness having been revealed by massed archers, the Hussite and Swiss peasant armies and Italian professional mercenaries. The increasing use of mercenaries rather than semi-amateur armies was one of the reasons why states faced growing economic problems. The rise of powerful states led, in most parts of Germany, to the destruction of their castles and to steady encroachments on their rights. Subordination to the rising princely states, voluntary or enforced, meant an end to their autonomy. Many knights were losing their land as they were forced to pledge it and many found the only answer to their problems lay in placing higher burdens on their tenants, adding to peasant discontent. Social barriers hardened visibly in the late fifteenth century, especially the distinction between nobles and non-nobles. The nobility began to close ranks as the sources of their status disappeared. For example, inter-class marriages, which had become common earlier, especially between noble men and the daughters of rich citizens, were frowned on.

As their military role disappeared, many knights, suffering from an identity crisis, turned to organized crime to sustain them, especially in the west and south west, where the states were weak, and this added to the serious law and order problem in the later fifteenth century. This culminated in the great rebellion of the knights in 1522, led by Ulrich von Hutten and Franz von Sickingen. It arose from a mixture of enthusiasm for the Lutheran religion — many knights, including Hutten and Sickingen introduced the new faith on their lands early — and an attempt to regain lost status. It began in August 1522 with a meeting of some six hundred knights at Landau, at which a fraternal union was established for six years. Sickingen then attacked the Archbishop of Trier with the stated aim of secularizing the see. The knights' hostility was focused against the higher clergy and against those knights who had capitulated and become servants of the rising states. The leaders appealed to German national sentiment in stirring up resentment against Rome's supposed plundering of German treasure and urged Luther to join them in a campaign to liberate the fatherland. They had a Utopian vision of a decentralized political and ecclesiastical system, which would restore the knights' usefulness. The rising was largely restricted to the south west but there was a real fear that it would spread and infect the nobilities of other states.

Sickingen held out in his castle against Hessian and Palatinate armies until April 1523. He was killed in the fighting while Hutten died later the same year in Switzerland. The collapse of the revolt was followed by a systematic razing of knightly castles. Thereafter the majority of the free knights lost their political power. In 1542 an institutional structure of three circles (*Ritterkreise*) was created for them in return for payments to the Emperor and some 1500 knightly families kept their status but they had to seek employment in the Church or in imperial or princely service. The larger states, including Austria, continued their attempts to subordinate the knights, using a variety of techniques, until the end of the Empire. Had it not been for the protection of the imperial courts, they would have disappeared as a distinct class much sooner.

The towns were also experiencing growing social and political tensions. In the early sixteenth century many saw a growing influx of new inhabitants from rural areas. The newcomers were usually denied citizenship and formed a voiceless urban proletariat and a large reservoir of discontent when economic activity declined. During periods of recession towns also stopped immigration, which in turn added to discontent in rural areas. Most German cities were governed by small groups of patricians, often guild masters or substantial traders. These tended to be unchanging circles of families; in the prosperous towns there was not the same pressure as elsewhere to become landed gentlemen. Only in a few cities, usually the seat of state governments, did a "new" middle class in the form of educated administrators, lawyers and teachers become significant. Friction between groups was endemic in some towns, for example between those who were *ratsfähig*, eligible for membership of the town council, or those who were *Bürger* and had the rights of citizenship and the rest. Some cities in the south and in Switzerland ruled substantial territories outside their walls and the magistracies often imitated princely rulers in seeking to increase their powers over their subjects. The fourteenth and fifteenth centuries saw many violent risings in towns, often with the object of forcing a clique of council families to admit "new men" to a share of power. From the late fourteenth to the early sixteenth century there were a number of rebellions by town dwellers excluded from the charmed circle of city government but expected to contribute with their money and lives to the defence of the city.[2]

Growing political tensions were also appearing in many states. Constitutional battles arose from attempts by rulers to lay the foundations of the state by equipping themselves with standing armies and trained professional bureaucracies. Among the leaders in this process were Trier, the lands of the Teutonic Order, Bohemia and Württemberg. In the fourteenth and fifteenth centuries there was a gradual evolution of feudal lordships into something recognizable as the modern state. Many princes were trying to consolidate their lands and take an essential step in state-building by imitating the electors in introducing primogeniture and ending the practices of division and appanage-creation. This was achieved in Württemberg in 1482 and Bavaria in 1506. New methods of government were appearing, with the use of written records and procedures and the employment of professional administrators. A new class of literate legally trained middle-class officials was appearing, a product of the universities of Prague, Heidelberg, Vienna or Leipzig, the last set up to cater for Germans thrown out of Prague during the Hussite troubles.

One of the most spectacular signs of the rise of the professional administrator was the great expansion in universities in Germany before the Reformation. Five universities existed before 1400, Prague, Vienna, Heidelberg, Cologne and Erfurt, and eight were added in the fifteenth century. In the fifteenth and early sixteenth centuries Germans continued to study at Italian and French universities but this was changing quickly. Although the Reformation increased the output of universities, such experts were scarce and the salaries available were very generous. The rise of the expert lawyer and administrator was seen as part of a general assault on traditional structures. Viewed with the same suspicion was the gradual intrusion of Roman Law. Justinian's code, glossed or amended in the Italian universities, undermined legal particularism. It replaced or existed alongside the traditional unwritten customary law and led to the creation of an apparatus of state courts alongside and gradually replacing the traditional noble and town tribunals.

Roman Law emphasized authority and enjoyed enormous prestige because of Renaissance admiration for the Ancient World and it was increasingly looked to when common and customary law did not provide an answer. It involved the new concept that law was not simply remembered but could be made and it increased the ability of governments to shape the future by issuing regulations. Ironically the initial demand for the reception of Roman Law did not usually come from rulers but from the educated laity, who wanted a more orderly judicial system — the reception of Roman Law was an expression rather than a cause of the crisis mentality of the time — but it contributed to the strengthening of the state and added to the professionalism of government. The impact of Roman Law was patchy and some areas, such as Saxony, were not touched by it but its piecemeal acceptance added to the feeling that the good old world was being swept away in a tide of innovation. The most practical manifestation was in the production of written law codes for cities and states (for example in Nuremberg in 1484 and Bavaria 1485–95), which was becoming common in the sixteenth century. In 1501 a corpus of imperial laws was published. Such codification was seen by some as a means of improving efficiency and achieving standardization. It was also seen by others as a cause of problems: in contrast to the good old days when there was only one law and everyone was happy, there were now dozens of laws and thousands of lawyers and everyone was miserable.

Alongside the beginnings of modern administration some states saw the simultaneous rise of parliamentary Estates (*Landstände* or *Landschaft*), claiming to share power with the princes.[3] The Estates originated in the feudal relationship: in return for the protection of the lord, subjects owed a duty to advise and aid him. Their role was strengthened by a thirteenth-century imperial law which obliged rulers to seek the consent of their nobility if they were planning to make substantial changes in their fiefs. In the later Middle Ages many became powerful, administering the prince's finances, guaranteeing loans, recruiting and maintaining troops bound to them by oath and pursuing diplomatic relations with other Estates and even with German and foreign rulers. The causes of the growing power of the Estates included shortage of money and rulers' inability to exist on their traditional incomes, divisions of territory, succession disputes and rulers' desire to associate the influential sections of their subjects with their actions. The financial needs of states were becoming very pressing and this acted as an important motor of change. An attempt was made to modernize the medieval obligation of feudatories to aid and advise the overlord in the form of regular taxation and an increase in the number of tolls, dues and fees. In many cases the Estates saw themselves as custodians of traditional modes of government.

Changes were also taking place in the shape of Germany. By the end of the fifteenth century it was again contracting as pieces around the periphery began to fall away. In 1460 Schleswig passed to Denmark and the Burgundian lands, Switzerland and the Netherlands drifted away over a number of years. People who had earlier been German were becoming Swiss, Dutch or Flemish. A number of imperial cities like Basle joined the Swiss confederation and many seriously considered joining. Schaffhausen became Swiss as late as 1501. From 1471 the Swiss did not attend the imperial diet and from 1495 they claimed exemption from the jurisdiction of the imperial courts. This was accepted *de facto* in 1499.

In 1410 the Teutonic Knights lost the battle of Tannenberg against the Poles, after which the Polish crown took sovereignty over Prussia and Danzig. In 1466 in the second Treaty of Thorn the Order had to cede the bulk of its territories to Poland. German power retreated further as the eastern Baltic became a battleground between Russia, Poland, Denmark and Sweden.

In Bohemia during the fifteenth century the Hussite heresy appeared as part of a national reaction by the Czechs against domination by a Latin German Empire. It brought to a temporary end German immigration into the region. There was a strong nationalist element in the German "crusades" against the Hussites between 1421 and 1430. The 1422 *Reichstag* at Nuremberg agreed to levy a common tax on the whole Empire to fund the war against the Hussites, the first imperial tax. After 1491 Bohemia was temporarily detached from the Empire when it passed into the hands of the Polish royal house. The Empire's influence in Italy also declined, though claims to authority there were maintained. This loss of non-German areas was symbolized in 1486 when the title of the Empire was formally changed to the Holy Roman Empire *of the German Nation*. Earlier its title had also included the *Welsch*, i.e. Italian, nation. By the middle of the fourteenth century the use of the phrase "German lands" to describe the Empire had become common.

What Germany lost were primarily non-German areas and this had some beneficial effects. The Empire acquired clearer boundaries and became more German in character, though it still contained substantial non-German minorities. There was a strong wave of German sentiment in the 1470s against Burgundian power, which was encroaching on the western borders of the *Reich*. German national feeling was also fostered by developments during the Renaissance, which promoted a new interest in German history and study of "German" heroes of the past. The German Renaissance, centred in the prosperous cities of the south west and Alsace, produced a new German culture, which was not a pale copy of Italian models. The Emperor Maximilian I supported a number of humanist writers like Konrad Celtis and Sebastian Brant, who also contributed to the growth of German national feeling.[4] Interest in figures like Arminius, or Hermann, the Germanic chieftain who had destroyed several Roman legions, and Charlemagne grew. In 1497 a German edition of Tacitus' *Germania* appeared. The idea of *translatio imperii*, the belief that the sceptre of imperial power had been transferred from the Romans to the Germans, was revived.

As the political cohesion of Germany began visibly to weaken and as her neighbours, particularly France, began to overtake her, a psychology of decline set in. Some Germans sought to compensate by adopting a grossly romanticized view of their own past, with great emphasis on the innate superiority of the Germans. The idea arose that the Germans were the *Urvolk*, the original people of Europe who had retained their "pure" blood and who spoke the original language of humanity, the *Ursprache*, as spoken by Adam and Eve. Much was made of the superior virtues of the Germans, their loyalty and honesty, which made them such an easy prey for foxy and devious Latins like the French. Such ideas fuelled anti- foreign sentiment, always a strong element in German national feeling. In the absence of a real all-German monarch on whom to focus their emotions, the Germans tended to focus their hatred against someone outside. In the fifteenth and sixteenth centuries the Italians and the Spaniards became the targets for such feelings. Anti-Italian feeling turned easily into anti-papal sentiment, expressed in the claim that the pope was robbing Germany, as was to become clear during the Reformation. From the seventeenth to the twentieth centuries the same role was filled by the French; the France of Louis XIV was to be seen as a rapacious thief of German land.

In the last decades of the fifteenth century this essentially negative nationalism was reinforced by more positive developments. The *Reich* began belatedly to acquire the common institutions of a state. There was also an increase in enthusiasm for the Empire, which developed from a revival of interest in Classical Rome, of which many Germans saw the Empire as the spiritual heir, and from growing discontent. The symbols of the Empire, eagles, the imperial crown and various coats of arms, were in widespread use. Groups such as the smaller nobility, the peasants and the urban poor, victims of change, looked to a revival of imperial power to protect them against their oppressors, landlords, guild masters, a greedy immoral clergy and princes beginning to make themselves absolute and depriving localities of their long-held rights. Emperors like Maximilian I and Charles V were seen by many as new messiahs leading a rebirth of the German nation and the Habsburgs employed propagandists to foster this idea.

The reign of Emperor Maximilian I (1493–1519) saw the culmination of many of these developments. He has been labelled the last medieval Emperor — others reserve this title for his successor, Charles V — responsible for the last serious attempt to rescue the Empire from the decline which was staring it in the face. His skilful propaganda contributed to the growth of a very romanticized view of his role. He was certainly similar to many of his predecessors in that he placed German affairs low in his order of priorities and devoted himself to the pursuit of dynastic interests in many parts of Europe, especially in Italy, which brought him into chronic conflict with the French. Maximilian's reign also saw a major political battle over reform of the structure of the Empire.

Discussion of the imperial constitution and calls for reform of the Empire had been growing in intensity among German rulers and intellectuals from the early fifteenth century on. In the course of that century a number of reform schemes were put forward. Some of these were by noted philosophers, such as Nicholas of Kues' *Concordantia Catholica* (1433), and some were anonymous, such as the *Reformation of the Emperor Sigismund* (dated 1439–1441). Cardinal Nicholas of Kues was Bishop of Brixen in the Tyrol. He travelled widely in Germany as papal legate between 1450 and 1452 and found a great deal wrong with the Church. These reform plans were part of the prevailing universalist spirit of the times and contained a common core of proposals, including regular meetings of the imperial diet, a permanent council of German rulers to share power with the Emperor, the creation of an effective peace-keeping apparatus in the *Reich*, a proper legal system, a standing imperial army maintained by regular taxation of all the states and an organized imperial civil service. Early attempts were made to bring in such reforms at the imperial diets of 1434 and 1437 and the Emperor Sigismund tried to strengthen his powers by creating a lasting alliance with the German cities but nothing came of these proposals as they met strong resistance from the electors. There were deep divisions between the crown and the princes on the type of reform needed and too many vested interests opposed to it. From the middle years of the century the initiative came increasingly from princes anxious to place more restrictions on the power of the crown as part of a reform package, in order to make it impossible for future emperors to recover their authority.

The country's territorial losses and growing internal lawlessness were seen as signs of obvious flaws caused by the weakness, especially in finances, of the monarchy. There were serious deficiencies in the coinage system and there was no organized imperial government or army to maintain law and order. The failure of monarchs to create an effective peace-keeping apparatus had serious effects on German political and economic life. The failure of King Wenceslas to maintain order was used to justify his deposition in 1400. There was a growing fear that the imperial title might pass to a foreign ruler and be lost to the German nation. Imperial justice was very weak, as reflected in the prevalence of private wars to settle differences under the graphically named *Faustrecht*, the law of the fist, the activities of self-appointed free courts, the *Fehmgerichte*, and the formation of leagues of cities, nobles and rulers to maintain order and settle disputes in their areas. Papal mediation was often more effective in ending disputes between the states than imperial jurisdiction. The towns were especially deeply concerned about public order. In 1488 a new league was set up in Swabia in the south west to resist encroachments by more powerful neighbouring states, especially Bavaria. This and other leagues were retrospectively authorized by the Emperor and were potentially a powerful vehicle for a revival of imperial power in south western Germany.

In the early fifteenth century attempts were made to re-establish an aulic court (*Hofgericht*) or a royal chamber court (*Kammergericht*), staffed with qualified jurists, as a supreme court for the whole Empire but they only lasted for a short time and their competence was limited by the general weakness of the crown. The aulic court worked only for brief periods, for example in the years 1470–5, when it was leased to the Elector of Mainz. The chamber court also functioned occasionally at Rottweil in Swabia. Recent research has gone some way to rehabilitating these courts, showing that they were not as totally ineffective as once thought. Although Frederick III made much of his jurisdiction, in reality it did not exist for the majority of his reign. The imperial diet met only infrequently against the opposition of the princes, who knew that it was usually only summoned when the Emperor wanted money. This situation led to appeals to the Emperor to take back lost rights and revenues and Maximilian's father Frederick III had tried this but without success.

When an imperial reform movement emerged in the 1480s Maximilian supported it in the hope that it would enable him more easily to exploit German resources in pursuit of non-German aims. He inherited from his father a package of dynastic claims and ambitions. Frederick III had a long but undistinguished reign, which lasted from 1440–93, though he handed power to his son Maximilian in 1486. His hold on the Austrian lands was never secure, he was forced to neglect German affairs and his reign was a period of instability. Traditional historiography has not been kind to him but he can be seen as the real founder of Habsburg power after the family had raised itself to prominence in Germany from minor origins. From early days the Habsburgs sought to elevate themselves above their fellow princes, for example by awarding themselves exclusively the title of archduke. Duke Rudolph IV of Austria claimed this title in 1358–9 on the basis of forged documents and it was confirmed by Frederick III. Thereafter the Habsburgs saw themselves as special, the arch-house, and their possessions as a special entity among the states of the Empire. Frederick III's adoption of the mystical device *AEIOU*, which in various translations is said to have promised Austria domination of the globe, was another sign of this, though the significance of the motto perhaps owes more to hindsight than reality.

Frederick did not want to be king/Emperor and it is not clear why the electors chose him — perhaps there was no other obvious candidate— but his election began a continuous Habsburg possession of the imperial title which lasted with one brief interruption (1742–5) until 1806. He was the last Emperor to be crowned by the pope in Rome; Maximilian proclaimed himself Emperor at Trent in February 1508, though he stated his intention of obtaining papal coronation in future. Charles V proclaimed himself Emperor and was subsequently crowned by the pope. After him German monarchs simply adopted the imperial title on their election. Frederick founded the first institutions of a distinct Austrian state and built up the power of his lands. This process was continued by Maximilian I, who benefited from good fortune. His uncle Siegmund, the ruler of the Tyrol, had no heir and handed over his lands, with substantial silver reserves, to Maximilian. Innsbruck became his "capital" and he used the revenues from mining to build up powerful infantry and artillery forces. As a result by 1500 Austria was probably the only German state with large enough dynastic resources (*Hausmacht*) to shoulder the burdens of the imperial title. In this way he helped to create the conditions for a potential revival of the *Reich* but at the same time he launched his family in pursuit of a number of wide-ranging ambitions, which distracted them from German affairs. They carried forward the long-established imperial ambitions in Italy. By marriage they acquired claims to Bohemia and Hungary. After the fall of Constantinople in 1453 they took over the old crusading ideal of liberating Byzantium.

The betrothal of Maximilian and Mary was a deliberate attempt by Frederick to link his house to the rising star of Burgundy. Charles of Burgundy also planned by this means to acquire a share of power over the Empire. When Frederick and the Duke of Burgundy met in Trier in 1473, Frederick had to slip away as the Burgundians were demanding too much. In spite of that and although the Burgundian state collapsed in January 1477 after defeat by the Swiss, the marriage went ahead. Maximilian immediately became involved in prolonged warfare against France, which also claimed the Burgundian inheritance, and the Netherlanders, who resisted his claims. Frederick III, after years of lethargy, showed remarkable energy in his old age and his successful prosecution of the war culminated in the Peace of Senlis in 1493, under which the Habsburgs kept the bulk of the Burgundian inheritance.

Although dead, the Burgundian state left behind a brilliant afterglow and the Habsburgs took over all its claims and sought to take over all its prestige by, for example, the adoption of the trappings of the Burgundian court including the Order of the Golden Fleece. Maximilian imitated Burgundian administrative techniques in his own lands and used Burgundian notions of chivalry in his propaganda to reinforce the message that the rising power of France in the West was a real threat to Germany. The re-creation of a powerful "middle kingdom" between Germany and France stretching from Switzerland to the Netherlands would not only give the Habsburgs a magnificent power base but could also be portrayed as a shield-wall for the *Reich*. Frederick also handed on to his son claims to Brittany. In 1515 Maximilian's grandson Ferdinand was married to the heiress of the Hungarian and Bohemian crowns, which, under agreements negotiated by Frederick III in 1491, fell to the Habsburgs on the death of Louis, King of Hungary at Mohács in 1526. If these claims could be made good against the Turks they would represent a great extension of Habsburg power.

All these ambitions and more were to be inherited by Maximilian's successor Charles V: in 1496 Maximilian married his son Philip to Joanna of Castile, heiress of Ferdinand and Isabella, the unifiers of Spain. A series of deaths made Maximilian's grandson Charles the unplanned universal heir to the possessions of Austria, Spain and Burgundy, adding the claims and ambitions of Castile and Aragon to those already pursued by the Habsburgs. Extensive possessions gave them extensive commitments and ambitions and Germany remained very much a side-show. Just at the time when Germany needed a monarch of her own she had to make do with a small share of someone else's. At the same time the Emperor was more than ever dependent on German resources, which were rarely forthcoming. In 1492 the *Reichstag* voted 94 000 *Gulden* to Maximilian for war against the French but only some 16 000 were actually paid over. Understandably the German princes were unsympathetic to the use of German blood and treasure in the pursuit of foreign ambitions even under Frederick III and realized that, if the Emperor became powerful as a result of foreign successes, any help they provided might simply be making a rod for their own backs. The majority of the princes were also motivated by a lively fear of becoming involved in wars of no direct concern to Germany, especially as there was before the reign of Charles V no formal provision in the German constitution for princes to come to the aid of a fellow prince under external attack.

The imperial reform movement reached its height in the 1480s and 1490s. The significance of the *Reichsreform* has often been distorted in the past in German nationalist historiography. It was not the culmination of a great campaign for change going back decades nor was it a step towards, or away from, the creation of a German nation state. From the outset there were two reform parties, one imperial, led by the Emperor, and the other led and organized by a group of princes. Their aims were broadly the same, to equip Germany with some of the institutions of government which it so obviously lacked, but the motives of the two parties were very different indeed. Maximilian planned to create a system which would guarantee him regular tax payments and military resources from the *Reich* plus a working regency system to run Germany in his absence on foreign campaigns. He also planned to establish a new supreme court which would make the princes more dependent on him.

The princely group saw reform as removing abuses, restoring proper balance to the imperial constitution, and dealing with practical problems, especially internal and external security. It was led and organized ably by a pupil of Nicholas of Kues, Berchtold von Henneberg, Archbishop-Elector of Mainz (1484–1504), a title which brought with it the post of arch-chancellor of Germany. This was the only ceremonial office held by an elector which gave its holder functions of real political weight, in this case control of the procedures and business of the imperial diet. Henneberg's party planned to give Germany an organized federal structure. The main instrument for the achievement of this was the proposed *Reichsregiment*, a standing committee containing representatives of the Emperor and the princes and equipped with considerable powers to act as a permanent executive to administer the *Reich*.

Henneberg drew his strongest support from the ecclesiastical states, the free cities and the small, poor and vulnerable states, especially in the west and south west, that is the weakest political units in Germany, which had most to fear from foreign intervention, a powerful Emperor and powerful princes. Henneberg was strongly opposed by Maximilian and the rulers of the stronger states, who had no deep interest in the Empire as long as there was no restriction on their freedom of action in their own lands. It was at this time that the concept of *teutsche Libertät* (Germanic liberty) was floated as propaganda against both imperial and princely reform plans. This was based on the totally spurious claim that the individual German states and territories had existed at some point in the remote past as sovereign entities and had then voluntarily subjected themselves to imperial control, while retaining their princely liberty. Particularism, the slow gradual devolution of the functions of government from a central authority to the individual states, was legitimized by this and resistance to attempts to restore centralized government could therefore be portrayed as the defence of the traditional freedom of the German rulers against a usurping power. Ironically, the claims of "Germanic liberty" were strengthened by Maximilian's own actions. As well as resisting the reform party, Maximilian employed an alternative policy of negotiating directly with the greater princes in order to sabotage Henneberg's plans. This was a tacit recognition that the Emperor and the greater princes were political and diplomatic equals.

The reform movement started in the Frankfurt *Reichstag* of 1486 and lasted into the 1520s.[5] It achieved some significant successes. In 1486 a general peace was proclaimed throughout the Empire, to last initially for ten years. This extended to the whole Empire the ban on all forms of violent self-help, which had earlier applied to specific places and times. At first only geographically and chronologically limited *Landfrieden* were enacted and the activity of the king's supreme court was intermittent. A peace covering the whole Empire (*Reichslandfrieden*) was first proclaimed at the Mainz *Reichstag* in 1235 and a temporary one-year *Landfrieden* was issued in 1467, involving an absolute ban on *Faustrecht*. In 1489 there was a further regularization of the procedures of the *Reichstag* (previously called the *Hoftag*), which was being summoned more frequently as the Emperor's need for money to finance his wars increased. The membership of the diet was fixed and lists were drawn up of those entitled to send delegates. It met in three houses or *curiae* and debated in secret. The towns had permanent representation in the *Reichstag* after 1489 but no vote until 1648. After the 1512 diet it was accepted that a vote of those present in the diet was binding on those who absented themselves. The principle of majority voting was already accepted in imperial elections.

Further major reforms came at the Worms `Reichstag` in 1495. Maximilian was very vulnerable, being simultaneously involved in several wars, and was forced to make concessions to the reformers. The peace of the Empire was declared perpetual. The Emperor and the German rulers signed a formal agreement to maintain peace and justice, a significant sign of how they were growing apart: *Kaiser* and *Reich* were becoming distinct and opposing concepts. Proposals were also put forward for the creation of a standing imperial army, to be financed by a general tax on all subjects under the control of the *Reichstag*. Nothing came of this. To deal with disputes, an imperial supreme court, the *Reichskammergericht* (imperial chamber court), an institution long needed in Germany, was re-established, equipped with a new ordinance and given a permanent seat in Frankfurt-am-Main. Maximilian was forced to concede a large measure of control over the new tribunal to the princes, who appointed some of its judges and, in theory, financed it. Initially it was regarded with great hostility by the towns and imperial knights, who had no say in its running, though very soon the latter group was able to win an important role in staffing the court. It was the first German central institution independent of the crown. It played a major part in the standardization and proper organization of justice in the Empire and the states in line with advanced judicial thinking at the time. In 1498 Maximilian set up a separate supreme tribunal under his total control, the imperial aulic council (*Reichshofrat*). The two courts were to remain in existence and rivals until the end of the Empire in 1806.

The Worms diet also instituted a regular imperial tax, the Common Penny, a universal progressive property and poll tax, to finance the *Reichskammergericht*. The funds, collected by the clergy, were to be administered by an imperial treasurer in Augsburg under the control of the *Reichstag*. A population survey was carried out to assess liability to the tax. As it turned out, this system could not be made permanent because of the opposition of powerful princes and in 1505 the *Reichsmatrikel*. the old system of matricular contributions, was restored. Under this each state's obligations to the *Reich* were laid down in proportion to its size. The tax was levied as Roman Months (*Römermonate*), so called because it was originally a tax raised to finance the Emperor's journey to Rome for his coronation by the pope. Under the *Matrikel* the collection and apportionment of imperial taxes were left to the state governments. This allowed traditional exemptions, for example of the nobility, to remain, unlike under the Common Penny. The diets of 1507 and 1510 also accepted the principle that subjects could be called upon to pay imperial taxes, an important constitutional point.

The 1497 diet issued the first imperial recess (*Reichsabschied*), a collection of the laws passed during the session, a recognition of the shared legislative authority of the Emperor and the *Reichstag*. The reform party pressed for the establishment of a *Reichsregiment*. Maximilian was able to block this but had to accept annual meetings of the diet, which was to become the supreme legislative authority in the *Reich*, making it a constitutional monarchy. By the meeting of the diet of Augsburg in 1500 Maximilian could no longer resist pressures in favour of the *Reichsregiment* and had to agree to its establishment. It was to consist of twenty members under the presidency of the Emperor or his nominee and was to include the seven electors and other members appointed by the German rulers. Plans were again floated for a standing army of 300 000 under the control of the *Reichsregiment*. In fact the *Regiment* only lasted until 1502 and in its brief life it was unable to achieve anything. The German rulers refused to provide funds for it, it had no bureaucracy to service it and no means of executing its decisions. Maximilian refused to accept any decisions affecting his own territories. He also refused to pay the yield of the Common Penny from his lands into the central treasury but appropriated it for his own use. He was as guilty of particularism as any of the German princes.

The final major achievement of the reform movement came in 1500 with the creation of the system of imperial Circles (*Reichskreise*) based on the constituencies electing members to the proposed *Reichsregiment*, regional unions of state designed to maintain internal order and external defence. By 1512 there were ten Circles in all. They covered the whole Empire except the Habsburgs' possessions in the east, Bohemia, Silesia and Lusatia, the lands of the imperial knights and a few other small territories. The Habsburgs' other lands dominated the Austrian Circle. The rulers in the Circles were supposed to hold regular meetings to concert arrangements to fulfil the functions of the organization. The majority never operated in the way intended.

Although it came after Maximilian's death, a list of major constitutional changes during the reform period should include the first capitulation of election (*Wahlkapitulation*), a list of promises and undertakings imposed by the electors on Charles V on his election in 1519. This document included, among other things, a formal guarantee by the Emperor to the German rulers of undisturbed possession of their lands and rights, even if these had originally been acquired as temporary grants from earlier monarchs. That was an open recognition of the federal nature of the Holy Roman Empire. Similar capitulations of election were given by all subsequent Emperors and became part of the law of the Empire.

In the light of the wide-ranging ambitions and lavish plans he pursued, Maximilian's reign must be judged unsuccessful. This was recognized by the Emperor in the instructions given while he was dying that his corpse was to be disfigured and was not to be embalmed before burial. Although his marriage policy was eventually to add Bohemia and Hungary to the possessions of his house, he failed in France and Italy. He introduced reforms in the government of his lands on which his successors could begin to build the institutions of an Austrian state but his assertion of monarchical power, involving infringement of the special rights of the various provinces and on the political power of the nobility and towns, aroused opposition. His death was followed by a period of disorder in various parts of his lands. In the Empire he failed to persuade the electors to elect his grandson Charles as king of the Romans, an office which enabled its holder to succeed to the imperial title without an election. This involved the Habsburgs in massive expenditure in bribes. The reform movement failed as neither the princely nor the imperial party gained its objectives; some argue that Germany was anyway too far advanced along the road of particularism for the trend to be reversed.

Arguably Germany was potentially far more united at the beginning of the sixteenth century than for centuries. The missing ingredient was a German religion and Luther seemed to provide this: he was an anti-foreign German nationalist who deliberately used the German language. A sign of the times came in August 1518 when Maximilian asked the *Reichstag* for money for a crusade. Instead the German states presented a list of their grievances against the papacy. The Worms diet of 1521 debated lavish plans to build on the foundations laid down in the *Reichsreform* but it was too late as the Lutheran Reformation was already sweeping the country.

3 The Reformation in Germany

The history of the German Reformation and its effects is readily available in a number of excellent works. Its analysis in this chapter will therefore be restricted to a few aspects. The role of Luther and theological elements in the Reformation will be examined only briefly. An excessively Luther-centric view is anyway dangerous as there were other movements at work at the same time which could have overtaken and swamped Lutheranism. More attention will be given to the mass movements associated with the Reformation and, in particular, to the effects of the events of the period 1517 to 1555 on German political and constitutional life.

These effects were momentous. Martin Luther certainly considered the Reformation a substantial break with the past: in a letter written in March 1542 to Jakob Probst he stated that Germany was finished and would never again be what it had been. Although it was deeply rooted in essentially medieval attitudes, the Reformation acted as a modernizing force in social, political and intellectual life. It was not, however, part of an early bourgeois revolution in the marxist sense, arising from the crisis of the feudal production system. There was nothing resembling the bourgeoisie in the modern sense in sixteenth-century Germany and the old medieval orders of society were not replaced by modern classes during the Reformation. [1]

The Reformation was a complex multi-level phenomenon, affecting Germany from top to bottom, the imperial and princely courts, the diets of the Empire and of individual states, universities, towns and villages. Within it a large number of different religious, political and social movements were at work, all seeking different ends but all united by the common theme of discontent with the prevailing situation and all reaching a decisive point at the same time. People at

30

all levels of society had grievances. There was social tension between lords and peasants, rich and poor peasants, nobles and middle-class people, guild masters and apprentices, urban patricians and guild members. Many princes were dissatisfied with the state of the imperial constitution, many educated laymen and clerics as well as ordinary people were profoundly unhappy about the Church and its theology and ordinary Germans had much to object to in the social and economic situation. All these different discontents were mingled together inextricably and it is impossible to attribute the troubles of the Reformation period to any single cause, economic, political or religious.

The Church had a political importance in Germany only equalled in the papal states. Its landholdings were huge and many of its prelates, archbishops, bishops, abbots, abbesses, deans and the heads of the Teutonic Order and the Order of St John, were political rulers of states as well as senior clergymen. Three archbishops were electors. Many prince-prelates employed subsidiary bishops to carry out religious functions while they devoted themselves to government. At a lower level clergymen drawing incomes from Church livings carried out educational, charitable, administrative and academic functions. Religious changes, when they happened, had a huge impact on the lives of ordinary Germans, not just the elites.

The period of flux which preceded and accompanied the Reformation, could have had several results, including the destruction of the Roman Catholic Church throughout Germany, a social revolution, a united Germany or a totally disunited Germany. In fact a combination of particular circumstances produced a very strange outcome. In the early years of the sixteenth century a national Germany was emerging throwing off earlier universalist pretensions and becoming more self-consciously German, though still, apparently, hovering between potential unity and a formal federal system. As it turned out, the Reformation was to produce a new factor of disunity. It ruined Charles V's plans to revive a strong Empire as the core of a revived Latin Christendom rescued from the ills of national and dynastic selfishness, which threatened its inner cohesion just when the Ottoman Empire was organizing itself for expansion under Suleiman the Magnificent. Charles' efforts could have succeeded as there was a yearning for *renovatio imperii* and disappointment over the unfulfilled potential of Maximilian's reign. But Charles refused to place himself at the head of the Lutheran movement while at the same time he tried to force the papacy to reform the Church. As a result he fell between two stools. Charles had too many obligations and was able to devote very little of his time to German affairs. At the height of his power after the victory over the Protestant rulers at Mühlberg in 1547, he was unable to make his will felt. Increasingly he left conduct of German and Austrian affairs to his brother Ferdinand, who preferred the policy of winning over the princes by concession rather than confrontation.

The Reformation also strengthened individual German rulers, both Protestant and Catholic, and further weakened the Emperor, whose efforts to increase his power in Germany were interpreted as part of the militant Counter-Reformation. The German princes were provided with ideological justification for their particularism. It is interesting that other European monarchs were also frightened by the potential of Charles' empire and some began to create a cult of imperial monarchy for themselves as a counter-measure, including Henry VIII of England and Francis I of France. Even Charles' brother, Ferdinand, effective ruler of the Austrian parts of the Empire, undermined imperial power out of fear that the imperial title would pass to Charles' son Philip of Spain and that "Spanish tyranny" would become a reality in Germany.

The Reformation produced a period of religious chaos and Luther eventually turned to the German rulers to restore order and take over the organization of the churches. As a result, state churches emerged, each with a prince or urban magistracy at its head, and the Protestant rulers acquired a substantial field of government in which they had no superior but God and were not even nominally subordinate to the Emperor. In many cases this was not immediately obvious as the period saw many great battles between princes and their subjects and parliamentary Estates, often involving the question of control of the resources of the newly reformed churches. The Reformation revived the idea of the restoration of power, ecclesiastical and political, to the local community; the idea that the German Protestant princes were able to seize the wealth of the Church and use it at will is wrong. The political power of many Catholic rulers was also increased as a result of the Reformation. The papacy was often glad to give them wide powers over the revenues and personnel of their churches in order to further the battle against heresy. Bavaria was a striking example of the successful use of the opportunities offered. By the second half of the century it was established as a major local power in southern Germany.

The social discontent which played a major role in the Reformation also helped the cause of particularism as it demonstrated the need for strong government which only the German princes could provide. The revolt of the imperial knights in 1522–3, although easily put down, seriously frightened the authorities. Chronic rural unrest, leading to the great peasants' revolt of 1524–5, major disturbances in many cities, serious economic and social problems and the perceived menace of the revolutionary Anabaptists, culminating in their seizure of Münster in 1535, were regarded as the outcome of a spiral of disorder and signs of the imminent dissolution of society which only the concentration of power in the hands of an authoritarian government could prevent.

The Reformation period also increased foreign influence in Germany as Catholic and Protestant rulers called on the help of their foreign co-religionists, setting a very dangerous precedent. German national pride suffered a number of severe blows with territorial losses to the Turks and to the French during the wars of religion, especially the bishoprics of Metz, Toul and Verdun, which opened up western Germany to French penetration, a constant feature of German political life until 1814.

Martin Luther, an Augustinian monk and from 1512 professor of theology at the Saxon university of Wittenberg, founded in 1502, is seen as the originator of the German Reformation. [2] The theatrical events of October 1517 in Wittenberg, Luther's attack on the sale of indulgences and his publication of the ninety-five theses, have been frequently described. Their significance is traditionally exaggerated. Perhaps a more decisive turning point came on 10 December 1520 when Luther, in response to an order to burn his works, burned books of Canon Law and the papal bull of excommunication at Wittenberg. The movement for change in the Church was already established before 1517 and Luther had published theological works anonymously in German before 1517, a sign of his German patriotism and wish to appeal beyond a purely academic audience.

Under different circumstances Luther might have been completely forgotten. Criticism of abuses in the Church was long-standing and was another aspect of the deep piety and enthusiastic popular religious observance in the fifteenth century. Orthodoxy was the rule. Heretical movements such as the Waldensians, Hussites and pre-Christian nature religions existed in Germany but they had few supporters. Spontaneous reform within the Church commenced well before 1517, for example in the restoration of the spirituality of the Benedictine Order which began in the early fifteenth century and proceeded with the support of many state and city governments.

Other leaders like Melanchthon, Bucer, Oecolampadius and Osiander, who did not give their names to Churches, were as important as Luther in consolidating the Reformation. Luther's historic reputation is based on a double distortion. In Catholic myth he was demonized as the man who, single-handed, smashed the unity of Christendom while in later German nationalist historiography he became a German hero, fighting alien forces undermining the fatherland. Luther contributed to the latter as he was certainly virulently xenophobic. He wrote of the Reformation as leading to the partitioning of Germany into Roman and free Empires and he consciously looked back to Arminius as a forerunner in resisting Roman tyranny over Germany.

His importance lay in his popularization of a clear theological alternative to Catholic doctrine and in the fact that he came to lead the first established Protestant Church. Luther, an idealistic, zealous and learned man, went through a deep personal religious crisis which led him to produce a new statement on Christianity. He was not modern. His attitudes had little to do with the Renaissance or humanism but were very characteristic of the late Middle Ages. Like most people living at the time, he had a deep fear of the tortures of hell, which the propaganda of the Church had made very real to them, and terrifying doubts about the possibility of salvation. [3] Much ink has been spilt on the question of whether Luther derived his ideas from earlier writers or in seeking psychological causes for his actions. Certainly there was nothing new about his basic ideas, which had been present as a kind of puritan element within Catholic theology for centuries. What made Luther important was the moment and circumstances in which he chose to publicize his views and the immoderate language which he used.

Although he made use of anti-clericalism to win support for his ideas and painted a very unflattering portrait of the pre-Reformation Church in his writings, he did not seek the regeneration of the Catholic Church by removing its abuses. He attacked what had become one of the fundamentals of the Catholic faith, the very essence of Catholicism, on which the entire structure of the Church was based, good works, and offered an alternative faith, by means of which a thorough rejuvenation of Christian society might be achieved. Scripture should take precedence over tradition in the Church. His basic position was that, since the Fall, man had been so utterly sinful that even to worship God was an act of gross presumption. The sacrifice on Calvary had assembled a reservoir of grace which enabled God arbitrarily to ignore the sinfulness of some men. This grace gave its recipients faith that they were saved, producing the key Lutheran doctrine of solafideism, salvation or justification by faith alone. Luther came to this conclusion at some point between 1515 and 1518. He later described how this realization, after a period of deep despair, made him feel reborn. The gates of paradise had opened for him and he had gone in.

For people unsure of salvation the new certainty offered by Luther was very appealing. All this was a perfectly tenable theological presupposition which, if taken to its logical conclusion, had the implication that man can do absolutely nothing to secure his own salvation and that therefore the Mass, the sacraments, the clergy and the whole visible Church could be dispensed with, except as a community of Christians. Luther also wished to admit the layman to what he saw as his rightful place in Christian life, which led to his doctrine of the priesthood of all believers. Certainly Luther was no believer in religious individualism; he sought freedom to interpret the faith for himself but not for everyone, although he was strongly influenced by the movement towards a more individual faith, with its emphasis on private worship and study, seen within the Church in the fifteenth century. Luther did not share the belief of, for example, the humanists, that political and social reforms would produce better men. For him man remained irretrievably sinful.

This system of ideas was complete in Luther's mind by 1512 though its implications were not worked out until the 1520s. When he was later forced to consider the organization of an external Church, the essential medievalism of his thinking became clear. He thought in terms of a collective act of praise in the vernacular with hymns and sermons, the election of clergy by congregations and the provision of local funds to maintain the clergy, charities and schools. On economic and social questions, which he considered trivial in the light of the imminent end of the world, he was very reactionary and was in no sense a father of capitalism. He believed that the disappearance of moral restraints in economic activity before 1517 was one of the causes of rising discontent and part of a general decay of old standards of behaviour. He held that many of the individual good works promoted by the Catholic Church were a waste of time and preferred organized communal good works. In his view, the resources of both state and Church, including monastic wealth, could be put to better use, particularly for welfare, charitable and educational ends. Here again, his well-documented links with late medieval humanism and the *Devotio Moderna* movement are clear.

When Luther chose to act in 1517 he was caught up in a great wave of undifferentiated enthusiasm at all levels of society. The process was initially gradual. The first impact was felt in very limited circles, in the universities and among urban intellectuals. The Church authorities at first ignored Luther's protests against the sale of indulgences, part of a massive financial transaction involving the Hohenzollern Archbishop of Mainz, the Fuggers and the Holy See. The ninety-five theses were published without Luther's knowledge in Nuremberg, Basle and Leipzig. The whole Reformation then exploded on the indulgence issue. The fact that there was such a huge popular demand for indulgences demonstrates the spiritual needs felt by the people; Luther provided an alternative answer to such needs. His ideas spread with remarkable speed and he became a German hero. This cannot be explained by the printing press alone. Personal links within clerical and intellectual networks were also very important. His appeal fell on very receptive soil, long fertilized by frustration at the mechanistic practices of the Church, virulent anti-clericalism, growing since the fifteenth century, a desire to return to a simple faith and a lovable Church and caring clergy, thought to have existed in the past. Luther represented a political as well as a religious challenge. There was also yearning for a German leader to solve Germany's problems. The Elector Frederick of Saxony (1486–1525) was being spoken of as a candidate for the imperial title at the next election and this idea was encouraged by the papacy nervous of the excessive power concentrated in the hands of Charles of Habsburg. This fact was to protect Luther for a long time. A German religion was perhaps the missing ingredient needed to cement the long-growing revival of German national sentiment.

Dissatisfaction with the state of the Church was widespread and long-standing. Criticism of the low standards of the Church in Germany came from the top to the bottom of society. There were calls for spiritual reform after the Great Schism of 1378, seen in growing calls for a Church Council, the Lollard and Hussite movements, pressure for monastic reform and groups such as *Devotio Moderna* and the Brethren of the Common Life, which tried to involve the laity more closely in the life of the Church. There were symptoms of growing religious individualism and the pursuit of personal piety rather than the mechanical worship of the organized Church, such as the rise of travelling evangelists and mass preaching and an increasing use of sermons. At its most extreme it gave rise to violent millenarianism and social revolutionary religious movements such as the

Taborites in Bohemia. The climate of opinion was changing with the Renaissance and the rise of humanism. The humanist movement was based on a dense and active network of groups and individuals all over Central Europe maintaining contacts with one another. They placed emphasis on the power of education to enable men to understand the world in which they lived. A greater proportion of the laity, especially in towns, were receiving an education and had access to new ideas.

At the Augsburg diet of 1518 a comprehensive list of the grievances (*Gravamina*) of the German nation was handed to the papal legate. This had been a frequent event in the fifteenth century. The Council of Constance (1418) tried to draft a Concordat regulating the relationship between the German Church and the papacy, including restrictions on Church taxation and indulgences and higher standards for the clergy but it did not come into effect. The *Reichstag* of 1439, 1445 and 1446 spelled out the grievances of the German nation against the papacy, proposed measures to limit papal interference in the German Church and called for a German Church council to deal with abuses. The 1521 diet of Worms, which condemned Luther for heresy, again listed over one hundred complaints against the papacy. Throughout the complaints changed little. Too many cases in Church courts were summoned to Rome in order to extract fees. Too many German benefices were given to foreigners. Church taxes were too high. Indulgences were scandalously abused. Charities and church buildings were neglected. These claims were, in reality, grossly exaggerated.

When Luther was declared an outlaw at the *Reichstag* at Worms in May 1521 he was taken under the protection of the Elector of Saxony, whose subject he was. Saxony was specifically excluded from the operation of the edict because of the political power of the elector. He was then effectively away from the public scene for two years, during which time his ideas spread rapidly from the students of the university of Wittenberg to the Augustinian Order, which adopted them as a weapon against their great rivals, the Dominicans, and beyond to the whole country. The reputation of Wittenberg as a university was made and it rapidly became the biggest in Germany. Monasteries emptied, clergy married and the Mass was abolished in many towns and on the estates of many nobles. The uniformity of Catholic worship was replaced by a bewildering variety of "reformed" Churches. Hundreds of independent centres of reformed doctrine, such as that of Martin Bucer in Mainz, later moved to Strasburg, appeared inside and outside Germany. Between 1517 and 1521 only four cities in the Empire banned Luther's writings and two of those were in the Netherlands.

The new ideas spread quickly among Germans in the Baltic and Scandinavia, Bohemia, Transylvania and the Low Countries. Had it not been for disputes over details of scriptural interpretation between Luther and Zwingli, which the Marburg debate of 1529 was unable to settle, Switzerland would also have gone Lutheran. This explosive spread was fuelled by Luther's enormous writing energy and power of communication, a charisma of the written word or "inspired journalism". The Lutheran press campaign, the circulation of Luther's sermons and pamphlets and the writings of a host of other reformers in hundreds of thousands of copies, was in itself a remarkable phenomenon and a sign of the fevered nature of the times. As important were the thousands of woodcuts, which spread the message of the Reformation, and later the Counter-Reformation, to the ninety per cent of the population who were illiterate. In spite of efforts by various authorities to stop their spread, because of fear of putting the scriptures in the hands of ordinary people and of religious disputes igniting unrest, pamphlets by and about Luther became a very profitable commodity, for which demand was high. They were cheap and easily concealed and distributed. In the absence of copyright laws and the effective collapse of censorship until the late 1530s, they continued to spread.

Luther's translation of the Bible, not the first in German but the first to achieve a mass readership, and a host of tracts and cheap news sheets appeared in numerous editions. Very soon Catholic counterblasts began to appear. In the ten years after 1510 the number of books alone printed in Germany quadrupled, with dozens of presses catering for a market which seemed insatiable, in spite of high prices. Germany was not again to experience a similar publications explosion until the late eighteenth century. In addition to the religious impact, this, along with the use of German in church services, was an important step in the final emergence of a literary High German (*Hochdeutsch*) based on the language spoken across central Germany from Mainz to Saxony, accelerating a process of linguistic standardization which had begun in the later Middle Ages. Without this, the political fragmentation of Germany might have led to the development of two or more mutually incomprehensible languages in north and south, as was to happen in the case of Dutch and German.

To most of his early supporters Luther was to prove a profound disappointment. He failed to fulfil their hopes and over the next eight years he was to lose the support of the peasants, the lower nobility, humanist intellectuals, who disliked his pessimistic view of mankind — in 1524 Erasmus published an attack on Luther's doctrines — and most of his fellow theologians. At the same time he won over a substantial section of the German princes and governments, which ensured the survival of his movement. By 1523 Luther was saying something rather different from what he had been saying in 1517. The notions of a personal interior religion, a Church free of state control and wide toleration of different religious views had gone and Luther had come to realize the need for a Church with a distinct clergy, external organization and state protection, if only to bring some order to the religious anarchy and threatened social revolution which his early actions had unleashed in Germany. Between 1525 and 1526 he accepted the Elector of Saxony's right to inspect and organize a state Lutheran Church, which began in 1527. The prince thereby became head of the Church and acquired control of a vital sphere of government, with a major role in education and the administration of charities, potentially substantial revenues and an important organ of propaganda, in which for the first time he was truly sovereign as he was supreme bishop by the grace of God and not acting as an agent of the Emperor.

The Church claimed total authority over major aspects of peoples' daily lives. Saxony was followed in installing a new state Church structure by other states, including Mansfeld, Brunswick-Lüneburg, Ansbach, Hesse, Mecklenburg, Anhalt, ducal Prussia and Brandenburg. State Churches on the Lutheran model were, however, initially the exception in the towns. Apart from a few like Nuremberg and Magdeburg, most German free cities, when they decided on their own form of Church, opted at first for the Zwinglian Zürich reformation and entered the Lutheran community only in the 1530s. [4] Some commentators have argued that Lutheranism, in contrast to the second-wave Reformation movement Calvinism, bred apolitical attitudes in its followers. This is oversimple and exaggerates the differences. Calvinism was to teach the duty of Christians to strive for the improvement of state and society in an effort to create a Godly community. Lutheranism urged an abstention from political involvement, preferring a cultivation of the inner spiritual life. It did not teach mindless obedience of authority, as those who sought to portray Luther as a proto-Nazi were later to claim. To Lutherans the spiritual was all-important and the secular incidental. Legitimate authority was to be respected as long as it did not infringe religious rights. It is significant that Luther later had to be pressurized into endorsing the Lutheran political alliance, the League of Schmalkalden.

Monocausal explanations of the early success of the Lutheran movement are unacceptable. Recent work has revealed clearly the importance of social, economic and political factors, alongside spiritual concerns, in producing an audience receptive to Luther's ideas. It is often impossible to disentangle one from the other. After 1517 movements for political and religious change came together. Detailed local studies have shown the enormous variation from case to case, particularly in the cities. [5] Anti-clericalism was a common factor: the clergy formed a substantial and usually privileged part of the population of many towns. Cathedrals and their surroundings were often special enclaves exempt from town jurisdiction. In some cases the Reformation movement began among the common people and was used by parties in internal political power struggles. In many towns the Reformation became a genuinely popular movement when it was taken up by non-citizen groups keen to topple the prevailing guild oligarchy and resisted by the traditional ruling groups, who clung to the old faith for political or personal reasons. In others, for example Nuremberg, it was adopted by the ruling elite and imposed on the masses, again as a political device. In some free cities Church fraternities and charitable funds were a major political issue where these were controlled by small elites and there was suspicion of corruption. Even before 1517 many cities had exercised some control over the Church and its associated charitable and educational institutions within their walls and the Reformation enabled them to take total powers. In a few, such as Cologne, the Reformation was eventually reversed but this was rare. More commonly towns acted as bases for the spread of the new faith into surrounding rural areas. Outside the towns the lower clergy, the lower nobility of the individual states and the free imperial knights played a major role in spreading Lutheranism, especially where their status was under attack from rulers, for example by assaults on the rights of the parliamentary Estates. Everywhere the clergy played a very important role. External factors were also important. Many of the small states bordering substantial Protestant states like Saxony and Hesse found themselves under strong pressure to adopt the new faith.

The popular movement for religious reform in the towns and cities spanned the whole Reformation period and continued for most of the century after the establishment of state churches. Out of sixty imperial free cities, only five of the smallest did not adopt the

Reformation and hundreds of other towns were involved, often long before their rulers. The movement has been intensively studied in recent years after long neglect by historians of the role of the cities in German history. The German city states embodied a tradition of urban self-government and communal pride also seen in Italy, Switzerland and the Low Countries. Levels of educational provision were usually high in towns and they often employed modern administrative techniques, for example written law codes, before the princely states. Many were suffering increasing demographic, economic and political problems in the early years of the sixteenth century, producing pressure on the established authorities.

The Reformation saw the last flowering of medieval urban republicanism in Germany. The ruling elites in many cities tried to strengthen themselves in imitation of princes and there were campaigns to win for the imperial free cities, equality with the electors and princes in the imperial diet. The larger free cities began to hold joint meetings, the town diets (*Städtetag*) to concert policy and lend weight to their grievances. The first was held in 1522 in Esslingen, which produced a *Recess* listing grievances and expressing opposition to a common imperial external tariff, the *Reichszoll*, an idea which had long been circulating. This attempt to unite the towns to increase their political muscle in Germany came to nothing; divisions were deep, a factor to be made worse by religious disputes, and too many pleaded poverty. The early sixteenth century saw more frequent riots in towns. Some free cities and many towns in princely states were facing growing encroachments on their rights from rulers modernizing and centralizing their governments and some took advantage of the troubled times to try to reverse this process and recover their autonomy.

Many of the princes and city governments which became "Lutheran" did not regard the schism in the Church as permanent but were compelled to step in and try to control a movement which was becoming essentially popular and threatening to become dangerously radical. It was in order to restore control that Luther left Wartburg Castle, to which he had withdrawn for safety after the diet of Worms, and returned to Wittenberg. In the early stages of the Reformation large numbers of autonomous religious communities (*Gemeinden*) sprang up spontaneously and there was a real fear that this movement would become political. It is also far too simple to see the princes' adoption of the new faith as motivated by greed for the Church's wealth or political independence from the Emperor. Some may have used Lutheranism for base ends but others, such as Luther's patrons the electors of Saxony and Margrave George of Ansbach, were sincerely motivated by a desire for religious reform and saw themselves as the divinely appointed instruments of such reform. There had long been disquiet on the part of many German governments over deficiencies in the Church and what was seen as the squandering of its resources. A strong movement towards state and city control of the Church had appeared in Germany long before 1517 and in some cases the Reformation completed the process of giving princes and city governments control over Church property and jurisdiction. German support for the conciliar movement in the early fifteenth century was strong in the hope that it would lead to reforms and a transfer of powers over the Church into the hands of secular authorities. Before 1500 the rulers of Jülich-Cleves, Austria, Saxony and Brandenburg, for example, had entered agreements with the papacy giving them considerable control over the Church in their states. The Emperor Frederick III gained the right to appoint to a number of important bishoprics within his lands. Secular rulers' ability to interfere in the running of the Church was enhanced by the fact that many high positions in it were held by members of the ruling families or their clients. The 1446 *Reichstag* gave the German rulers substantial rights over their Churches and by the 1448 Concordat of Vienna the papacy confirmed these rights. The pope was left with only vague powers of supervision. It did not, for example, have the right to fill German benefices with Italians.

There was no great rush to seize the wealth of the Church in the early stages of the Reformation. The majority of rulers remained concerned to preserve imperial law and some were very reluctant to act. For example the Elector of Brandenburg Joachim II began to take control of the Church in 1539–40 but initially only as an interim measure until a German Church council was convened. In the 1520s the majority of the "Lutheran" rulers were waiting for the calling of a German national synod to make final dispositions regarding the organization of the Church, including decisions on its property. Plans were circulating to use its revenues to maintain an imperial standing army, as well as for educational, charitable and religious purposes. The heavy additional costs facing governments caused by inflation and mounting military, administrative and diplomatic expenditure made the wealth of the Church very tempting but, unlike in England, the German Reformation did not lead to a wholesale looting of Church property. In some cases, when a ruler became lukewarm in his support of the new faith, defence of the Holy Evangelium passed to the Estates, who were sometimes able to prevent a squandering of Church funds and were prepared to pay their rulers substantial taxes to induce them to act as defenders of the faith. Eventually the position of most rulers was strengthened, even if it took time. [6] Church property was secularized and often taken into the prince's domain, providing extra income. It was frequently sold to the nobility. The elimination of the clergy from the parliamentary Estates and the state's enhanced access to the manpower, buildings and facilities of the Church were additional factors strengthening the state.

It was Charles V's inability to provide a national German solution for the problem, as he was urged to do by, for example, Johann Sleidan (known as Sleidanus) in his *Oratio* of 1544, which called on the Emperor to put himself at the head of the Protestant faith, which forced rulers to take the initiative into their own hands, especially when the Reformation threatened to become anarchic. Charles was absent from Germany during the decisive years, 1521 to 1530. When he returned after nine years in Spain he was at the height of his power and was horrified at the spread of heresy and the social unrest which had grown up in his absence. Recent studies have thrown a great deal of light on the so-called Radical Reformation, an inchoate movement of religious sects. [7] These, condemned by Luther as "false brethren" and "mad saints", sprang into existence independently of Luther's protest but were unwittingly encouraged by him. Luther was horrified by them and they had a substantial impact on the development of his ideas and attitudes.

They appeared very quickly in the first weeks of the Reformation in many parts of Germany and most had utopian social revolutionary programmes. Luther had no direct social teaching as such but what he said was easy to misunderstand, by those who had no privilege, as a general attack on privilege. He also helped to put the Bible in the hands of the semi-educated. The Radical Reformation attracted a mass following and by 1530 in terms of numbers of followers it was bigger than all other movements put together. The Radical Reformation was a Protean development but a number of generalizations can be made. The various movements on the radical wing of the Reformation were very similar. They usually appeared spontaneously. They covered a wide spectrum from the Spiritual and Mennonite movements, pacifist, contemplative and humane, to violent revolutionary sects seeking to initiate God's kingdom on earth by the extermination of the godless. The movement was not new but had existed as an undercurrent for centuries in the form of relics of pre-Christian religions, for example in witchcraft, or as heretical movements driven underground but not eradicated.

Groups known as the Peasant Biblicists or the *Illuminati* also predated Luther. These involved the sudden appearance of a charismatic leader, who claimed to have experienced visions and to have acquired special knowledge of some imminent huge catastrophe, which he or she had to pass on to the world. In the century before the Reformation several such leaders had quickly attracted a substantial following of disciples and taken on a very threatening character until put down. They were often lower class and violent and preached dangerous egalitarian and democratic ideas. The best known leaders of the Radical Reformation were Andreas Karlstadt, who had great influence in Switzerland, Gabriel Zwilling in Wittenberg and Thomas Müntzer. One of the most prominent groups to appear before Luther were the Zwickau Brethren in Saxony, led by the weavers Niklas Storch and Thomas Drechsel. This was influenced by the earlier Taborite movement in neighbouring Bohemia.

The best known of these sects was the Anabaptist movement, a very diverse and fissiparous collection of groups united only by the belief in regeneration by adult rebaptism. It had developed in the Netherlands and spread into the Rhineland before Luther appeared on the scene, a product of the deep economic crisis which was striking the Dutch urban poor and middle classes. During the Lutheran Reformation it experienced a final upsurge, attracting about ten thousand people concentrated in Switzerland and south and central Germany, again fuelled by a sharp recession from 1528 to 1534, which caused another wave of religious extremism. In 1529 the *Reichstag* banned Anabaptism. It culminated in 1535 in the seizure of the city of Münster by a group of revolutionary Anabaptists under "King" Jan of Leyden. For years before thousands of religious extremists had moved into the city from the Netherlands and neighbouring German states, producing a mounting political confrontation with the authorities. In 1532 Münster became officially Lutheran and in 1534 Anabaptism won hundreds of converts in a wave of millenarian hysteria. For some reason, it was believed the end of the world would begin in the city. The Anabaptist New Jerusalem held out against a siege for months during which terrible atrocities were committed. The *Reichstag* voted funds for its capture which happened in June 1535. This brief experience of the fiery breath of anarchy sent a shudder of horror through Europe and unleashed another wave of terrible persecution against the sects. The last serious outbreak of revolutionary Anabaptism occurred on the Lower Rhine in the late 1560s.

Although the majority of the Radical Reformation movements were docile, tolerant and egalitarian, they were viciously persecuted, being seen as a threat to all order, religious, social and economic. The development is well illustrated in the recently-studied career of Melchior Hoffmann, a fur dealer from south western Germany, who became a convinced follower of Luther and acted as a missionary of the new faith among the German-speaking communities in Scandinavia and the Baltic. In 1529 he broke with Lutheranism because it had become the faith of rich urban patricians in northern Germany. He went to Strasburg, which until 1534 was ready to tolerate a wide variety of different faiths within its walls. He gravitated into a spiritualist Anabaptist movement but quickly moved on to lead a group within the revolutionary wing, known as the Melchiorites, which had a substantial following among the lower classes facing severe economic and social problems. He was imprisoned from 1535, when the city turned against extremists, until his death in 1543.

The sects were deeply involved in the most important event of the Reformation period, the great peasant revolt in southern and central Germany in 1525–6, called the Peasants' War. It was the long-predicted culmination of long-developing movements in Germany and other parts of Europe, which had produced a series of major risings at the turn of the century, the most serious in Germany and Hungary. The best known outbreaks were associated with the *Bundschuh* in south west Germany before 1500 and the *Arme Konrad* in Württemberg in 1514. Both were wide-spread conspiratorial movements with known ringleaders. In the areas where the rising of 1525–6 was most intense, stability had already been undermined by a local war between the towns of the Swabian League and some of the aristocracy and the rebellion of a number of imperial knights (1522–3).

The Peasants' War took the form of risings all over southern and central Germany and was perhaps the greatest mass movement in German history. From the outset the rising adopted a defensive attitude. It began with meetings, petitions and calls for mediation and only later did it become violent. [8] It began in the summer of 1524 near Lake Constance and spread rapidly up the Rhine, into the Moselle valley, east into Austria and north into Saxony and Brunswick. A second wave of risings came later in 1525 and 1526 in the Rhine valley, Alsace, the Tyrol, Salzburg, Franconia and Thuringia.

Detailed research into the rising has modified older views which saw it as a uniform movement of the dispossessed. It was in no sense a national movement and remained provincial and localized, though certain common features were visible. The rising was most intensive in those areas where the rural economy was most advanced and where a man's land was always divided among all his children on his death, leading to overpopulation and serious land hunger. Significantly, Bavaria and most of northern Germany were spared. These were areas with stronger state governments, with fewer ecclesiastical states and free knights and where land-hunger was less acute than in the south and west. A variety of factors, including the proximity of towns, closeness to main roads and population densities, influenced village prosperity. Only peasants able to sell products directly on the market could take advantage of the price rise. Jurisdiction over villages in these areas was often shared between several lords, the Habsburgs, the Church and the nobility. The competition between them to impose a single lordship often added to the peasants' problems. The composition of the peasant "armies" varied from region to region. It was more than a large-scale riot but highly organized and led by men with military experience. It was joined by the poor and not-so-poor and leadership of the movement was taken over in some areas by townsmen, richer peasants who wanted to rise more quickly and enjoy higher status, and even officials and minor noblemen, who were casualties of the political and economic changes taking place and who used the grievances of the peasants to win over a following. Well-known examples of the last were Götz von Berlichingen, Florian Geyer and Tilman Riemenschneider, Mayor of Würzburg. Though it was an overwhelmingly rural phenomenon, many towns, especially those in decline or experiencing serious internal problems, played a prominent role, for example Mühlhausen in Thuringia. A series of urban risings in Speyer, Worms, Frankfurt, Mainz, Cologne, with echoes in the Netherlands and Poland, was sparked off by the rising.

In some of the towns of the south west there was a movement to secede from the Empire and join the Swiss confederation and they were accused of wishing to spread Swiss-style republicanism throughout Germany. The example of "free" Switzerland, where the peasants believed there were autonomous self-governing peasant communes, was important, especially in Swabia. In the Tyrol and Salzburg the movement took on a constitutional tone, with plans for the parliamentary Estates, the *Landschaft*, which contained peasant representatives, to retake political power. Some more extreme groups put forward radical utopian plans for a new German state of burghers and peasants under a paternal Emperor with the nobility reduced to the status of paid officials. It is on these aspects of the rising that East German historians have concentrated, who portray it as a failed bourgeois national revolution. From the outset a prominent role was played by Thomas Münzer, a charismatic leader who had emerged in the Zwickau Brethren in 1520, had quickly broken with Luther and who then went around among the peasants and workers in the Saxon mining areas preaching that the apocalypse was imminent and advocating a simple social Christianity based on the freedom and equality of all men. The peasants, he said, were to purge the world of the ungodly, especially the nobility, in preparation for the second coming. In Thuringia under Münzer and in the Tyrol under Michael Gaismair (or Geismair) a kind of primitive Christian communism also emerged within the movement but it was not typical.

The peasant revolt involved a complex mixture of economic, political, religious and social motives but it was at basis reactionary and restorative, growing out of a general yearning for a return to the "good old days". The peasants resented the growth of the intrusive and standardizing state, assaults on village self-government and the price rise. They sought to put the clock back to what was seen as a fairer world before their position had started to deteriorate. They opposed the village ordinances (Dorfordnungen), imposed by the state and supervised by its officials, which replaced the self-government of village communes based on traditional unwritten laws. Their support of a "moral economy" was part of a wider anti-monopoly movement arising from a conviction that the sufferings of the poor were due to the activities of wicked men, monopolists, usurers and engrossers. They called for "Godly law" (göttliches Recht) and return of the "old law"; the Reformation provided a link between the two. Godly law was to become a new universally applicable criterion of right and wrong, overriding the variety of local laws and conventions. The peasants were prepared to have their grievances judged by learned and pious men of the new faith, who would decide on the basis of Godly law.

The peasants also looked for the return of a powerful mystical Emperor who would step in to humble their oppressive landlords, the nobility and higher clergy, who, under pressure from falling grain prices and rental incomes since the late fifteenth century, sought to cushion themselves against economic change by exploiting their tenants more harshly. The measures adopted by lords seeking to increase their take from the peasants varied from place to place and included restricting their access to forests and pastures and employing jurisdiction as a source of revenue, major causes of grievance. No one seemed able to protect the peasants against restrictions on their freedom, increasing since the late fifteenth century, and the loss of their traditional rights. The main targets of peasant anger were not the higher lords but their agents in the localities, especially if they were based in the towns. Rural resentment of the towns was an important factor, made worse by a movement of urban capital into the countryside in the later medieval period, which ruptured long-standing personal ties. Divisions within the peasant community were also a factor, with landless labourers seeking to acquire a share of common land and the richer peasants seeking to stop them.

The most important statement of the peasants' "programme" was the Twelve Articles of Memmingen of February/March 1525. This was issued after three peasant "unions", those of the Danube valley, Lake Constance and the Allgäu, came together there. Subsequently many copies were printed in several widely spaced centres. It was a document full of biblical quotations, combining social, economic, political and religious demands. The notion of community (*Gemeinde*) was central to everything. The peasants called for community owner-ship of woods, waters and meadows, the abolition of rents, tithes and serfdom. They wanted a restoration of their traditional rights of access to common lands, forests and fisheries. They were horrified at the steady encroachment of the state on their lives, a state which claimed to own everything, the fish in the river, the birds in the air, the wind which turned the mill and the current in the river. They opposed the expansion of the state at the cost of village self-government and the spread of Roman Law, although they sometimes benefited from it.

Hostility to the legal profession was a powerful unifying element among the different strands of the peasant revolt. The damage caused to their lands by the lords' exercise of their hunting rights and increased taxes and tithes had long figured in lists of peasant grievances. Christian love and justice were to determine relations between lords and tenants: the lords should protect their subjects and they should in return pay him just dues. They condemned the failure of the clergy to give them the comfort they needed in hard times and demanded the free preaching of the gospel by clergy elected by the community and paid from the yield of tithes. Any surplus was to be used for purposes useful to the community. They stated that they had looked in the Holy Evangelium and could find there no justification for the things they objected to.

The peasant leaders' call for the creation of a great tribunal of princes and reforming clergy to judge their cause, of course, came to nothing and violence spread. It was very easy for the authorities to split the peasants and defeat them piecemeal. The risings were put down with great harshness from April 1525 into the summer of 1526 by German mercenary troops returning after Charles V's great victory at Pavia. The Swabian League and rulers of both faiths co-operated to crush it. In mid-May a great peasant "parliament" was held at Heilbronn, which put forward a number of draft proposals, some including plans for reform of the Empire, the significance of which has sometimes been exaggerated, but it only lasted a short time because of the approach of the Swabian League army, which on 14 and 15 May crushed the main peasant army at Frankenhausen. Other defeats followed. It is estimated that about 75 000 peasants were killed. For areas which were overpopulated this was not a catastrophe. In the subsequent judicial procedures many ringleaders were killed but the majority were given corporal punishments or fines. Collective fines were also levied against whole villages.

The defeat of the peasantry had significant long-term effects. Probably, except at a local level, there was no immediate sharp deterioration in their position, which was poor anyway. An attempt was made to avoid further trouble. In 1526 the imperial diet at Speyer considered the grievances of the peasantry, including the Twelve Articles, and a special committee was established to deal with this matter. This eventually put forward a number of proposals for reform, at the same time, significantly, taking the opportunity to attack abuses in the Church. It recommended that no more taxes should be paid from the German Church to Rome, restrictions on the operations of Church courts and steps to improve the quality of the clergy, including higher pay for them. For the peasants it suggested steps to remove their most obvious grievances, such as lighter labour services and improvements in the administration of justice. The report was rejected by the full *Reichstag*, which recommended firmer measures to deal with any future risings rather than steps to remove their causes. A few empty exhortations to lords to behave with more humanity to their peasants were widely ignored, except by the Swabian League, which tried to enforce them on its members.

The picture remained very varied. In some parts of Germany, for example the Tyrol, the peasantry was able to resist attacks on its position through its representation in the local Estates. Elsewhere governments, where they were strong enough to do so, took steps to remove grievances and to negotiate compromise settlements between peasants and lords. In most parts of Germany the bulk of the peasantry was effectively excluded from political, economic and social power before the rising and this was to remain the position until the nineteenth century. Their position deteriorated because of the growing burden of payments to the state, the lord and the tithe-owner but it would be very wrong to regard them as leaderless and voiceless after 1525. They could and did defend their rights in the imperial courts or, ultimately, by violence. It was widely accepted that the Emperor had a duty to protect subjects against the tyranny of their lords. Peasant communities, especially in the south west, funded appeals to the *Reichskammergericht* and often showed remarkable sophistication. If in sixteenth-century Japan villagers went in search of seven samurai, in Germany they went to find lawyers. Unrest was endemic in the German countryside until the French Revolution. The Church and the lower nobility were also badly hit by the rising and the main beneficiaries were the greater nobles and the larger secular rulers. The need to restore order gave the German rulers an excuse to increase their power while a growing determination to bring an end to religious chaos speeded up the movement towards state control of the Protestant churches.

There has been great debate about the links between the revolt and the Reformation. No doubt the general effervescence which accompanied Luther's protest encouraged the movement and aroused an expectation of change. At first Luther's attitude towards the rising was ambiguous. He had no sympathy with the peasants' social and economic aspirations, arguing that they had a duty to obey their lords. Their rebellion was a sin. Equally the lords had an obligation to protect their peasants. He considered that some of the peasants' grievances were justified and condemned lords whose maltreatment of their peasants had helped to cause the rising. He believed the peasants had been led astray by false prophets. He firmly denied that the peasants had any right to find their own religion on the basis of individual interpretations of the Bible or to use religious arguments to justify attacks on the social order. He is condemned for his famous strongly worded and bloodthirsty pamphlet of May 1525 against the peasants, urging the lords to put them down with brutality, which led to a hardening of attitudes. The first edition of this contained an earlier pamphlet calling for a mediated settlement but this disappeared from later printings and was forgotten.

This was probably not, as has been suggested, a sign of his political dependence on the ruling class but originated in his theological views.

Luther accepted a hierarchical society and the need for authority. In this he differed from Zwingli, who taught that subjects had a right, or a duty, to overthrow an authority which did not maintain a proper Christian order in the world. He put forward his famous doctrine of the two kingdoms (*Zwei-Reich-Lehre*), which drew a clear distinction between religious and secular spheres. Rebellion was wrong as no man could be judge in his own cause. Because of his innate sinfulness, man deserved a harsh life on earth but could console himself with the hope of bliss in heaven. Neither lords nor peasants were behaving in a manner suitable to prepare them for the imminent end of the world. It is anyway doubtful if Luther's whole-hearted support for the peasantry would have done them much good as the trends against which they were revolting were already too well-established. After the failure of the revolt the revolutionary sects were persecuted and driven underground and conservative state-run Churches came to dominate Protestant Germany.

The impact of the Reformation on German political life was profound. The religious and social tensions cut across political developments and contributed to the accelerating decline in imperial power and an even more decisive movement towards federalism in Germany during the reign of Charles V. [9] In the past attempts have been made to assign Charles' motives to neat categories, imperial, Habsburg/dynastic and Catholic. Men of his generation did not think in terms of such water-tight compartments. For example, Charles and his brother Ferdinand continued Maximilian I's policy of using imperial feudal rights and jurisdiction to try to extend Austrian political control among the little territories north of Lake Constance. Up to 1530 he was strongly influenced by his grand chancellor Mercurio Gattinara, a northern Italian in Burgundian service, then by Nicolas and Anthony Granvelle, father and son, also Burgundians, as first secretaries and later by his Spanish advisers. As his reign progressed he became increasingly Spanish in outlook, though he continued to regard the imperial title as providing a spiritual basis for the great empire he possessed and for his claims to universal monarchy. Charles inherited a whole complex of policies along with each of his various possessions and the balance between them shifted constantly during his reign. From Burgundy he took the policy of building a powerful "middle kingdom" between France and Germany, from Spain the crusading zeal of the *reconquista* and the expansionist ambitions of Castile and Aragon and from the Austrian lands a desire to make a reality of the German imperial title and ambitions in Italy and the Balkans. Common to all was a desire to stop the eastwards expansion of France and the westwards expansion of the Ottoman Turks. Charles made no attempt to create a super-state, to co-ordinate all his separate territories into a single structure of imperial power. It was probably impossible anyway. All his possessions suffered from having to share their ruler with other territories. This was particularly true of Germany.

Charles V was elected as Emperor by the unanimous vote of the electors on 28 June 1519 after spending 852 000 *Gulden* (*Fl.*) in bribes. The French king, a rival candidate, mounted a vigorous campaign to stop Charles' election, which included making large payments to German rulers. The election of the "German candidate" was popular and produced a wave of national enthusiasm. Charles was expected to act as a strong leader and defender of German national interests. Such hopes were soon disappointed. His reign in Germany must be regarded as a total failure, though there is a danger of judging it entirely from the perspective of 1556, when he abdicated. On more than one occasion he seemed close to asserting his authority in the Empire, though the problems facing him were formidable.

From the outset relations between the Emperor and the German princes were strained as the princes were afraid of Charles, not only because of his huge *Hausmacht* but because of the risk of Germany being dragged into foreign wars for him. This fear was seen in the imposition on the new Emperor of a restrictive capitulation of election (*Wahlkapitulation*) in 1519. Although this was modelled on the similar promises given on their accession by many German rulers, it went further than the usual undertaking to observe existing rights and agreements. Charles had to promise, among other things, to respect the rights and privileges of the German rulers, to appoint no foreigners to office within the *Reich*, to bring no foreign troops into the *Reich* and not to declare war without the consent of the electors. This last provision created the concept of the imperial war (*Reichskrieg*), a war declared and fought by the whole Empire. German and Latin were to be the only official languages of the Empire. The Emperor was obliged to consult the *Reichstag* or the electors on all imperial matters. All subsequent emperors and kings of the Romans had to issue a capitulation of election, which gradually extended these restrictions and became part of the law of the Empire alongside the Golden Bull, the perpetual peace of 1495, the religious peace of 1555 and the treaties of Westphalia of 1648.

The election of Charles marked a break in the imperial reform process which had begun under his grandfather but it revived soon after. Eighteen imperial diets were convened between 1521 and 1555, a large number compared with earlier and later periods, and at these the work of the imperial reform movement was completed, almost entirely in the manner desired by the princely party. A committee structure was established within the imperial diet, the *Ausschüsse*, to deal with specific items of business. This grew out of the earlier *ad hoc* committees set up to deal with petitions to the diet, the *Supplikationsausschüsse*. Provision was made for the calling by the arch-chancellor of Germany, the Elector of Mainz, of a delegate diet (*Deputationsreichstag*) of representatives of the Circles in an emergency, extended in 1555 into a standing committee with power to deal with any business left over at the end of a meeting of the full diet. This was to be abolished in 1603, when the electors vetoed its further operation and insisted that they alone should exercise decision-making functions between diets.

The functions of the Circles, increased to ten in number, were extended to include nominating judges to the imperial chamber court (*Reichskammergericht*), the maintenance of defence and internal peace, economic and coinage regulation, discussion of common concerns and the collection of taxes and recruiting of troops under the *Matrikel*. This was significant because it gave the states a pretext to extend their tax-levying powers. Imperial taxes were privileged as they overrode all constitutional conventions in force in any state. The later sixteenth century saw a sharp increase in the volume and frequency of imperial taxation to fund warfare against the Turks. Rulers habitually levied more than they were entitled to and used the surplus for their own purposes. Where financial control was exercised by Estates, either exclusively or jointly with the government, there was an incentive for rulers to switch the bulk of taxation from traditional land taxes to excises and taxes on consumption, which were easier to collect. All this led to increasing constitutional conflict in some states.

The leading rulers in each Circle were designated as convening princes (*kreisausschreibende Fürsten*), with the tasks of supervising the work of the Circle and calling assemblies of its members. This amounted to an active and viable federative political structure which could work, as was shown in 1544 when an imperial army was brought together to fight the Turks, but its operation always varied from area to area. It functioned best in the south west, especially in Swabia, where the Swabian League had created habits of co-operation between the states and the Circle became a real working union.

In 1532 the Regensburg diet accepted a common criminal code, the *Carolina*, which was to become the basis of the penal procedures of the states just as the ordinance of the imperial chamber court (*Reichskammergericht*) was supposed to be the basis for civil procedures. The last act of the reform movement came in 1559 with the issue of a coinage ordinance attempting to establish a common standard for the various coinages circulating in the Empire.

In 1521 a *Reichsregiment* was established, not, as Maximilian and Charles intended, a docile regency council to run the Empire in his absence but a body controlled by the German princes. It sat in Nuremberg until 1530 and put forward sensible schemes to give the Empire a professional civil service and military, economic and financial unity while preserving its federative nature. These plans were to remain on paper as the *Reichsregiment* was crippled by religious disputes and the rivalries of the greater princes. In 1526 it was responsible for the interim decision that questions of choice of religion were to be left to the individual rulers until a national Church council, vetoed by Charles in 1524, could be called together. This was to have major consequences; when Charles returned to Germany in 1530 Protestantism was already established.

Relations between the Emperor and the German princes did not improve as time passed. As Spain became increasingly the centre of gravity of Charles' *imperium*, the main source of money and troops, the prospect of a Spanish Emperor loomed larger. The phrase "Spanish tyranny" entered the German political vocabulary as a major threat to *teutsche Freiheit*. In his proposition to the 1521 *Reichstag* Charles stated that, in future, Germany should not have many masters but one. This was a silly statement as Charles had no means of enforcing his rule and it served only to antagonize those whose co-operation he needed to run the Empire. From 1521 to 1530 he was absent and left his brother Ferdinand as regent. The Nuremberg diet of 1522–3 called for a Church council and ordered Luther's supporters to remain quiet until it met. Action against the Lutherans was avoided out of fear of provoking a violent reaction, especially from the population of the towns. Religious polarization began early. In 1524 the Regensburg Union and in 1525 the Dessau Alliance were formed, unions of Catholic rulers, the main aim of which was to prevent disorder. In October 1525 Saxony and Hesse formed the Torgau Union, later joined by other Lutheran states in the north. In July 1524 Charles issued another mandate against Luther repeating the Edict of Worms and calling for its enforcement. Some members of the Swabian League began to burn Luther's works, which had only happened so far in the Austrian lands. This caused riots in a number of cities and was ignored in north Germany and most towns.

The 1526 diet in Speyer effectively gave the governments of the German states interim powers to make decisions on religious matters until a Church council was convened. This was tacit acceptance that individual states had to find a temporary religious settlement appropriate to local conditions in order to avoid spiralling disorder. In 1529 Ferdinand tried to reverse this, which led to the issue of a formal protestation by a small body of Lutheran rulers, princes and free cities, the Protestants, claiming a right to make decisions on religious questions and not to be bound by the decisions of the *Reichstag*.

Charles returned to Germany in 1530 after making peace with the pope. From 1530 to 1532 he was at the height of his power. Charles underestimated the religious conviction of the Protestants and believed that the whole thing was just a squabble over details. His main aim was to unite the Empire in the far more urgent task of fighting against the Turkish threat. In fact, the need to deal with the Turks constantly distracted Charles and played a major part in allowing Protestantism to survive and grow. He made energetic but vain attempts to preserve the unity of the Church. He saw the schism as easily curable and was ready to agree to the Mass in both kinds as an interim measure and put pressure on the papacy to carry out reforms in the Church and to call a joint council of the Church including the Protestants.

Several attempts were made to find a settlement. In the 1530 diet at Augsburg there was a serious attempt to find a compromise after the pope refused to call a council of the Church. The Protestants issued a statement of their faith, the Augsburg Confession, drawn up by Melanchthon in close consultation with Luther. This was very conciliatory, too conciliatory in the eyes of some Protestants. It left open the possibility of reconciliation with the Roman Catholic Church and made clear the differences between Lutheranism and the other sects. It was answered at once with a Catholic counter-statement which made clear the deep theological differences between Catholicism and Lutheranism. Papal and French agents helped further to sabotage the negotiations and the Lutherans refused absolutely to accept papal supremacy. There was also growing unrest among the Catholic princes because of the secularization of Church land and the gradual erosion of Catholic power in the Empire but Charles was able to find few allies among them. The prospect of an imperial victory so frightened even the Catholic rulers that they turned to foreign friends, especially France, for protection against their own sovereign.

In February 1531 the leading Protestant princes and Bavaria set up the League of Schmalkalden to defend the reformed religion *and* the rights of princes. It was eventually joined by seven princes and sixteen cities. Luther, after serious reservations about an act of defiance against the Emperor, accepted it. This was significant: earlier leagues, like the Swabian, had operated nominally as agents of the Emperor to preserve peace but the Schmalkaldic League was openly partisan and opposed the Emperor. Its formation provoked a lively debate among the Protestants, which highlighted divisions between the Lutherans and Zwinglians, about a right of resistance. The League was eventually justified by an assumed general right, shared by nobles and towns as well as princes, to resist a superior who behaved as a tyrant. This was an important step in the emergence of the states' claim to sovereignty. The League became an important political factor, an organized centre for the spread of Protestantism before the rise of Calvinism, especially important after the alternative Swiss centre faded away following the death of Zwingli. In 1534 the League restored the Lutheran Duke of Württemberg after he had been deposed in 1519 and his country occupied by Swabian League troops in the name of the Emperor. After his restoration the Lutheran Reformation was introduced. In 1542 the duchy of Brunswick-Wolfenbüttel was forcibly converted to Lutheranism and the duke imprisoned by the Schmalkaldic League.

The Turkish threat forced Charles to compromise again. The Emperor was absent from 1532 to 1545, when Ferdinand was again in charge. Ferdinand was elected king of the Romans, automatic heir to his brother, in 1531. He was the last German king or Emperor to be crowned in Aachen. One reason for this was his desire to remove Ferdinand from Spain, where he had been brought up and where he was more popular than Charles. His Interim of 1532 postponed action against the Lutherans and again provisionally accepted the existence of Protestantism. The Catholics were persuaded to accept that questions concerning the disposition of Church property were also, *ad interim*, to be decided by the state governments. Between 1538 and 1541 several colloquies were held in an attempt to find a compromise but all failed. At the same time Charles was working hard to exploit divisions within the Protestant camp, using for the purpose the Elector of Saxony's expansionist plans to absorb bishoprics on his borders and the landgrave of Hesse's bigamous marriage.

Friction between the Emperor and the Protestants was increased by other than religious factors. By 1541 Charles was resolved on war against the Protestants and their defeat seems to have become his prime aim, especially as the movement was again spreading and threatening Cologne, Münster, the Palatinate and the Netherlands, areas vital to Spanish communications in Europe. In 1538 relations between the Netherlands and the neighbouring Protestant German territory of Cleves-Jülich deteriorated sharply. Since 1521 the duke possessed a strategically and economically important area on the Lower Rhine and it was the ambition of his house to expand and convert his lands into a major state. In 1538, when the native ruling house in neighbouring Guelders died out, he tried to take the territory, which Charles also claimed. In 1541 the Netherlands government sent in troops to seize Guelders and to attack Cleves and Jülich. The duke was forced in 1543 to accept the Treaty of Venlo, agreeing to restore the Catholic faith in his lands and to an imperial occupation of his fortresses. The Peace of Crépy with France (1544) gave Charles a free hand. Under its terms Francis I of France had to agree to a joint attack on the German Protestants, the Turks and Geneva. Hungary was also pacified by 1547, freeing Charles' hands further. Since the death of King Louis of Hungary and Bohemia at Mohács in 1526 Charles' brother Ferdinand had been nominally king of both states but his possession was challenged by the Turks and the Transylvanians. Warfare, which threatened to spill over into Germany, continued until 1538 and again from 1540 to 1547, when it was ended by the Treaty of Adrianople.

The Council of Trent opened in March 1545, raising the possibility of redress of the Protestants' grievances. Subsidies and military aid were obtained from the papacy. Dukes Maurice of Saxony and William of Bavaria were prepared to ally with the Emperor in return for a promised elevation to the rank of elector. Maurice, head of the ducal or Albertine line of the Saxon ruling house, [10] initially remained Catholic when the electoral or Ernestine line adopted the reformed faith. The Emperor wooed him with promises of territorial gain. Here dynastic rivalry was an important factor in a religious decision, as it was in the case of the House of Brunswick. There were also deep divisions among the Protestant rulers. In 1546 Charles went to war against the Schmalkaldic League to execute an imperial ban against the Elector of Saxony and the landgrave of Hesse as punishment for their attack on Brunswick-Wolfenbüttel. On 24 April 1547 he inflicted a decisive defeat on the Saxons at Mühlberg, after which the elector and the landgrave were imprisoned. Charles again seemed to be in a position of unassailable power.

On the pretext that he had gone to war in order to suppress a rebellion and therefore had the right to tear up all existing agreements, he proposed a harsh settlement including a strongly Catholic religious settlement and a thorough-going reform of the government of the Empire. An imperial commission took over the government of free cities which had turned Protestant, the guilds, blamed for the rush of their cities into heresy, were deprived of their power and oligarchic city governments were installed, as had happened to Ghent after it revolted against Charles in 1540. An attempt was made to revive the Swabian League as an instrument of imperial power at a meeting of representatives of selected German rulers at Ulm in 1547, at which Charles announced that the new League would have himself and Austria as members and a common law court, army and treasury.

At the Augsburg *Reichstag*, which opened on 1 September 1547 and lasted ten months, there was a strong imperial military presence to make clear who was master now. This produced the religious Interim of 1548, a provisional settlement until the Council of Trent completed its work. Charles' plans to restore unity to the Church by compromise were ruined when he again fell out with the pope, who, worried at Charles' growing power, encouraged his opponents and moved the Council, which very few German prelates attended because of conditions in Germany, to Bologna. The Interim, while allowing communion in both kinds and married clergy, made no theological concessions to the Protestants and did nothing to remove abuses from the Church. It was therefore acceptable to neither side. It soon became clear, in the form of disturbances in a number of states and cities, that there was considerable popular support for the Lutheran faith. As a political system for Germany Charles proposed the creation of a perpetual *Bund* or confederation of states under imperial control, with regular taxes, a standing army and a permanent administration and law courts, all under the direct control of the Emperor. An additional Circle, the Burgundian, was created out of Charles' possessions in the Netherlands and Franche Comté as a means of extending his personal power into the Empire. This was to be in perpetual alliance with the Empire but largely outside its jurisdiction. Charles had no intention of subjecting his dynastic possessions to a structure of imperial government which might slip out of Habsburg hands. Had all this come into effect, it would have started Germany down a constitutional road very different from the one along which it had been proceeding for centuries.

There were other changes. Maurice of Saxony, labelled by the Lutherans the Meissen Judas, was awarded the lands and title of the deposed Elector of Saxony, whose sons were given small duchies carved out of Maurice's former possessions. There was a strange after-shock of all this in 1563–7, when the son of the deposed Elector John Frederick II allied with the last of the robber knights, Wilhelm von Grunbach, in a combined attack on Maurice to recover the electoral lands and title. It came to nothing. All this was seen by the German rulers as a breach of the Emperor's capitulation of election and an attack on the German constitution. Eventually Charles abandoned his far-reaching constitutional plans in the face of growing opposition.

In 1550 Maurice of Saxony deserted Charles and reconstituted an alliance of Protestant rulers against him. This entered the Treaty of Chambord with France in January 1552, under which Henry II, as defender of German liberty (*Vindex libertatis Germaniae*) provided military aid in return for Cambrai, Metz, Toul and Verdun, which considerably strengthened the French position in Alsace and Lorraine. The Schmalkaldic princes resumed war against the Emperor in the spring of 1552. A nominal imperial war against France was declared but a very limited effort was put into it. Some seized the opportunity of the disorder to pursue their own interests. For example, the Hohenzollern margrave of Kulmbach, Albert Alcibiades, in a pioneering exercise of the predatory habits which were later to characterize his house, tried in 1553 to seize Nuremberg, Bamberg and Würzburg. Maurice of Saxony was killed during the suppression of this. The Catholics remained neutral, including Ferdinand, installed by Charles as ruler of the Austrian lands in the partition of his empire in 1551, who signed a separate peace with Saxony in 1552. In 1551 Charles made public his intention to have his son Philip succeed Ferdinand as Emperor, which caused considerable concern among the German princes. This was an early sign of growing divisions between the Spanish and German branches of the Habsburg House, which were to become significant later. Charles was defeated and had to flee from the *Reich*. He abdicated from all his thrones in 1556, the first Emperor to do so.

In 1555 Ferdinand, given a free hand by Charles, who was in Brussels, very much a bystander, mediated the Augsburg Settlement, which brought the religious war in the Empire to an end and annulled the 1521 Edict of Worms. The diet which agreed to the settlement met after several postponements in February 1555. It made ritual noises about an eventual reconciliation of the two faiths but eventually accepted an agreement which recognized that its efforts were too late. The settlement recognized the primacy of the states but at the same time confirmed the imperial constitution, restoring the balance which

Charles V after 1547 had threatened to destroy. It also confirmed the *Reichsfrieden*: in future disputes between Catholics and Protestants could be settled only according to the law. One of the motives behind this was continuing nervousness about popular unrest caused by religious issues.

The basic principle behind the religious settlement was *cuius regio, eius religio*, the ruler had the right to determine the faith of his subjects, with some restrictions on the rights of the governments of free cities. The rights of dissenters to leave states with their possessions were guaranteed. Although Augsburg gave the Lutheran faith legal recognition in the Empire it also helped the Catholic cause. Calvinism and Zwinglianism were banned, a blow to many free cities in the south west, which had adopted these faiths, and further secularizations of Church lands were forbidden. The settlement embodied two incompatible principles, the preservation of the status quo and the right of the two legal religions to grow. Initially this did not produce problems.

By 1555 some of the fire had gone out of the Reformation, which was represented by less extreme figures like Melanchthon and Bucer. The creation of established Lutheran churches with a married well-educated clergy represented a substantial social change as this group, with its interest in status and property and therefore in stability, reinforced the middle classes.[11] In most of the free cities there was a return of stability by the middle of the century with the restoration to power of small patrician groups and tighter control of established churches. A new less dogmatic generation of German rulers was emerging, more attached to the ways of compromise in religion, concerned with the internal problems of their own states and anxious to avoid war. Typical was the pragmatic Ferdinand I, eager to meet the Turkish threat to his own possessions and preferring a quiet life in Germany.

4   Peace and Polarization: Germany 1555–1618

Traditionally the early part of this period of German history has not received much attention. It is seen as rather uneventful, a time of settlement after the troubles of the Reformation, and only becomes interesting again with the revival of tension caused by the advance of the Counter-Reformation, culminating in the outbreak of the Thirty Years' War. For Germany it was a period of peace and comparative stability at a time when other parts of Europe were engaged in warfare. The French wars of religion, the Spanish-Dutch war and the Turkish wars in Eastern Europe all touched the periphery of the Empire but Germany remained immune from serious trouble. During these years a number of well-established trends were consolidated. The federalization of the Holy Roman Empire continued, with measures enacted at a series of major *Reichstag* meetings. The Empire was a functioning political entity, which existed in its institutions and ceremonials. Descriptions of the situation after 1555 as "the glass peace", for example, are perhaps too influenced by hindsight. The settlement of 1555 created a remarkably successful *modus vivendi* between the Emperor and the princes and among the German states.

At the same time tensions seethed below the surface. All three major religions in Germany went in for proselytizing of varying intensity. This, and the readiness of all parties to look outside Germany to foreign friends, was a dangerous development. Within individual German states the extension of an absolutist system of government continued, culminating in some cases in serious constitutional struggles between rulers and Estates. Economic decline and stagnation deepened, marked particularly by the ossification of many German towns and cities partly as a result of the rise of the territorial states. A few states remained economically buoyant, for example Brunswick-Wolfenbüttel with its ample mineral resources in the Harz Mountains, but the majority accumulated mounting debts. As before, the urban picture was very mixed. The emergence and consolidation of a distinct Austrian state proceeded. All these trends came to a head in the Thirty Years' War, which accelerated and, in some cases, completed the processes.

The Habsburg successors of Charles V were very different from him. Ferdinand I, who was Emperor from 1556 until 1564 (although the electors accepted Charles' abdication and Ferdinand's automatic succession only in 1558) was more open and less inclined to heaviness and melancholy than Charles. He was also more German and more *politique* than his brother. At the Regensburg diet 1556–7 he tried to bring the two religious parties to conversations — a meeting was actually convened in Worms in 1557 — and he put pressure on the pope to permit clerical marriage and communion in both kinds in an effort to build bridges. At the same time he sought an internal revival of the Catholic Church. To this end he promoted the Jesuits in Germany in an effort to win people back to the Catholic faith by persuasion instead of force. Peter Canisius was especially successful in this work.

Ferdinand, strongly influenced by Spanish absolutist ideas, also continued the building of the Austrian state. In particular he saw the need to create strong central institutions to give some unity to a collection of disparate provinces. He had begun this process in 1527, while acting as regent for his brother, with the creation of the first all-Austrian organs of government. It should be noted that no clear distinction was drawn between Austrian and imperial institutions until 1620. The Austrian state grew gradually as an extra layer of administration spread on top of existing well-established provincial organs and, in that respect, could be regarded as unnecessary. He also moved the centre of gravity of the Austrian state eastwards from the Alpine core to Vienna, the more easily to control the newly acquired lands in Bohemia and to assert claims to the whole of Hungary, of which he held only a small strip.

Ferdinand was a careful ruler. In Bohemia he slowly extended his power by exploiting class and religious differences and building up a pro-Habsburg Catholic group among the nobles. Throughout he was conciliatory, a wise move as ninety per cent of the population were Protestant. His hold in the small territory of Royal Hungary, the only part of the kingdom not held by the Turks, was very weak. The powerful nobility was able to play off the Habsburgs against the Turks and keep their autonomy, as expressed in the diet. In some ways Ferdinand was oddly old-fashioned. On his death in 1564 his lands were partitioned among his three sons, creating three separate states. The senior line ruled the Austrian archduchies, Hungary and Bohemia. Inner Austria, Styria, Carinthia and Carniola formed a second unit and the Tyrol a third. This showed a conflict in his mind between state-building and the essentially medieval practice of creating appanages, though it has been argued that this device was seen as a means of preventing inheritance disputes before the principle of primogeniture was clearly accepted.

His successor as Emperor, Maximilian II (1564–76), has traditionally been seen as secretly inclined to Protestantism. He was, in reality, in matters of religion a *politique* like his father. He saw toleration as the only means of avoiding the destruction of the *Reich*. He challenged Spain's oppressive religious policies in the Netherlands, nominally still part of the Empire, although the 1555 settlement did not extend to the Burgundian Circle, of which they were part. He faced a growing problem within his own possessions from the parliamentary Estates, dominated by Protestant nobles, which were able to exploit the crown's problems with the Turks and financial weakness to demand political and religious concessions.

An influx of American silver was undercutting the production of Austria and Bohemia which, in any case, was facing growing technical problems. A decline in production was marked from the middle of the century. There were temporary recoveries but the trend was quite obviously downwards. The same was true of the Saxon and Thuringian mines. Lutheranism and Calvinism were spreading among the politically dominant Austrian aristocracy, which faced little challenge from the weak towns. The Estates in the Austrian lands, increasingly powerful from the 1530s, were able to extort major concessions in the late 1560s and early 1570s, which gave them control of taxation and considerable religious freedom. Austria came close to becoming Protestant. At the same time Maximilian undertook a major reform of the standards of the Catholic Church in his lands. In 1552 he brought in the Jesuits and set up universities for them in Vienna and Graz. In this he was strongly influenced by the example of Bavaria, where the Jesuits had their first German centre at Ingolstadt. Maximilian's policy seemed to stem from a desire to build bridges between the two faiths and end the schism between them. His reign was peaceful.

During this period the *Reich* was also remarkably tranquil. A serious effort was made to solve by compromise points of religious friction left over after the 1555 settlement. Speeches in the *Reichstag*, in a spirit of German patriotism, called for measures to preserve the Empire and the *Reichstag* voted taxes for the Turkish wars with little dissent. Apart from the Turkish threat, serious after 1576, other aspects of the international situation reinforced this. French influence and the French alliance with the Protestants were nullified by the wars of religion and only began to revive after the accession of Henry IV. Two elections of kings of the Romans, in 1562 and 1575, confirmed the Habsburgs' possession of the imperial title. The second such election, that of Archduke Rudolph, later Emperor Rudolph II, did lead to expressions of suspicion because he had been brought up in Spain, but only the Elector Palatine actually voted against him. Maximilian and Rudolph organized an active imperialist propaganda campaign, particularly through the clergy, calling for internal unity in the face of external threats and emphasizing the identity of the Empire and the House of Habsburg. Imperial propositions to the *Reichstag* were a useful vehicle for such appeals and were clearly intended for wide publication. As a result of cautious policies Ferdinand and Maximilian were able to build up considerable influence in the Empire. This was facilitated by the fact that the princes were no longer as afraid of the Emperor as under Charles V but were now more frightened of their neighbours, foreign powers and of being dragged into wars. Many rulers also faced internal constitutional problems with their subjects. In the second half of the sixteenth century many of the German Estates were reaching the pinnacle of their power and serious clashes between them and the nascent bureaucratic states took place.[1] At the same time the German princes were unwilling to support positive steps to strengthen the institutions of the *Reich*. At the diet of 1570 an imperial plan was floated for a new military system to give the Empire effective armed forces but this came to nothing.

There was no hard opposition to imperial authority as no single German ruler seemed willing or able to place himself at the head of such a movement. Moderation and pragmatism seemed the keynotes of the age. Dukes John III and John V of Jülich-Cleves sought to find a compromise or middle way between Catholicism and Protestantism, avoiding persecution and tolerating unorthodox practices. Their capital, Düsseldorf, became a centre of humanist ideas in the north west of the Empire.

With the legal acceptance of Lutheranism, Saxony's role as stand-ard-bearer of opposition waned and it was not to be taken up by the elector palatine until the emergence of militant Calvinism later in the century. Elector Augustus I of Saxony (1553–86) was a frugal ambitious ruler, who gave his state modest prosperity and educational reforms, including a new university at Leipzig. Another leading Lutheran state, Brandenburg-Prussia, also became passive. In 1525 Albert of Hohenzollern had begun the construction of a substantial state by secularizing the lands of the decaying Teutonic Order, of which he was master, and converting them into the duchy of Prussia, a fief of the Polish crown. The ban of the Empire was decreed against Albert but, because of circumstances, it was not put into operation. This policy was continued by his successor Elector Joachim I. Joachim II (1535–71) was, however, a puppet of the noble-dominated Estates. The *Junkers* were able to achieve political and social domi-nance, enserfing the peasantry, and destroyed the prosperity of the towns. The crown could do little to stop this due to financial weakness and other factors.[2] Other potential leaders of a princely opposition party, such as Hesse, lacked the means: on the death of Philip of Hesse, his possessions were divided into three separate states.

Matters began to change in the 1570s and 1580s after the accession to the imperial throne of a man unsuited to the tasks facing him, Rudolph II (1576–1612).[3] He was an extremely odd character, perhaps insane at times. He was deeply interested in art, including a large collection of erotica, and science, the latter covering the whole spectrum from the new astronomy to alchemy. He made his chosen capital Prague a major cultural centre for Europe. Resisting the mixing of religion and politics, he sought to draw the best from Catholicism and Protestantism to produce an amalgam acceptable to everyone. He spent long periods during the later years of his reign in self-imposed isolation in his palace in Prague, from where he con-ducted relations with the world through low-born favourites. This produced a serious vacuum in leadership in the Austrian lands and the Empire at a time of growing political and religious tensions in both.

Germany entered a period of confessionalism. Permanent religious/political networks, educational, personal, diplomatic and military, developed above the states as German life became increasingly confessionalized, a reflection of development taking place throughout the whole of Europe. Two Germanies began to emerge, with clear differences in culture and ideology. A new generation of young self-confident princes appeared, which had not experienced the earlier religious troubles. Most German states were essentially confessional, in that one religion was regarded as the basis of the entire political structure and toleration of other faiths was seen as inherently dangerous, an open door to treason and social disorder. In addition many aspects of government previously controlled by the Church, education, poor relief and marital law, were now in state hands.

The sixteenth century saw the foundation of a number of new universities, which, like the states, were confessional. The Lutheran and Calvinist universities were state-controlled while in the Catholic states the Jesuits and Benedictines remained important in their running. The administrative personnel in states were usually of one faith. There is evidence that some Catholic leaders, for example Philip II of Spain, believed in a kind of domino theory, to the effect that, if religious diversity was allowed to infect one province, it would spread like a disease and threaten all authority. On the Protestant side there was fear of a Catholic plot to exterminate them: memories of the St Bartholomew's Day massacre of 1572 lingered for a long time. A feeling of insecurity quickly spread fuelled by pamphlet warfare, in which vicious attacks by one faith on another were common although such material was illegal under imperial law. Typical of the atmosphere of suspicion caused by all this was the Protestant reaction to Pope Gregory XIII's reform of the calendar in 1582 to replace the outdated Julian calendar. It involved the disappearance of the days between 5 and 14 October and the year was to begin on 1 January instead of 1 March as previously. This was seen in Protestant areas as a plot to rob men of ten days of their lives and attempts by the Emperor to impose the new system throughout the *Reich* as imperial despotism. Protestant Germany refused to accept the new calendar until 1700 and the issue produced serious violence in some places. After riots in 1584 the city of Augsburg postponed the introduction of the new calendar until 1586 and many Protestants there clung to the old system.

Large areas of the *Reich* were affected by religious warfare in neighbouring countries, France and the Netherlands. In 1567 the Spaniards occupied Cleves-Jülich as part of their campaign against the rebellious Dutch provinces. Religious confrontation again became a serious problem in Germany. Each faith began a creeping encroachment on the territories of the other and extremists on both sides began to adopt deliberately aggressive policies. The Catholic Church, aware of divisions in the Protestant camp and the quietude and divisions of

Lutheranism, made a determined attempt to win back lost lands. In 1566 Austria and Catholic states in the Empire adopted the decrees of the Council of Trent, which had ended in 1563 and had confirmed traditional doctrine and practices, finally closing the door on compromise with the Protestants. Under Pope Gregory XIII a major Catholic renewal movement was launched in Germany with the establishment of the German Congregation in Rome and the despatch of a number of energetic nuncios, based in Munich, Cologne and Graz, who often operated without the Emperor's approval. A new harder line in religion became visible. The activities of the Jesuits in Austria, Salzburg, Bavaria, Mainz, Trier, Würzburg, Münster, Augsburg and Fulda increased, resulting, for example, in the expulsion of Protestants. The bishopric of Eichsfeld in Thuringia and the Lutheran state of Baden-Baden returned to Catholicism.

This was answered by a Protestant revival. In 1577 a conference of Lutheran theologians at Bergen Abbey near Magdeburg produced a clear statement of Lutheran doctrine, which breathed new life into the Church. In 1580 a declaration of agreement based on this was published, signed by fifty rulers, thirty-eight imperial cities and eight thousand clergymen. The state of Württemberg emerged as the powerhouse of revitalized Lutheranism, with the university of Tübingen as a centre. At the same time a militant Calvinist movement, inheriting the Zwinglian legacy, was spreading rapidly and became especially strong in the same areas as the earlier radical Reformation movements. At first it spread spontaneously from Switzerland, the Netherlands and France into the western areas of the Empire and from there to all parts. Under the 1555 settlement it was an illegal faith and was persecuted by many rulers, Catholic and Lutheran.

Solidarity between the two Protestant faiths was very limited, though initially in 1566, to avoid making a concession to the Catholics, the Lutheran establishment went along with the fiction that Calvinism was only a variant of the Augsburg Confession. It was tolerated or actively promoted by a number of princely and urban governments, beginning with the palatinate. Elector Frederick III converted to Calvinism in 1562, after a long search for religious truth, against very powerful resistance from his Lutheran subjects. The Palatinate was followed by Nassau, Hesse-Cassel, Saxe-Anhalt, Lippe, Cleves and, briefly, electoral Saxony. Unusually for something regarded as "the religion of rebels" the initiative for this often came from governments and met opposition from subjects. In the case of

Germany there was no necessary link between a particular religion and a particular class or political programme, though political troubles in some free cities in the early seventeenth century were attributed to the dangerous "democratic" spirit of Calvinism. The organization of the Calvinist Church in Germany was more authoritarian than elsewhere and the power of the ruler was more firmly entrenched. Some princes adopted Calvinism as a means of defeating Estates dominated by Lutheran establishments. This produced some odd results. In Lippe[4] the Calvinist Reformation was introduced by the ruling count between 1590 and 1610. It was resisted by the main city of the state, Lemgo, which obtained a verdict in its favour from the imperial aulic council. The city's Lutheran Church was retained under its own control. The opposite process took place in East Frisia, where the city of Emden went Calvinist under the influence of the neighbouring Netherlands, with which it had close ties, while the ruling prince remained Lutheran. In Brandenburg in 1613 the elector became a Calvinist while the state remained officially Lutheran. The co-existence of different faiths in a single state did not inevitably lead to conflict. Economic and political considerations often led to *de facto* toleration of minorities and the avoidance of extreme positions. There were cities in the south west where all three faiths established a pragmatic *modus vivendi*, though this was rare and such arrangements were usually fragile and susceptible to periodic friction. In many of the south German cities forcibly recatholicized after Mühlberg a system of *Parität*, the legal existence of two or more faiths in the same polity, was introduced in 1555. These arrangements were individually negotiated city by city and many were very complicated indeed and full of potential for trouble. In some a *Simultaneum*, an arrangement for shared use of a single church building, funds or other facilities by two faiths, was introduced, for example in Ravensburg and Augsburg.

Under the 1555 settlement it was unclear whether the religious status quo of that year was permanently established as far as the free cities were concerned or whether their governments had the right to change the established faith. This became important as circumstances changed, if religious issues became political, as they often did, or if waves of proselytizing zeal affected one side or the other, as was becoming more frequent in the last decades of the century. Demographic and economic changes could also alter the whole picture. Friction grew in Aachen, a Catholic city, when large numbers of Calvinists, many of them refugees from the Netherlands, began to move in, forming a majority of the city's population by the end of the century. Religion was not the decisive factor in determining the social and political structures in the towns; other factors were more important in this. The tradition of popular participation in government did not die away and even in the towns in princely states, called in German *Landstädte* to distinguish them from the free cities (*Reichsstädte*), some self-government remained. Many of the free cities were to experience chronic political instability from the Reformation until the eighteenth century.[5]

The causes of religious tension, apart from encroachment by one faith on the territory and rights of another, were breaches of the 1555 settlement, the continued secularization of Church lands in Protestant states and the advance of Protestantism among the free cities. The Augsburg Settlement had established parity in some cities but some Protestant magistracies had subsequently abandoned this unilaterally. The Ecclesiastical Reservation clause, which prevented Catholic prelates who became Protestants from converting their sees into secular states, was regarded by the Protestants as a barrier to their expansion. Catholic ruling houses, on the other hand, were able to expand by placing members in ecclesiastical posts. In a secret unpublished declaration at the time of the Augsburg Settlement, which did not become imperial law, Ferdinand I had guaranteed the religious liberties of Protestant nobles and towns in the ecclesiastical states, a breach of the principle of *cuius regio, eius religio* and a cause of great irritation to many bishops and archbishops.

Many of the twenty-six cathedral chapters, which elected bishops, contained, contrary to the Tridentine decrees, Protestant nobles, as the prebends and benefices available were a useful way of providing for younger sons. Where a chapter had a Protestant majority, it often wished to elect a Protestant prelate. If the see was then secularized, the prebends could be turned into fiefs. Some were elected and accepted as bishops by pope and Emperor if they gave guarantees that they would accept the decrees of Trent. For example, two sons of the Duke of Brunswick became bishops of Halberstadt and Osnabrück and this was a clear sign of the ambitions of the House of Brunswick to possess these territories. Even more spectacular, Albert of Hohenzollern secularized the east Prussian territories of the Teutonic Order. Saxony absorbed Merseburg, Meissen and Naumburg. It was obvious that Saxony, Brandenburg, Mecklenburg and Pomerania were casting covetous eyes on ecclesiastical territories within or near their borders, Magdeburg, Bremen, Verden, Schwerin, Minden, Halberstadt and Lübeck, and used the same procedure, having members of the ruling family elected to the sees in preparation for later annexation. This was another weapon in the ongoing campaign by the larger princes to extend their power over their smaller neighbours. Some of the sees did not have representation in the imperial diet but problems arose when other Catholic states refused to accept the right of Protestant prelates to control Catholic seats and votes in the imperial diet. There was a chronic dispute over the admission of Magdeburg from the 1570s until the outbreak of the Thirty Years' War.

Many Catholics realistically accepted that north Germany was lost to them but real trouble appeared when Protestants threatened to take over sees on the "border" between the two faiths, such as Cologne and Strasburg. Cologne was very sensitive indeed. It was an established ambition of the Bavarian Wittelsbachs to turn Cologne into a *de facto* permanent secundogeniture of their house, a device employed by other houses. In 1582 the Archbishop Elector of Cologne, Gebhard Truchsess von Waldburg stated his intention of becoming a Lutheran in order to marry. This would have seriously upset the balance of power in Germany, involving the loss of a Catholic electoral vote and of a substantial and strategically important Catholic outpost in the north west. The Estates of the archbishopric were strongly Catholic. Waldburg was deprived of his see in 1583 and Ernest of Wittelsbach, brother of the reigning Duke of Bavaria and already the holder of a number of important sees, was elected in his stead. War seemed likely as Spain and Bavaria were ready to support the new elector while the Palatinate supported the deposed Waldburg. The Dutch refused to become involved and eventually, after some localized violence in the electorate, Waldburg was bought off. Thereafter, members of the Bavarian house were to hold Cologne until 1761. Problems appeared in Strasburg between 1583 and 1604 because the cathedral chapter was divided between Catholic and Protestant parties. This eventually led to a double election of two bishops with useful international connections, a French Guise and a relative of the Elector of Brandenburg. Again war was avoided but the affair increased tension.

Rudolph II, like his immediate predecessors, was anxious to avoid trouble with the Protestant princes and feared the accusations that he was bringing Spanish influence into the Empire and threatening to drag Germany into Spain's wars. In 1579 Rudolph was betrothed to the Infanta Isabella, the daughter of Philip II, which revived hopes of an eventual revival of Charles V's empire, enlarged with Portugal and its possessions. This aroused great hostility in Germany and the marriage came to nothing. Rudolph was also unable to prevent direct papal contacts with German Catholic princes behind his back. In 1582 he apologized to the Protestant electors when the nuncio published a papal bull in Germany without his permission. Rudolph was increasingly out of step with his times. Within both religious camps aggressive "activist" parties were gaining strength and elbowing aside the moderates. By the later years of Rudolph's reign, especially after 1606, it was impossible to achieve anything concrete in the *Reichstag*, as it had become paralysed by religious squabbles. The Protestants complained, inaccurately, that the Catholic ecclesiastical states represented a solid bloc vote for the Emperor and demanded extra votes for themselves to balance it. They began meeting separately as a group before the opening of diets to concert policies. In 1598 a long and significant debate took place in which some Protestant states argued, contrary to the prevailing convention, that majority votes of the diet were not binding on all Estates of the Empire on non-religious as well as religious questions.

The imperial diet met only five times during the reign. The imperial deputation (*Reichsdeputation*), a small committee of the full diet, which became active in the 1570s, met more frequently. Other imperial organs like the imperial defence organization and the two supreme courts were also crippled by religious differences. In 1588 a long overdue inspection of the imperial cameral court was torpedoed when the Catholics refused to allow a Protestant to represent the Archbishop of Magdeburg on the inspecting commission. The Protestants complained in the *Reichstag* when the imperial courts found in favour of Catholic litigants appealing against a loss of rights and property to Protestant rulers and in 1600 they refused to participate any more in hearing appeals against cameral court verdicts, normally dealt with in the imperial deputation.

Rudolph became involved in a major war against the Turks between 1592 and 1606 but could obtain only limited help from the princes of the Empire or from the Estates of his own lands. A prominent figure at Rudolph's court, Andreas Haniwald, secretary of the imperial aulic council, was a strong Catholic imperialist and absolutist, who planned to rebuild his master's power in the Austrian lands by an alliance with the towns and peasantry against the nobles, who dominated the Estates, but this came to nothing. The only policy available to the Emperor's representatives in the Empire was co-operation with the Catholic party but this made the position of the majority of moderate Protestant princes around Saxony increasingly difficult and gave ammunition to the militant party growing up around the Wittelsbach elector palatine.

The Palatinate was emerging as the leading anti-imperial state, using Calvinism as a political weapon. It organized opposition to the Turkish taxes and mounted campaigns of obstructionism in the imperial diet. The Elector Palatine John Casimir (1583–92) opened his territory to Calvinist refugees. Unlike many of his fellow rulers he had no constitutional problems in his main territory as there were no Estates in the Lower Palatinate. A kind of Calvinist International was developing led by Prince Christian of Anhalt, a close adviser of the elector palatine. Its headquarters were in The Hague but it had major centres in the Empire, including the universities of Heidelberg and Altdorf and military academies established in 1606 at Sedan in the Calvinist duchy of Bouillon, ruled in the early seventeenth century by Turenne, a prominent Huguenot leader and uncle of the elector palatine, and in 1617 at Siegen in Nassau. It derived intellectual legitimacy from the work of a group of Dutch, French and German anti-absolutist writers, labelled by their opponents the *Monarchomachs* (king-killers). This "organization" maintained a network of contacts with sympathisers in many parts of the Empire, including members of the Austrian and Bohemian nobility, and other states.

The Emperor's position in Germany was further weakened by the clear ambition of another branch of the Wittelsbach family, the Duke of Bavaria, to become leader of the Catholic party not for religious reasons but as the basis for Bavaria's role as a regional power in southern Germany. The Duke of Bavaria, Maximilian I (1598–1651) issued propaganda offering the prospect of a Catholic Wittelsbach Emperor as an alternative to the Habsburgs. The emergence of a powerful Bavaria represented a serious threat to Habsburg influence. Since subjecting the nobility to their rule in 1495 and achieving primogeniture in the early sixteenth century a series of talented rulers had built Bavaria into a well-organized state. Albert V (1550–79) broke the power of his Lutheran nobility, who dominated the Estates, and created a powerful central administration in Munich in close alliance with the Catholic Church, over which the duke had substantial control. In 1570 a Spiritual Council (*Geistlicher Rat*) was set up, a joint body of laymen and clergy, which ran the Catholic Church. William V continued along the same lines. By a concordat signed in 1583 the papacy accepted ducal control of the resources and personnel of the Church. The relationship between Church and state was not always harmonious, as the bishops chafed under secular control, but in general it functioned well. The work was completed by Maximilian I, the most able of the three, whose long reign saw the creation of an advanced administration and the consolidation of absolutism. A new office, that of *Rentmeister*, was created. Its holders took charge of financial administration in the four *Aemter* into which the duchy was divided. Later they also took over judicial powers, leaving the noble governor or *Viztum* with little more than ceremonial functions. In 1591 all Bavarian officials were required to take an oath to the Tridentine decrees and to live as observant Catholics. This was later extended to all Bavarian subjects: the obligation to produce regular certificates of confession and attendance at the Mass was an effective instrument of social and political control. The court, which took part in a regular programme of Catholic ritual and observance, widely reported among the population, became a model of baroque piety, which added to its authority and standing in Catholic Germany. What had begun as an imposition quickly, thanks mainly to the skill of the Jesuits, became popular and Bavarians came to identify closely with their Church and dynasty. Good relations between the crown and the nobility were restored by the issue of new law codes in 1616 and 1618, which considerably weakened the rights of the peasantry. This helped to console the landowners for the loss of their political power in the Estates. Prussian absolutism was later to be founded on a similar bargain between the crown and the nobility of Brandenburg in 1653.

The Bavarian example was imitated by others, including the later Emperor Ferdinand II and the Archbishop of Salzburg. Archbishop Wolf Dietrich von Raitenau (1587–1612), was a strong ruler who eliminated the political power of the Estates and the cathedral chapter, ironically in order to strengthen his state against Bavarian and Austrian encroachments. In 1606 he forced the cathedral chapter to accept an agreement never to elect a Habsburg or Wittelsbach prince to the see. In 1612 a Bavarian army invaded Salzburg and arrested and deposed von Raitenau after border clashes.

Growing religious tension was accompanied by a revival of social problems, which added further to the atmosphere of instability in Germany in the last decades of the sixteenth and early years of the seventeenth century. There was a widespread belief that Germany had suffered a general moral decline, manifested in conspicuous consumption, excessive eating and drinking, profanity, libidinage, dishonesty and greed. The Turks were again seen as God's agents for the punishment of wicked Germans.

The Reformation period had seen important social changes, which added to a growing feeling of unease. Any disturbance of the social order was regarded as dangerous because of the built-in limits of the economy: one group could only acquire more by taking it from others, threatening the whole structure. The effects of the changes were extremely complex and difficult to reduce to simple formulas. Old concepts, such as the patriarchal household, including family and servants, as the basic unit of society and a society divided into traditional Estates, survived but there was an increasingly fluid situation within each Estate. There was certainly greater social mobility, especially in the towns, where the opportunities were greater. It was made possible by the expansion of education, the emergence of professional administrators and, probably the least important factor, changing economic opportunities. Attitudes were also changing. Although the supposed link between Protestantism, especially Calvinism, and capitalism has been exaggerated in the past, there was certainly a new attitude to work and accumulation after the Reformation. The Catholic clergy, as before, could not own or inherit property but Protestant clergymen could do both and marry, leaving heirs. The old view, that the lowest in society did physical work while the highest did no work, was changing. Work was no longer seen as something to be done only in order to acquire enough capital to make further work unnecessary but as valuable in its own right. Criticism of a nobility which did nothing to justify its status was becoming more common. Protestant nobles began to engage in trade and manufacturing, though usually only in the products of their own lands, without derogation, loss of status. New groups were increasing in wealth and social and political power, while older elites clung on to what they could of their former position, with varied success.

Changes in Church/state relations disrupted old systems, bringing about significant changes in the distribution of power, wealth and status in both Catholic and Protestant states. Political power and social power were not always in the same hands: in many free cities the old patricians, although forced to admit wider circles of citizens to a share of political power, clung on to their old social status. A visible raising of social barriers among the nobility and urban patricians in the last decades of the century was a reaction against a perceived excess of social mobility earlier. Some successful townsmen moved sideways to become land-owning nobles. Perhaps the most striking example of this was the Fuggers, who became counts of the Empire and princes of Babenhausen. Although there are dangers in exaggerating the extent of the change, economic classes in a modern sense were just beginning to emerge alongside the surviving traditional medieval orders. Yet it remained an oddly ambivalent world, with the same men practising proto-capitalist methods in order to enrich themselves while continuing to give lavishly to charity in the medieval style.

The economic situation was also becoming more difficult. It would be inaccurate to talk of a general economic decline in Germany in the later sixteenth century though changes were occurring which caused decline in some areas and growth in others. The general commercial situation in Europe continued to change to Germany's disadvantage and the German economies could not be isolated from developments elsewhere. There were marked signs of economic change and decline, especially in the cities. Stettin and its hinterland were badly hurt by the collapse of its biggest trading company in 1572. Many of the formerly prosperous free cities of the south were declining and experiencing pastoralization of their economies, adding new fuel to internal political divisions and sharpening religious divisions. There was a marked withdrawal of capital from enterprise and investment in land as many urban patricians became nobles. The position of the guilds was often a potent source of trouble. As cities began to experience decline, the guilds, where they were traditionally impor-tant, often tried to increase their power in order to defend the livelihood of their members. This bred conservatism and resistance to change, which could in turn make the economic position worse. It is significant that many of the few manufacturing bright-spots in late sixteenth-century Germany were in cities like Frankfurt, which had a textile industry free of guild control and open to new methods, or in small towns and rural areas outside the walls and beyond the control of guild-dominated centres like Cologne and Aachen. The first stages of mercantilism, state direction of the economy, caused further disruptions.

Economic stagnation was made worse by a number of years of poor weather, labelled the Little Ice Age, which lasted into the mid-eighteenth century. The inevitable crisis caused by population growth combined with the built-in limits of agricultural productivity had arrived.[6] Governments did not begin to regard overpopulation as dangerous until the eighteenth century; earlier the prevailing view was that population was the prime source of a state's strength. Germany, especially the western parts, began to experience the problems of overpopulation and food shortages. Large numbers of people lived an extremely marginal existence and a natural or family disaster could throw whole families into total destitution. Pauperism and vagabondage were increasing before 1618, adding to public insecurity. The years 1560 to 1600 saw a sharp increase in criminality, mainly as a result of the growth of robber bands. Epidemics of plague, malaria and other diseases hit Europe in the years before 1618. Malnutrition, and the sterility it produces, were chronic. All this, combined with the appearance of comets, created genuine fears about the future. As before the Lutheran Reformation, there was a mounting feeling of imminent catastrophe and growing millenarian hysteria.

The late sixteenth century was marked by serious peasant revolts and political and social conflicts, often violent, in towns and cities, *Reichsstädte* and *Landstädte*. Between the 1580s and the 1620s there was a wave of serious peasant risings, especially in the south west. The peasants were under growing pressure from land hunger and increasing demands from states and landlords desperate to increase their incomes. In some cases princes revived their campaigns to take over free cities, including the most important ones such as Hamburg, Bremen, Cologne and Frankfurt, in alliance with parties inside them. All this was a sign of deep social and political tensions. In some cities these expressed themselves in the form of violent anti-Semitism, which was never far below the surface, with the reappearance of old myths about Jewish ritual murders of Christian children.[7] Typical of all this was the so-called Fettmilch Rising in Frankfurt-am-Main between 1612 and 1614. This was named after a gingerbread baker Vincenz Fettmilch, who led a popular movement among the citizens which culminated in August 1614 in a vicious pogrom against the largest Jewish community in Germany leading to its expulsion. Other "outsiders" such as gypsies also suffered an upsurge of persecution and there was a large-scale witch craze between 1580 and 1600, followed by further waves during and after the Thirty Years' War, all part of the same phenomenon.

There are clear indications that these movements were sometimes deliberately exploited for political purposes by one faction against another and that the authorities in some places encouraged these outbreaks as a safety valve; it was easy to blame visible groups like Jews and witches for economic and climatic phenomena which were otherwise inexplicable. Superstition and survivals from pre-Christian times were not far below the surface, especially in rural areas. In 1631 Friedrich Spee wrote *Cautio Criminalis*, an essay on witch trials showing how ridiculous the whole procedure was, but its impact was only gradual.[8]

Added to all this were symptoms of the further development of the concept of the state in the modern sense, the beginnings of which had contributed to the pre-Reformation crisis. In the later sixteenth century theory and practical developments were proceeding rapidly hand-in-hand. Bodin's *Six Books of the Republic* (1576) put forward the concepts of the sovereign state: indivisible and unlimited sovereignty, the exercise of which could be restrained by divine and natural law, prevailing constitutional agreements or the fundamental laws of the state.[9] The impact of this in the *Reich* was limited, where the long-standing debate on the nature and origins of territorial sovereignty (*Landeshoheit*), the powers of the German princes, was more important. Most German rulers were very far from possessing sovereign power, though many aspired to it. Corporate and individual liberties and privileges remained powerful, though they were often customary and not written down. The growth of the state was, inevitably, at the cost of these rights and the constitutional disputes of the time showed a growing tendency on the part of princes to command rather than to negotiate. The state, it was argued, always knew best.

New administrative methods continued to exist side by side with more traditional systems but the trend was clear; experts were taking over and the old self-governing institutions saw their functions and status being eroded. As governments tried to deal with the effects of structural changes by means of legislation, the size and scope of government had to increase. The most common device chosen for this purpose was the *Polizeiordnung*, an untranslatable term perhaps best rendered as "administrative ordinance".[10] The notion of *Polizei* or *Policey*, which the ordinance was designed to further, can perhaps be best rendered as "good government", with emphasis on the duty of the Christian ruler to protect the good and punish evildoers. These regulations, designed to promote good order and morality, were issued in increasing numbers in the sixteenth century by most governments, from the free cities to the Empire, and covered ever wider aspects of the daily lives of the people. Poor relief, charities, education, public health, medical matters, fire regulations, the guilds, wage and price regulations and control of servants were all covered. Of growing importance in the later sixteenth century were sumptuary laws designed to prevent what was seen as a dangerous blurring of the lines between the different social orders. It was considered important to preserve visibly the status of each order by distinctions of dress. Without this, it was feared, the respect given by one order to another, the glue which held society together, would be eroded. The first imperial *Polizeiordnung*, including sumptuary regulations, was issued in 1530, laying down what clothes and furs each order could wear and how much each could spend on events like weddings and funerals. They were repeated in 1548 and 1577.

Political tensions in individual states were mirrored in Germany as a whole, as was illustrated in 1608 with the Donauwörth affair. This free city, which had a Protestant majority and a Catholic minority with certain defined rights, was in an area of the Empire of great religious sensitivity, where Protestant and Catholic states and cities were very close to one another, including Bavaria and the Calvinist Upper Palatinate. There was a long history of friction between the two groups in the city, in which the Catholic Bishop of Augsburg had played a provocative role. In 1608 it was annexed by Bavaria under the pretext of executing a verdict of the imperial aulic council (*Reichshofrat*) against the city government after a religious riot in 1607. The aulic council was seen as an instrument of Catholic policy, especially when its business increased because its rival, the imperial chamber court, was paralysed by religious disputes. This was not, as the Protestants claimed to believe, the beginning of the long-expected Catholic offensive but an attempt to uphold the constitution of the Empire and, at the same time, to win back something seen as legitimately Catholic. If there was a great Catholic offensive in Germany it came after 1618 not before but the affair caused great alarm.

The Donauwörth affair accelerated the formation of religious leagues in Germany, traditionally seen as an important step in the process leading to the Thirty Years' War. On 27 April 1608 the Calvinists walked out of the *Reichstag*, which stopped its work and prevented the grant of a tax for war against the Turks. At the same time the institutions of the religious conciliation system, in operation since 1555, ceased to function. On 14 May the Evangelical Union was set up, consisting of the Palatinate, Anhalt, Württemberg and a number of free cities, in other words very much the activist minority of the German Protestants and clients of the Palatinate. The membership was later extended in 1612–13 when Hesse-Cassel and Brandenburg joined and it also entered formal agreements with England and the United Provinces.

Frederick V became elector palatine in 1610. He was a very weak character, strongly under the influence of Christian of Anhalt. In July 1609 the Catholic League was established, led and financed by Maximilian of Bavaria. It grew out of the earlier Landsberg League

(1556–98), which had begun life as a non-confessional peace-keeping alliance similar to the Swabian League, taken over by Bavaria. Initially this was also very much a minority movement among German Catholic rulers, but it too expanded as tension grew. A number of ecclesiastical states joined it, including Mainz and Cologne, and Spain became its protector. The League was always much better organized than the Union, thanks to Bavarian control of it, and it quickly built up an effective army under the Walloon general Count Tilly. In 1616 Austria and Saxony, the leading Lutheran state, joined it, at which point Maximilian of Bavaria left it and founded another Catholic League with a few ecclesiastical states. He clearly wanted no rivals to his control. Neither the Union nor the League was ever designed to include all the Catholics or Protestants in the Empire. In reality both were vehicles for Bavarian and Palatinate influence and instruments of their ambitions to become regional powers in the south and west of the Empire. Religion was a useful means of disguising power politics and of attracting powerful foreign friends. Neither the League nor the Union was the spearhead of a crusade to rid Germany of Protestantism or to capture it entirely for one or other of the reformed faiths.

The formation of the German religious leagues has in the past often been quoted as evidence of the inevitability of a religious war in the Empire. This "tinder-box" theory, that Germany and Europe had divided into two armed camps and that only a spark was needed to set off the explosion, owes more to the analogy with Europe in 1914 than to a realistic assessment of the actual situation in Germany in 1618. It is interesting to note that Europe experienced a general pacification in the years before 1618, a peace of exhaustion. The end of the Anglo-Spanish War came in 1604 and the French civil wars, in which Spain was involved, ended in 1598. Spain and the Dutch signed a twelve-year truce in 1609 after the peace party under Oldenbar-nevelt came to power in the Netherlands, though the Orangist war party remained influential in north western Germany, maintaining garrisons in Emden and other strong points. Peace came in the Baltic region between 1613 and 1617. Turkish attacks on Austria, regular since 1593, stopped in 1615. Although the position in Germany was becoming more tense before 1618, the majority of German rulers were far more afraid of war than desired it. It was imperial policy to try to play down religious problems. The German religious leagues did not divide Germany into two religious armed camps but they were ominous in that they became vehicles for growing foreign influence in

Germany. This was a clear sign of development of a power vacuum in the Empire, which states like Bavaria and the Palatinate rushed to fill and into which foreign influence was drawn. The Protestant Union was linked to England and to the House of Orange in the Netherlands and the League to Spain.

This was shown very clearly in the Jülich-Berg crisis of 1609–10. The male line of the native dynasty of this substantial and strategically very important territory on the Lower Rhine died out. In order to forestall an imperial take-over, the territory was occupied jointly by the two rival candidates for the vacant throne, the Elector of Brandenburg, who became a personal convert to Calvinism — his state remained legally Lutheran — to win a marriage into the House of Orange and Dutch support, and the Count of Palatinate-Neuburg, a member of a junior branch of the House of Wittelsbach. He became a convert to Catholicism to win Habsburg and Bavarian support for his claims. Such opportunism points to a certain shallowness of religious convictions, at least among the main power-exercisers of the Empire.

The Jülich-Berg affair was important because it impinged on the vital interests of other European powers. The government of Spain was frightened that the territory so close to the Netherlands would fall into hostile hands and encouraged the Emperor to intervene judicially, as he had a right to do when a fief of the Empire fell vacant. The French likewise felt threatened if Jülich-Berg should come into the possession of a pro-Habsburg ruler and were prepared to march in to prevent this. A French intervention had the backing of England, the Dutch and the Protestant Union. There was a real possibility in 1610 of the Franco-Spanish War reviving and spilling over on to German soil. Although this did not happen due to the assassination of Henry IV in May 1610, which prevented an internationalization of the problem, and although eventually the affair was settled by the Treaty of Xanten in 1614, which partitioned the territories between the two claimants and guaranteed existing religious rights there, this event did illustrate very well the basic cause of the Thirty Years' War, mutual fear and misunderstanding, not religious polarization. It added to the growing fear on both sides, the Habsburgs and their enemies, that the other was about to launch a great attack which, according to growing war parties in several states, but most importantly in Spain and the Netherlands, had to be met with a defensive pre-emptive strike. In the final crisis which precipitated the war each side believed it was acting defensively.

The leaders of the Spanish war party were Oñate, Spanish ambassador in Vienna from 1616 to 1617, Baltasar de Zuñiga, Philip IV's first minister, in Madrid, Archduke Albert, governor of the Spanish Netherlands and his commander Spinola. They were on the Habsburg side the equivalents of the Elector Palatine and Christian of Anhalt.[11] When the Bohemian crisis broke there was a very deep difference of opinion, especially in the Spanish government, as to whether Spain should intervene. The war party argued that Spain could not afford not to intervene. A long debate followed on the costs and political repercussions of intervention in Germany and of not intervening. Among the horrors which might follow if Spain did not become involved were a Protestant Emperor, the loss of Bohemia to the Calvinists, a severe threat to Catholic Poland, and the loss of Alsace, which was vital to Spanish communications in Europe, the Spanish Road.[12] Opponents of war argued that Spain could not afford war until she had recovered her strength.

To the Austrian branch of the House of Habsburg the prospect of war was even more frightening. Like Spain it was in a weak state in the years before the outbreak of war, having been through a period of severe internal troubles. Between 1600 and 1612 Rudolf II played virtually no part in the government of his possessions. The noble-dominated Estates of his possessions took advantage of this to extend their powers. Calvinism spread rapidly, acquiring an institutional base in the Estates, towns, villages and schools, and their leader Georg von Tschernembl had close links to the Calvinist International described earlier. In 1608 the Estates of Upper and Lower Austria formed the Union of Horn and expressly reserved the right to use force to defend their rights, including religious liberties. They also entered a military alliance with the governor of the neighbouring Upper Palatinate, Christian of Anhalt. There was growing social tension as some of the nobles took advantage of their new power to extend their rights over the peasantry. The Austrian lands were afflicted with growing religious, social and political tensions and the monarchy seemed powerless to intervene. There was a major peasant revolt between 1594 and 1597, part of a wave of peasant risings in the south of the Empire at this time, and serious disorders in Habsburg Hungary. There were more serious risings in Upper Austria in 1632 and 1636.

Rudolph's brothers also took advantage of his weakness to build states for themselves within his possessions. In 1608 Archduke Matthias allowed himself to become the figurehead of a revolt of the

Hungarians and Austrians. As a result he became nominal ruler of Hungary, Moravia and Austria. Rudolph was only able to keep Bohemia by making massive political and religious concessions to the Estates in 1609, the famous Letter of Majesty. The Bohemian Protestants had sunk their doctrinal differences to form a bloc in 1575 and were powerful in the Estates. The Letter of Majesty allowed them to create a defence system to protect their rights. After Rudolph's death Matthias was briefly Emperor between 1612 and 1619. He was an ambitious mediocrity willing to use any device to gain power but in fact he gained only the trappings of power, not the reality. Though his main adviser, Cardinal Klesl, was a *politique*, he embarked on a more aggressive policy towards the Estates and Protestantism in the Austrian lands, leading to a marked sharpening of internal tensions. In 1614 he called representatives of the Estates of his lands together at Linz and asked for financial help. This was refused.

In the Empire he was even more powerless. Rudolph's inertia had encouraged the princes, including Bavaria and the Palatinate, to carve out little informal empires for themselves. In 1610 the electors met and claimed a right to govern the Empire in the absence, for whatever reason, of the Emperor. This casts serious doubt on the view of the Thirty Years' War as the culmination of a contest between imperial despotism and princely particularism. The opposite seems to have been the case. Rudolph and Matthias were incapable of acting as despots and it was the almost complete absence of imperial authority in the Empire, not rampant particularism, which gave the German rulers the motive and opportunity to look to their own state interests.

Another legend has in the past been considered a major cause of the war, the so-called Madrid-Vienna axis, a supposed close alliance between the two branches of the House of Habsburg to restore their power in Germany and Europe by means of a Catholic crusade. They are said to have had grandiose plans: Spain was to recover the Netherlands and humiliate France and Austria was to restore Habsburg authority in Germany. Together they would recatholicize Scandinavia, turn the Baltic into a Habsburg lake, revive Poland, creating a Vienna-Madrid-Warsaw axis, and launch an attack on the Turks to liberate Hungary and the Balkans and recover Constantinople.

In fact such an alliance between Madrid and Vienna was created by the war and was not a cause of it. Both states were very weak at the outset of war and needed peace. Though the Habsburgs' enemies habitually interpreted the relationship between Spain and Austria as very close, in fact there was, in spite of the family link, no real identity of interest between them. An alliance with France would have benefited each more than the alliance with one another. More than that, before 1618 there was very real mistrust and divergence of opinion between the two over policy in Germany, Bohemia, Italy and the Netherlands, especially as the last two were claimed as fiefs of the Empire, that is under ultimate imperial authority, though they were possessed by the Spanish branch of the family. The Austrian branch was very bitter when, at the partition of Charles V's empire, Spain emerged as the senior line, with the advantages of American silver, a stronger monarchy and an absence of Protestants. This was also a sign of the devaluation of the imperial title, though Philip II would have liked to have been Holy Roman Emperor.

As we have seen, the Austrian branch tended to follow a more *politique* line on religion and the Dutch revolt. Matthias had briefly flirted with the idea of taking over the role of figurehead of the Dutch rebels. The Austrians were greatly irritated when Spain assumed that German territory near the Spanish Road was a legitimate sphere of Spanish influence and acted in accordance with this assumption. This, plus Spanish interference in German affairs, added fuel to the "Spanish tyranny" argument of the German princes and made life difficult for emperors like Rudolph II, who needed German aid against the Turks. The Emperors' position was further damaged by the growing religious squabbles, in which Spain was seen as playing a role. Spain also took advantage of troubles in Rudolph's later years to increase her influence in Austria.[13] Philip II was always ready to give advice to his Austrian cousins, whether they wanted it or not. He was constantly annoyed at the Austrians' obsession with their Balkan ambitions and refused to give any help for their campaign in Hungary unless Spain was given overall charge of it.

The Emperor Ferdinand II, who succeeded Matthias, is traditionally portrayed as the Spanish candidate for the imperial crown but in fact his choice as heir to the Austrian lands after the sons of Maximilian II died out without direct heirs was a defeat for Spain, which also had a claim to the Austrian inheritance. Ferdinand was a member of the Inner Austrian or Styrian branch of the Austrian Habsburgs. He had ruled Inner Austria from 1595. He was an absolutist who, like Maximilian of Bavaria, used the Counter-Reformation for political ends, in particular to smash the noble-dominated Estates. The traditional Protestant view of Ferdinand as a bigot and tyrant is over-simple. While his personal zeal as an observant Catholic was undeniable, he was a rather lazy and easy-going man under the influence of his advisers. His main aim was to turn Austria into a powerful state with central institutions, religiously uniform for political reasons. As Matthias had no children he was recognized as the Habsburg candidate for the imperial title in preference to Philip IV and as heir to the Austrian senior line in 1617 by the Treaty of Graz, also known as the Oñate Treaty, which was kept secret for a long time. He had to buy off Spanish claims by promising to cede to them Austrian possessions in Alsace and imperial fiefs like Mantua in northern Italy, which seemed likely to become vacant soon. He succeeded to an Austria in ruins thanks to his cousins and the last thing he needed at his accession was a large-scale war.

His ambitions lay in Austria, not in Germany. Certainly he needed allies among the German rulers but had great difficulties in winning them. The Catholic League was not immediately available to him, as it was a Bavarian alliance and its leader, Maximilian of Bavaria, was very cautious in the early stages of the war, 1619–20, and only committed himself to Ferdinand when he had strong guarantees. What pushed Austria and Spain together was fear of the Calvinist activism already noted. This was not a factor in areas which were solidly Catholic or Protestant like Bavaria, Saxony, Scandinavia and Brandenburg but in areas where religious confrontation was or had recently been acute, including the Netherlands, England, Austria, France, Hungary, parts of Germany and Bohemia. It was in Bohemia that the Thirty Years' War began.

5 The Thirty Years' War and its Consequences

There was a time when it was fashionable to deny that there was any such thing as the Thirty Years' War: the whole thing was an invention of German nationalist historians in the nineteenth century. The fighting between 1618 and 1648 was a series of separate conflicts, often fought over issues which had little to do with Germany but which happened to spill over on to German soil and to involve German rulers. The war never involved the whole of the Empire. Many of those who fought in "German" armies were not Germans but Walloons, Scots, Spaniards, Dutchmen and Italians. There was a Bohemian phase, a Danish phase, a Swedish phase and a French phase, the first arising from a revolt in the Austrian Habsburgs' territories, the second and third a spilling over into Germany of the Northern War for domination of the Baltic and the last a part of the much longer struggle, fought on many fronts between the Habsburgs and their enemies, for hegemony in Europe. Although the fighting in Germany ended in 1648, it continued elsewhere until 1659–60.

It is easy with hindsight to challenge long-held assumptions about the war but, in doing so, one runs the risk of ignoring the way in which contemporaries viewed it. The war was seen by them as a continuous conflict which lasted for thirty years. Some contemporaries called it "the German war". Important German political and religious questions were at issue in it, not just in the propaganda of the belligerents. It therefore had some characteristics of a German civil war. The treaties of Westphalia which brought it to an end had important long-term consequences for Germany.

The war had its origins in the internal political problems of the Austrian state and, initially at least, there was no sign that it would

85

turn into a German or European conflict. It was the European implications of the Bohemian question which led eventually to the internationalization of the war. Bohemia was seen as one of the areas in Europe on the front line of religious confrontation. It was regarded as vital to the Habsburgs in maintaining their influence in German politics, particularly because of its vote in imperial elections, and in their struggles against the Turks. By extension it was crucial to the religious future of Poland and therefore to the Baltic. If it could be won for the reformed faith, Protestantism would gain a great accession of power in Europe.

In 1617 a majority of the Bohemian nobility, which dominated the Estates, elected Ferdinand of Styria, as the adopted son of Matthias, King of Bohemia in return for a confirmation of the privileges of the kingdom and an affirmation that its throne was elective. Relations between the new king and his subjects quickly deteriorated. Trouble had been foreshadowed during Matthias' reign, when the government attempted to stop the building of Protestant churches in certain areas and committed other infringements of the Letter of Majesty. There was growing polarization, as the majority of moderates in the Bohemian ruling class lost ground to extremist minorities of Catholics and Protestants, and a real danger of civil war. The resistance to Ferdinand was not exclusively Protestant but had the characteristics of a Bohemian nationalist movement, involving both Czech and German nobles of both faiths. The whole movement was portrayed as legitimate resistance to prevent the imposition of a tyranny. A coup attempt was launched from March 1618 by a minority of the nobility planning to depose the Habsburgs and install a Protestant dynasty. The Calvinist "International" became involved after an armed rising in May 1618 following the famous defenestration of Prague. After a mock trial of three crown officials held to be responsible for breaches of Bohemian liberties by a "court" of Protestant nobles, they were thrown out of a high window. Their survival was seen on the Catholic side as a sign of divine favour; a contemporary print showed angels, under the personal direction of the Virgin Mary, wafting them gently to the ground with heavenly parachutes. The Bohemian revolt was followed closely by another in the archduchy of Upper Austria.

In January 1619 a defensive alliance was signed between the Bohemian rebels and the Upper Austrian Estates, after which they began to raise an army. The leading element in this movement was the lesser nobility. The towns and the peasantry played little part and there was an undercurrent of class bitterness accompanying the whole thing. The nobility refused to arm the peasants as they were afraid of them. These divisions weakened the rebel cause from the outset and it was their constant aim to secure foreign help for their cause. Their initial appeals, including to the Turks, had no success but the insurrection gradually spread. In March 1619 Matthias died. The Estates of Upper and Lower Austria refused to accept Ferdinand as their ruler and they were quickly joined by the provinces of Silesia, Lusatia and Moravia. In June 1619 a rebel army came close to Vienna. On 26 August the Bohemian diet elected Frederick V, elector palatine, king. He accepted against the advice of the members of the Protestant Union and his fellow Protestant rulers, including his father-in-law, James I of England, who was trying to establish a reputation as the arbiter of Protestant Europe. It quickly became clear that Frederick was no more than a puppet of a party within the nobility. Ferdinand, in the meantime elected Emperor unopposed, did not immediately move to deal with the rebellions by force, though in reality he had little choice as he possessed no military resources to speak of. The recruiting and financing of troops had fallen largely under the control of the Estates of the Austrian lands, the most important of which were in open rebellion against him.

In spite of this, the Bohemian rebels were vulnerable and had to continue their efforts to internationalize the war. Frederick's coronation in Prague in November raised calls for a Protestant Emperor but only the Transylvanian prince Bethlen Gabor and the Duke of Savoy, who had ambitions on the Bohemian and even the imperial crown, were prepared to go beyond encouraging words to help Frederick. The Catholic League also did nothing to help Ferdinand until Spain entered the war in October 1619. This was after a long debate in the government, which the war party eventually won. They argued that, though Spain was in a financial mess, she had to intervene. Otherwise she ran the risk of lots of dominoes falling, including the total loss of the Netherlands, and ultimately the loss of the South American and East Indian colonies to the Dutch. In August 1618 the Orangists had come back into power in the United Provinces and Dutch interlopers were already making serious inroads in Brazil and the Far East.

Spanish armies from the southern Netherlands and Italy moved into Germany from November 1619 to early 1620, occupying the parts of the Palatinate to the west of the Rhine and giving rise to rumours that Spain planned to annex the whole of the Lower Palatinate. In July the League and the Union signed the Treaty of Ulm, which neutralized the west of the Empire, a sign of a desire to avoid war rather than launch crusades against one another. These events gave Maximilian of Bavaria the security he needed and he was ready to enter an alliance with Ferdinand in return for a promise of territory. In 1621 Bavarian troops occupied Upper Austria. The harshness of the occupation was to provoke a peasant revolt in 1626. It was not clear whether this cession of land would be as security for the costs of Maximilian's military aid or permanent. Maximilian was also given a verbal promise of a share of the Palatinate and an electoral title. In December 1619 Saxony also allied with the Emperor in return for the cession of Lusatia and a guarantee of the existing rights of Lutherans in the Empire. The allied forces won a speedy and overwhelming victory on the White Mountain outside Prague on 8 November 1620. There was a certain irony in the fact that at this battle the Bohemian army consisted mainly of Germans and Hungarians and the imperial army, apart from some Saxons, of Italian and Walloon mercenaries hired by the Catholic League. This was one of the only two occasions during the war when the Habsburg forces were able to combine. The other occasion was in 1634 at Nördlingen, another great victory, which prolonged the war and led to French intervention. The victory on the White Mountain ended the Bohemian revolt but began the real Thirty Years' War.

Detailed accounts of the course of the war are readily available in many places,[1] to which the reader is referred. There were two main theatres of conflict once the Bohemian phase ended, in the Rhineland, where Spain fought against France or her agents, and in other parts of Germany, where the Austrian Habsburgs fought against first the Danes and then the Swedes and their German allies.

Attention here will be focused on imperial policy in the war and the impact of the war on Germany. One issue is the question of imperial absolutism, the supposed ambition of Ferdinand II to deprive the German princes of their autonomy and to restore full centralized monarchical control over the whole Empire. There can be little doubt that Ferdinand did see an opportunity during the war to increase imperial influence in Germany not so much by force as by persuasion and conciliation. Ferdinand was certainly tough in restoring monarchical power in his own hereditary lands, where it was threatened by the nobility, but not in Germany. Three points are traditionally quoted in connexion with the imperial absolutism debate, the Edict of Restitution of 1629, the role of the imperial commander Wallenstein and the Peace of Prague of 1635.

The Edict of Restitution of March 1629, issued after the defeat of Danish intervention in the war, was as much political as religious in motivation. It proposed substantial changes, a great redistribution of religious and temporal power, which would have considerably strengthened Habsburg power in Germany. Under the edict all land secularized illegally since 1552 was to return to the Church including sees in north Germany. Tilly's army was used to enforce the decisions of special imperial commissioners administering the edict and members of the imperial family were appointed to vacant sees, which were occupied by imperial troops. Calvinism was outlawed and German rulers were reminded that, under imperial law, they were not allowed to make alliances with foreign states. All these decisions were issued as imperial decrees without reference to the *Reichstag*, which was profoundly worrying to all the German princes, Catholic and Protestant. The edict was an assertion of existing law but its enforcement by the imperial courts caused outrage among the German princes. It was an exercise of the imperial office not seen since after Charles V's victory in 1547 and was attacked as absolutism and Spanish tyranny. Significantly Maximilian of Bavaria refused to allow his troops to be used to enforce the edict. He also took the lead at a meeting of the electors in Regensburg in 1630, in which French influence was very visible, which demanded the abolition of the edict and refused to elect Ferdinand's son as king of the Romans. In 1631 Bavaria entered an alliance with France, showing the readiness of the German princes to turn to foreign friends when the Emperor threatened to become too powerful. At the insistence of the electors the Emperor was forced to suspend the edict in May 1635. In spite of this, the electors still refused to elect his son king and to give him military aid.

There is dispute about the significance of Albrecht von Wallenstein (1583–1634).[2] He rose rapidly to prominence after the White Mountain, which enabled him to buy up confiscated rebel lands at low prices. 1625 saw his emergence as the leading imperial general. In the spring of that year he offered to raise an army of 40 000 for the Emperor, financed with his own resources and equipped from his own enterprises, to meet the Danish intervention. This was an opportunity for Ferdinand to end his reliance on Maximilian of Bavaria and he appointed Wallenstein commander of all imperial troops in the Empire. Wallenstein's successes were immediate and spectacular and he was made commander in chief of all the imperial forces. Following a series of victories in 1626, northern Germany came under Wallenstein's control. In May 1629 Christian IV of Denmark came to terms in the Peace of Lübeck. The Emperor, not wishing to spread the war, was very generous to Denmark. In July 1629 the two duchies of

Mecklenburg were given to Wallenstein as a state of his own, as an alternative to paying him the huge sums the Emperor owed him. Against the advice of many of his counsellors Ferdinand deposed and dispossessed the two Mecklenburg dukes on the grounds that they had been allies of Denmark. This exercise of the imperial will again caused very unfavourable comment among the German princes, as did the appointment of Wallenstein as general of the Oceanic (Atlantic) and Baltic seas, with plans to establish an imperial navy.

All in all, Wallenstein provided the answer to Ferdinand's prayers, an army which won victories and which could support itself at someone else's cost. Ironically, his great success was his undoing. His great power worried everybody, including his nominal employer, the Emperor. The 1630 electoral diet, which forced Ferdinand to suspend the Edict of Restitution, also made him dismiss Wallenstein and after this the imperial armies were reduced. Unfortunately, Wallenstein's successes in the north precipitated the Swedish intervention in Germany, a revival of the northern wars which had racked the Baltic in the second half of the sixteenth century. Wallenstein's victories revived fears of a Vienna/Warsaw axis. Sigismund III, the Vasa King of Poland responsible for the virtual elimination of Protestantism in that country, was brother-in-law of the Emperor. He had been King of Sweden until 1598, when his attempts to recatholicize the country provoked a coup which deposed him. The Swedish invasion of Germany in 1630 was designed to meet the threat of an attempt to restore the Catholic Vasas by force. A series of imperial defeats, culminating in April 1632 in a Swedish occupation of Munich, led to the recall of Wallenstein as a commander with unlimited powers. Bavaria returned to the imperial alliance. Wallenstein again became too powerful and threatened to undermine the Emperor's carefully constructed system of influence in Germany. There were rumours that he was in secret negotiation with the Emperor's enemies with a view to changing sides and in February 1634 he was killed on imperial orders. His "state", including his substantial financial and manufacturing empire, collapsed. Command of the imperial forces passed to the Emperor's son, King Ferdinand of Hungary and Bohemia.

Some credit Wallenstein with a desire to restore a powerful Habsburg monarchy in Germany while others argue that he was motivated solely by great personal ambition, in particular to create a state for himself. Some dismiss him as old-style *condottiere*, a type of man Europe had already outgrown, a half-way stage between the private contractors who raised mercenary armies and the commanders of the state-controlled standing armies of the eighteenth century. Others do not regard him as a German but see him as a Bohemian patriot with political and economic ideas way ahead of his time. On balance the policies of Wallenstein seem to have stemmed from personal ambition rather than a desire to promote imperial absolutism.

The Peace of Prague was signed between the Emperor and the Elector of Saxony in 1635 after the massive defeat of the Swedes and their Saxon allies at Nördlingen on 6 September 1634. It took the form of a permanent alliance designed to keep foreigners out of Germany, not an instrument of imperial dictatorship, and other German rulers were subsequently invited to join it. Under the terms of the treaty all the princes were forbidden to enter foreign alliances. It also contained a plan for an imperial standing army to be financed by the princes but controlled by the Emperor. There was to be a general *restitutio in integrum*, a return to pre-1618 conditions, from which only Bohemia and the Palatinate were excluded. The Edict of Restitution was suspended and a new normal date for the division of Germany between the faiths was fixed at 1627. Calvinism was still not recognized as an official faith. The Catholic League was abolished, though Bavaria later reestablished it. The deposed dukes of Mecklenburg were restored. Bohemia was recognized as an hereditary possession of the House of Habsburg. The *Reichstag* and the *Reichskammergericht* were to be restored to regular activity.

The treaty was in reality a manifestation of German national feeling (*Reichspatriotismus*) against the foreigners who were ravaging the country. It was not an instrument of imperial absolutism: Ferdinand was in any case too old for such ambitions. Its main aim was to prevent Germany being dragged into war between Spain and France. In December 1636 Ferdinand's son was elected king of the Romans and succeeded his father as Emperor Ferdinand III in 1637.

By then foreign interference was too deeply established to be easily eliminated. As a result Germany did not have any chance to solve her constitutional and other problems by herself. In May 1635 France declared war on Spain and the final and most destructive phase of the conflict began, which lasted until 1648. The alliance system established in the Treaty of Prague did not have time to establish itself and little could be done to prevent the armies of France and Sweden, and their German clients, ravaging the country. Saxony, Brandenburg, Bavaria, the south west, Mecklenburg and Bohemia all became theatres of war. Many German states tried to save themselves by returning to neutrality but this could be as damaging as belligerency. Saxony and Brandenburg were both plundered by the armies of their nominal protector, Sweden. Bavaria abandoned neutrality in the last months of the war as the elector believed that the settlement being proposed by the French was not beneficial to Bavarian interests and was afraid of a French domination of Germany. His country was again devastated in the last campaign.

It soon became clear that the French and the Swedes were anxious to dictate a settlement to the Emperor and his allies. Sweden demanded money and territory for itself and an amnesty for all its allies among the German princes. French ambitions were more wide-ranging: Germany was a vital component in the French security system which Richelieu was seeking to create and they were already thinking of creating a permanent alliance system among the states of the Empire. The French also wanted substantial territorial concessions to strengthen their eastern borders. Their basic aim was a settlement which would for all time deprive the Emperor of the resources of Germany. In fact, during the long negotiations which preceded the Peace of Westphalia the Emperor was able to defeat such aims. Ferdinand III had some success in building up support among the German rulers and had some very able diplomats at the negotiations, which took place in two centres, made neutral for the purpose, Münster and Osnabrück, for some seven years from 1641. Actual intensive negotiations began in 1645 after the Emperor in August abandoned his claim to negotiate exclusively on behalf of all the states of the Empire.

Eventually the German states divided into Catholic and Protestant *corpora* which prevented individual states holding up the business because of trivia and made the negotiations much easier. The Emperor was able to play on fears of Swedish ambitions in north Germany and the Baltic on the part of Brandenburg, Denmark, the Dutch and the Hanseatic cities. The negotiations revealed a surprisingly large reservoir of imperial sentiment in Germany, especially among the weaker Catholic states, who were afraid of aggressive Protestantism backed by powerful foreign states, and among the electors disquieted by a campaign by some princes, backed by Sweden, to lessen their predominant position in the politics of the Empire. This was one reason why Sweden's favourite client state and the leader of a group of princes seeking radical constitutional changes, Hesse-Cassel, did not achieve what it sought, including the substantial territorial gains it had hoped for. It had to be content with little bits and pieces which did nothing to strengthen it. Catholic predominance in the south was restored by the abolition of the duchy of Franconia, created for the mercenary commander Bernhard of Saxe-Weimar out of the sees of Bamberg and Würzburg.

In particular Ferdinand was able to frustrate plans to include detailed changes in the imperial constitution in the peace settlement, including a permanent capitulation of election agreed by all the German rulers not just the electors, changes in the system of electing a king of the Romans and reform of the *Reichshofrat* to end the Emperor's exclusive control of it. An imperial diet was supposed to meet within six months of the peace settlement to deal with these matters but in fact it did not convene until 1653. These points were never settled and were to remain a source of friction in German politics until the end of the Empire. The only minor concessions made were that after 1648 the princes and towns would be able to comment officially on the contents of the *Wahlkapitulation* and that in future a king of the Romans could be elected only by a unanimous vote of the electors. As before, the election of an Emperor would require only a majority.

The fixing of the situation in 1624 as the basis for the religious settlement was also a minor victory for the imperialists, as was the renewal of the 1555 Ecclesiastical Reservation clause to prevent further erosion of the Catholic position in the Empire. Although a numerical minority, Catholics continued after 1648 to dominate the college of electors and to set the public tone of the Empire. It was accepted that there would always be a Catholic majority in the college of electors. The Bohemian vote, long in abeyance, was revived in 1708 to balance the newly created Hanoverian electorate and it was laid down that if, as happened in 1777, the Bavarian and Palatinate lines were amalgamated, an extra Catholic vote would be created. The Catholic Church remained an important element in the imperial structure. About a third of the Empire consisted of ecclesiastical territories and imperial counts and knights were able to find a useful niche in cathedral chapters. Abbeys and convents were a source of useful employment for younger sons and convenient stowing places for the unmarriageable daughters of the imperial nobility.

The treaties of Westphalia were signed simultaneously in Osnabrück between the Emperor and Sweden and in Münster between the Emperor and France and their allies on 24 October 1648. A Spanish-Dutch peace had been signed earlier in January. The treaties were important at two levels. They were international treaties in which France, Sweden, the Emperor and the electors, princes and towns of the Empire came to terms as equals. It was an attempt at a general and comprehensive settlement of all outstanding European problems, to be rounded off by the treaties of the Pyrenees in 1659 and Oliva in 1660. As such it lasted in its essentials until the French Revolution. It was also an agreement between the head and members of the Holy Roman Empire and among the members of the Empire themselves. The two treaties became a major element in the imperial constitution alongside the Golden Bull, capitulations of election and the religious peace of 1555. The constitution of the *Reich* was rebuilt in its final form; there was, in reality, no alternative to the structure established in 1648.

The treaties are enormous documents, most of them taken up with minor points of detail, mainly concerned with religion. There was an attempt at a comprehensive clarification of the constitutional situation: all existing customs and usages contrary to their provisions were specifically annulled. Perhaps the most important part was paragraphs 1 and 2 of Article VIII of the Treaty of Osnabrück, by which the Emperor recognized "German liberty". This confirmed the German rulers' free exercise of territorial sovereignty, *Landeshoheit*, a term used only from the middle of the seventeenth century. They were not given this by the treaties of Westphalia but their absolute possession of it was confirmed. From now on they exercised this right of government in their own name, not as supposed agents of the Emperor. Now only certain powers were specifically reserved by the Emperor, the *Reservatrechte*. These included the right to charter universities and grant titles of nobility and the Emperor's rights as feudal overlord. All Jews in the Empire were the Emperor's subjects. The princes also now had the right to make alliances among themselves and with foreign powers as long as such alliances were not aimed against the Emperor, the Empire or the peace of the Empire. This completed the process by which the princes secured a monopoly of diplomatic power for themselves. Not only was the Emperor no longer able to speak for them but their subjects, organized in Estates or in towns, could no longer enter agreements with "foreigners" without the prince's consent, as they had sometimes done earlier.

The composition of the *Reichstag* was laid down; it was to consist of three voting houses (*curia*) of electors, princes and, it was now accepted after long dispute, towns. This last provision was of more symbolic than real importance because most of the imperial cities were in advanced decline and the majority never bothered to send representatives to the diet. The subordinate role of the house of towns was shown in the fact that they could not initiate legislation and in joint meetings their representatives stood while those of the electors and princes sat. The legislative power of the diet was confirmed; its consent was required for everything which touched the Estates of the Empire, war and peace, taxes, duties, treaties which placed obligations on the Empire, the imperial fortresses, the movement of imperial troops and the imposition of the ban of the Empire, the ultimate punishment of a ruler, depriving him of land and titles and making him an outlaw.

There were important religious clauses. Calvinism was confirmed as the third official religion of the *Reich*. The princes were given the total *jus reformandi* over their churches. The amendment of the imperial constitution to accept the equality of the two faiths, long discussed before the war, was now accepted. The *Reichstag* was divided officially into two religious *corpora*, Catholic and Protestant, led by Mainz and Saxony, with an "alarm bell" procedure: any matter concerning religion could not be settled by majority vote but only by compromise. This was known as the *jus itio in partes* and would be described in the jargon of modern sociology as a consociational solution. This settled the important constitutional issue of majority voting raised at the 1598 diet. The rights of religious minorities were guaranteed not in a spirit of toleration but out of a desire to end religious confrontation and the use of religion as a political weapon. Article 5, Paragraph 35 laid down that 1624 was to be the key year in the religious settlement: members of any of the three legal faiths established in a state in 1624 could stay there. Those not covered by this provision were to be allowed to leave with all their property or, if they stayed, were not to be persecuted. Members of minority religions were to be allowed private worship in their own homes. Individual princes could, if they wished, extend toleration beyond this minimum level. Catholic rulers usually interpreted the settlement in a narrow sense, Protestants often more generously. All disputes between the faiths were to be settled by the imperial courts and the Emperor was declared protector of all three faiths. There was to be religious equality in the staffing of the two imperial high courts.

A less extreme view of religion was evident during the negotiations leading to the treaties. In both Catholicism and Protestantism there was a movement away from religious persecution and towards a more contemplative inward Christianity, which abstained from involvement in politics. In spite of this desire to see an end of the politicization of religion, which was held to be responsible for the horrors of the war, there remained a constant undercurrent of religious mistrust. Religion was still being used as a political weapon in the later eighteenth century, when Prussia and Austria posed as leaders of German Protestantism and Catholicism respectively. Clearly, after 1648 religious considerations were far from paramount in decision-making, if they ever had been. This was seen, for example, in the refusal of Catholic rulers to take any notice of the pope's objections to the settlement, but it would be misleading to talk of a comprehensive "secularization of politics" in post-1648 Germany. Many governments might have preferred such a development but it was hard to eradicate a confessionalism which had become so deeply rooted earlier. In fact many potential points of religious friction were left unsettled: most German states remained mixed in religion and some, for example the Palatinate, were very mixed.

The situation became more complex still if princes changed their faith or the ruling line changed, though it was very rare after 1648 for such rulers to try to convert all their subjects forcibly. When the Elector of Saxony became a convert to Catholicism in the late seventeenth century this was a purely personal change. Saxony remained a Lutheran state; the elector remained an official Lutheran and head of the Protestant *corpus* in the *Reichstag*, though actual leadership was increasingly provided by the deputy director, Brandenburg-Prussia. The settlement also contained all kinds of compromises, including the *Simultaneum*, the sharing of churches between two or more religions, and *Parität*, the fixed apportionment of public offices between two faiths, in a number of free cities. The town of Siegen in Nassau became the common capital of two states, one ruled by a Catholic line and one by a Protestant line of the House of Nassau. The two faiths could hold processions in the town only on certain days and using certain roads. One church in Protestant Frankfurt-am-Main remained Catholic as the Mass associated with imperial coronations was held there. The Catholic bishopric of Osnabrück, which had a predominantly Lutheran population, passed alternately between a Catholic bishop, elected by a cathedral chapter dominated by Protestant nobles, and a Protestant prince of the House of Hanover, who acted as head of state but did not exercise clerical functions.

There were major territorial changes with long-term implications for Germany. Brandenburg-Prussia, cheated of its legitimate claims to the whole of Pomerania, the more valuable western part of which containing the port of Stettin went to Sweden, gained the sees of Minden, Kammin and Halberstadt and the reversion to Magdeburg, which was taken up in 1680. Although substantial, these were not seen as enough and the Hohenzollerns remained determined to recover what they had lost. Some of these acquisitions added to the central block of Brandenburg territory around Berlin but left the two outlying blocks in the west based on Cleves and Mark, gained in 1614, and in the east, ducal or east Prussia, a fief of the Polish crown inherited in 1618. Saxony retained Lusatia, her reward for helping Ferdinand II put down the Bohemian rebels. This added to the prestige of the Saxon dynasty but was of little value in enhancing its potential as a power. Bavaria kept the Upper Palatinate, adding further to her already compact territory, and the Palatine electoral title with all its precendence and attributes. A new eighth electorate was created for the restored elector palatine, who kept the scattered and vulnerable territories of the Lower or Rhenish Palatinate. In a dispute typical of the Empire, Bavaria and the Palatinate both claimed the imperial vicariate, the regency during an imperial interregnum, which under the Golden Bull the elector palatine and the Elector of Saxony exercised and which came into operation in 1657 after the death of Ferdinand III.

All in all, the treaties of Westphalia contained nothing startlingly new. They rounded off trends visible for over four hundred years. They ratified the states' rights. They were not seen by the Germans as something revolutionary or as a conscious turning point but as a restatement of old rights. The political form of Germany until 1806 was dictated by it. After 1648 the Empire was a federative state. The treaties of Westphalia were not in themselves the cause of Germany's weakness and division but they codified in European public law the factors contributing to weakness and division since the twelfth century. Particularism became firmly established. Disputes as to whether the Empire was a federation or a confederation, that is a state in which a central government devolved some of its functions downwards to lower units or a state made up of a collection of sovereign units devolving some of their power upwards to a central government, is irrelevant as the *Reich* was unique and fitted into no pattern.

A major result of the treaties was to make foreign interference in German affairs a permanent and important factor. From 1648 onwards no major development could take place in Germany without arousing foreign interest. France and Sweden were guarantors of the treaties and on the basis of this assumed a legal right of interference in the affairs of Germany. Sweden became a state of the Empire through its possessions in the north, including Wismar, reputed to be the strongest fortress in the Empire. It also controlled the mouths of the Elbe and Weser rivers. French possession of the three bishoprics of Metz, Toul and Verdun, held since 1552, was confirmed. France also gained Breisach on the east bank of the Rhine, Austrian lands in Alsace, the Sundgau, and a protectorate over ten imperial free cities in Alsace. As was shown in his instructions for his negotiators at Münster of October 1645, the Emperor would have ceded the whole Breisgau, the area around Freiburg, as well in order to preserve the Austrian heartlands intact. As a result of these gains France possessed entry ports, which gave her an open door into Germany. Legally these territories remained part of the Empire but, unlike Sweden, France did not become a member of the Empire as that would have involved a recognition of the Emperor's nominal overlordship. The whole of Alsace and Lorraine was opened to French influence and it was to be easy for Louis XIV to turn protection into possession in the 1680s. France considered it vital to maintain a powerful voice in German affairs and kept diplomatic representatives at the imperial diet, after 1663 in permanent session at Regensburg. These were usually talented professional diplomats not the gilded aristocratic ninnies sent as representatives to less important embassies. It was the ambition of France to build up a system of clients among the rulers of the Empire and in the immediate aftermath of the Thirty Years' War many German princes rushed into Louis XIV's arms, seeking status, subsidies and protection against the Emperor in a French connexion.

After 1648 the majority of the German rulers were very nervous indeed and terrified of a resumption of warfare. France was able to take advantage of this feeling of vulnerability. There were, apparently, two methods of obtaining security available to the German rulers. One, already touched on, was the creation of standing armies. This was an option available only to the larger states; apart from Austria and Brandenburg-Prussia, only Bavaria, Saxony, Brunswick-Lüneburg (Hanover), Hesse-Cassel, Trier, Mainz, Cologne, Salzburg and Münster had respectable forces while many others had small ceremonial armies reinforced with militias and gendarmeries. Other states, for example Mecklenburg-Schwerin and Württemberg, would have liked to have joined the "armed estates" (*armierte Stände*), as they became known, but were unable to do so, mainly because of opposition from their parliamentary Estates. The other method of finding security was an alliance. After 1648 there was a rush into alliances, especially in the south and west, motivated by fear of the over-mighty Emperor and of being dragged into the Franco-Spanish war, which went on until 1659.

The first major shock came in 1651 when it seemed for a time that the north west and west might be engulfed in conflict after the Elector of Brandenburg invaded Jülich-Berg on the Lower Rhine from his neighbouring possession in Cleves, with a view to seizing it. The affair was settled by imperial mediation but sent a shiver through the Empire. From such small beginnings the Thirty Years' War had started. Shortly afterwards two defensive associations were formed, the Protestant Union, known as the Waldeck Union after the memorandum of Count George Frederick of Waldeck, a Brandenburg minister, which led to its establishment in 1654, and the Catholic Cologne Alliance of 1655. These two groupings had the same objectives, the preservation of peace and their members' rights. In 1658 many members of the two alliances came together with France in the League of the Rhine (*Rheinbund*), an alliance formed on the initiative of the Elector of Mainz with the same objectives. It involved arrangements for mutual military support against foreign and internal enemies of the members, including their own subjects. Its most spectacular mobilization under the latter heading occurred in 1664, when a league army, including French troops, helped the Archbishop of Mainz to reduce his previously autonomous city of Erfurt to obedience. This was legitimized by an imperial mandate to restore order in the city. In 1671 the city of Brunswick was seized by force by the Duke of Brunswick-Wolfenbüttel. Brunswick had never been an imperial free city but enjoyed complete autonomy. In the fifteenth century it had been invited to the *Reichstag* and had paid imperial taxes directly. There is some doubt about Erfurt's status but it too had in the past been treated as a free city. The League, which lasted until 1668, was a most useful instrument of French policy; it increased French influence in Germany and it ensured the neutrality of the Empire during the French invasion of the Spanish Netherlands, nominally part of the Empire, in the War of Devolution, 1667–8.

There were other foreign influences in addition to those of France and Sweden. Denmark, although much weaker than Sweden, was a force in the north. North western Germany was subject to Dutch and Spanish influence, the latter from the Spanish Netherlands. The period after 1648 saw mounting friction between the Dutch and the substantial prince bishopric of Münster, a Catholic outpost in a largely Protestant area. The energetic Bishop Christoph Bernhard von Galen (1650–78), who crushed the opposition of the Protestant city of Münster by force, recatholicized it, installed an absolutist system of government and created a sizeable standing army, fought the Dutch and pursued a policy of territorial expansion which threatened the stability of the whole region.

The Thirty Years' War had other major consequences for Germany. Its effects on the German collective consciousness were considerable. The war produced a deep feeling of insecurity as well as severe material deprivation, made worse by the post-war economic depression. It was attacked by Grotius in 1625 as a war without reason, far worse than the wars of barbarous nations. Although it was not, in fact, a pointless war, it was certainly seen by contemporaries as especially terrible in its length, viciousness and in the size of the armies involved. The common man was held to have suffered in it more than was normal. It bred a belief, which gained wide currency in Germany in the Neo-Stoicism of the Dutch phililogist Justus Lipsius, that hard times need hard remedies, a yearning for government. It helped further to legitimize the modern state and accelerated its emergence. It speeded up modernization through absolutism, a process already well-established before 1618. Absolutism as a system of government was both necessary and fashionable. Germany experienced some of the most disturbing manifestations of the so-called general crisis of the seventeenth century, a period of deep and dramatic changes lasting from about 1630 to 1670, which affected all aspects of life. The culmination of the period of instability which had been growing through the sixteenth century, with its implicit threat of civil war, it was a time of flux and chaos, uncertainty and fear. [3] Only strong government could save society from the terrible internal and external dangers which faced it. In particular the dangers of war, brutally illustrated by the Thirty Years' War, justified the taking of extra powers by governments.

A strong state was needed to regulate a society with an inherent tendency to anarchy and to control inevitable conflicts over the distribution of scarce resources. Only the monarch, elevated above the mass of the people thanks to his office, was able to understand the mysteries of government (*arcana imperii*). Subjects were, in contrast, unable to see beyond their narrow class or local interests. This contributed to the revival of the image of the monarch as the stern father of his people, with a duty to promote the common welfare by good *Polizei*. The model of classical Rome, with its supposed virtues of obedience, discipline and respect for authority, was held up before the people as an example to imitate. An important description of a good state in action was given in 1656 in the *Teutsche Fürstenstaat* (*The German Princely State*) of Veit Ludwig von Seckendorff, an experienced administrator.

Fashion also played a major role in the spread of absolutist ideas: the great success of Louis XIV's France was attributed by many contemporaries not to the large population, fertile soil and skilled ministers and generals of France but to its system of government and economic management. This bred a great desire to imitate the absolutism of Louis XIV and the grandeur and pomp of Versailles among many German rulers. From 1648 French culture and fashion were to be predominant among the upper classes in Germany. [4] The vogue of absolutism was also seen in the theatre, opera, literature, elaborate court ceremonial, architecture and garden design, in which order and discipline were given visible expression. Only Vienna, among the larger German courts, resisted the French wave and stuck to the Burgundian/Spanish ceremonial until the reign of Francis I (1745–65). Although none of the German rulers was able to reach the level of Versailles, many fine German palaces and gardens are products of this period, including Mannheim, the new residence of the elector palatine after the French destruction of Heidelberg in 1689, Karlsruhe in Baden, Schleissheim and Nymphenburg outside Munich, Herrenhausen near Hanover, Favorite near Rastatt in Baden, Monrepos near Ludwigsburg in Württemberg and Solitude near Stuttgart. These palaces were the stage for elaborate court rituals, "theatrical" representations of the supremacy of the ruler, which were such an important part of the political system. They also functioned as focal points, "capitals" for the emerging states. One beneficial result of this was the great cultural and architectural richness of Germany: even small capitals could, like eighteenth-century Weimar, become intellectual centres.

The new structure of government which was emerging in the German states showed common features, which is not surprising as it was often copied from foreign states such as France or Sweden — this imitation often went as far as the adoption of foreign titles for officials — or from other German states. Fiscal concerns were central. The war taught states many lessons on the management of their finances. Most emerged from the war heavily indebted. The 1654 *Reichstag* passed a general exemption (*Indult*) allowing them to write off three quarters of the accumulated interest on their debts. There was no prospect of the capital being repaid. Many governments had already issued unilateral *moratoria* on their debts during the war, which had damaged the financial system and contributed to the decline of towns. Now only a state which could cast the tax net as widely as possible and mobilize ample resources could survive and become considerable. A poor state would be a victim state. The emergency situation created by the war gave rulers, especially in the larger states, the excuse to by-pass their Estates.

In 1634 the Elector of Bavaria seized his Estates' funds without ceremony and elsewhere taxes were collected by force without the Estates' approval. Under absolutism this special war situation was to be prolonged into peace-time and to become the basis of government. War councils played an important part in the process of state-building. Initially their competence was limited to military matters but, in many cases, it was quickly extended into other fields. The Vienna aulic war council (*Hofkriegsrat*) was set up in 1556 but it had limited powers. More effective was the war council in Ferdinand II's Styria, which organized defence against the Turks in frontier regions. Although it operated at first in close co-operation with the Estates, it quickly became the heart of the government. In 1620 a war council was established as the key institution in the Bavarian government and this was later copied in Brandenburg, where the General War Commissariat, created in 1655, became the most important department, with competence in military and financial matters covering all the provinces of Brandenburg-Prussia.

The idea of the state as something distinct from the personal property of a ruling dynasty emerged slowly and was still incomplete in the eighteenth century. In practical terms the movement towards absolutism aimed at the greatest possible measure of uniformity and standardization. It also sought to concentrate power at the centre and to eliminate the intermediate corporate bodies, with which the prince had earlier shared power, the nobility, parliamentary Estates and self-governing towns. Middlemen and amateurs were to be eliminated. Absolutism meant simplification and standardization. Civil services and armies, under complete state control, became bigger, better-equipped and more professional, making them more expensive. This in turn made tighter centralized state control more necessary in order to increase revenues to fund them. In the electorate of Hanover there were seven separate Estates bodies representing the provinces from which it had been built up. Territorial sovereignty, recognized in the Westphalian treaties, was seen as a uniform set of prerogatives enjoyed by all German rulers which could override the constitutional agreements in force in any given state. Even when they survived, the Estates were often much weakened. A favourite device adopted by many rulers was to persuade them to dispense with regular full meetings, supposedly to save money, and to leave the conduct of affairs to small standing committees. These were usually easier to manage or intimidate. Urban self-government was weakened or eliminated by the introduction of a state official, often initially with limited powers, a procedure again supposedly made necessary by the war. Another device frequently adopted by rulers was the creation of a common central court of appeal for all their territories. This symbolized the unity of the state above provinces and was a useful way of by-passing courts controlled by the Estates. Another was the creation of ever-narrower inner cabinets or committees, which made the real decisions under the ruler's personal control while the privy council or *Hofrat*, in which representatives of the nobility often sat as of right, retained purely administrative functions. The Churches, both Catholic and Protestant, exercised wide supervisory powers in moral and family matters and often controlled education and charities. Increasingly they became little more than departments of the government, giving the state an information and propaganda organization with a branch in every village. Education, designed to teach obedience and the duties of good subjects, expanded. In some German states a comprehensive system of schools was created. [5]

In general, new methods and a new professional mentality began to prevail in the localities as well as at the centre, with orderly procedures. The state became more inquisitive, conducting censuses and land surveys and making regular inspections. Written reports and questionnaires replaced the often more haphazard practices of the older semi-amateur administrators. Proper accounting and the collection of accurate statistics, at a time when many noble Estates were floundering because accounting was a total mystery, became standard practice. Ordinances, once a comparatively rare device, began to rain down in ever-increasing numbers on the Germans. Absolutism and mercantilism, [6] its economic counterpart, involved growing state control of and intervention in the daily lives of the subjects. Nothing was regarded as being outside the competence of the state. In the person of the prince and his officials, the state defined the interests of the community as a whole, the common good (*das gemeine Beste*). As a result, it became real and immediate to the Germans to an extent not often seen elsewhere while the Empire became more and more remote and irrelevant to their lives.

Austria was in the lead among German states in the early stages of absolutism. Although the Emperor lost the war in Germany, he won it in his own hereditary lands, where his authority was considerably strengthened. Monarchical power in Austria and Bohemia, which had come close to being undermined in the early seventeenth century, was fully restored. Bohemia lost its nominally elective crown and became an hereditary possession of the Habsburgs. The resistance of the nobility was ended, helped by another major peasant revolt in Upper Austria from 1625 to 1626, which cemented the alliance between the crown and the nobility. In 1621 a new system of government was introduced, followed in 1627 by a new constitution, imposed by the crown, which destroyed the power of the Estates. Urban and village self-government was abolished. Much tighter state control of the Catholic Church was imposed and religious orthodoxy strictly enforced. Protestants were given twelve months to convert to Catholicism or to leave the country. The same was done in other provinces. Well over 100 000 Protestants of all classes are estimated to have emigrated from the Habsburg lands, which had a substantial political and social impact. A new multi-national nobility was imported and rewarded for their service to the crown with the lands and status of the defeated rebels.

In 1621 Ferdinand II declared the unity of his lands, although he immediately gave the Tyrol to his brother as a secundogeniture, and began the creation of Austrian state machinery separate from imperial organs. This gave him a more secure power base. He still had plenty of opportunities to exercise influence in Germany. It is wrong to assume that after 1648 Austria in some way turned its back on Germany in order to concentrate on war against the Turks in Hungary and the Balkans. Any idea that there was after 1648 a dichotomy in Habsburg policy between imperial and Austrian or dynastic interests is as false as it was in the time of Charles V: Austria retained important territories inside Germany, which was her back door when she turned her main attention to south eastern Europe. She could not afford to ignore it and allow it to come totally under the control of foreign powers. In addition, the situation after 1648 made the small states of the Empire even more dependent on the Emperor for protection. The Thirty Years' War left a legacy of fear among them of a general war of all against all and of more foreign intervention in Germany. This helped to create a large reservoir of imperial loyalty especially in the west and south west. The treaties of Westphalia did not reduce the Empire to a crowned Polish republic, as France and Sweden had wished. There were many loopholes in the treaties and vague points open to different interpretations which enabled Emperors to keep their influence in Germany alive.

Although the spread of absolutist methods of government was speeded up by the war, it would be a mistake to exaggerate its success. Most of the German states were too small for anything but an imitation of the externals of the Sun King's France and the old personal links between ruler and subjects in the little states could not easily be eradicated. Even in Bavaria and Brandenburg absolutism remained an aspiration as rulers tried to deal with remarkably flexible and resilient pre-absolutist structures able to adapt to the new system and, by outward conformity, to neutralize some of its effects. Many Estates retained some administrative and judicial functions and a role in recruiting and the collection and administration of taxes even if their political power was taken away. Similarly the nobility in most German states retained important administrative functions as well as social predominance.

Governments faced other problems: many Estates clung to the *Inkolat*, the rule that only natives of a province could hold office there. It was important for rulers to break this and to be able to choose their servants at will. Led by the Habsburgs, they often solved this by employing foreigners. They then had the problem of controlling the new officeholders, especially when they were nobles. New nobles too often adopted the habits and attitudes of the old. Within a century of the White Mountain the Bohemian nobility, descended from Ferdinand II's new ruling class, had acquired a corporate Bohemian identity. There were often divisions within the nobility, with the court nobility usually dominant. Factions at court, fluid alliances and groupings within the nobility and bureaucracy and intermarriage between old and new nobility were other factors which limited total monarchical power. It is not surprising that many states tried to keep the nobility out of the central financial administrations, which were usually the heart of the new administrative structures. New universities were founded and old ones expanded to train more professional administrators, teachers, lawyers and clergymen for state service. The freeing of universities from the straitjacket of clerical control initially benefited the Protestant states and was only much later copied in Catholic states. The Prussian university at Halle in Magdeburg, opened in 1694, quickly became the best university in Germany which helped to make Brandenburg-Prussia the intellectual capital of the Empire. Halle was overtaken only in the 1730s by the new university at Göttingen in Hanover.

Stronger government was needed to deal with the aftermath of the Thirty Years' War. There has been a long debate about the economic and social consequences of the war. It is very complex and the picture is still unclear. The first point which needs to be made is that much of the evidence was falsified in advance: town councils often exaggerated the damage they had suffered in order to obtain tax cuts. The same arguments had been used by several states in the later sixteenth century to try to obtain reductions in the level of imperial taxation. In 1594 the *Matrikel*, which apportioned imperial taxes between the states of the Empire, was revised to shift the burden of contributions on to the free cities.Thereafter they paid about a quarter of the total. The cities were usually better payers than the princely states though, with few exceptions, they all suffered from mounting debts long before 1618. [7]

Many deserted villages were attributed in folklore to the Thirty Years' War, when in fact they had been empty since the fourteenth century, though the war *did* destroy villages. In the course of the Black Death some parts of central Germany, for example Saxony, suffered an estimated population loss of fifty per cent. Rulers also exaggerated the effects of war in order to enhance their achievements in post-war restoration work: a good example is the work of Pufendorf as a historian of the reign of the Great Elector. Some commentators have adopted opposite and extreme views: some minimize the extent of the damage and population losses. [8] Some argue that the south German cities were successfully diversifying their economies before 1618 to meet changing circumstances, by moving, for example, into new textiles or luxury metalwork, and that this hopeful development was cut short by the war. This may be true of some cities but it was not a general development. The traditional German view was that Germany lost two thirds of her population and suffered massive economic damage in the war, which set her back a hundred years, excluded her from the race for colonies and commercial expansion and kept her weak and disunited when other states were carving out places in the world for themselves. It was easy and convenient for the Germans to blame the weakness of their country on the actions of foreigners.

In spite of these disputes there is some consensus on the effects of the war. [9] The general view is that the whole of Western Europe was struck by a period of economic recession, part of a general crisis, in the early seventeenth century. Economic decline in parts of Germany had started before 1618 and the war accelerated and completed it. The war was followed by a long recession in southern and central Europe as a whole, marked by stagnant population growth and stagnant or falling prices, and it took Germany between fifty and a hundred years to recover. Before 1618, among the problems besetting the German economy were a chaotic coinage, a multiplicity of tolls which hindered the movement of goods, disruption of the Rhine trade because of the Spanish-Dutch war, the Jülich-Berg troubles and religious persecutions. It is undeniable that the soldiery was usually brutal and destructive but the effects of the war were patchy. Not surprisingly, the costs of war fell most heavily on those areas directly touched by it. Large areas of the *Reich* suffered little while others were devastated.

The economic effects similarly varied. The war stimulated certain sections of the economy while disrupting others. There were some bright spots. For example, Hamburg did well, drawing trade from eastern Germany and taking advantage of disruption in the Netherlands to capture some Dutch trade with Spain and Portugal. Hamburg was very much the economic and diplomatic "capital" of northern Germany. Frankfurt-am-Main was also buoyant. The Saxon and Silesian linen manufacturies experienced expansion while those of south Germany collapsed. After 1648 capital was diverted into reconstruction and absolutist state-building. Extensive reconstruction work had to be undertaken all over Germany, for example in rebuilding destroyed towns and villages, and it diverted capital from other forms of investment. The contributions taken by the Swedes had a similar effect. These *were* spent in Germany but the contributions diverted resources from investment into consumption. During the war Germany suffered serious inflation, with many coinage debasements. Local booms caused by expansions in weapons production were short-lived. One effect of the war was a general diversion of state funds into military spending from areas seen as dispensable, such as education. After the war the reconstruction of agriculture absorbed a large share of the limited capital available. The loss of animals during the war caused serious long-term damage. Many of the gains of the sixteenth century were temporarily lost.

After 1648 Germany became an economic colony of Western Europe, exporting raw materials and importing manufactured goods which had earlier been made in the country. The mouths of the Rhine were controlled by the Dutch and other rivers by the Swedes, who continued to take illegal tolls on them after the end of the war. Sweden's status as a great power was based on very insubstantial foundations and the Swedes were concerned primarily with security and revenue-raising rather than long-term economic growth. For a long time after 1648 Germany's main Atlantic ports, Hamburg and Bremen, were troubled by internal political problems and constant harassment by Sweden and Denmark. This was part of a common pattern: the last attempt to establish an urban league took place in 1668 when Cologne and Regensburg were being threatened by their princely neighbours. It came to nothing. The last town diet was held in 1671. Towns like Lübeck and Rostock, which had thrived earlier, experienced the pastoralization of their economies seen earlier in the south. Germany was also hit by the silting of rivers, for example the Ems.

The situation was made worse by the rise of economic particularism combined with the economic management techniques later given the collective name of mercantilism. This involved state management and control of the economy, exercised through a variety of different techniques but all aimed at promoting manufacturing, excluding imports and accumulating wealth in the form of bullion. Most German states pursued interventionist economic policies designed to foster what they perceived as their own economic best interests, usually interpreted as the maintenance of a large population, which meant peasants. State attempts to plan the economy were generally unsuccessful, though there were some exceptions. Some of the measures undertaken in Brandenburg-Prussia, for example canal building, had beneficial effects in the long term. The basic problem was that mercantilism was based on a number of false assumptions about the nature of commerce and manufacturing, in particular that the amount of wealth in the world was fixed and that one state could only thrive by taking trade away from another. Mercantilists thought of the economy as an extension of warfare by other means. Also most states did not have the capital to invest in economic growth or were not prepared to divert it from other spending, especially for military purposes which seemed more pressing. Too often states funded huge enterprises like the giant textile factories in Berlin and Linz, which were totally reliant on the state as supplier of capital and as customer and were quite incapable of competing in open markets. All this caused further distortion and fragmentation of the German economy. A special significance has been given by some commentators to

Germany's failure to develop a substantial maritime trade. As a result, it has been said, authoritarian agrarian traditions remained predominant and German states did not develop the cosmopolitan democratic attitudes which business on the high seas supposedly promotes.

There is still dispute about the war's impact on population levels. It is difficult to sort out losses as a result of military action from those caused by disease — Germany was hit by a series of plagues between 1634 and 1639 — by the reduction of fertility resulting from malnutrition, and by malnutrition itself. Some of the population "loss" was in fact accounted for by the movement of people into fortified towns, which hit agriculture. The most commonly accepted view is that Germany's population fell from between fifteen and twenty-one millions to between ten and thirteen millions, a loss of between thirty and forty per cent, that is all the growth of the sixteenth century. The variations in losses between different regions of Germany were marked. Some areas, for example the Austrian lands and the north west, were barely touched and population levels were not affected. Economic and demographic damage as great or even greater was to befall certain areas, such as the south west and the Palatinate, during French invasions later in the century and it was to take even longer to recover from these. Population growth after the war varied from region to region but was rarely sufficient to act as an engine of economic expansion. In general high fertility resulting from earlier marriages and smaller demand for food produced rising birth rates but it took a long time to recover losses. Badly hit areas like Mecklenburg, Pomerania, Brandenburg and Württemberg took a century to reach their former population levels. Governments remained obsessed by the problems of underpopulation well into the eighteenth century. Resettlement began quickly after the war with large-scale population movements within the country. There was a large influx of immigrants from the Netherlands and Switzerland into the west and south after the decline of industries there. Dutch experts in new farming methods were attracted to Brandenburg, where they faced the hostility of the locals and had only a limited impact. There was also movement resulting from religious emigration, for example of Bohemian Protestants to Saxony, Austrian Protestants to Franconia, Waldensians from Savoy and Huguenots after the revocation of the Edict of Nantes in 1685, from which many German territories benefited.

In social terms, perhaps the most significant development was a reversal of the trend towards greater social mobility seen in the sixteenth century. There was a further intensification of the social reaction, which had started to appear in the late sixteenth century with a hardening of visible class barriers. The rise of a substantial independent middle class stopped. The majority of the towns, except the princely capitals which fostered employment and attracted population, stagnated. The fastest growing city after 1648 was Berlin, mainly as a result of the Great Elector's policies designed to attract immigrants. There were a few new towns, for example Erlangen, built in 1686 in Ansbach for Huguenot refugees from France, Mannheim, built on a strictly geometric grid pattern in 1689 as a new residence by the elector palatine, and Ludwigsburg, the residence of the Duke of Württemberg, built in the early eighteenth century. There was no strong economic middle class. The urban oligarchies were usually guild dominated, often corrupt and narrow of horizons. Religious and social exclusiveness was common, especially in the free cities. Ossification and stifling parochialism were characteristic. After 1648 large-scale textile production began at Nördlingen but by 1698 this had been destroyed by a revolt of the guild weavers.

Most states favoured, as far as possible, a simplification of social divisions. Except in the city states and a few princely territories such as Württemberg, the nobility of which were all free imperial nobles, and East Frisia, where the nobility was weak, noble dominance was reasserted. Noblemen moved into government service as administrators, diplomats and officers. It was not difficult to portray this as an extension of the old feudal obligation to aid and advise the ruler, though in some cases, for example Brandenburg-Prussia, this happened only after substantial pressure from the crown. Economic factors were very important; agrarian stagnation after the war hit land values and the yield from land, making nobles more willing to work for the state in order to maintain their status. Some states, such as the Mecklenburgs, had very large nobilities, members of which habitually sought employment in the governments of German and foreign states. Special training schools (*Ritterakademien*) were established for the nobility in many states. Another symptom of this development was an increase in the number of nobles taking degrees in German universities.

The most important element in the German middle class was made up of lawyers, teachers and administrators, dependent for their livelihood on the nobility and the princes. Dynasticism in offices was becoming increasingly common, with sons following fathers in posts. Officials enjoyed special privileges and in some states developed into a self-perpetuating elite like the French *noblesse de robe*. Although most German states did not develop the system of venality of offices seen in France, offices, and the fees and privileges which they produced, were seen as hereditary property. After 1648 the nobility remained socially and economically if not politically dominant and it remained the ambition of successful middle-class men to obtain noble status and land and to give up enterprise or a profession in order to live nobly on their estates. Where this was legally forbidden or was difficult, for example in Brandenburg-Prussia in the eighteenth century, middle-class confidence and esteem were damaged. This again represented the reversal of a trend seen in the sixteenth century.

A significant result of the war was the so-called Second Serfdom, the growth or intensification of serfdom in eastern Germany. The description is misleading as it was in fact not a second serfdom but the first in many parts of the Empire. For example, in 1652 legal serfdom was introduced in Lusatia. It was not a new system but the completion of a process which had begun long before the war and it varied from region to region. It resulted from a shortage of labour and new agricultural market opportunities. Many lords took advantage of the indebtedness of the peasants, made worse by the war, to increase their power over them. Many peasants had left their holdings because of the terrible conditions during the war. In north eastern Germany many landlords had taken advantage of this to take land into their demesnes and create great *latifundia*, an extension of *Gutsherrschaft*.

The hiring of temporary wage labour or giving generous inducements to persuade people to take over devastated farms and work the lord's land were possible answers to the shortage of people. The easiest solution to the labour problem was to tie the peasants to the soil by making them unfree and depriving them of the opportunity, readily available in post-1648 Germany, of moving to better conditions. Much of German agriculture was experiencing serious troubles before the war, with falling prices. The war delayed the fall but the general trend was downwards. The war also caused a disruption of grain exports from the East. The Prussian *Junkers* did well shipping grain through Danzig and Königsberg until about 1660. It was ironical that closer economic links between Eastern and Western Europe caused greater political and social divergence between them. The movement towards serfdom was speeded up by other developments. Some eastern landlords sought to diversify by promoting rural manufactures but this option was available to few and most had to find an economic life-buoy in more intensive cultivation of the soil. A new form of cultivation for the market, the Holstein *Koppelwirtschaft*, spread eastwards. The new methods, which involved dispensing with regular fallows by creating larger fields for mixed arable farming and cattle-rearing, needed more labour.

Free peasants survived in parts of eastern Germany, for example the *Köllmer* in east Prussia and Saxony, but they were the exception. In the west serfdom existed but in general it survived there only in the form of relics of unfreedom. There were some areas of peasant prosperity, including the north west, southern Bavaria and parts of the Black Forest, but the general position of the peasantry was depressed. A major factor determining the fate of the peasants was the role played by the state. The peasant was protected when the state intervened to restore the land which peasants had been forced to sell during the war, especially when noble land was exempt from taxation. In such cases the state was afraid of losing tax revenues. Bavaria and Hanover were good examples of this. Elsewhere the state was too weak or was unable for various reasons to intervene, as was the case in Mecklenburg, Brandenburg-Prussia, Pomerania and Bohemia. The lords built up substantial economic, social and political power, including judicial and police powers over their peasants, and the right of presentation to Church benefices. The reduction in the prosperity and autonomy of the towns of north eastern Germany was completed. The nobles had the right to import goods free of toll for their own use. They used this to undercut the economies of the towns. In 1653 a significant *Recess* or agreement was signed between the Elector of Brandenburg and the nobility of the Mark. Under this the nobility granted the elector taxation in order to finance a standing army, in return for which their economic and social privileges were confirmed. This was the beginning of the "historic compromise" between the Prussian crown and the *Junkers*, upon which the whole state was built. The emerging Prussian absolutist state was a life-belt for the Brandenburg nobility, especially welcome as international grain prices collapsed between 1660 and 1670.

Germany after 1648 was further away than ever from economic and political unity. Absolutism and mercantilism had become the typical German forms of government and economic organization. Germany was a cultural and economic colony of her neighbours, a prey to foreign political influence, foreign fashions and even a foreign language, as French became increasingly the preferred language of the upper classes. The greater German states were looking outside Germany for their expansion. By the middle of the seventeenth century the crisis of the late sixteenth and early seventeenth centuries was over and Germany entered a period of relative stability even more of a backwater than before.

6 Absolutism and Particularism: Germany after 1648

German history after 1648 was marked by three characteristics which were to remain dominant until the Empire ended in 1806. The first of these was the paramountcy of foreign influence. The other side of the coin was the growing tendency of the larger German states to seek an extension of their power outside Germany, Austria in Hungary and the Balkans, Saxony, the third largest German state, in Poland and Hanover in Britain. Bavaria dreamed of re-creating the Burgundian state by exchanging German territory for the Netherlands. Of the leading states only Brandenburg-Prussia saw serious opportunities for expansion in Germany by means of its "rounding off" policy (*Arrondierungspolitik*), trying to join together the various blocks of territory of which the state was composed, but in the eighteenth century Prussia also looked to Poland for territorial expansion.

The Empire was also seen as a European necessity, a vital component in the European balance of power, the disappearance of which would lead to an orgy of wars and conquest, as seen in collapse and dismemberment of the Spanish and Swedish empires. To contemporaries the Empire could still behave like a proper state to preserve internal peace and external defence. It was not regarded as simply a power vacuum to be fought over by the first-comers. Germany was part of a European states system which emerged after 1648 and, in a changed form, after 1714.[1] The German states, especially the medium-sized ones, possessed a kind of continent in microcosm in the Empire, in which they could behave like powers. Even pigmy states could engage in diplomatic wheeling and dealing. These factors produced a diplomatic situation of extreme complexity in Germany after 1648. It is often forgotten that the period after 1648, when the princes enjoyed, to all intents and purposes, total sovereignty, was a period of peace and cultural blossoming. This is perhaps not surprising as very few of the German "states" had the resources to act as European or even German powers, whatever the rights guaranteed them in 1648. For many "German liberty" meant the liberty to be unimportant. The majority remained weak and vulnerable and continued to be motivated more by fear than by a desire to throw their weight around. The lessons of the Thirty Years' War, in particular the extreme vulnerability of most German states, were not forgotten.

Germany contained states which were of European significance, possessing the resources in population and wealth plus the organization for power which, in combination, produced great-power status. After 1714 Austria, with a population within the *Reich* of about six millions, was a great power. The controls on her established in the Westphalian treaties were much less effective in the eighteenth century as the guarantors of the settlement, France and Sweden, were weaker after 1714–21. After 1740 Austria was joined as a great power by Prussia, whose population by then was about two and a half millions. In addition there were German "regional powers", strong enough, for various economic, strategic or military reasons, to be desirable allies of European great powers. These included Bavaria, Württemberg, Hesse-Cassel, Cologne, Trier, Mainz, Münster and the Palatinate.

The second dominant feature was what has come to be known as dualism, the emergence by the mid-eighteenth century of two German states powerful enough to dominate the whole country, Austria and Prussia. As early as 1708 the Venetian ambassador in Vienna, Dolfin, reported that the Emperor had made a serious mistake in allowing Prussia to adopt the royal title in 1701. As a result Prussia had taken over the leadership of the Protestant group of German rulers and was a potential rival for the imperial crown. In fact Dolfin was pre-dating a development which came later in the century but it was a perceptive observation.

The third trend visible after 1648 was a hardening of the dichotomy between the Emperor and the Empire. In 1727 the Emperor Charles VI protested in vain against the growing practice of the *Reichstag* of describing the states of the Empire as *das Reich* rather than the earlier formula "electors, princes and Estates". The concept of "German liberty" remained firmly established. Germany in the late medieval period was a complex patchwork of feudal rights and possessions and this continued to be the case in the period after 1648. Power and influence were shared among a host of institutions at all levels from the Emperor through the princes to the lower levels of administration. Within this system a trend established at least since the thirteenth century, the concentration of power at the middle level in the states, continued.

The Holy Roman Empire remained the political framework of the German nation until 1806. The Empire after 1648 has suffered from an almost universally bad press, especially in Germany. It is known in the form of belittling quotations about it, such as that of Samuel von Pufendorf, who in his pseudonymously published *On the State of the German Empire* (*De statu imperii Germanici*, Geneva 1667) described the Empire as irregular and monstrous. This famous quotation is always taken out of context. Pufendorf, professor of public law at Heidelberg and later the official historian of the Elector of Brandenburg, was an opponent of imperial power in Germany but a keen supporter of the Empire, which he wished to see converted into a true confederation of states. As well known are an anonymous Englishman's remark in the 1740s that it mattered as little who was Emperor as who was Lord Mayor of London and Voltaire's jibe that the Empire was neither holy, Roman, nor an empire. "Borussian" propaganda in the nineteenth century consistently portrayed the *Reich* as a barrier to the rise of Prussia, with its mission to unite and lead Germany. Too often forgotten are the verdicts of commentators like Leibniz and Rousseau, who saw great virtues in the Empire and recognized its importance to the stability of Europe. There have been too few serious studies, the Empire has been dismissed too glibly and there has been a tendency to regard the decline of Germany into impotence as complete by 1648: the Empire was already in its coffin then but the funeral was postponed until 1806.

There has also been a tendency to write off the imperial constitution as no more than the codification of weakness, a practice in which modern commentators are only echoing the views of some contemporaries. The Thirty Years' War and the period after it saw a heated debate among academics and polemicists about the exact nature of the German constitution. Speculation about the constitution and its improvement seemed to become particularly intense in periods of instability, war or post-war adjustment. For example, the religious troubles of the 1530s produced a lively debate on the issue of the German states' right of resistance against the Emperor, which expanded into considerations of the nature of the imperial constitution. The periods after the religious peace of 1555 and the Thirty Years' War saw similar peaks.

After 1648 friction between the Emperor and the princes, between princes and their subjects and between factions in the free cities all increased. The relationship between the confessions was still uncertain and the smaller states in particular were aware of their vulnerability. All this contributed to a lively interest in the nature of the *Reich*. Polemicists, often sponsored by the German governments, especially the Protestants, mobilized arguments drawn from history, political theory and law to attack or defend the position of the Emperor, the electors, the princes and the free cities. Opponents of imperial authority usually had as their target not the existence of the Empire but the supposed ambition of the Emperor to subvert the constitution and establish a despotism. Most German universities offered political science courses, including study of the history and constitution of the *Reich*, for future civil servants. A major problem with this debate was that the Empire was a bizarre growth quite unique in European history and impossible to fit into any morphology of state forms. Traditionally states had been categorized, according to the criteria laid down by Aristotle, as monarchies, aristocracies or democracies and their degenerated forms, tyranny, oligarchy and mob rule. The Empire fitted none of these; it was a mystery. The modern world has some analogues in the form of loose unions like the Commonwealth or the EEC. In the eighteenth century one jurist and avid collector and publisher of imperial law, J. J. Moser, came to the conclusion that it was empty hair-splitting to try to define the form of government of the Holy Roman Empire. Germany was ruled in the German manner and could not be subjected to academic analysis or measured against the forms of government of other states.

Many contemporaries believed the imperial constitution was perfect for Germany as it enshrined the virtues of German liberty, about which the Thirty Years' War was thought to have been fought. It combined the diversity which allowed each state to develop in its own way and at the same time gave a necessary measure of unity to the German nation. In the constitution a balance had been found which it would be dangerous to disturb, expressing as it did the true nature of Germany as it had evolved over the centuries. The post-1648 German political system was a mixture of different features, an exotic hybrid, the geological record of successive accretions: the relics of a unitary German monarchy, important survivals of a feudal political structure, the skeletal remains of an aristocratic limited monarchy and distinct traces of federal elements. The Holy Roman Empire had become a German habit. A system of checks and balances had developed over time, in which every interest group could be sure that, though it might never get its own way, it could be confident that its opponents never would either.

Because of its earlier development, Germany had a form of federative system which had evolved and had not been designed. The treaties of Westphalia, by codifying the duality of *Kaiser* and *Reich*, probably gave the Empire a new lease of life by clearly defining the powers of each. The imperial constitution was, apart from minor changes later, finalized in 1648. Under the Westphalian treaties an imperial diet was supposed to be called within six months of ratification to deal with outstanding constitutional issues. No diet had been held since long before the outbreak of the war and between 1613 and 1640 only meetings of the electors had taken place for the conduct of imperial business. The Emperor Ferdinand III was able to delay the next full diet until 1653. By then his position was much stronger and he was able to show, during the ceremonies at the opening of the diet in Regensburg, that the Habsburgs were still very much in the saddle.

In May 1654 this diet passed the last *Reichsabschied*, known later as the *jüngste Reichsabschied*, a collection of laws passed during its sittings, but this largely reaffirmed the constitution as it stood and did not include the permanent capitulation of election and other restrictions on imperial power which France and Sweden had intended in 1648. It did restrict the Emperor's right to create new princes with voting rights in the *Reichstag*. The next diet, which opened in Regensburg in 1663, remained in session for the rest of the life of the Empire until 1806 and did not produce an *Abschied*. It became permanent because the Emperor would not accept the constitutional reform plans of a group of princes, on which they were trying to make a grant of aid against the Turks dependent. It legislated by means of recommendations of the *Reich* (*Reichsgutachten*), of which almost 600 were produced between 1663 and 1717. The diet only left Regensburg in 1713 to avoid the plague and between 1742 and 1745, when it met in Frankfurt during the brief tenure of the imperial throne by the Elector of Bavaria.

One of the great virtues of the imperial constitution was its flexibility and looseness (characteristics which are sometimes seen as particular strengths of the British constitution). Made up as it was of a large number of different agreements and conventions, it was to be a bottomless well from which could be drawn arguments to support a wide range of constitutional positions. It could be adjusted as necessary, as in 1555 and 1648, to accommodate changes in the balance between the two elements, the imperial central authority and the states. The balance between the various power-exercising bodies at work within it provided opportunities for a wide range of possible developments. The system had the virtue that it placed no serious restrictions on the freedom of the individual states. There was no longer any threat of imperial despotism. The relative weight of imperial influence and the power of the individual states changed in a shifting and kaleidoscopic manner depending on the political situation inside and outside Germany.

In the opinion of many contemporary commentators the imperial constitution still contained the potential for development and reform. Emperor and Empire were not necessarily rigidly opposed and incapable of acting together. After 1648 there were brief revivals of imperial patriotism, seen in the Empire's opposition to the aggression of Louis XIV's France and during the last attacks by the Turks against Austria in the 1680s. German national feeling was visible during the imperial war, that is a war declared by the *Reichstag* and involving in theory the whole *Reich*, against France in the War of the Spanish Succession from 1700 to 1714. The Empire aimed to put the Emperor's son on the Spanish throne and to win back lost lands in the west: Strasburg remained a powerful symbol of German irredentism after its loss to France in 1681. Fear of the French later kept alive imperial sentiment in the west and south west.

A measurable decline in imperial loyalty and German national feeling began later in the eighteenth century. In the Treaty of Herrenhausen (1725) Hanover and Prussia made a secret agreement involving the possibility of a joint war against the Emperor in alliance with his foreign enemies. This was treason against the Empire. Prussia's behaviour, especially from the reign of Frederick William I (1713–40), marked as it was by a lack of respect for other states' borders and an increasing use of violence, was incompatible with the imperial constitution. Forced recruiting and plundering expeditions by Prussian troops gave rise to frequent complaints. It was clear that Prussia had taken a decision not to observe the common norms of behaviour in the Reich. In 1740 Prussia invaded Silesia beginning the War of the Austrian Succession, ending nearly a hundred years of internal peace in Germany. Austria was unable to recapture her lost province.

In 1756 Prussia began the Seven Years' War by an invasion of Saxony, a pre-emptive strike to ward off another Austrian attempt to retake Silesia. During the ensuing war most of the states of the Empire went to war against Prussia. Only Prussia's clients and allies, Hanover, Hesse-Cassel, Brunswick-Wolfenbüttel and Saxe-Gotha, refused to participate and the *Reichstag* refused to declare imperial war on Prussia. On 5 November 1757 a combined French and imperial army was defeated at Rossbach, an event exploited by Prussian propaganda to ridicule the Empire. The war ended in 1763 with Prussia still holding Silesia. This established dualism, shared informal control of the Empire between Austria and Prussia, neither strong enough to destroy the other. Dualism perpetuated the existence of the Empire but sustained it like a caliper on a paralysed limb, in a state of rigidity with movement made very difficult indeed.

The Empire had institutions which functioned. The imperial diet was an important political forum for Germany, in spite of the formality of its procedures and the obsession of many of its members with the petty rules of precedence so important to *ancien régime* minds. For example, there was extreme sensitivity to the distinction between the "old" princely houses which had held their seats before 1582 and the more recent "new" houses. The Wittelsbachs claimed to be the oldest house and on this basis took precedence on the bench of lay princes. To avoid troublesome squabbles about the Habsburgs' claim to the same distinction the Austrian representative sat with the ecclesiastical princes.

The diet contained representatives of about 150 "states" which enjoyed *Sitz und Stimme* (a seat and a vote) there. These included nine electors (the Duke of Brunswick-Lüneburg/Hanover was elevated to an electorate in 1697), about 45 free cities out of about 150 and about 60 lay and ecclesiastical princes, representing some one hundred separate territories. The imperial abbeys and free counties had collective votes but the imperial knights were not represented. After 1529 they paid "voluntary" donations to the Emperor in return for confirmation of their direct subjection to him. After the Thirty Years' War the *Reichstag* was an assembly of ambassadors representing virtually sovereign states and often one man represented several principals. In the later eighteenth century only about thirty representatives met regularly and the sessions of the diet were increasingly infrequent. Decision-making was difficult: members could hold business up while waiting for instructions from their principals and there were problems in achieving agreement between the three houses. The diet was inoperative between 1697 and 1701 and 1718 and 1723. As a result there was little imperial legislation especially after 1714, though a few important acts were passed.

In 1681 a new military system (*Kriegsverfassung*) was enacted, which enlarged the imperial army and passed the organization of it and the apportionment of the costs of its maintenance between different states to the Circles. The military role of the Circles was enhanced further in 1703 and 1706. Under this system it was possible for the smaller states to pay their larger neighbours to provide their contingents to the imperial army, thus avoiding the trouble and expense of maintaining their own little armies of a few hundred or even a few dozen men. This led to the *de facto* emergence of two distinct groupings among the German states, the armed, those with standing armies, and the unarmed (*armierte und nicht armierte Stände*). One problem was that the larger states were often unwilling to place their troops under any kind of imperial high command and insisted on keeping control in their own hands. This made imperial armies very unwieldy and inefficient. Only during the Spanish Succession War was an imperial command structure created. Typically, the imperial general field marshal's office had to have a Catholic and a Protestant member. After 1707 the Catholic post was held by Prince Eugene of Savoy. Another problem was that the armed states often found the provision of troops for smaller neighbours a useful means of extending political control over them and turning them into satellites, for example, if they fell into arrears with their payments for military substitution. Emperors from Leopold I were not anxious to see an imperial standing army created as it would certainly not be under their control.

In 1731 the *Reichstag* also passed an ordinance designed to place restrictions on the guilds, powerful institutions with a power base in many free cities and an organizational structure covering the Empire. Many state governments complained bitterly about their conservatism and obstructiveness. This led to a ban on some of the social and racial discrimination earlier practised by the guilds — members of the minority nationalities, the Wends and Sorbs, were excluded, as were the children of people engaged in a whole range of "inferior" occupations — and an increase in the number of apprentices entering crafts, including women in some. Another guild ordinance in 1772 attacked other abuses, including "Holy Monday", the widespread practice of extending the weekend by an extra day. Another law, the 1737 coinage ordinance, was an attempt yet again to bring order to a chaotic system, in which there were over 600 separate minting authorities and over forty German and foreign coinages circulated, and to establish a common standard. These acts depended for their operation on the willingness of the individual states to put them into effect. More significant than its legislative functions was the *Reichstag's* role as a major centre of German and European inter-state politics, as one of the "capitals" of Germany.

The Circles were another imperial institution which worked, at least partly. Each Circle was supposed to have regular meetings of the Circle diet to discuss matters of mutual concern, to appoint judges to the imperial chamber court, to pass legislation and to make provision for defence, internal order and the like. These meetings were supposed to be called by the convening princes (*kreisausschreibende Fürsten*), usually the most important rulers in the area. Those in the north were dominated by the larger states like Brandenburg and Saxony, or foreign powers like Sweden, and were the least effective. The most active were the Swabian and Franconian Circles in the south west. In the late seventeenth century the former, which contained a host of tiny states and free cities, developed a very successful system of co-operation reminiscent of the Swiss confederation. There was also effective defence co-operation between the exposed Circles of the south west, which began with the Frankfurt agreement of five Circles in 1697. This organized an army, which defended the Rhine frontier against the French during the War of the Spanish Succession and lasted into the 1720s. In all there were twelve associations between 1697 and 1748.[2]

At the same time the Emperor retained his reserved powers (*Reservatrechte*), which enabled him to exercise considerable influence. He possessed a range of privileges stemming from his personal feudal overlordship of the whole Empire, including formal enfeoffment of princes with newly acquired territories, a process essential if the holder was to exercise any representation in the *Reichstag* attached to the territory. Within the Empire only the Emperor could ennoble commoners or grant higher grades of nobility. He could grant pardons, exemptions from the jurisdiction of the imperial courts, legitimations of illegitimate children and university charters. He also exercised supreme judicial authority to judge the bodies and possessions of his feudal subjects. As protector of all three German Churches he had a voice in the election of new prelates. Some of these rights could only be exercised with the consent of the electors after 1711. Leopold I was also able to prevent the Empire from acting as a unit in diplomatic matters as was intended in the 1648 treaties; he simply assumed a right to negotiate on behalf of the Empire and presented the results to the *Reichstag* for ratification. As ruler of the Austrian lands he possessed diplomatic power: by means of subsidy treaties and alliances he could make his weight felt in Germany and he could offer some protection to the weak. The little German states and those close to the borders of Austria continued to look to the Emperor as a protector. The Emperor's influence was strong, especially in the south and west, among the smaller states throughout the Empire, particularly the Catholics, and among the imperial knights and counts, many of whom looked to Vienna for careers.

Even an interregnum following Ferdinand's death in 1657, when an imperial election was necessary because his second son, Leopold, had not previously been elected king of the Romans — his elder son, Ferdinand, who had, died in 1654 — did not lead to any substantial reduction in the Emperor's powers. During the long reign of Leopold I (1659–1705) imperial influence in Germany tended to stagnate, as the Emperor's efforts were devoted to consolidating Austrian power in the wars against Louis XIV's France and the Turks. Under Leopold Austria began a large-scale expansion eastwards. There was also a growing obsession with the future of the Spanish empire on the imminently awaited death of the sickly King Charles II of Spain (1665–1700). Leopold was very keen to possess Spain's Italian possessions. During this time Austria grew away from the Empire and neglected Germany, though there was a party in Vienna around the aulic chancellor Johann Paul Hocher, which continued to press the Emperor to take initiatives to restore his influence.

Imperial mercantilism (*Reichsmerkantilismus*) was one such scheme. In 1676 all French imports into the Empire were banned and in 1689 and 1702 imperial laws forbade all commerce with France. The bans were not enforced. In 1678 decisions were taken to float schemes for a common German economic policy and an imperial standing army. The idea of a common external tariff, associated with Christoph Royas y Spinola, Bishop of Wiener Neustadt, Peter Philip von Dernbach, Bishop of Bamberg, and the mercantilist writer Johann Becher, was revived. The yield from the tariff would be used to fund an imperial army. Of these plans only the much watered-down 1681 military constitution actually came into existence. Austrian propaganda in the *Reich* remained vigorous. An anonymous pamphlet of 1662 asked and answered a question: *What has Austria done for Germany? Austria has brought Germany to its Highest Flourishing.*

After the death of Leopold, his two sons, Joseph and Charles, held the imperial title in succession. Their reigns saw a conscious attempt to restore imperial influence in Germany, a process sometimes called the imperial reaction.[3] This reached its height during the reign of

Charles VI (1711–40), a man with an elevated conception of his imperial position, which he saw as far more than a collection of empty titles. He was determined to use his reserved powers to the full. His reign was in some ways a turning point as he was the last Emperor to make no real distinction between his position as Emperor and as ruler of the Habsburg lands. After 1740 there was a marked reversion to the situation of Leopold I's reign: the Habsburgs concentrated almost exclusively on Austria and its interests and abandoned attempts to control the Empire. They began to behave towards Germany like any other foreign power.

The imperial reaction began under Joseph I (1705–11). The wars against the French and the Turks in the later years of Leopold I's reign had revived imperial patriotism and the Emperor was able to benefit from this. For centuries this patriotism had become an increasingly insignificant and short-lived phenomenon with the rise of particularism, state egotism, but French policy helped to change this. French aggressiveness[4] in the 1670s and 1680s brought about a marked change of attitude among most German rulers; whereas previously they had regarded the Emperor as the main threat to peace and had looked to France for protection and for the promotion of their interests, for example in the League of the Rhine, they now saw the French as the main threat and looked to Vienna. States like Brandenburg, Münster and the Brunswick duchies, which had earlier operated a see-saw policy, moving between the French and the imperial alliance in pursuit of their immediate interests, moved back into the imperial orbit. German national sentiment grew as Germans became increasingly resentful of the trampling of the *Reich* by "the Christian Turks, the hereditary enemy of the German name". It was partly negative, focused against the hate-figure of Louis XIV, and partly positive in the form of growing attachment to the person of the Emperor.

In May 1674, during the Franco-Dutch War (1673–9), imperial war was declared against France, which had violated German neutrality. This was the first imperial war since Charles V's reign and the first of three in Leopold's reign. Peace was made between France and the Empire at Nijmegen in February 1679. Brandenburg, cheated of West Pomerania, in spite of its victory over the Swedes at Fehrbellin in 1675, became a secret ally of France. Louis XIV's *réunions* policy, under which the French, on the basis of documents "discovered" in archives, laid claim to and seized large areas of Germany as supposed feudal dependencies of territories belonging to the French crown in order to create a strong military frontier, aroused great hostility. In the 1680s and 1690s the French occupied large areas of Alsace and western Germany, including the city of Strasburg, which they had long coveted and which was seized by force in September 1681. When Louis XIV entered the city in October a large number of German princes were in his entourage. The loss of Strasburg was of great symbolic importance and its seizure was to fuel German nationalism in the nineteenth and twentieth centuries. Imperial propaganda also made much of it at the time, though it must be noted that the Habsburgs made similar use of some tenuous residual imperial rights to try to extend their political control in northern Italy and the south west of the *Reich*. Louis' persecution of the French Protestants after the revocation of the Edict of Nantes in 1685 also damaged his image in Germany.

The defensive League of Augsburg was set up in July 1686 and included the Emperor, Spain, Bavaria, Saxony, Sweden and the Circles of the south west. It was later enlarged when the Dutch and Britain joined. Imperial war was declared against France in 1688 and 1702. During the War of the League of Augsburg, also known as King William's War, the Nine Years' War and the War of the Palatinate Succession (1688–97) the French, again claiming German territory through the king's sister-in-law, the daughter of the elector palatine, invaded the western parts of the Empire. In the Palatinate they embarked on a campaign of deliberate incendiarism, in which hundreds of towns and villages were burned down. The damage was worse than that suffered during the Thirty Years' War. The reputation of France sank further. Southern Germany was again a theatre of war in the War of the Spanish Succession, during which the great majority of the German states fought against the French.

The Turkish siege of Vienna in 1683 gave a powerful boost to imperial patriotism. The lifting of the siege began a great offensive into Hungary and the Balkans, pushing the Turks back hundreds of miles. Under the terms of the peace treaties of Carlowitz (1699) and Passarowitz (1718) the Habsburgs gained substantial territories in the northern Balkans. These treaties and the treaties of Utrecht, Rastatt and Baden (1713–14), which concluded the Spanish Succession War, ended the threat from France and the Turks for a long time. The next threat to the stability of the Empire was to come from within Germany, from Prussia.

During this time loyalty to the Emperor could bring rewards: in 1697 it brought the House of Brunswick-Lüneburg an electoral crown.

Opposition to the Emperor could bring punishment. During Joseph's reign the electors of Bavaria and Cologne were placed under the ban of the Empire, involving the loss of their lands and titles, as a punishment for allying with Louis XIV. The tragedy of Bavaria was that, although it had substantial advantages, a compact state with an efficient centralized administration, it was too close to Austria and therefore did not have the freedom of action enjoyed by some other medium-sized states.[5]

Its rulers pursued a double policy to deal with the problem. They sought to have members of their house elected to as many ecclesiastical principalities as possible. Between 1583 and 1761 they were able to put a Wittelsbach on the throne of the electorate of Cologne, which was a base for further expansion. Clement Augustus, brother of the Elector of Bavaria, was Elector of Cologne between 1723 and 1761 and also held the bishoprics of Paderborn, Osnabrück, Hildesham and Münster. This policy was eventually ruined by biology: the Wittelsbachs did not produce enough male children. The second element in Bavarian policy was the French alliance. After 1670 the Bavarian Wittelsbachs were to remain the most loyal allies of France in the Empire for over a century. With French encouragement, they planned to take the imperial title: a Bavarian rival to the Habsburg candidate was first seriously considered as early as 1658. They derived little benefit from the French connexion and once came close to disaster because of it. In 1704 Bavaria was occupied by imperial troops, whose harsh behaviour provoked a peasant rising at Christmas 1705, put down with great brutality. The Wittelsbachs were restored to their titles and their ravaged lands in 1715 thanks to French intervention on their behalf.

During the Spanish Succession War Austria enjoyed a series of military successes thanks to the imperial commander Prince Eugene of Savoy, a brilliant general and diplomat. Austria made territorial gains in Italy and the Netherlands under the Treaty of Utrecht (1714) and in the Balkans under the Treaty of Passarowitz with the Turks (1718). The long French-inspired rebellion in Hungary was brought to an end in 1711 by the Treaty of Szatmar. By 1720 the Emperor's position in Germany was stronger than for ninety years. Habsburg power in Europe was at its apogee and Charles VI was stronger than Ferdinand II at the height of his success in the Thirty Years' War.

Personal factors also played a role in the imperial reaction. Joseph I suffered from the crown prince syndrome, the growing frustration of waiting during his father's long reign for his turn on the throne. He wished to imitate Louis XIV and make himself the Austrian Sun King. During his reign the sun symbol became part of the Habsburgs' iconography. Statues, pictures and medals were lavishly used for propaganda purposes, as they were by all rulers, to demonstrate the semi-divine status of the Emperor. During the War of the Spanish Succession Charles VI had been a candidate for the Spanish throne supported, initially, by the anti-French coalition. It appears that his brief experience as King of Spain affected his attitudes. He was very aware of the dignity of his imperial titles. During his reign the memory of Charles V was consciously and deliberately cultivated. He went in for substantial building activity, for example extensions to the Hofburg Palace in Vienna. Baroque architecture reached its height under the Fischer von Erlach, father and son, and Johann Lukas von Hildebrandt. The Charles Church in Vienna made prominent use of the pillars of Hercules, a symbol of Habsburg power used by Charles V. Only a shortage of money prevented the building of a summer palace at Schönbrunn bigger than Versailles. At one time Charles planned to turn the monastery at Klosterneuburg near Vienna into the Austrian Escorial, a centre for the government of the whole Empire in imitation of Philip II's complex outside Madrid. He retained many Spaniards at his court to run the former Spanish possessions acquired by Austria at Utrecht.

Charles's reign was significant for two things, the Pragmatic Sanction and the imperial reaction. It was only in his later years that the Sanction acquired real significance. During Leopold's reign the last collateral Habsburg line, the Tyrolean, died out and all the Austrian Habsburg lands came together in his hands. They remained a collection of provinces united only by a single ruler and it was not clear what would happen to them if the male line died out. Dynastic stability was a factor of central importance in the states system of the time, as witnessed by the numerous wars of succession. The Pragmatic Sanction was drawn up in 1703. It was initially a secret family agreement declaring all the Austrian possessions an indivisible whole. This was significant: it has been described as the first codification of the Austrian state idea. It also designated the order of succession in the female line. In 1713 Charles altered it by a unilateral declaration to make any daughter he might have, in the absence of a son, heiress to everything in preference to his brother's daughters. The Sanction became an important item of European diplomacy when Charles' sons died as infants and his elder daughter, Maria Theresa, emerged as heiress. This arrangement was not accepted by all German or

European states and in the later years of Charles' reign a possible partition of the Austrian empire was beginning to obsess Europe, as had the fate of Spain in the later seventeenth century. It became a major aim of Charles' policy after 1730 to obtain guarantees of the Sanction from German and European states. Charles was not stupid. He did not place great faith in a piece of paper but hoped to link it to alliances, to make other powers dependent for their own security on the survival of a strong Austria. Prince Eugene is supposed to have said that a strong army and a full treasury would be a better guarantee. It is unlikely that Eugene would have said anything so obvious. Charles knew this well and made determined efforts to reform the administration and finances but he had a tendency to look for magic answers, such as commercial companies, rather than to carry out the thorough-going reform of the whole Austrian system, which was what was really needed. The financial administration of the state remained decentralized like the general administration.[6]

The reforms were not very successful and poor finances were to dog Austria. During the wars of Leopold I's reign very heavy state debts had been accumulated and Austria had become very dependent on Jewish financiers to arrange these. In 1703 one of the largest of these, the Oppenheim firm, collapsed, causing serious problems for the government. It is ironical that the successes of 1714–18 gave Austria great possessions but also gave her great commitments which she was barely capable of bearing. Charles VI also did little to advance the creation of a modern administration in his lands. He appreciated the individual traditions of his various possessions, Austrian, Bohemian, Hungarian, Netherlands and Italian. He made no attempt to set up a unified administration for his territories. The Estates survived with a major administrative role. Austria had a semi-amateur system of government and remained a half-formed absolutist state. Major reform and modernization were only undertaken after 1740 by Charles' daughter Maria Theresa. If the Sanction was the first codification of the Austrian state idea, the practice lagged sadly behind.

Charles' desire to obtain the *Reich's* support for the Sanction and to increase Austrian influence in Germany, using the reservoir of imperial powers still available, were motives behind the imperial reaction in addition to the personal ones already mentioned. Personalities also played an important role. While he was king of the Romans, heir apparent to the imperial title, Joseph I had gathered round him a group of younger men anxious to see a revival of

Austrian power in Germany, in the belief that Germany would not be neglected as Austria's "back yard". The main figures were Prince Eugene of Savoy and Frederick Charles von Schönborn, the imperial vice-chancellor. Both men were to occupy powerful positions when Charles VI became Emperor. Both favoured an extension of Austrian power in Germany, though for different reasons, Eugene purely in pursuit of Austrian state interests but Schönborn for more complex reasons.

Schönborn was a member of a family of small imperial counts, a class among whom imperial loyalty was traditionally strong, from Franconia, an area where imperial influence survived more persistently than in most parts of Germany. The family was consistently imperialist and its members had risen to high positions in the Church and the imperial diplomatic service through their loyalty. There were many other examples of families from similar backgrounds who rose to high office through service to the Habsburgs, for example the Metternichs from the Rhineland, but the Schönborns were the most successful. They were the main rivals of the Wittelsbachs for ecclesiastical preferments, using the growing family property holdings as security for loans to pay the necessary bribes.

Frederick Charles was appointed imperial vice-chancellor by his uncle, Lothar von Schönborn, who was Archbishop and Elector of Mainz. Schönborn was himself a Catholic priest and coadjutor (that is automatic heir) to the Bishop of Bamberg. The old-fashioned Borussian view saw him as an agent of political Catholicism but that was oversimple. Certainly he saw a serious threat to the survival of the Empire from the rising Protestant north German states, especially Hanover and Prussia, strengthened by their territorial gains from Sweden in the Great Northern War of 1700 to 1721, whose rulers he mocked as "theatre kings". Schönborn was afraid that the end of the Empire was close and he had a terrible vision of what would follow: the weak, including the small and ecclesiastical states, would fall prey to the strong. Germany would again become the battlefield of foreign powers and would be divided up among them and the more powerful German states. He did not see imperial power and the states' rights as exclusive but complementary: each was an essential element in the German constitution and, without Austria and the Emperor, he believed, there would be no Empire and no German liberty.

In 1709 he wrote a long report on the state of the Empire after taking over his office. He found imperial feeling at a low ebb: the Emperor lacked power, imperial jurisdiction was flouted and the imperial diet was crippled by petty squabbles. He suggested remedies to restore the loose ties of the Empire, urging his master Joseph I to exploit the reservoir of loyalty where it still existed, in the Circles of the south west and the Upper Rhine and among the Catholic and small states. A reactivation of imperial justice would, he argued, be a valuable instrument in this. He also urged the Emperor to construct an alliance system with those states who were still loyal. His aim was to build up an Austrian/imperial party in Germany.

Schönborn's office was in the gift of the arch-chancellor of the Empire, the Elector of Mainz and its holder acted as the elector's agent in Vienna as head of the imperial chancery (*Reichskanzlei*), the main administrative organ of the Empire. The power deriving from the position depended very much on the man who held it. By 1711 it was not what it had been, having been neglected under Leopold I and held by Austrians with no real interest in German affairs. As a result it had suffered a steady loss of power to the exclusively Austrian offices of state, especially the aulic chancery (*Hofkanzlei*) set up in 1620 by Ferdinand II. In Vienna Schönborn faced strong opposition from Austrian statesmen, who resented the intrusion of a German into what they regarded as the secrets of the House of Austria. Particularly strong opposition came from the head of the *Hofkanzlei*, Philip Ludwig von Sinzendorf. He pursued purely Austrian aims and saw the Holy Roman Empire as a barrier to Austrian progress. His policy was that Austria should abandon all imperial pretensions and seek allies among German states on exactly the same terms as other foreign powers and not try to exploit residual imperial powers, which were, in his view, worthless. Schönborn opposed this approach. He believed that if purely Austrian interests came to predominate in the *Reich*, this would only hasten its disintegration: Austria would be acting in exactly the same way as other states seeking to win something from the decline.

Schönborn was able to claw back some of the influence lost earlier by his office, including the establishment of a special weekly imperial conference (or cabinet meeting) and admission to the Inner Cabinet when imperial affairs were discussed. He was also able to persuade the Emperor that Germany could prove a valuable accession of power to the House of Austria if correctly exploited and that imperial authority could be used as an instrument of Habsburg dynastic power. In this he was pushing at an open door in view of Charles VI's own views. The many policies which Schönborn pursued contributed to the imperial reaction, which reached its height in the late 1720s.

It took various forms. Schönborn was well aware of the value of public relations. He hired scholars and writers to produce imperialist propaganda and sponsored the publication of collections of imperial laws. His main aim was to stop the growth of Prussian power, which he described as a gnawing worm in the bowels of the Empire. Prussia was seizing every chance to encroach on the rights and lands of its weaker neighbours, raising the threat of a new dictator in the Empire and a rival for the imperial crown. In particular he was anxious to keep Prussia out of southern Germany. In this he had one spectacular success: he was able to sabotage Prussian plans to buy the small Ansbach/Bayreuth territories in Franconia held by a cadet line of the Hohenzollern family. He also encouraged cases against Prussia in the imperial courts: at one time there were over forty cases pending against her. The imperial resident in Berlin had the unpleasant job of delivering imperial rebukes, some of which amazed contemporaries by their tone. Such rolling phrases of majesty had not been used against a senior prince of the Empire for a long time. A Prussian representative in Vienna warned his master that the Emperor would tolerate no infringement of his authority: Charles VI had ambitions to imitate Caesar Augustus and the grandeur of the first Roman Empire.

The main agency of the imperial reaction was the supreme judicial authority, exercised through the imperial aulic council (*Reichshofrat*), which was seen as the last remaining jewel in the imperial crown, the only institution which after 1648 gave the Emperor a realistic opportunity to increase his influence in the *Reich*. The council experienced the last major exercise of its power during the imperial reaction. Its rival, the chamber court (*Reichskammergericht*), was wholly paid for by the princes through special contributions and it suffered from a chronic financial starvation. A new ordinance for the chamber court was issued in 1654, including measures to speed up its procedures, but their effect was limited. By the eighteenth century it was inefficient and slow. Many stories circulated about it, all variations on the theme that periodically all the accumulated papers in the court were thrown up into the air and those which fell face up were dealt with. As a result of recent detailed research the court has been rehabilitated and its older essentially negative image must be modified in the light of this. Many litigants, especially the Protestant nobility of northern and western Germany, still thought it worthwhile to seek redress there. It was to experience a marked revival in the later eighteenth century.

The aulic council was established by the early eighteenth century as the highest tribunal of the Empire. Litigants had a choice between the two imperial tribunals and the aulic council experienced a substantial increase in its business from the late seventeenth century onwards. It had a very wide competence outside the Austrian lands. It was a civil court, the highest criminal court of appeal and the highest feudal tribunal with jurisdiction over the grant of privileges, declarations of majorities, the confirmation of succession arrangements, wills, contracts, adoptions, wardships and legitimizations. In the eighteenth century the Empire was still a collection of feudal territories with overlapping and competing jurisdictions, in which states with firm borders and unchallenged central authority were emerging only slowly. The jurisdiction of the aulic council was important in regulating the mechanism and keeping order.

One of the strengths of the aulic council was that it was entirely at the disposal of the Emperor: he appointed its members and paid their salaries and issued regulations for the court without reference to the German states. Successive Emperors firmly resisted all attempts by the princes to obtain a say in its management, personnel or competence. Judicial power was held to belong to the Emperor alone and it was the function of the aulic council to advise him on the exercise of it. Jurisdiction was shared with the *Reichstag*, in only one matter, the imposition of the ban of the Empire, when the imperial diet had to confirm a verdict of the aulic council. A committee of the *Reichstag*, the *Reichsdeputation*, was set up in 1654 to deal with the appeals against the verdicts of the imperial courts allowed under certain limited circumstances but this did not come into existence until the eighteenth century, when such appeals began to flood in. The council saw itself as a guardian of imperial rights and a strong *esprit de corps* developed under Charles VI. Charles also carried out a major reform of the aulic council and appointed talented lawyers as presidents.

The council was attacked by its enemies as an instrument of Habsburg despotism, religious and political, and there was a constant campaign by leading princes to place restrictions on it. A frequent accusation against it was that it was partial to Catholics. In the Westphalian treaties the Emperor had agreed to appoint a fixed number of Protestant members but this was not always done, often with the excuse that suitable candidates were not available or that Protestant councillors became converts to Catholicism. One commentator, Hippolitus a Lapide, a propagandist in Swedish pay and a bitter enemy of the House of Habsburg, in his *De Ratione Status in Imperio Romano Germanico* (1640) described it as "the most poisonous spring for the destruction of German liberty". These attacks came to a head under Joseph I and Charles VI and were made more violent by the perceived influence of Schönborn and the large number of converts to Catholicism in prominent positions in Vienna. 1711 saw the first imperial election for fifty years (Joseph I had been elected king of the Romans during his father's lifetime) and this gave the princes a chance to vent their long-accumulating grievances, especially against interference by the aulic council in the internal affairs of their states.

An increasing part of its business at this time was concerned with constitutional disputes in individual German states, of which there were many as the struggle to impose absolutist systems of government reached crisis point in many states. Paragraph 180 of the *Reichsabschied* of 1654 was a major cause of trouble. Under this all subjects were obliged to contribute financially to the costs of *necessary* military arrangements undertaken by their rulers as part of the defence system of the Empire, regardless of any contrary constitutional agreements. This was further extended in Leopold I's capitulation of election in 1658, which limited subjects' rights of appeal to the imperial courts and placed restrictions on the Estates. Under these provisions the princes had a mandate to impose taxes at will, arguing that they were privileged imperial taxes which subjects had to pay. The principle that subjects had to contribute to imperial taxes was established in the fifteenth century. In the 1670s and 1680s a group of absolutist rulers, known as the Extensionists (*Extendisten*), tried to obtain an extension of these provisions to dismantle the last remaining rights of subjects. This campaign was resisted by the Emperor and the aulic council on the grounds that the word *necessary* in paragraph 180 meant necessary for the defence of the Empire, not what the prince thought necessary.

Constitutional disputes flared up again in the early eighteenth century and the aulic council became involved in many of them. In the little state of Nassau-Siegen the council was responsible for the deposition of the ruling count, William Hyacinth, who was an insane despot. In East Frisia a civil war broke out in the 1720s over disputes between the prince and the Estates. The aulic council was deeply involved in attempts to deal with the problems. In the case of Mecklenburg-Schwerin a tyrannical ruler, Duke Charles Leopold, was deposed and an imperial provisional administration installed after 1719. Later the council played a major role during constitutional disputes in the substantial duchy of Württemberg. A large number of small states and cities had their form of government influenced by decisions of the *Reichshofrat*. Among the most striking examples are the city of Hamburg, which in 1712 was given a new constitution after decades of internal strife. Hamburg was also saved from Danish attempts to seize it. The *Reich*, however weak, could still exercise judicial authority. A complete victory of absolutism in Germany was prevented and the aulic council helped to keep alive, however weakly, an older tradition of popular participation in government. It also helped to keep alive in some parts of Germany the idea of German unity at a time when the individual states were taking control over more and more of the people's daily lives.

More important perhaps, during the imperial reaction in the 1720s the aulic council was able to help to contain a serious religious dispute in Germany. After 1648 religion slowly declined as a major factor in German politics and toleration spread, largely for pragmatic reasons. This was accompanied by the appearance of more spiritual trends in both Churches. In the Protestant Churches Pietism was a powerful movement from the later seventeenth century. Founded in the 1670s by Philipp Jakob Spener, a Lutheran minister in Frankfurt-am-Main and later in Berlin, this preached a tolerant and undogmatic Christianity based on individual or group contemplation combined with good works. It attracted a substantial following but was not all-conquering. This secularization of attitudes, which developed among rulers and intellectuals, was slow to break through among some sections of the clergy and the mass of the population. In states like Brandenburg-Prussia, where toleration was officially fostered for demographic and economic reasons, the mass of ordinary Lutherans, often tacitly encouraged by their pastors, looked askance at strangers of a different faith and made life difficult for them.

Many of the free cities, in which parity of faiths had been introduced in 1648, experienced constant religious friction. Religious dispute at the academic level was a German hobby, leading to the production of a huge theological literature. It was no coincidence that the Enlightenment in Germany was more concerned with religion than the movement elsewhere and often centred on questions of toleration rather than political matters. After the settlement of 1648, which, like that of 1555, contained too many compromises and too many points of potential friction, further intermixing of the religions continued. There was some cooling off in the face of a common enemy, France, but many Protestant princes continued to be afraid of a Catholic Emperor and looked to France for protection. Religion still mattered in the early eighteenth century and religious concerns were never far from the surface, resulting from a combination of sincerely held beliefs and defence of vested interests, for example the Protestant Succession in Britain, the special position of the German ecclesiastical princes, fears, probably baseless, of a Protestant Emperor among Catholics and the continuing close interconnection between religion and politics in German life.

In the early years of the eighteenth century there was a sharp revival of religious confrontation. The basic cause of the religious crisis of the 1720s was the so-called Ryswick Clause, article four of the Treaty of Ryswick (1697), which ended the War of the League of Augsburg. France occupied the Palatinate from 1688 until 1697 and during that period many Catholic churches were built or reopened in the electorate. The area was already the scene of a long-standing bitter dispute between Lutherans and Calvinists over incomes and property. Under the Ryswick Clause, these Catholic rights were to remain in existence after 1697. This left many potential flash-points, including a large number of church buildings where the *Simultaneum* operated, that is the sharing of a single building by different faiths. Serious trouble began in 1715: a Jesuit professor at Heidelberg wrote a pamphlet attacking Luther. The Palatinate Calvinist Church also brought out a new catechism dedicated to the elector, who had become a personal convert to Catholicism, containing very uncomplimentary remarks about the pope and pointed references to the links between Roman Catholicism and tyranny. In July 1715 an imperial decree was issued forbidding the publication or distribution in the Empire of any material containing attacks on other Christian sects. The troubles in the Palatinate simmered on until 1718: in that year the elector moved his residence back to Heidelberg, where he wanted to use the impressive Church of the Holy Spirit, the burial place of his predecessors, as his Catholic court chapel. The *Simultaneum* was already in operation there, with the Calvinists using the nave and the Catholics the choir. A wall had been built between them. The Calvinists refused to leave, even though they were offered a brand new church. Eventually the elector seized the church with troops and tore down the wall. This began the crisis.

The time was ripe for trouble. The bicentenary of the beginning of the Reformation fell in 1717, an event marked with lavish ceremonial in all parts of Protestant Germany.[7] As a result of a number of developments the German Protestants felt under threat. The conversion to Catholicism of the Elector of Saxony in 1697 and the inheritance of the Palatinate by a Catholic line of the house in 1685, were seen as a great loss, although in the case of Saxony the conversion was personal and not official. The early eighteenth century also saw a revival of religious persecution in a number of ecclesiastical states, in answer to which some Protestant rulers had taken reprisals against their Catholic populations, including Hanover and Prussia. The Palatinate crisis broke in the middle of this. Through the involvement of the Protestant organization in the imperial diet, the *corpus evangelicorum*, the dispute rapidly escalated until all the greater Protestant states were involved plus their foreign allies. The rapid involvement of foreign powers was a dangerous development. The *Reichstag* became paralysed by the dispute, which promoted the rise of extremists on both sides. Vicious pamphlet warfare developed and there was a serious threat of war. The Prussian government's reprisals against Prussian Catholics were very harsh and were encouraged by Hanover, which was playing a clever game, hoping to use the religious issue to drive wedges between the Emperor and Prussia.

The Emperor, as protector of the three German Churches, refused to take sides and referred the whole matter to the aulic council, which ordered all the parties involved to stop illegal actions. Prussia in 1720 received edicts which caused amazement. The King of Prussia was treated as a recalcitrant vassal and his offences were catalogued in detail, including the perversion of the imperial constitution, failure to pay contributions to the maintenance of imperial armies, attacks on his neighbours, forced recruiting in neighbouring states, the creation of a huge army which was a constant threat to his neighbours and a desire to make himself independent of the Empire, among others. These firm imperial actions played a major part in solving the religious crisis. Gradually the fire went out of the issue and the extremists became increasingly isolated. There was great fear of war, especially among the smaller states in both religious camps. Hanover and Prussia needed imperial support to enjoy their gains from the Northern War against Sweden and were concerned at the spread of Russian power in the Baltic. Eventually the persecutions faded away. The dispute lingered on into the 1730s but religion was losing its power to divide. It is significant that events like the expulsion of over 20 000 Protestants from Salzburg in 1731-2 were seen as relics of a Gothic past even by Catholics.

By 1730 the imperial reaction was over. The reasons included the decline of Schönborn's power in Vienna as Austrian interests reasserted themselves. In 1728 he became Bishop of Bamberg and Würzburg, which made necessary long absences from Vienna. As a result conditions in the imperial chancery became increasingly chaotic and there were accusations of massive corruption. In 1730 he offered the Emperor his New Plan, under which his own bishoprics were to form the core of an alliance and military system based on the ecclesiastical states. A chain of fortresses from the Austrian Netherlands to Austria would give the Emperor a base from which to restore his power in Germany. This was too expensive and anyway Austria had too many pressing commitments elsewhere to be able to devote effort to Germany. In 1734 Schönborn resigned as imperial vicechancellor.

By then Austrian policy was increasingly concerned with the Pragmatic Sanction: purely Austrian interests were becoming paramount as the whole future of the Austrian state was coming into question. The late 1720s had seen the dangerous polarization of Europe into two alliance systems, with Spain, the Emperor and Russia allied against Britain, France and Prussia. Both groups were bidding for allies among the German rulers. In this dangerous situation the Emperor had to buy friends. The danger to the existence of Austria was becoming very real in the 1730s, when France again emerged actively in European affairs, having recovered from the damage she had suffered in the War of the Spanish Succession. During the Polish Succession War (1733–8) southern Germany was again a theatre of war and the Empire suffered further losses. France took Lorraine. The French revived their traditional policy of collecting clients among the German states, offering them the bait of a share of the Austrian lands in the forthcoming partition of the Habsburg state. This policy was especially successful with the Bavarian Wittelsbachs, who became the centre of a group of powers hoping to make territorial gains from a dismemberment of Austria, which would have left the Habsburgs only with Hungary. The electors of Bavaria and Saxony had claims to Austrian territory through their marriages to the daughters of Joseph I. France wanted the Austrian Netherlands, Spain coveted Naples and Sicily and Savoy had long desired the duchy of Milan.

The *Reichstag*, except the Elector of Bavaria, accepted the Sanction in 1732, after energetic Austrian diplomacy. This could be seen as the last triumph for Schönborn but it destroyed Charles VI's freedom of action. The Emperor had to bid for allies among the German princes as a petitioner in competition with other powers and he could not at the same time pose as head of the Empire and an impartial judge over them. It is interesting that from 1726 onwards Charles was signing treaties with German rulers as Archduke of Austria not as Emperor. This marked the symbolic end of the idea of the Empire above parties and was the beginning of the end for the imperial idea. Austria's prestige suffered badly during an unsuccessful war against Turkey (1737–9), in which it lost many of its earlier gains.

On the death of Charles VI in 1740 Frederick II of Prussia launched his invasion of Silesia. The Wittelsbachs achieved a long-held ambition when the Elector Charles Albert of Bavaria was chosen as Emperor in 1742, though he was little more than a puppet of the Prussians and French. The weakness of Austria meant that even traditional friends like Mainz felt compelled to vote for the Wittelsbach. Austria managed to survive thanks to the energy and skill of Maria Theresa. The main problem of the time was not the rise of Hanover and Prussia, as Schönborn believed, but the alienation of Austria from the Empire. The Pragmatic Sanction hastened this and ended the imperial reaction.

7 Dualism and Reform: Germany after the Seven Years' War

After 1740 there were clear signs of change in Germany. New ideas were beginning to spread even if there were very few new institutions. Certain basic characteristics and trends affecting the whole country can be isolated. As always there were exceptions to all generalizations.[1]

The Empire continued to provide a political framework for Germany but the political fragmentation of the country into a collection of virtually sovereign states continued and the Empire was losing what little unifying power it had possessed. There was a brief revival of interest in imperial institutions when Charles Albert, the Elector of Bavaria, was elected Emperor in 1742, but following his death in 1745 the title reverted to the Habsburgs in the person of Francis I, husband of Maria Theresa. By the reign of Joseph II (1765–90) the imperial title was seen as little more than an adjunct of Habsburg dynastic power, but still a significant one. While a young man, Joseph was instructed in the details of the imperial constitution by academic tutors, who emphasized its importance.

The growth of dualism, the emergence of Prussia as a second German great power alongside Austria, continued rapidly. This was significant as each saw the other, rather than as earlier a foreign state like Sweden or France, as the main enemy. German issues therefore became central to German politics. This was part of a general shift in the focus of European politics as a whole away from the Netherlands, the Baltic and the Rhine to the Franco-British competition for overseas empires and to Eastern Europe. Russia was a rising power while Poland was becoming an "empty area" to be exploited by its neighbours. That Germany did not become such a vacuum was because of the existence of the Empire and Austro-Prussian dualism.

The emergence of dualism was gradual. The first serious confrontation between the two German powers was in the imperial diet of 1653–4, when Prussia began to take over leadership of the Protestant anti-imperial party earlier held by Saxony and the Palatinate. In the 1670s and 1680s Brandenburg, like many other states, pursued a flexible foreign policy, switching between a French and imperial alliance as its interests dictated. Already before 1740 Vienna was coming to be seen as the centre of gravity of the Catholic and Berlin of the Protestant *Reich*.

A clear sign that dualism was established came in 1745 when Austria was forced to accept the Prussian seizure of Silesia. Frederick II's invasion of Silesia in December 1740 was a bold gamble which came off. He took advantage of the recent accession of the young and inexperienced Maria Theresa with the stated aim to make a name for himself and to end the "hermaphrodite" nature of his state between an electorate and a real kingdom. There was a very shadowy Prussian claim to Silesia but in reality it was simply a highly desirable strategically important province with a large mainly Protestant population of about a million, fertile soil and developed manufacturing, which lay conveniently on Prussia's borders.[2] During the ensuing War of the Austrian Succession (1741–8) Austria faced a hostile coalition of Prussia, France, Bavaria, Cologne, Sweden, Saxony, the Palatinate, Spain and Naples intent on dismembering her. The nadir of Austria's fortunes seemed to come in January 1742 when Charles Albert, Elector of Bavaria, already crowned King of Bohemia in December 1741, was elected Holy Roman Emperor Charles VII. This marked the attainment of a long-standing Wittelsbach ambition, for which Charles Albert had prepared by trying to make Munich a German cultural centre, even including an attempt to revive the Bavarian dialect of German as a standard high language.

Prussia and France had plans to enlarge Bavaria with Bohemia and a clutch of secularized bishoprics to give it a large territorial base to sustain a permanent possession of the imperial title. A meeting of some of the more important princes at Aschaffenburg in 1741 also put forward plans for a substantial reform of the imperial constitution involving a further major reduction in the Emperor's powers. Charles VII's career as Emperor was brief and sad. Bavaria was occupied by Austrian troops and he had to stay in Frankfurt. He died suddenly aged forty-seven in January 1745. A series of Austrian victories changed the German situation and Maria Theresa's husband, Francis Stephen of Lorraine, was elected Emperor Francis I, with Prussia and the Palatinate dissenting, in September 1745. Francis devoted most of his time to his duchy of Tuscany, which he had received in exchange for his native Lorraine, and Maria Theresa, the most able of the Habsburgs and a woman of strong moral convictions, was personally responsible for imperial policy. Much to her disgust, she was forced temporarily to accept her loss of Silesia by the Peace of Dresden in December 1745.

Prussia's possession of Silesia was challenged again in the Seven Years' War, in which Maria Theresa and her allies sought to eliminate Prussia as a European and even a German power. In spite of victories, Austria was unable to win back Silesia. An imperial army took the field, to be defeated by the Prussians at Rossbach in 1757. The army immediately became an object of ridicule in Germany though it was reorganized after Rossbach and, attached to the Austrian army, fought creditably in the later stages of the war. Prussia's possession of Silesia was again recognized by Austria at the Peace of Hubertusburg in February 1763. Significantly, the *Reich* was not involved in the negotiations leading to Hubertusburg; it was in the interests of neither of the German great powers to involve the other states.

The war left a damaging legacy: the imperial courts ceased temporarily to operate, the coinage was chaotic and religious friction was stirred up again. During the war both sides employed religious propaganda in order to influence German and foreign opinion. Prussia's accusations that Maria Theresa was mounting a crusade to eradicate Protestantism were given some credence. The Habsburgs regarded Roman Catholicism as a useful vehicle for their influence in Germany and Maria Theresa let it be known that her aim was not only to regain Silesia but also to punish wickedness and promote the Catholic faith. In his *Considerations on the Present State of Political Forces in Europe* (1738) Frederick argued that it was always the object of the imperial court to establish Habsburg despotism over the *Reich* and sweep away the democratic system which had prevailed in Germany since time immemorial. Frederick II portrayed himself as a new Gustavus Adolphus, protecting German Protestantism against the Counter-Reformation ambitions of the Habsburgs. When Maria Theresa attempted to have the ban of the Empire decreed against Frederick the Protestant princes in the *Reichstag* refused to consider this on the grounds that it was a religious matter. Frederick II was the first German for a long time to record substantial achievements and his reputation as a Protestant champion and a German hero grew with the development of pro-Frederick (*fritzisch*) sentiment even in the German states with which Prussia was at war.

After the war informal control of Germany was shared between Prussia and Austria. Both had major non-German interests and both behaved like foreign powers, as France had in the past, building up clientage blocs among the smaller German rulers. Neither was a wholly German state and neither looked to Germany as a main area for expansion. Both looked increasingly eastwards, where tempting gains seemed to beckon with the decay of the Turkish empire and Poland. In 1772 the first partition of Poland took place.

Prussia's ability to defeat Austria and retain Silesia was a result of the state-building activities of its rulers after the Thirty Years' War, in particular Frederick William the Great Elector (1640–88) and King Frederick William I (1713–40). The "Borussian" writers of the nineteenth century grossly distorted the significance of their work, portraying it as preparation for a Prussian leadership role in Germany, culminating in the unification of 1871. Although this was long ago discredited, an adulatory attitude towards Prussia can still be found in some German historiography in the later twentieth century. This can effectively conceal the true significance of the "rise" of Prussia; a succession of talented rulers pursued the same policies as most of the rulers of the larger states in Germany but pursued them with more consistency and ruthlessness than most. They concentrated in particular on the creation of a powerful army. After 1648 the possessions of the Hohenzollerns were scattered vulnerably across northern Germany from the Rhine to the Memel, creating a serious problem of defence. Territorial fragmentation, a factor which in the case of other states, for example the Palatinate, was a source of weakness became for Brandenburg-Prussia an incentive for state-building. As a result Brandenburg-Prussia's political weight in Germany and Europe grew rapidly and it became a model to be copied by others.

In the course of a century an authoritarian militaristic state was established in Prussia; the rationalization of the long-term damaging effects of this was another aspect of the Borussian legend. Prussian rulers were obsessed with the acquisition of extra land and population as the only genuine sources of strength for a state. Prussia had a great deal of empty land available. In the case of Prussia the will to become a great power was more important than the resources; eventually the exercise of will enabled the state to seize the extra resources it needed. In pursuit of this the Hohenzollerns were prepared to press all claims, however shadowy, for example in the case of Silesia, and adopted a predatory policy towards their neighbours. They also opened their state to useful refugees and followed a pragmatic policy of religious toleration for this purpose. Some 15 000 Huguenots came after the revocation of the Edict of Nantes in 1685 and about 20 000 Protestants from Salzburg in 1731. Internally ruthless efforts were devoted to the centralization of government and the husbanding of resources for military purposes. It is argued that a Calvinist spirit played an important role in all this. In 1613 the Elector John Sigismund became a convert to Calvinism but, because of the opposition of the nobility and people, he was unable to convert his state, which remained Lutheran. This personal conversion was important in several respects. It gave Brandenburg important international links, especially with the Dutch. Calvinism came to represent the "Prussian" idea. The Great Elector and Frederick William I employed a small Calvinist elite as their main agents; it was easy to maintain cohesion in a small group which formed a religious minority faced with the hostility of the traditional ruling class it was in the process of displacing. A small Calvinist Church developed covering the whole state and not, like the Lutheran establishment, rooted in the separate provinces. Toleration produced intellectual freedom and an openness in Brandenburg-Prussia not seen in most other German states. It became an early centre for the Pietist movement within Protestantism and the university at Halle, under the influence of the Pietist educationist August Hermann Francke, became the best in the Empire.

King Frederick William I was responsible for substantial achievements in building the state. Under him Brandenburg-Prussia acquired an army out of all proportion to its size and resources. He is said to have personified the Calvinist Pietist spirit most spectacularly. He reacted strongly against his father's expensive and showy court — the only permanent achievement of Elector Frederick III (1688–1713) had been the assumption in 1701 of the title of king — and installed a regime of thrift, discipline and hard work which came to be identified as archetypal Prussian virtues. He deliberately employed foreign or non-noble civil servants because the native nobility continued to oppose the changes he wished to introduce but, by a mixture of persuasion and compulsion, he was able to begin the conversion of the nobility into military and administrative servants of the state. Such service later became a jealously guarded badge of status among the Prussian aristocracy.

Frederick II (1740–86) was prepared to take risks which would have horrified his less imaginative father and he was not restrained by Frederick William's lingering imperial patriotism. His gamble of 1740 brought magnificent dividends. Silesia was the making of Brandenburg-Prussia. Frederick also made substantial gains from the first partition of Poland in 1772. He reversed his father's policy of employing non-nobles, convinced that the nobility had to be preserved as natural officers and administrators, and encouraged it by a range of measures, including a monopoly of certain land, cheap credit and substantial powers of local self-government. He also did not press his attempts to abolish serfdom on noble lands beyond persuasion. The unchallenged domination of Prussian society by the aristocracy was to have important effects later.

In addition to the quality of its rulers, the rise of Brandenburg-Prussia was due to other factors. A substantial measure of luck played a part: the Great Elector, Frederick William I and Frederick II had long reigns. The elder son of the Great Elector, Charles Emil, died in 1674, leaving a single heir. This avoided the possibility of a division of the Hohenzollern lands. They were fortunate that their potential rivals in the north were distracted from Germany and abandoned the expansionist policies they had earlier pursued there. Saxony was unfortunate in that two talented rulers, John George III (1680–91) and John George IV (1691–4) died prematurely. The next elector, Augustus, known as the Strong (1694–1733) was elected King of Poland in 1697. Thereafter it was the ambition of the Saxons to make themselves hereditary kings and to create a powerful state there. The Saxon-Polish union eventually brought economic benefits but did not enhance Saxony's power and after the Seven Years' War it abandoned foreign commitments and concentrated on internal rebuilding and reform. Brunswick-Lüneburg, another rising state in the late seventeenth century — its senior line acquired an electoral title in 1692 and the two main territories of the House of Welf, Lüneburg and Calenberg, were united as the electorate of Hanover in 1705 — was distracted from Germany by the acquisition of the British throne in 1714. After that Hanover was very much a side-show. Sweden's power in northern Germany was destroyed in the Great Northern War (1700–21). Other possible rivals, such as Denmark and Hesse-Cassel, lacked the opportunities and resources to challenge Brandenburg-Prussia.

As well as marking the arrival of Prussia as a great power, the Seven Years' War also roused general expectations of change in

Germany: a period of instability, which had lasted since 1740, seemed to have come to an end in 1763. Strangely for the "Age of Reason", there was in some quarters in the 1760s a millenarian atmosphere, with predictions of an imminent spiritual revolution, the greatest overturning since the Reformation, which would sweep away ignorance and allow the victory of Reason. The war was followed by a pause in the struggle between Prussia and Austria, which was only to become serious again in the late 1770s as a result of Joseph II's policies. 1764 saw the election and coronation of Joseph as king of the Romans. The failing health of his father, Francis I, was the main reason for the election. This event, attended by considerable pomp and ceremonial, was widely seen as a new beginning for the *Reich* and a symbol of its new unity. Joseph was the first king or Emperor elected by all the electors without dissent and no new restrictions were placed on him in his capitulation of election. These facts were commented on by some contemporaries as an optimistic sign for the future.

The Seven Years' War also contributed to political change in Germany, as a result of which the predominant form of government in Germany became enlightened or reforming absolutism. Under its influence many German states underwent substantial modernization. Prussia and Austria were able to recover from the devastation of the war and to consolidate their power. This in turn enabled the Holy Roman Empire to survive as the dualism of the two great powers guaranteed its existence. They were strong enough to prevent foreign domination of Germany but neither was strong enough to destroy the other.

There is continuing controversy about the nature of enlightened absolutism, whether any such thing ever existed and, if it did, the reasons for it. It was partly a result of the new ideas circulating in Europe from the late seventeenth century, with a much more optimistic view of man's capacity to change the world in which he lived in contrast to the essentially pessimistic assumptions which underlay much of classic absolutism. Man was seen as possessing an ability to change his fate and to be capable of progress and even perfection, which could be achieved by the application of Reason. The Enlightenment was a cosmopolitan international movement. It concerned itself primarily with cultural and philosophical questions. Initially its impact was intellectual rather than political but it did eventually have political results. It is a good illustration of the power of intellectual ideas to produce change in society though it would be dangerous to exaggerate the extent to which these new ideas overcame the resistance of vested interests, the stubbornness of popular religious enthusiasm and the innate conservatism of rural societies.

The alliance of absolutism and the Enlightenment was very much a marriage of convenience. Enlightened absolutism involved no change in the form of government — like "pure" absolutism it was based on the principle of everything for the people but nothing by the people — but, as new ideas spread, there were significant changes in perceptions of the objectives of the state or a reordering of priorities between the different tasks of government. Governments were now seen as having a duty to promote the happiness of their subjects as well as security and order. Concepts which had long been circulating among limited groups of intellectuals, such as the implied contract between ruler and ruled and the ruler's duty to promote the welfare and happiness of his subjects as a community, began to gain a wider following. These were not foreign imports into Germany but were rooted in the natural law teachings of Christian Thomasius (1655–1728) and Christian Wolff (1679–1754), both professors at Halle university. Wolff in particular developed social contract theory, from which he justified an extension of the power of the state: when man entered the contract, he gave up his freedom in return for justice, peace and order. Their explorations of the notions of the promotion of the common good and the happiness of mankind as duties of the state were also important in legitimizing authority. Also very influential were journals like Christoph Friedrich Nicolai's *Allgemeine deutsche Bibliothek*, founded in 1765. There was a "publications explosion" after 1770, a huge increase in the number of new journals being published, accompanied by a proliferation of reading circles and the like, a development often encouraged by the princes. In 1740 260 journals were founded, between 1770 and 1780 718 and between 1780 and 1790 1 225. Censorship in Germany was patchy and the press was often freest in the tiny states and the largest ones. There were oddities: Joseph II's government censored religious works of superstition but allowed the publication of free-thinking works. The journals were overwhelmingly philosophical and religious in content, catering for the two leading hobbies of educated Germans, and only marginally political.

Another important aspect of the German Enlightenment was the campaign of "popular enlightenment" (*Volksaufklärung*), which sought to overcome the social exclusivity of knowledge by making available the teachings of the Enlightenment to the adult common man, the

Volk, defined by contemporaries as those with a limited education, especially the rural population. From the mid-eighteenth century academic economists, the cameralists, became increasingly concerned with agricultural improvement and governments encouraged the formation of private societies to promote the new agriculture. The products of individuals, societies and governments offered advice and instruction on a fascinating variety of economic, social, veterinary, agricultural and health matters. What distinguished them from the mass of advice which rained down on the Germans from their governments was the undisguised intention to change mentalities, to teach the practical application of reason in daily life and to educate the people away from an unthinking acceptance of traditional attitudes and practices, which was seen as the badge of unenlightenment.[3]

There were also practical reasons for enlightened absolutism. After the Seven Years' War governments were faced with new and pressing problems, for which the old solutions were no longer effective. Marked economic expansion began again in the German states about 1740 with the onset of sustained population growth. The population of Europe as a whole began to rise from about 1750, there were inflationary pressures and governments were faced with the problem of meeting the higher costs of administration and warfare. Military considerations were as central to enlightened absolutism as they had been to traditional absolutism. The Seven Years' War, in its great length, world-wide nature and the size of the forces involved, caused huge losses in money and manpower. Prussia was especially hard-hit, losing at least 180 000 soldiers, largely a result of Frederick II's tactics of deliberately seeking confrontation with the enemy, and massive civilian losses.

The need for substantial internal reconstruction and another round of modernization and state-building was obvious. The inherent strains in absolutism were also becoming clear, especially the fact that it had achieved at best a partial modernization, administrative and military reform, but remained politically and socially conservative. This was a problem which was never resolved and there was always an ambivalence or even a lack of logic in enlightened government, a desire to change some things but not others. A second wave of modernization was needed and it was carried out in some German states.

The achievement of Frederick II in Prussia was not to change the basis of the Prussian state but to make the system work more efficiently and to try to apply reason to its working. It was the modification of his father's system which enabled Frederick and Prussia to survive the near-disasters of the Seven Years' War. Frederick was also responsible for important economic, judicial and educational reforms.[4] The years after 1763 saw a massive opening up of new land for cultivation by drainage, clearances and deforestation, with particularly beneficial results in the new land acquired in the first partition of Poland. Judicial torture was abolished in 1754, an example followed in other states, though some retained it into the nineteenth century. The use of cruel punishments, except for desertion from the army, also declined sharply. Frederick abolished serfdom on the royal domains but was unable to persuade the majority of the nobility to do the same on their lands. His attempt to deal with the financial problems of his state by means of the fiscal experiment of a general excise on the French model was not very successful and very unpopular. Of greater significance was his creation of the Prussian Giro Bank in 1765, which issued notes. It was to be twenty years before this was copied in Austria in the form of the Vienna Commercial Bank.

Frederick's codification of the civil law, the *Allgemeine Landrecht*, was also a significant reform and characteristic of enlightened absolutism. The first draft produced by Frederick's commission was ready in 1784. Its main framers, Carl Gottlieb Svarez and Ernst Ferdinand Klein, were strongly influenced by natural law theories and saw a law code as a substitute for a written constitution. It contained restrictions on royal powers but these were deleted from the final version published in 1794. During the drafting of the code Frederick consulted "public opinion" in the form of the noble-dominated Estates. As a result the code retained relics of the *Ständestaat* (society of rigidly defined orders) in the form of noble privileges. Such compromises between the progressive and the reactionary were common in many states. The code was not revolutionary but of great symbolic importance. It regulated relations between the government and the governed and laid down the rights of various social groups.

Prussia under Frederick II typified the partial modernization characteristic of enlightened absolutism. In general, reform at the top did not deeply affect the corporate structure of society and the old pre-absolutist institutional structures were not destroyed. Alexis de Tocqueville summed up the enlightened absolutist state well as "a modern head on a Gothic body". The state remained an alien corporation set over the people but not of them.

A similar process of reform was seen in Austria under Maria Theresa and Joseph II, who attempted to modernize the country after Austria came close to dismemberment in the Austrian Succession War.[5] Both were strongly influenced by the Prussian model. In the later years of Charles VI's reign Austria had gone to sleep and stagnated and there was an urgent need to catch up. Earlier reform had too often taken the form of tinkering and improvisation. Under the influence of Friedrich Wilhelm Haugwitz, a rational root-and-branch reform of the administrative, financial, judicial and military organization of the Habsburg lands was carried through. In the process Austria was converted into a state, not just a collection of provinces sharing the same ruler. The opposition of the Estates and other institutions of the old system was simply brushed aside. A second bout of reform and modernization followed the Seven Years' War. Joseph II tried to complete the process in a great rush, bringing several parts of his lands near to open revolt. A sharp reaction followed the death of Emperor Leopold II in 1792.

Perhaps in the past there has been too much concentration on the "great" German enlightened despots and not enough study of the smaller states. There was enormous variation within Germany but educated Germans came to regard enlightened despotism as their own particular and superior form of government, based as it was on reason not force. Some lesser German rulers also tried to put into effect the ideas of the Enlightenment. Most are not remembered by history but they were often able to achieve more than their better-known colleagues because they were not distracted by great power pretensions and could devote themselves more assiduously to internal affairs. States like Baden and Saxe-Weimar were, by the standards of the time, well-governed. After 1763 there were significant enlightened reforms in Saxony under the regent Maria Anthonia and the Elector Frederick Augustus III, who assumed power in 1768. The existence of the Empire helped: even though weak, it acted as an umbrella protecting the small states.[6] Even in the ecclesiastical states there was a new spirit of enlightened Catholicism, typified in the movement known as Febronianism, which advocated the formation of a reformed German national Church free of all papal control. One motive behind this appeal to the old tradition of "German liberty" by the German bishops was hostility to Joseph II's infringements of the rights of the Church in Austria.[7]

Enlightened absolutism also did nothing to strengthen national feeling. Its emphasis was exclusively on the prince and the state. The power of the individual state was further enhanced as it came to be seen as a source of progress as well as the preserver of order. The later eighteenth century also saw definite signs of a kind of local nationalism or patriotism appearing in Germany. The motivation behind these campaigns was the promotion of dynastic loyalty. The main concern of those in power was to preserve their position not to change Germany as a whole. Prussia was supremely a state: it had millions of non-Germans in its eastern provinces after the partitions of Poland but all subjects were equal in their subordination to the state and their right to enjoy the protection of the state and no distinctions were drawn on the basis of language or nationality. During Frederick II's reign the Prussian clergy were used to promote this and there are examples of the same policy at work elsewhere. Frederick's attitude to Germany was ambivalent. In his instructions for teachers in Prussian high schools he laid down that German history and politics were to be taught. In his *Ode to the Germans* (March 1760), however, he drew a clear distinction between Prussians and Germans and congratulated the former on their fortune in being able to leave a devastated Germany and find a better homeland for themselves. Well into the nineteenth century German writers used the word "nation" indiscriminately with reference to Germany or Prussia, Bavaria and so on.

There was no group or class in Germany strong enough to rival the princes as leaders. The old parliamentary Estates had either disappeared or had been emasculated. The Church, especially in Protestant states but also in many Catholic states, was virtually a department of state used to run the education system, teach obedience as a religious duty and spread the state's propaganda. The peasants, the overwhelming majority of the population, possessed only the negative power to resist change. The majority of peasants in the east were serfs. In the west many were facing growing economic difficulties. A sharp population rise produced growing land hunger and the period after 1770 saw the first major waves of emigration, especially to North America but also to Russia and south eastern Europe. There were also substantial internal migrations within Germany. There were signs of growing discontent against feudal relics, such as hunting rights, but there was no articulated or organized peasant movement. The majority of free cities were inward-looking and sleepy, ruled by conservative oligarchies anxious to keep political power within their own charmed circle. In most the economy was stagnant and dominated by the guilds. Only a few cities like Hamburg, Bremen and Frankfurt, which experienced economic expansion in the later eighteenth century, were prosperous and cosmopolitan, but they tended to look away from Germany into the Atlantic or France. Even in these more open cities power remained in the hands of a small elite and religious toleration was limited.[8] Localism remained very powerful. In spite of that, it was to be in the great commercial cities and some of the larger princely capitals that a new middle class began to emerge in the later eighteenth century.

Real power in Germany remained in the hands of the nobility and the rising and expanding class of officials. The administrations of many German states were in the hands of highly educated and trained bureaucrats, often strongly influenced by enlightened ideas. Administration was becoming increasingly professional. In 1770 a system of examinations for aspirant bureaucrats was introduced in Prussia, though it was not always strictly enforced because of Frederick II's preference for noble servants. In the later eighteenth century a strong *esprit de corps* grew up among the upper ranks of the administrators. They began to see themselves as members of a corporation, servants of the state rather than the prince, with a duty to defend the general welfare not only against vested interests but also against tyrannical rulers. Sometimes enlightened government is too closely identified with the person of the prince when in reality the impetus for progressive change came from reforming civil servants trying to push through reforms against the opposition of timid or conservative rulers or colleagues. In spite of absolutism, active politics were something which went on within the small ruling class and often involved real clashes of principle.

Although the Enlightenment did not provide a political blueprint, in later years of the eighteenth century, from about 1770, it began to take on a political tinge. By subjecting the contemporary situation to critical eyes, Enlightenment ideas opened the door to a movement for political change. Long-accepted institutions came to be questioned and measured for their usefulness or otherwise against criteria established by the Enlightenment, which asked the basic question: "Is it reasonable that. . .?" This test could be, and was, applied to monarchy, old privileges and customs, the mercantilist economic system, witch-trials, which continued into the 1770s, religious exclusiveness and the old colonial system, among others. There were also growing divisions of opinion about what exactly Enlightenment was.

In the German context religious issues were a major theme in the political debate. There were mounting attacks on irrational survivals in some free cities and ecclesiastical states, such as the use of the catechism to teach a political message, that it was sinful to disobey one's prince, to refuse to pay taxes or to neglect one's duties to social superiors. Many secular princes longed to get their hands on Church lands, which they saw as wastefully administered under the dead hand of the Church. There were among the ecclesiastical states some very glaring exceptions to enlightened despotism and attacks on clerical abuses did not all stem from self-interest. There were also more frequent attacks on religious exclusiveness and evidence of a more tolerant atmosphere in the later eighteenth century. Writers came out in favour of ending legal disabilities on the Jews. There were rationalist attacks on superstition in the Church, a questioning of the value of monasticism, campaigns against the Jesuits, culminating in the suppression of the order in 1774, and calls for tighter state controls on the Church.

Joseph II of Austria showed the way by his policies of religious toleration and various measures of modernization of the administration of the Church. In October 1781 he introduced religious toleration and subsequently introduced a series of measures which amounted to a nationalization of the Church. Joseph shared the view, common in Protestant Germany, that religious clergy were idle and useless and, by providing charity, encouraged idleness in the people at large. He closed a large number of monasteries and convents which had gone into sharp decline from the middle of the century. His attacks on the Church were very unpopular with the majority of the Austrian people, over whom the Church still had a powerful hold. Joseph's actions were especially significant. The Church had played a major role in the growth of the Austrian state from the sixteenth century. The carefully constructed system of baroque religious observance and imagery known as *Pietas Austriaca*, under which the Catholic Church and the dynasty mutually reinforced one another, was very important. This alliance was intensified by the wars against the Turks in the late seventeenth century, which were officially portrayed as crusades. Strict religious uniformity was enforced; only in Silesia, and the small portion of it left to Austria after 1745, was Protestantism tolerated. At the same time, the Habsburgs resisted outside interference with their control of the Church. Charles VI banned all appeals to Rome and the activities of the Church courts were severely restricted. Maria Theresa, although a pious Catholic, sharply reduced the clergy's influence on education and censorship and introduced limited religious toleration in Moravia. This was mirrored in other German states. For example, Bavaria banned further land transfers to the Church in 1764.

The institution of monarchy was also being questioned from both reactionary and progressive wings of opinion. Enlightened rulers were faced with hostility from a range of vested interests for carrying out too much reform and from progressives for carrying out too little. Some rulers saw the writing on the wall: perhaps the best-known example is the advice given by Joseph II in letters to his sister and her husband, the Queen and King of France. He warned them that they must either reform from above or there would be enforced reform from below. The concept of the monarch as first servant of state was available for use against unsatisfactory princes as new standards against which a ruler's performance could be measured emerged. The Duke of Württemberg Charles Eugene (1737–93) was attacked as a typical small-state despot because of his tyrannical treatment of his Estates in the early part of his reign. In the 1780s the rulers of Hesse-Cassel accumulated a huge fortune from their notorious trade in mercenaries, which made them an object of contempt, though they were not the only German rulers who engaged in this business. This also tended to overshadow the substantial achievements of the landgrave Frederick II in reconstructing his country after the devastation of the Seven Years' War.

Some commentators were concluding before the French Revolution that monarchy was dispensable if it did not make itself an instrument of reform. This was symbolized in literary attacks on tyranny, such as Schiller's *Don Carlos* (1787). Here the figure of Philip II of Spain, brutal, bigoted, suspicious and capricious, embodied everything which was wrong with tyrannical monarchy. Schiller's suggested solution was an enlightened prince relying on the guidance of an enlightened minister, Don Carlos and Posa.

Often the practical solutions suggested for bad government were, to say the least, naive: the ruler was to be carefully educated from birth. Bad princes were to be prevailed upon to abdicate and declare republics. The subjects of a bad ruler should pray hard for a better one next time. Other more realistic commentators favoured the creation of the *Rechtsstaat*, the state based on law, in which the powers of the government would be clearly defined in a written law code, which was actually happening in some German states.

A few rulers took the next logical step, abandoning monarchical absolutism once the people were held to be ready for responsible self-government. The best example is Joseph II's brother Peter Leopold,

Grand Duke of Tuscany, probably the greatest of the enlightened rulers but too little known. He was responsible for a large number of beneficial reforms in the Habsburg secundogeniture Tuscany, culminating in the proposal to set up the beginnings of a democratic system of government. This plan was vetoed by Joseph II, who feared the impact of the example in the Austrian lands. Peter Leopold became the Emperor Leopold II in 1790 but died two years later. His premature death was a severe blow to enlightened reform in Austria as there was a sharp reaction under his son and successor Francis II.

Some contemporary commentators believed that the logical next step, self-government, could be achieved through a modernized form of the old Estates. There was a minor renaissance of some of the German Estates in the late eighteenth century, with a revival of interest in constitutionalism, though most progressives condemned the Estates as totally reactionary, representing self-centred oligarchies and providing no foundation for democracy or Liberalism.[9]

Political debate was sharpened by serious economic and social problems which hit Germany after the Seven Years' War. During the war inflation was rampant in Prussia and other states and it was followed by the first severe depression since the first decade of the century. During this slump dozens of companies in the Netherlands and the German states, which had expanded rapidly during the war, went bankrupt. Another more severe economic depression came in the early 1770s. 1771 and 1772 saw serious harvest failures, leading to high mortality and unemployment.[10] This was the first serious subsistence crisis since 1708–12 and even well-organized states, which normally maintained full grain stores to meet emergencies, had problems, especially as some had sold grain to France to make a windfall profit before the full effects of the crisis were felt in Germany. The population was growing rapidly and strains in the economy were becoming very obvious. The population of Germany rose from an estimated twenty millions in 1750 to about twenty-four in 1800. In some parts, especially the Rhineland and the south west, overpopulation was becoming a serious problem. Prussia, which saw the fastest growth, was fortunate in having large areas of underpopulated land available. Other areas, such as Alpine Bavaria, saw no population growth, which would suggest that the rise was caused by specific local factors rather than general climatic, economic or medicinal change. The main cause was probably earlier marriage, made possible by the spread of manufacturing in rural areas, which gave country-dwellers alternative sources of income and freed them from traditional dependence on agriculture. The decline of the guilds, which had also artificially delayed the marriage of apprentices, also played a part.

If food supplies did become more secure because of climatic improvements and increased output, as some historians argue, it did not improve life for the majority of Germans but simply kept them alive to become chronically poor. The growth of a substantial underclass, in both town and country, was the subject of considerable contemporary comment. Pauperism again became a serious problem. It is estimated that after 1763 as many as a quarter of the population of Germany lived close to destitution. In spite of absolutism and the rain of *Polizeiordnungen* which had fallen on Germany, marginal groups were never eliminated from society. Mendicants and other dangerous classes, groups regarded as threatening and useless, like gypsies, itinerants and those without a fixed place in the social order, were becoming a growing menace in the countryside. The political division of the Empire made the apprehension of criminals who escaped from one jurisdiction to another very difficult. Only notorious criminals, for whose capture large rewards were offered, were likely to be caught. The widespread use of banishment, which amounted to social death, as a punishment added to the numbers of the dangerous classes. In towns and cities a growing number were in receipt of some form of poor relief. Work was seen as the best remedy for such problems and the period after the war saw a sharp increase in the number of workhouses and the like, where the indigent were confined.

At the same time new attitudes to the economy were beginning to appear with the spread of the theories of Adam Smith and the Physiocrats. These involved the revolutionary idea that, if each individual were free to pursue his own best interests, the whole of society would gain by the mysterious operation of the Hidden Hand. There was a dawning realization that poverty and other social ills were not caused by fecklessness but by flaws in the social system. The individual's ambition and desire to possess were reasonable and desirable and should be encouraged as a contribution to the common good. Economic progress was to be achieved by removing restraints on the economy. There were calls for the free movement of land, capital, labour and goods, all of which flew in the face of the prevailing economic and social system. The first translation of Smith's *Wealth of Nations* into German appeared in 1776 and his ideas quickly gathered a substantial following among academics. The basic ideas underlying the science of economic management began to change as leading exponents of cameralism, taught in most German universities, adopted the view that excessive state regulation of the economy was hindering rather than fostering its growth. The universities of Königsberg and Göttingen became centres for the diffusion of Smith's ideas and they began to exercise a growing influence on the generation of young men entering the German bureaucracies at this time. Political objectives remained predominant: states wanted to make more people work and people work more.

In practical terms the impact was limited. In order to be successful, a free market economy has certain prerequisites, productive agriculture and manufactures, a strong independent economic middle class and ample capital resources. Before the French Revolution such conditions were only to be found in a few areas of Germany, for example the northern Rhineland, where the old economic system was already breaking down. There was nothing resembling a German national economy at the time but rather a series of economic zones over and above individual states. The main problem was the high cost of transport but the fragmentation of the economy was a major cause of its weakness; barriers between and within states, especially in the form of toll stations, slowed down economic movement. There were at least thirty such barriers on the Rhine.

The economic picture in rural areas was also, with a few exceptions, bad. German agriculture was, in general, very inefficient as the great majority of those engaged in it were subsistence farmers. The backwardness of agriculture was a major barrier to modernization. The predominant crop, grain, was unsuitable to conditions in many parts of Germany but the peasants were very resistant to innovations. There was great reluctance to adopt new crops and techniques, though the famine of the early 1770s hastened acceptance of the potato. Rural economic individualism was very rare as there were few incentives or opportunities to improve cultivation even when urban markets were easily available. In areas where the peasants' tenure was favourable, such as the south west, land hunger and high rents and taxes made improvements difficult.

Some form of personal unfreedom was the predominant situation of the majority of the peasantry, though there were enormous variations from place to place and complex gradations of serfdom from hereditary *Leibeigenschaft*, the harshest form common in the eastern lands, through various forms of *Erbuntertänigkeit* (hereditary unfreedom) to little more than ceremonial relics in parts of the west. The institution of serfdom was coming in for attack for both economic and humanitarian motives. The system was portrayed as inefficient and wasteful of time, energy and enterprise. Many governments tried to carry through a conversion of services into money rents and to give peasants secure leases. There were problems everywhere arising from the peasants' deep conservatism, which led them to view all change with deep suspicion, and their lack of capital to invest in new methods. Unfortunately attempts to abolish serfdom also created problems. Governments often prevented reform by stopping landlords evicting their peasants in order to farm the land more efficiently. The state had a vested interest in restricting the mobility of the population to keep its taxpayers and recruits under control. Any proposed reform came up against the very difficult problem regarding the ultimate ownership of the serf's land: did it belong to the lord or the peasant? Attempts by enlightened monarchs like Frederick II and Maria Theresa to persuade lords to commute labour services into money rents by example had very limited success. Frederick abolished serfdom on royal domains and brought in a system of leases for the holders of royal lands under which the peasants were protected against abuse. Joseph II abolished serfdom in Austria in 1781, building on his mother's work, but this had to be withdrawn in 1790 by his successor as it was far too sweeping and revolutionary. A return to a voluntary approach had little real effect

The picture in manufacturing was little better. The guilds, with their power base in many free cities, represented a substantial force and could not easily be brushed aside. There were many strongly-worded attacks on their stultifying practices, especially after the temporary abolition of the powers of the French guilds in 1774. In Germany imperial legislation gave the states the right to reform the guilds and remove abuses, but few dared to challenge such a powerful vested interest and the guilds continued to play a major role in German manufacturing until the middle years of the nineteenth century.[11] Governments were also nervous about challenging the guilds because of the growing social tensions in many towns, usually caused by economic problems.

In some areas manufacturers migrated outside towns to escape guild restrictions. Such was the case in the north west, where vigorous textile and metal-working centres developed including Monschau in Jülich and Verviers in the Austrian Netherlands. A mixed system became common, with certain basic processes, for example spinning and weaving, carried on in peasant households under the putting out system and finishing processes in large centralized workshops. This proto-industrialization advanced rapidly in some areas; in 1789 over half the population of Berg was in non-agricultural employment.

The first mechanized factories were also operating before the French Revolution. There were large textile works, foundries and glassworks employing thousands in Berlin, Linz, Vienna, the Rhineland and Saxony but they were the exception. State-run industries remained very important to the economies of many states but few were strong enough to survive without state aid. The aim was that they would eventually become self-sufficient but this was rarely achieved. Too often governments did not allow their enterprises enough time to grow before beginning to raid their funds. Over-regulation was a constant problem, with civil servants interfering in enterprises following the fashionable economic nostrums of the time. Private consumption was very restricted. The state, usually the army, remained the main consumer of manufactured goods. Among private individuals only the nobility, the higher clergy and richer townspeople disposed of significant purchasing power. State-encouraged economic growth was not always a total failure and state enterprises, though they rarely reached the objectives set for them, may well have helped to alleviate some of the damaging effects of the economic backwardness of Germany. Some state initiatives were reasonably successful: Frederick II was responsible for significant improvements in the economy of Prussia, in particular in agriculture, which helped to sustain a larger population. He left a full treasury, a favourable trade balance and expanding output. The Austrian economy also improved under Maria Theresa and Joseph II: new lands were settled and commerce and manufactures were promoted, though Austria, like most German states, accumulated very large debts in the later eighteenth century.

If change in the German economy was slow, social change was speeding up in Germany after 1770 in the sense that the traditional distribution of economic, political and social power between the different social classes was coming under challenge. Social change is traditionally understood as *progressive* change, that is movement away from a closed and rigid social system towards a more open one in which social mobility is easier. The period saw challenges to the entrenched social position of the nobility and urban patriciates, which was not held to be reasonable. The nobles no longer played a vital role in society but still enjoyed privileges, usually including a monopoly of land designated as noble, tax exemptions, patrimonial jurisdiction and police powers over their peasant "subjects", ecclesiastical patronage, hunting rights, social predominance and guaranteed access to certain fields of employment. One problem was that nobility was still seen as the main source of status: too much wealth made in trade or public service was effectively sterilized by the purchase of titles and land to give noble status. The period saw the beginning of a challenge to this, as the middle classes grew in size and confidence and began to question the special rights of the nobles.

The old order, based on the notion of a division of society into well-defined Estates, was beginning to change well before the French Revolution although no well-defined new system, based on modern classes or individualism, had appeared to replace the older social order. Germany had entered a period of flux or transition, the outcome of which was unclear. The absolutist state, with its desire to simplify the social order and its downgrading of the old feudal relationships, was an important agent of this change. There were also new attitudes on the status of women and the role of the family.

The old *Ständestaat* was based on the concept of social inequality; the new idea of equality before the law was beginning to develop to challenge it. The growing self-confidence of a new middle class was measurable. There were enormous variations between state and state and town and town but certain trends were clear. There was a large "old" conservative middle class in the smaller towns and cities, with many of its members enjoying special privileged status, like the clergy and university staff and students, and a "new" progressive middle class alongside and often overlapping with it. A party of movement, of progressive opinions, was appearing. An early expression of this was found in the Patriotic societies, devoted to discussion and work for the good of the fatherland, which spread in the 1760s. Secret societies also played a part. The first German Free Masonic lodge was set up in Hamburg in 1737 to be followed by hundreds more. The reading circles which proliferated in the later eighteenth century were sometimes a cover for secret activities. The growth of these societies symbolized the development of a completely new form of voluntary association very different from the old institutions like the Estates, guilds and Churches, which had earlier determined peoples' view of their place in society but which were now becoming visibly weaker. They often went in for a great deal of rather silly ceremonial but they allowed mixing under circumstances of equality of nobles and non-nobles which boosted growing middle-class self-confidence. With the publications explosion, they contributed to the development of a middle-class consciousness (*bürgerliche Öffentlichkeit*), which envisaged a society of equal citizens rather than of *Stände*.

Central to the thinking of this group was the notion of mobility, social and physical, manifested in a desire to travel, something earlier restricted to a few. Status had to be earned and could not be possessed, like noble status, purely because of an accident of birth. The Patriot societies and other progressive associations were open to all those who were of a proper background and had the correct attitudes; once admitted, all members were held to be equal. A more favourable view of commerce and its practitioners began to appear in literature after a long period when the merchant was looked down on by members of the university-educated professional middle class. The concept of the citizen (*Staatsbürger*) with civic rights (*bürgerliche Rechte*) and the right to participate in the life of the state was well established. This right did not belong to all men but had to be earned by the possession of certain qualities and certain behaviour, increasingly identified with middle-class virtues and summed up in the word *Bildung* (education and cultivation).

Access to university education and the emergence of the concept of all-round education contributed to growing pride in middle-class achievement. Another factor was the rise of an all-German middle class, a group of mobile educated and professional people, including academics, students, officials, officers, diplomats, musicians and projectors, whose links with their *enges Vaterland* (narrow fatherland, the individual state in which they lived) weakened as they moved around the *Reich*. One feature of all this was a growing knowledge of and interest in the history of Germany and a better appreciation of how it had developed to its "monstrous" state.

A recent study of the French Revolution[12] has drawn attention to the great intensity and mobilizing power of a new form of patriotism which emerged in France after the Seven Years' War. This produced a new concept of citizenship which took precedence over regional, class or group loyalties, taught that all patriotic citizens had a duty to involve themselves in state affairs and began to breach the walls between the state and private spheres so typical of the *ancien régime*. While various factors produced a more restrained situation in Germany, it is clear that something similar existed there in the later eighteenth century. When the French Revolution broke out, many German intellectuals saw this as an attempt by the French to win for themselves by force what the Germans had already won by thought, in itself significant. By the beginning of the eighteenth century French fashions and habits had taken Germany by storm. This was true of all Europe but was especially strong in Germany and was commented on unfavourably by patriots. By the end of the century there were changes in German literature, a kind of intellectual revolution which led to a weakening of French influence. At first there was no national political content but this gradually changed. Although it was still very much a minority movement, the numbers of those who saw themselves as patriots or *Vaterlandsfreunde* were increasing. The concept of the good citizen or patriot was political, social and moral: he was seen as having a duty to act as a model in his personal life, to involve himself in the community (*die gemeine Sache*) and to work for the common good of the fatherland, rising above the narrow class, occupational, religious or regional group to which he belonged. The Patriot movement represented a kind of political Third Way between the corporative state of Estates, regarded as reactionary, and the enlightened absolute monarchy and a middle culture between the frenchified courts and nobility and traditional regional *altständisch* culture. It was based on the involvement of the people, by which was understood the middle classes, in the state and in that lay the roots of popular sovereignty, democracy and modern nationalism.

If this was something recognizable as early nationalism, it was cultural rather than political, based on the notion of the linguistic spiritual *Kulturnation*, an "inner Germany", which would survive even if there was no *Staatsnation*, political unity. There was a growing movement to promote the use of the German language. Christian Thomasius used German rather than Latin in his lectures in the late seventeenth century, a revolutionary step at the time. Between 1774 and 1786 the German dictionary of J. C. Adelung was published in several volumes. One element in growing middle-class self-confidence was seen in a reaction against French fashions and resentment of the social predominance of the French language, which was seen as light and trivial. A mixture of class and national resentment was growing up.

In Germany the issue was complicated by the fact that every German had two states, the territorial state and the *Reich*. "Fatherland" could mean either of these or the German nation as an abstract cultural entity without borders. German patriotism was therefore innately ambivalent: it could lead to support for the untrammelled freedom of the individual states (*Staatssouveränität*) to liberate the reforming urges of progressive rulers, or for a revitalization of the imperial constitution as a barrier against the despotism of an unenlightened prince. A majority of the German patriots accepted that the essence of a good political system was one in which the only limits on freedom were those made necessary by the common good and in which there was some mechanism to restrain or moderate the exercise of power. This could include enlightened public opinion formed by a free press, written constitutions or law codes, creating the state based on law (*Rechtsstaat*), intermediate powers, such as parliamentary institutions and privileged corporations, or the imperial laws and tribunals. All could act as a barrier to tyranny.

Political debate in Germany became more lively under the impact of the American Revolution, between 1763 and 1783.[13] Some German thinkers were beginning to break out of Aristotelian concepts of the state and society as inseparable and were moving towards Liberal notions of the minimal state and self-regulating society, though it all remained in the realm of ideas. Up to that point the majority of progressive thinkers in Germany had admired the British constitution as a model. The American constitution was seen as the first practical application of things which had previously existed only in theory or were mistakenly believed to exist in England, such as the division of powers, popular sovereignty, a society without a nobility, equality before the law, the absence of an established Church, a federal system, a republic (a form of government which in Europe was known from Poland and Venice and was equated with weakness and decline), a written constitution and a free economy. America was far enough away from Europe to be romanticized. Not many commentators advocated the imitation of the American example in Germany, which was anyway seen as not needing a revolution but only more reform under its enlightened rulers.

Another effect of this quickening debate was that the new ideas were being answered by spokesmen for an articulate and intelligent conservatism, based on an organic view of the state and society and respect for traditions. J. J. Moser rejected enlightened absolutism as a false panacea for states (*Univeral-Staats-Medizin*), which would destroy traditional rights. These writers offered a defence of strong monarchy, the nobility and religious exclusiveness, among other things. Noble privilege was defended with the claim that the nobility was vital to the stability of the whole social order and, not being motivated by ambition and greed, provided the natural servants of the crown. This was a view strongly held by Frederick II.

The years after 1763 saw the foundations of the bodies of ideas which were to blossom in the nineteenth century into organized political Liberalism and Conservatism. The practical effects of the debate were limited and the changes which have been described affected only a tiny group at the top of German society. The great majority of Germans remained largely unaffected but there was a mounting atmosphere of expectation of change in the 1770s and 1780s.

The German question continued to concern the rest of Europe. French influence remained important and was accompanied by growing Russian influence, arising from intermarriage between the Romanoffs and German dynasties. In the years after the Treaty of Aix la Chapelle of 1748 Russia became an official guarantor of the imperial constitution, replacing Sweden in that role. Germany remained very much a side-show in European affairs. Internally it seemed to have settled down into a state of equilibrium, only occasionally troubled by small problems. Among these was the Württemberg constitutional dispute in the 1760s, which saw the last major intervention of the imperial aulic council in the internal affairs of a substantial state of the Empire. The Protestant constitutional establishment there was guaranteed by Hanover, Prussia and Denmark. In 1759 the prominent jurist and leader of the Estates, Johann Jakob Moser, was imprisoned by the duke, who was trying to bring in an absolutist system of government. In 1764 military force was used against the Estates when they protested against the duke's illegal taxation. After litigation the case was settled in favour of the Estates in 1770. Thereafter the Duke Charles Eugene became an enlightened ruler and promoted commerce and education. He abandoned military ambitions and was seen as a model ruler by the end of his reign.[14]

Another minor problem was the so-called Potato War (or War of the Bavarian Succession) 1778–9. This arose out of the succession problem in the Wittelsbach electorates, Bavaria and the Palatinate, which had run out of male heirs. The Bavarian male line died out in 1777 and its territory was inherited by the elector palatine, who also had no male heirs. Joseph II, who claimed a share of the inheritance as husband of the sister of the last Elector of Bavaria, was very eager to gain Bavarian territory. The whole thing could have been settled between Prussia and Austria to their mutual benefit but mistrust between them was too great. Eventually the whole inheritance passed to a cadet line of the Wittelsbachs. Frederick II was very nervous about the Austrian threat to Prussia and Joseph II's need to demonstrate his power. After a brief "war", in which the two armies avoided meeting one another, the whole matter was settled with French and Russian mediation by the Peace of Teschen in 1779.

Rivalry between Austria and Prussia deepened as a definite attempt to revive Austrian power in Germany to rival Prussia was launched. Habsburg candidates, including some of Maria Theresa's large brood of sixteen children, were elected to a number of important ecclesiastical positions. Joseph II's brother Maximilian Francis took over the sees of Cologne and Münster in 1784. Austria also revived an old scheme, to persuade the Elector of Bavaria to exchange his German possessions for the Austrian Netherlands. In addition to this Joseph had a comprehensive plan to extend Austria deep into southern Germany by exchanging Württemberg and Baden for Austria's Italian possessions, Tuscany and Modena. In the 1780s Joseph tried to revive lapsed imperial rights of presentation to benefices in imperial abbeys and foundations, of which there were almost 300 in the *Reich*, using the aulic council for this purpose. This did nothing to add to the Emperor's popularity in the German Catholic Church. Joseph also proposed a reform of the imperial courts, ignoring the rights of the princes in this matter. The reform was suspected to be a cover for attempts to ensure that the verdicts of the *Reichshofrat* were more uniformly in Austria's political interest and the suspicion was well-founded.

Such actions raised questions about the role of the Emperor. From the 1770s onwards there were calls for reform of the Holy Roman Empire, which even Germans were beginning to see as old-fashioned, but the demand was for a rationalization of the constitution not the abolition of the Empire or the creation of a united German state. National feeling expressed itself in calls for a strengthening of the *Reich* against the larger states, including Austria, which seemed ready to sacrifice the smaller states for their own narrow interests. The partition of Poland was seen as a dreadful warning of what could happen in the *Reich*. The large states were not interested in changing a system which suited their interests. One reason for this was growing fear of Austrian "tyranny" in the Empire, a fear encouraged by Prussian propaganda. This manifested itself in challenges to Austria's right to speak on behalf of the whole *Reich*. One expression of growing disquiet was a revival of the notion of *Drittes Deutschland*, the Third Germany, also known as trialism, the idea that the states which made up Germany without Austria and Prussia should come together in a closer arrangement to defend their independence against the two German great powers. The idea of the *Trias* was refloated in the 1780s by Baden, as a scheme of reform for the *Reich*. This proposed the division of Germany into three states, Austria, Prussia and a confederation of the rest. The period saw growing pressure for a long-overdue inspection of the *Reichskammergericht*, a sign of the desire of some of the smaller states to revive the institutions of the Empire as a means of saving it from the mounting egotism of the large states. In 1775 the *Reichskammergericht* was reformed to speed up its procedures and in 1782 extra judges were appointed, initiating a period of intense judicial activity with the backlog of old cases cleared up and a flood of new litigation.

The *Fürstenbund* (League of Princes), set up by Frederick II in 1785, had its origins in these developments. The League was designed to give Prussia German allies in case Austria tried to attack her after Frederick's death. It was also part of Frederick's scheme to create a Prussian sphere of influence in northern Germany, a security zone under Prussian control to guarantee the survival of the state under a weak ruler. The League was also a symptom of a growing constitutional crisis in the Empire. It began as a movement among some of the medium-sized princes to build a union of the Third Germany and it was only later taken over by Prussia for its own ends, when its original purpose was abandoned. Its stated aim was to preserve the status quo in the German constitution and article four of its act of association committed its members to seek a reform of the imperial supreme courts and to defend them against imperial encroachments. Frederick cynically used the defence of "German liberty" and anti-Catholicism as political weapons in his campaign. Prussia was able to portray the Bavarian exchange scheme as an attack on the *Reich* constitution. The League was joined by Hanover, Saxony, a number of small states and some ecclesiastical states alienated by Joseph II's attacks on the Catholic Church in Austria. Although Prussia was exploiting the Empire for its own purposes, there was a genuine hope among some of the smaller states that it would lead to real *Reichsreform*, calls for which were becoming more frequent.[15] The League was also a sign of reviving suspicion of the Emperor's intentions: Joseph II was seen as a violent and ambitious ruler, who used the Empire for Austrian purposes. The League made a partition of Germany between Prussia and Austria impossible as it amounted to a guarantee of the status quo, though this was not Prussia's intention. Frederick had the role of a national leader thrust upon him. The establishment of the *Fürstenbund* added to the constitutional debates and new questions were asked about the relationship of the Emperor and the Empire.

Disenchantment with the situation was typified in an anonymous pamphlet of 1787, which asked *Warum soll Deutschland einen Kaiser haben?* (Does Germany need an Emperor?) and concluded that the office was now redundant as the whole Empire was against the tide of the times. Such a view was unusual. Politically-informed Germans looking at their country in the later eighteenth century found much to bemoan but also much to praise. Typical was F. C. von Moser's anonymously published study of the German national spirit of 1765 (*Von dem deutschen National-Geist*), which contrasted the potential strength of Germany and the low esteem it enjoyed among its neighbours. Some reacted to the situation with resignation, others with a desire to change things; very few thought in terms of sweeping away the *Reich* and replacing it with something else. For one thing, it was difficult to define acceptable alternatives. There was a widespread view that Germans were singularly fortunate in the constitution of their country, which allowed a wide measure of freedom to the individual states and to individual Germans, while protecting certain basic rights against encroachments. Imperial law guaranteed to all subjects freedom to practise one of three legal religions somewhere in the Empire, freedom of movement within the Empire to all who were not tied to the soil, the right to inherit property anywhere in the Empire, the right to justice in properly conducted courts and the right to security of person and property under the law. Already in the second half of the eighteenth century the modern notion of freedom was beginning to grow up alongside the older tradition of liberties; in the eyes of many commentators the imperial constitution was flexible enough to accommodate and protect both. At the same time the old medieval universalist view, which had seen the *Reich* as the leading state of Christendom and the Emperor as its secular head, was passing away and was being replaced by a new universalism more in tune with the enlightened spirit of the age, a combination of patriotism and cosmopolitanism which saw the advancement of Germany as beneficial to the whole of humanity.

8 The End of the Empire: Germany and the French Revolution

There is still debate among historians whether the French Revolution modernized Germany or brought a period of progress to a sharp end. Before 1789 most of the German states were changing and, though generalization is as always dangerous, certain trends were visible. In many states major reforms had been achieved during the period of enlightened absolutism, resulting in marked improvements in the lives of subjects. Germany was still administratively progressive and economically and socially backward but things were changing. Economic individualism, secularization and social mobility were beginning to appear. Cultural developments were a significant sign of changing attitudes. There is no evidence of mass discontent with government in the majority of the German states but critical middle-class public opinion was becoming an important factor. This was reflected, for example, in attacks on the abuse of power by governments and in propaganda in favour of individual freedoms put forward by writers, though such ideas remained vague and unco-ordinated and there was still nothing resembling an organized opposition party with a coherent political programme.

In the years immediately before the revolution the pace of reform had begun to slow down in many states as opposition from vested interests grew. Important changes also took place in the two leading German states. With the death of Frederick II in 1786 Prussia entered a period of stagnation and in the last year of his reign Joseph II of Austria was facing rebellion in many of his provinces. All this sharpened debate within the ruling and educated classes about the nature and functions of government, in Germany as a whole and in the individual states.

Karl Friedrich Häberlin (1756–1808), an academic lawyer, a practitioner in the *Reichskammergericht* and a diplomat in the service of Brunswick, was a leading advocate of *Reichsreform*. He regarded the imperial courts as the last barrier against despotic government and praised the imperial system for giving Germans a measure of freedom and security, the like of which was only enjoyed by the English. August Ludwig von Schlözer (1735–1809), one of the fathers of German Liberalism, was a pioneer of political journalism in Germany as well as an academic historian and his journal *Statsanzeigen* had the largest circulation of any such publication in Germany. Otto Heinrich Freiherr von Gemmingen (1755–1836), a diplomat, playwright and author, while Badenese envoy in Vienna published a pamphlet *I am a German and want to remain a German (Ich bin ein Deutscher and will ein Deutscher bleiben)*. Wilhelm Ludwig Wekhrlin (1739–92) was a bold and active journalist of advanced views and publisher of a number of magazines, the most famous of which was *Das graue Ungeheuer*. In November 1783 Wilhelm von Edelsheim, chief minister of Baden, put forward a scheme for a union of the Third Germany, excluding the two great powers, plus an institutional reform of the *Reich*. One of the best-known advocates of *Reichsreform*, including a thorough-going modernization of the judicial system, was Karl Theodor von Dalberg, coadjutor of Konstanz and later the last Elector of Mainz.

It is interesting to hypothesize what would have happened had these trends continued. As it was, everything changed after the French Revolution. A French cartoon of 1793 showed the sans-culottes feeding the bread of liberty to various European rulers, including the Emperor, on the points of their bayonets. After 1789, as a result of their military victories, the French took over direct or indirect control of Germany and became the dictators of developments there. Germany experienced an imported revolution.

The years 1789 to 1814 were a very important transitional period in the history of Germany, which experienced rapid kaleidoscopic change.[1] This period saw sharp departures from existing developments and had important long-term effects which deeply influenced developments in the nineteenth century. It witnessed the destruction of the existing German political framework and, at the same time, developments which made it much more difficult to construct a new one. The main changes, in outline, were: the end of the Holy Roman Empire, a further strengthening of Austria, Prussia and the medium-sized states and a rapid modernization of government in many states. A distinct German nationalism emerged, strengthened by the rise of the Romantic Movement. There was also an acceleration in the growth of Liberalism, another important factor in nineteenth-century Germany.

The French Revolution did not burst on Germany from a clear sky. The soil was well prepared and a psychology of expectation was well established. There had been growing debate, at the intellectual level, on a variety of social, economic, political and religious topics from the 1770s onwards. Whereas the American Revolution had caused only a mild flutter, events on Germany's doorstep in the summer of 1789 clearly had a greater effect: they raised the temperature of the debate, although the immediate practical results were very small. Interest remained the preserve of a small group within German society. There was nothing approaching a mass revolutionary movement: in general mass movements were something conspicuously absent from German public life in the eighteenth century. The majority of Germans were apolitical, leading some to talk of a German "spectator psychology": they stood by and watched with interest but did not see the relevance of events in France to their own lives. They were *gedankenvoll aber tatenarm* ("full of theory but short of action"). In spite of superficial similarities between the two countries, there was no spontaneous revolution in any part of Germany.

The first reason must be sought in the character of revolutions.[2] Revolutions happen as the result of a combination of unusual circumstances and cannot be made to occur as an act of will, however much some people might want to bring about radical changes in society. A combination of predisposing factors is necessary. These include an economic crisis so severe as to approach what is called a universal crisis, the existence of a revolutionary class, mass discontent and acts of provocation by the government. A combination of these could turn urban demonstrations against food shortages or peasant riots into a revolution which causes political, economic and social power to migrate irreversibly from one group to another. The old ruling group is eliminated in one way or another and the material base of political power shifts.

In France the revolution originated as a revolt by the privileged nobility against their exclusion from political power and attempts by the royal government to reform the administration, especially the taxation system, as glaring faults had been revealed by the national bankruptcy following French involvement in the War of American Independence. The movement was taken up by elements in the middle class, excluded, in their eyes unfairly, from influence and office. This merged with a wave of urban and rural rioting arising from basic economic grievances, which produced mass pressure at the seat of government in Paris. The French government's response was inconsistent, a mixture of concession and repression. The discontented middle class, instead of trying to reform the existing system, saw an opportunity to overturn it and became a revolutionary class. In 1789 they began by establishing a constitutional monarchy, carried through a series of policies designed to modernize France and took the first steps in a great transfer of property. Once they were in power, divisions among revolutionaries led to growing extremism, the killing of the king, the establishment of a republic and the Terror.

Such developments were unthinkable in Germany, which consisted of hundreds of vested interests. The political, social and economic facts of life in each German state were different: well-run states, politically more advanced than France in 1789, bordered petty tyrannies. It is easier to decide why there was no revolution in, for example, Hesse-Cassel, than in Germany as a whole. Many German rulers were seen as the caring fathers of their people and were personally popular. Radicals like the journalist Christian Schubart might mock the worship of princes but his was an untypical voice. Above all Germany lacked a Paris: there was no similar great concentration of population and political power. Germany had a large number of capitals and centres, economic, political and cultural.

Social conditions were also quite different in the two countries. In most German states the aristocracy was entrenched in power as well as privilege. The states were usually based on an alliance of the crown, the nobles, the urban oligarchies and the bureaucracy. The last were motivated by a desire to improve their states not to revolutionize them. In most states there was still a relatively static society, more traditional and stable and less open to new ideas than that of France. The bulk of the middle class was more conservative and there was, in most cases, no bourgeoisie in the French sense. There was no revolutionary class prepared to give leadership and political direction to a large reservoir of inarticulate discontent, especially among the peasantry and among the poor in towns and cities. The peasants in western Germany were in general much better off than those in France. "Feudalism" survived only in the form of relics, which were in some cases actually beneficial to the peasants. Many states protected them against excessive exploitation and they had recourse to the imperial courts. They often had alternative sources of income. There was little middle-class landownership and the patriarchal relationship between lord and peasant survived. The peasants' position was much worse in the east but there they were usually too cowed to rebel. There was in Germany a legacy of civic apathy, the product of absolutism and Lutheranism. In spite of changes taking place before the revolution life for most Germans was still organized by the state, the Church, the school, the guild and the extended family. There was a cultivation of negative virtues, such as stability, loyalty and obedience, rather than initiative and individualism. Habits of deference from those who traditionally obeyed towards those who traditionally ruled were deeply-rooted.

It is not surprising, therefore, that most ordinary Germans regarded events in France in the summer of 1789 with indifference. There was tremendous publicity in favour of the revolution, seen by most German intellectuals as a new dawn, a triumph of reason and the rights of man, the victory of liberty over tyranny, intolerance, injustice and oppression. Like the Reformation, whose great liberating work it continued, it was seen as universally relevant and not just a French event. In educated circles there was a general welcome for the written constitution, the abolition of clerical and noble privilege, equality before the law and a career open to talents: it was said, apparently without irony, that the French were trying to establish a state based on sound Prussian principles. Many intellectuals travelled to Paris to "drink at the well-springs of liberty." Louis XVI was now seen as an enlightened ruler on the German model. Revolution and reform initiated from the top were seen as alternative answers to deal with the same problems. Therefore a revolution was quite unnecessary in Germany. In the absence of other political outlets in Germany, enthusiasm for events in France acted as a kind of safety valve.

Of major German intellectuals only a few, including Goethe, opposed the revolution from the beginning. Support in Germany was further stirred up after 1790 by a well-organized French propaganda machine with centres in Strasburg, Basle and Vienna. It also spread through Masonic lodges and reading clubs. It would, however, be wrong to think that enthusiasm for the revolution in Germany was the work of foreign agitators, as German governments tended to do: the conspiracy theory was the easiest explanation of the revolution for conservatives to understand.

There were some more tangible echoes of the revolution in the spring and summer of 1789 and in 1790. There were several peasant and urban riots in various parts of Germany, especially in the

Rhineland. These outbreaks of violence were products of pre-existing problems. Imitation of events just over the border was a new outlet to express long-standing grievances against landlords, employers and governments. The economic troubles which had contributed to the revolutionary crisis in France also affected western Germany. There was agitation among the better-off peasants in areas where serfdom was only an irritating relic, especially the hunting rights retained by the lords. Such outbreaks were isolated and easily dealt with. After 1780 there was a sharp rise in grain, especially rye, prices, from which the free peasants benefited, though real incomes generally fell. The years 1790 to 1806 have been seen as the Golden Age of the Baltic, with huge grain exports and unprecedented prosperity. There was, therefore, less pressure for evictions, which had been a major cause of social grievance in previous decades. Emigration also acted as a safety valve for overpopulation in the west. In the towns there is some evidence that riots arose from economic grievances or from party squabbles within the oligarchies, in which one group used the mob against another.

In Aachen the guild artisans rioted against the introduction of new machines. There were isolated risings in other parts of Germany, usually arising out of local grievances: for example in the Tyrol there were anti-conscription riots and in Breslau and other centres in Silesia troubles caused by losses in the local linen industry because of English competition. The most extensive outbreaks were in Saxony, again arising out of local peasant grievances. The ringleaders used French revolutionary propaganda in their appeals but the troubles faded away when the Saxon government behaved sensibly and made concessions. Only in Austria did the situation approach the universality of crisis which preceded the revolution in France with a serious economic crisis, food shortages, war, unpopular military recruiting and political revolts.

Enthusiasm for the revolution among the majority of German intellectuals did not last long. The growing extremism of the revolutionaries, leading to poverty, civil war, attacks on religion and the Terror, understandably caused wide revulsion. The poet Schiller, given honorary French citizenship in the early days of the revolution, renounced it as an expression of his growing disgust at the violence in France. The French became the object of patronizing attitudes: they were considered to be incapable of fulfilling the promise of their own revolution. One result of this was an idealization of the early stages of the revolution, which, it was believed, had established a modernized state, an emancipated society and unparalleled national unity. In the early years of the nineteenth century German Liberals believed that the French had let their revolution slip into anarchy, by implication a mistake which Germans would not have made.

This disillusionment was increased by a change in French foreign policy. After initially declaring a break from the immoral diplomacy of the old regime, symbolized in the Partition of Poland, and denying any ambitions on the territory of its neighbours, the declaration of peace to the world, the French revolutionary government changed to a policy of seeking the natural frontiers of France, including the river Rhine, which would mean swallowing millions of Germans. The French also embarked on a policy of ideological expansion with promises of help for peoples struggling to be free. Friction between France and German states began from 1790 as the French started to interfere with the rights of the Empire in certain enclaves of German territory within the borders of France, including the extension to them of the abolition of feudalism enacted in France. The French were ready to pay compensation to those who lost as a result but it led to appeals to the Emperor for help from the German rulers involved. The French for their part became increasingly irritated at the activities of counter-revolutionary *émigrés* concentrated at Koblenz and Brussels. There was growing concern on the part of some German governments, seen in attempts to set up *cordons sanitaires* to keep out "the liberty influenza" by preventing the import of French revolutionary propaganda. Some speakers in the *Reichstag* in 1792 proposed a revival of the Circle associations as a means of guaranteeing the integrity of the Empire.

At first most German rulers had seen no threat from the revolution, which they believed was due to the incompetence of Louis XVI, who had not made concessions in time to save a fundamentally sound system of government. Gradually the conspiracy theory came to hold the centre of the stage: the revolution was seen as the work of wicked men and Freemasons. All those wanting change were tarred with the same brush, though the party of movement in Germany was very divided and fragmented. The name "Jacobin" was applied to all those who criticized the existing order. Progressive bureaucrats had to keep their heads down as a rain of repressive edicts fell on Germany. Other measures included the restoration of the death penalty, rigorous censorship, bans on meetings and tighter controls on the universities. Strict censorship was imposed in Prussia in 1794. 1790 also saw the beginning of a spate of conservative propaganda against the revolutionaries, including the use of sermons. There was a general clamp-down on Freemasons and Illuminati, a symptom of the powerful conviction that the revolution was the result of a Masonic plot. Austria also entered a period of reaction which was to last for fifty years. Ironically, the reforming Emperor Joseph II had created a secret police and other organs of repression to use against opponents of his reforms and reactionaries. These were turned against progressives under Francis II. This was seen clearly in the so-called Jacobin trials in Austria.[3]

The whole picture changed radically in April 1792, when the first revolutionary war began. The war arose from the French internal political situation, not from any desire by foreign tyrants to destroy the revolution. The French Revolution broke out when Eastern Europe was involved in the Russo-Turkish War, which began in 1787 and lasted until 1792, and the Russo-Swedish War in the Baltic from 1788 to 1790. As a result there no desire for a war in the West in Austria and Prussia.[4] There were deep divisions among the revolutionaries and political tensions in France were made worse by the rise of a powerful party of moderates, seriously worried by the extremism which the revolution had called forth. There was, apparently, a real danger of a counter-revolution. The moderate revolutionary Gironde party, under pressure from Left and Right, chose a policy of fireworks abroad instead of fireworks at home, a forward foreign policy to keep out of power the more extreme Mountain party and the royalists. They believed a war would "cleanse" the revolution and force traitors to reveal themselves. In April 1792 the National Assembly, in an atmosphere of super-heated patriotism, approved a declaration of war against the Emperor. The Gironde played on old-established anti-Austrian sentiment in France. The alliance with Austria, in existence since 1756, was seen as a cause of the decline of France and this sentiment had been increased by the frivolous behaviour of Queen Marie Antoinette, the sister of Joseph II and Leopold II.

In reality the French government had no war aims but dreamed up theories to justify its aggressive foreign policy, including the gaining of the so-called natural frontiers of France and the liberation of peoples groaning under tyranny. The second theory was embodied in the so-called liberty decree of 19 November 1792, which offered French aid to all peoples striving to recover their liberty. Very quickly the war became its own policy-maker. Its importance in French internal politics continued, as it increasingly determined policy, created economic and political crises, drove the revolution to extremes and made a military dictatorship more likely. Europe became increasingly terrified of a revived France, especially when the Jacobins came into power and embarked on a policy of ideological warfare. This led to a series of coalitions against the French. France engaged in the search for defensible frontiers, which led her to try to subordinate the whole continent.

The actions of the French helped to push together Prussia and Austria. The German states did not want war. Indeed, France and the West were not the main focus of attention for the leading states. Austria and Prussia continued to see one another as the main enemy. Prussian intervention in the Netherlands in 1788 to put down a rising against the Orange stadholder and in Liège in August 1789 in support of a rising against the bishop were anti-Austrian moves. Prussia was also an ally of the Turks. In 1789–90 Prussia had been planning to attack Austria and dismember her when she fell apart as a result of Joseph II's blundering. King Frederick William II yearned for territorial expansion to avoid living under the shadow of his uncle, Frederick II. Austria continued to pursue her own ambitions, including a revival of the Bavarian exchange scheme based on a plan to give the Wittelsbachs a new state made up of secularized ecclesiastical territories. From the summer of 1791 fear of France pushed the two into uneasy co-operation. They were encouraged to fight the French by Russia, which hoped in this way to divert their attention from the Balkans and Poland.

At first after the outbreak of war the allies drove back the French and seemed on the point of invading France but between September and November 1792 a great turning point came. Robespierre and the Jacobins came into power and initiated a much more efficient war effort with great ideological fervour. Great French victories were won at Valmy and Jemappes, after which they occupied the Austrian Netherlands and the Rhineland. A declaration of imperial war against the French was passed by the *Reichstag* in March 1793 but there was no great enthusiasm for it. Prussia in particular was anxious to withdraw from the war in order to digest her gains from the second partition of Poland.

Under Jacobin influence in the period 1792–5 French policy still at least paid lip service to ideals, seen in mottos such as "War on the chateaux, peace to the cottage" and attempts to win over the people of the occupied areas by, among other things, attacks on the old ruling groups, the establishment of revolutionary clubs and the planting of liberty trees.

1794 saw the fall of Robespierre in the Thermidorean reaction, after which power passed to the Directory, which established the policy to be continued by Napoleon after he seized power in France in 1799. This was essentially pragmatic and dropped all pretense of idealism, seen in a new motto, "War must feed war". This signalled a return to more traditional policies, the exploitation of Germany for the benefit of France, the creation of client states (called sister republics), the levying of requisitions and contributions in return for the French alliance and protection and, eventually, outright annexation. One reason for the change of French policy was disillusionment with the lack of enthusiasm for the French among the "liberated" peoples. As Robespierre said, "No one likes missionaries with bayonets." When the French first invaded the Rhineland in late 1792 the old regime collapsed and most of its leaders fled. There was no resistance and the overwhelming reaction of the people was indifference, a tribute to the success of absolutism in teaching obedience. Commissioners and commanders on the spot later reported strong anti-French feeling but this was ignored: French internal politics were the dominant factor in determining policy towards the occupied areas.

Important was the influence of Director Reubell, an Alsatian, who was very keen on the annexation of the Rhineland by France for defensive purposes and this was probably the ultimate aim of French policy from the beginning. The French tried to set up a puppet government, based on members of the Jacobin Club under the former librarian of the Archbishop of Mainz, Georg Forster, a man highly honoured because he had sailed around the world with the English explorer Captain Cook,[5] but it had little support except among French officers and pro-French intellectuals. Much attention has been paid to the German "Jacobins" by later German historians looking for the roots of twentieth-century political systems but their significance at the time was minimal. Men like Forster, Dorsch, a defrocked priest, Böhmer, former head of the Protestant grammar school in Worms, and Rheinhard, a teacher in France since 1787, were very untypical of the Rhineland population. A few industrialists in the Aachen region were pro-French, as they wanted to sell their goods into the French market. The brief Mainz Republic, 1792–3, was a provisional government run by Germans but it enjoyed no popular support at all and depended for its operation on French military power. After Forster himself visited France, he came back very disillusioned, saying "There is no virtue in the Revolution."

Although there was very little active resistance, there was a strong anti-French element in the officials of the former rulers, guild masters and priests and a large reservoir of sentimental loyalty to the old princes. During 1793, when the French were temporarily driven out of Rhineland, the old rulers flocked back to an ecstatic welcome from the people. When the French returned and took permanent possession in 1794, their attitude had changed. They now believed that the people had been so stultified by tyranny that they had to be forced to be free. This bred a strange attitude among the French towards the Germans, like that of colonial administrators towards "natives". Also, the main concern of the French after 1794 was to exploit the resources of the occupied areas for the benefit of the French war effort. Apart from this, one searches in vain for any coherent French policy towards Germany. The decision to annex the Rhineland was taken as early as 1793 but was not put into effect for years. Much of the policy was improvised by generals and commissioners on the spot. In 1794 the princes, higher clergy and nobility fled again. There was some resistance from the guilds, especially in Aachen and Cologne, and from the clergy. Many of the anti-clerical policies of the French were gratuitously provocative and helped to make them more unpopular with a pious population. In general the people were again totally quiet.[6]

After 1794 the French system was introduced in the Rhineland in a piecemeal fashion, including the abolition of the guilds, the full French legal, judicial and administrative systems and the abolition of feudalism in all its forms. This produced expectations of change elsewhere in the German states not occupied by the French. In Baden, for example, the commutation of labour services into rents had begun in 1785 but had stopped during the reaction of 1790. The Badenese peasants expected that the process would continue when their state became an ally of France and that the poor would gain big farms. This did not happen, as the French, after the failure of the Mainz Republic, preferred to run their satellite empire in co-operation with officials and representatives of the old regime. Increasingly, financial considerations became dominant as the French economy was in ruins by 1794. The revolutionary paper currency, the *assignat*, had lost value, causing rapid inflation. The Rhineland was a rich area and the French looked to it as a place where they could find solutions to their problems. They were increasingly willing to collaborate with the old order, the nobility and the old bureaucracies. This was especially true under the Napoleonic regime, which was very much an amalgam of the revolution and the old regime. In France Napoleon ruled through the so-called "notables", the richest men in each *département*.

The French occupation of the Rhineland also led to territorial changes in Germany east of the Rhine. In 1794 Prussia, anxious for peace, short of money, worried about a war on two fronts, against the French and against Polish rebels, and afraid of Austria and Russia combining against her, began negotiations with the French to pull out of the war. In April 1795, by the Treaty of Basle, Prussia and France came to a separate peace, under which the whole of Germany north of the Main river was neutralized. Prussia sought to justify the treaty by a vote of the *Reichstag* of 22 December 1794 calling for peace negotiations with the French, which the Austrian government chose to ignore. Prussia was already thinking in terms of a north German confederation of states under its leadership within the Empire. Prussia agreed at Basle to cede to France its lands west of the Rhine and it was promised compensation inside the rest of Germany for losses in the Rhineland, although these were a small part of the whole. As a result, Prussia was able to concentrate on her concerns in Eastern Europe. For ten years she remained passive and isolated. For ten years she effectively abdicated from participation in German affairs.

From the summer of 1796 into 1797 the south German states also began to come to separate terms with the French after their invasion of south Germany. The *Reichskrieg* ended. Germany became very much a side-show as the main theatre of war shifted to Italy, where Napoleon Bonaparte was making his name as a successful general commanding an army able to support itself without money from France. He was able to pursue an independent diplomacy without much reference to his supposed masters in Paris. In 1797 he negotiated a provisional settlement with the Austrians, finalized in October 1797 in the Peace of Campo Formio. By this Austria agreed to give up Belgium, Lombardy and, in a secret article, the Rhineland, in return for French permission to seize the republic of Venice. Again the principle was stated that German rulers who lost territory in the Rhineland were to be compensated in the rest of Germany. The details of this were to be worked out later.

Nine states were nominated by the imperial diet to represent the Empire in negotiations with the French and they were mandated to preserve the integrity of the *Reich*. A congress of ambassadors of these nine and other leading German states sat in Rastatt from December until April 1799 to do this but in reality it was a farce: from this point on the future of Germany was decided exclusively in Paris. Dualism was in abeyance as the only two German states strong enough to defeat France had either been defeated, Austria, or was neutral,

Prussia. Both had already entered secret agreements with France unknown to the other states. The lesser German states lined up to obtain territory which was now in the gift of the French. There was a lively trade in bribes in Paris, in the course of which the French foreign minister Talleyrand made a fortune.

The Rastatt conference finally collapsed when the French envoys were murdered by Austrian troops on 28 April 1799 but by then the War of the Second Coalition had already broken out. Napoleon came to power in France in November 1799 by a coup to prevent a restoration of the monarchy. He took over the German policy already established under the preceding regime, the Directory, the traditional French policy of sowing jealousy and division among the German rulers, dividing Austria from the rest, seeking an alliance with Prussia and strengthening the Third Germany to make it a satellite of France. He was very successful: he achieved more perfectly than before the aims of Louis XIV. As in the reign of Louis, many German princes fell over themselves to embrace the conquerer. French policy was increasingly based on buying the co-operation of the princes as the easiest way of achieving what they wanted. In the process Germany became a "great French prefecture": the French had access to German financial and human resources and was able to deny those resources to their enemies.

The Napoleonic period saw important changes and substantial if partial modernization in Germany — some historians write of a "Napoleonic revolution" or "the revolution of the princes" — but these developments were not the result of any coherent plan. The modernizing reforms which took place were incidental and a means of cementing Germany's colonial states. In addition, the French "settlement" took place in a period of continuous warfare, involving frequent political and geographical changes which gave the whole thing an air of impermanence. There was no period of prolonged peace and stability which might have made lasting changes possible. Certainly Napoleon had no intention of doing anything to foster German unity: he said that if the Germanic Body (a typical French belittling term for the Holy Roman Empire) did not exist, the French would have to create it expressly for their own purposes. His original aim was to preserve the *Reich* as the best way of reorganizing it in the French interest, for example by the creation of new electorates. The election of a Protestant Emperor was another possibility considered.

The main result of the Napoleonic reorganizations was a great territorial redistribution which led to the elimination of the majority of the ecclesiastical states, the free cities and the small states. Germany was reduced from something over three hundred to some forty states in a series of boundary changes presided over by the French, who used their power to tie German states more tightly to them. The main gainers were the south German states, especially Bavaria, Baden and Württemberg. The first major changes were rushed through at French dictation, the document known as the *Reichsdeputationshauptschluss* of 1803.

In December 1800 the last Austrian army in the field was defeated at Hohenlinden and in February 1801 France and Austria, on behalf of the Empire, signed the Peace of Lunéville. This confirmed the terms of Campo Formio, that France would annex the Left Bank of the Rhine and that the German states which lost territory would be compensated in the rest of the Empire. Austria also had to cede land in Italy but was allowed to annex the republic of Venice, Istria and Dalmatia to make this more palatable. Under the Peace of Amiens between France and Britain of March 1802 the House of Orange was to be compensated in Germany for its lost lands in the Netherlands. On 7 March 1801 the *Reichstag* accepted the terms of Lunéville and commissioned the Emperor to negotiate the details on behalf of the whole Empire. Francis refused. The Empire had to write its own death certificate. This led in October 1801 to a recommendation by the diet that an imperial deputation (*Reichsdeputation*), a committee of the diet, should be set up to work out the details. The Emperor agreed and the deputation, consisting of Mainz, Saxony, Prussia, Bohemia, Bavaria, Württemberg, Hesse-Cassel and the master of the Teutonic Order, met in August 1802. Its report, the *Reichsdeputationshauptschluss*, was published on 25 February 1803. Again the whole thing was a sham; all the decisions had been reached in advance in an agreement between France and Russia signed in June 1802 — the Russian imperial family was related to a number of German reigning houses and protected their interests — and between France and individual German states.

On paper the imperial deputation was to carry out a modernization and rationalization of the constitution and the internal boundaries of the *Reich*. In reality it simply legalized expropriation. At last rulers could legitimately seize territory they had long coveted. This showed that the Holy Roman Empire, even in its weakness, had been able to preserve Germany from a great dismemberment. The majority of free cities and small states were mediatized, simply absorbed by their neighbours. Attempts were made in the *Hauptschluss* to preserve existing rights in mediatized territories but there was effectively no mechanism to enforce this. The most spectacular feature of the 1803 settlement was the secularization of the ecclesiastical states. Only Mainz, the Teutonic Order and the Order of St John avoided this and in the case of Mainz it was only a postponement. The Trier and Cologne electorates disappeared and that of Mainz was transferred to Regensburg. Four new electorates, Baden, Württemberg, Hesse-Cassel and Salzburg, were created. Salzburg only lasted until 1805, when it was transferred to Würzburg.

Very few princes, the most prominent the Elector of Saxony, spoke out against the secularization. Most welcomed it as a marvellous opportunity. In the period before the French Revolution many German rulers had attacked the small states as bastions of misgovernment and corruption, which some were, but this was mainly an excuse for seizing them. Some, such as Prussia and Bavaria, did not wait until the discussions were complete and began seizing free cities and the land of knights and counts as early as 1791 and 1796. The secularization had been long prepared for in France and the Empire by propaganda campaigns against the supposed inadequacies of government in the ecclesiastical states, portrayed as centres of obscurantism. There were well-documented precedents for the whole procedure in the treaties of 1648, when secularization had similarly provided compensation. The majority of the governments at the same time began to seize Church property, Catholic and Protestant, both in newly acquired lands and in their former territories. This great dissolution of the monasteries led to a massive property transfer, the effects of which have not been sufficiently researched. In general it seems, initially at least, to have had damaging effects on education and the provision of charity. The position of the nobility in the ecclesiastical states also suffered as their traditional rights, for example in cathedral chapters, were lost.

The next major step came in 1806 with the establishment of the Confederation of the Rhine (*Rheinbund*), the abolition of the Holy Roman Empire, the creation of more French satellite states and the defeat of Prussia by the French. In 1805 a coalition of Austria and Russia was defeated at Austerlitz by France and her German allies, including Bavaria, Baden and Württemberg. The whole of non-Austrian Germany was either neutral or allied to France in this war. Under the Peace of Pressburg which followed, the clients of France made further gains involving more major territorial revisions. Prussia, Bavaria and other states were further enlarged. The south German states also proceeded to mediatize the imperial counts and knights. Although they kept their lands, they were no longer direct subjects of the Emperor. Bavaria also seized the free city of Augsburg. The other free cities were gobbled up later. The Confederation of the Rhine was established, a league of states under French protection.

Napoleon at first thought in terms of a small version of the Empire with common institutions, including a federal assembly, a constitution and a common law code but the German states were very hostile to this. Some, especially Bavaria, opposed the whole idea and wanted total sovereignty and independence. The idea of a constitution was raised several times during the life of the confederation but nothing ever came of it. Under several articles of the Act of Association France, as Protector of the Confederation, retained substantial rights of interference in the internal affairs of the member states. Finally the confederation came into existence on 12 July 1806 in the form of a perpetual alliance of sixteen sovereigns and France, which took over the defence and foreign policy of the whole alliance. A common army under total French control was established. In return for French protection all members provided men and money to the French war effort. Prussia, Austria, Denmark, Sweden and the north German states, accepted as a Prussian sphere of influence, were specifically excluded from the confederation. France wanted no rivals to her control.

After the defeat of Prussia in 1806 the French set up three artificial satellite states, the kingdom of Westphalia and the grand duchies of Frankfurt and Berg, ruled by Napoleon's brother Jerome, his brother-in-law Eugene Beauharnais and a French general, Murat. They joined the confederation, which was later expanded in the north until at its greatest it had thirty-seven members. As states joined the confederation, they left the Holy Roman Empire on the grounds that it could not protect its members and was no longer an effective bond, as its courts were useless and its diet paralysed. The abolition of the *Reich* was prepared for by a long propaganda campaign against it as a feudal Gothic survival. Its days were numbered when, in December 1804, Napoleon declared himself Emperor of the French. He had earlier dreamed of becoming Holy Roman Emperor himself. In 1803 he offered the title to the King of Prussia but he was not interested. Eventually a French ultimatum was issued to Francis II threatening war if he did not abandon the imperial title. On 6 August 1806 Francis II gave up his imperial crown and the Holy Roman Empire ended.

The end of the Empire did not produce a spectacular reaction in Germany. By then every reason for its continued existence had disappeared. A Nuremberg bookseller, Palm, published a pamphlet *Germany in her Deepest Humiliation*, as a result of which he was shot after a French court martial trial. Later he became a hero of German nationalism. This fact shows how little the Germans seemed to regret the end of the *Reich* which had lasted for over a thousand years.

The effects of the period of French control varied from area to area. After 1794 the Rhineland became effectively an integral part of France although the formal annexation came later. As a result the area experienced rapid modernization. Between 1801 and 1810 it enjoyed stability and prosperity. French rule became popular with the middle class and the area became a great nursery of Liberalism and free trade ideas in the nineteenth century.

The southern states, Bavaria, Baden and Württemberg, and the artificial states like Westphalia, Berg and Frankfurt experienced, in varying degrees, a period of so-called neo-absolutism or late absolutism. It was Napoleon's intention to make Westphalia a model of French good government, an example for the rest of Germany, but the demands of the French war effort took precedence here as elsewhere and its resources were regularly raided. The southern states had reform thrust on them. All faced two problems: they had to meet the very heavy commitments in men and money to France. As a result the indebtedness most had suffered before 1789 became much worse and radical financial and administrative reform became vital. They also had to absorb substantial new territories with widely different social, legal, economic and religious backgrounds. The easiest way of dealing with both was to scrap everything and impose a single new standard system for the whole new state. This produced, among other things, rapid modernizations of administrative and legal systems, the introduction of more efficient taxation involving new land surveys and the end of tax exemptions, the abolition of religious discrimination, the emancipation of the Jews and attacks on the power of the guilds. Bavaria, under its chief minister Montgelas, Württemberg and Baden experienced major reforms. Often French practices were adopted as the best available model, involving centralization of government, some form of the prefect system, judicial reforms and the introduction of clear and rational common legal systems.

The Code Napoleon of 1804, embodying equality before the law and freedom of the individual and of property, was a rational and easily exportable system and, in some form or another, it was widely adopted and in some parts of Germany it remained in force until 1900. The reforms were carried out by bureaucrats, sometimes only waiting for a chance to revive the work of enlightened despotism. Their efforts often came up against vested interests, such as the nobles, urban oligarchies and peasants, and change had to be tempered to accommodate political realities.[7] The abolition of "feudalism", for example, was not always welcome to the peasantry, who often lost benefits and found their feudal dues being converted into taxes. Shortage of capital continued to deprive most peasants of the benefits of emancipation. For example, in 1803 the Bavarian government gave peasants the right to buy out their landlords' rights but most were unable to do so. Only where governments made available long-term low-interest loans was a class of free small farmers created.

Some states, with French encouragement, introduced unitary constitutions on the French model as symbols and instruments of the unity of the newly constructed states. It would be a mistake to see this as a liberal step, though it laid the foundations for the growth of a Liberal constitutional movement later in the nineteenth century. The parliaments established under the new constitutions often became a platform for the older vested interests not for the people. Even in the French-ruled states like Westphalia there was no increase in popular participation in decision-making. German states were in a transitional phase; documents spoke interchangeably of *Bürger* (citizen) and *Untertan* (subject) without apparent awareness of any contradiction. The French period modernized the states and strengthened the power of the established authorities. The French period also legitimized the old order in another way. Grievances about new burdens of taxation, conscription and the economic problems arising from the Continental System (Napoleon's attempt to bring Britain to her knees by shutting Europe to British commerce) for example, could be shifted against the French rather than the native rulers. This led to a romanticization of the old order. Anti-French nationalism grew as a result but the chances of achieving German unity were reduced as the new states, enlarged under French patronage, were much stronger and more confident and self-sufficient. Disillusionment with the French Revolution also produced in many a turn to idealism and the pursuit of spiritual rather than material improvement, individual development rather than collective political action.

In terms of economic change the effects of the French period varied from place to place. It speeded up changes which had begun before

1789 and which were important preparatory steps for further economic modernization in the nineteenth century, including a weakening of the guilds, a releasing of land and capital and a freeing of labour. There was economic progress in some parts of Germany and changes in the nature of the economy and in the location of centres of economic activity. The period saw a decline of the Atlantic economy and, as new industries, textiles, coal and iron, became the basis of economic life, the rise of new inland centres in Belgium, north eastern France, Alsace, the Ruhr and northern Italy, the modern Golden Triangle of Europe. The industrial revolution was not to occur in Germany until the 1850s but some areas had entered the preparatory phase by 1815. The Rhineland in 1815 was further ahead of the rest of Germany than in 1789 after twenty years of French administration and it remained a centre of economic growth after 1815. Among certain groups in the Rhineland there was a strong desire to remain French in 1814–15 and the region kept French law until 1900. The middle class there was larger and enjoyed greater opportunities for economic activity than in most other parts of Germany. Elsewhere land and office remained much more attractive than enterprise. Napoleon's Continental System, introduced in 1806, might have had beneficial effects on the economies of the German states but it did not last long enough and resulted in a loss of British and other overseas markets for German goods and severe damage to German ports. It also operated as an instrument of French economic domination. An important result of the Continental System was the mechanization of the continental cotton industry, of which France was the main beneficiary.

The two leading German states, Prussia and Austria, also experienced change as a result of the French period. In both cases this arose indirectly. In the case of Austria the changes were very limited and took the form mainly of defensive reforms designed to modernize the army. One leading minister, Philip von Stadion, was in favour of more far-reaching reform but opposition was too powerful. The conservative anti-Josephine forces remained in power after the reaction of 1792, symbolized in the person of Metternich.

The Prussian Reform Movement (1806–19) was important, though again it is necessary to beware of the Borussian legend, the idea that during this period Prussia was equipping herself to lead and unify Germany. There was certainly nothing in Prussia's behaviour before 1806 to suggest this. Prussia withdrew from the French war in 1795 in order to concentrate on Poland, a sign of her growing concern with non-German interests. Her basic concern remained the same, to prevent any one power, Austria or France, from becoming too strong in Germany. The old view that Prussia stagnated totally after the death of Frederick II has been modified. The impetus for reform did not die away and enlightened ideas lived on in the bureaucracy. Between 1795 and 1806 Prussia experienced a prosperous and peaceful period, with a boom in grain exports and a flowering of culture. A code of written laws, the preparation of which had begun under Frederick II, was introduced. This marked the beginning of the *Rechtstaat* in Prussia. The relationships between the classes and between the government and the governed were regulated in great detail by the code. As in other states, there was some reaction after the French Revolution and the pace of reform slowed down. Many later leaders of the reform movement had to keep their heads down during this period. Prussia made substantial territorial gains as a client of France but her policy has, accurately, been described as "precarious and self-deluding non-alignment".

In November 1805 Prussia entered a secret agreement with Russia and came close to issuing an ultimatum to France demanding her withdrawal from Germany, Italy, the Netherlands and Switzerland. It was decided not to present it when news of the French victory at Austerlitz arrived. Instead she renewed her alliance with France and agreed to enforce a blockade against British imports, in return for which she was given Hanover. In October 1806 she woke up to the danger that France was becoming too strong and chose to attack her in alliance with Russia. The Prussian army had not been reformed since Frederick II had reconstructed it after the Seven Years' War. It was much inferior to the army of Frederick William I, which was responsible for the brilliant successes of the 1740s and 1750s. In particular there had been no changes to take account of the military revolution which had taken place in France after the revolution. On 14 October 1806 Prussia suffered a massive defeat at Jena. This was followed by a rapid French occupation of the country. In the subsequent peace settlement she had to sign away all her territory west of the Elbe, her Polish lands and her territory in south Germany. The most striking aspect of the whole affair was the total collapse of morale in Prussia after 1806, symbolized in the governor of Berlin's proclamation to the people in the name of the king after Jena, stating that the first duty of the citizen was to keep quiet (*Ruhe ist die erste Bürgerpflicht*). However well administered the state was, the majority of Prussians saw it as an alien corporation set over them. As in the

Rhineland in 1792–3, its defeat was not seen as a concern of the people.

This disaster gave the reformers a chance. They were able to capture the king's ear. The reform movement was not a result of popular demand, a factor singularly lacking in Prussia, and the whole thing was restricted to a small section of the ruling class, especially within Prussia's excellent civil service, which contained highly-educated and highly-motivated administrators. Its leaders were Stein, Hardenberg, Humboldt, Scharnhorst and Gneisenau.[8] They drew their ideas and aspirations from a variety of sources, including the Enlightenment, the early ideals of the French Revolution and Adam Smith's theories on free enterprise. There was a strong centre of support for the movement in Königsberg and east Prussia, where there were many Liberal nobles, a tradition of opposition to the crown and links to the wide world through trade. The reformers had been able to carry out reforms before 1806, including the freeing of the peasants on the royal domains and the new Polish lands, a reduction in noble privileges, cuts in internal tolls and a reduction of the restrictions on the transfer of land.

The basic desire of the reform movement was to take the logical next step from enlightened absolutism, that is to involve the people in the running of the state and in this way to interest them in its fate. This was seen as the only way of reviving Prussia faced with the great power of revolutionary France. Their stated aim, in the words of Stein's Nassau memorandum of June 1807, was to "reawaken a spirit of community, the employment of dormant or misapplied energies and unused knowledge, to create harmony between the views and desires of the nation (presumably Prussia) and those of the administrative authorities of the state, to bring about the revival of patriotism and the desire for national honour and independence." Some reformers combined with this a desire to create some kind of German union, though their ideas were vague. Most of the reformers evinced considerable devotion to the idea of a united Germany but they did not put forward concrete proposals as to how this was to be achieved. Most of the leaders were non-Prussians, though this was not unusual as there was a common market for men of talent in eighteenth-century Germany: Stein was an imperial count from the Rhineland, a member of a class and from an area where loyalty to the Holy Roman Empire remained strong in the late eighteenth century. Another major leader, Hardenberg, was a Prussian patriot, who pursued the policy of making north Germany a Prussian sphere of influence.

The reformers had a comprehensive scheme of change to transform Prussia, including the abolition of serfdom, full free enterprise, the end of guild powers and of restrictions on the transfer of land, equality of all before the law and major reforms in the army and government. They were unable to put these ideas into practice in full. The reasons for this failure were many: the reformers suffered from the inherent weaknesses of any movement seeking change in a despotic political system. The king was a weak and hopeless ally and they faced strong opposition from articulate and influential vested interests, especially the nobility.

The reform had a partial achievement: it carried through a renaissance and modernization of Prussia, which enabled it to over-come the stagnation which had followed the death of Frederick the Great in 1786. Prussia went on to join the coalition which defeated France in the years 1813–15. Noble privilege remained but it was no longer the monopoly of a small closed elite. The French period saw a further opening up of the land market. The economic crisis after the Seven Years' War produced many bankruptcies among noble estate owners and much land had come on to the market but non-noble purchasers could only buy it using subterfuges. The reform period removed artificial barriers to the transfer of land between the classes, leading to the emergence of a "modernized Junkerdom", a class of legally privileged large landowners sharing power with the bureaucracy. No strong landowning peasantry was created by the reform (and this had been one of its aims) and marked divisions between east and west remained. Urban self-government was intro-duced. Important reforms were also carried out in the army. Another major legacy of the reform period was a group of reforming civil servants who remained in post after the leaders of the movement had fallen. They had to be careful during the period of reaction which followed the defeat of Napoleon but they kept alive progressive ideas into the nineteenth century and were to be responsible for further measures of modernization in the 1820s and 1830s.

To sum up the results of the French period: as was the case with the Thirty Years' War, the period was not a great turning point or watershed. Like the Thirty Years' War it accelerated and intensified movements already begun before 1789, the modernization of states and of the German political structure. As a result of the changes of the period Germany, as under absolutism, experienced a further burst of partial modernization, especially in administration. But again there was no real social or political modernization. Germany entered the nineteenth century still bureaucratic in government and noble-dominated socially. In 1815 a new Germany was set up as a loose confederation of thirty-nine sovereign states with no ruler over them, a kind of streamlined or modernized Holy Roman Empire. Its vital function in maintaining the European balance of power was written into the Treaty of Vienna.

We have seen Germany develop from a medieval feudal monarchy to an informal federation, which ended in 1806, after which, until 1815, it was no more than a geographical expression. The basic problem throughout the period examined was to reconcile unity and diversity. A *modus vivendi* was found after 1648 but the end of the Holy Roman Empire in 1806 revived the problem. The period also saw the steady growth of foreign interference as Germany was a vital component of the European balance of power. A major feature was the rise of the state and the triumph of absolutism. This was reinforced in the eighteenth century by the Enlightenment, which also gave birth to modern Liberalism and Conservatism. This led to an idealization of the state and a lack of initiative and popular participation in decision-making. Germany remained politically retarded into the nineteenth and even the twentieth century. Economically Germany declined to become an economic backwater of Europe marked by a weak middle class and the social and psychological legacy of serfdom, especially in the east. A state with its physical and psychological centre of gravity in the east, Prussia, was to found a new *Reich*, very different from the first, in 1871.

Notes

Unless otherwise stated, the books are published in London.

Chapter 1. Introduction

1. See F. R. H. Du Boulay, *Germany in the Later Middle Ages* (1983) and J. Leuschner, *Germany in the late Middle Ages* (Amsterdam, 1981).
2. K. Leyser, "A recent view of the German College of Electors", in *Medium Aevum*, 23, 1954, 76–87, a review article.
3. M. Todd, *The Northern Barbarians* (Oxford, 1987): the Elbe was a distinct boundary between very different terrains even in the prehistoric period.

Chapter 2. Germany on the Eve of the Reformation

1. G. Strauss, *Manifestations of Discontent in Germany on the Eve of the Reformation: a collection of documents* (Bloomington, 1971) and (ed.), *Pre-Reformation Germany* (1972).
2. C. R. Friedrichs, "Capitalism, Mobility and Class Formation in the Early Modern German City", in P. Abrams (ed.), *Towns in Societies* (Cambridge, 1978) 187–213.
3. See F. L. Carsten, *Princes and Parliaments in Germany* (Oxford, 1959) for details.
4. See the first two chapters of A. G. Dickens, *The German Nation and Martin Luther* (1974) and N. Cohn, *The Pursuit of the Millenium: revolutionary millenarians and mystical anarchists of the Middle Ages* (3rd edn, 1970).

5. H. Baron, "Imperial reform and the Habsburgs 1486–1504", in *AmHR*, 44, 1939, 293–303, S. W. Rowan, "Imperial taxes and German Politics in the Fifteenth Century: An Outline", in *CEH*, 13, 1980, 203–17, S. W. Rowan, "A Reichstag in the Reform Era", in J. A. Vann and S. W. Rowan (eds), *The Old Reich* (Brussels, 1974).

Chapter 3. The Reformation in Germany

1. A. Friesen, *Reformation and Utopia* (Wiesbaden, 1974), R. Scribner, "Is there a Social History of the Reformation?" in *Social History*, 4, 1977, 483–505.
2. J. Atkinson, *Martin Luther and the Birth of Protestantism* (2nd edn, 1982).
3. G. Strauss, "Success and failure in the German Reformations", in *PandP*, 67, 1975, 30–63, on the deep attachment of the German people to superstitious and irrational religious practices.
4. T. A. Brady, *Turning Swiss: cities and empire 1450–1550* (Cambridge, 1985).
5. G. Strauss, *Nuremberg in the Sixteenth Century* (revised edn, Bloomington, 1976), S. E. Ozment, *The Reformation in the Cities* (New Haven, 1975), B. Moeller, *Imperial Cities and the Reformation* (Philadelphia, 1972), T. A. Brady, *Turning Swiss: cities and empire 1450–1550* (Cambridge, 1985), H. Baron, "Religion and politics in the German imperial cities during the Reformation", in *EHR*, 52, 1937, 405–27, 614–33, L. G. Duggan, *Bishop and chapter* (Rutgers, 1978), R. Po-chia Hsia, *Society and Religion in Münster 1535–1618* (New Haven, 1984).
6. It has recently been argued by P. S. Fichtner, *Protestantism and Primogeniture in Early Modern Germany* (New Haven, 1989) that in one respect the Reformation set back the consolidation of the states because Protestantism taught the duty of fathers to care equally for all their children. This led to a revival of the practice of dividing territories to create appanages for younger sons.
7. G. H. Williams, *The Radical Reformation* (1962), C. P. Clasen, *Anabaptism. A Social History* (Ithaca/London, 1972), M. A. Mullett, *Radical Religious Movements in Early Modern Europe* (1980).
8. R. Scribner and G. Benecke (eds), *The German Peasant War of 1525: New viewpoints* (1979). See also T. Scott, "The Peasants' War: a

Historiographical Review", in *HJ*, 22, 1979, 693–720, 953–74, P. Blickle, "Peasant revolts in the German Empire in the late Middle Ages", in *Social History*. 4, 1979, 223–39.

9. K. Brandi, *The Emperor Charles V* (1939), R. Tyler, *The Emperor Charles V* (1956), J. M. Headley, *The Emperor and his Chancellor* (Cambridge, 1983), H. Koenigsberger, *The Habsburgs and Europe 1516–1660 (Ithaca, 1971)*.

10. The Saxon Wettin lands were divided in 1485, with the Ernestine line taking the electorate with its capital at Wittenberg, and the Albertine Thuringia.

11. A. J. La Vopa, *Grace, Talent and Merit. Poor Students, clerical careers and professional ideology in eighteenth-century Germany* (Cambridge, 1988).

Chapter 4.   Peace and Polarization: Germany 1555–1618

1. H. J. Cohn, *Government in Reformation Europe* (1971), M. Raeff, *The Well-Ordered Police State* (London/New Haven, 1983).

2. F. L. Carsten, *The Origins of Prussia* (Oxford, 1954) and *A History of the Prussian Junkers* (Aldershot, 1989). R. Brenner, "Agrarian Class Structure and Economic Development in Pre-Industrial Europe", in *PandP*, 70, 1976, 30-75, a major article which began a debate on the differences between the nature of peasant communities east and west of the Elbe river. H. Wunder responded with reference to conditions in Germany in *PandP*, 78, 1978, 47–55. There is further material in T. H. Aston and C. H. E. Philpin (eds), *The Brenner Debate* (Cambridge, 1987).

3. See the excellent study by R. J. W. Evans, *Rudolph II and His World* (Oxford, 1973).

4. G. Benecke, *Society and Politics in Germany 1500–1750* (1974).

5. J. Whaley, *Religious Toleration and Social Change in Hamburg 1529–1819* (Cambridge, 1985), G. L. Soliday, *A Community in Conflict: Frankfurt Society in the Seventeenth and Early Eighteenth Centuries* (Hanover, New Hampshire, 1974).

6. J. de Vries, *The Economy of Europe in an Age of Crisis 1600–1750* (Cambridge, 1976).

7. R. Po-chia Hsia, *The Myth of Ritual Murder. Jews and Magic in Reformation Germany* (New Haven, 1988).

8. D. W. Sabean, *Power in the Blood: popular culture and village discourse in early modern Germany* (Cambridge, 1984).

9. J. H. Franklin, *Bodin and the Rise of Absolutist Theory* (Cambridge, 1973).
10. M. Raeff, *The Well-Ordered Police State* (London/New Haven, 1983).
11. J. I. Israel, *The Dutch Republic and the Hispanic World 1606–1661* (Oxford, 1982). There is an important series of articles by P. Brightwell: "The Spanish system and the twelve years' Truce", in *EHR*, 89, 1974, 270–92, "The Spanish Origins of the Thirty Years' War", in *ESR*, 9, 1979, 409–31, "Spain and Bohemia: The Decision to Intervene 1619" and "Spain, Bohemia and Europe 1619–21", in *ESR*, 12, 1982, 117–41 and 371–99. R. A. Stradling, *Europe and the Decline of Spain* (1981).
12. G. Parker, *The Army of Flanders and the Spanish Road 1567–1659* (1972).
13. R. Chudoba, *Spain and the Empire 1519–1643* (Chicago, 1952).

Chapter 5. The Thirty Years' War and its Consequences

1. G. Parker (ed.), *The Thirty Years' War* (revised edn, 1987), P. Limm, *The Thirty Years' War* (1984), T. K. Rabb, *The Thirty Years' War* (2nd edn, 1981), H. Langer, *The Thirty Years' War* (New York, 1980), G. Benecke, *Germany in the Thirty Years' War* (1978).
2. There is no modern biography of Wallenstein in English. Golo Mann, *Wallenstein* (5th edn, Frankfurt, 1971) is in German.
3. T. K. Rabb, *The Struggle for Stability in Early Modern Europe* (New York, 1975), P. Clark (ed.), *The European Crisis of the 1590's* (1985), G. Parker and L. M. Smith (eds), *The General Crisis of the Seventeenth Century* (1978), T. H. Aston (ed.), *Crisis in Europe 1560–1660* (1965).
4. P. Goubert, *Louis XIV and Twenty Million Frenchmen* (1970).
5. J. Van Horn Melton, *Absolutism and the Eighteenth-Century Origins of Compulsory Schooling in Prussia and Austria* (Cambridge, 1988).
6. C. Wilson, *Mercantilism* (1958), D. C. Coleman, *Revisions in Mercantilism* (1969).
7. C. R. Friedrichs, *Urban Society in an Age of War: Nördlingen 1580–1720* (Princeton, 1979).
8. S. H. Steinberg, "The Thirty Years' War. A New Interpretation", in *History*, 32, 1947, 89–102.
9. E. Sagarra, *A Social History of Germany 1648–1914* (1977), H. Kamen, *The Iron Century. Social Change in Europe 1550–1660* (1971).

Chapter 6. Absolutism and Particularism: Germany after 1648

1. J. Black, *The Rise of the European Powers 1679–1793* (1990).
2. J. Vann and S. Rowan (eds), *The Old Reich* (Brussels, 1974).
3. M. Hughes, *Law and Politics in Eighteenth-Century Germany* (Woodbridge, 1988).
4. R. Place, "The Self-Deception of the Strong. France on the Eve of the War of the League of Augsburg", in *French Historical Studies*, 6, 1970, 459–73.
5. J. Black, "The Problem of the Small State: Bavaria and Britain in the Second Quarter of the Eighteenth Century", in *EHQ*, 19, 1989, 5–36.
6. J. W. Stoye, "Emperor Charles VI: the Early Years of the Reign", in *TRHS*, 5th series, 12, 1962, 63–84.
7. J. Whaley, *Religious Toleration and Social Change in Hamburg 1529–1819* (Cambridge, 1985).

Chapter 7. Dualism and Reform: Germany after the Seven Years' War

1. T. C. W. Blanning, *Reform and Revolution in Mainz* (Cambridge, 1974), J. Gagliardo, *Reich and Nation: the Holy Roman Empire as Idea and Reality 1763–1806* (Bloomington/London, 1980), K. Epstein, *The Genesis of German Conservatism* (Princeton, 1966), C. J. Friedrich, "The Continental Tradition of Training Administrators in Law and Jurisprudence", in *JMH*, 11, 1939, 129–48.
2. W. Hubatsch, *Frederick the Great of Prussia* (1975), D. B. Horn, *Frederick the Great and the Rise of Prussia* (1964), G. Ritter, *Frederick the Great: a historical profile* (1968), G. P. Gooch, *Frederick the Great* (1947).
3. A. Ward, *Book Production, Fiction and the German Reading Public 1740–1800* (Oxford, 1974), J. Van Horn Melton, "From Enlightenment to Revolution", in *CEH*, 12, 1979, 103–23.
4. See H. Rosenberg, *Bureaucracy, aristocracy and autocracy: the Prussian experience 1660–1815* (Cambridge, Mass., 1958).
5. E. Crankshaw, *Maria Theresa* (1969), C. A. Macartney, *Maria Theresa and the House of Austria* (1969), G. P. Gooch, *Maria Theresa and Other Studies* (1951), D. Beales, *Joseph II*, vol. I, "In the shadow of Maria Theresa, 1741–1780" (Cambridge, 1987).

6. Helen Liebel, *Enlightened Bureaucracy versus Enlightened Despotism in Baden* (Philadelphia, 1965), C. W. Ingrao, *The Hessian Mercenary State* (Cambridge, 1987).
7. Febronius was the pseudonym of Johann Nikolaus von Hontheim, suffragen Bishop of Trier.
8. Mack Walker, *German Home Towns: community, state and general estate 1648–1871* (Ithaca, 1971).
9. R. R. Palmer, *The World of the French Revolution* (1971) and J. Godechot, *France and the Atlantic Revolution of the Eighteenth Century* (New York, 1971).
10. Wright, *Serf, Sovereign and Seigneur* (Minneapolis, 1966).
11. H. Kisch, "Growth Deterrents of a Medieval Heritage: The Aachen-area Woollen Trades before 1790", in *JEcH*, 24, 1964, 517–37.
12. S. Schama, *Citizens* (1989).
13. G. Parry, "Enlightened government and its critics in eighteenth-century Germany", in *HJ*, 6, 1963, 178–92.
14. There is useful material on this in Mack Walker, *Johann Jakob Moser and the Holy Roman Empire of the German Nation* (Chapel Hill, 1980).
15. H. Gross, *Empire and Sovereignty. A History of the Public Law Literature in the Holy Roman Empire* (Chicago/London, 1973).

Chapter 8.   The End of the Empire: Germany and the French Revolution

1. G. P. Gooch, *Germany and the French Revolution* (1920), J. M. Diefendorf, *Businessmen and Politics in the Rhineland 1789–1834* (Princeton, 1980), M. Hughes, *Nationalism and Society. Germany 1800–1945* (1988), chapter 3, G. A. Craig, "German Intellectuals and Politics 1789–1815. The Case of Heinrich von Kleist", in *CEH*, 2, 1969, 3–21.
2. R. R. Palmer, *The World of the French Revolution* (1971), J. Godechot, *France and the Atlantic Revolution of the Eighteenth Century 1770–1799* (New York, 1971), G. Best (ed.), *The Permanent Revolution. The French Revolution and its Legacy* (1988).
3. E. Wangermann, *From Joseph II to the Jacobin Trials* (1959).
4. T. C. W. Blanning, *The Origins of the French Revolutionary Wars* (1986).

5. G. A. Craig, "Engagement and Neutrality in Germany: The Case of Georg Forster", in *JMH*, 41, 1969, 1–16.
6. T. C. W. Blanning, *The French Revolution in Germany* (Oxford, 1983).
7. Mack Walker, "Napoleonic Germany and the Hometown Communities", in *CEH*, 2, 1969, 99–113.
8. G. S. Ford, *Stein and the Era of Reform in Prussia* (Princeton, 1922), W. M. Simon, *The Failure of the Prussian Reform Movement 1807–1819* (Ithaca, 1955), M. W. Gray, *Prussia in Transition* (Philadelphia, 1986).

Suggestions for Further Reading

Unless otherwise stated, books are published in London. Only works in English are listed. Readers who wish to consult works in German are recommended to look at the relevant volumes in the excellent series published by the Siedler Verlag, Berlin, "Das Reich und die Deutschen" and "Die Deutschen und ihre Nation". They are up-to-date and have full bibliographies:

H. Bookmann, *Stauferzeit und spätes Mittelalter. Deutschland 1125–1517* (1987).

H. Schilling, *Aufbruch und Krise. Deutschland 1517–1648* (1988).

H. Schilling, *Höfe und Allianzen. Deutschland 1648–1763* (1989).

H. Möller, *Fürstenstaat oder Bürgernation. Deutschland 1763–1815* (1989).

General Works

Macmillan History of Europe:

T. Munck, *Seventeenth Century Europe 1598–1700* (1990).

J. Black, *Eighteenth Century Europe 1700–1789* (1990).

Longmans General History of Europe:

D. Hay, *Europe in the Fourteenth and Fifteenth Centuries* (2nd edn, 1989).

H. G. Koenigsberger (et al.), *Europe in the Sixteenth Century* (2nd edn, 1989).

D. H. Pennington, *Europe in the Seventeenth Century* (2nd edn, 1989).

H. S. Offler, "Aspects of Government in the Late Medieval Empire" in J. R. Hale (et al., eds), *Europe in the Later Middle Ages* (1965).

J. Hale, *War and Society in Renaissance Europe* (1985).

D. Waley, *Later Medieval Europe: from St. Louis to Luther* (revised edn, 1975).

B. Guenee, *States and Rulers in Later Medieval Europe* (1985).

M. Jones (ed.), *Gentry and Lesser Nobility in Late Medieval Europe* (1986).

H. Trevor-Roper, *Renaissance Essays* (1985. Including essays on Maximilian I as an art patron and the outbreak of the Thirty Years' War).

H. G. Koenigsberger, *Early Modern Europe 1500–1789* (1987).

G. R. Elton, *Reformation Europe 1517–1559* (1963).

C. Wilson, *The Transformation of Europe 1558–1648* (1976).

J. H. Elliott, *Europe Divided 1559–1598* (1968).

G. Parker, *Europe in Crisis 1598–1648* (Glasgow, 1979).

J. Stoye, *Europe Unfolding 1648–1688* (1969).

G. N. Clark, *War and Society in the Seventeenth Century* (Cambridge, 1958).

J. Black, *The Rise of the European Powers 1679–1793* (1990).

J. Miller (ed.), *Absolutism in Seventeenth-Century Europe* (1990).

O. Hufton, *Europe: Privilege and Protest 1730–89* (1980).

W. Doyle, *The Old European Order 1660–1800* (Oxford 1978).

G. Rudé, *Revolutionary Europe 1783–1815* (1964).

G. Best, *War and society in Revolutionary Europe 1770–1870* (1982).

H. Kellenbenz, *The Rise of the European Economy* (1976).

J. de Vries, *The Economy of Europe in an Age of Crisis 1600–1750* (Cambridge, 1976).

——*European Urbanization 1500–1800* (1984).

P. Kriedte, *Peasants, Landlords and Merchant Capitalists. Europe and the World Economy* (Leamington Spa, 1983).

R. Ehrenberg, *Capital and Finance in the Age of the Renaissance* (1928).

C. Lis and H. Soly, *Poverty and Capitalism in Pre-Industrial Europe* (Hassocks, 1982).

S. Woolf, *The Poor in Western Europe* (1986).

Y-M. Bercé, *Revolt and revolution in early modern Europe* (1987. Study of the violence endemic in early modern societies.)

R. Mackenney, *The City State 1500–1700* (1989).

General Works on Germany

G. Barraclough, *The Origins of Modern Germany* (revised edn, 1988). (Still very valuable survey of German history from Charlemagne to Adolf Hitler).

J. B. Gillingham, *The Kingdom of Germany in the High Middle Ages* (Historical Association pamphlet, 1971).

H. Fuhrmann, *Germany in the High Middle Ages 1050–1250* (Cambridge, 1986).

A. Haverkamp, *Medieval Germany 1056–1273* (Oxford 1988).

F. R. H. Du Boulay, *Germany in the Later Middle Ages* (1983).

H. Holborn, *A History of Modern Germany*, vol. I, The Reformation (1959), vol. II, 1648–1840 (1965).

C. T. Atkinson, *A History of Germany 1715–1815* (1908, old but useful for the wealth of factual detail. Often described by its author as "the charnel house" after a reviewer said it failed to breathe life into the dry bones of eighteenth-century German history).

R. Vierhaus, *Germany in the Age of Absolutism* (Cambridge, 1989). (A translation of a well-reviewed German survey of the period 1648–1763, first published in 1978.)

G. Benecke, *Society and Politics in Germany 1500–1750* (1974. Not quite what the title suggests, mainly a detailed study of the small territory of Lippe, but an important step in the revision of traditional views of the Holy Roman Empire).

F. Heer, *The Holy Roman Empire* (1968. Glossy, descriptive and rather sentimental survey).

J. W. Zophy (ed.), *The Holy Roman Empire: A Dictionary Handbook* (1980).

JMH, 58, 1986, Supplement, "Politics and Society in the Holy Roman Empire 1500–1806" (a collection of important essays).

J. J. Sheehan, *German History 1770–1866* (Oxford, 1990).

F. L. Carsten, *Princes and Parliaments in Germany* (Oxford, 1959).

——*Essays in German History* (1985).

——*The Origins of Prussia* (Oxford, 1954).

——*A History of the Prussian Junkers* (1989).

E. Sagarra, *A Social History of Germany 1648–1914* (1977).

P-C. Witt (ed.), *Wealth and Taxation in Central Europe* (Leamington Spa, 1987).

C. McClelland, *State, Society and University in Germany 1700–1914* (Cambridge, 1980).

R. Aris, *A History of Political Thought in Germany from 1789 to 1815* (1936).

F. Hertz, *The Development of the German Public Mind* (1962).

M. Geisberg, *The German Single-Leaf Woodcut 1500–1550*, 4 vols, 1973.

D. Alexander, *The German Single-Leaf Woodcut 1550–1600*, 3 vols, 1975.

——*The German Single-Leaf Woodcut 1600–1700*, 2 vols, 1977.

J. R. Paas, *The German Political Broadsheet 1600–1700*, vol. I, 1600–1617 (Wiesbaden, 1985). (Part of a projected ten-volume work.)

A. Nitschke, "German politics and medieval history", in *JContH*, 3/2, 1968, 75–92 and W. Ullmann, "Reflections on the Medieval Empire", in *TRHS*, 5th series, 14, 89–108. (Two articles examining the distortions in earlier treatments of medieval history in Germany.)

Germany on the Eve of the Reformation

G. Strauss, *Manifestations of Discontent in Germany on the Eve of the Reformation: a collection of documents* (Bloomington, 1971).
——(ed.), *Pre-Reformation Germany* (1972. A valuable collection including essays on the medieval background and the imperial reform movement).
S. W. Rowan, "The Common Penny 1495–9", in *CEH*, 10, 1977, 148–64.
C. Tilly (ed.), *The Formation of National States in eastern Europe* (Princeton, 1975).
G. Benecke, *Maximilian I* (1982).
H. J. Cohn, *The government of the Rhine Palatinate in the fifteenth century* (Oxford, 1965. A pioneering work on modernization of administration in one German state).
P. Dollinger, *The German Hansa* (1970).

The Reformation

G. Hoffmeister (ed.), *The Renaissance and the Reformation in Germany* (1977). (Collected essays.)
R. Po-chia Hsia (ed.), *The German People and the Reformation* (1988).
F. Lau and E. Bizer, *A History of the Reformation* (1968).
P. Chaunu (ed.), *The Reformation* (Gloucester, 1989). (A collection of essays by sixteen international historians covering all aspects of the Reformation.)
H. Daniel-Rops, *The Protestant Reformation* (1961).
M. A. Mullett, *Luther* (1986).
K. Randell, *Luther and the German Reformation* (1989).
A. G. Dickens, *The German Nation and Martin Luther* (1974).
——*Reformation and Society in Sixteenth-Century Europe* (1966).
——*Martin Luther and the Reformation* (1967).
R. Bainton, *Here I Stand. A Life of Martin Luther* (1950).

E. G. Rupp, *The Righteousness of God: Luther Studies* (1953).

R. W. Scribner, *The German Reformation* (1986).

——*For the Sake of Simple Folk* (Cambridge, 1981).

J. Atkinson, *The Trial of Luther* (1971).

——*Martin Luther and the Birth of Protestantism* (2nd edn, 1982).

G. Strauss, *Nuremberg in the Sixteenth Century* (revised edn, Bloomington, 1976).

——*Law, Resistance and the State: the opposition to Roman Law in the Reformation* (Princeton, 1986).

——"Protestant dogma and city government. The case of Nuremberg", in *PandP*, 36, 1967, 38–58.

——"Success and failure in the German Reformation", in *PandP*, 67, 1975, 30–63.

R. Po-chia Hsia, *Social Discipline in the Reformation. Central Europe 1550–1750* (1989).

T. A. Brady, *Ruling Class, Regime and Reformation at Strasburg 1520–55* (Leiden, 1978).

J. M. Estes, *Christian Magistrate and State Church* (Buffalo, 1982. A study of Johannes Brenz, the main reformer of Württemberg).

T. Scott, *Freiburg and the Breisgau* (Oxford, 1987).

——"Community and Conflict in Early Modern Germany", in *EHQ*, 16, 1986, 209–16. (A review article.)

L. J. Abray, *The People's Reformation. Magistrates, Clergy and Commons 1500–1598* (Oxford, 1985. A study of Strasbourg).

L. Roper, *The Holy Household. Women and Morals in Reformation Augsburg* (Oxford, 1989).

The following collection of essays and articles are valuable:

A. G. Dickens, *Reformation Studies* (1983). (Some on Germany but most dealing with England.)

F. H. Littell (ed.), *Reformation Studies* (1962).

E. I. Kouri and T. Scott, *Politics and Society in Reformation Europe* (1987).

K. von Greyerz (ed.), *Religion, Politics and Social Protest: Three Studies in Early Modern Germany* (1984).

K. von Greyerz (ed.), *Religion and Society in Early Modern Europe 1500–1800* (1984).

R. W. Scribner, *Popular Culture and Popular Movements in Reformation Germany* (1987).

J. D. Tracy (ed.), *Luther and the Modern State in Germany* (Kirksville, 1986).

*   *   *

H. A. Oberman, "The nationalist conscription of Martin Luther". in C. Lindberg (ed.), *Piety, Politics and Ethics* (Kirksville, 1984).

H. Robinson-Hammerstein (ed.), *The Transmission of Ideas in the Lutheran Reformation* (Dublin, 1988). (A collection of essays on the various means by which the Reformation message spread.)

E. L. Eisenstein, *The Printing Press as an Agent of Change*, 2 vols (Cambridge, 1979).

P. A. Russell, *Lay theology in the Reformation: Popular pamphleteers in South West Germany 1521–5* (Cambridge, 1986).

C. Andersson, "Popular Imagery in German Reformation Broadsheets", in G. P. Tyson and S. S. Wagonheim (eds), *Print and Culture in the Renaissance* (1986).

G. Strauss, *Luther's House of Learning. The indoctrination of the young in the German Reformation* (Baltimore, 1978).

*   *   *

S. E. Ozment, *The Reformation in the Cities* (New Haven, 1975).

B. Moeller, *Imperial Cities and the Reformation* (Philadelphia, 1972).

T. A. Brady, *Turning Swiss: cities and empire 1450–1550* (Cambridge, 1985).

H. Baron, "Religion and politics in the German imperial cities during the Reformation", in *EHR*, 52, 1937, 405–27, 614–33.

L. G. Duggan, *Bishop and chapter* (Rutgers, 1978). (A study of the bishopric of Speyer to 1552.)

R. Po-chia Hsia, *Society and Religion in Münster 1535–1618* (New Haven, 1984).

J. Kitch (ed.), *Capitalism and the Reformation* (1967).

H. J. Cohn (ed.), *Government in Reformation Europe* (1971).

P. S. Fichtner, *Protestantism and Primogeniture in Early Modern Germany* (New Haven, 1989).

*   *   *

G. H. Williams, *The Radical Reformation* (1962).

C. P. Clasen, *Anabaptism. A Social History* (Ithaca/London, 1972).

M. A. Mullett, *Radical Religious Movements in Early Modern Europe* (1980).

R. E. McLaughlin, *Caspar Schwenckfeld. Reluctant Radical* (New Haven, 1986).

C. A. Pater, *Karlstadt as the Father of the Baptist Movement* (Buffalo, 1984).

S. C. Karant-Nunn, *Zwickau in Transition 1500–47* (Columbus, 1988).

T. Scott, *Thomas Müntzer. Theology and Revolution in the German Reformation* (Cambridge, 1989).

*   *   *

R. W. Scribner and G. Benecke (eds), *The German Peasant War 1525: new viewpoints* (1979).

P. Blickle, "Peasant revolts in the German Empire in the late Middle Ages", in *Social History*, 4, 1979, 223–39.

*   *   *

B. P. Levack, *The Witch-Hunt in Early Modern Europe* (1987).

G. Scarre, *Witchcraft and Magic in 16th and 17th Century Europe* (Basingstoke, 1987).

R. Po-chia Hsia, *The Myth of Ritual Murder. Jews and Magic in Reformation Germany* (New Haven, 1988).

*   *   *

K. Brandi, *The Emperor Charles V* (1939).

R. Tyler, *The Emperor Charles V* (1956).

J. M. Headley, *The Emperor and his Chancellor* (Cambridge, 1983).

H. G. Koenigsberger, *The Habsburgs and Europe 1516–1660* (Ithaca, 1971).

S. Fischer-Galati, *Ottoman Imperialism and German Protestantism 1521–55* (Oxford, 1959).

R. A. Kann, *A History of the Habsburg Empire 1526–1918* (Berkeley, 1977).

K. J. Dillon, *King and Estates in the Bohemian Lands 1526–64* (Brussels, 1976. A detailed analysis of Ferdinand's policies in Bohemia, showing his skill in extending royal power in the face of considerable opposition).

Germany 1555–1618

H. Kamen, *The Iron Century* (1971).
——*European Society 1500–1700* (1984).
P. Clark (ed.), *The European Crisis of the 1590's* (1985), esp. H. Schilling, "The situation in German towns".
G. Parker and L. M. Smith (eds), *The General Crisis of the Seventeenth Century* (1978).
T. H. Aston (ed.), *Crisis in Europe 1560–1660* (1965).
O. Subtelny, *Domination in Eastern Europe. Native Nobilities and Foreign Absolutism* (Gloucester, 1986. Includes material on extension of Habsburg power in south-eastern Europe.)
C. H. Carter, *The Secret Diplomacy of the Habsburgs 1598–1625* (New York, 1964).
R. Bireley, *Religion and Politics in the Age of the Counter-Reformation* (Chapel Hill, 1981. A balanced study of Ferdinand II).
M. Prestwich (ed.), *International Calvinism* (Oxford, 1985).
M. Greengrass, *Conscience and Society: Calvinism in Early Modern Europe 1560–1635* (1988).
——*Continental Calvinism* (1989).
R. J. W. Evans, *The Making of the Habsburg Monarchy 1550–1700* (Oxford, 1979).
——*Rudolf II and His World: a study in intellectual history 1576–1612* (Oxford, 1973).
H. Rebel, *Peasant Classes* (Princeton, 1982: a detailed study of the peasantry in the Austrian archduchies between 1511 and 1636).
T. Robisheaux, *Rural Society and the Search for Order in Early Modern Germany* (Cambridge, 1989). (A detailed study of villages in the small territory of Hohenlohe in the later sixteenth century, a neglected period.).
G. Parker, *The Army of Flanders and the Spanish Road 1567–1659* (1972).
——*The Military Revolution* (Cambridge, 1988).
C. V. Wedgewood, *The Thirty Years' War* (1938)
S. H. Steinberg, *The Thirty Years' War and the Conflict for European Hegemony* (2nd edn, 1977).
——"The Thirty Years War. A New Interpretation", in *History*, 32, 1947, 89–102.
G. Pagès, *The Thirty Years' War* (1970. A translation of the original French edition of 1939.)
P. Limm, *The Thirty Years' War* (1984).
T. K. Rabb, *The Thirty Years' War* (2nd edn, 1981).

H. Langer, *The Thirty Years' War* (New York, 1980).

G. Benecke, *Germany in the Thirty Years' War* (1978. Documents).

J. V. Polisensky, *The Thirty Years' War* (1971. Translation from the Czech).

——*War and Society in Europe 1618–48* (Cambridge, 1978).

——"The Thirty Years' War", in *PandP*, 6, 1954, 31–43.

——"The Thirty Years' War and the Crises and Revolutions of Seventeenth-Century Europe", in *PandP*, 39, 1968, 34–43.

G. Parker (ed.), *The Thirty Years' War* (revised edn, 1987. A very valuable up-to-date survey of all aspects of the conflict by experts).

R. A. Stradling, "Olivares and the origins of the Franco-Spanish war 1627–1635", in *EHR*, 101, 1986, 68–94.

J. I. Israel, "A Conflict of Empires: Spain and the Netherlands 1618–1648", in *PandP*, 76, 1977, 34–74.

M. Roberts, "The political objectives of Gustavus Adolphus in Germany 1630–2", in *TRHS*, 5th series, 7, 1957, 19–46.

*　　*　　*

W. Coupe, "Political and religious cartoons of the Thirty Years' War", in *Journal of the Warburg and Courtauld Institutes*, 25, 1962, 65–86.

The Consequences of Thirty Years' War

J. H. Shennan, *Liberty and Order in Early Modern Europe. The Subject and the State 1650–1800* (1986). (A study of the rise of the modern state. It draws the bulk of its illustrations from France and Russia but includes material on central Europe and makes general points which are valid for Germany).

——*The Origins of the Modern European State 1450–1725* (1974).

T. K. Rabb, *The Struggle for Stability in Early Modern Europe* (New York, 1975).

——"The Effects of the Thirty Years' war on the German Economy", in *JMH*, 34, 1962, 40–51.

H. Kamen, "The Economic and Social Consequences of the Thirty Years' War", in *PandP*, 39, 1968, 44–61.

G. Benecke, "The Problem of Death and Destruction in Germany in the Thirty Years War", in *ESR*, 2, 1972, 239–53.

*　　*　　*

R. J. W. Evans, "Culture and Anarchy in the Empire 1540–1680", in *CEH*, 18, 1985, 14–30.

M. Raeff, *The Well-Ordered Police State* (London/New Haven, 1983. The author, earlier a specialist in Russian history, compares the growth of the state in Germany and the Russia of Peter the Great).

S. Stern, *The Court Jew. A Contribution to the History of Absolutism in Europe* (New York, 1985).

D. Ludloff, "Industrial Development in 16th and 17th century Germany", *PandP*, 12, 1957, 58–73.

C. R. Friedrichs, *Urban Society in an Age of War: Nördlingen 1580–1720* (Princeton, 1979).

H. Powell, *Trammels of Tradition: Aspects of German life and culture in the 17th century and their impact on the contemporary literature* (Tübingen, 1988).

J. Whaley, *Religious Toleration and Social Change in Hamburg 1529–1819* (Cambridge, 1985).

G. L. Soliday, *A Community in Conflict: Frankfurt Society in the Seventeenth and Early Eighteenth Centuries* (Hanover, New Hampshire, 1974).

M. Fulbrook, *Piety and Politics. Religion and the Rise of Absolutism in England, Württemberg and Prussia* (Cambridge, 1983).

Post-1648 Germany

J. Vann and S. Rowan (eds), *The Old Reich* (Brussels, 1974: a collection of essays on different aspects of the Empire, itself an important stage in its "rehabilitation").

G. Strauss, "The Holy Roman Empire revisited", in *CEH*, 11, 1978, 290–301. (A review article.)

H. Gross, *Empire and Sovereignty. A History of the Public Law Literature in the Holy Roman Empire* (Chicago/London, 1973).

*   *   *

H. W. Koch, *A History of Prussia* (1978).

E. J. Feuchtwanger, *Prussia: Myth and Reality* (1970).

R. von Thadden, *Prussia: The History of a Lost State* (Cambridge, 1987).

F. Schevill, *The Great Elector* (Chicago, 1947).

R. A. Dorwart, *The Prussian Welfare State before 1740* (Cambridge Mass., 1971).

——*The Administrative Reforms of Frederick William I of Prussia* (Cambridge Mass., 1953).

J. P. Spielman, *Leopold I of Austria* (1977).

L. and M. Frey, *The Question of Empire: Leopold I and the War of Spanish Succession 1701–5* (New York, 1983. A factual uncontroversial survey).

J. W. Stoye, *The Siege of Vienna* (1964).

C. W. Ingrao, *In Quest and Crisis. Emperor Joseph I and the Habsburg Monarchy* (West Lafayette, 1974. A rather negative view of Joseph's policies in the Empire).

R. H. Thompson, *Lothar Franz von Schönborn and the diplomacy of the electorate of Mainz* (The Hague 1974. A detailed study of the activity of the Archbishop of Mainz in German and European politics. Such studies are rare in English).

J. A. Vann, *The Swabian Kreis. Institutional Growth in the Holy Roman Empire 1648–1715* (Brussels, 1975).

——*The Making of a State. Württemberg 1593–1793* (Ithaca, 1985).

M. Hughes, *Law and Politics in Eighteenth-Century Germany* (Woodbridge, 1988).

R. Hatton, *George I, Elector and King* (1978).

Germany after the Seven Years' War

K. Epstein, *The Genesis of German Conservatism* (Princeton, 1966. An off-putting title for an excellent survey of the impact of enlightened ideas in Germany).

G. Parry, "Enlightened government and its critics in eighteenth-century Germany", in *HJ*, 6, 1963, 178–92.

C. B. A. Behrens, *Society, Government and Enlightenment: The Experiences of 18th century France and Prussia* (1985).

R. Porter, *The Enlightenment* (1989).

H. P. Liebel, "The Bourgeoisie in South-West Germany 1500–1789: a rising class?" in *International Review of Social History*, 10, 1965.

* * *

C. A. Macartney, *The Habsburg and Hohenzollern Dynasties in the seventeenth and eighteenth centuries* (1970).

H. M. Scott (ed.), *Enlightened Absolutism* (1989).

J. G. Gagliardo, *Reich and Nation: the Holy Roman Empire as Idea and Reality 1763–1806* (Bloomington/London, 1980).

——*Enlightened Despotism* (1968).

S. Andrews (ed.), *Enlightened Despotism* (1967).

M. Walker, *Johann Jakob Moser and the Holy Roman Empire of the German Nation* (Chapel Hill, 1980).

H. Liebel, *Enlightened Bureaucracy versus Enlightened despotism in Baden 1750–92* (Philadelphia, 1965).

H. Strakosch, *State Absolutism and the Rule of Law: the struggle for the codification of civil law in Austria 1753–1811* (Sydney, 1967).

J. Stroup, *The Struggle for Identity in the Clerical Estate* (Leiden, 1984. A study of enlightened clergy in Hanover and Brunswick and their opposition to absolutism).

C. McClelland, "The Aristocracy and University reform in Eighteenth-Century Germany", in L. Stone (ed.), *Schooling and Society. Studies in the History of Education* (Baltimore, 1976).

*   *   *

G. Ritter, *Frederick the Great: a historical profile* (1968).

G. P. Gooch, *Frederick the Great. The ruler, the writer, the man* (1947).

C. Duffy, *Frederick the Great. A Military Life* (1985).

H. Rosenberg, *Bureaucracy, aristocracy and autocracy: the Prussian experience 1660–1815* (Cambridge Mass., 1958).

W. O. Henderson, *Studies in the economic policy of Frederick the Great* (1963).

——*The state and industrial reform in Prussia 1740–1870* (Liverpool, 1958).

*   *   *

G. P. Gooch, *Maria Theresa and Other Studies* (1951).

E. Crankshaw, *Maria Theresa* (1969).

C. A. Macartney, *Maria Theresa and the House of Austria* (1969).

D. Beales, *Joseph II*, vol. 1, "In the shadow of Maria Theresa, 1741–1780" (Cambridge, 1986).

P. G. M. Dickson, *Finance and Government under Maria Theresa 1740–1780* (2 vols, Oxford, 1987). (An exhaustive analysis, very technical in places.)

T. C. W. Blanning, *Joseph II and Enlightened Despotism* (1970).

S. K. Padover, *The Revolutionary Emperor: Joseph II* (1934).

P. P. Bernard, *The Limits of Enlightenment: Joseph II and the Law* (Urbana/London, 1979).

P. P. Bernard, *Joseph II and Bavaria. Two Eighteenth-Century Attempts at German Unification* (The Hague, 1965. Apart from the bizarre subtitle, a straightforward account of Joseph's Bavarian exchange scheme).

*   *   *

W. E. Wright, *Serf, Sovereign and Seigneur. Agrarian reform in Eighteenth-Century Bohemia* (Minneapolis, 1966).

R. Okey, *Eastern Europe 1740–1980* (1982).

K. Roider, "Origins of Wars in the Balkans 1600–1792", in J. Black (ed.), *The Origins of War in Early Modern Europe* (Edinburgh, 1987).

A. Klima, "Industrial developments in Bohemia 1648–1781", in *PandP*, 11, 1956–7, 87–97.

F. Spencer, "An eighteenth-century account of German Emigration to the American colonies", in *JMH*, 28, 1956, 55–9.

W. H. Bruford, *Germany in the Eighteenth Century: the social background of the literary revival* (Cambridge, 1935).

A. Menhennet, *Order and Freedom. Literature and Society in Germany from 1720 to 1805* (1973).

C. McClelland, *State, Society and University in Germany 1700–1914* (Cambridge, 1980).

J. Van Horn Melton, *Absolutism and the Eighteenth-Century Origins of Compulsory Schooling in Prussia and Austria* (Cambridge, 1988. Shows how government plans to use education as an instrument of social control did not always work out).

A. J. La Vopa, *Prussian School Teachers 1763–1848* (Chapel Hill, 1980).

——*Grace, Talent and Merit* (Cambridge, 1988. A study of poor students, usually the sons of Protestant clergymen, who obtained university scholarships in the eighteenth century, illustrating Pietism and the Enlightenment).

J. Gagliardo, *From Pariah to Patriot: The changing image of the German Peasant 1770–1840* (Lexington, 1969).

J. W. Van Cleve, *The Merchant in German Literature of the Enlightenment* (Chapel Hill, 1986).

T. C. W. Blanning, *Reform and Revolution in Mainz 1743–1803* (Cambridge, 1974).

C. W. Ingrao, *The Hessian Mercenary State 1760–85* (Cambridge, 1987).

A. Fauchier-Magnan, *The Small German Courts in the Eighteenth Century* (1958. A translation from the French, a general survey drawing examples from the Württemberg courts).

G. W. Pedlow, *The Survival of the Hessian Nobility 1770–1870* (Princeton, 1987). (A study of the way in which the nobility of Hesse-Cassel successfully adapted to change and retained their privileged position.)

The Impact of the French Revolution

R. R. Palmer, *The World of the French Revolution* (1971).

J. Godechot, *France and the Atlantic Revolution of the Eighteenth Century 1770–1799* (New York, 1971).

G. Best (ed.), *The Permanent Revolution. The French Revolution and its Legacy* (1988).

T. C. W. Blanning, *The French Revolution in Germany. Occupation and Resistance in the Rhineland 1792–1802* (Oxford, 1983).

——*The Origins of the French Revolutionary Wars* (1986).

S. S. Biro, *The German Policy of Revolutionary France.*, 2 vols (Cambridge Mass., 1957. A full, factual, rather dull and sometimes inaccurate survey).

F. Venturi, *The End of the Old Regime in Europe 1768–76* (Princeton, 1989).

H. T. Mason and W. Doyle (eds), *The Impact of the French Revolution on European Consciousness* (1989).

G. D. Holman, *Jean-Francois Reubell* (The Hague, 1971). (A biography of the member of the Directory and leading exponent of annexationist policies.)

G. P. Gooch, *Germany and the French Revolution* (1920).

——"Germany's Debt to the French Revolution", in *Studies in German History* (1948).

A. Ramm, *Germany 1789–1919: A Political History* (1967).

*   *   *

F. Wangermann, *From Joseph II to the Jacobin Trials. Government policy and public opinion in the Hapsburg dominions in the period of the French Revolution* (1959).

C. A. Macartney, *The Habsburg Empire 1790–1918* (1968).

*   *   *

G. S. Ford, *Stein and the Era of Reform in Prussia* (Princeton, 1922).

G. A. Craig, *The Politics of the Prussian Army 1640–1945* (1964).

G. Ritter, *The Sword and the Sceptre.*, vol. I, "The Prussian Tradition 1740–1890" (Coral Gables, 1969).

P. W. Schroeder, "The Collapse of the Second Coalition", in *JMH*, 59, 1987, 244–90. (This contains useful material on Austrian policy in Germany.)

F. Crouzet (et al., eds), *Essays in European Economic History 1789–1914* (1969. Contains: G. Adelmann, "Structural Change in the Rhenish Linen and Cotton Trades at the Outset of Industrialization".

F. Crouzet, "Wars, Blockade and Economic Change in Europe 1792–1815", in *JEcH*, 24, 1964, 567–88.

H. Freudenberger, "State intervention as an obstacle to economic growth in the Habsburg monarchy", in *JEcH*, 27, 1967, 493–509.

* * *

O. Connelly, *Napoleon's Satellite Kingdoms* (London/New York, 1965).

W. M. Simon, *The Failure of the Prussian Reform Movement 1807–1819* (Ithaca, 1955).

J. M. Diefendorf, *Businessmen and Politics in the Rhineland 1789–1834* (Princeton, 1980).

* * *

F. L. Ford, "The Revolutionary-Napoleonic Era: How much of a watershed?" in *AmHR*, 69, 1963–4, 18–29.

Central European History, 22/2, 1989: special issue "The French Revolution in Germany and Austria".

Index

Michael Hughes is a senior lecturer in history in the
University College of Wales, Aberystwyth. He has
researched and taught the history of Germany, from
the Reformation to the Third Reich, for over twenty
years. He is also author of *Nationalism and Society:
Germany 1800–1945* and *Law and Politics in
Eighteenth-Century Germany.*